The Rainbow Road
from Tooting Broadway
to Kalimpong

THE COMPLETE WORKS OF SANGHARAKSHITA include all his previously published work, as well as talks, seminars, and writings published here for the first time. The collection represents the definitive edition of his life's work as Buddhist writer and teacher. For further details, including the contents of each volume, please turn to the 'Guide' on pp.523–32.

FOUNDATION

1. A Survey of Buddhism / The Buddha's Noble Eightfold Path
2. The Three Jewels I
3. The Three Jewels II
4. The Bodhisattva Ideal
5. The Purpose and Practice of Buddhist Meditation
6. The Essential Sangharakshita

INDIA

7. Crossing the Stream: India Writings I
8. Beating the Dharma Drum: India Writings II
9. Dr Ambedkar and the Revival of Buddhism I
10. Dr Ambedkar and the Revival of Buddhism II

THE WEST

11. A New Buddhist Movement I
12. A New Buddhist Movement II
13. Eastern and Western Traditions

COMMENTARY

14 The Eternal Legacy / Wisdom Beyond Words
15 Pāli Canon Teachings and Translations
16 Mahāyāna Myths and Stories
17 Wisdom Teachings of the Mahāyāna
18 Milarepa and the Art of Discipleship I
19 Milarepa and the Art of Discipleship II

MEMOIRS

20 The Rainbow Road from Tooting Broadway to Kalimpong
21 Facing Mount Kanchenjunga
22 In the Sign of the Golden Wheel
23 Moving Against the Stream
24 Through Buddhist Eyes

POETRY AND THE ARTS

25 Poems and Stories
26 Aphorisms and the Arts

27 Concordance and Appendices

COMPLETE WORKS 20 MEMOIRS

Sangharakshita
The Rainbow Road from Tooting Broadway to Kalimpong

MEMOIRS OF AN ENGLISH BUDDHIST

EDITED BY KALYANAPRABHA

Windhorse Publications
169 Mill Road
Cambridge
CB1 3AN
UK

info@windhorsepublications.com
www.windhorsepublications.com

© Sangharakshita, 2017

The right of Sangharakshita to be identified as the author
of this work has been asserted by him in accordance
with the Copyright, Designs and Patents Act 1988.

Cover design by Dhammarati
Cover images © Clear Vision Trust Picture Archive
Typesetting and layout by Ruth Rudd
Printed by Bell & Bain Ltd, Glasgow

**British Library Cataloguing
in Publication Data:**
A catalogue record for this book is
available from the British Library.

ISBN 978-1-909314-85-6 (paperback)
ISBN 978-1-909314-86-3 (hardback)

CONTENTS

Foreword, Kalyanaprabha ix
Map xv

1 Giants and Dragons 1
2 The Children's Encyclopaedia 15
3 Learning to Walk 26
4 'Here Comes the Boys' Brigade' 34
5 Evacuated 45
6 The Veil of Isis 54
7 The Pendulum Swings 68
8 Buddhism and the LCC 75
9 The Misfit 91
10 Passage to India 107
11 With the Swamis in Ceylon 116
12 Maitreya, the Coming Buddha 130
13 The Three Worlds 138
14 Coincidences 146
15 The End of the Beginning 152
16 Jumping in at the Shallow End 158
17 Direct Action Day 165
18 All-India Religions Conference 173
19 Two Meetings and a Marriage 178
20 Anandamayi, the Blissful Mother 183

21	The Three Untouchables	193
22	Meditations in the Mango Grove	204
23	The Divine Eye	211
24	The Going Forth	219
25	A Question of Identity	227
26	Śramaṇa Versus Brāhmaṇa	231
27	The Temple of the Virgin Goddess	237
28	The Road to Trivandrum	243
29	What Happened to the Offerings	247
30	The Town of the Three Rivers	255
31	'What Is Your Caste?'	263
32	The Three Lawyers	271
33	Other Friends	282
34	Outings and Activities	288
35	The Path Within	300
36	'Krishna Has Come!'	308
37	Ramdas, the Servant of God	319
38	At the 'Abode Of Bliss'	328
39	The Vision in the Cave	335
40	The One-Eyed Guru	349
41	Sandalwood Country	364
42	'Tiger, Tiger...'	375
43	Disappointment at Sarnath	381
44	Through the Curtain of Fire	392
45	At the Shrine of the Recumbent Buddha	402
46	'Here the Blessed One was Born'	414
47	With the Newars in Nepal	424
48	Academic Interlude	442
49	In the Land of the Great Disciples	457
50	Facing Mount Kanchenjunga	467

Appendices

1	Introduction to *Learning to Walk*	475
2	Chapter One: Original Version	479

Notes   505
Index   509

A Guide to *The Complete Works of Sangharakshita*   523

FOREWORD

In the Buddhist world the name Sangharakshita conjures up the idea of 'Buddhist teacher', and the words 'Buddhist teacher' no doubt have connotations of their own. It is not so usual for Buddhist teachers to write their memoirs[1] and some might think that the founder of a new Buddhist movement would have had more important things to do. Yet Sangharakshita's memoirs run to several volumes. A Foreword to the first of them must surely account for that.

In his introduction to *Learning to Walk* (see Appendix 1) Sangharakshita explains the circumstances under which, in 1959, he began this record of his life. It was not because he himself felt any particular need to write about it. Rather, it came about in response to the urging of Jivaka, a somewhat unusual guest who was staying with him at the Triyana Vardhana Vihara, the monastery in Kalimpong in the eastern Himalayas that Sangharakshita founded in 1957.

What was to become *The Rainbow Road from Tooting Broadway to Kalimpong* was not by any means complete when the author put it aside to work on other literary projects and there was a gap of ten years (during which he moved to England and started the Friends of the Western Buddhist Order) before he returned to the task once more, taking up his pen in 1972 to continue where he had left off – in the middle of chapter 32. By then – in fact even whilst he was writing in Kalimpong – he had come to realize 'the significance of what I was doing'. But just what was – or is – that significance?

In an essay entitled 'A Room with a View'[2] Sangharakshita refers to Martin Amis' *Experience* (published 2000), a collection of memoirs written in response to the death of his father, novelist Kingsley Amis. Martin Amis suggests that in modern times the autobiography – or at least, what he calls 'high autobiography' – is replacing the novel as the dominant literary genre. And perhaps a memoir – while not strictly speaking the same as autobiography – can nevertheless be included in the category to which Amis refers.

But if autobiography is replacing the novel there must be something they have in common so that one can do as well what the other has hitherto done. What do both the novel and the autobiography most essentially have in common? What both the novel and the autobiography have in common is that they deal with the lives of human beings, showing in particular the significant events of those lives, the greatest novels being those best able to show how events form and shape character and how character impacts on events through the choices made and actions taken. Embedded in all this we see, of course, the Buddha's great teaching of *pratītya-samutpāda*, conditioned co-production, at work: this being, that becomes, with the arising of this, that too arises – but applied to the complex psychological world of human beings. It is those novels that are able to show the deeper patternings of human existence and to show it in a way that we recognize, making plain what before we only half knew or didn't really know at all, that become the greatest novels of all – and no doubt the same may be said of autobiography. What Sangharakshita himself saw as the significance of what he was doing, he does not say, but this is surely at least one aspect of that significance: we are able to see for ourselves something of how events impacted on Dennis Lingwood, later Sangharakshita, and how Dennis Lingwood and Sangharakshita impacted on events and on the lives of others. As he himself explains, the degree of distinctness with which any particular memory remained in his mind gives some indication of the intensity of the original experience and of the 'nature and ultimate extent of the influence exerted ... on the development of character and formation of opinion'.[3]

An aphorism of Sangharakshita is that religion 'cannot be taught it must be caught'[4] and it has been central to his exposition of the Buddha's Dharma that the spirit of Buddhism can best be caught through *kalyāṇa mitratā* or spiritual friendship. It is through coming to know a friend more and more deeply that we see directly how the Dharma expresses itself in his or her life so that the Dharma is then not just a matter of words and ideas, not abstract principles to be cogitated upon, but something living, a transforming spirit, one could even say a magical power whose effect becomes intensified as a person goes for Refuge more and more deeply to the Three Jewels, and which to the receptive friend becomes more and more apparent the deeper the friendship goes, opening up for him or her new vistas of experience and understanding.

In *A Rainbow Road*, and in the subsequent memoirs, we are drawn in to Sangharakshita's life through the medium of his memories. To read them is to come to know him more deeply. To immerse oneself in them can become, one might even say, an experience of *kalyāṇa mitratā*. We are able to see the world through his eyes; find out how he responded to events, and how he saw them – what was his perspective – and how, through his experiences of life, he grew.

Sometimes what shaped his life came from a conscious decision – like the decision to leave school at the age of fifteen, or later on, in India, to sever his connection with the Ramakrishna Mission. But often we are left with the impression that there are other, deeper forces at work, something acting on his life from some quite mysterious level of existence: there are hints of this in the very first chapter, 'Giants and Dragons', which deals with his early childhood, and we see it again, for instance, in his discovery of *Isis Unveiled* in the public library in Torquay, and the *Diamond Sūtra* in an obscure second-hand bookshop in London, books that were crucial to his development. There is the strange coincidence that the signals unit to which he was conscripted when he was nineteen was sent of all places to India. And then there is his great heart's wish for ordination as a Buddhist monk which finally found fulfilment in his *śrāmaṇera* ordination at one of the great Buddhist pilgrimage places, Kusinara, the site of the Buddha's Great Decease.

Through the pages of *The Rainbow Road* we are invited to step into a life that began quite humbly in Tooting, London. We are afforded glimpses of Mother and Father, of sister Joan, of some notable aunts and one or two uncles, of school, friends, confinement to bed with disease of the heart, and of growing up during the Second World War. We learn that Sangharakshita's was a temperament that in adolescence expressed itself in 'violent oscillation between extremes' – a sensibility of such intensity that it was only through coming into contact with the

Buddha's teaching that he found a refuge which, as he once remarked, perhaps saved him from insanity. He discovered the Buddha's teaching around his seventeenth birthday. What he writes of this experience is worth quoting in full:

> When I read the *Diamond Sūtra* I knew that I was a Buddhist. Though this book epitomizes a teaching of such rarefied sublimity that even *arahants*, saints who have attained individual Nirvāṇa, are said to become confused and afraid when they hear it for the first time, I at once joyfully embraced it with an unqualified acceptance and assent. To me the *Diamond Sūtra* was not new. I had known it and believed it and realized it ages before and the reading of the *sūtra* as it were awoke me to the existence of something I had forgotten. Once I realized that I was a Buddhist it seemed that I had always been one, that it was the most natural thing in the world to be, and that I had never been anything else.

It is from this point, from this recognition of the truth of the Buddha's teaching, and his own relation to it that Sangharakshita's life moves on with a single central theme that becomes stronger and deeper, its implications ever clearer through all the ensuing multifarious experiences, spiritual and mundane.

It is indeed a rare life with its undistracted interest from so early on in religion and higher culture, and with its one-pointed dedication to the realization of the Buddha's teaching. At the same time Sangharakshita shares with us experiences we quickly recognize, for they are common to human life: experiences of love and of loss, of hopes and disappointments. He writes of childhood illness, the ending of his parents' marriage, the bombing of the family home, the intensity of first loves, the excitement of travel, the ups and downs of friendship, the pain of rejection, and disappointment with the spiritual community. His memoirs communicate to us so directly that it is through human life and only through human life and experience that the Buddha's teaching may be realized.

But *The Rainbow Road from Tooting Broadway to Kalimpong* can also be enjoyed simply as literature. (The *Times Literary Supplement* likened his 'deft prose' to that of E. M. Forster.) His observations of life in India in the 1940s in all its colourful variety, as well as the ubiquitous caste-ridden atmosphere of the great subcontinent, are an education in themselves. His description of the ascetics and religious people – both charlatans and the genuinely highly developed – are fascinating, and his sensitivity to landscape and the natural world is described with all the vividness of one with poetic sensibility.

These memoirs may be read in conjunction with other writings emanating from the time, in particular the early poems and articles.[5] In *The History of My Going for Refuge*, we find further reflections on some of the crucial turning points in his spiritual life that are described in this memoir.[6]

Finally a note on the title. As Sangharakshita explains in Appendix 1, the memoir first appeared (minus the first ten chapters) as *The Thousand-Petalled Lotus*, but this had not been his original choice of title. Windhorse Publications brought out a new edition with the first ten chapters reinstated in 1997 under the title *the Rainbow Road*. But in fact *The Rainbow Road* had been the working title. In the 1997 edition the last five words of the title were transferred to a subtitle. Now, however, for the *Complete Works* edition we are able to restore to this first volume of memoirs the title and subtitle as originally envisaged by the author: *The Rainbow Road from Tooting Broadway to Kalimpong: Memoirs of an English Buddhist.*

I hope you will find in the pages that follow much to interest you, and that you will enjoy, as I have done, the humour, be moved by the pathos, and even find yourself glimpsing new vistas of possibility for your own life of which you have never dreamed.

Kalyanaprabha
Great Malvern
18 June 2016

Sangharakshita in India and Ceylon 1944–1950

You asked, 'What is this transient pattern?'
If we tell the truth of it, it will be a long story;
It is a pattern that came up out of an ocean
And in a moment returned to the ocean's depth.[7]

Omar Khayyám
(1048–1131)

I
GIANTS AND DRAGONS

On Sunday mornings, when the weather was fine, Father used to take me to see my grandmother, pushing the perambulator with the cream-coloured silk awning through two or three miles of south-west London streets.

As soon as he had swung open the front gate I used to run up the path and rattle the shining brass letter box until someone came to let us in, all the time peering eagerly through the coloured glass panels of the big green front door. The hall never failed to interest me, and never did I pass through it without pausing to look up at the Nepalese kukris and Chinese swords and chopstick-sets with which the walls were decorated, and rarely could I refrain from ringing the Tibetan ritual handbell that stood in a corner behind the door.

What most of all drew my attention was the big Chinese picture on the left-hand wall. This Father had lifted me up to look at ever since I was a baby and it was thus among the most familiar objects of my childhood. Almost square in shape, it depicted an august and mysterious personage seated cross-legged on a kind of throne. He was arrayed in loosely flowing robes and behind his head was a nimbus. His features, which were markedly oriental, with slant almond eyes that gazed into the far distance, were expressive of a remarkable combination of benignity and power. This enigmatic being was surrounded by half a dozen figures, some making offerings, others playing on musical instruments. None of them was more than a tenth of the size of their master, whom for this reason I called the Giant.

Running into the sitting room, I found objects to gaze at, and even to handle, which were hardly less wonderful than those in the hall. The Chinese cloisonné vases were as fine as any of those which, in later years, I saw in Tibetan temples and at the houses of wealthy Chinese friends, and the exquisite shape of some of them has been in my experience unique. One great flagon-shaped pair with gold dragon handles depicted houses, gardens, and human figures. Even now, at a distance of more than forty years, I can still see a favourite figure in blue gown and black cap standing pensively among the toy hills.

Round each of the other vases, all of which were a deep rich blue, coiled a five-clawed imperial dragon with white beard and tusks, red horns, black eyes, purple mane, and scales picked out in gold. Each dragon had its jewel and spat flame in its defence. Of these mysterious beasts it never occurred to me to feel afraid, and certainly they were never for me, as they are for the Christian tradition, symbolical of evil. It was therefore without astonishment that I learned, in later life, that to the Chinese the dragon had been for thousands of years the symbol of the yang, the bright, masculine, creative principle of the universe, even as the phoenix, with which I was unacquainted, was the symbol of the yin, the dark, feminine, destructive principle.

On the mantelpiece was a small sedent bronze image which, when able to talk, I learned to call the Empress Dowager. When I shook it, it rattled. This figure, the features of which I remember as well as those of any living face, I now know represented not the last Manchu ruler of imperial China but the 'Goddess of Mercy', Kwan Yin, the feminized Chinese version of the bodhisattva Avalokiteśvara, one of the most popular figures of the Indian Buddhist pantheon. The rattling noise must have been produced not, as I then supposed, by a stone, but by one of those holy relics which the Buddhists of China, like those of Tibet, frequently sealed in images.

In grandmother's kitchen there hung, on opposite walls, the portraits of two men, one in naval the other in military uniform. The man in the first, which was considerably larger, wore a walrus moustache and must have been about thirty. The man in the second picture, which was slightly yellowed, had a small trim moustache and seemed to be in his early twenties. At that time it puzzled me very much to be told that both men were my grandfather, for Nana, as we called her, had been twice married and twice widowed. By each marriage she had had two children, a boy and a girl, Father being the eldest. It was her second husband who was responsible for introducing into the house the exotic objects described. Of partly Portuguese descent, he had travelled widely, at one time serving in the Merchant Navy. At the time of the Boxer Rebellion he was working for the Imperial Chinese Government on the construction of railways and, having a mania for curios, took advantage of the sack of the Summer Palace at Beijing to add to his collection.

Grandfather was also a photographer, it seems, for there was an album of photographs taken at the time of the rebellion. Kneeling on the ground, hands pinioned behind their backs, were rows of naked rebels, some with their severed heads already at the executioner's feet. My sister and I spent many happy hours looking at these pictures, until one day Nana realized that they were not the most suitable thing for children to see.

About Nana's first husband, my own grandfather, I knew even less than I did about her second. This was partly because he had died so young that Father had no recollections of him to share with me. All I knew was that he came of a good Suffolk family, being the youngest of eight brothers, and that after their marriage he and Nana, the daughter of a Norfolk smallholder, had gone to live at Woolwich, where Father was born. Grandfather was then working in the War Office, on account of his fine copper-plate hand being assigned the responsibility of writing out the commissions that went to the Queen for signature. On his sudden death from pneumonia Nana was left to support herself and two small children, one of them still a baby. Being a woman of great strength of character she met the situation courageously and from odd reminiscences of hers in later years I gathered that at different times she had worked as charwoman, parlourmaid, and housekeeper. After five or six years of this hard life she had married again and come to live in Tooting.

Between Father and his sister, who was also my godmother, existed a very strong affinity. Besides inheriting Nana's heavy eyebrows, blue-grey eyes, and aquiline nose, both of them were, like her, outspoken in opinion and firm in adherence to principle. But whereas Auntie Noni was exceptionally self-possessed, and could make the deadliest remarks with the utmost coolness, Father was hot-tempered in the extreme and almost morbidly quick to take offence. Since he was of a generous and forgiving nature his anger never lasted long, however, and by the time I was born his temper was more or less under control. Indeed, he was an unusually good man. Unselfishness was second nature to him, and it was long before I met anyone who so consistently and so cheerfully put the happiness of others before his own. Auntie Noni, who was unmarried, idolized him. This was perhaps natural. Unfortunately, she was also in the habit of singing his praises to Mother and reminding her, on every possible occasion, what a good man Father was and how lucky she was to have married him. This last remark was always conveyed in a tone which suggested that having such a man for a husband was a miracle for which Mother ought to go down on her unworthy knees and render thanks to heaven.

Unlike Mother, both Father and Auntie Noni had a very lively sense of humour and were excellent raconteurs. Father's stories, which he told me when I had been put to bed, were usually about his own life, especially his schooldays and his experiences in the trenches during the Great War. In this way I learned how he had given a false age in order to enlist, how he had lived under shellfire, and how he had seen comrades blown to bits and had been himself badly wounded, as well as how he had woken up in a hospital tent without the use of his right arm, which was permanently disabled. While convalescing in the Church Lane Hospital, Upper Tooting, he met Mother, who was working there as a VAD. One of his more amusing stories was about her helping him clamber over the hospital wall at night when he had stayed out after hours. They were married in 1919, when Father was nineteen and Mother perhaps twenty. Six years later, in a nursing home in Stockwell only a stone's throw from the spot where the English Buddhist monk Ananda Maitreya had died two years earlier, I was born.

At the time of my birth my parents were living in Nana's house in Tooting, where they occupied the upstairs flat. They had moved there some months earlier when, on learning that my mother was pregnant, Nana had shifted to Southfields. Brick-walled and slate-roofed, with a dusty privet hedge, lace-curtained windows, and highly polished front door, this modest terrace property was one of the hundreds of thousands which, standing back to back in interminable rows, help to make up the vast maze of mutually intersecting streets that is suburban London.

What I take to be my earliest memory, however, finds me not outside the house but inside it, in my parents' bedroom. Lying at night in the big double bed, where I had been put to sleep, I used to stare up at the foliated stucco ceiling-piece, the size and shape of a cartwheel, from the centre of which depended the unlit gas-bracket. As the motors passed up and down the main road at the top of the street their headlights swung round the ceiling-piece like great bright spokes round a shadowy hub. If the motors were going south, towards the coast, the spokes swung clockwise; if north, to the city's heart, in the opposite direction. With the clanging of distant tram bells and the low roar and rumble of the other traffic in my ears, I used to lie in the darkness and watch the spokes turning now this way, now that, and now both ways simultaneously as two motors crossed each other, until lulled to sleep.

As I grew older I naturally became dissatisfied with passive contemplation. 'Mother, can I go out to play?' was my constant cry. The natural playground of the London child is, of course, the street, but there I was not allowed to play until after I had started school. In the meantime, therefore, I played on the black and white tiles of the porch and behind the dusty privet with my sister Joan, fifteen months younger than myself, and a girl of my own age who lived up the street. Sometimes we played so noisily that 'the lady downstairs' had to tap gently on the window of her front room to quieten us. When it rained, or when I was not allowed to play 'out in the front', my refrain was, 'Mother, can Frances come in to play?' Usually she could. Our favourite indoor game was 'dressing up', for which we ransacked the house for old lace curtains. As a special treat we were sometimes allowed to borrow the embroidered veil in which Father and I had been christened, and then great was our joy, for instead of playing mothers and fathers, as we usually did, we could play at weddings. In my case this love of dressing up persisted much longer than it did with the girls, and even at the age of eight I could spend hours in front of the wardrobe mirror experimenting with different styles of dress. Jersey and knickerbockers were not my real costume, I felt, and almost desperately I swathed and draped myself in lengths of material, searching in vain for my true vesture. The only times I felt satisfied were when, with the help of a Red Ensign, I achieved a toga-like effect which, though not exactly right, was to some extent what I desired. Gravely holding grandfather's silver-mounted amber cane, I would then stand gazing at my reflection with solemn pleasure.

Halfway up the street, on the other side of the road, stood the school Father had attended as a boy and to which, at the age of four, I too was

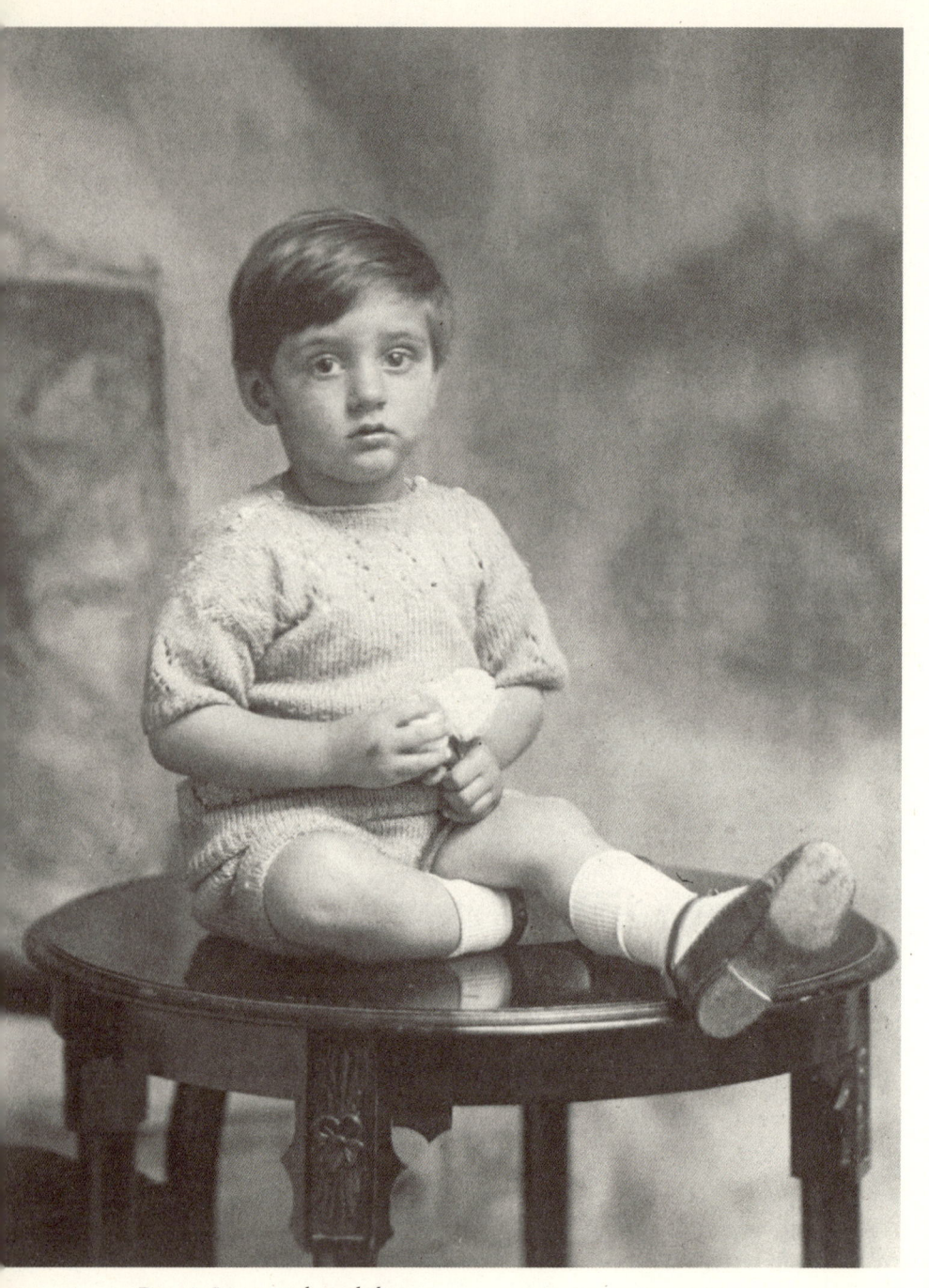

Dennis Lingwood aged three

6 / GIANTS AND DRAGONS

sent. Ever since I could remember I had seen its turquoise green cupolas against the sky, and heard its bell ringing twice a day. Nevertheless, on the day of my admission I was so frightened that I ran home at the first opportunity. This reluctance to study did not last long and I spent in the Infants' Department four not unhappy years – the longest period of continuous schooling I was ever to receive.

After tea on weekdays, all day Saturday (though not usually on Sunday), as well as practically every day during the holidays, we were free to play in the street. Frances, Joan, and I continued to share our games, for though we knew many other children we formed a self-contained little confederacy and were happiest playing with one another. We never played all our games on one day. As I look back it seems that our games had their cycles and that conkers and marbles, spinning-tops and hopscotch, came and went in accordance with laws as immutable as those of physics or chemistry. On or about a certain day in August, for example, all the children in the neighbourhood would begin making grottoes, any attempt to set them up earlier, or to prolong their existence for more than three weeks, being regarded as extremely reprehensible. These grottoes, which were always built on the pavement against a wall, consisted of shells or small stones arranged in the form of a square, within which could be set flowers, small pieces of crockery, and any bright or curious object. After constructing the grottoes we had the right to sit by them and demand coppers from the passers-by.

Another event that loomed large in our year was Derby Day, when throughout the afternoon and evening and until late at night a continuous stream of cars, buses, coaches, and horse-drawn carts and carriages, all packed with happy and excited racegoers, would be flowing past the top of the street along the main road between London and Epsom. Waving red, white, and blue streamers, swarms of excited children would be standing on the kerb, their parents generally hovering behind to see that they did not fall under the wheels of the vehicles. When, races over and bets lost and won, the stream of traffic set more and more steadily in the homeward direction, our excitement reached its climax. Each brightly lit coach that swung slowly past us would be greeted by a shout of 'Throw out yer mouldies!' whereupon the beerily jovial occupants would fling into our midst handfuls of coppers for which we scrambled and fought until the next coach came along. At intervals, with the crack of a whip and the jingle of beribboned harness, there would pass by, in all the glory of innumerable gleaming pearl buttons, a Pearly King and Pearly Queen. They were always stout and elderly, while the Queen, who was generally stouter than the King and laughed with even greater heartiness, invariably wore a wide black hat with enormous ostrich plumes that nodded and danced at every step the pony took.

Yet another annual event was Guy Fawkes Day. As soon as it was dark, Joan and I, Mother and Father, and sometimes Nana and Auntie Noni too, would file downstairs into our tiny back yard where the guy had already been propped up in the middle of the concrete. After Father had sprinkled him with paraffin he was set on fire, whereupon the flames would leap up, the smoke swirl, and the darkness be lit up with a ruddy glare in which our faces would glow crimson and our voices sound strangely different. Sparklers, which we could run about with in our hands, and Roman Candles and Golden Rain, which had to be set at a distance on the ground, would then be ignited. Catherine wheels would go whizzing round, broadcasting a shower of rainbow sparks, and red and green rockets spring hissing up into the night. Squibs and crackers exploded at our feet. In less than half an hour our Guy Fawkes would be blazing merrily. Ten more minutes and its head, charred features no longer recognizable, would collapse into the flames, sending up a shower of orange-gold sparks. Within the hour the bonfire would have burned itself out and the last flames have subsided, leaving only a mass of glowing embers. Standing silent in the darkness, our shouts and laughter hushed, we would look up through the misty air and see that the stars had come out in the chill November sky.

To what extent London children keep up the old customs, or are familiar with the traditional sights and sounds, I do not know. Perhaps they still hear the muffin-bell in the distance, still see the knife-grinder pushing his grinding-wheel through narrow suburban streets and the rag-and-bone man offering tortoises and goldfish in exchange for scrap iron, old clothes, old newspapers, and broken china. But I am sure none of them ever saw the lamplighter on his rounds. Even before we left the house at Tooting the old gas streetlights, which on rainy days were reflected in a strange iridescence from the wet pavements, had been replaced by electric standards. As late as eight o'clock at the height of summer and as early as four o'clock in the depths of winter, the old lamplighter would come down the street. Having set his ladder against the arm of the lamp-post he would climb up, open the window of the glass shade, light the mantle, adjust the flame and climb down, shoulder his ladder and be off down the street to the next lamp-post. I am sure there is hardly anything lonelier in the world than a deserted street in a big city, dimly lit at intervals by gas lamps.

Not that Joan and I were ever allowed out alone after dark. But sometimes in the summer, when it was fully light at six o'clock, Mother would send us to the Broadway to meet Father. Tooting Broadway, where the statue of Edward VII in royal robes dominated the public conveniences from its marble pedestal, and where the trams lumbered past with a dreadful grinding of wheels and shrieking of brakes, was to us the hub of the universe. It was, indeed, one of the biggest traffic junctions and busiest shopping centres in South London, though Father could remember how, at the beginning of the century, the High Street had been a country road with green fields on either side. Waiting inside the vestibule of the Tube, Joan and I used to feast our eyes on the gilded baskets of colourful hot-house fruits hanging in the windows of Walton's the Fruiterers. Every time a blast of hot air struck us from the escalator shaft, which meant a train had come in, we craned eagerly forward, searching for Father among the crowd pouring through the gate. As soon as we saw him, bareheaded and attaché case in hand, coming towards us with his rolling, rather nautical stride, we would dash forward and, seizing hold of a hand apiece, lead him home in triumph.

Once in the kitchen, I would open his case and take out the newspaper, which was always the *Daily Herald*, for unlike the rest of the family Father was a staunch supporter of the Labour Party. His only concession to conservatism was to take the *Sunday Express*, a paper Nana also read. Later on, I do not know why, he changed to the *People*. My own interest in the *Daily Herald*, which I read spread out on the floor, it being too big for me to hold at arm's length, was strictly non-political. I was interested in following the adventures of Bobby Bear. Only after informing myself of the latest exploits of this hero did I turn to the news. It was from Father's newspaper, I think, rather than from any school primer, that I learned to read.

The first real book I ever handled was the family Bible, with its tooled leather cover and worn gilt clasp, which was so big and heavy that I could hardly lift it. Imitating Father, I called it 'Grandmother's Bible', the volume having formerly belonged to Nana's mother, who was, however, still living, and whom I saw only once. The rich blues, reds, and yellows of the illustrations, which depicted such subjects as Daniel kneeling in the lions' den among skulls and ribs and Samson with the ass's jaw-bone in his hand, had long been familiar to me. One rainy day, when I was five or six years old, it occurred to me that instead of merely looking at the pictures I could read the text, whereupon I promptly spelled my way through the first and second chapters of Genesis.

If the Bible gave me my first experience of prose, it was from a prayer book that I had my first taste of poetry. In the sitting room cupboard, among Father's books, I discovered at the age of six or seven a volume entitled *Prayer and Praise at Eventide*. From the inscription on the flyleaf I gathered that it had been presented to my paternal grandfather by his mother. Opening it, I came on the lines

Stay, pilgrim, stay!
Night treads upon the heels of the day.

This was the first time I had ever met a metaphor and I can still recall the shock of delight the experience gave me. Though I read the rest of the volume, even the prayers, none of it had for me the magic of those two lines.

Nana visited us once a week on the day she came from Southfields to Tooting to see her old friends, collect her rents, and do a little shopping. Auntie Noni came less often. With the exception of Father's friends and their wives, nearly all the other visitors were Mother's relations. The most frequent and regular of these were Auntie Kate and Auntie Jessie.

Only the creator of the Aunts in *The Mill on the Floss* could have done them justice, though neither of them had either the formidability of Aunt Glegg or the airs and graces of Aunt Dean. Auntie Kate, who could not quite be called stout, had a watery blue eye with a twinkle in it and wore her hair in a bun kept in position by large hairpins. Her nose, which being the family nose could only be called long, was red at the end and shiny, for despite the expostulations of Mother and Auntie Jessie she refused to powder. Their epithet for her was 'old-fashioned', which was hardly matter for astonishment since she was the eldest of the sisters and had already married and given birth to a son when Mother, who was the youngest, was still in the cradle. Auntie Kate was in fact an old-timer in many ways. Even the sweets she brought us were of a kind that must have been on the market in Dickensian times. Her sense of humour, too, was nineteenth-century, and when on holiday at the seaside she used to send all her friends and relations comic postcards depicting enormously fat women in bathing costumes and with exaggeratedly prominent posteriors. Yet Auntie Kate was a victim of melancholia, and in later years used to spend her evenings reading *Jack the Ripper*, after which she would put out the light and sit alone in the dark.

Auntie Jessie's epithet was 'stately', even as Mother's was 'vivacious'. She had a full bosom, kind brown eyes, a musical voice, and was always redolent of scent and powder. Moreover she was quiet and gentle, with a touch of sadness in her expression. Unlike Auntie Kate she relished a ribald joke well enough to laugh at one but not well enough to tell one, and while laughing she always put her hand up to her mouth as if to hide a blush or her rather prominent false teeth.

On visiting days the two aunts usually arrived early in the afternoon; but sometimes they came at eleven o'clock, on which occasions Auntie Kate would scandalize Mother and Auntie Jessie by producing her own lunch, cold meat and pickled onions, out of a brown paper bag. After discussing haberdashery and husbands, and drinking innumerable cups of tea, the three sisters would try on one another's hats, for they all frequently bought new ones, and at each meeting at least one hat was produced which at least one sister had not seen. This ritual accomplished, Auntie Kate and Auntie Jessie would pull on their gloves, pick up their handbags and, after kisses all round, depart to catch the tram home.

At that period Auntie Kate lived, as indeed she had always lived, at Fulham, and twice or thrice a year Mother and I visited her there. As we crossed over Wandsworth Bridge and passed the rows of meanly decent houses where, at six o'clock on a cold December night, one might well be tempted to murmur

The winter evening settles down
With smell of steaks in passageways[8]

Mother would point out to me one house, bigger than the rest, which held a special place in her affections. This was the house where she had been born. Sometimes the sight of the old home revived memories, and then Mother would tell me about the grandfather who had been born in Hungary and could speak only a little broken English and in whose sweetshop she used to help as a girl, and about the father who had been a clarinettist and whom she had sometimes accompanied to recitals on the Continent. She also talked about her brothers and sisters, thirteen in number, not all of whom I had seen. Uncle Dick, the youngest, who like his father was a clarinettist, had gone to India at the age of sixteen and joined the Governor of Bengal's band. This brother was the innocent cause of one of the cruellest disappointments of my boyhood. When I was six he returned to England on leave. The news of his arrival threw me into a fever of excitement, for I assumed he would be accompanied by a whole retinue of Indian servants, and never having set eyes on an Indian before I looked forward to his coming to the house with the keenest anticipation. Alas! as the kitchen door opened, and I craned my head forward for a glimpse of the

Dusk faces with white silken turbans wreathed[9]

which I hoped to see beaming over his shoulder, all I saw were the very European features of Uncle Dick, Auntie Dolly, and my two small cousins.

At Christmas time representatives of both Mother's and Father's families would be invited to the house, though Mother often complained that 'her side' was being neglected. Preparations for the festival began with the purchase of large quantities of holly and mistletoe from a barrow at Tooting Broadway, where the brightly-lit shop windows already glittered with tinsel and where, during Christmas week, the slow-moving crowds of cheerful shoppers thronged the pavements more and more densely every night. The peak was the last Saturday before Christmas, when with the help of Nana's expert eye we bought the turkey, and when the last stir was given to the Christmas pudding. In the kitchen and the sitting room Father would put up paper chains, which we sometimes made ourselves from slips of coloured paper, as well as Chinese lanterns, bunches of balloons, and paper bells. There was also a Christmas tree, which we decorated with iridescent globes of coloured glass saved from year to year, candles of red, blue, green, and yellow wax, and strings of tinsel. The lower branches were hung with presents, while at the top of the tree glittered a large tinsel star.

Aged five

On Christmas Day itself, the first thing I did was to empty the stocking hanging at the foot of the bed and open the parcels heaped on a chair at my bedside. In the toe of the stocking there was always a tangerine. The remainder of the morning was spent in the sitting room, where there were dishes of nuts and packets of figs and dates and where, at noon, Joan and I would be given a glass of port wine to drink with our mince pie. As the turkey had to be roasted for several hours, Christmas dinner was a late meal. Flushed and triumphant, Mother would emerge from the scullery amidst clouds of steam bearing the turkey – a sprig of holly stuck in its breast – before her on a large oval dish. After dinner presents were untied from the tree and distributed. In the evening Father sometimes played his favourite gramophone records, among which I remember an operatic aria sung by Caruso, of whom he was very fond, and Gershwin's *Rhapsody in Blue*. From the way in which the clarinet climbed the scale in the opening bars of the latter piece I called it 'the aeroplane'.

Birthdays were celebrated in much the same way, though on a considerably reduced scale, turkey and Christmas pudding being replaced by a birthday cake with the appropriate number of candles, while instead of an assembly of grown-ups there would be a small gathering of children. But for me Christmases and birthdays alike always ended in disaster, for I would get keyed up to such a pitch of excitement that, however tired, I could not bear the thought of going to bed. The result was that Father had to exert his authority and send me off to my own room in tears. Even so early in life did I have to learn that

Every sweet with sour is tempered still.[10]

2
THE CHILDREN'S ENCYCLOPAEDIA

One cold bright December morning, when I was eight years old, I opened my pyjama jacket, pulled my vest up to my chin, and stood on a chair in front of the window so that the doctor could peer more closely at my chest. It was covered with dull red spots. Making me turn round he scrutinized my back. The same dull red spots! 'Scarlet fever,' he said briefly. 'He'll have to go to hospital.'
Though I had had measles and whooping cough, as well as influenza, this was the first time it had been necessary for me to be removed to hospital, and I was filled with apprehension. Besides, it was only a week before Christmas, and I was deeply disturbed by the prospect of missing any of the customary festivities. To assuage my fears, a copy of *Alice in Wonderland* was taken prematurely from its hiding-place in a cupboard with the assurance that, if I was a good boy and went to the hospital without making a fuss, I would definitely be home in time to open the rest of my presents on Christmas morning. When the ambulance arrived, therefore, I left quite cheerfully, clutching the *Alice in Wonderland* and declaring loudly that I would be back in four or five days.

Perhaps I would not have gone so quietly had I known that I should be away for five weeks and that, even when I did eventually return, it would be to an existence quite different from the one to which I was accustomed, and that I should be allowed no festivities of any sort for several years.

The ward where I found myself in bed an hour later contained about forty boys of different ages, all with scarlet fever. At first I took refuge behind the *Alice in Wonderland*, now my sole memento of home. But soon my nervousness abated, I became used to the disciplined routine of hospital life and started making friends with some of the other boys. Our day began very early. Long before the short winter day had dawned two cheery cleaners, clad in pink gowns and white aprons, would clatter in with mops and pails and proceed to swing the castored truckle beds out into the centre of the ward with a single heave of their brawny arms. When they had swept, scrubbed, dusted, and polished every square inch of wood and metal, so that wood shone like glass and metal gleamed like silver and gold, beds would be pushed into position against the wall and the patients given their breakfast. Having never been interested in food, I remember of the hospital meals only the unpleasant thickness of the china mugs from which we drank our well-diluted milk. Breakfast finished, faces and hands were washed, ear-passages and nostrils cleaned. Finally, our beds were made, the coarse white sheets being turned back halfway down the bed and tucked in so tightly that the mattress curved like a bow.

Christmas morning found me eagerly untying the parcel Father had left in the hall the night before. Though it contained all manner of good things, including books and toys, I remember best of all the two sour red plums he had tucked into a corner of the box. In spite of our protests, and even tears, we were not allowed to keep our presents, all of which went into the common toy-box in the bathroom.

While the cheerful faces and friendly voices of the two cleaners are still vivid in my mind, of the nurses, with the exception of the ward sister, I remember nothing. They were, as no doubt they had been trained to be, machines for taking temperatures and administering medicines, though human hearts must have beaten somewhere beneath those starched bosoms. The ward sister was very pretty, and severe almost to the point of spitefulness. She it was who, every evening before we went to sleep, pencil in hand, and with the face of a Medusa, held an investigation into the state of our bowels during the day, giving a tick in the register if they had moved and a zero and a glass of syrup of senna if they had not. Constipation, we were made to feel, was a criminal offence. On one occasion, when I had tremblingly admitted for the third day in succession that I had had no motion, she scolded me harshly and told me to go to the lavatory and sit there until my recalcitrant bowels had moved.

Fortunately not all my hospital experiences were as unpleasant. On my return from the chickenpox ward, where I was isolated for a week with three or four other boys, I was allowed to spend most of the day out of bed. One morning the other convalescent boys and I were taken downstairs into the courtyard where we played for an hour in the pallid brightness of the winter sunshine under the guardianship of the oldest patient, a lad of twelve. When confined to the ward we amused ourselves sliding up and down the highly polished floor in our stockinged feet. But my pleasantest memory is of the hours we spent singing together 'Underneath the Arches', 'Shanty Town', and the rest of the Flanagan and Allen songs, then at the height of their popularity.

While I was in hospital only one boy died. We had been aware for several days that he was more seriously ill than other patients, for when the doctors came screens were placed around his bed, and once to our horror we saw several yards of rubber piping disappearing behind the green curtains of the screens. One day two figures, muffled in red cloaks and hoods, came and sat with him for an hour. That night, when only a dim blue light burned in the ward, and the night sister sat writing at the table, I saw shadowy figures flitting between his bed and the door. They seemed to be carrying something heavy. In the morning, when the screens were dismantled, we saw that the boy was no longer there.

On the day of my discharge one of the nurses took Mother aside and told her that my exceptionally high pulse-rate, which had always been attributed to my well-known fear of doctors, might be due to some other cause. She advised her to take me to our own doctor and have my heart thoroughly tested. Alarmed, my parents had this done without delay, and it was discovered that I apparently had valvular disease of the heart. Years later there was considerable controversy between medical men over the cause of my complaint. According to some of them it was due to my having had rheumatic fever in very early childhood. Our own doctor, however, to whom I had been taken for every cough and cold since I was born, maintained that I had never had rheumatic fever. In my own opinion the disease was functional, that is, of psychological origin. After I went to India and took up the practice of Buddhist meditation, which calms the mind and helps resolve complexes, there was a marked improvement in my condition.

Whatever the origin of the disease might have been, about the way in which it was to be treated the general practitioner had in those days no doubts. I was ordered to bed, where I had to remain flat on my back. Thenceforward I saw only the nasturtium-patterned walls of my room where, hour after hour for two years, I watched the eyes of the owl clock moving backwards and forwards with a sharp click-clack as the pendulum swung to and fro.

Since I had to be kept absolutely quiet, no visitors were admitted. I saw only the doctor, who at the beginning came thrice a day, the district nurse, and my parents. Once Joan, finding the door open, peeped in with a scared face. A few months prior to my catching scarlet fever I had been promoted to the Junior Department at school and my teacher, a red-faced, kind-hearted little woman, unwilling to suffer my education to be discontinued, offered to teach me spelling and arithmetic in her spare time. But when it was found that these lessons agitated me they were stopped.

During the whole period of my confinement my parents were continually occupied by two problems: how to keep me quiet and how to keep me occupied. The first problem, the solution of which was the more urgent, inasmuch as my life was thought to depend on it, could be solved by such measures as not allowing me ever to sit up in bed by my own exertions, and by excluding visitors and shutting out noise. The second, it was soon discovered, could be solved by providing me with books and magazines, and I promptly developed a habit of avid and incessant reading which never afterwards left me.

Soon after my incarceration began, Father brought into my room an armful of books from his own library and arranged them in the little bookcase on the wall, on top of which stood the model yacht *White Eagle* given me by Nana for my seventh birthday. Some of Father's books I had already read. In addition to *An Outline of English Church History* and a pocket *Johnson's Dictionary*, both of which like *Prayer and Praise at Eventide* had belonged to my grandfather, there were Harrison Ainsworth's *The Tower of London*, E.W. Hornung's *Raffles*, Walter Besant's *The World Went Very Well Then*, *Peter the Whaler*, *Tom Brown's Schooldays*, Kingsley's *Hypatia*, Charlotte Brontë's *Jane Eyre*, and an illustrated English Reader, beside others now forgotten. This odd collection of books, every one of which I read and reread, laid the foundations of my education, for neither before nor after my illness was I able to learn at school anything that could be considered either useful or interesting.

Like the baby cuckoo which keeps its sparrow foster-parents flying to and fro all day with food for its insatiable maw, I gave my parents no respite from the search for reading matter. Immediately after breakfast Father would dash round the corner to the newsagent's and bring me back a boys' weekly, one of which was published every day. My favourite was the *Wizard*, published on Monday, with the *Adventurer, Hotspur*, and *Rover* following not far behind. The *Champion*, which appeared on Thursday, stood low in favour, for it consisted mainly of stories with a sporting background, while the famous *Gem* and *Magnet*, which contained nothing but rather silly stories about boys in Eton jackets and masters in billowing gowns (the gowns always 'billowed' in these stories), I considered not worth reading. My preference was for the exotic. The indefatigable writers who, week after week, turned out the latest enthralling instalment of the serials which I followed with so much interest, catered for the natural boyish craving for adventure by exploiting three distant parts of the globe – Darkest Africa (tom-toms and cannibalism), the Wild West (cattle rustling and scalping), and the Mysterious East (tongs, opium-fiends, six-inch fingernails, and throwing-hatchets). One serial, however, had a Dyak headhunter for hero, while in another Tibetan lamas in tall hoods, and with steel-devouring termites concealed in the seams of their robes, came to England and gained hypnotic control over a champion football team as a means of raising money for their government.

Of all the stories it was the ones about the Mysterious East that most excited my interest and stimulated my imagination, and I had not been many months in bed when I wrote a story of my own set in the same opium-laden atmosphere of warring tongs and international smuggling rings, where fatal hatchets suddenly flashed through the air from silken sleeves, and men who had talked were dragged out of the river by the police. This story was my first literary effort. No doubt Father read it, and perhaps he thought that vicarious escapes from sudden and violent death were not the best thing for valvular disease of the heart, and I did no more writing.

Out of the dozen or so books he had given me, my greatest favourites were *Jane Eyre* and *Hypatia*. I can still see the narrow black figure of Mr Brocklehurst astride Mrs Reed's hearthrug, still hear him ordering

Jane's naturally curly hair to be shorn as a rebuke to worldly vanity, after which awful sentence his wife and daughters (exquisite satire!) come rustling into the room in all the splendour of their silk and satin and glory of false fronts and flowing ringlets. No less vividly do I remember the haughty Miss Blanche at the piano, Mr Rochester making his unconventional declaration, and the mad wife escaping from her chamber at midnight to rend Jane's bridal veil. In fact almost every incident in this extraordinary novel, which ten years later I could still read with enjoyment, is printed indelibly on my mind.

Much less vivid is *Hypatia*, which as literature merely flutters its wings where *Jane Eyre* soars with ease, though strong impressions of this tale of the best of Paganism and the worst of Christianity in naked conflict still remain. My sympathies were very much with the last of the Neoplatonists, and I was unspeakably shocked when the Christian mob, incited by Cyril the archbishop, tore her to pieces on the altar steps of the great basilica beneath the very eyes of Christ. But even more deeply than by this tragic incident was I impressed by Hypatia's address to her students, in the course of which I heard for the first time the thunder-roll of Homeric verse, and by the description of her lying rigid upon her couch while her soul flew alone to the Alone. This was my first acquaintance with mystical religion and was never to be forgotten.

Religion in any form had not, indeed, occupied a very prominent place in my early life. Though baptized soon after birth into the Church of England, to which Father's family belonged, I had never been made to comply with any form of religious observance. For a short while Joan and I attended Sunday school at the nearby Congregational Church, sitting on a hard bench against the wall in the bottom class and feeling extremely bored. More interesting was my first service, from which I returned to tell my parents that I had seen the Holy Ghost. Enquiry revealed that this phenomenon was in fact the minister, who had appeared in a white surplice.

My parents' indifference to religious observances was due, I think, not so much to any deficiency of religious instinct on their part as to the lifeless formalism which seemed to have blighted all the churches, chapels, tabernacles, and meeting houses of Tooting. The only sign of spiritual life to be discerned in our neighbourhood were the grey-haired Salvation Army lasses who, in poke bonnets and with banners bearing such legends as 'JESUS DIED FOR YOU', stood under the leadership of an aged captain outside the Trafalgar public house every Sunday morning and in cracked voices sang doleful hymns to the squeak of a concertina and the rattle of tambourines. Father always gave them a copper, for though, like most Londoners, he could not agree with their religious opinions, he respected them for their integrity and for the nobility of their social work.

Only once do I remember seeing a clergyman in the street. This was the Congregational minister, who, like Mr Chadband, wore black and was a fat yellow man who looked as though he had a good deal of train oil in his system. Probably this clerical elusiveness helped give me the feeling which, during the present century, has become almost universal in Protestant countries, that religion is the business of the clergy and that its manifestations are confined in space to the churches and in time to Sunday mornings and evenings. At any rate, no clergyman was ever known to visit the house, and only after removal to another part of Tooting did we become the object of ministerial solicitude.

When orthodoxy decays heterodoxy flourishes, and in the absence of more solid spiritual nourishment Father turned to the Ancient and Mystical Order of Druids, of which he became a member, and to Dr Coué's New Thought, while Mother turned to the Rechabites. My first experience of a religious gathering took place under the auspices of this obscure sect, whose principal tenet was teetotalism. I accompanied Mother to a meeting at the suggestion of one of her friends, the mother of a class-mate of mine, who said, 'Oh, Gerald simply *loves* Rechabites!' I did not love them. All they did was to sit gloomily around a table in a small room in Balham while an elderly man read aloud from a black Bible, after which they drank cups of strong tea. Perhaps they said prayers too, but I do not remember any. Mother was probably as dissatisfied as I was, for she soon stopped going. When I was older she dabbled in Spiritualism and attended séances with a friend. Later she joined the Baptist Church at Streatham, which for a time occupied an important place in my own religious life, and still later, under her son's guidance, she became mildly interested in Buddhism.

Beneath these changes in religious affiliation her basic attitude remained unaltered. Nothing that anyone was reported to have said or done, however wicked, ever roused her indignation or made her feel, even when she had herself been wronged, that they should be punished by human hand. In her opinion the consequences of one's actions were inescapable, and he who did evil inevitably suffered. At the same time she never alluded to God, whom one born a Christian might be expected to regard as a rewarder of good and punisher of evil, from which I conclude that she believed in a principle not unlike the Buddhist karma, according to which pleasant and painful sensations arise in natural dependence upon pure and impure mental states respectively without the intervention of any external agency.

Having nothing to do except read, the rapidity with which I could devour a book became quite alarming: I must have held the world record for a boy of my age. How many words one issue of the *Wizard* or *Hotspur* contained I no longer recollect, but I remember boasting to Father, who had fondly imagined that one of them sufficed me for a whole day, that it had lasted twenty-five minutes exactly by the owl clock. Instead of being pleased with my precocity he looked dismayed. It was rather as though the baby cuckoo, after swallowing a particularly fat and juicy worm, which its overworked foster parents had thought would satisfy its demands for the day, should immediately open its beak and declare it was still hungry. Fortunately the problem was solved by the next-door neighbours. This kind-hearted couple, a printer and his wife, who had passed their *Everybody*'s over the fence to us every week for several years, now gave me a complete set, in sixty-one parts, of Harmsworth's *Children's Encyclopaedia*. This was a sizeable morsel even for a digestion like mine, and it kept me fairly quiet for the remainder of the two years.

Alfred Harmsworth, afterwards Lord Northcliffe, has sometimes been ridiculed on account of his enthusiasm for popular education; but I fervently blessed him for the *Children's Encyclopaedia*. All sixty-one parts (including the Index) were at my bedside day and night, and rarely was I seen without one of them in my hand. Thanks to Mr Harmsworth I was no longer alone in my little room with the nasturtium-patterned wallpaper, the owl clock, the model yacht, and my one dozen oft-read volumes. I could now speak with the good and wise of all ages; I could follow Nature into her innermost recesses and explore all her secrets, from the constitution of the heavens to the structure of a crystal. The pageant of history from its first dawnings in Egypt, China, and Babylonia, passed with all its kings and princes, its priests and nobles and common people, before my eyes. The buskined and unbuskined heroes of ancient and modern tragedy trod my bedside rug for their stage. Perseus slew Medusa the Gorgon, Hercules performed his Twelve Labours, and Jason went in search of the Golden Fleece, in my sight. Shining presences of marble and bronze rose as though to music and stood before me in the naked glory of their perfectly proportioned Hellenic manhood; pensive Italian madonnas smiled. The cross on which Christ was crucified, the tree beneath which the Buddha attained Enlightenment, had their roots in the floor of my room, wherein, as into a garner, the harvest of the ages was gathered unto me for the making of the bread that would keep my soul alive. The body was forgotten, and my imagination, now possessed of 'infinite riches in a little room', rejoiced in the freedom of all the heavens of the spirit.

Though not a page of those sixty-one parts remained unread, it was inevitable that some subjects should interest me more than others. My favourite sections, to which I turned most frequently, and over which I lingered longest, were the ones dealing with art, with history, and with literature – or rather, with the history of literature, for, the *Children's Encyclopaedia* being not a thesaurus of select classics but an outline of knowledge in all its branches, the only species of literature actually represented was Poetry, to which a separate section was devoted.

Strangely enough the Philosophy section, which discussed abstract ideas such as Truth, Beauty, Goodness, and Justice, all of which the editor had stoutly capitalized, failed to awaken in me the love of wisdom, though I studied with interest the lives of the great philosophers, as well as those of the Buddha, Mohammed, Zoroaster, Confucius, and Lao-tzu. Archaeology, however, fascinated me, especially that of Ancient Egypt, and I never wearied of looking at the picture of a pharoah with red-brown face in profile, his hair done up in slender braids, the double crown of Upper and Lower Egypt on his head, and the crook and flail, symbols of protection and punishment, crossed over his linen-clad breast; nor of gazing at those pages from the *Book of the Dead*, with their green Osiris and black-headed Anubis, or at the fresco of the fowler poised, sling in hand, upon his little boat among the reeds and lotuses, while the ducks flew up above his head.

The section which attracted me least was Popular Science, perhaps because I had no means of performing even the simplest of the experiments described. Neither was I particularly interested in the circulation of the blood or in the internal combustion engine. Perhaps at this period I was more strongly attracted by Beauty than by either Truth or Goodness. Certainly I was never tired of looking at what were to me the most precious parts of the whole *Encyclopaedia* – the numerous plates, some of them in full colour, which illustrated the history of art, especially of painting and sculpture, in Ancient Greece and Rome, Italy, France, England, Germany, Spain, and Holland. Though every picture gave me pleasure, I admired most of all the works of the Renaissance artists, especially the deific sublimity of Michelangelo and the dancing delicacy of Botticelli.

Towards the end of the second year of my confinement my parents started giving even more serious thought to my condition than before. If I was no worse, neither was I noticeably any the better, and they could not help wondering whether I was doomed to lifelong invalidism, like white-faced Auntie Fanny at Besthorpe, who had not been outside her room for twenty years. In these circumstances it was only natural that they should feel the advisability of having a second medical opinion. Another doctor, therefore, was called in, and after examining me he confirmed our own physician's diagnosis and recommended continuation of the regimen already prescribed. Still dissatisfied, Father made arrangements for me to be examined by the famous heart specialist Dr Mackenzie. As he bore me into the consulting room, Dr Mackenzie asked, 'Why are you carrying him? Let him walk!'

'He can't walk,' explained Father, for to such a degree had I lost the use of my legs that I could not even stand.

'Can't walk!' roared the cardiologist, 'He must be *made* to walk! Put him down! Put him down!'

Whether his diagnosis agreed with that of the other doctors I have no knowledge. All I know is that he told Father in the strongest possible terms that I should be got out of bed immediately and allowed to run about. Twenty years later, in Calcutta, I met a Bengali doctor, also a heart specialist, who had studied under Dr Mackenzie. After hearing my story he told me that this great cardiologist had revolutionized the method of treating diseases of the heart and that after considerable initial opposition his findings had won general acceptance. At my Bengali friend's request I allowed him to examine my heart, which he pronounced perfectly sound.

When Dr Mackenzie gave his unexpected verdict, he was regarded as daringly, even dangerously, heterodox by the majority of the members of a profession which attaches as much importance to its own special form of orthodoxy as the most zealous religionists do to theirs. In this conflict of expert opinion Father had no means of judging who was right and who wrong. Eventually, after much anxious thought, he took the responsibility into his own hands and resolved to follow a middle course. No doubt this was a difficult decision, the making of which required not only common sense but courage; but in neither of these two qualities was Father at any time deficient. Mother, in her distress, consulted an occultist. Gazing into a crystal ball, he said that he saw me ascending a flight of golden stairs and disappearing over the top.

3
LEARNING TO WALK

It was late spring when, wrapped in a blanket in Father's arms, I looked out of the scullery window down at his tiny garden. Though I did not see there Primavera in person, with Venus, Cupid, Flora, Zephyr, and the Three Graces, as in Botticelli's picture, the prospect could hardly have been more delightful if I had. Pansies and marigolds, stocks and antirrhinums, looked up at me from their built-up bed at the far end of the yard. On the wire netting to the right hung red and yellow nasturtiums and the tiny stars of the virginia creeper. To the left, surrounded by pieces of crazy paving, stood a small pond, the dark waters of which showed every now and then a red-gold gleam as a goldfish rose to the surface. From the aviary I could hear the chirp and twitter of the green budgerigars.

Thereafter, instead of lying in bed, I spent the day reclining on a bed-chair in the kitchen, where I once again saw Nana and Auntie Noni, Auntie Kate and Auntie Jessie, and other visitors.

The next step was to get me up and walking. Since two doctors were of the opinion that if I attempted to stand I would immediately collapse, perhaps dying on the spot, this had to be managed with extreme caution. However, when at last I succeeded in standing on my own two feet I did not collapse. Instead, I sprained both ankles, since they were too weak to support me. Due to these sprains it was three weeks before I could renew the attempt; but renew it I did and eventually succeeded in standing, somewhat shakily, beside the bed-chair. As I seemed none the worse for the experiment, I was allowed to take a step or two. This I did clinging to the furniture and after a few weeks' practice could walk slowly across the room without much difficulty.

Seeing how pale my long confinement had made me, and being himself a great lover of the open air, Father bought an invalid chair and started taking me out in it on as many fine days as possible. Sometimes we went as far afield as Mitcham Common. On one such excursion, when Father was picking buttercups and cornflowers a short distance away, I saw a lizard sunning itself on the matted grass beneath a gorse-bush. Now I had always loved these little reptiles and before my illness had once or twice caught them on Wimbledon Common. The sight of this one, with his slim chocolate-brown body, cocked head, and beady eyes over which the thin secondary eyelid would every now and then be drawn, filled me with excitement. Forgetting my invalidism I leaped out of the chair and ran towards him. Father yelled a warning and rushed back, but by the time he reached me I was lying unconscious on the grass. This misadventure put me back into my room for several months, and when I emerged for the second time the whole procedure of standing up and learning to walk had to be repeated. Though our outings continued, and though I was permitted to walk about in the house, from that time onwards I could not so much as raise my hand quickly without an anxious voice immediately saying 'Be careful!' or 'Go slowly!'

As might have been foreseen, the intense love of art which I had imbibed from the art section of the *Children's Encyclopaedia* developed, by a natural transition, from passive enjoyment to active creation, and when I was neither being propelled over Mitcham Common by one parent nor pushed around Tooting Broadway by the other I would either draw or paint. My first drawing was an imaginary head of Cleopatra, complete with uraeus; the second, King George V in coronation robes. These were followed by sketches of Queen Elizabeth I, one of my favourite characters in history, whom I often drew, and of Mary Queen of Scots, both betraying the hand of the beginner in the face, but very carefully executed as to ruffs and stomachers, crowns and jewels. Early paintings included one of that old friend of my childhood the Chinese dragon, rampant in all the splendour of purple mane and crimson claw, an Egyptian landscape showing palm trees against a sunset on which I lavished all the reds and oranges and yellows in my paintbox, and portraits of King Henry VIII and his mother Elizabeth of York. These and other products of my joint devotion to art and history were shown to visitors and duly admired and the feeling became general that I was going to be an artist.

Despite his fear lest I should over-exert myself, Father never forgot his hope that I would one day be able, if not to leap and run, at least to walk like other boys. After a few months of divided allegiance to nature and art, I was allowed to spend more and more time on my feet and less and less in the wheel-chair, which eventually could be dispensed with altogether. I was even allowed to play in the street. This welcome improvement in my condition made a marked difference not to me only but to the whole family. We could all go to Southfields on Sunday afternoons. Mother and I could continue our long-interrupted trips to Fulham where, during my illness, Auntie Kate and Auntie Jessie had established themselves together in a new house. Nana and Auntie Noni could join us on visits to the Zoo. Best of all, my emancipation enabled us to revive the family custom of spending Sundays on Wimbledon Common.

After we had alighted from the bus, a leisurely walk across a mile of purple heather brought us to our favourite picnicking place. This was a grove of birch half a mile from the Windmill, the well-known shape of which was visible through the trees. All about us were other little birch groves, with here and there an oak. To the rear stood a small dark wood where the trees spread their branches above a dense undergrowth of bracken and cool green fern, and where the notes of birds sounded almost eerily in the stillness. Spreading out a groundsheet, we sat or lay in the hot sunshine, the scent of grass and clover in our nostrils and the humming of bees in our ears. Besides roaming in the wood, where snails with beautifully coloured shells could be picked from the underside of a rotting log, I had of course to keep up acquaintance with my old friends the lizards, catching two or three of them on every visit. Some were bottle green with black markings and yellow-green underparts; some fawn with brown markings and vermilion underparts; and some black with brown and white markings and cream underparts. Father constructed for them a box with sliding glass panels which I called the Lizardry.

Since I fed them several times a day they soon lost all fear of me. In fact I found them very easy to tame. Like most reptiles they liked to have their heads stroked and used to shut their eyes with pleasure whenever I gave them this satisfaction. Toads also had a great fascination for me. My favourite toad, whom I poked out of his hiding-place in the bole of an old tree, where I had seen his eyes shining in the darkness, learned to recognize my voice and would hobble out from behind his log whenever I called him.

Now that I was walking about my parents naturally started thinking it was time for me to return to school. After an absence of more than two years, therefore, I again went twice daily to the huge brick building down the street. By special permission of the headmistress, I arrived five minutes later than the other children and left five minutes earlier. This was to guard against my being bullied by boys who might have been tempted to take a mean advantage of my defencelessness. Though it was at first assumed that I was far behind the other pupils, I was admitted to the top class of the Junior Department, which most of the boys and girls who had been with me in the bottom class had now reached. Soon after my admission the half-yearly examinations were held. To everybody's astonishment the boy who had not attended school for so long stood twenty-first in a class of about forty. In the next examination I stood sixth and in the one after that came out top of the class, where I remained for the rest of my school career. On account of such precocity I speedily became a favourite with the headmistress, a tall, stout woman whose head was covered with tiny grey curls, and she allowed me to join the small group of children who sat at a table in the hall making rugs.

With my class mistress I was on even friendlier terms. Like her husband in the Senior Department upstairs, she had once taught Father. Though she was older than the headmistress, her hair was a glossy chestnut, and she wore dark blue or brown silk dresses with low V-necks. Whenever she lost her temper, which happened frequently, her face and neck would flush crimson to her very bosom. She it was who gave me such a distaste for Tennyson that it was years before I could enjoy him again. Every child in the class had to learn by heart a verse from 'The Lady of Shalott'. Mine was the one beginning 'She left the web, she left the loom.' Learning poetry by heart I did not mind very much. What hurt me was the way in which we had to chant it in unison, with an exaggerated stress on certain words.

She *left* the web, she *left* the loom,
She *made* THREEEE PACES THROUUUUUGH THE ROOM.

This was called giving expression to the poem.

Even worse was the way in which the worthy woman explained each verse.

'*Who* left the loom?' she would demand in ringing tones, sweeping the class with a fiery glance.

'Please, ma'am, the Lady of Shalott,' the small voice of one of the brighter pupils would dutifully reply.

'And *what* did she make?' No answer.

'WHAT did she make?' The V-neck was flushing dangerously. After a pause a hand would go up and a timid voice say, 'She made three paces.'

'Yes,' our teacher would boom with grim satisfaction, 'she made three paces THROUGH the room. And when she had made three paces THROUGH the room what did she do?'

This question would floor us and the danger-signal would start flashing again.

'She looked out of the window,' ventured someone at last.

'She did NOT look out of the window, you blockhead! Can't you read the poem? SHE LOOKED DOWN TO CAMELOT!!'

Thus the catechism would proceed. In this way we got through the whole poem in the course of about half a term. Probably most of the pupils could not have got through it in any other way; but I have sometimes felt that it might be better not to teach poetry at all than to teach it like this.

But for her sins against 'The Lady of Shalott' Mrs Ainsworth has long had my forgiveness. Like all the other teachers she was, despite her warm temper, a kind-hearted woman who had devoted the best part of forty years to a profession in which the labour is great and rewards few. In my progress and welfare she always took a keen interest. As a mark of special favour I was given the task of making tea for the teachers during the morning and afternoon breaks; for, not being allowed to run about in the playground with the other boys, I had in any case nothing to do. Several of the teachers used to provide out of their own meagre salaries midday meals, as well as clothes and shoes, for about a dozen very poor boys and girls, and I had sometimes to keep an eye on boiling peas and potatoes.

When a year had passed in this pleasant fashion I was promoted from the Junior to the Senior Department where, though classes were still mixed, we had masters instead of mistresses, it being no doubt assumed that we now needed a firmer hand.

Like Mrs Ainsworth downstairs and her husband, my new class teacher had taught Father, whom he still remembered. Smoky Joe, as the class affectionately called him (his name was William Smoker), had wavy iron-grey hair and a kind face with lean brown chaps and a humorous mouth. The most striking thing about his appearance, however, was his suits, which could be described only as loud. One was bright ginger, another deep mauve. Changes from one colour to another were of great interest to the class, and when he entered the classroom in a new suit, perhaps even louder than any of its predecessors, we would almost raise a cheer. His method of teaching was, I believe, very good. At least he treated us like intelligent beings who could be induced to understand rather than as morons who could at best be made to memorize. Occasionally he would bark at us, but he never became really angry and never called for the cane and punishment book more than once or twice a term. Though I was with him for only a year he occupies an honoured place in my history, for more than anyone else so far encountered did he encourage my interest in art and literature. To him I now started bringing the drawings and paintings which I was still industriously producing. Being art master for the whole Senior Department he was able to give me not only appreciation, which I never lacked, but hints in matters of technique, wherein I was very weak indeed. He also gave me the freedom of his cupboard, from which I used to borrow a book during breaks, encouraged me in the writing of essays, and gave me my first opportunity of addressing an audience.

At about the same time I developed a love of music. Our music master, a German with a portly figure and fine tenor voice, threw himself with gusto into the task of teaching us the songs of Purcell, Sullivan, and other composers, playing the piano with one hand while conducting with tremendous vigour with the other. My first experience of orchestral music came when all the pupils in the Senior Department were taken to a special children's concert at the Methodist Central Hall at Tooting Broadway. Before the concert began the conductor introduced each instrument in turn to the audience, after which he spoke to us about the compositions we were to hear. The overture *Fingal's Cave* made a deep impression on me, and from that afternoon I had, as it were, an orchestra playing in my brain. Between the orchestral items a stately soprano in an evening gown warbled arias. At the end of every song she descended the dozen or so steps of the rostrum with great dignity and sailed out through a side door. In acknowledgement of our prolonged applause she reappeared, ascended the rostrum, bowed and again descended and disappeared. Since our applause continued, this performance was repeated three or four times. I am sure she had never before had so many calls. But this was not so much because we had enjoyed the arias as because we wanted to see her ascend and descend the rostrum again. By the end of the afternoon the children, not one of whom had attended a concert before, were wildly enthusiastic.

The German music master, who had also played his part in making the concert a success, was very ardently pro-Nazi, and he and Smoky Joe, who was no less strongly anti-Nazi, had many a heated argument in the masters' common room, whence their loud angry voices could be heard down the corridor and even in the hall. This was, for me, the first rumbling of the approaching storm.

Useful though it was at break-time, Smoky Joe's cupboard was not the only source upon which I drew for books. Even before returning to school I had borrowed from the Tooting Public Library, using Father's ticket until I was old enough to join. One of the first books to be carried home was Donnelly's *Atlantis*, which opened for me yet another new world. But being still interested mainly in art, archaeology, and history, for some time I confined myself to John Addington Symonds's *The Renaissance in Italy* and Mandell Creighton's *History of the Papacy*, each in six or seven volumes, as well as to the bulky tomes of Mommsen and Maspero. Ancient Egypt and Renaissance Italy indeed cast a spell upon me, and for many months I had no time for any other places or periods.

About the same time that I was thus borrowing books, I started buying them. Ever since my recovery Father had regularly taken me to a curio shop at Clapham Common, not very far from my birthplace, and had sometimes bought curios for the small collection which, with Nana's help, I had begun to build up. On the way we used to pass a second-hand bookshop. Soon boxes and shelves of books, of all sorts and conditions, attracted me more powerfully than suits of armour and old china, and I started visiting the bookshop alone. For me at that time there was no greater adventure than a trip to Clapham Common with a shilling or two in my pocket for second-hand books.

Besides allowing us to spend our Sundays on Wimbledon Common, my emancipation from bed and bath chair made seaside holidays again possible. Our favourite resort was Shoreham, a former fishing village on the south coast, where we always stayed with the white-haired septuagenarian widow of a sea captain. With its heavy green plush tablecloth, and curtains of thick lace, Mrs Bareham's dining room was almost as old-fashioned as Auntie Kate's. All four walls were covered by photographs of sailing ships, portraits of the deceased sea captain and his son, and huge framed certificates of membership of the Order of Buffaloes, the captain having been many times president of the Shoreham Lodge, as yet another certificate testified. Every inch of space on the piano, the low cupboard, and the side tables, as well as all the little shelves on the many-tiered bamboo mantelpiece, was crowded with china bric-a-brac. Under a glass bell in the corner, standing side by side, were a large stuffed seagull and a child's doll.

On fine mornings we all sallied forth together after breakfast, Joan and I armed with our buckets and spades. Across the toll-bridge we went, along the mud-flats where dazzlingly white swans stood cleaning themselves with orange bills, past Bungalow Town with its stony gardens in which sea-thistle and red poppies grew between the pebbles, through the double row of bathing huts before which old sailors sat chewing tobacco on capsized boats, and down the scrunching pebbly slope that led to the beach. As we approached, the sea-breeze would blow more strongly in our faces, the smell of the ozone grow more unmistakable, the hush-hushing of the sea louder, until at last we saw, perhaps a quarter of a mile below the gently sloping flats of glistening grey sand, the long silvery line of the sea's edge. Afternoons were always spent on the Downs. But the place to which I resorted most often, and with the greatest delight, was the square-towered Norman church, where I spent hours in the churchyard deciphering the barely legible inscriptions on the tombstones.

What my parents thought of my enthusiasm for old churches I do not know, but it had its roots in something deeper than mere archaeological interest. As I stood within their ancient walls, on the spot where, century after century, hearts and voices had been lifted up in prayer and thanksgiving to the Highest, and saw the light slanting red, blue, yellow and green through the stained glass window above the altar, I felt myself breathing an atmosphere of holiness, purity, and peace as tangible as the stones of which the place was built. Whether at Shoreham or Chichester, Norwich or Westminster, thereafter I never missed an opportunity of visiting the shrines of England.

4
'HERE COMES THE BOYS' BRIGADE'

A few weeks after we had returned, sunburnt and happy, from one of the Shoreham holidays, we left the old house where I had spent all the eleven years of my life, and moved to a semi-detached council house on the Streatham side of Tooting.

The removal took place in early autumn. What afterwards became father's garden, complete with lawn, flower-beds, and vegetable plot, was then a wilderness. Large yellow-green leaves from the old fig tree behind the house carpeted the ground. Weeds grew shoulder high. Halfway down the garden, which was more than a hundred feet long, stood a line of ragged blackcurrant bushes, round which Joan and I were soon playing cowboys and Indians. At the far end, underneath the back fence, was a rhubarb bed. Along the fence on the left grew loganberries which had not been pruned for years. But best of all I remember the chrysanthemums, which grew red and yellow and bronze all over the garden. So many of them there were that all that autumn the air was filled with their acrid scent. Indeed, whether because I had never seen chrysanthemums growing in such profusion before, or because there is a subtle relation between scents and moods, or because they symbolized something I felt but could not express, those frost-bitten blossoms growing so rankly in the neglected garden were one of the major emotional experiences of my life.

One afternoon, not long after our removal, Joan and I heard Mother excitedly calling out to us from the front gate. A strange red glare overspread the whole south-eastern horizon and was reflected above the housetops far up into the sky, where it shaded off into an angry pink. Every now and then a flame would leap up or a wisp of smoke drift black across the crimson. As we watched the glow, which certainly came from no common house fire, icy fingers of fear for a moment touched our hearts. That evening we learned that the Crystal Palace had been burned to the ground.

The following spring I wrote my first poems. The actual writing of them I do not remember, but I quite clearly recall handing a certain red notebook over the fence to the plump, pigtailed girl next door whom I had told about the poems. With this girl, as well as with her elder sister and younger brother, I had become friends during the winter. My parents had become acquainted with hers. Norah's mother, a Somerset woman, was a paragon of respectability. On Sabbath mornings, sedate in her Sunday best, she could be seen sallying forth to the Methodist Central Hall, which she also attended during the week, being very prominent at prayer meetings and flower shows. Norah and Peter usually accompanied her. At home the children were allowed to play only hymns on the piano. They were frequently scolded, and Joan and I often heard the whack of a cane, followed by a shriek, from the other side of the fence. Norah's father, who was in the police force, fared no better. A hulking, red-faced fellow, he was always being driven out of the house with a broomstick by his plump, pious wife, whose terms of endearment as she thwacked him were clearly audible. After she had withdrawn, slamming the back door shut behind her, he would go and sit beside the chained watch-dog, who, also being regularly beaten, would wag its tail in silent sympathy. In this domestic warfare the children took sides, Norah and Peter supporting their mother, and Phyllis, the eldest, their father. Even at that time Phyllis bitterly hated her mother and as she grew older did her best to defend the pusillanimous policeman from the onslaughts of Methodism militant, sometimes carrying the war into the enemy's camp. With all three children Joan and I were on friendly terms and thus it happened that Norah, who was the nearest to me in age, came to be reading my poems that spring.

What I was reading at this time I do not know. Perhaps most of my time was devoted to painting. Certainly it was in the course of the same year that my parents, for the first and last time, discussed the advisability of sending me to an art school. The seventeen-year-old daughter of one of Mother's friends studied at the Slade School of Fine Art and one day she sent me, through Mother, a portfolio of life-drawings. They were all male and female nudes, complete with carefully drawn genitals. Mother and Father seem to have decided that such studies might not be good for my morals, for, though I drew and painted as industriously as ever, there was no more talk of sending me to an art school.

That Christmas I met with a book that swung me, almost violently, from art to literature. Among the presents at my bedside on Christmas morning was a blue-bound copy of *Paradise Lost*, the title of which had stood high on my latest book list. That morning I had the greatest poetic experience of my life. If it was the reading of Spenser that made a poet of Keats, it was that apocalypse of Miltonic sublimity that made of me, from that day onwards, if not a poet yet at least a modest practitioner of the art of verse. Thereafter I knew no rest until I had planned an epic of my own. What the subject was I do not know, but I remember that it was in blank verse divided stanza-like into blocks of nine lines each and opened with the appearance of a very Miltonic angel in my bedroom. Other poets whom I read, admired, and imitated included Keats, Mrs Browning, and Housman. The first I read in a little pink leather and gilt volume of selections, enjoying most of all the sonnets and the descriptions of Circe from *Endymion* and of the deposed Saturn from *Hyperion*. Mrs Browning's *A Drama of Exile* and *The Lay of the Brown Rosary* I admired inordinately, chanting the latter aloud in my delight to the four walls of my bedroom. Many of the lyrics of *A Shropshire Lad* also made a strong appeal to me, especially the one beginning

> Loveliest of trees, the cherry now
> Is hung with bloom along the bough,[11]

which seemed almost the last word in consummate beauty of expression. Rossetti's poems I knew, at that time, only by the quotations in William Sharp's study of the poet,[12] but meagre as these were the intensely fused sensuousness and mysticism of which they breathed went to my head like some subtle and dangerous perfume. For many years Milton and Rossetti were my favourite poets.

Hard on the heels of my epic, of which I wrote only 900 lines, came a medieval drama with 'chanters' (borrowed from Thomas Hardy?)

and a whole succession of lyrics. Nor was prose neglected. The same period saw the beginning of a 'History of the Reign of Queen Elizabeth', of which I wrote twenty or thirty foolscap pages, a short story about Ancient Egypt in the style of Joan Grant's *Winged Pharaoh*, and 'The Life of Siddhartha Gautama the Buddha' which when finished I copied out in purple ink on my best notepaper.

Meanwhile at school, which I continued to attend, though having a much longer walk every day than before, the curriculum had been disrupted by several events of interest. The first of these had transformed me into a pirate. Included in the Senior Department's Christmas entertainment was a staging of Gilbert and Sullivan's *The Pirates of Penzance*, the rehearsals for which kept us busy for several months. Though I had played Sir Walter Raleigh in an Empire Day playlet while in the Juniors, as well as acted the part of Shylock, in which I had drawn much applause by the way I sharpened my knife on the sole of my foot as I declared 'I will have my pound of flesh,' this was the first time I had ever been a pirate. Mother and Father feared the excitement might upset my heart, especially as in one scene the chorus of pirates had to dance a few steps, kicking their legs into the air as they did so. Moreover, on the day of the performance, which was attended by parents, I did not get to bed till one o'clock. However, I was none the worse for the experiment with piracy.

Another disruption was caused by the Golden Jubilee celebrations of the LCC, in which all London schools naturally participated. Our contribution was a topography of south-west London, a subject in which Smoky Joe had done a considerable amount of research. The topography was written page by page on the blackboard from which it was painfully copied by all the children in the class, Smoky Joe having told us that the neatest copy would be sent to the Jubilee exhibition at County Hall. Among other topographical facts I learned that Tooting was named after one Tut, an Anglo-Saxon chief who had sailed up the River Wandle (whence Wandsworth, the name of our borough) and founded a settlement; that Tooting Bec was so called from the Abbey of Bec in Normandy, to which lands there had been gifted shortly after the Conquest; that Nelson had been born at Merton and that Daniel Defoe had worshipped in a Dissenting Chapel at Clapham. When, later on, we were taken to the exhibition, I saw my copy of the topography, finely bound, occupying the place of honour in the middle of the hall.

The last of the disruptive events is hardly on the same scale as its predecessors, though it had consequences which to me were not unimportant. For this one Smoky Joe was in a way responsible. While he corrected the exercise books on Friday afternoons it was my task to speak to the class. One day I spoke on 'My Curios', which by that time included a blue silk Chinese robe embroidered with carp and lotuses, a pair of ivory chopsticks complete with knife and silver toothpicks in a silver-mounted ivory case, bamboo nose-ornaments from Borneo, a thunderbolt, pieces of gum tree (all gifts from Nana), a Chinese monkey with a bag on his back, a little old woman carrying loads, a teak bat carved with peacocks, two halberds from the Tower of London, two Chinese executioner's swords in green leather scabbards, a sixteenth-century Dutch tile depicting Jacob's Ladder, a Moroccan dagger, a Song Dynasty bowl, precious and semi-precious stones (all from Father), an Indian wire bracelet, a rosary, and sundry foreign coins (from other sources). There was also a small brass incense burner in the shape of the famous Kamakura Buddha, bought at a Brighton curio shop with my own money, in which I regularly burned sticks of very sweet incense – my first act of Buddhist worship. Smoky Joe asked me to turn the substance of my talk into an essay, and it was this essay which, on its being shown to a visiting inspector, led to my being transferred to a better school.

The institution in which I now found myself was, of course, better than my old school in the opinion of my parents and teachers, in fact of the world generally; but not necessarily in mine. The real source of my education was still the Tooting Public Library. But I donned without protest the uniform of the new school – green cap and blazer with grey flannel trousers – and every day made the slightly longer journey to and from its more exclusive precincts.

On the day of my admission the headmaster sent me to join my class, where a history lesson was in progress. All the double desks were full except two, one of which contained a very blonde girl with roses-and-cream complexion and china-blue eyes, while in the other sat a swarthy girl with black hair and brown eyes. These, as I afterwards found, were the beauties of the class and inseparable friends. Seeing my hesitation, the master called out good-humouredly, 'Take your choice! Which of these two young ladies would you prefer to sit beside?' There was a general titter from the class; the fair one blushed, the dark one smiled.

'If they sit together I can have a desk to myself,' I replied. This arrangement was quite satisfactory to the two beauties who had, before my entrance, been separated for talking during the lesson, and I accordingly took my seat at the desk which the fair one promptly vacated.

Despite the fact of my being two years behind in the course, the headmaster had decided that I should join a class higher than that to which my age entitled me. In the subjects which interested me most, history, English, and art, I at once went to the top. In mathematics, which I hated, I stayed somewhere near the bottom. Physics, French, shorthand, typing, and bookkeeping were all new to me, but I soon caught up with my classmates. Chemistry, also a new subject, I disliked; but the crusty old chemistry master, a great rapper on knuckles with the ruler, fortunately was much more a stickler for copperplate handwriting, and neatness in the illustration of experiments, than he was for knowledge of chemistry, and always gave me good marks.

Being still excused games, I spent the games period in the art room. The art master, a small, grey-headed man in sweater and sandals who flirted with the girl students and swore at the boys, was not just an ordinary teacher who 'took art' but a real artist, the first I ever met. 'Bloody Christ!' he would mutter whenever a student submitted a drawing, 'What do you call this?' With him I soon became well acquainted, sometimes contriving, with his connivance, to be sketching in the art room when I should have been doing geometry elsewhere. He was good enough to correct my drawings, showing me exactly how to make an eye gleam or a petal look soft, things which even Smoky Joe had not taught me.

Even more interesting was a teacher who joined the staff after I had started attending the school, and left before we were evacuated. He was a short, well-built, youngish man with flaming red hair, red moustache, and red beard. Apparently he had only three interests or enthusiasms in life: George Bernard Shaw, atheism, and chess. Thanks to him we read, that is to say listened to, perhaps a dozen of G. B. S.'s plays. During the history period he read *Caesar and Cleopatra* or *St Joan*, during geography *The Devil's Disciple*, presumably because its action takes place in the wide open spaces of America, and the rest of Shaw's works during English lessons and on Friday afternoons. In my case this unorthodox method of instruction proved entirely successful.

Though I have long since forgotten everything else I learned that year, the memory of these marathon reading sessions, when on hot summer afternoons we had only to sit and listen while he read steadily through the two stout volumes of the Collected Plays, is still fresh and vivid. Atheism was generally inculcated during the morning scripture lessons which, being nominally a member of the Church of England, he was obliged to take. Chess came in the afternoon, during the last period, and usually continued long after the rest of the school had gone home to tea. Playing twenty or thirty boys simultaneously, moving in a matter of seconds from one board to the next, he invariably defeated us all. Alas! after a few months he was transferred to another school, whether because of the scripture lessons, or because his appointment had only been a temporary one, we never knew.

With my fellow students I had very little personal contact. Except for my best friend Clement, who was only six months older than I was, all the other boys in the class were senior to me by two years, and the meaningless obscenity of their conversation disgusted me. Besides, shortly after our removal to the new house, I had joined the Boys' Brigade, and for the next four years membership of this organization fully satisfied my gregarious instincts.

At six o'clock one cold November evening, when it had already been dark for more than an hour, Mother and I found ourselves looking, from the opposite side of the road, at the as yet unlit hall in which Brigade meetings were held. Seeing our hesitation, a sixteen-year-old sergeant, in the blue and white Brigade uniform, detached himself from the group of boys talking at the gate and coming over to us asked if he could be of any assistance. Before many weeks had passed I was as keen a member as any in the company. Meetings were held several times a week and I was never absent. On Fridays there were the weekly parades, for which brasses had to be cleaned, leather polished, and piping whitened. After the inspection we were drilled, going through such simple manoeuvres as marching up and down the hall, turning about, halting, and forming fours. All meetings opened and closed with prayer.

The 'officers' who drilled us consisted of the captain of the company, a lieutenant, and two staff officers. The captain, whom the regular members called Skipper, was a short, flaxen-haired, brisk little man who worked for a well-known shipping line, on whose behalf he occasionally attended shipping conferences in Rome, Amsterdam, and other places.

Besides being our captain, he was superintendent of the Sunday school and held various offices in the Baptist church to which we were attached. The lieutenant, known to us as Reg, and the two young staff officers, brothers who had been christened Roland and Oliver, were all teachers in the Sunday school, Reg being, in addition, a sidesman of the church. In due course I started attending not only the parades but also the Sunday morning Bible class, the Wednesday evening prayer meeting, the Thursday evening Morse and semaphore class, and the Monday evening band practice, at which I thumped a side drum.

The company was a small one, never more than sixty strong. Like similar groups the world over, it had a hard core of enthusiasts who could be relied upon to turn up for all meetings with the regularity of clockwork. One of the reasons for which I became one of the band of fifteen or twenty stalwarts whose unflagging devotion it was that, next to the zeal of the captain and officers, kept the company going, was that it satisfied my natural human craving to belong to a group. Another was that the strongly ethical tone of the BB, as we affectionately referred to our organization, with its emphasis on clean living, team spirit, sense of responsibility, service, and fear of God, struck chords in my heart which even poetry and painting were powerless to vibrate. This was all the more the case inasmuch as I saw the qualities of which the BB thought so highly exemplified not only in Skipper and the officers but also, to a lesser degree, in many of the boys. For the latter, therefore, I had a far stronger feeling of brotherhood than for my foul-mouthed associates at school.

But the strongest reason for the almost fanatical punctiliousness with which I discharged the obligations of membership was the one of which I was then least aware. Among the members was a friendly, affable, good-looking boy about two years senior to me, and for him I at once developed an ardent affection. This early love, to which I remained faithful throughout the whole of my BB career, as well as for some time afterwards, was one of those dumb adolescent attachments which nobody seems to notice, least of all its object. If on raw winter evenings, when more often than not it was raining, or even snowing, I hastened through the dimly lit streets with eagerly beating heart, it was not only because of the thought of the cheery voices that would greet me as I entered the brightly lit hall, but with the hope of seeing, and fear of not seeing, that dearest of all faces. Since Sid was as faithful a member as I was, I rarely had to suffer the pangs of disappointment.

But though we met several times a week and were on the best of terms we never became close friends. Strangely enough, this was a deprivation which I never felt. Being utterly happy merely to see his face and hear his voice, it never occurred to me to desire a more intimate relationship.

In accordance with the constitution of the movement, which had been founded as a means of encouraging young men and boys to lead Christian lives, every company of the BB was attached to a church, the priest or minister in charge of which became the honorary 'colonel'. The Baptist church to which our company belonged was a fairly new, red brick building, complete with steeple, which stood facing Mitcham Lane about half a mile from the top of the road down which I lived. On the opposite corner, also facing Mitcham Lane, stood the Anglican Parish Church. The congregation which filled the red-brick building on Sunday mornings and evenings consisted mainly of prosperous artisans, small shopkeepers, white-collar workers, and other representatives of the petty bourgeoisie from Lower Streatham. During the years in which I was a member of the BB it had as its pastor a man of deep and fervent piety and great preaching ability. Thanks to his ministrations, as well as to the labours of the more devoted of the laity, the congregation grew steadily and the church flourished.

The close connection which existed between the BB and the churches to which the companies were affiliated encouraged, and indeed was intended to encourage, a more active participation on the part of its members in organized religious life. In my case the progression from the church hall, in which Friday evening parades were held, to the church itself, occurred quite naturally. Our Sunday morning Bible class began at ten o'clock and lasted an hour. We sang hymns of the more virile type such as 'Onward Christian Soldiers', sat with bowed heads through extempore prayers, and listened to a talk of the jocular-muscular variety by Skipper. When these proceedings were over I strolled into church with the other boys as a matter of course, taking my place with them in the gallery, where I sat near Sid.

Below us, at the far end of the church, was a huge pulpit, the size of a small room, from which the pastor not only preached but conducted the service. On either side of this structure were the choir stalls; in front of it was the Lord's Table, whereon always stood a vase of flowers; behind it, the organ. From the back rows of the gallery, where the BB usually sat, only the first two rows of the downstairs pews were visible.

Though we sometimes yawned and fidgeted during the long sermon, the BB boys always conducted themselves with proper reverence.

In the gallery I met Mr Young, the elderly stonemason in a very stiff white collar who was sidesman for that part of the church. As he gave each of us in turn a handshake and a hymn-book, his deeply lined face lit up with a warm smile. He and Skipper, who was a member of the choir, were both firm believers in the necessity of making a joyful noise before the Lord, and during the singing of the hymns their two voices, raised as in competition, would be heard high above the lusty voices of the rest of the congregation. Mr Young always prolonged the concluding note of each verse much longer than anyone else, frequently ending with a screech that was apt to be rather disconcerting to the newcomer.

He it was, I believe, who invited me to attend the Sunday school, where I joined his class, of which Sid and a few other boys were already members. For some reason or other he took the keenest interest in my spiritual welfare and with great conviction told the rest of the class that the Lord had chosen me out for a great work. Being as he was a Bible Christian of the fundamentalist type, his interest took the form of strong encouragement in the prayerful study of the Word of God. Every quarter he gave me a little book of daily Bible readings of which I regrettably made less use than he had hoped. Occasionally he called on me at home, where he met Father and Mother, who respected him very much for his rugged, almost gnarled and knotted, piety. After my evacuation he sent me the Bible readings by post.

Another member of the church who, though for a shorter period, wrought for me in the Lord, was a plump, almost burly youth of eighteen or nineteen with crinkly hair and a suave, soft manner, called Ben. His attack on the problem of salvation was not quite so frontal as that of my older preceptor. Having started a boys' club, where we played table tennis on Wednesday evenings, he invited two or three of the more promising members at a time to his house for tea. After a substantial repast, over which his mother presided, we found ourselves, one by one, on our knees in the drawing room, with Ben, also on his knees, loudly praying beside us. When his prayer, in which he offered up our sinful souls to Jesus, was over, we had to offer them up on our own behalf. In this workmanlike manner he converted a number of boys, for having eaten his excellent tea we felt it would not be good manners to refuse to be saved.

Besides Sunday school and the club, I attended, for a time, the prayer meeting for young men which was held weekly in the vestry. This was the sort of evangelical equivalent of a confirmation class, though here less emphasis was placed on doctrine than on devotion and it was hoped that some, at least, of those who attended would become active church members.

One of the main functions of these meetings was to encourage us in the practice of extempore prayer, to which the Baptists, like most dissenting churches, attached great importance. Kneeling on the ground before our chairs, on the seats of which we rested our elbows, we prayed aloud in turn in such words as we were able to muster. Most of the boys, if not all, borrowed the pious phraseology of their elders, and, with a little practice, were able to offer up prayers with the same unfeeling facility with which they wrote essays at school.

Hymns were sung to the accompaniment of a rather ancient piano harmonium, which Sid was always glad of an opportunity to play, and there was a Bible reading. Either Reg or Mr Young usually spoke, but once we studied Bunyan's *Holy War* for several weeks in succession with a speaker from another church. On one occasion our own pastor addressed us on the imminence of the Second Coming and Last Judgement, speaking with such eloquent earnestness that I could not help glancing out of the open window at the peaceful summer evening sky, half expecting to see there angels descending in the van of the Lord.

Yet despite membership of the BB, regular attendance at church and Sunday school, and frequent prayer meetings, the development of my religious convictions was not really influenced at all. This was due partly to the very nature of Baptist Christianity itself, which made not reason but the emotions its chief target, and partly to the fact that I had started thinking for myself in matters of religion. Only once did I have a serious argument. This occurred at one of the vestry prayer meetings, when a boy of my own age maintained that salvation was by faith alone and I declared it was by faith and works. Usually I was satisfied with a temporary emotional exaltation, returning home after a particularly moving sermon with my heart on fire with devotion to the Person of Christ. But at night, when I said my prayers, I still said them, as my habit was at that period, to the Buddha, Christ, and Mohammed in turn, it being my naive conviction that by this means I should be sure of gaining the ear of whoever happened to be the true saviour.

5
EVACUATED

3 September 1939 was a Sunday. As usual we sang hymns and listened to prayers in the Bible class, afterwards filing into church where, after exchanging a few words with Mr Young, we took our customary seats in the gallery. Only one hymn, I think, had been sung when a sidesman ascended the pulpit steps and handed the pastor a slip of paper. Slowly rising to his feet, the pastor announced, not the number of the next hymn, but the fact that our country was at war with Germany. Adding that members of the congregation would no doubt wish to return as quickly as possible to their homes, with a short prayer and a blessing he dismissed us. As we left the church the first air raid warning sounded.

The emotion which filled my heart as I hurried home was neither fear nor sorrow, but exhilaration. Now that the worst had happened the misery of suspense was ended, and it was with something like exultation that I felt my own insignificant life, like a straw on a stream, being gripped by the irresistible current of national events and swept I knew not whither.

For a year Father and the men of his generation had been accustoming themselves to the thought that the war they had fought to end all wars, to ensure peace to their sons and their sons' sons for ever, had failed. For a second time the lights were going out all over Europe.

At home, at Southfields, and at Ewell, where Father's step-brother Uncle Charles now lived with his wife Auntie Kath, there were anxious family conferences. During the Crisis, in September 1938, the tension had been unbearable, though when Chamberlain stepped with a tired smile from the aeroplane at Hendon waving a piece of paper the general feeling, in our family at least, had been not only one of relief but of defeat. Like many other women, Auntie Kath wrote Mr Chamberlain a letter of thanks and hysterical adulation, receiving in due course a courteous reply. But as the months went by gas masks were issued, Anderson shelters dug in back gardens, and sandbags stacked in front of the doors and windows of public buildings. The BB started a first aid class, Father joined the ARP as a stretcher-bearer, and Joan was evacuated to a farm near Chichester.

During the first few weeks of the war all was in turmoil. But as weeks, then months, slipped by without anything happening, the life of the nation seemed to return from a state of emergency to something very much like normality, and the initial feeling of exhilaration began to subside into one of boredom. Gas masks, which we at first religiously took with us wherever we went, buying fancy cases for them to replace the original plain cardboard box, were left at home in cupboards. Father complained that at the ARP headquarters, where he was on duty day and night, there was little to do except play cards in the canteen. As for me, the greater part of the school having been evacuated to safer parts of the country in the previous March and August, I had only skeleton classes to attend twice or thrice a week. Since nothing was taught but algebra and trigonometry I soon ceased to attend them, and with the help of Cardinal Newman and Dr Johnson, Sir Francis Bacon, Heine and the Greek tragic poets, devoted myself more seriously than ever to the task of self-education.

By the summer of 1940 the war had entered its second phase, and it became clear that London would soon know the horrors of aerial bombardment. Fresh arrangements were made for the evacuation of schools and Father insisted that this time I must go.

After a seven-hour journey the train stopped at about three o'clock in the afternoon at Barnstaple, a small town in north Devon. Clement and I, who had resolved to stick together, were taken to the Vicarage, a large house in the best part of the town. From what could be heard of the billeting officers' talk, as they discussed the allocation of evacuees, we gathered that the most difficult part of their work that afternoon would be to find a brace of boys acceptable to Mrs Smith, the Vicar's aunt. Clement and I were selected as the least likely to give her any trouble.

In view of what we had overheard it was not without qualms that we followed the billeting officer through the iron gate, up the pathway through the very neglected garden, to the blue and white building that was to be our home.

Before many days had passed we had settled down at the Vicarage and were being treated almost as members of the family which, for such a big house, was a very small one. The Vicar, who in his college days had played rugby, was a very tall, powerfully built man with thinning iron-grey hair and pallid, puffy face which, in contrast to his black suit, showed hardly less white than his clerical collar. Once he had dealt with a truculent beggar by lifting him by the seat of his trousers and the scruff of his neck and throwing him bodily over the front gate. Mrs Smith, his aunt, was a tiny, sharp-tongued woman of seventy-two who was living, so she declared, with only half a lung. Extremely witty and very fond of repartee, she quickly took a liking to me, for, unlike the Vicar, who merely listened with a smile, I could not only take her catches but return them. Poor Clement, a frank, honest, open-hearted youth who blushed easily, she did not particularly like, for though well-mannered he was clumsy in the extreme and whenever she directed her witticisms against him he became embarrassed and confused. To such an extent, indeed, did she succeed in entangling him in his own words that once, when he had something of moment to impart, he first wrote it out and then read it aloud to her in the kitchen like a speech, a procedure which set the mischievous old creature's eyes twinkling in amusement.

Mr Smith, the Vicar's uncle, was a small choleric old gentleman, almost completely bald, who, even with the aid of a stick, moved about with extreme difficulty. He liked to talk about his experiences during the Great War when he had been a special constable in the East End of London. If half the stories he told us were true, it was much more dangerous to walk the streets of Bermondsey after dark than to wander alone in Darkest Africa. At any rate he had sufficient confidence in the ferocity of the female East Enders to declare, with a chuckle, that the best method of executing Hitler would be to let half a dozen of them tear him to pieces with their fingernails – a suggestion of which the prudent Vicar neither approved nor disapproved.

The only other member of the family was the cook, Mrs Levy, a plump, raven-haired Jewess whose husband, an architect, had died in a Nazi concentration camp. She was a cultured woman and talked to me about German literature. Sometimes, not without tears, she spoke of her murdered husband and of the beautiful home from which they had been driven by the Gestapo. Clement, who was very fond of children, used to play with her daughter Sybil, aged five, who soon became very attached to him. But one day Mrs Smith's short temper and sharp tongue proved too much for the overworked refugee woman and after a painful scene she indignantly departed with Sybil in a taxi, taking her luggage with her in seventeen suitcases. The mode of her conveyance and the number of her suitcases scandalized Mrs Smith, who was, apparently, accustomed to servants leaving on foot with small bundles. 'Seventeen suitcases!' she exclaimed, shaking her white head in horrified amazement, 'Whoever heard of a servant having seventeen suitcases!'

Besides being allocated to billets, the evacuees were distributed among the Barnstaple schools, in whose overcrowded classrooms we now pursued our studies. Partly because of its unfamiliarity, partly because my own reading was so far in advance of the curriculum, I developed a hearty dislike for the school which Clement and I attended. The only master (there were no mistresses) I found in the least sympathetic was the art master. In his classroom, where I also learned bookbinding, I spent my happiest hours. There it was that I produced what was to be my last work of art, an ink drawing of Herod on his throne and Salome kneeling before him with the head of John the Baptist on a trencher. The fact that the nipples on Salome's breasts were clearly delineated gave the Barnstaple boys cause for obscene comment; but the art master, who had doubtless seen such things before, paid no more and no less attention to them than to the rest of the picture, which he commended highly.

Life at the Vicarage, though certainly neither austere nor puritanical, was naturally rather staid. Amusements were few, though in a moment of abandon Mrs Smith once suggested that we might play croquet with her on the lawn. At five o'clock in the afternoon, when school was finished for the day and we had had tea, Clement and I, now inseparable, used to escape down the road into the countryside. On Sunday mornings we accompanied Mrs Smith to church, where the Vicar conducted the service and preached. Whether due to the modest vestments, or to the murmured plainchant, or to the fact that the Vicar was by ordination a successor of the Apostles of old, I perceived in the little Anglican church an atmosphere of sacredness which in the Baptist church, for all its cheerful piety, I had never felt.

During our first week at the Vicarage Clement and I had been allowed to listen to news broadcasts, for having relatives in London we were naturally anxious to know whether they were likely to be in danger or not. As the news became daily more ominous, however, we had to leave the dining room a few minutes before these broadcasts began. Mr and Mrs Smith probably wished to spare us the shock of hearing of any sudden reverse. But one day, as soon as the eight o'clock broadcast was over, they called us back to the dining room and with serious faces and solemn voices broke to us, as though it had been the death of a near relative, the news of the fall of France.

> Another deadly blow!
> Another mighty Empire overthrown!
> And We are left, or shall be left, alone;
> The last that dare to struggle with the Foe.
> 'Tis well![13]

Clement and I had not been able to follow the vicissitudes of the War very closely, for the Smiths had interdicted newspapers as well as broadcasts; but we could understand that what had happened was an unparalleled catastrophe. Even had we failed to understand, Mr Churchill's famous 'blood, toil, tears, and sweat' speech, broadcast a few days later, would have convinced us that our country's plight was even more disastrous than it was in November 1806, during the Napoleonic Wars, when Wordsworth wrote his sonnet – more disastrous than it had been for a thousand years.

Nevertheless, living as I did as much in imagination as reality, I was at that time no less concerned with a war that had been fought 3,000 years earlier than the one in which I was personally involved. Clement and I had discovered a stationer's shop which not only stocked new books but displayed outside its door a caseful of second-hand volumes. My first bargain was Chapman's Homer's *Iliad*. Though the poem had long been familiar to me in prose translation, and though I knew all the episodes, it was a new poem that burst upon me that afternoon as I sat out in the brilliantly sunlit garden reading the glorious old fourteeners in the shade of an ash willow. My second bargain was the First Part of Goethe's *Faust*, which produced on me an effect so tremendous, and awoke echoes at a depth so profound, that I was quite unable to analyse its nature and say in what the effect consisted.

We had been exactly one month at the Vicarage and I was beginning to feel at home, when Mrs Smith broke to us, very gently, the news that we were being transferred to another billet. A week before there had occurred an incident which might have had something to do with this unexpected change. One morning, at the time we usually left for school, the rain was streaming down so heavily that Clement and I, who had neither raincoats nor umbrellas, decided that we had better remain at home. When, later in the morning, Mr Smith discovered that we were still in the house he became furiously angry and, with dreadful imprecations for being 'afraid of a little rain', drove us out into the downpour with his stick. On our arrival at school half an hour later, drenched by the storm, we reported the matter to the headmaster, who, seeing how wet we were, sent us back. Whether or not this unpleasant incident was the real cause for our having to leave the Vicarage, all that Mrs Smith told us was that since they now had no servant and had to do all the housework themselves – even the Vicar helping to dry the dishes – and since she had, as we knew, only half a lung, it was impossible for them to look after us any longer.

My first memory of our new billet is of our eating eggs and bacon in the kitchen and the landlady, a thin sharp-featured woman of forty with lank black hair, saying 'It's better than what they gave you at the Vicarage, I'll warrant,' for being a good Wesleyan she had all the chapelgoer's hatred for the Church. Clement, who felt much more at ease than he had done for a long time, wishing to please her heartily agreed, thus winning a grim smile. But I, unwilling to abet in this way any impeachment of the hospitality of our late hosts, remained silent. This did not satisfy Mrs Williams, who repeated her remark, which this time received a non-committal reply.

The four-roomed house in which I now spent my second month as an evacuee was situated in a working-class district on the outskirts of the town. At the end of the little street, behind a heap of slag, lay two or three green fields, the tip of a tongue of countryside that protruded into the urban area. Across these fields Clement and I walked every day to school, which backed on to the green strip. Through the fields meandered a stream. Tall bulrushes and water-flags grew on its banks, where I always lingered to look into the dark waters for the big brown fishes which could sometimes be seen gently moving their fins above the mud.

Since the house was small, with neither front nor back garden, we were allowed to go out more freely than had been the case at the Vicarage. On Saturdays Clement and I used to spend the day at Bideford, a large town twelve miles from Barnstaple. Since I was saving my pocket money to buy books, and since Clement had spent all his buying ice-creams for the landlady's two small boys – thus winning more grim smiles and the remark that he, at least, was not mean with his money – we walked the whole distance. On our first visit, which had taken place in our Vicarage days, I had located a second-hand bookshop. Here we spent the whole of every visit, though Clement would doubtless have preferred to see a football match or wander about the town. What delighted me most about it was the number of eighteenth-century calfskin quartos and folios, especially the folio Shakespeare in a dozen or more volumes. Confused and excited by this profusion of riches, I hurried from shelf to shelf, and from room to room, unable to open one book without being immediately attracted by another. When, at five o'clock, it was time to depart, I hastily made my purchases hardly knowing what I was buying.

I also joined the Barnstaple Public Library, which, judging from the number of eighteenth-century editions it contained, must have been originally a private collection. Here I found Johnson's *Works* edited by Arthur Murphy in twelve or thirteen leather-bound volumes, on which I greedily seized. Such was my devotion to my hero that I not only read *The Rambler* and *The Adventurer*, which I admired inordinately, but even his tragedy *Irene*, the verses of which stuck like glue. Since I now devoured collected works and multi-volume editions with ease, I also set to work on Hoole's *Orlando Furioso*, reading a volume a day till it was finished. So omnivorous was my intellectual appetite at this period that one Sunday I read, in addition to the usual instalment of Hoole, Diderot's *Memoirs of a Nun* and all seven of Aeschylus' tragedies. At this time I was utterly devoid of discrimination. Every book I read thrilled and captivated me and left upon my mind a vivid impression.

One day Mrs Williams took us by bus to the coastal town of Ilfracombe, where she had once lived with her first husband, a seven-foot giant who committed suicide. After wandering the narrow streets that ran up and down the cliff face, I plunged into the nearest second-hand bookshop, emerging a couple of hours later with Boswell's *Life of Johnson*, an illustrated book on Rossetti as a painter, and a leather bound duodecimo volume dated 1723, in Latin and English, entitled *The Secret Instructions of the Jesuits*. Perhaps it was at Ilfracombe that I also bought *Religio Medici* and *Hydriotaphia*, which I admired so much that I imitated the second of them in an essay entitled 'Of Tombs and Sepultures'. This, apart from an abortive attempt to imitate Hardy, was the sole literary product of my sojourn at Barnstaple, which was about to end.

Kindled by the incident of the eggs and bacon and aggravated by the incident of the ice-cream, Mrs Williams's dislike for me had grown more bitter every week. She disliked my preoccupation with books, which she thought unnatural, my manner of speaking, which she jeeringly said was more like that of a man of forty than a boy of fourteen, and my habit of not spending money – except on books, which to her way of thinking was no better than not spending it at all. The thought that though I had ten shillings in my purse I would not spend one penny of it on sweets or ice-cream, either for myself or others, infuriated her. One day her dislike flared into open resentment. During tea Reggie, the older of her two young sons, a boy of eleven who naturally took his cue from his mother, spoke to me with such insolent rudeness that, unable to bear the affront, I made him a sharp retort. Mrs Williams's eyes flashed. 'No 'vacuee is going to talk to my son like that,' she declared, after saying exactly what she thought of me. It was not her cold, hard anger that rankled with me so much as the way in which she spat out the term ''vacuee' as though it was the supreme insult. From that day onwards it was open warfare between us. On my side there was either contemptuous silence or a barbed retort; on hers, incessant bitter, jeering abuse. The situation was made worse by her liking for Clement which, in the absence of her young soldier husband, was by that time warmer than it should have been.

Having a thin, weak body, I was ashamed to take off my shirt in front of others. Consequently I always washed in the bathroom. But Clement, who had a good physique, being now nearly sixteen, always stripped to the waist and washed in the kitchen. I often saw Mrs Williams watching him, her hard eyes glittering with lust. Knowing that a few of the older evacuee boys slept with their landladies, whose husbands were also in the Forces, I had no difficulty in interpreting the signs.

Eventually my life in Mrs Williams's house became so unbearable that I asked the street billeting officer, who had accompanied us from

London, to find me another billet. She heard me sympathetically but did nothing. I therefore decided to telephone Mother. At the beginning of the war Uncle Charles and his family had been evacuated to Torquay, in South Devon, where his firm was engaged on vitally important war work. Mother had recently gone to stay with him, for the Blitz had started and Father had refused to allow her to remain in London any longer. When I told her that I was unhappy she promised to come to Barnstaple immediately.

What passed between Mother and Mrs Williams, or between Mother and the billeting officer next day, I never knew, but from the look on her face as she emerged from her interviews with them I saw that she had spared neither. On her arrival she had found that the strain of life as an unwanted, indeed hated, ''vacuee' had seriously affected my health. Though I had telephoned her only in the hope of getting my billet changed, she decided to take me back with her to Torquay, a decision which I did not question. My only regret at leaving Barnstaple was that two volumes of Johnson's works were still unread.

6
THE VEIL OF ISIS

Torquay, as the illustrated brochures of its numerous hotels informed the visitor, was the Riviera of England. Only in Torquay did tropical palms grow in the open air. Only in Torquay could one shut one's eyes against the blinding brilliance of the sunshine and imagine that one was in the south of France, or Italy, or even India. Barnstaple and Bideford were old-fashioned towns of the south-west, towns in which men talked of Drake as though the Armada had been defeated yesterday, and I had not found their atmosphere congenial. But Torquay was different. Barnstaple and Bideford were provincial; Torquay was cosmopolitan. They stood on grey rocks and looked west towards the grey Atlantic; it was built on red rock and gazed south towards

> The blue Mediterranean, where he lay,
> Lulled by the coil of his crystálline streams.[14]

Perhaps it was no coincidence that my introduction to the Wisdom of the East, my first confrontation with the Veil of Isis, should have occurred at Torquay.

On the day after our arrival Mother had me admitted to the nearest school. This decision of hers I accepted far less quietly than the one which was responsible for my being with her in Torquay at all. In fact, I was still arguing when we reached the school gate. Being now fifteen I wanted to get out into the world, to find a job and work. But Mother's

With mother, and sister Joan (right), probably in Torquay

mind was made up, and being wise enough not to argue she countered all my protests with a quiet 'You must finish your education first.'

My last school, which was of the 'open air' variety, was a cheerful, friendly place, and the leniency with which I was excused lessons I did not like soon reconciled me to a further period of Babylonian captivity. Though it had both masters and mistresses, all of whose gowns 'billowed' in true *Gem* and *Magnet* style, my dealings were mainly with the mistresses. Of these, the English mistress, to whose class I was assigned, turned out to be the most sympathetic to my literary aspirations. She was a good teacher, but quite unable to maintain discipline, and the class ragged her unmercifully. So great did the uproar sometimes become that her friend the history mistress, who was as short and fat as the English mistress was tall and thin, would have to come from the classroom next door and restore order. Either because I was well behaved and gave no trouble, or because she divined in me a passion for literature such as she had found in no other boy, the pale harassed woman soon became not only a kindly critic but almost a friend. On my essay on 'The Disestablishment of the Church of England', a subject which gave me the opportunity to air my knowledge of the word 'antidisestablishmentarianism', said to be the longest in the dictionary, and which I had learned from Smoky Joe, she wrote: 'Your command of English is excellent; but you have a tendency to use long words for their own sake. Remember that the best word is the one which most clearly and simply expresses your meaning.' In spite of her sensible advice, it was several years before I could bring myself to sacrifice 'antidisestablishmentarianism' and its 'proud compeers' on the altar of chastity of style.

With her encouragement I began writing, in imitation of Lamb's *Tales from Shakespeare*, a synopsis of *The Spanish Tragedy*; but the synopsis threatened to become longer than the play itself and I gave up after thirty pages. When I left she gave me a copy of Tennyson's *Complete Poems*, thus breaking down the prejudice set up by Mrs Ainsworth's well-meaning attempts to 'teach' 'The Lady of Shalott', and paving the way for a rich enjoyment of that long-neglected poet.

As there was no room for me in Uncle Charles's house, where Nana was also staying, Mother found me lodgings in a nearby street. Mrs Baker, my landlady, was an elderly woman so short of stature and broad of feature that she looked as though she had been depressed by some gigantic thumb. She spoke very loudly, with an extremely broad Devonshire accent, repeating each phrase two or three times before passing on to the next, as if convinced that every morsel of her conversation was so valuable that the listener should be given as many opportunities as possible to take it in. She was a good cook, but insanely house-proud, and never wearied of directing my attention to the excellence of her possessions. Never, when referring to any object in the house, did she use the definite article: it was always *my* sitting room, *my* table, *my* dinner, *my* electric light, *my* radio, *my* curtains. Her husband, whom she nagged and scolded incessantly, was a retired lighthouse-keeper. A placid, good-humoured man with a cheery red face, he would wink at me behind his wife's back as she waddled back into her kitchen after a more than usually violent outburst.

Every afternoon I had tea at Uncle Charles's house, which was just round the corner from Mrs Baker's, and on Sundays I went to lunch and stayed for the rest of the day. Though they had given me a very cold reception on the night of my arrival, my aunt and uncle had quickly thawed and once Mother had been forgiven her 'foolishness' in bringing me back with her all was well between us. With Auntie Kath, who was six or seven years older than Uncle Charles, I had indeed always been on good terms. An intelligent woman with charming manners who had been head librarian at Mudie's, she was extremely thin, with large eyes, rouged cheek-bones, and a mass of dark frizzy hair. In Torquay she always dressed in slacks. Mother and Nana used to shake their heads over her housekeeping and it was rumoured she could not cook. Moreover she had an abnormally hearty appetite and consumed huge quantities of food. 'Oh I do love a good tuck in!' she would exclaim as, with shining eyes, she sat down to a meal, frequently attacking it before anyone else was seated. On our visits to Ewell Joan and I had liked her none the less for her peccadilloes, and in Torquay, where she sometimes discussed modern literature and religion with me, I always enjoyed her company. Uncle Charles, who at thirty was already more than half bald, was the chief accountant of a famous British firm. Constant overwork had made him irritable, and there were sometimes rather vicious squabbles between him and Auntie Kath. Though he was as parsimonious as she was extravagant, and moreover inclined to be sadistic, I had always liked him because he was the only uncle young enough to romp and play with me when I was a small boy.

On Sunday afternoons we all went for a walk in the woods near Babbacombe Downs, where we waded ankle-deep in damp dead leaves, picking up dry sticks for the evening fire. Autumn had already come to South Devon. Sometimes, invigorated by the clear crisp air, we followed the precipitous cliff paths far up the coast, pausing wherever there was a gap in the slowly crimsoning forest to look down at the blue-black sea moaning far below. Every now and then fragments of damp white mist would come flying in over the cliff-top. As autumn gave place to winter, the hips and haws showed more and more vividly scarlet among the naked briars.

Before I had been in Torquay many months Uncle Charles was having to spend more and more Sunday afternoons working on his files. Since Mother had returned to London in early autumn, and since Nana did not think it right to leave Uncle Charles alone in the house to make his own tea, Auntie Kath and I sometimes went for our walks alone.

The first thing I did after Mother's departure from Torquay was to leave school and start looking for a job.

Parkes' Coal Company, in whose office in Torquay's main thoroughfare I soon found a situation, was a small concern dealing in coal, coke, and anthracite. Despite the war-time shortage of fuel, business was brisk, for Torquay was a town of hotels, all of which were faced with the problem of keeping their guests warm during the winter. Many a time during the next two months I was to lift the receiver and hear the voice of an irate hotel proprietor demanding to know why the promised twenty tons of whatever it was his furnaces consumed had still not been delivered. One or two proprietors were so utterly unreasonable in their expectations that whenever their voice was heard shrieking from the receiver the whole office groaned. The worst offender, however, was an eccentric baronet who, not long after I had settled in Kalimpong, wrote me incoherent letters on Buddhism without knowing that he had once shouted at me over the telephone for not sending his weekly bag of coke on time. The last arrow in the quiver of an offended customer was always the threat to transfer his or her custom to the rival concern over the road, between which and Parkes' competition was all the more fierce because our senior partner had once been their manager. Their customers must have made the same threat, for during the winter several big hotels were exchanged between us.

Parkes' office was situated above a sweetshop, with the girl assistants in which I speedily became acquainted, for though not then rationed, chocolate and sweets were often difficult to obtain. The office consisted of the big general office in which the head clerk and the rest of the staff had their stools, the partners' office, a dusty record room where we prepared tea, and a cubby-hole on the next floor where the monthly accounts were made out, two afternoons a week, by an ancient Dickensian clerk in a stiff collar with rheumy eyes and a perpetual dewdrop depending from his nose. When I joined the firm the staff in the general office consisted of Mr Williams the head clerk, a cheerful bald-headed man in spectacles, his assistant, a C3 youth waiting to be called up who swore softly at the partners, the customers, the War, and the world in general as he typed delivery bills on a specially equipped typewriter, and two or three youths a little older than myself who all left before I did. The senior partner was a small, smiling, self-satisfied westcountryman of sixty who was always rubbing his hands together; the junior partner a pink-faced, hefty young Scotsman whose name was identical with that of a well-known brand of whisky.

My duties were at first very simple. I answered the telephone, made tea, and delivered bills to the nearer hotels. Not having been able to learn to type by the touch system at school in London, I now adopted the two-finger method, with the help of which I was soon sufficiently proficient to type the numerous letters that the senior partner was in the habit of writing out in longhand just before it was time for me to go home. Office hours were from nine till six, with an hour for lunch, but I usually had to stay till eight o'clock. My wages were ten shillings a week.

Not long after joining Parkes' I signalized my newly-won independence (more apparent than real, for Father still paid all my expenses, allowing me to spend the whole of my wages on books) by moving into more congenial quarters. Now that I had been with her for two or three months Mrs Baker so much regarded me as a member of the family that she included me in all the naggings and scoldings administered to her long-suffering husband. This I did not much mind. But her habit of refusing to allow the electric light to be switched on until at least an hour after dark was a more serious matter. Even though she knew her husband was itching to read the newspaper, and that I was impatient to write down the poems I had composed in the bus coming home, she would sit chuckling in her chair, exclaiming over and over again how pleasant it was to sit in the dark and what a pity that her electricity would have to be switched on so soon. Probably she was not sorry when I left, for ever since the morning that she had found a copy of Swedenborg's *Heaven and Hell* under my pillow she had looked upon me with a feeling akin to horror.

However appropriate the cheerless term 'lodgings' may have been for my room at Mrs Baker's, it was certainly not applicable to the quarters I occupied for the remainder of my stay in Torquay. True I paid – that is, Father paid – a small sum weekly for bed and board, but the kindness and consideration with which I was treated, and the friendliness of every member of the family, made me feel that I had found a second home. Mr French, the head of the family, was a burly inarticulate man of forty of whom, except at weekends, I saw little. His time was divided between the dairy in St Marychurch where I stayed, and the farm from which he supplied the shop with milk, butter, and eggs. In the course of our only serious conversation he solemnly averred that he believed in the literal historical existence of Adam and Eve and seemed astonished that I did not. His wife was a quiet, rather stout woman with greying hair and a toothy smile who had been a teacher. Gwen, Mrs French's unmarried sister, was about thirty-two but looked several years younger. She had light brown hair with a streak of gold in it, grey eyes, a pleasant husky voice and a much gayer and happier temperament than her more serious sister. Mary, the French's only child, was a fair-haired little girl of five who, for some obscure reason, took a great liking to me almost at first sight. Though by no means fond of children, I could not help liking her in return, and even unbent so far as to allow her to sit on my knee. Being unable to articulate properly owing to some defect, she expressed her feelings towards me by laughing heartily whenever we met. With both Mrs French and Gwen I was soon on a more intimate footing than I had ever been with anyone outside the immediate family circle. For Gwen, indeed, I developed a very deep attachment. What was stranger, she became extremely fond of me.

My late hours at Parkes' Coal Company during the week, and my walks with Auntie Kath on Sunday afternoons, left me with much less time for reading than I had enjoyed either in London or at Barnstaple. Yet I continued to read in a week more than the average boy of my age read in a year. Some of the books I consumed at this time exercised a decisive influence on my whole life and thought. Among my discoveries was Schopenhauer, in whom I at once recognized a kindred spirit. Classical authors included Plato (in the complete Bohn translation), Aristotle, Theocritus, Longinus, Demetrius, Tyrtaeus, and Lucian, but my most ardent admiration was for Seneca and the Emperor Julian. The ethical sublimity of the Roman moralist struck for the first time a chord which has vibrated in me ever since. Strange to relate, it was not from the Bible or *The Holy War*, but from the *De Beneficia* and *De Consolatione*, that I learned not only to love the good life but to strive after it. Why I admired the writings of the Emperor Julian is not clear to me. Perhaps it was the 'archetypal' semi-orientalism of his religion that appealed to me, for I was becoming more and more attracted to the exotic in literature.

Neither the Torquay nor the Barnstaple Public Library had a section devoted to the literatures of the East. But at Torquay, after the Russian and other minor European literatures, half a dozen volumes did their best to represent the vast riches of Chinese, Japanese, Sanskrit, Persian, and Arabic prose and poetry, philosophy and religion. As soon as I saw these books there flashed upon me, like a revelation, the thought, 'Why should I limit myself to Europe?'

Of the Torquay Public Library's oriental section, the whole of which I probably read, I now remember only *The Yoga of the Bhagavat Gītā* by Sri Krishna Prem, an English Vaishnavite with whom I subsequently corresponded, *Noh Plays of Japan*, and the *Dabistan*. But from that day there grew upon me the conviction, afterwards immovably implanted in the centre of my consciousness, that regionalism or nationalism in literature or art, philosophy or religion, is an anachronism. Why should not the cultured Englishman be as familiar with Li Po in translation as he is with Shakespeare in the original, or the German philosopher as well acquainted with the doctrines of Nāgārjuna as he is with those of Kant? Why should not the West be as receptive to Eastern culture in the twentieth century as she was to Graeco-Roman art and literature in the fifteenth? Whether he is born in Europe, Asia, Africa, America, or Australasia, and whether he be a Buddhist, Christian, Muslim, Hindu, Zoroastrian, Jew, Confucian, Taoist, Shintoist, Animist, or atheist, the true citizen of the world should aim at a broad acquaintance with all that is best in the whole cultural and spiritual heritage of mankind.

Having exhausted the Torquay Public Library's stock of oriental literature, I turned to the stationers and booksellers opposite Parkes'.

Here I found, in the Everyman series, *Hindu Scriptures* and Kalidasa's *Śakuntala*.[15] In the first, a volume of selections from Hindu religious literature, I particularly admired the Vedic hymns, especially those addressed to Ushas, the Dawn; the Upanishads I found obscure. Compared with the plays of Marlowe and Ben Jonson, all of which I had read while still with Mrs Baker, *Śakuntala* seemed rather poor stuff – even after making all possible allowance for the difference, really not very great, of dramatic convention. In India Kalidasa is always compared with Shakespeare; but when, willing to revise my early judgement, I read *Śakuntala* again seventeen years later, I was obliged to ratify it instead. However, the lovely imagery of the *Meghadūta* or 'Cloud-Messenger', a long lyric poem, delighted me immensely. Shortly afterwards, in the same bookshop, I found *The Song Celestial*, Sir Edwin Arnold's famous verse translation of the *Bhagavad Gītā*. This gave me even greater satisfaction. Indeed, I used to read the eleventh book, 'The Vision of the Universal Form', in a state bordering on ecstasy.

> Then, O King! the God, so saying,
> Stood, to Pritha's Son displaying
> All the splendour, wonder, dread
> Of His vast Almighty-head.
> Out of countless eyes beholding,
> Out of countless mouths commanding,
> Countless mystic forms enfolding
> In one Form: supremely standing
> Countless radiant glories wearing,
> Countless heavenly weapons bearing,
> Crowned with garlands of star-clusters,
> Robed in garb of woven lustres,
> Breathing from His perfect Presence
> Breaths of every subtle essence
> Of all heavenly odours; shedding
> Blinding brilliance; overspreading –
> Boundless, beautiful – all spaces
> With His all-regarding faces;
> So He showed! If there should rise
> Suddenly within the skies
> Sunburst of a thousand suns

Flooding earth with beams undeemed-of,
Then might be that Holy One's
Majesty and radiance dreamed of![16]

Whether I appreciated such lines more as poetry or religion would be difficult to say. Sometimes it happened that when I thought I enjoyed a poem, I really responded to a religious teaching, and when I thought I responded to a religious teaching I in fact enjoyed a poem. But of my reaction to the work that now brought me face to face with the Veil of Isis there could be no uncertainty.

One Saturday afternoon, as I was changing books, I noticed on a door in the Reference Room the words 'Moyse Collection'. On my application to the librarian the door was unlocked and I found myself in the midst of the biggest and richest collection of books I had yet seen. Resisting the very strong temptation to describe in detail the excursions into the Greek and Latin classics, Old English texts, and Elizabethan drama which I thenceforward made on Saturday afternoons (for the books belonging to this collection had to be read on the spot), I shall confine myself to two volumes which were my stepping-stones to higher things. The first of these was Hartmann's *Paracelsus*. Though the work interested me deeply, I was still more interested by its constant references, usually in footnotes, to *Esoteric Buddhism*, a work of which I had never heard. Coming upon it one afternoon not far from *Paracelsus*, I promptly read it. Much more vividly than the vague sense of widening horizons which it gave me do I remember its constant references, also in footnotes, to another work of which I had never heard: *Isis Unveiled*. This was not available in the Moyse Collection, but I discovered it soon afterwards in the Lending Department and bore the two bulky volumes back with me to St Marychurch.

How shall I describe their effect upon me? Though in itself almost entirely negative, it proved to be more far-reaching in its consequences than any book I had previously encountered. Within a fortnight I had read both volumes twice from cover to cover. Impressed, bewildered, thrilled, excited, stimulated as I was by their staggeringly immense wealth – their 'inexhaustible truckloads,' as Maeterlinck called them – of information on every conceivable aspect of philosophy, comparative religion, occultism, mysticism, science, and a hundred other subjects, the realization which dawned most clearly upon me, and which by the time

I had finished stood out with blinding obviousness in the very forefront of my consciousness, was the fact that *I was not a Christian* – that I never had been, and never would be – and that the whole structure of Christian doctrine was from beginning to end thoroughly repugnant to me. This realization gave me a sense of relief, of liberation as from some oppressive burden, which was so great that I wanted to dance and sing for joy. What I was, what I believed, I knew not, but what I was not and what I did not believe, that I knew with utter certainty, and this knowledge, merely negative though it was as yet, gave me a foretaste of that freedom which comes when all obstacles are removed, all barriers broken down, all limitations transcended.

The effects of this great emancipation were for the time being insignificant. In an attempt to give it a positive content I plunged into Swedenborg's *Arcana Celestae*, into the study of Hebrew, into the *Key to Theosophy*, into Rosicrucianism; but not until a year later, in London, did I find that for which I was searching. *Isis Unveiled* could not help me. Indeed, the title originally chosen by the author had been 'The Veil of Isis'; but the publishers, alive to the publicity value of the suggestion of secrets revealed, changed this to the title under which it subsequently became famous. It is a curious fact that though I at first assumed that the author, H. P. Blavatsky, was a man, by the time I had finished it I knew, intuitively, that *Isis Unveiled* had been written by a woman. Though it was an incomparably greater Hand that lifted for me the Veil of Isis, she has my undying gratitude for having brought me where I could see it face to face.

At Parkes' Coal Company my position had been steadily improving. As one by one they left I took over the work, first of the two or three youths, then of the C3 swearer, and finally of Mr Williams. The last in the coal office had become the first. Instead of handing over calls to more experienced members of the staff, I now took orders, soothed irate hotel proprietors, and explained the current coal situation. When customers called at the office, I accepted payments, issued receipts, and assured them that their next consignment would be delivered without delay. (Among the callers was Agatha Christie, who was on our books under her real name.) Twice or thrice a week I went to our petrol dump, the keys of which were now in my keeping, watched while the drivers filled the tanks of their lorries, and took dippings of the amount remaining with a notched steel yard. On Friday afternoons I paid the foreman, drivers, and delivery men their wages at the coalyard adjoining Torquay station.

My biggest job, however, was the daily typing of delivery bills on the specially equipped typewriter, the intricacies of which I had now mastered. On busy days this kept me hard at work from two in the afternoon until six in the evening. After being typed the delivery bills had to be checked by the senior partner. As we were supposed to close at six, and as this part of the work sometimes took two hours, the checking should have started at four. But in the days when the C3 youth officiated at the typewriter, it was the senior partner's pleasant habit to waste the whole afternoon gossiping and then, at six o'clock, to sit down with a gay smile to do the checking. My indispensability now enabled me to put a stop to this imposition. At four o'clock I would look at the clock above the mantelpiece and remark that I wanted to leave 'early' that evening. This was office parlance for 'not later than six-thirty'. After I had done this three or four times the hint was taken and the checking of orders sometimes started as early as three o'clock.

Our shortage of staff reduced the junior partner, who having put more money into the business had more prestige to maintain, to the practice of some strange subterfuges. One of these I witnessed several times before understanding its significance. Whenever, owing to my preoccupation at the typewriter, he had answered the telephone himself, he would gently lay down the receiver, quietly rise to his feet, and having stolen tiptoe across the room to the far corner would stand there for a minute as if lost in thought. Then springing suddenly to life, he would stride rapidly to the telephone, crashing his heels into the floor as he did so, and picking up the receiver shout 'Hullo, hullo! Yes, speaking!' in loud cheery tones.

Though I worked very hard during my last two or three months in the coal office I was quite happy there, and while not actually liking the work, took an interest in it and did it to the best of my ability. My wages had more than doubled, for after the departure of the C3 youth I asked for a rise, and after the departure of Mr Williams the partners gave me another of their own accord. Higher wages to me, of course, meant more books. After the hints about wanting to go 'early' I was often able to leave the office at six, instead of at eight as before, which left me more time in which to enjoy the pleasant company of Mrs French and Gwen. It also gave me time for the study of the Rosicrucian literature which I now received every fortnight from San José, California.

In Torquay 'suited and booted' – his first – and only – bespoke suit was bought by Nana for £3

The advertisements of the Ancient and Mystical Order Rosae Crucis (AMORC) are well known to the readers of the occult, spiritualist, or universalist type of periodical. They even appear in newspapers and magazines. How my eye was first caught by one of them I do not recollect; but evidently the prospect of being initiated into the ancient mysteries appealed to me, for I was soon spending a substantial portion of my wages on the various dues. Of the rather nebulous contents of the green folders which came every two weeks in plain covers, thus greatly intriguing Mrs French and Gwen, both of whom wondered who the mysterious correspondent in the United States could be, only vaguely beautiful impressions now remain. The memory of a certain 'initiation' remains vivid, however, because it was the occasion of my hurting, quite unintentionally, the feelings of my two friends.

This 'initiation' consisted, as far as I can remember, in lighting a number of candles in front of a mirror and then gazing with concentration into the mirror until the Rosy Cross appeared. Now since there was no electric bulb in my room, I was supplied with candles, by the light of which I used to read at night. Not wanting to ask for an extra supply, for the ceremony had to be kept secret, I bought a packet on the way home from the office. At lunch the next day the sisters gently reproached me for buying candles myself instead of asking for them, for while cleaning my room they had noticed the remains of the packet I had purchased in a half-open drawer.

As spring gave way to summer, Auntie Kath, Uncle Charles, Nana, and I began spending either the mornings or the afternoons on Sundays down on Babbacombe beach. Never, in England, did I enjoy such perfect weather in such perfect surroundings. Behind us the red sandstone cliffs rose sheer for three or four hundred feet. Before us lay the shimmering, intensely blue width of the sea, from which the sun struck little sparkles of gold. Between the two stretched a ribbon of dazzlingly white beach, and overhead, from horizon to horizon, the quivering blueness of the sky.

But when Father, who throughout the Blitz had worked day and night as a stretcher-bearer, came to Torquay for a short holiday, I started feeling homesick. After giving notice to the partners, who spent my last days gloomily reconciling themselves to the prospect of having a girl in the office, and bidding an affectionate farewell to Mrs French and Gwen, I returned to London after an absence of one year.

7
THE PENDULUM SWINGS

The two and a half years which followed my return from Torquay were among the most important of my present existence. Every aspect of my being, from the lowest to the highest, sought eagerly for the fullest possible unfoldment and expression, so that my life was during this whole period a chaos of conflicting impulses. My love of art, of literature, of music, already sufficiently ardent, became a ruthless passion. Books, never chewed or merely tasted, were now indiscriminately swallowed whole in a fruitless attempt to satisfy an appetite frightful in its ravenousness. My senses, practically dormant until then, suddenly awoke and clamoured for satisfaction. For the first time in my life came psychical and mystical experiences. Though heights were touched, existence for me consisted not in progress but in a perpetual violent oscillation between extremes. Small wonder that the heroes of this period were stricken, tormented, demoniacal figures – Strindberg, Nietzsche, Beethoven.

The London of 1941 was not the London of 1940, any more than the youth who returned from Torquay was the boy who had been evacuated to Barnstaple. The Blitz lay between. In nearly every street great gaps showed in the rows of houses as noticeably as missing teeth in a human face. The populace, though in the mass cheerful, confident, and determined, now that frightfulness had done its worst, and failed, was in individuals beginning to exhibit signs of strain.

How great a test of endurance the Blitz had been was clear from Father's tales of the period when, night after night, he and the rest of his squad had rescued the trapped and the injured, and removed dead bodies from the wreckage of bomb shelters, sometimes from blazing buildings, while bombs were still falling in other parts of the city and while the earth rocked and quivered beneath them and the anti-aircraft guns pounded away as, in the blackness of the sky, the searchlights darted hither and thither trying to pick out the tiny dark shapes of the bombers. His worst experience, however, had been not during but after an air raid, when his squad helped remove the bodies of the scores of people, mostly women and children, who were drowned the night a water main, struck by a bomb, had burst and flooded the tube shelter in which they had taken refuge.

Yet even the Blitz had not been without its comic aspect. Once, during a particularly heavy bombardment, when the singing of shrapnel filled the air, Father left the house in such haste that he forgot to put on his steel helmet. Noticing it on its peg in the hall a minute later, Mother seized it in her hand and heedless of the shrapnel ran bareheaded up the street crying, 'Phil, Phil, you've forgotten your helmet!'

At the time of my return to London the Blitz had not quite petered out, and from the few air raids I experienced I was able to imagine what it must have been like at the height of its fury. Not that I had never heard bombs falling before. At Torquay, one night, six or seven had been dropped in a line, the first a hundred yards from the house, the last in an open field five miles away. Each time the whistle had seemed shriller and the crash more deafening than before; but instead of falling nearer, as I thought, the bombs were in fact falling further away and the last, being the biggest and loudest, seemed the nearest. Indeed, it seemed to explode directly over my head. The following morning Gwen and I went to see the damage done by the nearest (and smallest) bomb, which had destroyed two houses and injured several people.

In London, of course, the whistle and crash of bombs was only part of the proceedings. Much worse were the ear-splitting detonations, four or five at a time in quick succession, of the nearby ack-ack guns, especially of the Mobile Unit which sometimes operated from the top of the road. Much practice had made the gunners expert, and many a time did Father and I, standing out in the garden, see the enemy planes falling in flames to the ground. With so much artillery fire the danger from flying shrapnel was no less than that from falling bombs, but long experience of the Blitz had intensified the strain of Anglo-Saxon fatalism in the English character, and though few took unnecessary risks the general attitude was 'If your number's on it, you'll get it; if it isn't, you won't.' Within a few weeks I had become as phlegmatic as other Londoners. At breakfast on mornings after particularly noisy raids Father used to relate how, thinking I must have been disturbed, he had looked into my room during the night and found me fast asleep.

The worst experience which awaited me on my return to London had nothing to do with the Blitz. One day, while reading the newspaper, I became aware that my parents were talking to each other as I had never heard them talk before. Like all husbands and wives they had quarrelled occasionally, but never had such bitter words been exchanged between them. Horrified, I listened from behind the newspaper.

'Yes, and you brought your son back from Torquay to spy on me!' exclaimed Mother in a fury.

'Son, tell your mother whether I brought you back or whether you came of your own accord,' said Father in an injured, sorrowful voice. Without lowering the newspaper, I burst into tears. Father waited until my sobs had subsided, then took away the newspaper and gently repeated the question. He looked worried and miserable. Mother's averted face was hard and cold.

'I came of my own accord,' I said amidst sobs.

Much as this incident lacerated my feelings at the time, I soon ceased to think about it. The storm having perhaps cleared the air, relations between Father and Mother were again harmonious and I was busy reviving old connections and forming new ones.

Having exhausted such resources of the Tooting Public Library as appealed to me, I began to rely more and more on its counterpart at Streatham. In addition to Gnosticism, Rosicrucianism, and Neoplatonism, I took up the study of Chinese history and culture, began reading biographies of the great composers, started teaching myself Arabic and New Testament Greek, and opened up a campaign against philosophy by storming two of its strongest citadels: Kant's *Critique of Pure Reason*, which I read thrice, and Hegel's *Philosophy of Religion*.

Attempts to revive my old connections with the BB were less successful. Where our hall had once stood was a large empty space and several piles of rubble. For two weeks I attended parades and Bible classes in the hall of the Anglican church across the road, whose company and ours were now amalgamated; but most of the old familiar faces were gone and the atmosphere was different. Besides, having realized in Torquay that I had never believed in Christianity, the hymns and prayers now seemed empty and unreal. Perhaps Skipper sensed the change in me. Or perhaps I was anxious to share my new understanding. Whichever it may have been, I have a vague recollection of trying to convince him of the necessity of an impartial study of all religions and of our both feeling, at the end of the discussion, that we now stood very far apart.

As air raid warnings became rarer, Mother and I started going out together, making trips to the National Gallery, where a single masterpiece was on exhibition at a time, and to Westminster Abbey. Once we went to Westminster Cathedral with Auntie Kate, who lit candles and said prayers while Mother and I watched the priests officiating at the high altar, and once we went to see Mother's eldest brother, whom I had never met. But even more than churches and museums, which were my passion rather than hers, Mother loved shops and restaurants. Her most serious complaint against Father had always been that from one year's end to the next he never took her out for an evening's entertainment. Though by nature sociable, he preferred his own fireside, or a quiet hour at the public house with friends, to the artificial glitter and hollow gaiety of the fashionable West End restaurants, or the tawdry pseudo-Gothic splendours of the local cinema.

Having no children of school age, and being under forty-five, Mother had been required to register for part-time national service. Either shortly before or shortly after my return from Torquay she and her friend Margaret joined the Education Department of the LCC. The branch in which they worked, then conveniently located in the deserted buildings of a nearby kindergarten, was responsible for the supply of equipment to evacuated schools. So much did Mother like this work, and so capable an administrator did she prove, that within a few months she was transferred from the part-time to the full-time staff and promoted to assistant head of the branch. This meant that she no longer had time to cook lunch, so at twelve o'clock each day she and I and Margaret went to a restaurant at Tooting Broadway. With us came Mother's chief, the head of the branch, a small, unobtrusive, kindly man of about fifty-five.

With Father on duty at the ARP headquarters, in the evenings Mother and I were generally alone. As she sat silently mending socks and shirts hour after hour there would sometimes escape from her a sigh of sheer weariness which, though it pierced me to the heart, I ignored and went on reading. If she ventured a remark I answered with a grunt. After leaving England I bitterly regretted this selfish behaviour, the memory of which filled me with grief and shame. Never in my life was the aesthetic so inimical to the ethical. If she wanted to listen to the Forces Programme I curtly told her that it would disturb me; but if I wished to listen to Bach or Beethoven, which gave her a headache, I switched on the radio without caring for her feelings. Later on, Joan and I always quarrelled about the radio, which I took into the sitting room, where there was an extra plug-in, whenever I wanted to listen to the Promenade Concerts. Since Joan was good-natured and I bad-tempered she usually gave in to me, but if one of her favourite crooners was on the air she insisted on her rights. On such occasions I did sometimes give in, though with a very bad grace; but if a symphony or concerto which I particularly wanted to hear was being broadcast over another wavelength I would go to any lengths of rudeness and ill-temper to get my own way. With Mother there was never any dispute. Besides being accustomed to me having my own way, she was naturally of a gentle, patient disposition. Once, in a moment of exasperation, she exclaimed, 'You're just like your father – obstinate as a mule!' But such outbursts were rare. Thus it was that she submitted to evenings of sheer boredom without a word of complaint, darning socks and turning the wrists and collars of shirts with war-time economy, while I read philosophy and religion or listened to classical music on the radio.

Though I had responded to classical music ever since that afternoon I had heard *Fingal's Cave* at the Methodist Central Hall, only after my return from Torquay did it become an addiction. Bach's *Toccata and Fugue in D Minor*, which seemingly explores the heights and depths of the universe, occupied in my experience of music a place analogous to that of *Paradise Lost* in my experience of poetry. Stunned, overwhelmed, annihilated by those majestic chords, I went about for several days in a kind of waking trance. As soon as I came to my senses I tried to translate my experience of the music into poetry. Later on, in fact, I wrote in imitation of Baudelaire's 'Les Phares' a poem on all the great composers from Bach to Delius, as well as a dramatic idyll on Beethoven.

My enjoyment of music was far more intense than that of poetry had ever been. This was partly due to the very nature of music, which unlike poetry is pure feeling devoid of all cognitive content, and partly to the fact that at this period I craved constant emotional intoxication. My two favourite composers, that is to say those by whom I was most strongly stimulated, were Beethoven and Tchaikovsky. When the violence of my feelings had subsided I preferred Mozart and Haydn, while Bach remained a constant favourite.

Whether the intensity of my enjoyment of music contributed to my first mystical experience, which came at about this time, I am unable to say. But a Beethoven overture or a symphony by Mozart used to affect me so powerfully that for several days I would hear the music ringing again and again in my ears. So intense, indeed, would my concentration on these inner sounds be, that not only did they sound as loud and clear as when I had heard them with my physical ears over the radio, but I would practically lose consciousness of my body. This state of semi-trance which music sometimes induced in me seemed to be of the same order as the two experiences which, appropriating a conveniently vague term, I have called mystical.

Both occurred several times. The first had indeed come to me, though not very intensely, even before my evacuation. Like most of my other mystical experiences, it is associated in memory with the place at which it occurred. One day, on my way to the Tooting Public Library, I as usual had to cross the road at Amen Corner – so called because in ancient times, when the choir of the parish church performed the annual ceremony of 'beating the bounds,' they broke up at this spot, which marked the boundary of the parish, with a loud 'Amen'. As I crossed from one side of the street to the other I suddenly awoke to the complete absurdity of the mind being tied down to a single physical body. Why could I not look at the world through the eyes of the man standing on the opposite pavement? Why could I not know his thoughts as easily as I knew my own? As these questions flashed upon me I felt my consciousness desperately struggling to free itself from the body and project itself into all the bodies walking round Amen Corner. Though its efforts were unavailing and it sank back exhausted I thereafter had a feeling of being imprisoned. When years later I read in the *Śūraṅgama Sūtra*, a famous text of Buddhist idealism, the dialogue in which the Buddha makes his disciple Ānanda realize, step by step, that his consciousness is neither inside the body nor outside it, nor yet somewhere between, being in its true nature universal, I felt I was treading on familiar ground.

The other experience was even more striking. As I was walking down the main road towards Tooting Broadway, it suddenly seemed as though

I was moving in a world of ghosts. The whole street with its houses, shops, and people suddenly receded into the infinitely remote distance. The roar of the traffic faded into an intense silence. My own body felt light, airy, insubstantial, and it seemed I no longer walked on the solid pavement but floated, clearly conscious, through an immense void. This void was simultaneously coterminous with my own consciousness, so that it also seemed that I was floating through myself. Though this experience, which was much more vivid than the first, generally lasted for the time it took me to walk a hundred yards, its after-effects persisted much longer; for upwards of an hour the objective world, though again visible, seemed strangely unreal, as if it had no business to be there and might disappear at any second. My subsequent study of Buddhist literature confirmed this experience too. When I read in the *Laṅkāvatāra Sūtra* and other works that one must meditate on the world as being in reality like a dream, I at once understood what was meant.

After two or three months at home I began to feel that I should work again. This time Mother raised no objection. At the suggestion of Sid, Mother's chief, I applied for a clerical post in the Public Health Department of the LCC and after a rather perfunctory interview entered the service of the biggest municipality in the world.

8
BUDDHISM AND THE LCC

How many storeys County Hall Main Block consists of I do not remember, but they contain six hundred rooms and twelve miles of corridor. North Block and South Block, between which one passes on the way to the Main Block, though each containing the same number of storeys cover a much smaller acreage. The Public Health Department occupied the whole of the fourth floor. The branch to which I was allocated, and in which I worked for two years and four months, was tucked away in the north-east corner next to the office of the Medical Officer of Health, who was the head of the whole department. It consisted of four rooms: a small one overlooking an inner courtyard for the Chief, his deputy, and his personal assistant (myself), a large room for the woman and girl clerical assistants, the number of whom varied from six to eight, a room for the three matrons, and a waiting room.

The Chief was a short, cheerful, easygoing man in his early forties. Unlike most of the other members of his grade he was of working-class origin and instead of joining straight from university had worked his way up from the lower ranks. His deputy was a dull, colourless man in his late thirties with a pale unhealthy complexion and astonishingly bass voice. Of the women and girls in the general office all except two either left after I joined or joined before I left.

The two exceptions were Thelma and Miss Cook. Thelma, who remained twenty-nine for the whole time I knew her, though she celebrated several birthdays, was a bold-eyed, black-haired wench who darkened her naturally swarthy complexion by the liberal application of reddish-brown pigment. In my memories of her she invariably wears a cabbage green costume, though I suppose she must occasionally have worn something else. Originally a punching machine operator, she still belonged to the technical grade, but through intrigue had managed to get herself transferred to a post in the higher clerical grade. Between her and the long-suffering Miss Cook there was a deadly feud.

Miss Cook, the cousin of a famous counsel, was the seniormost member of the general office, having joined the service before most of the girls were born. Of slightly 'Jewish' physiognomy, she liked to relate how her friends called her an old Jewish matriarch. Short-sighted, with her grey hair tumbling about her face, she peered at papers over the tops of her spectacles. Always much better dressed than any of the girls, she sometimes appeared on Saturdays in voluminous black taffeta that rustled loudly as she moved.

Between Miss Cook and me relations were cordial. Once, when I had been rather impudent, she banged me over the head with a file; but this act of exasperation only cemented our friendship. During the Chief's lunch hour she would sit on the edge of my desk and talk to me. Her favourite topics were the Kabbala, the poetry of Swinburne, and her experiences as a worker in the Social Welfare Department. Though I was sixteen and she sixty-five, this rather Victorian old lady never hesitated to describe the seamiest aspects of life in the East End, with which, indeed, she had a very extensive acquaintance. Due to the matter-of-fact way in which she spoke of rape, incest, prostitution, and venereal disease, I was able from that time to discuss these subjects without embarrassment.

Miss Gretton, the Head Matron, could hardly have been less than fifty-five and might well have been considerably more. Her hair, which sometimes showed white at the roots, was a kind of carroty-brown, and round it she wore a green velvet fillet. Her face was a mask of powder, rouge, lipstick, and mascara, all heavily applied. On her fingers, the long nails of which gleamed bright scarlet, she wore numerous rings, the most noticeable being mounted with a thick silver plate, about two inches square, engraved with what she claimed were Hebrew characters. Her dresses, which she wore very short, were full of the most vivid reds, greens, and violets. In the office she never put her arms into the sleeves of her coat, but sat with it draped around her like a cloak. At her throat were several strings of artificial pearls. When she stood, she looked so round-shouldered as to be almost a hunchback. Nothing was known of her origins, but on the strength of the fact that her private nursing home had been bought by a member of the royal family she apparently considered that she belonged to the aristocracy. To women of the working class who came for interviews she could be unspeakably rude. Middle-class women were treated with haughty condescension. To titled women she was all graciousness.

The two other matrons, who had been in charge of big London hospitals, were between sixty-five and seventy. Both were white haired and plainly dressed, and neither wore make-up. Though of rather severe demeanour they were quiet, ladylike, and courteous.

The Civil Nursing Reserve, as the branch was called, had been formed by the Ministry of Health as a means of supplementing the nursing staff of hospitals in London and the Home Counties, where air raid casualties had imposed a severe strain upon the resources of all such institutions. Its work consisted in the recruitment, training, and allocation of personnel. These simple functions were not, however, discharged without considerable friction between the various agencies involved, as well as between members of the staff of each agency. In the CNR the friction was mainly between the Chief and Miss Gretton. This was only a reflection of the antagonism which ran through the whole department.

Unlike certain other departments, Public Health was divided into a hierarchy of four grades as rigidly defined and (with the exception of the MOH, a professional man with administrative functions) as mutually exclusive as the four castes of Hindu society: technical, clerical, administrative, and professional. Between the matrons, who belonged to the professional grade, and the heads of branches, who belonged to the administrative grade, went on a continual cold war. The matrons, while jealously guarding their supreme authority on all 'professional' matters, were constantly trying to usurp functions which were strictly administrative, an encroachment that the administrative staff vigorously contested. These skirmishes usually resulted in victory for the administrative side, by whom the line of demarcation between the two spheres of jurisdiction was better understood and more scrupulously respected.

After the question under dispute had been carried up to the MOH for decision, a defeated matron would airily remark, 'I thought it was a professional matter,' or, if the encroachment had been particularly flagrant, 'I don't know what difference it makes if I deal with such a small matter, even if it is administrative.' Sometimes, of course, the question under dispute was such that the wisdom of Solomon could hardly have decided whether it was administrative or professional.

The CNR being one of the principal battlegrounds in this departmental war of the frogs and the mice, it was not long before I started playing my own very minor part in the strategy. More important to me during the first few weeks of my service, however, were two quite non-official incidents, both of which stand out in vivid colours against the drab background of paper-littered desks, tall filing cabinets, and dimly-lit corridors.

Needing an envelope, I went across to the general office. It was the first time I had been there, and since the place was full of women and girls I naturally felt rather hesitant. Approaching the nearest desk I asked, 'Could you spare me an envelope?' (I pronounced the initial vowel of the word as a short 'e', as though the syllable rhymed with 'hen').

'Oh, you mean an *awnvelope!*' laughed the red-headed girl behind the desk, gaily handing me the controversial piece of stationery. I retreated in confusion.

The second incident occurred some time later. One lunch hour I wanted to consult the index of CNR members. The red-headed girl was alone in the office, reading a book. My heart thumped painfully. 'What are you reading?' I asked, to make conversation.

Instead of replying she blushed deeply and covered the open pages of the book with her two hands.

'Let me see,' I insisted, approaching her desk. Blushing more furiously still, she took away her hands and looked up at me in smiling confusion as I examined the book. It was Santayana's *Egotism in German Philosophy*. Her conquest of me was complete.

Sonia, as I was soon permitted to call her, was a medium-sized girl of twenty-two with strawberry blonde hair. Though not thin she was slightly built with small, undeveloped breasts. She had a heart-shaped face and a fair complexion. Her eyes were violet, nose perfectly shaped though slightly freckled, and mouth wide but not full. Next to her voice, the clearest and most musical I had ever heard, the most striking thing about her was the frank, generous, open expression of her face, on which I never saw even the slightest trace of ill-nature.

Whether derived from her Anglo-Irish father or her Franco-Russian mother there was, however, a marked strain of fecklessness in her make-up. Her stockings were laddered, her shoes dirty, her coat unbrushed, and she signed the late book more often than any other member of the staff. Later, when we were on confidential terms, she told me, with her usual frank gaiety of manner, 'I could never marry anyone with less than £5,000 a year. When Daddy was alive Mummy had that amount and she could *never* make both ends meet.' This confession did not come as a rebuff to any proposal of mine. She had been proposed to by an admirer earning, unfortunately, only £2,000 a year. During the time I knew her she had, in fact, five suitors, one of whom proposed almost as often as he saw her. But as she seemed not particularly fond of any of these shadowy figures, speaking of them only with compassionate amusement, it never occurred to me to feel jealous.

The confession referred to belongs to a period much later than the incident of the book. Meanwhile I enjoyed cosy chats with her behind one of the big filing cabinets, where I helped her make the morning coffee and afternoon tea whenever it was her turn to perform this duty. None of the other girls, with whom I was soon on first-name terms, ever commented in my presence on what must have been obvious to them all. But Thelma's jealous eyes were always on Sonia and me, and she tried hard to make me flirt with her.

My own regular duty was to open the letters which, twice a day, a departmental messenger put into my in-basket. This was not such a simple task as it looked, for after a few weeks the Chief left it to me to decide which letters could be dealt with by the general office and which needed his personal attention. In the latter case I called for the case papers. This often led to friction between Miss Cook and Thelma.

Miss Cook, who had the nose of a bloodhound for missing papers, after an unsuccessful search through all the files would look over the tops of her spectacles at nobody in particular, and declare, 'They must be on somebody's desk.' The girls perfunctorily searched their desks for the missing papers. 'There are no papers, Miss Cook,' Thelma would say at last. 'She's a new case.'

'No, no!' Miss Cook would exclaim, becoming excited. 'I know the name. R. L. V. Smith. She came up seven months ago in connection with that Nicholson case. There *must* be some papers somewhere.'

'I tell you there are no papers, Miss Cook,' Thelma would retort angrily. 'She's a new case. Give her to me.'

But once convinced there were papers Miss Cook never gave up the search till they were found. For the rest of the day she would go about muttering 'R. L. V. Smith, R. L. V. Smith. Now where can her papers be?' Several hours later the stillness of the general office would be rent by a triumphant cry: 'Here they are; she had them all the time!'

'Miss Cook, how dare you touch my desk!' Thelma would shout, breaking off from a personal telephone conversation that had already lasted an hour and a half. But Miss Cook, her chubby face wreathed in smiles, was already out of the door and streaking across the corridor to the Chief's office.

Thelma's uncooperativeness was part of a deliberate policy. Just as Miss Gretton, with whom she was on the best of terms, constantly tried to usurp administrative functions, Thelma did her utmost to keep the whole work of the general office in her own hands, and the two women worked together. Their intention was to trap the Chief. Had the letter from R. L. V. Smith been handed over to Thelma she would have quietly attached it to the case papers hidden on her desk and gone with the whole correspondence to Miss Gretton. Between them the matter would have been settled, even though it might require an administrative decision, or involve a matter of principle.

If Miss Cook either wearied of her search or, convinced that she had made a mistake, returned the letter to me with the remark that there were no case papers, the Chief dealt with it on its own merits. Meanwhile Miss Gretton and Thelma, knowing that the letter had been received, would immediately take the very action it should have prevented. Later, when the muddle came to light, the Chief would be accused of taking action on a letter without reference to the previous correspondence and Miss Cook blamed for not making a thorough search for the case papers. Thus only Miss Cook's obstinacy stood between the Chief and disaster.

Once she pursued papers for three weeks. Even when the Chief, convinced that there could be no previous correspondence, ordered her to surrender the letter that put her on the trail, she defied him and went on with her search. The missing papers were eventually discovered when she ransacked Thelma's desk for the fourth time. Where they had been in the meantime no one ever knew.

Sometimes Thelma would try to draw a red herring across the trail. After detaching the more important correspondence, she returned the rest of the case papers to the file; but Miss Cook was rarely deceived, for she seemed to have a memory not only for every set of case papers but for each individual letter that had ever passed through her hands. Another ruse was to file case papers out of alphabetical order. This move Miss Cook countered by checking the entire contents of the box files, of which there were several hundred, at least once a week.

After the morning post had been opened and Miss Cook was hot on the scent, the Chief and I simply talked. In addition to official business, which occupied only part of our time, we discussed philosophy, religion, and literature. In those days the great Trollope revival was beginning to sweep the reading public, and the Chief was among its most ardent supporters. Rarely did he go out to lunch without one of the minor works of his favourite author tucked beneath his arm. Since fiction was the branch of literature which I had cultivated least, I was slightly scornful of this enthusiasm, and the merits and demerits of Trollope were vigorously debated between us. In an effort to convince him of the truth of my system, which was then Neo-Hegelian, I started writing, in the manner of Proclus' *On the One*, a series of theses. After the ninetieth thesis I gave up, entangled in my own ideas.

At ten o'clock came the usual pleasant interlude behind the filing cabinet in the general office, at the end of which I departed with three cups of coffee. As soon as he had gulped down his, the Chief would hitch up his cuffs and, with a cheery remark to me, tackle the contents of his in-basket with vigour. I followed his example. The lunch hour I usually spent in quest of second-hand books. After a hurried lunch at a cheap Italian restaurant, I hastened along York Road to my favourite shop, the proprietor of which always gave me a cordial welcome, for I was his best customer. I also patronized a stall in the Dip, a rather suspicious market area to which there was access from York Road through a long dark tunnel that reeked of stale beer. In between the brewers' drays one would occasionally descry human refuse in the form of decrepit prostitutes and drunkards, some of whom would hoarsely beg for a copper. From these lunch-hour expeditions I rarely returned without one or two newly-purchased volumes, so that it was not long before Father had to order for me yet another bookcase.

The instant I re-entered the office, the Chief hastily donned hat and coat and dashed out with his latest Trollope, flinging at me as he went an admonition to 'hold the fort'. Hardly had his footsteps died away along the corridor than the door would open to Miss Cook, whose lunch hour coincided with mine. 'What do you *think*?' she would exclaim, 'I found those missing papers under ...' Whereupon I would have to listen to her latest adventures among the filing cabinets. Occasionally I was honoured by a visit from Miss Gretton, who once or twice dangled her legs over the edge of my desk and tried to look like a lorelei on a rock. Shorter than Miss Cook's, her visits were made with the object of ascertaining whether the Chief had overstayed his lunch hour. So if it was three o'clock, I had to be careful to observe that he had not left the office till two. Thus her plan of throwing out in front of the MOH a casual remark about his never returning before four o'clock would be frustrated.

The latter part of the afternoon was devoted to dictating letters. When the Chief was ready, I telephoned the typing pool and asked them to send someone along. If the stenographer who appeared a few minutes later happened to be about sixty, the Chief would acknowledge her greeting with a scowl and a grunt and plunge at once into his dictation. If she was sixteen (there were no intermediate age groups) he would exclaim, 'Hullo, we haven't seen you for a long time! How are you?' After the blushing miss had said that she was all right, thank you, and answered other questions of a personal nature, she would be asked if she was sure she was quite comfortable, whether the chair was not too hard or the table too low, or the light insufficient, after which, with many cheerful smiles, the day's dictation would begin.

On Saturday afternoons I crossed Westminster Bridge and walked through Whitehall and Trafalgar Square on my weekly pilgrimage to the bookshops in Charing Cross Road. Though attracted most of all by the second-hand bookstalls where poets could still be bought for sixpence and philosophers for a shilling, I also penetrated the more sophisticated establishments where beings of indeterminate age and sex, in velveteen trousers and with long hair, dispensed Marx and Freud, Dylan Thomas and D. H. Lawrence, at much higher prices.

With Charing Cross Road as my base, I explored Soho, the Strand, Leicester Square, Shaftesbury Avenue, and Piccadilly Circus. The whole of this area was then overrun with American troops. They lounged at street corners, leaned against public buildings, clung to the railings of latrines, and jigged and ambled along the pavements. So numerous were they that they outnumbered the civilian population five to one. Plump and soft with good living, sometimes obese, they stood or strolled with their hands in their pockets, caps askew, and tunic buttons undone. A passing officer would be saluted with a casual flip of the hand and a familiar 'Hiya, Joe!' Most of them had hanging on to them two or three little painted harlots, not professional prostitutes but 'enthusiastic amateurs' of fourteen or fifteen eager to sell their skinny adolescent bodies to any GI who would give them a 'good time'. In every street huge white-helmeted military policemen, heavily armed, kept grim watch upon the corruption that seethed and bubbled around them.

Younger members of the LCC Staff Association occasionally organized Saturday afternoon lectures and debates. Though these functions attracted me much less strongly than the bookshops of Charing Cross Road, I yielded to the persuasions of a youth who worked further down the corridor and attended two or three of them. This same youth, who was an ardent Communist, had already lent me a textbook of Dialectical Materialism. 'What do you think of it?' he eagerly enquired when I returned the book. But my Neo-Hegelianism had been offended by the author's dogmatic assertion that Marx had found Hegel standing on his head and had set him on his feet. I therefore replied, 'I think it's Marx who is standing on his head, not Hegel.'

At my first Staff Association debate, which was on the motion 'India should be granted immediate independence,' I took an instant dislike to the Chairman, an angular, masculine young woman with a high bony forehead who obviously thought that she was well on her way to becoming chairman of the LCC. When, shortly afterwards, an attempt was made to draw me more deeply into such activities by inviting me to read a paper, I therefore chose the subject 'The Inferiority of Women', interlarding my address with copious extracts from my favourite Schopenhauer diatribes against the 'weaker' sex. After I had read my paper there was a stunned silence. No doubt those rather leftist young members of the Staff Association had never before heard anything so shamelessly reactionary. But they had nothing to say in rebuttal of my arguments. Next day I read the paper to Sonia, who, despite my entreaties, had not attended the meeting. She merely laughed and exclaimed, 'Oh you're mad, quite mad!'

That summer I spent a week at Besthorpe, the tiny Norfolk village in which Nana had been born and where Father had spent several years of his boyhood. It was my third visit, and I stayed in great-grandmother's thatched cottage, now occupied by Uncle Arthur, Auntie Dolly, and Cousin Ezalda. Though I made a trip to Norwich, where I visited the cathedral, the Castle Museum, and the tomb of Sir Thomas Browne, I spent the best part of my time writing letters to Sonia. These letters, the first and the last love letters I ever wrote, were long, literary, and idealistic. In one of them I compared my love to that of Dante for Beatrice. Both my aunt and my cousin were intensely curious to know the reason for this frantic epistolary activity, for I wrote twice a day; but for all their teasing the secret remained unrevealed.

What Sonia thought of my declarations I never knew. The courage I had felt at a safe distance of a hundred miles from my beloved evaporated in her presence. Sonia herself seemed afraid even to allude to the subject. Though she was gay, friendly, and charming as ever, she seemed nervous when we were alone together, as though apprehensive of a sudden violent demonstration of passion. Sometimes she looked at me with a pleading expression, like that of a rabbit fascinated by a snake. On all subjects other than the one we both avoided I talked to her with the frank egotism of the lover; told her my ideas and ideals, ambitions and aspirations. She listened with a smile, laughing whenever I said anything more than usually outrageous, but always with a strange, half-frightened look in her eyes. Her usual comment was, 'You're a genius, no doubt, but absolutely mad.'

Return to London meant, almost as much as a return to Sonia, a renewal of acquaintance with the bookshops of Charing Cross Road. Expanding my sphere of operations, I began penetrating into two or three little courts which opened from it on the right. In one of these I discovered the oriental bookshop which, though well known to all serious English students of Eastern philosophy and religion, had been until then unknown to me. Unlike the other bookshops with their sixpenny and shilling boxes on either side of a wide open door, it was an aloof, reserved, almost mysterious place. In a single box outside the empty window on the left were some damaged specimens of the lighter sort of theosophical literature. The window on the right contained expensive books on the occult sciences. The door between was shut fast. Only after I had several times stopped to thumb the damaged volumes did I venture inside. The interior of the shop was even less like that of a bookshop than the exterior. Through a door at the back of the shop could be seen an octogenarian gentleman, in very powerful spectacles, sitting at a desk. Above the mantelpiece behind him hung a life-size photograph of Mme Blavatsky.

At John Watkins, which thereafter I visited frequently, I bought the two books by which I have been most profoundly influenced. These were the *Diamond Sūtra*, which I read first in Gemmell's then in Max Müller's translation, and the *Sūtra of Wei Lang (Huineng)*. If, when I read *Isis Unveiled*, I knew that I was not a Christian, when I read the *Diamond Sūtra* I knew that I was a Buddhist. Though this book epitomizes a teaching of such rarefied sublimity that even *arahants*, saints who have attained individual Nirvāṇa, are said to become confused and afraid when they hear it for the first time, I at once joyfully embraced it with an unqualified acceptance and assent. To me the *Diamond Sūtra* was not new. I had known it and believed it and realized it ages before and the reading of the *Sūtra* as it were awoke me to the existence of something I had forgotten. Once I realized that I was a Buddhist it seemed that I had always been one, that it was the most natural thing in the world to be, and that I had never been anything else. My experience of the *Sūtra of Wei Lang*, which I read in the original Shanghai edition of Wong Mou-Lam's translation, though taking place at a slightly lower level, was repeated with much greater frequency. Whenever I read the text I would be thrown into a kind of ecstasy. Basically, of course, the teaching of the two *sūtras* is the same, though it cannot be denied that Wei Lang's doctrine of the identity of *prajñā* and *samādhi*, Wisdom and Meditation, has been productive of much confusion of thought, not only in Far Eastern Zen circles, but in their modern Western counterparts.

The realization that I was a Buddhist came in the later summer or early autumn of 1942. At about the same period I had for the first time experiences of the type which are generally known as psychic. Whether these started before or after reading the *Diamond Sūtra* I do not remember. The latter alternative is the more likely as, after a longer or shorter interval of time, a spiritual experience is often as it were echoed on the lower intellectual, emotional, or psychic, or even physical, plane. All these experiences, perhaps seven or eight in number, occurred in my office in County Hall, generally when I was alone. Without any warning a whole series of future events would suddenly unroll themselves like a cinematograph before me. These events, which I saw not with the physical eyes but with what the Buddhist tradition terms the 'divine eye', appeared as clear, vivid, and distinct as anything

I had ever seen by normal means. They were always previsions of what would happen in my immediate surroundings from half an hour to one hour afterwards. I therefore knew in advance who would come into the office, how they would stand, what they would say. Never did anything foreseen fail to occur. Later, in India and elsewhere, I met a number of people, including Europeans, who were much concerned with the development of psychic powers. While such powers undoubtedly can be developed by anybody who is prepared to submit to the proper training and discipline, Buddhist tradition is unanimous in maintaining that the better course is to direct all one's energies to the attainment of Enlightenment and to allow psychic powers to come, if they do come, of their own accord.

From the office I now often went straight to the theatre, having under the Chief's tuition developed a love for the stage which I never in the slightest degree felt for the screen. I saw, among other plays, *Ghosts*, *Hedda Gabler*, and *The Way of the World* at the Duke of York's, *The Master Builder* and *An Ideal Husband* at the Westminster, *Othello* at Wimbledon, and *Twelfth Night* and *Lady Precious Stream* at the Open Air Theatre in Regent's Park. But more deeply than by any of these dramas was I moved by Leslie French's ballet *Everyman*. Though I had read the old morality play several years before, along with *The Fall of Lucifer* and *The Harrowing of Hell*, it now struck me with the force of a thunderbolt. Perhaps for the first time in my life I realized that Friends and Kin, Wealth and Possessions, must all be left behind, and that only our Good Deeds can go with us when Death summons us to make our last journey. So deeply was I impressed that when I tried to write an appreciation of *Everyman* I found my feelings too strong for expression. What, then, would have been the effect of this drama on the unsophisticated audiences of the Age of Faith for whom it was staged, not as an evening's entertainment, but as part of a religious ritual! Only in Tibetan Buddhist literature did I ever again hear that thrilling note of intense pathos, of direct, naked sincerity of religious utterance – so different from the sanctimonious tones of conventional piety – which reverberates through *Everyman*.

With the growth of my interest in the Wisdom of the East visits to, and purchases from, John Watkins became more and more frequent. To the study of Buddhism was annexed that of Taoism and Confucianism, Hinduism and Islam, Sufism and Christian mysticism. My enjoyment of literature was enriched by the discovery of Chinese and Persian poetry, in both of which fields I read as widely as my dependence on translations allowed. Next to Buddhism I was most attracted by Taoism, and among the Taoist classics it was the *Dao De Jing* for which I conceived the strongest admiration. This wonderful distillation of concentrated spiritual wisdom I read in six or eight translations, gaining from each one a new appreciation of its inexhaustible riches of meaning. To me the best translation was Chu Ta-Kao's, which moreover led me, via an advertisement on its back cover, straight to *The Middle Way* and eventually to the London Buddhist Society.

After becoming a subscriber to this journal, which I read with avidity, I wrote two articles on Buddhism. In view of the way in which I subsequently emphasized that our basic allegiance should be not to this or that school, but to the whole Buddhist tradition, it is significant that the first of these articles was entitled 'The Unity of Buddhism'. The second, which was too long to be published, dealt with the Three Characteristics of Existence, otherwise known as the Three Signata – another major preoccupation of later years.[17] Clare Cameron, the editor of *The Middle Way*, had already written to say that she was glad to welcome a new subscriber so well versed in Buddhism, which kind words I did not really deserve. To her, therefore, the articles were submitted. The letter which I wrote on this occasion gave rise to a correspondence which has continued, despite interruptions, for many years.

In the spring Sonia was called up. We parted, as we had met, in the general office. With the intention of allowing the rest of the staff time to depart, I had waited for a few minutes after office hours before crossing the corridor for our last minutes together. To my dismay Thelma was still at her desk. As though in mockery of the look of chagrin which must have appeared on my face, she called out, with pretended archness, 'If you want me to leave the room you'll have to carry me out in your arms!' Never had I so hated a woman. Ignoring her, I turned to Sonia, and after a few minutes of ordinary talk, during which my eyes were eloquent of all the love, desperation, and anguish my tongue was prevented from uttering, we parted with mutual good wishes and a conventional handshake. Thelma's jealous eyes watched us closely from over the filing baskets and followed me to the door.

Hardly knowing what I did, I boarded the homeward tram at the foot of Westminster Bridge and sat on top with grief more acute than I had yet known clutching at my heart. At Clapham Common I suddenly decided to alight. For several months I had been aware of growing estrangement between Mother and Father and instinctively I shrank from returning in a state of such black and bitter sorrow to a home where the peace and consolation I needed were no longer to be found. Instead, like some stricken beast returning to its hole to die, I took refuge in the familiar premises of the second-hand bookshop.

Exactly two hours later, by the clock tower at the tram stop, I emerged. As I boarded the Tooting Broadway tram I realized, with a shock of astonishment, that during the whole of that time I had not once thought of Sonia. Yet though, as it seemed, Nature had not meant me for a lover, I never forgot her. From the letters which came from the ATS training camp to which she had been posted I learned that though well she was unhappy. But that her unhappiness had the same cause as mine she gave me no reason to believe.

Summer passed quickly, and with it my last season as a civilian. After a holiday at Torquay with Joan, who had taken her School Certificate and now lived at home, I was called for my final medical examination. To my amazement I was classified B2. 'There's nothing wrong with your heart,' declared the cardiologist to whom, in view of my history, I had been sent by the general board.

'But I was in bed for two years!' I protested, outraged. With a slight frown he again applied his stethoscope to my chest and back. 'Absolutely nothing wrong,' he repeated, after an examination which seemed to me even more perfunctory than the first. 'Your heart's perfectly sound.'

I left the hospital in bewilderment, not knowing whether to feel delighted at this sudden revelation that I was not a semi-convalescent, but a healthy young man, or dismayed at the prospect of being conscripted. Father was at first equally astonished, but after discussing this unexpected development we agreed that the permanent advantage of good health more than outweighed the temporary inconvenience of a year or two in the army. Consequently we went to the public house where Father now spent most of his evenings and celebrated the news with several rounds of drinks.

My only worry was the thought that I might not be able to finish the novel on which I had been working since the middle of September.[18] So, giving up other interests, I spent all my weekends and evenings shut in my room, where I rapidly filled notebook after notebook. Poetry, of course, could not be so easily relinquished. Ever since joining the LCC I had composed poems in tram and tube while travelling between Tooting Broadway and Westminster. Those composed during the morning journey were written down as soon as I arrived at the office; those composed during the evening journey as soon as I reached home.

One October evening, while I was hanging up my hat and coat in the hall, I heard Father's voice calling me from the sitting room. Alarmed by his unusual agitation I sprang to the open door. Father was standing in the middle of the carpet with an almost berserk expression on his face. Mother sat quietly weeping; near her sat Sid, looking glum and uncomfortable. Joan was sobbing with her head on the mantelpiece.

'Your mother wants to leave us!' Father burst out, before I had time to realize the terrible significance of the scene.

Now that the worst had happened, I knew that I had been expecting it for a long time; but I did not know what to say.

'Do you want to see your mother again?' Father demanded of Joan with unusual roughness.

'No, no, I never want to see her again!' replied my poor sister with renewed sobs. She had been at home only two months and for her the blow had fallen without warning.

Mother began to sob as if her heart would break, wailing, 'Oh, don't talk like that, dear!' But Joan only repeated her words with greater vehemence.

Turning to me, Father asked, 'Do *you* want to see your mother again?' His tone suggested that I could give no other reply than Joan's. Moistening my lips with my tongue, I replied, 'Yes, of course I do.' At these words both Mother and Joan sobbed more violently than ever.

'Well,' said Father, slightly taken aback, 'I won't stand in your way.' Even in anger he was a just man.

How the miserable scene ended I do not know. Sid, who was acquainted with Father, having visited the house several times, tried to make amends at his departure by saying, 'I can't say how sorry I am that this has happened.' But these humble words were of no more avail than the falling of a drop of water upon a red-hot iron plate.

For the rest of the evening we sat in wretched silence. At nine o'clock Joan kissed Father with a bright 'Goodnight, Dad!' and walked out of the room past Mother without a word. Mother's face, whiter and more miserable than I had ever known it, smote me to the heart. After bidding Father goodnight I therefore went over to her and kissed her with a 'Goodnight, Mum!' as usual.

The next few weeks were the worst I had ever known. Three times Mother tried to leave and three times she broke down at the last minute and was unable to go. The ties of twenty-four years were not so easily broken. The intervals between these attempts were periods of unprecedented strain for all of us. Mother was terrified that Father would commit suicide. Once, on my return from the office, I found her sitting at the bottom of the stairs almost crazy with apprehension. From the kitchen I could hear the sound of Father's feet as he paced like a madman up and down the room.

'What's the matter?' I asked. But Mother was becoming hysterical, and she could only repeat, in a whisper, 'Go in to him, go in to him,' in a manner that chilled my blood.

Softly opening the door, I asked, 'Are you all right, Dad?' Father stopped pacing and sat down wearily, passing his hand across his brow. 'Yes, it's all right now, son,' he replied quietly.

Wherever Father went I accompanied him, for Mother would plead, 'Don't leave him. He might do himself an injury.' Usually we went to the public house, where Father drank heavily, and where, to keep him company, I drank heavily too. At night I lay in bed anxiously listening to Mother's and Father's voices as they talked downstairs. Whenever one of them was raised, however slightly, my heart thumped with fear. Only when I heard Mother coming upstairs to her room in the early hours of the morning would I be able to sleep. However, as the weeks went by they talked more and more quietly, as though what had happened was a burden they both had to bear. Then one Saturday afternoon I came home from the office to find that Mother had gone.

At the end of November, a few days after the novel had been finished, came my calling-up papers.

9
THE MISFIT

Leatherhead, where the Signals Unit to which I had been instructed to report was stationed, was a quiet old-fashioned country town in the heart of Surrey. As we approached the crossroads on the far side of the town the traffic-lights abruptly changed from green to red. Ernie, the ginger-haired Cockney who had travelled down with me, remarked how odd it was that a town with no traffic should need traffic lights. We were both more than a little nervous. Turning left past the cinema, as a friendly policeman had directed, we passed a field and a row of small houses. Next came a hospital which I recognized as one of those to which the CNR allocated nurses. Before we could reach the end of the road the November rain, which had been threatening all the morning, started falling steadily. Despite our reluctance we quickened our pace and, passing the remaining villas, turned right into a country lane. After a dozen yards the land became a cart track and we were ankle deep in mud. Perhaps we had lost our way! After anxious consultations we pressed on between the tall hedges until, turning a bend, we saw a khaki-clad figure standing on guard beside a gate.

An hour later, feeling very conspicuous in our civilian suits, we were seated at a scrubbed wooden table in the dining-hall, with about forty other men, eating sausages and mash, followed by apple pie and custard. 'Grub doesn't seem too bad in this hole,' muttered Ernie, busy with a second helping of pie. But the sight and smell of the tubs of greasy water in which we afterwards washed our plates outside almost made me vomit.

The camp was both small and new. It consisted of an eight-roomed house, obviously requisitioned, and two rows of army huts, some still under construction, that had been laid out in the grounds to one side of the house. The dining-hall, which faced the huts, was built alongside the house and communicated with the back door of the kitchen. To the left of the huts, in view of the gate, stood the structure we soon learned to refer to as 'the ablutions'. The trampling of army boots had left no trace of the garden, and in between the huts, as well as between the huts and the house, were avenues of mud. The camp was surrounded by six feet of barbed wire.

In the afternoon Ernie and I were issued with uniforms that did not fit, boots that felt too large, and rifles that seemed much too heavy to lift, together with sundry other articles for which we did not think we would have any particular use. My hair, rather long by army standards, was cut. We were then taken to a hut containing a dozen army cots, two of which were unoccupied, and told that we belonged to 'C' squad and were to take orders from the corporal in charge.

For the next three weeks I felt as though my soul was petrified. Thought, emotion, and will were suspended. I carried out my duties and obeyed orders mechanically, without any mental reaction. It was as though the integrity of my inner being could be safeguarded only by means of a temporary paralysis that not only prevented it from reacting to army life but made it impossible for army life to act upon or influence it in any way. Had this defensive mechanism not come into operation the futility of the existence into which I had been so abruptly plunged might have driven me mad.

Our day began at five o'clock. Still half asleep, we stumbled from the huts and through the darkness towards the light that fell through the door of 'the ablutions'. Unless we arrived very early it was necessary to queue up for our wash and shave, as the number of taps was limited. Porridge and poached eggs were eaten as dawn broke. The rest of our time until parade was spent making up beds for inspection, polishing brasses, applying green blanco to webbing, and cleaning rifles. At eight o'clock we fell in outside the house. After the RSM had run his eye over our rather straggling line, the two corporals were given their orders. With a sudden change of manner from the obsequious to the bullying, they turned smartly from the RSM to their respective squads, barked out a command, and marched us off to the strip of newly asphalted road which was our parade ground.

These drill periods were a nightmare. Had we been allowed simply to march, the foot drill with which we started would not have proved difficult to learn. But apparently intimidation was the army method. We were bawled at for not holding our heads high enough or swinging our arms high enough or sticking our chests out far enough. The main principle of the drill seemed to be that what the squad did was always wrong. One morning an elderly recruit, formerly a teacher, became so exasperated by the corporal's constant hectoring that he snapped, 'It's no use you shouting at me like that, my man, I'm doing my best!' But bad as foot drill was, rifle drill, which we started a week later, was far worse, and our new instructor a fiend compared to short, fresh-complexioned Corporal Smith.

Corporal Halford was a small, ape-like Welshman whose habit it was to masturbate in front of the inmates of his hut every night before going to bed. His manner was simultaneously oily and ferocious, his expression somewhere between a leer and a snarl. It was his practice to threaten the squad with detention, pack drill, fatigues, and other punishments in a low, menacing tone and then suddenly startle it with a command that cracked like a whiplash. The threats were supposed to reduce us to such a state of nervousness that when the command came we jumped. By this method he certainly put a finer polish on our foot drill. But his efforts to teach us rifle drill only reduced the squad to suppressed laughter and himself to snarling ferocity. One of the recruits was a bald-headed businessman who, since a uniform could not be found to fit him, was still wearing black jacket and pin-stripe trousers. 'I'm so sorry, corporal', he said with a giggle one morning, 'I just can't seem to manage the bloody thing.'

He spoke for most of us. The rifles were not only large and heavy but extremely difficult to handle. The smallest recruit, in fact, asked the RSM if he could have a shorter weapon. It would be hard to say whose astonishment was the greater, the RSM's at this strange request or the little recruit's on learning that rifles were all the same size. 'Just like the army,' he grumbled, 'they might as well give us all the same size boots.'

Bad as the rest of the squad was at rifle drill, Ernie and I were far worse. As we often remarked to each other, ability to handle a rifle seemed in inverse ratio to one's IQ.

In the afternoon, Corporal Smith, who was in charge of our hut, taught us 'naming the parts of the rifle'. Unfortunately he was unable to pronounce certain sounds. 'Male thread', for example, was always 'male tread'. At first we carefully reproduced all his mispronunciations. He also taught us how to take the rifle apart for cleaning, how to use the pull-through, and how to load and unload. Next to striking an officer, we gathered, the most serious offence one could commit in the army was to lose one's rifle.

Every other afternoon we had an hour's PT on the lawn behind the house. These periods I was soon able to evade. The gruff old MO who had inoculated us had merely said, 'If you collapse during PT fall out and report sick!' But thinking it safer to fall out first I told the corporal I had been excused PT on medical grounds. When there was nothing else to do, we were ordered into our jeans for fatigues. This we liked best of all. Ernie and I quickly discovered that provided we carried something in our hand and walked past NCOs with a brisk, purposeful air, we were never molested. Many an afternoon did we spend walking about the camp with the same piece of wood or the same empty bucket.

Unless we happened to be confined to barracks, our evenings were our own. Ernie and I could not escape from camp quickly enough. Usually we went into Leatherhead immediately after tea and spent the evening in the Forces Canteen. On the way back to camp I sometimes telephoned Mother, who was then living at Clapham.

But the best part of the day was the hour or two before lights out. With the beds made down and the mouth of the stove glowing fiery red, the bleak bare hut looked almost comfortable. In twos or threes our fellow inmates returned, most of them redder in the face, louder of voice, and more uncertain of step than when they went out. Lying or sitting on our beds, or on our neighbours' beds, we talked and laughed in the warm, friendly, uninhibited atmosphere of the barrack room until our 'personalities', that had been crushed flat by the corporal's boots all day, began to revive, and our individual idiosyncrasies to bloom like exotic flowers.

Ernie, who at first occupied the bed adjacent to mine, had naturally become my best friend. A month younger than I, he did not look more than fourteen. Despite the sharpness of his features his face wore an expression of such guilelessness and innocence that even the hearts of NCOs were touched. He was, however, by far the shrewdest person in the whole camp and on more than one occasion was I staggered by the almost supernatural quality of his cunning. The hut soon discovered that he possessed a pair of well-developed breasts, the fame whereof spread throughout the camp and reached even the Colonel's ears. At first Ernie was very ashamed of these features, scowling whenever they were made the subject of comment. But he quickly learned that they could be turned to advantage. More than one of our married friends was deeply disturbed at the sight of Ernie sitting on the end of his bed playing with his shapely white breasts. Not that he had the slightest intention of granting any favours. 'Don't go away,' he would mutter out of the corner of his mouth, whenever any of his admirers showed signs of becoming too importunate. 'That dirty bugger's after me again.'

Four of the other inmates of the hut were of our own age. Laurie, a calm, smiling, good-natured boy with a slight squint, preferred to go about alone. Alice, so called after a famous actress whose surname was the same as his own, was distinguished by his ability to drop off to sleep at a moment's notice at any time in any position. A fat, owlish youth, his pulse rate was thirty-two, the lowest of which I ever heard. Mike, clean-limbed and handsome, found it impossible to adapt himself to army life. At first defiant and disobedient, he eventually became openly rebellious and in the end got into very serious trouble. He was the type the army breaks. Smeed, who arrived later and whom we never called by his first name, was a slow, moon-faced youth much interested in railway engines who was neither liked nor disliked.

The idiosyncrasies of our elders, having had in some cases twice as much time for development, were naturally more marked. Pinkie, the schoolmaster who had snapped at Corporal Smith, was never seen off parade without his pipe. His hobby was collecting bus and tram routes; his favourite reading, timetables. He knew, stop by stop, the route of every bus and tram in London and the Home Counties. To him a holiday meant a ride over one of the longer and less familiar routes.

Batty Tatty, or Tat – undersized, weedy, and pimpled – had a loud voice and the music hall type of Lancashire accent. He spent the whole of every evening deeply absorbed in a large album that contained only photographs of himself from the age of two months upwards. A strange combination of simplicity and cunning, he was utterly selfish, and though the butt of all, became the friend of none. Harry 'the Ticker', who had asked the RSM for a shorter rifle, was so called for his constant cheerful grumble, which was so incessant as to resemble the regular ticking of a watch. He and Alice apparently had an elective affinity for each other, for they were always together. Fish, a Jew of uncertain age, took himself so seriously as to become an object of ridicule. His greatest fear was that he might have to cut short his black, wavy hair, which was thin on top and dyed; his greatest sorrow, when he was made to hand in his greatcoat after having it altered by his tailor. Pete and Eddie were even more inseparable than most chums. The former was the fattest, the latter the tallest and thinnest, inmate of the hut. Though very obviously himself an Anglo-Indian, Eddie always spoke of 'the bloody wogs' with contempt and loathing. Behind his back the hut was unimpressed. 'He's a bloody wog himself,' we chuckled.

The hut's chief topic of conversation was sex. Ernie and I and the rest of the youngsters, who had nothing of our own to contribute, listened while the older men discussed the size, shape, and mechanics of their respective organs, their sexual experiences, the different modes of copulation, and the sexual physiology of the female, all in the most exhaustive detail. But once our natural curiosity was satisfied, we found this incessant preoccupation with sex both boring and disgusting and turned away to discuss more interesting subjects among ourselves.

In the course of my fourth week at camp my numbed faculties began to revive. For some days I had been composing Persian-style quatrains as we marched up and down our parade ground. These poems, more than 300 of which were eventually written down, came up crocus-like through the crust of despair that overlaid my heart. The current of my inner life, frozen ice-hard since the day I joined the army, thawed and began to flow. As a mountain stream discovers a path round the boulders it is powerless to displace, I awoke to the fact that, although military life might for a time divert, it could not permanently deflect, the master current of my being. Though it could waste my time, it could not destroy my interests. I resolved I would allow the army neither to make me nor break me. Since it was stronger than I, I would observe its ridiculous regulations and obey the orders of its idiotic minions, but with all the strength and integrity of my soul I would loathe, despise, and utterly repudiate the army and all it stood for.

The nature of our unit eventually made it easy for me not only to carry out this resolution but actively to pursue my own interests. Full-time military training had quickly yielded to half-time, the mornings or afternoons thus gained being devoted to learning Morse. The 'technical' corporals who now took us in hand were notoriously indifferent to matters of discipline, and between them and the 'military' corporals smouldered ill-concealed hostility. Corporal Smith left our hut to take charge of a new intake, his place being occupied by Tom, a handsome young giant of a technical instructor whom Ernie's breasts at once captivated. After our return from Christmas leave drill and fatigues were discontinued, and after a fierce battle between the technical and military NCOs we were even excused guard duties.

The arrival of a Regular Army sergeant seemed at first to augur trouble. He did, indeed, inveigle the CO, a former bank manager, into ordering a company parade in full marching order. But the sight of us lined up outside in the lane with our packs askew and our rifles at different angles was so ludicrous that the experiment was not repeated. Besides, the technical side was reinforced by the arrival of a fat, friendly CSM and a small, grizzled, blasphemous QM, who lounged about in canvas shoes with their hands in their pockets, buttons undone and without caps. Though their informal presence soon made it obvious that our duties would not be military in the narrow sense of the term at all, the unit's indispensable minimum of Regular Army NCOs did their utmost to make camp life conform to the traditional pattern.

From the point of view of the work we did later, our being in the army was an accident. Nothing the military NCOs taught us proved of the slightest value. Packs and rifles proved mere impedimenta. Futile exhibitions of Regular Army infantilism such as company parades wasted time that should have been devoted to improving our knowledge of the work to which our country had called us. The officers and the RSM, of course, knew this long before we did, and the very perfunctory military routine they had included in our training was no more than a token recognition of the fact that the unit was part of the army. Yet to the last we were harassed by pettifogging Regular NCOs who made life as difficult for us as they possibly could.

Corporal Halford's behaviour over the question of leave was a case in point. After a few of us, including Ernie and myself, had twice or thrice gone home on weekend passes, he warned us, as though in friendly confidence, that the RSM strongly objected to this, and that those who offended in future would be transferred to the Signals Depot in Oswestry, a name as dreadful to our ears as that of Sheol to the ancient Hebrews. This information disturbed us profoundly. The married men saw their opportunities for sexual intercourse curtailed. Ernie and I and the rest of the youngsters felt that without an occasional brief spell of freedom our existence would be intolerable. For several days the inmates of every hut debated the subject with gloomy faces. Some felt Halford's warning had saved us from disaster; others that he was bluffing; most, that it would be better not to take any chances. That weekend nearly everybody remained in camp. Ernie and I uneasily went home as usual.

Not long afterwards the RSM held a question-and-answer meeting. NCOs were excluded. Halford, however, was kind enough to warn us against asking questions about leave. After the RSM had answered innocuous enquiries about promotions, widow's pensions, and medical treatment, one long-suffering married man, greatly daring, rose to his feet and hesitantly asked the question which was uppermost in our minds: 'How often should we apply for a weekend pass?'

'As often as you like,' replied the RSM. 'In fact,' he continued crisply, 'unless you happen to be on guard duty I would advise you to apply every week. Now that you've started your technical training you'll naturally be feeling a bit of a strain. After a day or two at home you'll come back to your duties all the fresher. No need for anyone to be in camp at weekends except the guard.'

The technical training, then recently begun, had in fact proved a considerable strain on almost all the older men. For some, the learning of the Morse code was in itself difficult enough. (Ernie had learned it in the Boy Scouts, I in the BB.) But that was merely a beginning. As we gradually progressed from receiving at a speed of five words a minute to a speed of ten, and from ten to fifteen, several, unable to stand the increase of nervous tension, fell by the wayside and were transferred to general duties. Ernie and I, who soon led the class, long afterwards ruefully agreed that it would have been better for us to have fallen too. For whereas throw-outs who worked in the office were eventually promoted NCOs and WOs, we remained signalmen for ever. But in those early days, not knowing what was in store, we zealously pursued the path of our own undoing.

Stimulated by the encouragement of Tom and the officers, our speed steadily increased, and we were soon far ahead of the rest of the class. Though each did his best to surpass the other, we invariably passed our speed tests together. Our enthusiasm was largely due to consciousness of our enhanced prestige. The last in the drill squad had become the first in the technical class. The despair of the Regular Army corporals were the delight of the Morse instructors. When, one afternoon, we both blocked for one minute at a speed of thirty-one, faster than which even Tom could not transmit, we felt that our theory that the worse you were at squad drill the greater was your intelligence had been fully vindicated.

Meanwhile spring had come. The laburnums we passed on our way in to town had burst into yellow flame, while the young leaves of the copper-beech trees showed a chocolate-veined redness against the late afternoon sky. Ever sensitive to change of season, but most of all to the advent of spring, I felt strangely exhilarated. Since our promotion to the Set Room, whence for security reasons all but the instructors and operators were strictly barred, we enjoyed more weekend passes and afternoons off than ever. Father, always pleased to see me home again, jocosely remarked that in *his* army days leave had not been so easy to get. Mother seemed to spend Saturday afternoons waiting behind the front door of her flat, for it always flew open even before I had finished ringing the bell. Though more subdued than before, she seemed happy and contented. She and Father had agreed on a divorce. With Sid, who sometimes came to tea, my relations were cordial, for it was impossible not to like the quiet, friendly, inoffensive man. Joan, too, now reconciled to Mother and on good terms with Sid, was also a frequent visitor. Tall and well developed, she worked in a bank; but her ambition, of which Father heard with dismay, was to join the ATS. Sometimes I went to see Nana and Auntie Noni, on one occasion spending the afternoon rambling with Auntie over Wimbledon Common, where mile after mile the purple-black heather showed patches of tender green, while along the edges of the wood fern-shoots stood among last year's yellow-brown bracken like little green croziers.

Our evenings Ernie and I usually spent in the crowded bar of the King's Head with Tom, who taught us to drink black and tans but took good care we did not have too many. Sometimes we wrote letters and played table tennis with the ATS in the Forces Recreation Room in the High Street. Once or twice I took Ernie to Ewell, only two or three stations along the line. Auntie Kath, who had returned from Torquay with Uncle Charles after the Blitz, was friendly and voluble as ever. On learning that she had herself cooked us scrambled eggs and chipped potatoes the rest of the family was dumbfounded. 'Were they eatable?' I was asked in obvious disbelief.

One Saturday afternoon Ernie and I climbed to the top of Box Hill. Far below us tiny fields of different shades of green and brown made a patchwork to the horizon, gradually softening into haze. In between were hedges, trees, and farms. Here and there a pond flashed molten gold in the sun. Just below the horizon showed the dark smudge of towns. As we lay in the hot grass, the earth as it were lifting us up to the embraces of the sun which swam in a great sky of cloudless blue, I read a few chapters of *Thus Spake Zarathustra*. Intoxicated by those ardent words, I wanted to shout them out in the face of the sun so that they might echo from end to end of the sky. But after shutting my eyes for a minute against the blinding brilliance of the light, I saw they were already written in quivering scarlet letters across the blue.

In Leatherhead my favourite spot was the garden of a tea-shop. Blackbirds, bright-eyed and yellow-billed, hopped on the lawn, and pink and white petals drifted from the fruit trees onto the pages of my book. I was reading at the time, with equal delight, Donne and Herrick. An unusually felicitous line went through me like a spear. Sometimes, closing the book, I would fall into a muse and try to shape the rhythms and the images that were ringing in my head into verses of my own. Later, on the outskirts of the town, I discovered a mile or two of river, overhung with willows, up and down which kingfishers flashed crimson and blue. Sitting beside the shallow, sunlit water, at the bottom of which sticks and stones were clearly visible, I read *The Middle Way*, in which my article 'The Unity of Buddhism' had appeared a few months earlier.

Having learned about its activities, and seen my name in the pages of its journal, I was naturally desirous of coming into closer contact with the London Buddhist Society. One warm Saturday afternoon, therefore, I found my way to the rooms it then occupied over a restaurant in Great Russell Street. I had finished looking at the books and was talking to the librarian when in came a pixie-like figure with a square-cut fringe and voluminous tweed cloak. This was Clare Cameron. When I introduced myself to her she was astonished at seeing a boy instead of the middle-aged man she had imagined. For my part, I recognized in her one of those rare spirits who, in the words of the Indian poet, are tender as a flower and hard as a diamond. I liked her instantly. After she had introduced me to the founder-president, Christmas Humphreys, a correct gentlemanly figure in a lounge suit, a recording of Bach's 'Sheep May Safely Graze' was played and the meeting began.

Thereafter I attended meetings as often as I could. Usually not more than a dozen people were present. One afternoon an air raid warning sounded while we were meditating, for in a last desperate bid for victory, before the final crash, Germany had started its indiscriminate launching of VIs against the civilian population of London and the Home Counties. But either out of Buddhist equanimity or British phlegm we continued to meditate, not stirring even when, a few minutes later, the windows rattled with the blast of an explosion.

Among the members with whom I became acquainted was R. L. Jackson, a short grizzled man in sports jacket and baggy flannels who had obviously had a hard life and whose conversation, like his writings, was larded with quotations from the English poets. It seemed odd that he should address the president deferentially as 'Mr Humphreys' when the latter called him simply 'Jackson', treating him in an off-hand, patronizing sort of manner. Perhaps I had assumed that class distinctions would not be recognized within in the Society. Nearer my own age was Arnold Price, with whom I could discuss Buddhism more freely than with anybody else. One evening we progressed, arguing, through every public house between Great Russell Street and Waterloo Station – perhaps not the most seemly behaviour for either the future translator of the *Diamond Sūtra* or the future *bhikṣu*.

A more Buddhistic occasion was that on which Humphreys took us all to a vegetarian restaurant for dinner, in the course of which he gave an amusing description of how he had tried to translate one of his own poems into French. Clare Maison, whom I took part of the way home afterwards, was like most of the women members a great admirer of the president. As we stood on the draughty tube platform waiting for her train, she told me about her efforts to collect material for a biography of Ananda Maitreya, the first Englishman to return to England as a *bhikṣu*.

By this time I was sufficiently adjusted to life in the unit to be able to pursue my study of Buddhism unperturbed by the un-Buddhistic surroundings. The books I borrowed from the Society's library I usually read sitting on the quiet banks of the river, where I also wrote two or three poems afterwards published in *The Middle Way*. Memories of *The Systems of Buddhistic Thought* and *Thirty Stanzas on Representation Only*, both of which influenced me deeply, are inseparably connected with those of dragonflies, gauze-winged and sapphire-bodied, delicately poised on the surface of the water, over which played reflections and shadows of willow leaves. This was perhaps as it should have been. Was not the Buddha-nature reflected in every natural object, in every flower and stone and blade of grass?

Back in the Set Room I pondered on the new, yet strangely familiar, teachings with which I was gradually becoming acquainted. Sometimes, neglecting my task of intercepting unidentifiable transmissions, I sat with headphones over my ears, hands resting on the dials, and simply gazed out of the window at the sky. At the end of every hour I wrote 'Nil to report' in the log before me. On the lawn outside a new intake practised charging with fixed bayonets at a dummy on which the heart and stomach were indicated by red patches. The sergeant was satisfied with their performance only when, with rage-distorted features and blood-curdling yells, they rushed like madmen upon the dummy and eviscerated it with gleeful ferocity.

In May the Buddhist Society celebrated, as it did every year, the full moon day of the Indian month of Vaiśākha, anniversary of the Birth, Enlightenment, and *parinirvāṇa* of Gautama the Buddha. The meeting must have been held on a Saturday or a Sunday afternoon, for I was able to attend. Mother, who had been studying some elementary books on Buddhism, accompanied me. As we sat at the back of the hall waiting for the meeting to begin, a short stout gentleman of Mongolian appearance, in a dark suit and carrying an attaché case, entered the hall and disappeared into an adjoining room. Five minutes later he reappeared in orange robes. This was U Thittila, the first Buddhist monk I had seen. Later, when I was myself 'in the robes', I heard that narrowly formalistic Burmese Buddhists had severely criticized him for his supposed misconduct in wearing ordinary European clothes when not actually performing his religious duties. English Buddhists saw the matter in quite a different light. Throughout the Blitz U Thittila had worked as a stretcher-bearer, on several occasions risking his life to rescue people trapped beneath fallen masonry. Finding that the voluminous drapery of his robes hampered his movements he sensibly exchanged them for more practical garments. People who knew him said he practised what he preached. I have always been glad that it was from him that I first took the Three Refuges and Five Precepts, with the recitation of which the meeting opened, U Thittila intoning them in Pāli and Humphreys leading the responses. At the end of the meeting I introduced Mother to Humphreys and Clare Cameron, both of whom were among the speakers. U Thittila, again in his dark suit, hurried away. The V1s were still falling and he most likely had a job to do.

A few days later Clare Cameron invited me to have tea with her at her Bayswater flat. On the way up to the bright pleasant kitchen I caught a glimpse of her husband, Thomas Burke, at work in his book-lined study. If at our first meeting she had impressed me as being tender *and* hard, I now saw that Clare appeared not only very young but very old – a combination of elf and sibyl. Her physical age might have been anywhere between thirty and fifty. But what struck me most was the way in which her whole face lit up from within when she smiled – lit up through a faint network of tiny lines and wrinkles that testified that, for her, understanding had not been achieved without suffering. She looked frail as gossamer. But I soon realized that she was the only person in the society with enough strength of character not to be dominated by Humphreys.

In the course of my first visit she gave me a copy of her book of poems *A Stranger Here*. A week or two later, taking my courage in both hands, I showed her what I thought were the best of my own verses. As we walked through Kensington Gardens she gave me the benefit of some very sound criticism. Ten years later, when I published *Messengers From Tibet and Other Poems*, I dedicated it to her in token of my gratitude and admiration.

Several times that June, as I sat twiddling knobs and dials in the Set Room, I saw the black cigar-like shape of a V1 streaking through the sky in the direction of London. Once, watching one of these sinister objects, I heard the engine cut off and saw it suddenly nosedive into a field. The explosion that followed rattled the windows. But dangerous as I knew them to be I little thought that one of them would be responsible for the destruction of my own home.

After leaving camp at one o'clock on Saturday afternoon as usual, I alighted from the tram at the bottom of our road at two-thirty. It was one of those bright, clear summer days which make a disaster seem all the more horrible in contrast, as if Nature cared nothing for the misery of man. As I stepped onto the pavement I noticed that tiles were missing from the roofs of several houses and a few windows broken. Obviously a 'rocket' had fallen somewhere near. As I climbed the hill the damage became worse. Whole roofs had been blown off and hardly a pane of glass was intact. Our own house was still out of sight round the bend at the top of the road. Fear gripped my heart, but I did not quicken my pace. The house only three or four doors down from ours was half destroyed. Several people stared at me curiously as I passed. Turning the bend I saw, to my intense relief, Father standing outside the gate in conversation with a neighbour. His bicycle was propped against the kerb. Behind him the whole front of the house gaped open; the downstairs ceiling sagged dangerously.

'Seems rather badly damaged,' I remarked. 'When did it happen?'

'About an hour ago,' Father replied quite cheerfully. 'The dust was still settling when I arrived.'

'Where were you at the time, then?'

'Oh, I had just stopped at Jack and Hilda's on my way back from work, just to see if they were all right. As soon as I heard the explosion I jumped on my bike and came here.'

Had Father returned at one o'clock, as he usually did on Saturdays, instead of at one-thirty, he would surely have been killed, as the rocket had exploded on our very doorstep, where the dent it had made was later found. Father's anxiety about the safety of my uncle and aunt had saved his life. Mother was, of course, at Clapham; Joan had joined the ATS three weeks previously. Had Mother not left us, had Father not returned late, had Joan not joined the ATS, and had I arrived an hour earlier, the whole family would have been killed at lunch. Friends and relations were deeply impressed by what appeared to have been a providential escape for all of us. Norah and Phyllis, who had been at home when the rocket fell, were both seriously injured. Two or three people in the house opposite were killed.

That afternoon and the following day Father and I salvaged whatever we could from the ruins. A few pieces of furniture and one or two carpets were still usable and the contents of drawers and cupboards largely intact. Though it was dangerous to do so, I insisted on climbing up the remaining stairs to see what had happened to my books. Out of 1,000, about 400 were either destroyed or very badly damaged. The undamaged ones, which fortunately included most of the more valuable volumes, I removed and stacked on the lawn with the rest of the salvage. The floor of my room then collapsed.

Father having managed to borrow a truck, we removed the remnants of our home to Ewell, it having been understood between Uncle Charles and Father since the beginning of the war that the house of each would be at the disposal of the other in case of need. After returning to camp on Sunday night, I saw the CO on Monday morning and was granted a week's compassionate leave. From Leatherhead I went straight to Joan's camp, which was in a nearby town. She, too, was granted compassionate leave and the pair of us, now both in khaki, travelled up to Ewell. Somehow we felt very young and yet terribly old. Joan, who had taken the news in a calm, matter-of-fact way, now told me about her work. Though barely seventeen, she regularly took a two-ton lorry from the south coast all the way up to Scotland, driving at night, in convoy, and without lights. Father was, of course, very glad to see her, and the three of us spent the week at Ewell together quite happily. Uncle Charles's firm having again evacuated its staff, this time to Somerset, we had the house to ourselves.

Not long after my return to camp rumours began to circulate about the unit having been posted abroad. The married men fervently hoped they were unfounded; but in Ernie and me and the rest of the youngsters vague nomadic longings stirred. Though for security reasons our destination was not revealed, the rumours were at first tacitly then expressly confirmed, until the whole camp was restless, excited, and there was no talk save of our impending departure. Tom, who was on confidential terms with one of the officers, told Ernie and me that our destination was definitely India. But with such a buzz of speculation around us, some saying it would be Gibraltar, some Singapore, and some even America, it was difficult to feel sure. Besides, that I should be going to India, the land in which the Buddha had lived and taught, seemed too good to be true. For the first, though by no means the last time in my life, did I have an obscure sense of some mysterious Destiny shaping my ends. I had thought the army would cut me off from Buddhism. What if it should now prove the means appointed to bring me closer to it than I had dreamed would be possible?

At the beginning of August we were given a week's embarkation leave. Much of this time I spent arranging what was left of my library and tying my manuscript books in bundles. Two or three rare volumes, as well as the thick black notebook containing my most recent poems, I left with Clare. One or two days were spent with Nana in Somerset, where she was staying, not very happily, in the same village as Uncle Charles and Auntie Kath. When I said goodbye she clung to me tearfully as if she would never let me go. Both knew we would never meet again. Back in London, I took Sonia to see *Swan Lake*, dined out once or twice with Mother, and spent a few evenings at the local public house with Father. The final leave-takings were restrained and casual.

Three or four days later we entrained for the north. Most of the journey I spent writing poetry. But the bleak northern landscape, with its barren fields and squat stone hedges, fascinated me, and every now and then I lifted my eyes from the notebook and gazed out of the window. In the late afternoon on the second day the train stopped at the foot of a huge rock which, rising sheer for several hundred feet, tapered into the walls, battlements, and turrets of an ancient castle. Two or three hours later, rifles in hand, packs on our backs, and kitbags balanced on one shoulder, we stood on the quayside of the Glasgow docks waiting to file up the gangway into the bowels of the enormous grey troop-ship.

Two days later, as the convoy passed the northern coast of Scotland and swung out into the Atlantic, I celebrated my nineteenth birthday. England had been left behind, perhaps for ever. But where were we going? Five days later, in the middle of the Atlantic, halfway to America, we still did not know the answer.

10
PASSAGE TO INDIA

'D' deck, somewhere on which the unit was quartered, was the fourth deck down. Ernie and I were crowded together with scores of other sweating naked bodies under the harsh glare of electric lights while around us the whole ship quivered and shook with the constant heavy pounding of the engines. Practically the entire space from hatch cover to bulkhead was occupied by long clamped-down tables where we ate during the day and on which some of us slept at night. Kitbags were stacked in corners and packs and water-bottles stowed away between the girders and the deckhead. Though stifled by the heat, most of us caught colds through our habit of sleeping as close as possible to the blowers. Prickly heat was made worse by our having to wash and bathe in warm sticky sea-water using gritty yellow sea-soap that refused to lather. Like the rest of the troops Ernie and I spent most of our time on the passenger and boat decks, elbowing our way aft through the slowly milling khaki mass. At night, stupefied rather than asleep, we lay on tables or benches or the deck, or hung side by side from the deckhead in hammocks. Loud snores and heavy breathing filled the darkness, in which glowed two or three small red lights. Dreaming feverish dreams, we could feel ourselves being still shaken by the mighty pulsations of the engines. In the morning, tired and sticky, we got up with relief and went for a latherless wash and shave in sea-water.

Not knowing when I would again see a library or bookshop, I had squeezed into my kitbag *The Light of Asia, Selections from Hegel, The*

Penguin Book of English Verse, and a few other pocket volumes selected chiefly on account of their convenient size. The unit had won exemption from ship's duties on the grounds that it had work to do in the Set Room that had been rigged up in the monkey island; but atmospheric disturbances and the ship's dynamo made reception impossible. Since the only remaining call on our time was the ten o'clock lifeboat drill, I was therefore free to spend most of the day reading. Probably because of the conditions under which we were living, I read such poems as 'Heaven-Haven', 'The Haystack in the Floods', and 'Cynara'[19] with a strangely troubled intensity of emotion. Every day I composed in my head and then wrote down two or three short poems. These eventually formed a sort of verse diary of my impressions of the voyage.

One morning we awoke to find the ship in blue waters. The convoy had altered course two or three days earlier, and we had passed Gibraltar in the night. From then onwards my poems were usually descriptive of the scenes we passed. Alexandria, a distant streak of gleaming whiteness between sea and sky, led to a poem on Alexander the Great, the desert to one beginning, 'The first camel I saw was a white one', and so on. At Port Said, which we reached at nightfall, everyone crowded excitedly to the rail to see what was, after five years of blackout, the marvellous sight of buildings outlined with thousands of yellow lights. Red and blue neon signs flared with unearthly splendour against the sky, the biggest and brightest of them an advertisement for Dewar's Whisky, seeming for once like the dazzling epiphany of another world. Most beautiful of all, the lights nearest the quayside picked out in the black depths of the dock waters inverted palaces of rippling gold.

As slowly we squeezed our way down through the Suez Canal, the banks seeming in places hardly wider than the ship itself, I never tired of watching the great foam-serpent at the water's edge as it raced abreast of the ship with an eager undulating movement. Sometimes I stared so long and hard that I could scarcely believe it was not a real live dragon keeping me friendly company like a faithful dog, instead of just the bow wash striking against the side of the canal.

At Suez we were allowed ashore. Though I had not been seasick the earth felt strangely firm underfoot. After a visit to the local restaurant, a low wooden shack where we ate eggs and bacon with an unusual amount of elbow room, Ernie and I spent half an hour exploring the dock area before finally climbing back on board. Aden, which we saw at twilight, was an enormous ash heap at the foot of which ant-like figures crawled about among the cinders. But this dismal sight once left behind, day after day there was only the blue-black wrinkled expanse of the Indian Ocean, where porpoises played astern and flying-fish skimmed like silver arrows over the waves and where, at night, the phosphorescent wake streamed out through the darkness behind us a pale and ghostly green.

What would India be like? Long before the horizon thickened into land I started asking myself this question. The *Children's Encyclopaedia* had left vague memories of marble palaces and bewhiskered Rajput princes. Missionaries on furlough, appealing for our coppers at Sunday school, had given impressions of a land of mud huts where they lived in constant fear of martyrdom at the hands of fanatical grass-skirted savages. Uncle Dick had spoken of rickshaws. Regular Army NCOs who had been stationed in India described it as the hottest, poorest, filthiest country on earth and the 'wogs' as the very dregs of humanity. It seemed difficult to fit the Buddha and his teaching into any of these backgrounds.

What gradually hove in sight through the drizzle of a late September morning (we were in the midst of a different set of seasons and had run into the tail end of the monsoon) was a stretch of Bombay dockside under a low grey sky. As we edged nearer through the dingy water, more like ochre-coloured liquid mud than anything else, oblong boxes grew by degrees into huge warehouses of corrugated iron. Here and there a crane hung idle against the sky. The odd knots of blue-clad figures on the quay did not seem to be doing anything in particular. There was no noise. The whole place seemed half dead. Only the kites, rising and falling in endless spirals overhead, seemed more or less alive.

From the back of the lorry that took us to the station we had a glimpse of tree-lined streets, bullock-carts, and thin dark figures in flapping off-white garments. On the journey to Delhi, which we made in bogies with hard wooden benches instead of upholstered seats, ghastly poverty whined around us whenever the train stopped. Emaciated women in filthy rags pushed rusty tins through the windows and pleaded with gentle insistence for alms. Spindly-limbed children with enormous protruding bellies clamoured for coins and scraps of food. Gauntly naked men, in an attempt to excite pity, pointed to deformed or missing limbs. Half the beggars seemed blind or halt or maimed. One, quite naked, moved from carriage to carriage exhibiting testicles swollen to the size of footballs. Horrified at the sight of poverty such as they had never imagined could exist, most of the BORs handed out small coins and food at every station. The Indian troops a little further down the train, doubtless more accustomed to such sights, leaned grinning from the windows and gave nothing. Even more dreadful than the poverty was the apathy, the patient hopeless resignation, apparent on the faces of the beggars. Their shoulders were bowed and their heads bent in uncomplaining acceptance of their lot. It was God's will, they seemed to be saying, God's will be done!

The camp outside Delhi consisted of a dozen buildings with thatched roofs and dazzlingly white walls surrounded by sand and scrub on which the sun blazed down from a sky more deeply and darkly blue than I had ever known. In between the barracks, shading them from the glare, could be seen the bushy, light green foliage of the *margosa* trees. Grey-brown squirrels with three white stripes down their backs raced chattering up and down the smooth trunks, sometimes pausing in between flicks of their bushy tails to cling motionless for an instant with bright beady eyes. Crows in pearl-grey cravats perched on the roofs, while overhead hovered more kites which, effortlessly rising and falling hour after hour, described great sweeps whenever their outstretched wings were caught by an air current.

Owing largely to the heat, at that time of year so intense that the landscape quivered, army life in India had developed a pattern of its own. There were no general duties. In our case there were no parades or military duties of any kind either. All the menial work of the camp was done by Indian bearers. Operators were on duty only half the day, one week mornings one week afternoons, the rest of the time being their own. In the Set Room, where most of us wore nothing but shorts and canvas shoes, a quiet drowsy atmosphere prevailed. Only an occasional muffled shriek from somebody's headphones disturbed the stillness. Very little work was done. Most of my time was spent scribbling poems on scraps of paper. Sometimes I watched the bulgy-eyed, semi-transparent orange geckoes suckered onto the wall. Every now and then one of them would make a loud clicking sound. Once a praying mantis, vivid green and with a face like the head of a safety pin, whirred onto my set and perched there motionless. At ten in the morning and four in the afternoon would come the licensed cake-wallah. A good part of our pay was spent each week buying little sweet cakes covered with multi-coloured icing, three or four of which we always took with our mugs of dark, bitter-tasting tea.

In the lofty-ceilinged barrack room it was comparatively cool. Seven or eight charpoys, wooden bedsteads with a network of coarse fibre rope instead of springs, stood with their heads against the wall. Six-foot bamboos, lashed to the legs of the charpoys, supported the mosquito-nets, whereunder much of our time was spent in the traditional recumbent posture of the British soldier in India. A door, through which I could see the scrubby yellow landscape and intensely blue sky, opened onto a veranda which ran the whole length of the building. Here the dhobi-wallah, the cake-wallah, and our own bearers, in green, brown, and blue lungis, would squat on their heels quietly chatting, occasionally glancing up through the doorway with bright, furtive eyes. For the first week Myers's trilogy *The Near and the Far*, which I had borrowed from a room-mate, absorbed my whole attention. With its background of sophisticated court life at Agra and Delhi during the reign of Akbar it was a fitting introduction to the glory and grandeur that had been Mogul India.

Half a mile from camp was a small bazaar. Here, in a tiny restaurant exhibiting the blue-wheeled 'in bounds' sign, Ernie and I sometimes sat among the cracked wall mirrors at a marble topped table, drinking iced Vimto through double straws. When he came to take our order, the proprietor cheerfully wiped the table with a filthy rag. In a shop which sold magazines, stationery, and picture postcards I discovered a couple of shelves of books. As is usual in Indian bookstalls, pornography and religion rubbed shoulders. An English translation of the *Bhagavad Gītā*, which I purchased for a few annas, was keeping company with *The Adventures of Erotic Edna* and *Hindu Art of Love (Illustrated)*. Later, especially in South India, I often found articles on God-Realization and frankly-worded advertisements for aphrodisiacs printed side by side in the same magazine. India believed, apparently, in impartial catering for all tastes.

When I had been on morning duty I usually spent the afternoon and evening in the city. Sometimes I walked several miles along the Agra–Delhi road before getting a lift from a passing army truck. The flat, rocky landscape, barren save for the tender green of stunted thorn trees, had a delicate austere beauty which touched me more deeply than anything

I had seen in England. Lush meadows and leafy woods seemed, in fact, rather vulgar in comparison. It was an aloof, aristocratic landscape which somehow suggested centuries of culture and refinement. Usually neither a house nor a human being was in sight. Once or twice I saw a figure that might have come from the Old Testament standing motionless on a rock while little white goats with black and brown markings and blunt faces streamed among the nullahs nibbling at tufts of wiry grass.

The contrast between the red sandstone walls of the Lal Khila, or Red Fort, massive enough to enclose a town, and the row of white marble palace buildings that overlooked the River Jumna from the rear battlements, struck me as tremendously effective. Is not this wedding of strength and grace, of the stupendous and the delicate, one of the greatest charms of Mogul architecture? While I would not attempt to erect a personal preference into an objective aesthetic judgement, its austerely beautiful mosques and tombs, its palaces and forts, have often satisfied me more deeply than the prodigal richness, the unrestrained exuberance, of their Hindu counterparts. Indeed, they have often satisfied me more deeply than their Indian Buddhist counterparts. As I stood in the multi-columned Diwan-i-Khas, or Hall of Private Audience, where at the feet of emperors a shallow stream had once flowed over a gem-studded silver bed – flowed the length of the building and out under the pierced marble screens into the private apartments – I felt the truth of the Persian couplet inscribed in flawless calligraphy above the windows overlooking the tree-tops and the slow, sad river: 'If there is Paradise upon the face of the earth, it is here, it is here, it is here.'[20]

In Sher Shah's mosque, which I also visited, red sandstone and white marble had united to create a building with all the majesty of a fort and the beauty of a palace. The contrast between the austere squareness of the façade and the soaring curves of the lofty lancet arches by which it was pierced thrilled me with exquisitely painful pleasure.

From the grass-grown ruins of the Purana Khila, or Old Fort, not far away, I peered down over ancient weathered battlements at a sea of darkly massed tree-tops. The sun was setting and the dusky tender greens and burnt reds of the landscape now glowed softly in a flood of pale amber light. Suddenly a flock of parakeets flew across the tree-tops, tiny spurts of greenness against the dark tangle of the vegetation below.

Occasionally, restless for I knew not what, I spent the afternoon wandering round the arcades of Connaught Circus. Hawkers squatting on the pavements offered cheap flashy curios at exorbitant prices. In the windows of the ivory marts elaborately carved boxes and statuettes were displayed against Persian carpets. Once, crossing the road to the next block, I saw in the distance the three onion domes of the Jamma Masjid, or Friday Mosque. Before long I found a bookshop. Rimbaud's poems, one of the first books I bought, delighted me even more than Baudelaire's, which I had read shortly before leaving England. Perhaps this was because of their tropical brilliance of colouring, which seemed in perfect keeping with my present surroundings. Certainly 'I have seen the dawn arisen like a flock of doves' was truer of India than of England. The collected poems of Sarojini Naidu, the Nightingale of India, though lushly rhetorical, interested me so much that I wrote on them an article, published in *The Poetry Review*, entitled 'Krishna's Flute'.[21] No doubt it was not their poetry which appealed to me so much as their vivid pictures of India. For all its poverty and filth the great subcontinent had already begun to cast upon me, as upon so many other Englishmen, the subtle spell of its unrivalled fascination.

At night, aching from the peregrinations of the day and feeling somehow frustrated, I ate ices in a milk bar or hung around the corner waiting for the driver of the 'liberty wagon' which would take us back to camp. As we rushed through the blackness of the night along the deserted highway, with the wind fresh in our faces and the sky thick with brilliant stars, it seemed, after the heat and dazzle of the day, that life had no purer enjoyment to offer. Alighting at the top of the road, I walked back to the barracks, past the old gymnasium on the left and the distant lights of the KOYLI camp over to the right, while millions of cicadas throbbed and shrilled and sang from the grass and jackals howled and barked in the far distance.

Among the books I had bought in Connaught Circus was an English translation of the *Aparokṣānubhūti*, a treatise by the great non-dualist Hindu philosopher, Shankara. In it was described a method of meditation by dissociating oneself successively from the body, the mind, and the empirical ego. At night, seated cross-legged inside the mosquito curtain while the other inmates of the room slept, I practised according to the instructions given in the book. 'I am not the body, I am not the mind,' I reflected, 'I am the non-dual Reality, the Brahman; I am the Absolute Existence-Knowledge-Bliss.' As I practised, body-consciousness faded away and my whole being was permeated by a

Army life: off duty

great peaceful joy. One night there appeared before me, as it were suspended in mid-air, the head of an old man. He had a grey stubble on scalp and chin and his yellowish face was deeply lined and wrinkled as though by the sins and vices of a lifetime. 'You're wasting your time,' he exclaimed, with a dreadful sneer. 'There's nothing in the universe but matter. Nothing but matter.'

'There is something higher than matter,' I promptly retorted, 'I know it, because I am experiencing it now.' Whereupon the apparition vanished. Years later, during my second visit to Nepal, I saw the same Māra, as it must have been. I recognized him at once, and he no doubt recognized me.

According to the guidebook, the Laxminarayan Temple was the most important Hindu shrine in New Delhi. But the driver of the ekka, or horse-drawn carriage I hired to take me there, did not seem to know where it was. Perhaps he knew it by its popular name, Birla Mandir, after the multi-millionaire who had donated the funds for its construction. Perhaps he wanted to take me by a circuitous route and charge for a whole afternoon's hire – a common trick with ekka drivers. Whichever it was, after jolting along for two hours in the little two-wheeled trap, I found myself not in the temple in New Delhi but in a *dharmashala*, or pilgrims' rest house, in Old Delhi, about six miles away. Here I was finally rescued by a friendly, English-educated young Indian, the first to whom I had spoken, who not only accompanied me all the way back to New Delhi but took the trouble of showing me round the temple precincts.

The Laxminarayan Temple, an imposing building in a sort of neo-Hindu style of architecture, stood in spacious grounds where pink cement paths ran between small artificial ponds. Inside there was a great deal of marble of various colours, and a bewilderingly large number of gods and goddesses, one painted bright blue and another with an elephant's head. Stranger still, there was a shrine dedicated to Guru Nanak, the founder of Sikhism, who I had always thought was not a Hindu but a Sikh. Behind the temple extended a garden where noisy crowds sauntered among pink cement elephants and looked into artificial caves, the mouths of which were painted to resemble the open jaws of mythological beasts. The bright pinks and greens and yellows of the coloured cement reminded me of the little iced cakes we bought from the cake-wallah.

Retracing our steps, my Indian friend and I passed between two more pink elephants into a side garden. Fronting the road from behind its own iron gate stood a temple of modest dimensions and distinctive architectural style. Removing my shoes, I ascended the two or three white marble steps and for the first time in my life found myself in a Buddhist temple. Facing me from the far end was a life-size image of the Buddha. Before it, on the white marble altar, candles burned among offerings of flowers. Incense hung in the air. The stillness was intense. After buying a copy of the *Dhammapada* and other literature at the stall inside the entrance I explored the rest of the enclosure. On a patch of lawn outside the tiny bungalow next door two or three bright yellow robes had been spread to dry in the sun. To my romantic imagination it was as if the golden petals of some gigantic celestial flower had fallen on the grass. In the hope of being able to meet a Buddhist monk I tried the door. It was locked from within. The windows were shuttered. There seemed to be no sign of life in the place at all.

11
WITH THE SWAMIS IN CEYLON

Though the headquarters of the unit were in Delhi, there were branches in Calcutta, Madras, and even farther afield. Shortly after my visit to the Birla Mandir I learned that two or three operators were to be posted to the Ceylon branch. Perhaps the sight of the Buddha-image, and of the yellow robes drying in the sun, had made me nostalgic for Buddhism, for I at once volunteered to go. Three days later, with a technical sergeant and another operator, I was on my way.

Kollupitiya, where the Ceylon branch was located, was a suburb of Colombo. Branching off from the main coastal road, which ran from the city down to Mount Lavinia and the southern tip of the island, a lane wandered between coconut palms into a small compound. On the right stood the Western-type house in which we worked and ate; to the left, the palm-leaf bungalow where we lived. Over the compound wall was the railway line, along which overcrowded trains dashed with white-clad passengers clinging on to doors and windows and even sitting on the roof. On the other side of the track ran a narrow strip of rocky beach, while below the beach lay the sea, off which there blew, night and day, a strong wind.

Colombo was smaller and more Westernized than New Delhi. Before many days had passed I knew my way about the main streets, was a regular visitor to the roomy premises of the Forces Canteen, and had penetrated into the Sinhalese quarter. I never tired of looking into the jewellers' windows, which were alive with the rainbow colours of the precious and semi-precious stones in which Ceylon abounds. Half the shops in town seemed to belong to jewellers. There was at least one good bookshop, though. Here I found, and promptly purchased, Romain Rolland's biographies of the Bengali saint Sri Ramakrishna and his famous disciple Swami Vivekananda. Years later, when my enthusiasm for the Ramakrishna-Vivekananda literature had waned, I was to wonder why they had attracted me so powerfully. Perhaps it was because they demonstrated that the spiritual life, far from being practicable only in the remote past, could be, and in fact had been, lived in modern times – perhaps because they indirectly encouraged me not merely to study but actually to practise the teaching to which I was already committed, the teaching of the Buddha.

Be that as it may, I had hardly started reading the two biographies when, looking one day for Buddhist temples on the fly-blown map of Colombo that hung on the wall in the unit, I saw against a black dot the words 'Vivekananda Society'. Excited by the discovery, I could not rest until, with much difficulty, I had located the place. It consisted of a small building with a library and reading room. Nobody there seemed able to tell me anything about Ramakrishna and Vivekananda, but a stout, elderly man with a very black complexion gave me the address of a monastery at Wellawatta, where there was a branch of the Ramakrishna Mission, and the name of the swami or Hindu monk in charge.

Wellawatta, the suburb in which the ashram, or monastery, was situated, lay only two miles south of Kollupitiya. For much of the way the road was lined with giant flame-of-the-forest trees, the orange-red blossoms of which littered the pavement. As I walked past the big suburban villas, Chinese restaurants, and Sinhalese toddy shops, over a bridge, and then past rows of palm-leaf boutiques and dilapidated cement doll's houses, I felt intensely excited. What would the swami be like? Did he know English? Would he agree to see me? To teach me? One of the books on Indian philosophy I had been reading stated that a holy man should never be approached without an offering. But the boutiques contained only green bananas (or plantains as they are called in the East), which in my ignorance I thought were unripe, and I was therefore forced to turn into the by-lane in which the monastery was situated empty-handed.

I need not have worried. After I had waited a few minutes on the inner veranda a door opened and there emerged a tall, rather portly man in salmon-pink robes. In excellent English, though with a strong accent, he asked what he could do for me. Gaining confidence from the friendly expression on his plump face, I told him about the events which had led me to the Vivekananda Society and thence to the monastery. All the books I had recently read, I explained, had emphasized that without a teacher no spiritual progress was possible. Could he help me? What the swami said in reply I do not remember, but he invited me to visit the monastery whenever I liked. Before I left a servant brought a plate of fruit cut into tiny cubes and some Indian sweetmeats. Nothing was said about my having omitted to bring an offering.

Thereafter I spent nearly all my evenings at the ashram, as I discovered the monastery was called. This was possible partly because of its nearness to the unit, and partly because of the nature of the shift system under which the two dozen or so operators who made up the unit's Colombo branch worked. At first we had four hours on and eight hours off duty alternately, right round the clock, with no day off. Thus I had the afternoon and evening free three days out of four. Later the system was changed. For a twenty-four hour period we had four hours on and four hours off duty alternately, after which we were free for twenty-four hours. Except that I sometimes operated the link with Delhi, my duties were the same as before. Earphones clamped to my head, left hand resting on the high-powered receiving set, I scoured the air for the faintest signals, listening carefully, and logging anything that sounded suspicious. Sometimes I wrote poetry – penning stanzas when I should have intercepted. Jock, the tall Scots technical sergeant who was in charge of the office, had no interest in life other than work and looked after the operators like a father. The OC, a captain, we saw only on pay days, when he sat at his table bareheaded so that we would not have to salute him. The military atmosphere was, in fact, completely lacking. There were neither parades nor inspections. So little did regular army imbecilities interfere with my studies and literary work at this period, that apart from the V-Day celebrations, which were quiet enough, I have only the vaguest memories of unit life. In the copper-coloured light that suffused the atmosphere every evening, turning the vegetation in the compound a deep rich green, all worldly preoccupations seemed to dissolve.

The ashram at Wellawatta, which nestled among coconut palms only a stone's throw from the beach, consisted of three units – hall, shrine-room, and residence – enclosing a little square of garden. The veranda of the residential quarter, which made up two sides of the square, faced inwards onto beds of fragrant flowering shrubs. Here I sat in the cool of the evening and discussed Indian philosophy, religion, and culture with the two resident swamis. Swami Siddhatmananda, the ashram president, who had received me on my first visit, was a Bengali. Joining the Ramakrishna Mission as a youth, he passed through the regular stages of probation and noviciate and in accordance with the Mission custom was posted, after ordination, to centres in India and abroad. Besides running the ashram he supervised the schools which the Mission conducted in different parts of Ceylon. Swami Vipulananda was a Tamil, that is to say, a native of the Tamil-speaking region of South India. Of medium height, and so dark as to make the whites of his eyes very noticeable, he spoke English with a delightful South Indian burr. A renowned scholar who specialized in the history of Tamil music, he had become a swami very late in life. Despite his obvious frailty, he was still active as Head of the Department of Tamil in the Ceylon University. My contact with these two swamis, who in many respects complemented each other, was of inestimable value to me, and my debt to them is very great. From them I imbibed not only something of the spirit of Indian culture but also, what was more important, an enthusiasm for the spiritual life.

Before many weeks had passed I was as much an inmate of the ashram as it was possible to be without sleeping there. Knowing that an understanding of Indian culture was at least partly dependent on a familiarity with the Indian way of life, Swami Siddhatmananda not only expounded the Vedanta but invited me to dinner. Helped on by kindly words of encouragement from him and Swami Vipulananda, I learned to sit cross-legged on a little wooden plank and to eat rice and curries with my fingers from a large circular brass tray placed directly on the stone floor. The cook, who watched my efforts with amusement, remarked that I ate like a crow. By this he meant that my fingers, instead of being loose and flexible, stabbed at the food with the sharp, jerky movements of a crow pecking with its beak. Later, after several years of practice, I was to hear that remark in many parts of India. In fact I used to tell the swamis that I found it more difficult to eat with my fingers than to understand the metaphysics of Shankara, the great exponent of Non-Dualist Vedanta.

One of them was a meat-eater and one a vegetarian, and since they came one from the north-east, where sweets are favoured, and one from the south, which prefers sour food, I tasted dishes of many kinds. Moreover, I sampled not only the Indian but also the Sinhalese type of cooking. Just as in Europe every country, so in India every province, has its own distinctive food habits. Bengalis have a weakness for sweetmeats. Tamils take chillies by the handful. Gujeratis put sugar into their curries and spices into their tea. Punjabis are fond of curd preparations. Malabaris love tamarind. While in the north-west the staple diet is wheat, the rest of the country lives on rice. An appreciation of the culinary variety to be found in India provides, perhaps, a good basis for the understanding of its cultural and religious diversity.

Another good basis for understanding is music. In Delhi, I had sometimes listened to Indian music, both popular and classical, for it was my conviction that what a man belonging to one culture has produced could, by virtue of their common humanity, be appreciated by a man belonging to another. At first the sounds meant absolutely nothing to me. But gradually I was able to distinguish something like a melody. At the ashram musical items occupied more than half the programme at all meetings and celebrations, to which flocked chiefly the music-loving Tamils. After the speeches, nearly always of extraordinary length, the platform would be cleared for the musicians. All sat cross-legged on the carpet with their unfamiliar instruments tucked into their thigh or laid across their knees or upright before them. On and on they played, hour after hour, while the audience, which apparently never tired, followed their movements with gleaming eyes and smiles of approval, giving vent now and then to exclamations of delight at some particularly brilliant display of virtuosity. To me the most interesting were the violinists, thin elderly men who played with closed eyes and beatific expressions, holding their instruments high in the air and twisting and swaying their bodies in time with the music. On one occasion a woman played on the musical glasses, an ancient Tamil instrument, striking them smartly with her palms and producing clear, bell-like notes of an astonishing purity.

As I had done in Delhi, I at first always strove to distinguish the melody. But Swami Vipulananda, who was both musicologist and connoisseur, advised me to listen instead to the tablas, the small round side-drums, and to try and follow the rhythm. Though I was never able to appreciate all the subtleties of Indian rhythm, the most highly developed in the world, I soon found that this method enabled me to appreciate Indian music to a much greater extent than before.[22]

Such gatherings were also the means of introducing me to the devotees and friends of the ashram, with one or two of whom I had already become acquainted. My greatest friend was Chelliah, a thin, youngish Tamil with great doe-like eyes whose hair had already started thinning. The swamis used to remonstrate with him on account of his strict vegetarianism, for he was very anaemic. When his first child, a boy, died soon after birth, Swami Vipulananda told him roundly, 'Your so-called religion has killed your son.' He listened with a bright apologetic smile and said nothing.

One day he took me inside a small wayside temple, dedicated to Ganesha, the elephant-headed god. I was rather shocked by the dust and cobwebs, the old beer bottles on the altar and the casual manner in which the priest, a filthy Brahmin, performed the ritual. When I told the swamis about it they admitted that the condition of most of the smaller temples in India was equally bad. Chelliah, however, who seemed quite oblivious to the squalor, said his prayers with evident devotion. In this he was characteristic of his race and religion. Few Hindus will admit that the untidiness of a temple or the slovenliness, or even immorality, of a priest, need be an obstacle to one who genuinely desires to worship God. In the ashram chapel, where pictures of Ramakrishna, Vivekananda, and Sarada Devi, the Holy Mother, occupied the place of honour, marble slabs shone like glass and brass altar vessels as gold.

Though many Tamils came to the ashram, which in fact was the cultural and religious centre of the more educated and well-to-do section of the Indian community, I never met there a single Sinhalese. One day I asked Swami Siddhatmananda why no *bhikkhus*, or Buddhist monks, ever attended the lectures. They did sometimes come, he said, but always insisted on standing at the back of the hall, as in Ceylon it was not the custom for monks to sit with laymen. Moreover, since the enjoyment of music was prohibited for them they had to leave as soon as the musical items began. Under these circumstances collaboration was difficult.

With one Sinhalese monk, however, they were on very friendly terms. This was Walpola Rahula, the famous political monk, then at the height of his fame. Even before meeting him at the ashram I had heard much of his doings, for the Ceylon Buddhist sangha, or monastic order, was rent into two factions, one enthusiastically supporting him, the other violently opposing. The *Dhammapada* I had bought in Delhi defined a *bhikkhu* as one who had control over his hands and feet; but as I watched him talking to the swamis, who sat relaxed and composed, I could not help noticing the constant agitation of his whole body, especially of his legs, which he jerked up and down as if to relieve some acute nervous tension. Though obviously a man of uncommon intelligence, he gave not the slightest indication of spirituality.[23]

Sometimes I accompanied the swamis when they called on their friends. With one, a prominent advocate, I discussed Tamil mystic poetry. Swami Vipulananda took me to the university, where I met several of his colleagues, some of whom used to give lectures at the ashram. Once we attended a semi-political meeting at which a small excitable South Indian named Ponnabalam, who often came to see the swamis, spoke for more than two hours in Tamil, a language which, according to a story which Swami Vipulananda related to me, sounded like the rattling of stones in a brass pot. Ponnabalam was later to make a name for himself in Ceylon politics as the leader of the Tamil community.

More interesting was the convocation of Vidyalankara Pirivena, a famous Buddhist monastic college five or six miles from Colombo, where I heard the Indian philosopher-statesman Dr Radhakrishnan deliver the convocation address. As we drove to the gate I noticed that the traffic, consisting of several hundred cars, was being very efficiently controlled by the nods and smiles of a single yellow-robed figure.

'Why don't they have a policeman?' I asked.

'Oh, one *bhikkhu* can do the job better than a dozen policemen,' I was told. 'No one would dare to disobey a *bhikkhu*.'

Inside the gate stood a small temple. To my astonishment it contained, not an image of the Buddha, as I had expected, but figures of various Hindu gods. 'These are just for the lay people,' explained the *bhikkhu* who had received us, with a superior smile. '*We* never worship them.' As we edged our way to our seats a very fat, dark monk sitting at the end of the row in front turned round and regarded me with curiosity. This was Jagdish Kashyap, who four years later became my teacher in Pāli and Buddhist philosophy.

At the ashram a day or two later I again saw Dr Radhakrishnan. A slim erect figure in long black coat and white turban, he had the features of a Mogul emperor. When Swami Siddhatmananda told him I was deeply interested in Indian philosophy he gave me a sharp astonished glance. But I did not venture to approach, for my eyes, which had been for several days badly inflamed, were now extremely sore, and the lids so gummed together I could hardly see.

The most interesting person I met through the good offices of the swamis was the Yoga Swami of Jaffna, in northern Ceylon. Since Swami Vipulananda, who always spoke of him with the deepest respect, had already roused my interest by recounting well-authenticated stories of the holy man's extraordinary powers, it was with considerable excitement that I learned of his unexpected arrival in Colombo.

One evening the swamis took me to see him. Swami Vipulananda prostrated himself before the Yoga Swami with great humility, which astonished me, for though I was accustomed to seeing people prostrate themselves in front of the swamis, I had not yet seen either of them pay such respect to anyone else.

The Yoga Swami reclined in an armchair. The perfect whiteness of his long hair and beard contrasted with the blackness of his short, powerfully built body. But his most noticeable feature was his eyes, which were of extraordinary size and brilliance. He seemed to be about eighty. Swami Vipulananda, who was over sixty, afterwards told me that the Yoga Swami had not changed at all in fifty years, and that old people had said the same thing when he was a boy. Though no one knew exactly how old he was, he was believed to be not less than one-hundred-and-sixty. Summer and winter he wore only a short white loincloth, being completely indifferent to heat, cold, and wet.

After exchanging a few words with Swami Vipulananda in Tamil, the Yoga Swami turned his great lustrous eyes on me and began speaking in broken English. During our conversation I had an uncanny sense that he was following my every thought. This feeling was intensified by the way he sometimes answered questions I had not formulated. Of our conversation I remember only him saying that he had been born in a Christian family and named John, but had reverted to Hinduism. Every now and then he ran his hand up and down my arm, squeezing it as he did so and muttering, half to himself, 'Very good boy, very good boy,' and 'Very good chair, I can sit in this chair. Very good boy. Very good chair.' When the servant came with cut fruits he solemnly distributed them to us, saying as he did so, 'This is my body; take, eat.'

The attraction I now felt for the spiritual life was stimulated not only by what Hindus call *satsangh*, personal contact with saints, but by reading. In the course of the seven months I spent in Ceylon I either bought, or borrowed from the ashram, nearly all the Ramakrishna Mission publications. Once, after I had read a volume of biographical sketches of Sri Ramakrishna's dozen or so disciples, representing almost as many types of spirituality, Swami Siddhatmananda asked me to name the disciple whose life I was most desirous of emulating.

'Swami Saradananda,' I replied without hesitation.

'Why?'

'Because he combined intense external activity with perfect internal tranquillity.'

Later I realized that the archetype of this ideal was the wise and compassionate bodhisattva, of whom an ancient Buddhist text says:

> Like a fire his mind constantly blazes up into good works for others;
> At the same time he always remains merged in the calm of the trances and formless attainments.[24]

Swami Siddhatmananda, with whom I studied some of the works of Shankara verse by verse, also took the trouble of procuring rare books for me from South India.

Not all my reading was Vedantic, though. Shortly after my arrival I joined the Colombo Public Library. Kierkegaard's *Fear and Trembling*, the reading of which constituted my introduction to the putative father of Existentialism, impressed and astonished me by the way in which it pared both philosophy and religion down to the quick of experience. Poetry was rather neglected, though I continued to write it on duty; but Bridges' *The Testament of Beauty* gave me, as the *Symposium* had done much earlier, glimpses of a world wherein the true and the beautiful are one. From odd corners in obscure stationers' shops I unearthed books and pamphlets on Buddhism published in Ceylon. Unlike the Ramakrishna Mission literature they were dry and dull, and more than one appeared to suggest that Buddhism had been spiritually dead for 2,000 years. 'Buddhism as Personal Religion', however, a lecture delivered in Ceylon by the Indian Buddhist scholar Dr Beni Madhab Barua, exercised a permanent influence on my understanding of the Buddha's teaching.[25]

With so much study of religious literature, all of which, whether Hindu or Buddhist, emphasized the importance of meditation, I was naturally eager to continue my own experiments in this line. They had begun in Delhi, where I had practised the technique of 'dissociation' described by Shankara in his *Aparokṣānubhūti*. Sitting cross-legged inside my mosquito curtain, I had reflected that I was not the body, not the mind, not the empirical ego – I was the non-dual Reality Itself, the Absolute Existence-Knowledge-Bliss. Now, having progressed as far as I could by this method, I decided, without saying anything to the swamis, to take up the practice of *prāṇāyāma*, or 'breath control', as outlined in Swami Vivekananda's *Raja Yoga*. Once again, therefore, I sat cross-legged beneath my mosquito curtain while others slept, this time inhaling, retaining, and exhaling my breath in accordance with the prescribed technique.

After a few days various abnormal experiences started occurring. Generally it was as though tremendous forces descended into me from an infinite height with a terribly disintegrating effect upon my whole being. Sometimes I felt I was being slowly lifted up into the air, then dashed violently to the ground. Since these experiences did not lead to peace of mind, happiness, or illumination, I soon gave up practising *prāṇāyāma*. But the experiences continued. For about three more weeks they disturbed me, sometimes interrupting my sleep seven or eight times in the course of a single night. It seemed that I was getting shocks of tremendously high voltage from a great dynamo of spiritual electricity the assaults of which I was powerless to resist. So violent were these shocks, and so extraordinary the experiences which accompanied them, that I sometimes prayed, to whom I knew not, 'O Lord, take them away and let me rest!'

Hindu yogis whom I subsequently met told me that without a highly qualified guide the practice of *prāṇāyāma* was extremely dangerous. Some declared that by writing on a subject in which he was himself so imperfectly versed, Swami Vivekananda had done a great deal of harm. A few, among them one of exceptionally high attainments, were emphatic that this form of Raja Yoga is of no spiritual value whatever.

Despite the time and energy I devoted to them, Vedantic study and Yogic practice could not disturb my basic loyalty, which was to Buddhism. With the unit cook, a devout old Sinhalese who dressed in a belted sarong, shirt, and jacket, and wore his hair in a bun, I visited the large new temple at Bambalapitiya. In the central shrine were three enormous Buddha-images, one standing, one recumbent, and one sedent.

Though the incense-laden atmosphere of the place, with its masses of fragrant temple-flowers and groups of little guttering candles on long marble-topped tables, was more congenial to me than that of the ashram chapel, the brightly painted images were too much like gigantic wax dolls to inspire me to devotion.

In April 1945 I applied for a week's leave and made a pilgrimage to the Dalada Maligawa, the Tooth Relic Temple at Kandy. Leaving Colombo in the late afternoon, the train wound slowly up to the last capital of the kings of Ceylon through picturesque mountain scenery. As night fell, tiny orange fires gleamed from the darkness of the jungle slopes. Soon after eight the moon, almost at full, soared from behind the black shoulder of the mountain and at once the whole landscape gleamed silver. By the time we reached Kandy the moon stood high in the sky. I drove through the moonlit streets to the Buddhist College hostelry where I was to stay. Around my thatched bungalow the sanded compound was a pool of dazzling whiteness. Refreshed by a wash, I sauntered out past the whitewashed bulk of the giant reliquary that, strangely insubstantial, sparkled on the right-hand side of the path, and strolled as far as the mustard yellow gateway. Nothing but the uncanny brightness and silence of the night! On the opposite side of the road the pointed octagonal roof of the temple library was silhouetted against the starry sky.

Next morning, without understanding quite how it happened, I found myself in the hands of a guide, a skinny elderly man who spoke the same broken English and wore the same greasy bun and hybrid costume as the unit cook. It was full moon day, he told me, and if we hurried we would be able to get into the temple before the crowd. On the way we met a little wizened monk of about ninety bowling along in a rickshaw. My guide at once dropped on to one knee and joined his hands in salutation. The rickshaw stopped. A brief conversation ensued, of which I understood not a word, but the monk looked at me with a friendly smile and nodded.

'He High Priest,' said my guide, when the rickshaw had passed on. 'He say we go side door ten o'clock open.' For this favour, which meant that I would be allowed inside the shrine before the main entrance was opened to the worshippers, my guide seemed to think it only right that I should make an offering.

'What would the High Priest like?' I asked dubiously.

'He very fond plum cake. You give one pound English plum cake he much happy. He like nothing on earth like English plum cake.' I handed over a note, the first of the many that were to pass between us that week.

The approach to the temple enclosure was lined with beggars even more horribly diseased and deformed than those I had seen in India. Frescoes hardly less horrible depicted sinners being impaled, roasted, or sawn in two in the hells. The double-storey wooden shrine with its beautiful downward-sweeping roof was jammed into a small courtyard between other buildings. As it was only nine o'clock we stood to one side and watched the worshippers buying flowers at the stalls from which, on entering the courtyard, I had purchased a garland of jasmine. Looking up under the projecting eaves of the shrine, I caught a glimpse of gallery ceilings brightly painted with intricate lotus patterns.

During the half hour we waited the cobbled space filled with white-clad figures, all holding above their heads little trays of flowers. As more and more worshippers surged in those at the front were pushed up the temple steps and pressed against the low brass door, on the upper leaves of which were embossed the sun and the moon. As the minutes passed I became aware of an undercurrent of excitement in the crowd, by this time so densely packed that the dark, glistening heads had disappeared beneath the sea of uplifted flowers. Every now and then would go up from the white mass of men and women on the temple steps a wail as of unutterable desire. It was as though I saw humanity clamouring for admission on the threshold of the Divine.

At 9.30 a side door opened and a dark finger beckoned. In and up we went, so quickly that I had no time to admire the carved and painted interior. The noise of the crowd faded to a murmur. Behind a massive steel grille stood, heaped with thick gold chains, a bell-shaped reliquary higher than a man. Above the altar outside the grille was suspended a silver canopy. From the ceiling, also of silver, hung little diamond ornaments like stars. Gold and silver images, miniature reliquaries and sprays of flowers, some studded with rubies, glittered about the base of the reliquary. The whole chamber was a blaze of gold and silver and jewels. Beside the altar stood an impassive figure in yellow robes. When I had offered my garland, and gazed my fill at the reliquary, he showed me a tray of chased silver three feet in diameter. My guide whispered that this meant another offering. As we left the chamber the door below was opened and the crowd streamed past us up the stairs with their trays of flowers.

In the octagonal library, formerly the throne room of the Kandyan kings, I was shown ancient palm-leaf manuscripts, some of them the gift of Sir Edwin Arnold, the famous Victorian poet, orientalist, and newspaper editor who had written *The Light of Asia*. After scratching the name of the temple with an iron stylus on a strip of palm-leaf, which was rubbed with ink to make the Sinhalese characters visible, another impressive yellow figure opened a drawer and looked at me with what was almost a smile. Without any prompting from the guide I dropped a note onto the little pile of paper currency inside. In Ceylon monks are not allowed to handle money.

After a week in the hills among the temples and monasteries of Kandy, I returned to Colombo, where I found the swamis preparing for the arrival of a very senior monk who was president of an ashram in the Himalayas, and a member of the Governing Body of the Mission. 'He is a great disciplinarian,' they informed me. 'Discipline' for me having acquired a rather unpleasant connotation I awaited the arrival of the visitor with interest but also with apprehension.

Swami Pavitrananda was tall and thin and almost grotesquely bony. His eyes burned darkly in their hollow sockets. When he spoke it was in a low, intense voice that was almost a whisper and with impressive earnestness. The two other swamis emanated a mild glow of spirituality; but he was a consuming fire. Like a moth by a flame, I was immediately attracted, for his very look showed me that if he was a disciplinarian it was not to others but to himself. He was, in fact, of an extremely affectionate disposition. In Calcutta a few months later, I often heard other members of the Mission speak of him as 'a very loving soul' (Bengalis never say 'affectionate'). In me he at once took great interest and we had many conversations. Unlike the other swamis, he did not speak about philosophy or literature or music, but only of the spiritual life. The need for simplicity, purity, humility, and devotion were his sole topics. He often spoke of the necessity for renunciation, and of the happiness of a monk's life, compared with which worldly happiness was as dross. As I listened my heart burned within me. Whether he asked me if I wanted to be a monk, or whether I asked him if he thought it possible for me to take up monastic life, I do not remember, but from that time onwards I was resolved upon a life of renunciation.

In my next letters home I told my parents that I was thinking of staying on in India after demobilization and becoming a monk. Since they were aware of my interest in Eastern religions, the news may not have been entirely unexpected. At any rate, they raised no objections. My father replied that my life was my own and that I must do with it what I thought best, my mother that she hoped my becoming a monk would not prevent me from seeing her sometimes.

Before leaving Colombo, Swami Pavitrananda invited me to stay with him at Almora in the Himalayas, and advised me to visit Belur Math, near Calcutta, the Mission's headquarters. As soon as Vaiśākha Pūrṇimā Day, anniversary of the Buddha's Enlightenment, had been celebrated by the ashram with the usual lengthy speeches and marathon musical items, I therefore applied for a transfer to Calcutta on compassionate grounds, stating that I had an uncle living there whom I wanted to meet.

12

MAITREYA, THE COMING BUDDHA

Unlike Delhi and Colombo, which are much smaller, Calcutta has a definite individuality, so that for all its poverty, putrefaction, and decay it is possible to love or at least to feel at home in it. The unit occupied two large houses at Ballygunge, a select residential suburb. Pomelo trees, their fruits hanging almost as big as footballs among the leaves, grew against the whitewashed garden wall, on the other side of which stretched half a mile of common. City-bound trams rattled past the bottom of the road every twenty minutes. Since duties were as light, and discipline as lax, as in Colombo, it was possible for me to make a speedy contact with the Ramakrishna Mission Institute of Culture, about half an hour's tram ride distant, the address of which had been given me by Swami Siddhatmananda.

   This organization, which then occupied the upper portion of a house in Wellington Square, became my centre of operations. Though the monk in charge, a rather Mongoloid Bengali, had welcomed me quite cordially, it was his assistant who became my friend. Kantaraj, who had originally been a follower of the Jain religion, was a diminutive South Indian with a dark bearded face and an astonishingly bass voice. Though working devotedly for the Institute, he was perfectly indifferent to culture. Books he touched only to dust and catalogue. His sole passion was service. He was prepared to render any service, however menial, to any person at any time, and despite any personal inconvenience. So well known was he for this characteristic that elderly and infirm swamis always preferred to stay at the Institute, and if the authorities at Belur Math wanted something done in Calcutta it was Kantaraj to whom they telephoned. He was the embodiment of cheerful asceticism. While most of the swamis working in Calcutta permitted themselves little luxuries, Kantaraj refused to own so much as a pair of shoes.

With him for guide, I visited Belur Math, a collection of buildings standing twelve miles out of town in spacious grounds on the banks of the Hooghly. The temple, all pinkish stone, was a rather pleasing structure of composite architectural style. Inside had been installed a life-size white marble statue of Sri Ramakrishna so oddly naturalistic, and so devoid of symbolic value, as to seem unsuitable as an object of worship. Perched along the river bank nearby were three queer little whitewashed temples. At one time or another, I met all the swamis in charge of the various offices and institutions. Cultured, intelligent, and friendly as they were, constant preoccupation with the material interests of the Mission seemed to have given them a strong tincture of worldliness. The novices, very likeable youngsters, were more ambitious to conquer America with their oratory than subjugate their own minds through spiritual practice. Swami Vipulananda's words came to me: 'We are nothing compared with the older generation of swamis.' Only the septuagenarian president, Kantaraj's guru, whose eyes shone with something of the lustre of the Yoga Swami's, gave me the impression of being wholly occupied with higher things.

Once we went from the math to Dakshineshwar by boat, the boatman pushing hard against the current with a long pole. Having shown me the room in which Sri Ramakrishna had spent the greater part of his life, Kantaraj wanted to take me inside the precincts of the temple. But a Brahmin priest came rushing forward and declared that Muslims and Christians could not so much as enter the great paved courtyard in front of the main building, a rather ugly brick structure. Indeed, there was a notice to that effect on the wall. In vain Kantaraj expostulated that Sri Ramakrishna had not recognized distinctions of caste and creed. The priest was adamant. The Mission, of course, was in no way to blame, as it had no control over the temple management, but it was interesting to see how little the teaching of Sri Ramakrishna had penetrated the heart of orthodox Hindu Bengal.

Only after visiting not merely Belur and Dakshineshwar, but most of the other Mission centres in and around Calcutta, did I go and see

Uncle Dick, who was my mother's youngest brother and a member of the Governor of Bengal's band. Despite the rickshaw-puller's attempts to mislead me, I found his quarters quite easily, for they were situated in a lane that debouched into the road alongside Government House. Soon I was spending almost as much time with Uncle Dick and his family as I was at the Institute. By September we were on such good terms that when Audrey, his second wife, decided to go to Darjeeling for a few weeks with Gillian, the youngest child, Uncle Dick suggested that I should accompany them.

After the heat of the plains Darjeeling, 7,500 feet above sea level, felt at times bitterly cold. Uncle Dick's chalet, perched on the hillside below a smaller, whiter, azure-domed Government House, despite blazing fires was often so chilly that I shivered. When the low grey cloud dispersed, however, and the sun poured in with a fierce, dry brilliance from the heavens, one felt warmer in the precipitous, traffic-free streets than within doors.

Every morning, after a late breakfast, Audrey, Gillian, and I went for a walk along the town's famous promenade, the Chowrasta, where Gillian had a pony ride. At eleven, appetites sharpened by the crisp mountain air, we were having coffee and cream cakes at Plievers, a fashionable rendezvous for the European and would-be European élite. Among the hard-faced, high-voiced memsahibs whom we encountered there, in the street and at tea-parties, were several who had been at school with Audrey. In the absence of their husbands, who sweated under office fans in the plains, they were squired by American officers. One of the chief ornaments of this frivolous, gossipy, superficial set was a stout, elderly woman in blue trousers and red bandana, who had become a Muslim to marry her second husband, the first having refused her a divorce, and who was currently trying to marry a third according to Buddhist rites and emigrate with him to Australia.

The climax, or rather anticlimax, of my attempts to participate in the brittle gaiety of hill station life was the Government House ball to which, unwillingly, I escorted Audrey and the short bosomy friend who had been trying to teach me to dance. As I sat at one side of the ballroom with four or five gaily dressed women (partners were scarce), watching Audrey spin past with one uniformed American, and a thin, very much dyed and painted woman of fifty-five vigorously doing a sort of rumba with another, I was suddenly seized by an overpowering sense of unreality such as I had sometimes experienced in England. The dancers became ghosts, the ballroom vanished, the music faded into the distance, and I was left alone in a great void with a strong feeling of disgust and revulsion.

Unreal though it appeared, it was not the phenomenal world itself that disgusted me, so much as the spectacle of an existence so entirely devoid of meaning, so utterly divorced from the primal simplicities. The sight of the short, sturdy hill-folk, with their cheerful, red-cheeked Mongoloid faces, so different from the sad countenances of the plains, aroused in me no such feelings. For them life did have a meaning, even if it merely consisted in the fact of their earning a livelihood by means of the broad, cone-shaped basket which most of them, both men and women, wore slung from the forehead by a hempen band. But the painted women who danced on the ballroom floor were puppets, jerked into spasmodic movement by the threads of trivial interests and base desires, and for them, ghastly simulacra that they were, life had no significance, and their dance was the dance of death.

On the mornings that Audrey complained of headaches I walked alone round Observatory Hill, where already trees stood leafless in the mist. Not having seen the snow ranges, I looked out eagerly for them every time the white cloud masses drifting past on the precipitous farther side of the deep, haze-blue valley seemed about to leave the sky clear. After waiting and watching for nearly an hour I happened to raise my eyes and there they were, seemingly halfway up the blue, more jaggedly white and splendid, and bigger and bolder and closer, than I had ever imagined mountains could be. Despite their size they rose clear of the bastions of cloud with an ethereal lightness that made them seem almost to float in the midst of the air.

Shortly before my departure I hired a pony and rode over the ridge into the nearby village of Ghoom. Though seemingly meek and docile enough when I had selected him at the pony-stand at the end of the Chowrasta, no sooner were we well out of town than my mount did his best to unseat me, first by galloping furiously and then by rubbing himself against a railing that overlooked a sheer drop of several hundred feet. But I clung grimly on and soon we were in the thick of the swirling white mist of Ghoom, pierced here and there by the shadow-like shapes of pines. Turning off from the main street, down which ran the track of the little toy railway, I rode through the drizzle between rows of low, open-fronted shops which sold nothing but knives and daggers, up a track leading away from the town to a spur swept by icy blasts. Through the mist came a curiously muffled sound of drums and horns. Presently the white walls and curved red roof of the Tibetan monastery, which was my destination, rose vaguely through the prevailing greyness.

Inside the temple all was gloom, for light filtered in only through the open door behind me and a kind of well in the roof. As my eyes became accustomed to the semi-darkness, I saw hanging in two rows from the ceiling, so as to form a sort of aisle, great cylinders made up of silk flounces of different colours. At the far end of the chamber a lamp flickered above rows of brass and silver bowls. Only gradually did I grow aware of the atmosphere of the place, a peculiar combination of stillness and vibrancy which I have since come to recognize as characteristic of Tibetan temples.

As I stood and gazed, I slowly made out, above the bowls and the lamp, first a great pair of hands, laid flat one above the other, then an enormous trunk with a swastika on the breast, and at last, more than twenty feet from the ground, the broad gently smiling face of the image. In the forehead gleamed a huge precious stone. This was Maitreya, the Coming Buddha. Later I learned that the founder of the monastery, the great Tibetan saint and yogi Tomo Geshe Rimpoche, had installed the image of the Lord Maitreya there as a prophecy that the time of his advent, as well as of the world-wide dissemination of Buddhism, was at hand. To me the great figure portended the dedication of my own life to the service of the Dharma.

Returning to Calcutta, where the Pujas – the month-long autumn religious festivals – were about to begin, I was at once conscious of breathing a religious atmosphere very different from that of Tibet. A tall, very dark Bengali whom I had met at the Institute took me to Kalighat, the most famous temple in Calcutta. From this place, a cross between a market and a shambles rather than a temple, I emerged with a crimson mark on my forehead and a garland of crimson flowers round my neck, bewildered by the jostling crowd, the reek of blood, and the stench of decayed flowers trodden into a pulp underfoot. With Kantaraj I went at night round the city to see the illuminated tableaux depicting the ten-armed goddess Durga slaying the Buffalo-Demon, from whose decapitated body emerged the head of a man. The painted and garmented clay figures were life-sized and very realistic. Different organizations and localities competed to produce the best tableau, and though the images would be worshipped for three days and then immersed in the river, the artistry lavished on them was immense. At Belur Math I saw the Kumari-Puja, the ceremonial worship of the Mother Goddess in the form of a living eight-year-old Brahmin girl. As I watched the priests waving lights before the small motionless figure, Kantaraj whispered in my ear that since Bengalis believed that a girl who had been thus worshipped would die young, it was necessary to find a penniless Brahmin and buy his consent with a large sum of money.

After the Pujas the Institute resumed its regular activities. The Calcutta intelligentsia included at that time a number of brilliant figures, several of whom I met not only after lectures but at their homes. Most, if not all, were sympathetic towards Buddhism, and two at least were Buddhist scholars of international renown. Dr Beni Madhab Barua, whose lecture on 'Buddhism as Personal Religion' I had admired in Colombo, was a diminutive, dark-suited Bengali Buddhist from Chittagong, in what is now Bangladesh, the people of which claim descent from the original Indian Buddhist community. With him I discussed points of Buddhist doctrine. Generously overlooking my ignorance, he discoursed not only in a genial, informative manner but with a profundity that I had till then only encountered in books. Dr Satkari Mookherjee, an authority on Buddhist logic, was an incredibly thin Bengali Brahmin with dry, claw-like hands and an aloof, abstracted manner. I also met Benoy Kumar Sarkar, who like many Bengali intellectuals had married a European, Dr Nalinaksha Dutt, editor of the ancient Buddhist manuscripts discovered at Gilgit in Kashmir, and a lean, long-haired Tantric scholar of the traditional type who had worked with Sir John Woodroffe. Less learned, but infinitely more charming, was silver-haired Dr Kalidas Nag, who from the readiness with which he consented to preside over meetings of all kinds, from archaeological conferences to primary school prize distributions, had acquired the title of 'Calcutta's permanent president'. No speaker ever pleased an audience more than Dr Nag; but when, amidst prolonged applause, he smilingly resumed his seat, no one was ever able to say about what he had been speaking. It seemed his mission in life simply to radiate amiability.

Kantaraj was an indefatigable guide. Having shown me the Mission's centres, from temples to maternity homes, he took me to all the parks, shrines, museums, and learned institutions in the city. One evening we went to see Swami Vivekananda's second brother, a valetudinarian who, sitting on a wooden bedstead in a dark, dirty room in the dilapidated ancestral home, railed bitterly against the Ramakrishna Mission. From his conversation I gathered that the youngest brother had become a Communist. We also paid a visit to the Sri Dharmarajika Vihara, headquarters of the Maha Bodhi Society of India, the most prominent Buddhist organization in the country. In the shrine above the lecture-hall I met a yellow-robed figure with suspicious eyes and an abrupt manner, whom Kantaraj introduced as the Sinhalese incumbent of the vihara. Unlike the Mission centres, both this and the other Buddhist temples and monasteries we visited seemed to be in the grip of a strange inertia.

Besides Kantaraj, there was Phani Sanyal, a thin, ascetic graduate then staying at the Institute, whom I sometimes accompanied on his weekly visits to the Udbodhan Office. At this centre, from which the Mission's Bengali publications were issued, Sri Ramakrishna's wife, popularly known as the Holy Mother, had lived for a number of years. Her room, now preserved as a shrine, was the purest and most peaceful place in Calcutta. While Sanyal meditated I simply steeped myself in its tranquillity as in a pool of limpid waters.

One of our expeditions, though, almost ended in disaster. For several days Calcutta, always politically turbulent, had been the scene of angry student demonstrations. Two or three youths were killed in the police firing. Fearing further trouble, Kantaraj advised us not to go out that evening; but Sanyal, who took no interest in politics, felt sure that peace had been restored to the city. We were only halfway down College Street, the main artery of university life, when we saw the bodies of the dead students being taken in procession from the Calcutta General Hospital. It was too late to turn back. Shouting anti-British slogans as they came, thousands of white-shirted demonstrators overwhelmed us like a tidal wave. Trying to look as though I had not noticed the procession, I kept a tight hold of the tail of Sanyal's shirt as, fighting to keep our balance, we slowly worked our way forward. Faces black with hatred scowled at me savagely as they passed. One demonstrator, seeing I was English, seized me roughly by the shoulder and tried to shove me out of his way; but so densely were we packed that I hardly staggered. Had we done anything except go straight through the procession I would undoubtedly have been torn to pieces, for nothing so much rouses the blood-lust of the Bengali mob as an individual in retreat. Not until we had reached a crossing two miles further down the road, not far from our destination, did we win clear of the procession. On our return to the Institute late that night we found the swamis almost frantic with anxiety for our safety. Kantaraj, who was more alarmed than anyone else, took us severely to task for our foolhardiness.

In November, the dropping of atom bombs on Nagasaki and Hiroshima having ended the war with Japan, the unit was ordered to Singapore. Before leaving, I presented most of my books to the Institute library. Even so, it was with a very weighty kitbag, haversack, and tin trunk that I staggered up the riveted steel plates of the incline into the hot interior of the waiting amphibian.

13
THE THREE WORLDS

After three stormy days in the Bay of Bengal, where the small craft bobbed up and down on the waves like a cork, we sailed through the smoother waters of the Malacca Straits and down to Singapore. We were still a mile from harbour when we saw the quayside aswarm with thousands of ant-like figures. These were Japanese prisoners of war. Some, stripped to the waist, were unloading cargo. But most, lined up as though on parade, were apparently waiting to go aboard the steamers that had been sent to repatriate the defeated army. Driving through the streets of Singapore we saw more prisoners, this time in squads of a hundred, marching down to the docks. At a command from their NCOs they saluted smartly as our lorry passed.

The five or six suburban villas allocated to the unit had been occupied by Japanese officers, from whom we inherited not only household effects but servants. The latter were short, slender-bodied Malays with light coffee complexions who always wore singlets and colourfully striped sarongs. Perhaps they had stayed on, serving with the same smile now one and now another set of victors, ever since the original dispossession of their wealthy Chinese masters.

An advance guard of wireless mechanics having already rigged up a Set Room in one of the villas, we were soon back on duty. But the war had ended and there were no longer any 'unidentifiable transmissions' for us to intercept. This the CO evidently knew, for we worked only four hours a day. There were no night duties.

In Singapore, 1946

    We had not thumbed our way into Singapore more than once or twice before we realized that it was a city of Chinese. All the European-style shops and restaurants in the centre of the town were owned and managed by these cheerfully industrious people. The slender handsome boys with their pale gold complexions and black slant eyes who, in white singlets and shorts, pedalled the tricycle rickshaws with a loud ringing of bells, were Chinese. Their friendly but independent bearing was in marked contrast to the behaviour, alternately obsequious and blustering, of the Indian rickshaw-pullers. Chinese, too, were the tiny silken-trousered prostitutes who, scenting business, walked stiff-legged along the pavements with little jerky steps. The few Malays one encountered were either doorkeepers, domestic servants, or bearers in restaurants. The Chinese quarter of the city, with its perpendicular shop signs, restaurants with wooden stools out on the pavement, sleek-haired women in black silk trousers and wooden clogs, grey-bearded old philosophers in long black gowns, and swarms of fat yellow children, was, like the Chinese quarters of cities all over the world, simply a slice of China. It even smelt Chinese.

Despite their commercialism, or perhaps even because of it, most Chinese of all, in a sense, were the three 'Worlds' – the New World, the Great World, and the Happy World. In one of these amusement parks, a few days after our arrival, I sat with Ernie, who had joined us from Delhi. All the food and drink available was a bottle of orangeade and a few peanuts. The bill came to three Straits dollars. But before a month had passed the ever-resourceful Chinese businessmen had pulled all the necessary strings, and the shops in each of the three 'Worlds' were crammed with luxury goods and the restaurants redolent of every kind of food. Night clubs and cabarets flourished. I contented myself by buying writing brushes and incense. The latter, rather to the disgust of my room-mates, I burned every night before going to sleep.

By the time life at the 'Worlds' reached its pre-war gaiety, provision had been made for all possible tastes, from the grossest to the most refined. Once or twice I visited the traditional Chinese theatre. Buskined actors in costumes of gorgeous brocade declaimed and sang in unnaturally falsetto voices. Whenever there was any movement on the stage a furious clashing of cymbals would break forth, accompanied by the thudding and shrilling of less familiar instruments. Performances were interminable, seeming to last the whole afternoon and evening. As in Elizabethan and Jacobean England, the female roles were played by boy actors.

Though the music was to me simply a noise, my experience of Indian classical music convinced me that with proper study I would eventually be able to enjoy it no less than its Western counterpart. If I could appreciate Chinese poetry and painting, why not Chinese music too? At the same time, perhaps owing to my lack of technical knowledge on the subject, I could not help feeling that a people's music was closer to its soul, hence more recondite, more difficult of access, than were its sister fine arts.

At the other end of the scale was the all-in wrestling. Gigantic Sikhs, long hair tied up in topknots and lithe bodies glistening with oil, struggled and strained beneath the arc-lamps with heavy, muscle-bound Chinese. Negroes, Malays, and Europeans all competed. Alf, the ex-miner room-mate who had persuaded me to accompany him, leaned forward in his seat following every hold and throw with intense excitement. Unable to appreciate the finer points of the art I felt bored. The reactions of the audience were to me of greater interest than the tricks of the wrestlers. Whenever a joint cracked a hiss of satisfaction would go up from the crowd. At the sight of blood it howled with delight. In the ringside seats wives of high-ranking army officers applauded vigorously.

The Indian quarter, a small island in the sea of Chinese humanity, was the dirtiest and most unsavoury section of the entire city. Shop signs were mostly in Tamil, for although no part of India was without its representatives, most Singapore Indians were of Dravidian stock. As I was about to turn into a side street in which I hoped to find the Singapore centre of the Ramakrishna Mission, I noticed a red 'out of bounds' sign. After a wary glance up and down the main street for military policemen, I slipped into the turning and was soon vigorously rattling the collapsible gates of the Mission building. The monk in charge must have been astonished to see a young British soldier. After a few minutes, however, we were chatting easily. He was a stout, elderly man of medium height. Kantaraj had told me that by reason of his absolute imperturbability he was known to the Mission as Buddha Maharaj. Certainly there was something Buddha-like not only in his unruffled demeanour but in the expression of cheerful benignity which irradiated his face. Even his eyes smiled.[26]

He listened to the story of my association with the Mission centres in Colombo and Calcutta with great interest, occasionally interposing a question about this or that swami he had known; for since the Japanese occupation he had heard no news of them. Neither had the Mission received any news of him. Only from the letter I wrote to Belur Math shortly afterwards did they learn he was still alive. At one time, Buddha Maharaj told me with a smile, the building had been requisitioned by the Japanese Army. Soldiers had bivouacked even in the shrine. On the return of the British, he had been called for interrogation, for unlike the Chinese, who remained basically loyal, the Indian community had actively collaborated with the Japanese. Through the intervention of an army officer who was acquainted with the Mission's work in India, he was released after a few hours.

Thereafter I was a regular visitor to the ashram. Buddha Maharaj told me much about the grim days of Japanese occupation. He also spoke of Subhas Chandra Bose, the 'Commander-in-Chief' of the so-called

Indian National Army, to whose bloodthirsty tirades I had sometimes listened in from Delhi. Though he did not explicitly admit the fact, he had evidently served under him as a sort of chaplain to the forces. Apart from a servant, the only other inmate of the ashram was a young Tamil novice. Visitors were rare. Among them, however, was a prominent Chinese Buddhist with whom, despite our great difference in years, I was speedily on terms of friendship.

Tan Keng Lock was a Chinese businessman who for many years had played a leading part in Singapore Buddhist activities. Before the war he had founded the International Buddhist Union, an organization which aimed not only at bringing together Buddhists of all nationalities, but also at a wider dissemination of the Buddha's teaching and a purification of certain aspects of popular Chinese Buddhist practice. During the Japanese occupation he had suffered terribly. His elder son had been arrested by the secret police and was never heard of again. There was not a Chinese family, he told me, of which at least one member had not been tortured to death. Other Chinese friends not only confirmed this report but described in harrowing detail the different methods of torture. One of the milder ones was to pump several gallons of water into the victim and then jump on his stomach. The superstitious believed that the YMCA building, which had housed the secret police headquarters, was haunted by the ghosts of the thousands done to death within its walls. Under such a regime Buddhist activities were out of the question. Two English books on Buddhism had, however, been published by a Japanese scholar attached to the cultural branch of the administration. Whether he considered that the behaviour of his fellow countrymen accorded with Buddhist principles was not made clear.

Besides inviting me to his own home, where we discussed Buddhism over glasses of orangeade, Tan Keng Lock showed me several Chinese temples. Though different in many ways from their Sinhalese counterparts, they exhaled the same atmosphere of peace, for over all brooded the same golden presence with the half-closed eyes and gently smiling lips.

He also took me to pay my respects to various prominent Chinese monks. The Venerable Siak Kiong Hiup, a small figure in black silk robes, lived alone with his sacred books and images in a quiet street not far from one of the 'Worlds'. Whenever he bowed, which was often, one saw on top of his shaven head the scars left by the candles which, in accordance with Chinese Mahāyāna tradition, had been burned there at the time of his ordination. These scars signified his readiness to suffer for the sake of all sentient beings. Active, friendly, humble, and courteous, he was indeed a good example of a bodhisattva monk. Tan Keng Lock told me that a number of Chinese Buddhists came to him for scriptural study. Though he could not speak a word of English, and I knew no Hokkien, we became good friends, and I like to think that even in the absence of Tan Keng Lock, who interpreted, we would have understood each other.

The Venerable Phoe Thay, who lived in a small monastery outside the city, might have been the original 'Laughing Buddha'. Unlike the Venerable Siak Kiong Hiup, he wore yellow robes of Sinhalese pattern which allowed for the exposure of his enormous stomach. His face was the merriest I had ever seen. In illustration of certain abstruse teachings which he was explaining to Tan Keng Lock, he bounced into an inner room. Suddenly a little ticket-window in the wall popped open to show his laughing face, which he kept covering with a corner of his robe. Disappearing for a second, he returned to the window with a large black begging-bowl. With another burst of laughter he clicked the window to and the interview was ended. Tan Keng Lock, who had followed the performance with great interest, afterwards told me that the fat monk was a man of high spiritual attainment and well versed in meditation.

Having made the acquaintance of the Chinese Buddhists, I was eager to get in touch with the other Buddhist communities. From either Buddha Maharaj or Tan Keng Lock I learned of the existence of a Sinhalese temple on the outskirts of the city. Here, in the tiny reception room, I met the Venerable M. M. Mahaweera, a placid, somewhat inscrutable person who for a number of years had been the incumbent. Apart from Walpola Rahula, who talked only politics, and a monk in Kandy who wanted to go to America, he was the first Theravādin monk I had met who knew English well enough to discuss simple doctrinal questions.

Perhaps because of my Western preconceptions, life at the temple seemed not tranquil but merely stagnant. Two or three Sinhalese and one or two Chinese Buddhists were the only visitors. Consequently I went there much less often than to the ashram. On one of my visits, however, the Venerable Mahaweera smilingly told me that three learned Sinhalese monks had arrived and would be staying with him for two or three weeks. This was an opportunity not to be missed. The monks were the famous trio Soma, Kheminda, and Pannasiha. They had been invited, it transpired, to work in an institute of Buddhist studies in eastern China; but finding it impossible to cross the Communist-held territory which lay between them and their destination, had decided to retrace their steps and were now on their way back to Ceylon. Bhikkhu Soma, who bore the brunt of my questioning, was a frowning thickset man of mixed Dutch and Sinhalese descent. Like Kheminda, he was of Christian origin and had worked in the Post Office before ordination. The expression of his features, which were deeply marked with signs of inner stress and strain, was one of grim determination, as though for him the moral and spiritual battle was still being fought. Though strongly adhering to the 'fundamentalist' Theravāda Buddhism of South-east Asia, he was not indifferent to ecumenical issues. In reply to a question about the more 'developed' Mahāyāna Buddhism of China, Japan, and Tibet, he declared it could be accepted only to the extent that it agreed with the original Pāli scriptures handed down in Ceylon. For a Theravādin, to whom development meant degeneration, and who usually rejected the Mahāyāna *in toto* as a complete betrayal of Buddhism, this was quite a generous concession. On the subject of the monastic life Bhikkhu Soma's views were even less conventional. Discussing an incident that had occurred during the voyage (an attempt, it seemed, had been made to seduce him), he declared that the true monk should rise above temptation rather than run away from it and that he should, if necessary, be able to look at a naked woman without desire.

The subject I was most eager to discuss with him, however, was not the acceptability or unacceptability of the Mahāyāna, or even the right way for a monk to look at a naked woman, but meditation. Producing a slender booklet on *ānāpānasati*, or mindfulness of the process of respiration, which I had bought in Ceylon, I asked if he could recommend the method it described. Bhikkhu Soma's reply was unhesitating. It was the best of methods, he said, the method employed by the Buddha on the eve of his Enlightenment. In fact, having himself derived great benefit from it, he had translated the canonical text in which it was expounded into English, together with its commentary. A copy of this work, together with two or three other books he had published, he presented to me.

That night, for the third time since leaving England, I sat beneath my mosquito net meditating while others slept. (The unit had been shifted to a group of houses in another suburb and there were now five or six of us to a room.) This time success was immediate. My mind became at first buoyant, then filled with peace and purity, and finally penetrated by a 'quintessential, keen, ethereal bliss' that was so intense I had to break off the practice. Obviously, the conditions under which I was then living were not ideal for meditation. I therefore resolved to continue the practice later, when they had become more favourable. This resolution I kept. Though the Theravāda sectarianism of Bhikkhu Soma and the author of the slender booklet was the antithesis of my own acceptance of the entire Buddhist tradition, in all its ramifications, I remain grateful to them for having introduced me to a practice which was for long the sheet anchor of my spiritual life.

14
COINCIDENCES

Whether by coincidence, or due to some mysterious shaping of my ends, within a month of the experiment with meditation I encountered the person with whom, a year later, I was to embark on a systematic practice of the method.

Rabindra Kumar Banerjee was a tall, well-built Bengali in the prime of manhood. From the moment Buddha Maharaj introduced us to each other we were friends. Like me, he was in khaki, but on his epaulettes he wore the tricoloured insignia of the Indian National Congress. Being of a frank, communicative nature, with more than a touch of naive boastfulness, it was not long before he was telling me about himself without either restraint or reserve. Politics were the passion of his life. Though respecting Gandhi for his moral character, he did not believe that independence could be won by non-violent means. His hero was Subhas Bose, who had broadcast his intention of wading through a sea of blood to Delhi. In fact, in the days when the future 'Commander-in-Chief' of the Indian National Army was President of the Congress he had worked under him as a volunteer. After Bose's arrest and subsequent dramatic escape to Axis territory he had joined the Royal Indian Air Force in order to work as a saboteur. After his discharge he had apparently been associated not only with the Congress but with the more explicitly orthodox right-wing Hindu Mahasabha. At the time of our meeting he was a member of the Mobile Medical Unit which the Congress, as an expression of goodwill from the people of India to those of Malaya, had dispatched to render free medical aid to the towns and villages of the interior, where drugs were still in very short supply.

Though born in an orthodox Brahmin family, he was an avowed enemy of the caste system, and neither believed in nor practised any form of social discrimination. Religion he violently condemned, probably because it was at that time identified in his mind with the inhuman social system sanctioned by the tradition to which by birth he belonged. Nevertheless, discerning beneath his anti-religious outbursts a strong ethical motivation, I not only spoke to him about religion but lent him books on Vedanta to read during his trip, which was to last three months, in the hope that these would prepare his mind for the eventual reception of Buddhism.

While he was away I made another important spiritual contact. On one of my visits to Tan Keng Lock I noticed, at the lower end of the road in which he lived, a noticeboard announcing the presence of the Singapore Lodge of the Theosophical Society. Despite my indebtedness to *Isis Unveiled* I had subsequently developed, for reasons now forgotten – if reasons there ever were – a strong prejudice against Theosophy. A prose poem I composed during the voyage to India had spoken of 'an evil, Theosophical face'. But now curiosity proved stronger than prejudice. The welcome that I received on my first visit to the Lodge, and the pleasant friendly atmosphere of its meetings, soon drew me in, and though I never joined the Society I participated as fully as possible in all the activities open to non-members. What attracted me most of all, perhaps, was the way everybody practised Brotherhood, the first of the three objectives of the Theosophical Society. Never before had I seen the members of so many different races, nations, and religions associating on terms of perfect equality and friendship, and the sight impressed me profoundly. Several of the members were occidentals, including the president, who was a young Canadian businessman, and the treasurer, an English merchant.

Though making a number of Indian and Chinese friends, I became most intimately associated with Rie, a second-generation Dutch Theosophist, and Sten, her Swedish husband. This was partly because Rie, like many Theosophists, was drawn more strongly to the Buddha than to any other religious teacher, and partly because it was round them that Lodge activities revolved. Though not very young, they had only recently married. In physical and mental characteristics alike they

With Rabindra Kumar Banerjee (left) and Swami Bhaswarananda (right), Ramakrishna Mission Boys Home, Singapore, May 1946

were well matched. Tall, slim, and fair, each lived only for Theosophy. Both were strict vegetarians. Indeed, they claimed that even their cat had learned to abstain from fish and meat, and that she brought her kittens not mice but lumps of cucumber, of which she was herself very fond.

At first I confined myself to attending lectures and borrowing books from the Lodge library. Apart from the writings of Annie Besant and C. W. Leadbeater, which I found of greater value than my prejudices had led me to expect, I read the series of works on the Hindu Tantra that Sir John Woodroffe had written in collaboration with Indian pandits and published under the pseudonym of 'Arthur Avalon'. Though tending to obscure fundamental differences between the Hindu and the Buddhist Tantric systems – differences which I myself at that time did not appreciate – those minutely accurate volumes were in many ways a revelation. Hinduism, evidently, was not to be equated with the well-diluted Vedantism of the Ramakrishna Mission.

While I was discovering Theosophy and the Tantra, the Lodge discovered a lecturer. What made the members think that a soldier of twenty-one would be a good speaker I do not know. To my own astonishment, if not to theirs, my first lecture was a success. Ideas, I found, wove themselves Persian carpet-wise into intricate patterns, and these patterns dipped themselves in colourful words, without the slightest difficulty. Nervousness I experienced only before rising to speak. After this initial effort I was in great demand as a lecturer not only at the Lodge but also at the ashram, where Buddha Maharaj gave me useful hints on public speaking. Tan Keng Lock, who with my encouragement had already revived his organization under the name of the Buddhist Union, arranged for me to speak under its auspices in Chinese temples.[27] Lodge audiences generally contained a fairly high percentage of young people, several of whom would ask questions. At temples, where the lectures had to be translated into Hokkien, I found myself confronted by rows of devout old Chinese ladies in black silk jackets and trousers sitting on little wooden stools. Some of them told their beads while I spoke. At the end of the meeting they hobbled forward one by one and bowed politely to the speaker. Lodge meetings ended with tea and biscuits. But at the temples the Venerable Siak Kiong Hiup would bow us into a room wherein a table stood spread with Chinese vegetarian delicacies.

Partly because of the example of the Chinese monks, who unlike the Sinhalese *bhikkhus* abstained from meat and fish, and partly as the result of my discussions with Rie and Sten, I decided to become a vegetarian. In making this decision I was not influenced by the Hindu argument 'Purity of food leads to purity of mind.' It appeared to me that the killing of animals for food was not consistent with the Buddha's teaching of universal compassion, so that one who claimed to be a practising Buddhist ought logically to be a vegetarian. Though fish was given up only some months later, meat was renounced immediately. The Indian cooks at the unit's new quarters smirked when I refused my portion of beef or mutton. 'He must be a Brahmin,' they jeered among themselves. In the mess my eccentricity passed without comment. Since meat and vegetables were usually cooked together I often had to go without a meal. On such occasions I fell back on the hard American army biscuits and tinned cheese, which stood in the centre of the table untouched by my carnivorous companions.

One application of Buddhist principles led to another. I soon realized that I was opposed not only to meat-eating but to violence in any form and that I ought never to have allowed myself to be conscripted. When, at the end of a Lodge meeting, a young Indian member asked if a Buddhist could be a soldier, I frankly admitted that he could not, adding that I hoped soon to be able to extricate myself from an anomalous situation.

About the morality of the War Crimes trials then being conducted in Singapore I was for a long time in doubt. Did they represent a stern determination to see that certain principles of conduct should be held inviolate even in time of war, or were they a hypocritical abasement of the conquered in the name of justice? If Tojo should be brought to trial, why not Truman? Granted that the Japanese committed atrocities, but who released the atom bomb? A popular song exhorted the Americans to 'Remember Pearl Harbour'. No doubt a similar song warned the Japanese not to forget Commodore Perry. Any attempt to pin responsibility for the war onto one nation seemed likely to lead to a *regressus ad infinitum* of accusation and counter-accusation. Besides, did not the Allies profess Christianity, and had not Christ taught his followers to forgive their enemies? In the end I decided that with Hiroshima and Nagasaki weighing so heavily in the balance it would be unwise for the victors to lay claim to a monopoly of moral sensitivity.

Back in London, English Buddhists were also debating the ethics of the trials. Clare Cameron wrote that many of them had been deeply shocked when Humphreys flew to Japan to take part in the Tokyo War Crimes trials as junior prosecuting counsel. I too felt that his acceptance of such an assignment was hardly in keeping with his character as president of the Buddhist Society and the upholder, presumably, of the ideals for which it stood. But when I wrote and told him this he curtly replied 'The Japanese don't think so and I don't see why you should.'

Another friend from the Buddhist Society was Arnold Price, who also continued to write. He was living in a caravan named 'Mahayana', earned a livelihood by doing carpentry jobs in the villages through which he passed and was still hard at work on the Chinese language. Were any Chinese Buddhist texts available in Singapore? Tan Keng Lock and the Venerable Siak Kiong Hiup, whom I consulted, eventually produced copies of three important canonical texts, two of them running into numerous volumes, which were promptly dispatched to 'Mahayana'. In another letter Arnold waxed enthusiastic over *Peaks and Lamas* by

Marco Pallis, a writer of whom I had never heard. 'You must read it if you get a chance,' he declared. By one of those strange coincidences which have occurred often in my life, I saw the book a few days later in the Singapore public library. Tibetan Buddhism, of which the author wrote from first-hand knowledge, evoked from me an immediate response. Coming events were casting their shadows before. Marco Pallis was later to become not only a close personal friend and valued adviser but the generous provider of the means of carrying out more than one cherished project. Meanwhile I read his book with avidity, being especially moved by the song in which Milarepa, the Tibetan poet-saint, hails his broken pot as his guru because it has taught him the law of impermanence.

Whereupon occurred another coincidence. In Dwight Goddard's *Buddhist Bible*, which I borrowed from the Lodge library, I found an abridged version of *Tibet's Great Yogi Milarepa*. It would be difficult to find a more powerful incentive to the leading of the spiritual life than this masterpiece of religious biography. As I read it my hair stood on end and tears came into my eyes. If I had any doubts about the nature of my vocation they were now dispelled, and from that time onwards I lived only for the day when I would be free to follow to its end the path that, as it seemed, had been in reality mine from the beginning.

15
THE END OF THE BEGINNING

Banerjee returned to Singapore full of indignation against the other members of the Medical Mission, who, instead of distributing the medicines and drugs free to the sick and suffering, had sold practically the entire valuable stock to the proprietors of pharmacies, thus making small fortunes for themselves. The intensity of his indignation did him credit, for it was the recoil of a truth-loving nature from an exceptionally despicable kind of dishonesty. But I could also see that the misconduct of the doctors provided him with the opportunity of indulging a strongly marked tendency to censoriousness. This in turn constituted a basis for unconscious egotism. He was one of those people who, being themselves strong enough to resist temptation, are unsparing in their condemnation of weaker souls, not realizing that their harshness is only a less easily recognizable expression of the very evil against which they are inveighing. These conclusions I of course did not confide to him; for though he was prepared to correct himself the minute anyone convinced him he was wrong, to convince him was extremely difficult.

Buddhism was, of course, often mentioned, and I believe he attended one of my lectures; but though admiring its repudiation of the caste system he was still too deeply committed to Forward Bloc ideology to be able to feel much sympathy for so pacifist a teaching. Like many Bengalis, he felt that by placing a premium on non-violence Buddhism had weakened India politically. Discussion therefore usually ended with our agreeing to differ. But if he was rock, I was water; and subsequent events showed that my words had not been entirely without effect.

Meanwhile, being interested mainly in nationalist politics, especially in the doings of Subhas Bose, whose fate was then the subject of fierce controversy, he investigated the history of the Indian National Army and the so-called Provisional Government of Azad Hind, former members of both of which still lurked in Singapore. He also collected literature pertaining to the struggle for independence. Through him I met several associates of Bose. One was a quiet, pleasant young schoolmaster, who had been nominated Minister of Education and Culture. Another was a Tamil girl who, at the age of sixteen, had been a sergeant in the Rani of Jhansi regiment. When we met, she and her sister were not only destitute but greatly distressed by the unwelcome attentions of a horde of Indian sepoys who seemed to think unprotected girls lawful prey. Banerjee promised to arrange jobs for them in India and at the time of his departure asked me to continue supplying them with tinned foodstuffs. The literature he collected consisted mostly of books banned in India, such as the speeches of Subhas Bose, which he gave me to read. Though I could not but sympathize wholeheartedly with the cause of Indian independence, the tin soldier militarism of the plump, bespectacled Bengali leader was not to my taste. But the friendship between Banerjee and myself, being an attraction of opposites, seemed only strengthened by such differences of opinion. When, after spending two months in Singapore, he embarked for India, we solemnly contracted to meet in Calcutta as soon after my demobilization as possible.

The last months of my army life were in some respects the most exasperating of all. Before the unit had been many weeks in Singapore it became obvious that its work had really ended on VJ Day. Why, then, were we in Singapore? At first we attributed the transfer to the usual army imbecility. But it soon transpired that we were there to do the work of a certain colonial power, which was finding it by no means easy to re-establish its dominion over territories won back from the Japanese. Post-war Asia was in no mood to swallow another dose of white imperialism. Ernie and I and a few other young unpromoted operators felt very strongly that if the war had been fought for freedom then why, now that it was won, should we be called upon to help suppress the freedom movement in a country which, having been liberated from one oppressor, had no desire to see him replaced by another? Besides, England was yielding to demands for independence within her own empire. Why should she be a party to the brutal suppression of a similar demand in territories not her own? We therefore decided on a policy of unconfessed non-cooperation. In our logbooks we either wrote 'Nil to report' or, when this appeared too obviously suspicious, logged one of the wanted call-signs and then allowed it to be blacked out by atmospherics. The officers who scrutinized our logbooks must have realized something was amiss. But having no means of checking the reliability of our work they kept their misgivings to themselves.

Objectionable as the task assigned to the unit was, it was the lone dyke that prevented us from being engulfed by the circumfluent waters of regular army inanity, which often enough swirled perilously near. The CSM who was posted to the unit soon after its arrival in Singapore quickly had us out of our comfortable quarters in the villas, which were allowed to stand empty, and under canvas. The monsoon had just started. Torrential rains beat upon the rotten leaky tents and came soaking and streaming in at a hundred places. For more than a month we lived in the midst of mud and cold and damp. Most of us caught chills, several influenza. That, of course, did not matter: we had been made to realize we were in the army!

Conditions in the next camp, where we lived in human habitations set amidst beautiful flowering trees, were much better; but either because the owners demanded that they be derequisitioned or because the brass hats who occupied suites at the Cathay or the Raffles Hotel decided they were too good for us, we did not enjoy them for long. The third and last camp was situated in a rubber plantation in the middle of the island. Outside the gate was a Chinese village. Though we continued to live in tents, the inconvenience was less keenly felt, partly because the monsoon had ended, and partly because the officers now lived under canvas too.

Life was at first almost idyllic. Around us, so thickly planted that one could not see through them to the end of the plantation, rose the straight, slender trunks of the rubber trees, with their grey-green foliage, in the shade of which I sometimes wandered if the tent became too hot and stuffy. When not on duty in the Set Room, which was temporarily housed in the huge half-cylinder of a Nissen hut, we helped erect the rough frame buildings which eventually became our new mess, canteen, recreation room, and 'ablutions'.

Prisoners of war also worked in the camp. These included two slim, self-effacing young Japanese officers. Whenever we gave them cigarettes they clicked their heels and bowed smartly. Both were extremely fond of Western classical music and often, when the strains of Bach or Beethoven came floating through the canteen door, they could be seen unobtrusively listening. There was also a party of Koreans, slow-moving and unintelligent, though simple and harmless enough. They were farm labourers who had been forcibly impressed into the Japanese Army. Every afternoon, when their duties for the day were done, they unconcernedly soaped one another's sturdy, thick-limbed orange bodies, as they stood naked round the pump.

We had not enjoyed the amenities of the new camp for more than a few weeks, when the dyke burst and the waters came pouring in.

A brigadier who inspected the camp was outraged by its lack of discipline. There were far too many men off duty. There were not enough parades, no fatigues, and, the supreme horror, no rifle drill. Tents were out of alignment, guy-ropes unwhitened. Fire-buckets had not had rings painted on them. Several pieces of litter were discernible. The men were improperly dressed. Operators strolled about the camp instead of 'proceeding in a smart soldierly manner'. Beds were not made up during the day, nor mosquito nets taken down. And so on and so on. The CO was severely reprimanded and told that discipline must be tightened up at once. These instructions were as balm to the soul of the CSM. Though we were spared any rifle drill, there were now daily parades, regular and more strict tent inspections, and frequent fatigues. What did it matter that they were all quite unnecessary? We were in the army!

But most of us had been in it long enough to know that, provided one did not refuse to obey an order, it was possible to get away with almost anything. Some reported sick. Others wrote home to their MP complaining about conditions in the unit. Satirical poems appeared on the noticeboard. In the end, despite a number of petty annoyances, there was no observable improvement in the discipline of the camp. In fact, by giving genuine cause for grievance, discipline had in reality been undermined.

That we could not be immediately repatriated and demobilized was obvious to the least intelligent. We were prepared to be patient and wait our turn. But we were not prepared to be harassed by artificially created work and meaningless restrictions simply in order to gratify some pettifogging brass hat's desire to throw his weight around. We refused to be victims to the Moloch of discipline. Some of us went so far as to make it quite obvious by our behaviour that now the war was over we regarded ourselves as being in the army only in a very nominal sense. I was one of these. Not a minute more than necessary did I spend in the camp. The CSM always looked at me sourly as I went out of the gate. Once he checked me for wearing a white shirt. But it was regulation khaki issue that had faded in the wash. I wore this shirt when, in anticipation of the unit's disbandment, a group photograph was taken.

'Who is that man in the white shirt?' roared the CO at the CSM after this souvenir had been developed and printed.

Special Communications Unit 14, Singapore, May 1946. Dennis Lingwood in white shirt, second row from back.

On Vaiśākha Pūrṇimā Day I went to the CO and said that I was a Buddhist and wanted the day off.

'The day off, eh?' said Pringy, as we called him, twirling his moustaches. 'Well, we can't lay on a liberty truck just for one man, can we, Sergeant-Major? You'd better give your fatigue party the day off and let them go into town too.' The CSM glowered.

156 / THE RAINBOW ROAD FROM TOOTING BROADWAY TO KALIMPONG

My original intention had been to be demobilized in England, spend some time with my parents and my sister, and then return to India. But a letter from a friend who had once accompanied me on a visit to Bhikkhu Soma, and who had gone home with a similar intention, caused me to change my mind. Escape from England was impossible, he wrote, as it was the Government's policy to discourage any drainage of manpower away from the country. I therefore decided to abandon my hopes of seeing the family and take the law into my own hands. I would apply for six weeks' leave in India, once again making Uncle Dick my excuse, and then, when the period was up, instead of returning to Singapore I would simply disappear. Technically of course I would be deserting. But about this I had no qualms. In fact, if not in law, the war was over. Whatever duty I had to my country I had done, and my life was now my own, to do with as I wished.

Had it not been for the relief afforded by my activities in Singapore, the period of suspense which followed this decision would have been intolerable. More than once, in sheer desperation, I was on the point of taking to the jungle and working my way up to Thailand on foot. The nearer the day of liberation drew, the more violent became my desire to escape from the pettiness and futility of army life. But at last, one morning, as in a dream, I found myself in the QM's store handing in my rifle, my webbing, and the rest of the much-hated equipment that had never been of the slightest use. Though nobody else then knew it, I was never to see that equipment again. Since the day that Ernie and I had trudged up the Leatherhead lane there had been no sweeter moment.

16

JUMPING IN AT THE SHALLOW END

One of the first things I did in Calcutta was to contact Banerjee. We met at the Institute of Culture, where I introduced him to Kantaraj. On his return from Singapore he had bought a partnership in a small retail coal business, on behalf of which he travelled in and around Calcutta in quest of orders. Ever rapid in transition from one extreme to the other, he now denounced politics as a menace to society and declared that religious and cultural activities alone constituted the true means of India's upliftment.

Here at last was common ground. But though we discussed long and earnestly the question of the kind of life we proposed to lead together, and the type of work to which we aspired to dedicate our energies, in the face of the vast difference which existed between our respective temperaments and backgrounds it was impossible for us to come to any immediate conclusion. I wanted to work for Buddhism and, if possible, become a Buddhist monk. He, for all his repudiation of social orthodoxy, was still at heart very much the Bengali Brahmin, and his appreciation of Buddhism was in my eyes nullified by his point-blank refusal to consider it anything but a branch of Hinduism.

In this he was by no means guilty of mere intransigence. Like all English-educated Caste Hindus, the depth of his emotional commitment to Hinduism was so great that he belonged to it even when he rebelled against it, so that to repudiate it for the sake of another religion would have meant a tearing up of roots such as no one born into a more youthful and secularized tradition can imagine. However much

Buddhism may appeal to him, no Caste Hindu finds it easy to renounce his 3,000 years of cultural and spiritual tradition, especially when that tradition affirms his own 'sacred, innate priority' over the Untouchable mass. Small wonder, then, that in an attempt to make the best of both worlds he should maintain, against all evidence, that Buddhism and Hinduism are one. Years later, in a heroic act of renunciation, Banerjee cut himself free of all such emotional entanglements. Meanwhile, as we argued at the Institute, the problem of the next step to be taken remained unsolved. So for the time being he continued his quest for customers, while I remained with Uncle Dick.

Despite my three years in the army, I found the pleasures of family life thoroughly insipid. My last month in European society was in fact memorable for the disgust rather than the delight it inspired. At the Saturday Club, where I dined one night with Uncle Dick and his friends, a member described how an Anglo-Indian dancer had been stabbed to death in her bath by an Indian servant and then raped. The coarse jests which followed nauseated me. 'Your nephew doesn't seem to like our stories,' sneered the narrator of the incident to Uncle Dick.

From Audrey's brother-in-law, a high-ranking police officer, I heard a story which I liked even less, and which made me ashamed of being English. It concerned the Dacca communal riots which had occurred more than twenty years earlier. In great detail, and with every evidence of satisfaction, Dave described how, step by step, *agents provocateurs* had stirred up Hindu against Muslim, and Muslim against Hindu, until half the city had been set ablaze and hundreds murdered. Much as the story shocked me, I was still more horrified by the laughter which followed. Uncle Dick, Audrey, and Audrey's sister Gladys were kindly, good-natured people. But Dave's story of how the police, in order to prevent the two Indian communities from forming a united front against the government, had resorted to tactics which can be described only as vile, seemed to fill them with nothing but amusement. Did they, then, have a double standard of morality, one for use among themselves, the other to be employed in dealing with Indians?

The longer I stayed with Uncle Dick the more ethical questions of this sort perplexed me. I was also troubled by problems of philosophy. What was the nature of causality? How was true knowledge possible, and in what did it consist? From questions such as these, which hammered on my brain as remorselessly as the falling of waterdrops on the head in the famous Chinese water-torture, which eventually drives its victim mad, I was distracted by an unexpected turn in events.

Several years before, the Institute had published a three-volume work entitled *The Cultural Heritage of India*. This having gone out of print, a revised edition in seven volumes was being planned. One day the Secretary Swami, who had some inkling of my aspirations and wanted to attach me more closely to the Mission, spoke to me about this project and made a proposal. Would I like to live with them and assist in the preparation of the new edition? Though I should have preferred to work with a Buddhist organization, the proposal was not without its attractions. Kantaraj, Sanyal, and several other inmates of the Institute were my friends. The type of work in which I was being asked to collaborate was extremely congenial. Besides, did not the swami's offer, which was communicated in a graceful and friendly manner, afford a means of escape from the mingled boredom and disgust of life with Uncle Dick and Audrey into the infinitely richer and more ample life of the real India? Might it not eventually provide a cultural springboard from which to leap and lose myself in the waters of the life spiritual?

The only difficulty was my relation with Banerjee, which had rapidly developed into a strong mutual attachment. Like the blind man and the lame man in the parable, we complemented each other to such an extent that neither felt capable of moving without the other. Besides, Banerjee had been cheated by his partner and, being as disgusted with business as I was with the social life of the English in India, was ready to devote himself to some kind of religious or cultural activity. Why should we not work together for the Institute? The Secretary Swami, to whom I put this counter-proposal, at first demurred that my friend would not be of much use in a purely literary undertaking, but when I urged on him Banerjee's willingness to be of service, and when he understood it would not be possible to have one of us without the other, he agreed that the arrangement should be given a trial. After taking my aunt, uncle, and cousins out for a farewell dinner, I therefore shifted to the Institute. From then onward I had no connections whatever with the European community.

As no separate room was available to us at the Institute, Banerjee and I slept on the floor of the sitting room. One night I awoke to see an evil face with a knife gripped between the teeth peering at me through the window. Though I saw the face for only a few seconds it created a strong impression, reminding me of all the dark and hostile forces that were lurking outside our small, self-contained world of religious and cultural activities waiting for an opportunity to break in. Thereafter our bedding was unrolled on the floor of the inner room I used as an office.

To keep me occupied until work on *The Cultural Heritage of India* was started, the Secretary Swami gave me letters to type. He also asked me to prepare the annual report of the Institute. Though such tasks were not uncongenial to me, I could not help feeling irritated at his method of work. Often a whole afternoon was spent over a single line of writing. Thus the work advanced with a slowness that my youthful impatience found extremely exasperating.

Banerjee, who was trying to extract money from his former partner, was out most of the day. In the evenings we discussed religion. More often than not he harangued the dozen or so student inmates of the Institute about politics while I read St John of the Cross or Meister Eckhart. Once, in fulfilment of a promise made in Singapore, he took me twenty miles out of Calcutta to the Bengali village, all coconut palms and fishponds, where his widowed mother lived with his uncles, brothers, sisters, cousins, and various other members of their large joint family. This was the first time I had stayed in an Indian household. It was also the first time Banerjee's home had admitted a European guest. Seven years earlier, he told me, his mother could never have brought herself to tolerate my unclean presence. But the war had to some extent broken down the old rigid social barriers. Now she actually welcomed me. True, I was not allowed into the kitchen, and Banerjee was desperately anxious that I should make a show of carrying water with me whenever I went to the latrine (toilet paper being regarded as an abomination); but despite such vestiges of Hindu orthodoxy, I felt quite at home in the peaceful atmosphere of the asymmetrical tiled cottage, with its cowdunged floor, large wooden bed platforms, and shining brassware.

Only subsequently did I learn that their allowing me to stay with them was an act of social heresy for which Banerjee's family ran the risk of being ostracized by the whole village. The fact that I had taken food in the house automatically polluted not only the building itself but every occupant. Until the prescribed ceremonies of purification had been undergone, no Caste Hindu could enter the house or touch any object that had been touched by a member of the household without becoming polluted in turn. To the orthodox Hindu pollution is as tangible and contagious as leprosy. By what means the village was placated after my departure I do not know, but there is little doubt that my visit cost the ladies of the family at least several ceremonial ablutions.

Since the typing and drafting I did for the swami occupied only a small part of my time, I was free to go out as much as I liked. Towards the end of February, when I had been nearly a month at the Institute, Kantaraj took Banerjee and me to Belur Math for Shivaratri, the 'Night of Shiva', a festival observed especially by ascetics, whose patron the god Shiva is considered to be. In accordance with custom, the swamis spent the whole night singing and dancing round a great bonfire. On a tigerskin-covered throne not far from the blaze sat a naked, ash-smeared figure with long matted hair. At intervals he rose to his feet and pranced round the fire waving his trident and shouting 'Shambhu! Shambhu!' in loud, raucous tones. Kantaraj whispered to me that this was Shiva. According to Western conceptions it was merely a swami impersonating the Deity. But Hindus believe that he actually takes possession of the impersonator, who is therefore honoured for one night as Shiva himself. Certainly the awe-inspiring figure with the trident was not human. Perhaps it was a case of mediumistic possession similar to that of the Tibetan 'oracles'. A concoction of bhang or hemp, used throughout India by sadhus to induce this condition, was flowing freely, and Shiva had no doubt imbibed it plentifully. Despite the remonstrances of Kantaraj, who feared it would make me drunk, a group of youthful novices pressed on me a glass of sour, greyish-white liquid with the laughing assurance that it was only milk. However, the drink produced no ill effect. At two o'clock I went to bed, leaving the swamis shouting and singing round the bonfire. Next day Shiva was again an ordinary monk.

There was also time for visits to the Maha Bodhi Society. One day the *bhikkhu* in charge, who seemed to live almost alone in the headquarters building, asked me to type some letters. On another occasion he sent us to Writer's Building on official business. Before long we were spending as much time for the Society's work as for that of the Institute. One day His Holiness, as the *bhikkhu* informed us he should be styled, asked us in an almost uncouthly abrupt manner why we did not join the Society as full-time workers. We could see for ourselves how short-handed they were, he said, and the General Secretary, who was in Ceylon, would undoubtedly agree gladly to our enrolment.

Though the offer did not take us by surprise, Banerjee and I did not feel like giving His Holiness a reply before we had had time to consult Kantaraj. With life at the Institute we were for several reasons dissatisfied. There was no sign of the editorial work being started. As a matter of fact, it did not start until years afterwards. Moreover, Banerjee, who was almost pathologically sensitive to slights, both real and imagined, had become convinced that the Secretary Swami despised him as one who, having failed to make a success of either politics or business, had taken refuge with me at the Institute because he had no alternative. His loud, emphatic assertion of how distinguished his family was, and how successful he could be if he cared, only excited the very suspicions they were meant to crush and made him look ridiculous. My protests that no one at the Institute despised him only infuriated him. Being myself respected, he said, I did not care if he was not. Whatever the Secretary Swami's true feelings might have been, it had become clear that if for me there was little work at the Institute, for Banerjee there was none at all, and that his presence was tolerated only on my account. But the real explanation of our decision to quit lay in an incident that had occurred some days earlier.

The premises the Institute occupied in Wellington Square were not its own. A Bengali couple, however, had donated in memory of their son a large block of flats in Russa Road. Here, when the building had been remodelled, was to be located the Institute's permanent home. Meanwhile, eviction suits had been filed against the tenants, most of whom refused to budge until they had found alternative accommodation. Saroj, a plump jolly novice of thirty-seven who had been a solicitor, was in charge of these proceedings.

One morning we found him weeping bitterly in the sitting room. The Secretary Swami, he explained between his sobs, exasperated by the law's delay, had ordered him to hire a gang of hooligans and drive out the tenants by force. In vain he had fallen on his knees and pleaded that he had joined the Mission to purify himself of sins, not to commit fresh ones. The swami was adamant. By foul means, if fair ones were of no help, the tenants must be dislodged. Banerjee and I were deeply distressed. The students, none of whom liked the swami, denounced him indignantly. Kantaraj was silent. Saroj was still sobbing bitterly when he was again summoned upstairs to the swami's room. Two hours later, dry-eyed but with an expression of intense misery on his face, he reappeared, took his umbrella from the stand, and without a word slowly went out as usual to the lawyer's office.

Later it transpired that the Secretary Swami had given him a good lecture on Nishkama Karma-Yoga or disinterested action as a means to God-realization. Referring to the *Bhagavad Gītā*, the famous dialogue between Sri Krishna, the incarnate Godhead, and his disciple Arjuna, he had reminded Saroj that pity was a weakness to be overcome. The *ātman*, the Spirit, was one and indestructible in all men: who then could hurt another, who be hurt? Had not Sri Krishna himself exhorted Arjuna to fight and slay? One who performed his duty, whatever that might be, with mind fixed on God, committed no sin. In fact, such disinterested performance of duty constituted one of the four great paths to Salvation. This sermon opened my eyes to the sinister implications of Hindu philosophy, and I recoiled from the Mission like one who, when a lamp is lit, sees that he had been about to step on a snake in the dark.

17
DIRECT ACTION DAY

In the Maha Bodhi Society's Headquarters Block, immediately behind the shrine and lecture-hall, Banerjee and I occupied a dark, dingy room on the ground floor. On the night of our arrival we were awoken by intolerably sharp stinging sensations all over our bodies. Switching on the light, we saw that hundreds of fat red bugs had swarmed out of the cracks in the wooden bed-platforms and were marching up and down the sheets and over the pillows. Thereafter we slept on the flat roof. In the incredibly filthy kitchen, cockroaches were no less numerous. Apart from the shrine, which though unused was kept reasonably clean, the whole place exhaled an atmosphere of dirt and decay that was somehow not only physical but moral. The ragged tablecloth in the dark, airless dining room was foul with the stains of several months and stank abominably. The black, hairy cook, who wore only a soiled white loincloth, despite daily ceremonial ablutions managed always to look unclean. Even the shifty-eyed accountant in the office was a crumpled, unwholesome object.

His Holiness alone was well-groomed and immaculate. Freshly shaved, his bald head agleam with scented oil, and clad in a bright new yellow robe, he sat at his desk rapping out orders. With his bold eye and brazen manner he looked like a saffron-coloured crow, the crow being in Indian folklore the most impudent of birds. To callers his first question was 'Well, what have you brought me today?' His drawers were filled with boxes of chocolates, fountain pens, and other presents. But though not very monk-like in his behaviour he was shrewd and businesslike and evidently managed the Society's affairs with commendable efficiency. Banerjee and me he treated extremely well. Unlike the Secretary Swami at the Institute, he had enough common sense to assign each of us the work for which he was best suited. I typed and read proofs in the office. Banerjee went calling on government officials. When a white face was needed to open ministerial doors His Holiness dispatched me too. Before long our relations with the bold, efficient *bhikkhu* were quite cordial. Like most capable men he was extremely ambitious. 'You'll see,' he used to tell us, 'within two years I shall be General Secretary of the Society.'

One day he took us to the Maha Bodhi Orphanage. This institution occupied a small double-storeyed house near Park Circus in a predominantly Muslim locality. The ages of the thirty-odd inmates ranged from five to fifteen, the younger boys being the more numerous. Later we learned how the Orphanage had been started. During the previous year's Hindu–Muslim riots, His Holiness had gone out with an escort of armed police picking up off the street boys whose parents had been killed. With the same intrepidity he had rescued Dr Beni Madhab Barua and his family, who had been marooned in a Muslim neighbourhood. At the Society's headquarters, situated in the predominantly Hindu College Square, he had sheltered ninety Muslims from the fury of the Hindu mob. Once, with a short laugh, he told us how he had rescued both Hindus and Muslims and accommodated them in different parts of the same Buddhist building. For these exploits, as well as for the competent though unsentimental manner in which he cared for the orphans, it was impossible not to admire him.

A few days later it transpired that his taking us to see the Orphanage had not been without a purpose. In his brusque, direct way he told us to shift from the headquarters building to the Orphanage. Banerjee was to be in charge of the boys, as the resident *bhikkhu*, a meek young Bihari, was not sufficiently strict, and they were getting out of hand. I was to attend the office every day, returning to the Orphanage in the evening.

This arrangement worked very well. Within an hour of our establishing ourselves among them, Banerjee, who was nothing if not a disciplinarian, had the boys well under control. One of his first actions was to make them turn out the contents of their small tin boxes. To our astonishment we discovered that a number of them possessed lewd pictures of women. These were destroyed. Besides dividing the boys into classes and teaching them, Banerjee drilled them every morning and improved their diet. Before long the Orphanage had a distinctly military atmosphere. Meanwhile I was typing letters for His Holiness, who was at that time dabbling in municipal politics, and learning to edit the *Maha Bodhi Journal*. In the evening I studied books on Buddhism that I had borrowed from the Society's library, brushed up my Hindi and Bengali, which I practised on the boys, and discussed religion with Banerjee. Sometimes these discussions led to quarrels, for my friend, who was beginning to feel the first loosening of his Hindu roots, sometimes reacted violently to my assertions.

Much of our spare time was naturally spent with the two other inmates of the Orphanage. These were the Bihari *bhikkhu*, who occupied the room next to ours, and an aged German lady who lived in a tiny room downstairs. When we first saw the *bhikkhu* we thought him a model monk. Though still in his early twenties, his deportment was perfect. Invariably quiet and composed, he walked with a grave, dignified gait, and his eyes were ever modestly downcast. We had not been many days at the Orphanage before we discovered that, though friendly and inoffensive, he was by no means the saint for which we had at first taken him. One of his weaknesses, in fact, so incensed Banerjee that, in defiance of all Buddhist tradition, he gave him a good beating with a stick as soon as he found it out. Far from resenting this high-handed treatment, the poor little monk became meeker than ever.

The German lady, Miss A. Christine Albers, then over eighty, we found living in a state of privation that appalled us. Though paralysed and practically bedridden, and even with the aid of a stick barely able to drag herself to the door of her room, she had been left without care or attention of any kind. In consideration of past services to the Maha Bodhi Society, the Trustees allowed her to stay at the Orphanage rent free; but there was no provision for her maintenance. Her sole income was the ten rupees she received every month from the Tagore family, in which she had been governess. Out of this meagre sum she bought greens and potatoes, which she boiled over a small charcoal brazier at her bedside. To add to her troubles, the cook pretended not to hear her feeble cries for water, while the boys thought it a great joke to startle her with loud shrieks whenever she hobbled to the door so that she lost her balance and fell down. Banerjee, who had all the Bengali's traditional reverence for womanhood, was as shocked by the poor old creature's plight as I was. The boys were punished for molesting her, the cook ordered to do her bidding. Before long we had made her fairly comfortable. Supported by Banerjee's strong arm, she was soon able to stagger the few steps from her room to the back yard, where she liked to sit on the step in the late afternoon sunshine. As she was by nature warm-hearted and communicative we soon learned her story.

Coming as a young woman from Germany to the United States, she had joined the Theosophical Society, then recently founded. In 1893 she attended the World's Parliament of Religions at Chicago and after hearing Swami Vivekananda and Anagarika Dharmapala lecture, decided to devote her life to educational work among Indian women. Since the beginning of the century she had lived in Calcutta. Apparently at one time she had conducted a small private school, besides doing tutorial work. She also made mention of some adopted daughters. How she had been connected with the Maha Bodhi Society was never quite clear, but she always spoke of the General Secretary, Devapriya Valisinha, with affection, declaring that had he been in Calcutta he would never have allowed her to be ill-used. Frail as she was, she continued to write little poems and articles for the *Maha Bodhi Journal*. She was, in fact, a considerable poetess. When, some years later, I heard of her death, I promised myself that I would some day publish a selection from her voluminous but unequal output. She was also of strongly psychic temperament. From her earliest years, she told me, she had been able to see and converse with spiritual beings. Sometimes she spoke of her mystical experiences. Dwelling often in what she called the Black Light, which was, according to her, much higher than the White Light, she seemed for all the privations she had undergone astonishingly happy and contented. When she spoke of spiritual things her whole face became radiant with joy. It was obvious she lived much more out of the body than in it. Most remarkable of all, she was utterly incapable of speaking ill, even by way of suggestion, of anyone she knew. Herself wholly good, she saw nothing but good around her.

We had been barely three weeks at the Orphanage when the world of politics, which we had hitherto been able to ignore, suddenly irrupted in a most disturbing manner into our small world of cultural and educational activities. After two centuries of British rule the great subcontinent was to be free. But the price of freedom was bisection. Already the creation of the twin dominions of India and Pakistan had been agreed upon.

The Punjab and Bengal were also to be divided. What, then, would be the fate of Calcutta? Would it, too, be divided, or would it fall intact into the hands of one or other of the two claimants? Determined to uphold Pakistan's right to the city by violence if necessary, the Muslim League declared 20 March Direct Action Day. This was the signal for fresh outbreaks of communal rioting. Though less serious than those of the previous year, in which the boys had been orphaned, they were sufficiently horrible. For a week we were shut up in the Orphanage, which was to some extent protected by its high brick walls. Only after dark did Banerjee and the cook, disguised as Muslims, steal out by the back door to buy provisions from the nearest bazaar. At night one of us always kept watch. Sometimes gangs of Muslim cut-throats hammered furiously on the gate. Once three or four of them climbed the wall and dropped into the courtyard. Almost suffocating with fright, we heard them whispering together in the darkness below. But for some reason or other they decided not to attack and went away.

Responsible as we were for the lives of thirty boys, besides those of Miss Albers and the cook (the *bhikkhu* had left some days earlier), Banerjee and I were day and night in a state of nervous tension. One of the greatest sources of strain was the uncertainty. Though we had a strangely vivid sense of murder being committed all around us, no reliable news of the actual course of events was available. The Orphanage was situated in a predominantly Muslim locality and it was reasonable to suppose that those members of the Hindu minority who had not fled at the first sign of trouble were being butchered. So much, indeed, we learned from the terrified occupants of the house across the lane, with whom, every evening, Banerjee exchanged signals from the shrine. The Orphanage being known as a Buddhist institution, we were at first confident that it was in no danger of attack. But as the days passed we became more and more uneasy. Christians, too, had felt safe, yet had not those in the adjacent lane been murdered while they slept, despite the large white crosses chalked on their doors?

One morning, a week after Direct Action Day, two incidents revealed the peril in which we stood. Banerjee had ordered the boys to keep away from the windows. But one of them, unthinkingly, not only leaned out but spat into the lane below. The gob of phlegm fell directly onto the head of a passing Muslim. Glaring up at the boy and shaking his fist, this son of the Prophet shouted 'Never mind, we're going to cut all your throats tonight.' Banerjee could not forbear giving the culprit a few blows, but the damage was done, and we were all thrown into a state of great perturbation. The boys became quiet as mice. Some wept silently.

Half an hour after this incident I looked out of the shrine window to see three men knocking on the door of the Hindu house opposite. From their demeanour they seemed to be friends come to enquire after the safety of the occupants. Slowly, cautiously, the door opened and a middle-aged man in a white shirt and dhoti appeared. A few words were exchanged, a knife flashed in the air, and before I could realize what had happened the visitors had vanished and a dead body lay bleeding in the street. This time we were completely unnerved. There was not a moment to be lost. After hurried consultations, it was decided that as the only person not likely to be attacked on the way – I still went out in Western dress – I should go immediately to the headquarters and ask His Holiness to communicate with the police.

Never shall I forget the sense of mingled freedom and apprehension with which I walked through the frightful silence of the deserted streets. Hooligans talking quietly in doorways eyed me curiously as I passed. Once or twice I saw a dead body. Within forty minutes I was safe inside the headquarters building. After a brief talk with His Holiness I telephoned the Calcutta police. One of the Assistant Commissioners, whom I requested to evacuate the boys from the Orphanage under armed police escort, assured me that the city was quiet, that no incident had been reported for twenty-four hours, and that we were in no danger. In vain I protested that only an hour earlier I had seen a man killed. The police, I was informed, knew of no such incident. When I insisted on the truth of my story, I was curtly told not to spread rumours. Now thoroughly roused, I telephoned the Commissioner and made an angry complaint. Within twenty minutes half a dozen police, armed with rifles and machine guns, drove up to the door. Off I sped to the rescue. As I left, His Holiness told me that under no circumstances was I to bring back Miss Albers. 'Leave her where she is,' he snapped, 'she's a memsahib. The Muslims won't kill her.'

Two trips were needed to complete the evacuation. On the second trip we brought Miss Albers, who obviously could not be abandoned. Seeing a pair of hard eyes watching from the big Ajanta-style horseshoe window of the shrine upstairs, I left to Banerjee the responsibility of carrying the old lady indoors and hurried on ahead to justify our flagrant disregard of His Holiness's express commands. 'Take her away!' he shouted. 'I won't have her here!' But Miss Albers had already been installed in the office and since, with Banerjee about, it was difficult for His Holiness to have the harmless old creature thrown out bodily, he had no alternative but to bite his lip in silent rage. The servants, however, were forbidden to help her. Again defying orders, my friend and I prepared for her reception a small dark cubby-hole next to the dining room.

Within a week the riots subsided into an uneasy calm. But His Holiness's unaccountable hatred for Miss Albers showed no sign of abating. Whenever, hearing the voice of someone known to her, she hobbled into the office for a chat, he would roughly order her to be gone. Once or twice only did the poor woman protest, 'Oh why are you so cruel to me, Reverend?' she would ask reproachfully, letting fall a tear. But beyond these words, uttered in a plaintive, sorrowful voice, she made no complaint to anyone.

With thirty boys in the building, the headquarters' routine was to some extent disrupted. Banerjee spent most of his time keeping them out of mischief. I resumed work in the office. Owing to our having espoused the cause of Miss Albers, whom we considered it our duty to protect, relations with His Holiness became rather strained. We were not sorry, therefore, when an elegant middle-aged Frenchwoman, in white gloves, cape, and broad-brimmed hat, descended one day on the Society and requisitioned our services for an exhibition of photographs of Cambodian Buddhist art that she was arranging at the Royal Asiatic Society of Bengal.

Suzanne Karpelles, with her rather prominent nose and large, intelligent black eyes, was the embodiment of gracious authority. It did not seem to occur to her that her wishes could ever be disregarded. Though she treated her two 'boys' with great courtesy and kindness, she was evidently a person not to be trifled with, and we both stood a little in awe of her. While helping to pin up photographs and write descriptive labels we naturally spoke of the pitiable conditions of Miss Albers. Madame Karpelles expressed a wish to see her. When we broke to Miss Albers what we thought would be the welcome news that she had a visitor the old woman reacted with unexpected violence. 'I can't see her! I can't see her!' she exclaimed, throwing up her hands wildly. 'Why did you bring her? She's always dolled up to the eyebrows and I've nothing decent to put on.' Alas, it was only too true! In our eagerness to please we had overlooked the fact that Miss Albers' entire wardrobe consisted of three ancient knitted dresses and a pair of worn cotton gloves bursting at the seams.

Banerjee was still showing visitors round the exhibition when His Holiness was invited to send a representative of the Society to speak on Buddhism at the Dharma Parishad, or All-India Religions Conference, to be held in Ahmedabad that April. As I had already lectured in the Society's hall, he decided to send me. Before I left, Banerjee and I had several serious discussions. The worldly, unspiritual atmosphere of the Society's headquarters, where we had a constant sense of something unpleasant going on behind the scenes, depressed and disgusted us. Moreover, His Holiness's promise to recommend to the General Secretary that we should be officially enrolled as full-time workers had not been kept, and our position in the Society was undefined. We therefore agreed that, while in Ahmedabad, I should get in touch with other Buddhists attending the Parishad and try to make arrangements for us to join an organization more conducive to our spiritual growth.

'Do your best for both of us!' shouted Banerjee as the train bearing me on the first lap of my 1,500-mile journey slowly steamed out of the station.

18
ALL-INDIA RELIGIONS CONFERENCE

The Dharma Parishad was one of the first of those inter-religious gatherings which, during the decade after independence, became such a feature of Indian cultural life.

Under a huge *pandal*, or framework of bamboo poles covered with white cloth, between two and three thousand people squatted from ten in the morning until four in the afternoon each day listening to the apparently interminable flow of lectures. On the platform, furnished with mattresses and bolsters instead of chairs, were crowded four or five dozen representatives of different religions and sects, as well as the organizers of the Conference. Since most of the speeches were in Gujerati, of which I understood not a word, I spent the greater part of the first session looking about me.

Practically all the delegates, it seemed, were Hindus. Christianity was represented by an English missionary, who squatted uncomfortably, his pink face and sandy hair oddly conspicuous; Islam, by a bearded moulvi in a black coat. Near the microphone sat two or three Jain *munis*, their white garments and the gauze masks they wore over mouth and nose giving them a strangely surgical appearance. There was also a Zoroastrian from Bombay, his peculiarly convoluted 'cow's-hoof' headgear glittering with gold thread. Nowhere could I detect the familiar yellow robe. Buddhism, from the numerical point of view alone one of the greatest of the world's religions, seemed to be most inadequately represented by the twenty-one-year-old ex-soldier from the Maha Bodhi

Society. While I was speculating on the possible explanation for this meagre representation of all religions other than Hinduism, I was jerked back to awareness of the proceedings by the sound of my name booming from the loudspeakers. It was my turn to contribute to the flow. As I rose to my feet a warning voice said 'Only ten minutes!' Another hissed vehemently in my ear, 'Say that Buddhism and Hinduism are the same!'

Though next day I wrote out the substance of my speech for publication, it has now almost faded from memory. But I spoke for twenty minutes instead of ten, and I did not say that Buddhism and Hinduism were the same. While I was prepared, in such a gathering, to stress points of agreement rather than differences, I drew the line at echoing, even in the supposed interests of inter-religious amity, an assertion that I thought false. Hinduism had yet to learn that tolerance is an acceptance of differences in religious conviction, rather than the forcible assimilation of one tradition to another. All over India, during the last twenty years, people knowing nothing of Buddhism, who never in their lives opened a Buddhist text, have told me with an air of authority, 'Buddhism is the same as Hinduism.' It may be. But uninformed insistence on the point betrays either a pathological basis or plain intellectual dishonesty.

Despite the speaker's recalcitrance, the speech was well received, and when I sat down the plump Gujerati organizers thumped me vigorously on the back and whispered words of congratulation. The rest of the day, indeed the rest of the week, was taken up by speeches in Gujerati and Hindi, most of them on Hinduism, and all more than an hour long. Once again I looked about me.

The representatives of Hinduism were indeed a motley crowd. While a few were dressed in snowy white, some wore red, brown, or orange garments. The predominant colour was the light salmon-pink of the orthodox Vedantic ascetics. Most of the monks were shaven-headed, but several had allowed both hair and beard to grow to enormous length. Worshippers of Shiva were swathed in row upon row of giant brown *rudrākṣa* beads and smeared with ashes; devotees of Vishnu wore a single row of tiny white beads of sacred basil, while their foreheads were adorned with a variety of red, white, and yellow sectarian marks. Some looked brutal and belligerent; others had features of striking refinement and intellectuality. Just in front of me sat three plump, silk-clad figures who, from the multitude of their bangles and anklets, I at first took for women. However, they were followers of the Vallabha sect, male followers of which are required to emulate Radha, the mistress and principal devotee of Sri Krishna, not only in internal devotional attitude towards the incarnate Lord, but externally in dress and demeanour. One of its sub-sects goes so far as to practise castration.

With representatives of so many rival sects on the platform there had naturally been a fierce dispute for precedence. By general consent this had in the end been conceded to His Holiness the Shankaracharya of Puri, incumbent of one of the four chief maths established by the great non-dualist philosopher Shankara, as the tradition to which His Holiness belonged was admittedly the most ancient. This dignitary therefore sat enthroned on a tigerskin-draped dais to one side of the platform. A short, plump man of about seventy, he sat motionless through the entire proceedings. His salmon-pink robe seemed to consist of a single piece of cloth, which was not only twisted about the body but draped over the head. Forehead and arms were marked with ashes in three horizontal bars. Round his neck hung massive ropes of *rudrākṣa* beads and a magnificent crystal rosary. More *rudrākṣa* beads were wound about his head, apparently to keep the robe in place. His left hand supported a silver staff, round which was twisted a strip of salmon-pink cloth. Before him on a small table stood a pair of silver sandals, a silver phallus of the god Shiva, and the rest of his regalia. Whenever he entered or left the *pandal* he was preceded by a master of ceremonies who shouted '*Jagatguru Śrī Śaṅkarāchārya-ji Ki Jai!* Victory to the World Teacher His Holiness the Shankaracharya!' To which the crowd dutifully responded 'Jai! Victory!'

In the course of one of the sessions, however, His Holiness's dignity was sadly compromised. One of the speakers was a short, corpulent monk of rather unpleasant countenance. Though I understood nothing of his speech, which was in Gujerati, I could sense the displeasure of the crowd. Presently there were angry murmurs, then shouts. Later I was told that not far from the *pandal* the corpulent monk had recently built a Gita temple. In it he had installed an image of the *Bhagavad Gītā* in the form of a goddess with four arms. To worship this image, which of course meant paying money to the temple, was according to him equivalent to reading, understanding, and practising the whole teaching of the sacred book it represented. Not everybody agreed that religion could be simplified in this way, and there had been strong opposition to the new temple. Apparently the founder was now taking advantage of the Parishad to attack his critics. So intemperate were his expressions that a section of the crowd, enraged, surged forward and tried to pluck him from the platform. His disciples sprang to the rescue. The microphone was overturned. In an instant the platform was a battlefield. The little Shankaracharya skipped down from his throne with astonishing agility. The master of ceremonies hastily swept the regalia into a dirty cloth. Non-combatant delegates jumped to their feet. But as quickly as it had begun the fracas subsided. His Holiness climbed back on to his throne; the regalia was again displayed; the delegates resumed their seats, and the cause of the disturbance concluded his speech on a more conciliatory note.

The best received address was given by a quite different type of person. He was an old blind ascetic who was led forward to the microphone by a youthful disciple. Like most of the orthodox Hindu delegates he spoke sitting cross-legged. Despite his blindness he spoke so impressively, and his rugged, unattractive presence radiated such power, that a hush fell upon the audience. Like most Hindus, though they might for a time be deceived by the emotional and intellectual imitations of religion, they recognized the authentic utterance, the genuine ring, of spiritual experience when they heard it. His speech ended, the blind ascetic followed his disciple out of the *pandal*, indifferent to the applause.

Several of the delegates, including myself, had been accommodated in the classrooms of the local high school, then closed for the summer holidays. As the custom is in non-Westernized Indian society, lunch was served at nine o'clock, so that we could sit through the day's proceedings without a break until tea-time. To this arrangement I could adapt myself. Indian food I was already accustomed to taking. What troubled me was the lack of a bathroom. The other delegates squatted one by one under a cold tap in the courtyard, changing from wet to dry clothes without any offence to decency. Both my English reluctance to take a bath in public and the nature of my dress made it impossible for me to follow their example. After wrapping a dry sarong round the waist over the wet one the latter can be allowed to slip to the ground. But one cannot follow this procedure with two pairs of trousers. Even when my room-mate, a cheerful, expansive monk in early middle age who, having mixed much with Europeans understood their difficulties, came to my rescue with a spare piece of white cloth, I draped it so self-consciously that some of the delegates remarked, wonderingly, 'He doesn't know how to take a bath.' I realized that without giving up Western dress, full adaptation to the Indian way of life was impossible.

The same cheerful monk lent me a brass water-pot, for had I been seen going in the direction of the latrines without one I might have been ostracized by the more orthodox delegates. He also attempted to constitute himself my guru. On the first evening of our acquaintance he explained to me the new method of meditation he had discovered. Rather reluctantly, I allowed him to press his thumbs against my eyeballs until they hurt unbearably.

'What do you see?' he demanded.

'A lot of coloured lights,' I replied truthfully.

'Yes, it's the Light of the Self!' he exclaimed triumphantly. 'You must meditate on that.'

In the classroom opposite camped the Shankaracharya. Though at first fearful of approaching so august a personage, I eventually plucked up enough courage to ask my room-mate if he thought an audience could be arranged. He thought it could. In fact, he spoke himself to the master of ceremonies, and late the same evening I was ushered into the presence of His Holiness.

By the flickering light of a single oil-lamp the small, familiar figure looked far more impressive than in the glare of the crowded *pandal*. Peering through the semi-darkness I could make out the tiger-skin, the crystal rosary, and the silver staff of office. So exalted a personage was apparently never seen except in full regalia.

I was given a seat immediately in front of the throne-dais. We had not conversed for more than a few minutes when I discovered that for all his apparent orthodoxy His Holiness was a kindly, unpretentious person who could be liked as a man, quite apart from the respect due to him on account of his high religious office. Most of his life, he told me, had been spent as a chartered accountant in Madras. Only after retirement had he become a monk. At the end of the audience, which lasted half an hour, he gave me his card and invited me to correspond. In the course of the next few years we not only exchanged a number of letters but also met once again in circumstances of unusual interest.

19
TWO MEETINGS AND A MARRIAGE

The Dharma Parishad was almost over when one of the organizers told me that another Buddhist delegate had arrived and would be presiding over the day's proceedings.

The first time we found ourselves on the platform together the new arrival and I eyed each other dubiously. What he thought of me I never knew. My first impressions of him were somewhat mixed. Despite his age and corpulence Pandit-ji, as the organizers respectfully called him, was both strong and active. His brow was noble and intellectual, but counterbalanced by crafty eyes and weak, self-indulgent mouth. Though affable and condescending in the extreme, his manner was very much that of the *grand seigneur*. From his scholarly presidential address, delivered with a cultured accent in impeccable English, I understood that though representing Buddhism he was himself a Hindu. This double allegiance puzzled me, for I had not then grasped the fact that the average Hindu considers he understands any other religion better, and is therefore more truly qualified to represent it, than its own professed adherents.

As the only two Buddhist delegates Pandit-ji and I, despite my misgivings, inevitably became acquainted. When the Parishad had ended and I had shifted from the school to the office of the convening organization, he and his companion, a well-fleshed, lethargic young Bengali named Sudhir, took me out with them on excursions. Together we visited a temple of the Narayana Swami sect, which has a considerable following in Gujerat. From the opposite banks of the river we viewed the low, red-tiled roofs of the Sabarmati Ashram, from which, for many years, Mahatma Gandhi had directed the struggle for independence. Once Pandit-ji took me back with him for lunch to the imitation marble villa of the millionaire Ahmedabad mill-owner with whom he and Sudhir were staying. Though the meal was served in Indian style, it transpired that the sons and daughters of the house were rather Westernized. The old scholar, who had once been their tutor, was asked his opinion of the latest divorce. His courteous and compliant reply showed that, whatever he really thought, he had no intention of giving offence.

For all his grey hairs, Pandit-ji's energy was prodigious. One day he told me he had arranged for Anandamayi Ma's fifty-first birthday to be celebrated in the Town Hall. The name was new to me. On my questioning him he told me, with a solemn air, that she was a great saint and yogini who had thousands of disciples all over northern India. Her peculiarities were numerous. One of them was that despite the entreaties of devotees she never stayed longer than a few weeks in any one place. Her entourage had to be ready to leave at a moment's notice, for sometimes, when the spirit moved her, she simply walked out of the ashram or *dharmashala* at which they were camping without giving any warning. In fact her movements were quite unpredictable. No one ever knew what the Blissful Mother would do next. From the complacency with which Pandit-ji related these facts I inferred that in his eyes, as in those of most Hindus, such irresponsibility was a sign of high spiritual attainment. To me it seemed more likely that Anandamayi had a shrewd sense of the dramatic.

However, being interested in anyone with a reputation for sanctity, I enquired where she was at that time staying. Mentioning the name of a certain town, Pandit-ji said that having already spent a couple of weeks there she was expected soon to be on the move again. But where she would go next no one knew. She might come to Ahmedabad, which she had already visited once. Or perhaps she would go to Dehra Dun. She might even return to Benares, where a large ashram was being constructed in her name on the sacred banks of the Ganges. He himself, Pandit-ji confided, wished to meet her again at the earliest opportunity. As soon as he heard she had reached Dehra Dun, the place she was most likely to visit next, he and Sudhir intended to hasten to her feet. Would I care to accompany them? Anandamayi was very sympathetic towards Buddhism, and had in fact given her approval of his project of reviving an organization for the propagation of the Dharma in India which he had started many years earlier. She would assuredly welcome me. Perhaps, under Anandamayi's guidance, he and Sudhir and I could work together for the revival of Buddhism in India.

When Pandit-ji unfolded a plan he was irresistible. Vista upon entrancing vista opened up as though by magic. Touched by the wand of his imagination, possibilities were transformed into actualities, and impossibilities into reasonable expectations. Even afterwards, when it became clear that none of his grandiose schemes had ever progressed beyond the fund-raising stage, I had to struggle hard to prevent myself from being carried away by the old man's eloquence.

On the day we discussed the celebration of Anandamayi's birthday I could not but be persuaded. Indeed, with Banerjee's parting words ringing in my ears, I had been casting about for contacts with Buddhist organizations ever since my arrival in Ahmedabad, and Pandit-ji's offer opened a door. But so long as we were waiting for news of Anandamayi's arrival in Dehra Dun our plans could be no more than tentative. Meanwhile, a meeting in honour of her birthday was held at the Town Hall, where at my suggestion Pandit-ji also arranged for the celebration of the Vaiśākha Pūrṇimā a few days later. It is significant that the thrice-sacred Buddhist festival had never been celebrated in Ahmedabad before.

At the end of the Vaiśākha meeting, at which both Pandit-ji and I spoke, I was approached by a handsome, golden-skinned youth of my own age who was so taken by the idea of an Englishman being a Buddhist that he insisted on my paying a visit to his home. In vain I demurred. Without giving me time even to tell Pandit-ji where I was going, he caught me by the hand and before I realized what had happened we were hurrying through the narrow, crowded streets of the old walled city. On the way my newly acquired friend told me he was a student in a Bombay medical college.

Before long I found myself for the second time inside an Indian home. Ashok's father, a lawyer, seemed to think it the most natural thing in the world that his son should bring a friend home to spend the night with him (for the masterful youth had already decided I was to stay) and after the exchange of a few friendly words left us to our own devices.

Ashok's hospitality was such that I could not but feel at ease. He arranged a hot bath, which I took in a bathroom full of highly polished brass vessels of various shapes and sizes, lent me a shirt and lungi, and took my own clothes away to be washed and ironed. By the time we sat down to dinner I was a member of the family. From the cage-like kitchen, where he squatted on the floor in front of a low, cowdung-plastered brick range, the Brahmin cook flipped paper-thin chappatis straight from the fire onto our round brass plates. Ashok had arranged for us to sleep on the roof. As we climbed to the top of the building, which was built round a square well, with inward-facing verandas on all four sides of each storey, I noticed in the corner of every landing a large built-in urinal of white porcelain. Despite the exposed position of these conveniences, I saw Ashok and the rest of the family using them without the slightest self-consciousness. Out on the roof the night was brilliant with the moon. After we had lain talking for a couple of hours I dropped off to sleep. Once during the night I awoke to find a dazzlingly bright golden face immediately above my own, but whether Ashok's or the moon's I could not tell.

This visit, which at Ashok's insistence I repeated, helped while away the time until the whimsical Anandamayi should have made up her mind what to do next. Not that I was either lonely or bored. People came almost every day to see me, and besides excursions with Pandit-ji there were invitations to the houses of other friends I had made. One of these was a dark, diminutive coal merchant, at whose house I usually lunched, and who was always at hand to supply anything I needed. Another was a lawyer with literary pretensions. At our first meeting he presented me with autographed copies of half a dozen slim volumes, all published at his own expense. As the custom is in India with books of a religious nature, the author's photograph figured prominently in every one of them. Back in my quarters I examined these gifts with interest. It would be difficult to say whether style or subject matter struck me as being the more odd. The first was strained to the highest pitch of perfervid bombast; in the second, the author's first wife having died young, apostrophes to the Deity were strangely mingled with laments for the loss of connubial felicity.

Once, at the invitation of the rather youthful bridegroom, I attended a Hindu wedding. When the procession, led by a hired brass band, reached the bride's house, where the ceremony was to be performed, a heated argument ensued between the representatives of the two families. The subject under dispute, I was informed, was the number of the bridegroom's friends to be admitted to the marriage feast. The bridegroom insisted on twenty; his future father-in-law, who was of course the founder of the feast, declared he could feed no more than twelve. Guests at a European banquet would feel embarrassed, if not insulted, to hear the question whether they were to be fed or not discussed with so much feeling in public. But in Gujerat, if not elsewhere in India, disputes of this kind were all part of the traditional marriage observances.

Whether twelve or twenty of us eventually took our seats on the dining room floor I no longer remember. Ever anxious not to offend socio-religious susceptibilities, my mind was occupied by the hints on Hindu etiquette just given me by the bridegroom. Above all, he had said, I must on no account touch my plate with my left hand. If I did so, even by accident, the other guests would regard it as a grievous insult and might even get up and leave the room. The result of this friendly admonition was that throughout the meal I remained fearfully conscious of my left hand, which seemed to have grown unnaturally large and heavy, for despite my efforts to hold it behind my back it had apparently developed a will of its own which impelled it ever and anon in the direction of my plate.

The sudden arrival of the news that Anandamayi was in Dehra Dun threw Pandit-ji, Sudhir, and me into a flutter which her going there in accordance with a previously announced programme could never have occasioned. Travelling via New Delhi, in less than two days we had made the journey from Ahmedabad to Dehra Dun, a distance of about six hundred miles, and were alighting from the bus at Kishengunj, an outlying suburb halfway between Dehra Dun town and the hill station proper. On the opposite side of the road I saw an open gate surmounted by a lofty semicircular arch on which was inscribed 'Sri Sri Sri Ma Anandamayi Ashram'.

20

ANANDAMAYI, THE BLISSFUL MOTHER

My first impression of the Blissful Mother was perhaps the most favourable. Entering the small meeting-hall of the ashram, where fifteen or twenty people squatted circlewise on the floor, I saw in the centre of the group a queenly figure in white who I at once knew must be Anandamayi. Either because of the way in which she wore her hair in a topknot, or because of her simple dignity of demeanour, her poise, and the smile that played faintly about her lips, despite her femininity she at once struck me as being strangely Buddha-like in appearance. At the same time I became aware that an intense peace, purity, and coolness, of a quality such as I had never before experienced, was not only pervading the room but as it were blowing from her like a delicate fresh breeze. As Pandit-ji, Sudhir, and I took our seats a few heads were turned in our direction, but our coming disturbed the tranquillity of the place no more and no longer than the dropping of three small pebbles ruffles the still surface of a pool. This was perhaps fortunate, as it gave me time to take in the scene more fully than might otherwise have been possible.

A long-bearded monk seated opposite Anandamayi was reading aloud from what appeared to be a sacred book. Every now and then the Blissful Mother would interpose a few words of comment. Her voice, which came as though from a great distance, was so low that in their eagerness not to miss a single word the listening semicircle was bent forward with an expression of concentrated attention. Occasionally, Anandamayi concluded her comments with a delicate ripple of laughter, the effect of which seemed to spread in ever-widening circles through the audience in the form of a profound satisfaction. As both reading and exposition were in Bengali, which I did not understand, my attention soon wandered. After a few moments I noticed that a woman in a white sari kept turning round and regarding me with mild, cow-like curiosity. From the lightness of her complexion I judged her to be either a Bengali or a Kashmiri, probably the latter.

At twelve o'clock, exactly half an hour after our arrival, the long-bearded monk closed his book. Some kind of devotional song was sung, and the meeting was over. People rose stiffly to their feet. Pandit-ji led me forward to Anandamayi, who alone had remained seated. In response to my salutations, which I made with folded hands, she inclined her head with a gracious smile. I noticed that her face, which from a distance had seemed beautiful, was deeply lined, especially round the eyes. There was an unpleasing squareness about her nose and chin. Yet despite these defects of feature the Mother's expression, indeed her whole appearance, was one of indescribable charm. After Pandit-ji, with the greatest deference, had exchanged a few words with her, and she had nodded queenly assent to some suggestion of his, we left her to go and seek our lunch.

This we found half a mile up the road in the house of Pandit-ji's brother-in-law, who had not been expecting us. A bald-headed, Westernized Bengali in European dress, he was, I subsequently learned, the son of Dr Gyanendranath Chakravarty, the famous Vice-Chancellor of Lucknow University, and of the still more famous Yashoda Ma, whose name was already familiar to me as the guru of the English Vaishnava Ronald Nixon, better known as Sri Krishna Prem. Despite the gentle cordiality of his welcome, there was clearly a mixture of hesitancy and restraint in his attitude towards Pandit-ji, and I was hardly astonished when, after regrets for the smallness of the house and the shortage of accommodation had been offered and received, Pandit-ji, Sudhir, and I left with well-filled stomachs to seek a lodging elsewhere. Thereafter I saw him only once or twice, for he never went to Anandamayi's ashram and Pandit-ji hardly ever visited him. Nevertheless, during our stay at Kishengunj I was able to learn from him much about his parents, both of whom were reputed to have been great yogis, his father in fact having been his mother's guru. From my correspondence with Sri Krishna Prem I already knew that Yashoda Ma had been a Vaishnava of the Bengal

School of Sri Chaitanya, to which Anandamayi also in a sense belonged.

It was early afternoon when we walked back towards the ashram, and the fine dust on either side of the road glared so intensely white in the blazing sun that our eyes ached. Despite his umbrella, Pandit-ji's face shone with perspiration, which dripped in great beads from the straw-coloured ends of his heavy white moustache, while the network of purple veins stood out grossly on his scarlet nose, cheeks, and forehead. His energy was undiminished, however, and though his breath was coming a little wheezingly he insisted on turning in at the gate and stalking up the drive of every bungalow we passed to enquire if there were rooms to let. What the caretakers, or the startled European couple whose afternoon siesta Pandit-ji rudely broke in upon with his rappings and bangings, thought of the strangely assorted trio on their doorsteps I do not know. But Pandit-ji's forehead was of brass. With an air of lordly condescension he demanded to know who the owners were and whether they were in residence, whether the place was to let, or for sale, as if he had come on purpose to buy it and had the money ready in his pocket.

After we had knocked in vain at nearly a dozen doors, the caretaker of a rambling whitewashed building, apparently deserted, said that if we could find a tent he would allow us to pitch it in a large mango garden which stood on the other side of the road between Anandamayi's ashram and the brother-in-law's bungalow. This concession was due to the fact that, having learned from a neighbour the owner's name and that he was away, Pandit-ji had represented himself to the caretaker as an old friend of the family. After the success of this ruse, to discover a tent was by no means beyond the crafty old scholar's resources, and by the time the sun had declined, the west reddened, and the air cooled, our canvas home had been put up among the mango trees. The last golden lights of day struggled through the rich green foliage. While Sudhir collected sticks and blew upon the smoky fire, Pandit-ji's squint-eyed servant fetched water from the canal. Pandit-ji himself, now in a fine humour, waxed eloquent to me on the advantages of living in the midst of nature and satisfying one's hunger with fruits and nuts like the sages of old. As he thus discoursed, his hands were busy opening the tins of jam, butter, biscuits, pineapple chunks, and chicken that he had purchased in the bazaar.

Devotional meetings were held twice daily at the Sri Sri Sri Ma Anandamayi Ashram, and since we had come to Kishengunj for the sole purpose of meeting the Blissful Mother we were naturally regular in attendance. These meetings invariably took place in the hall where I had first seen her, a rectangular room that occupied the greater part of the ground floor and was capable of accommodating nearly a hundred people. To me the morning sessions, lasting from 10 till 12, were the less interesting. Not more than a dozen or fifteen disciples and devotees attended, and though they opened and closed with devotional songs most of the time was occupied, as it had been on the morning of our arrival, with readings from a Bengali religious book by the same long-bearded ascetic, supplemented by occasional low-toned comments from Anandamayi. A skinny youth with a crane-neck, prominent Adam's apple, and long black hair, was writing down, I soon noticed, every word she spoke. I also noticed, on the occasions when my attention wandered from the irregular semicircle on the floor to the four white walls of the room, that most of the life-sized framed photographs that hung there were of Anandamayi, and that while in some of them she had an expression of supernatural dignity, in others she displayed an archness, almost a coquettishness, of expression which I felt rather inappropriate. In yet another, dishevelled hair fell across the laughing face of a wild woman. Evidently the Mother, or Ma in Bengali, as the devotees always called her, was a creature of many moods. The two or three pictures that were not hers included a plump youthful Krishna, with dusky blue complexion and peacock's feather in his thick wavy hair, and Sri Chaitanya in ecstasy.

From these wanderings my attention would often be recalled only by the light tapping of small hand-drums by the crane-necked youth that preluded the closing song. *Prasad*, or sacramental food, would then be distributed. This had been placed in front of Anandamayi on a tray at the beginning of the proceedings. As it could not be considered *prasad* till she had partaken of it, her personal attendant, an untidy Bengali young woman, lifted two or three sweets to her mouth – for we had not been at Kishengunj for many days before Pandit-ji explained to me, with an air of great solemnity, that for a number of years Anandamayi had neither fed nor washed herself with her own hands. Usually, after merely touching her lips the sweets would fall to the ground, where they would be scrambled for by the more enthusiastic devotees.

Western poets have familiarized us with the idea that each of the four seasons has its own prevailing mood. Indian aesthetics attributes a mood to every period of the day and night, and the ragas, or melodic themes of Indian music, which are classified in accordance with a similar scheme, may be played only at the particular hour that matches the prevailing mood. Whether for this reason, or because of the greater press of devotees, or the suffocatingly close atmosphere of the crowded room, or the heady perfume of flowers that opened only at night drifting in from the garden, the evening sessions, which lasted from four o'clock until eight or nine, were not only more interesting than those of the morning but quite different in character.

If the prevailing mood of the morning programmes was peace, that of the evening ones was excitement. Reading and exposition were forgotten, the whole period being given up to Hindi, Bengali, and Sanskrit devotional songs. These were sung to the accompaniment of a harmonium (now, to the disgust of purists, the mainstay of Indian amateur orchestras), a brace of small hand-drums, and several pairs of diminutive but nerve-tingling cymbals. Most of the songs, or bhajans as they are called, had the same subject as the photographs on the wall: Anandamayi. Only a few celebrated the praises of Rama, Krishna, and other divinities. Quite clearly, the Mother had become in her own lifetime the centre of a minor cult, a phenomenon by no means unusual in India.

Though I have described them as devotional songs, practically all the bhajans that the devotees sang with such full-throated fervour every evening were in fact little more than strings of names and epithets sung over and over again, one repetition by a soloist alternating with one by the whole congregation in chorus, a little more rapidly each time and with gradually mounting enthusiasm for at least fifteen or twenty minutes at a stretch, sometimes for more than an hour, depending on the degree of fervour the soloist was able to evoke in the congregation and the congregation in the soloist.

One of the bhajans addressed to Anandamayi consisted of the single word 'Ma' repeated a dozen times:

Ma, Ma-a, Maaa; Ma, Ma-a, Maaa;
Ma, Ma-a, Maaa; Ma, Ma-a, MAAA!

This was a great favourite among the 'inner circle' of disciples. The crane-necked youth, who at the same time officiated at the harmonium, would sing it with passionate abandon, head flung back, body swaying and jerking violently, eyes either tightly closed or fixed beseechingly on Anandamayi, and Adam's apple bobbing vigorously up and down. To me the spectacle of grown men and women singing *Ma, Ma-a, Maaa* like so many kittens crying for their mother was a gross caricature of religious devotion, and I was not astonished when, later on, I learned that several of the younger male members of Anandamayi's entourage had lost their mothers at an early age.

Since I had read books on Bengal Vaishnavism, besides visiting the famous Gaudiya Math, headquarters of the movement in Calcutta, it was not long before the aim and the technique of these *bhajan* sessions became clear. According to the tenets of this school, the highest attitude which the devotee can adopt towards Krishna, for them the chief divine incarnation, is that of the forsaken mistress towards her beloved. This attitude is exemplified in the highest degree by Radha, the cow-girl of Brindaban, whose illicit amour with the youthful Krishna is the central theme of the vast theological and devotional literature of Bengal Vaishnavism, as well as by the more historical Sri Chaitanya or Gouranga, the sixteenth-century Bengali founder, or rather inspirer, of the movement, to whom the introduction of public singing of the divine names by large numbers of people is attributed. As among certain Christian revivalist movements in the West, tears, horripilation, and swoons are regarded as evidence that the degree of emotional exaltation requisite to the manifestation of the divine grace in the form of a vision, tactile experience, or audition of the object of devotion, in this case Krishna, has been attained. Music being the most powerful excitant of the emotions, and the special psychological effects produced by the different melodic themes, rhythms, and musical instruments having been for ages past well understood in India, it was natural that for devotees of the type that gathered round Anandamayi the singing of bhajans should be the central spiritual exercise and principal means of approach to the Divine.

Probably because of the fact that the congregation was by Bengal Vaishnava standards small and the evening *bhajan* sessions short, the mounting devotional fervour and excitement of the devotees always fell a little short of that climax of uncontrollable emotion, of absolute abandon and self-forgetfulness, towards which they were unconsciously working. Even so, the atmosphere of the room was frequently so highly charged that its stepping-up by a single degree, one felt, would be sufficient to sweep the whole congregation off its feet.

This was the case particularly when Anandamayi sang, which was neither often nor without much entreaty. Not that her style of singing was at all emotional. High, clear, not very strong, and seeming to come not only from the depths of her being but from a great distance, her voice would rise and fall now very slowly, now a little more quickly, as in alternation with the congregation she sang over and over again the words *Sita-Ram, Sita-Ram*, her own smiling freedom from any trace of excitement contrasting in the most striking manner with the convulsive movements and agonized expressions of her disciples.

One Sunday evening, however, when the congregation was a little larger and more susceptible or perhaps the weather a little warmer than usual, the cunningly contrived sequence of melodic themes, the gradually rising tempo, the incessant clapping of hands and swaying of bodies in time with the furious tapping and banging of the drums, and above all the ringing high-pitched tintinnabulation of the cymbals, in the end so rapid as to form one continuous stream of delirium-inducing sound, succeeded in working up the emotions of the devotees almost to the desired point of release. Another fraction of a degree higher and all restraints would be down.

Abruptly, but without haste, Anandamayi rose to her feet. The mere thought that she was about to dance precipitated the long-desired climax. Screaming, sobbing, blinded by tears, the devotees leaped to their feet and began wildly gyrating round the room, most of them prancing like madmen and flinging their arms into the air with loud shrieks. Though the bhajans, many of which I liked and enjoyed, had pleasantly stimulated my own feelings, I now sat petrified, not only untouched by the surrounding hysteria but with a sense of complete isolation from the type of religion it represented. A stout, blue-turbaned Sikh with a noble white beard, utterly overcome by his feelings, staggered round the room uttering shriek after piercing shriek, collapsed, rolled over and over on the ground biting the carpet and foaming at the mouth and eventually lay sobbing and quivering in the middle of the room.

Anandamayi, who all this time had remained motionless with both arms slightly raised, now quietly resumed her seat. Gradually the excitement subsided. The last sobs and groans died away. Trembling and in a state of exhaustion, the devotees sank to the floor and began mopping the perspiration from their brows. After a few minutes, the harmonium began preluding the closing *bhajan*, wits were collected, and on a more subdued note the proceedings came to an end.

A person more out of place in these perfervidly devotional surroundings than the rationalist Jawaharlal Nehru could hardly be imagined. But not long afterwards he was induced to pay the Ashram a visit. The idea originated with Pandit-ji, who claimed to have been Nehru's tutor, and Anandamayi gave her consent. At the old man's insistence, the rather protracted negotiations that preceded the visit were kept a closely guarded secret, and apart from the Blissful Mother herself no one in the ashram knew anything about the matter until the last moment, a circumstance that occasioned much angry heart-burning among the younger members of the 'inner circle', who considered themselves entitled to a share in all counsels.

Nehru was then holidaying in Mussoorie, at a house belonging to one of his sisters, and in a few days' time was due to return to New Delhi for talks with the Viceroy, Lord Mountbatten, regarding the forthcoming transfer of power from His Majesty's Government to the Indian National Congress. Pandit-ji's plan was that, on his way down to Dehra Dun, Nehru should stop at the ashram for half an hour's talk with Anandamayi. In the interests of secrecy no written invitation was sent. Instead, telephone calls were made to Mussoorie from a public call-box in the bazaar, and after unsuccessful attempts to get through, preliminary skirmishes with secretaries, and inconclusive replies from aides, the great national leader was personally contacted, the invitation conveyed with all the tact and diplomacy at Pandit-ji's command, the invitation accepted, and Pandit-ji enabled to emerge from the telephone booth, where he had stood for more than an hour, his face radiant with satisfaction and triumph.

At eleven o'clock one morning in the first half of June, therefore, a small motorcade drew up at the ashram gate. Pandit-ji, who had been expectantly hovering there for nearly an hour, at once constituting himself master of ceremonies introduced me to Nehru. We silently saluted each other with folded hands. Pandit-ji, who with his voluminous Bengali-style shawl draped toga-like under one arm and across the opposite shoulder had the air of a Roman senator receiving the emperor at his country seat, then conducted his former pupil into the hall, where Anandamayi was waiting to receive him. Behind followed Nehru's daughter Indira, a slim youngish woman wearing a crimson sari and very high-heeled shoes, the redoubtable Sardar Vallabhbhai Patel, and members of the staff.

Though the crane-necked youth and others belonging to the inner group had not been let into the secret until almost the last moment, they certainly had no intention of allowing themselves to be any longer excluded from the proceedings. Nehru had therefore to sit through half an hour's *bhajan*. Since I was seated on his left this gave me an excellent opportunity of surreptitiously studying him. He sat elbows on knees, with back bent, shoulders hunched and eyes fixed on the ground. His pale face wore an expression of intense weariness, strain, and anxiety. Not once, during that half hour, did he show by so much as an eyelid's flicker that he was paying the slightest attention to the *bhajan*. In fact, he appeared completely abstracted from his surroundings. Patel, who was almost directly opposite me, sat massively erect, no less immobile than Nehru, gazing into space with an expression of monumental gravity that was almost gloom.

As soon as the *bhajan* was over Nehru had a short private talk with Anandamayi in her room, after which the motorcade resumed its journey.

Pandit-ji, who was one of the few ashramites present, told me that Nehru had asked Anandamayi how to obtain peace of mind and that she had replied 'Rest within.' The visit had not really been a success. Nehru had given no indication of being impressed by Anandamayi to the degree that Pandit-ji had hoped he would be. But this by no means discouraged the sanguine old man, who, after generalizing about the extreme subtlety of spiritual influences and how they worked most powerfully when least perceptible, was soon happily discoursing in a way which suggested his brain was busy with grandiose schemes in which he and Anandamayi were the powers behind the Congress throne.

However little Nehru's visit fulfilled Pandit-ji's larger expectations, it certainly had the advantage of momentarily enhancing his prestige at the ashram. This gave him an opportunity for airing his scheme for a Buddhist, or rather Buddhistic, organization under Anandamayi's patronage. The Dharma Vijaya Vahini, or 'Army of Conquest by Righteousness', as, in the language of Aśoka, it was to be called, had apparently already been once founded by Pandit-ji and was now to be resuscitated through our joint efforts.

Despite flashes of doubt – for although I accepted Pandit-ji's assurances that Anandamayi was personally sympathetic I could not fail to perceive the indifference of her followers – I plunged with enthusiasm into the work of remodelling the Vahini's prospectus. This entailed lengthy doctrinal discussions with Pandit-ji, who held strongly to the view that Buddhism was of Upanishadic origin. More practical matters, such as the recruitment of workers, were also discussed. This gave me an opportunity to suggest the name of Banerjee, of whom I had already spoken more than once, and with whom I had been in regular correspondence ever since my departure from Calcutta. But so gently did I throw out my line that the fish failed to notice the bait.

A day or two later, however, I received a despairing letter from my friend saying that he had no money and was being treated in an unbearably humiliating fashion by His Holiness. His appeal for help ended 'A friend in need is a friend indeed.' Feeling that it was now no time for hints, I frankly proposed to Pandit-ji that Banerjee should be invited to Kishengunj to cooperate with us in our work. Though demurring at first, he eventually gave his consent. Overjoyed, I hurried to the post office and wired my friend a hundred rupees for the journey.

21
THE THREE UNTOUCHABLES

There are some people so devastatingly frank that their advent in any small, self-centred group long accustomed to seeing itself only through its own eyes has an effect as of tearing off a veil. Banerjee was of this type. It was therefore to be expected that his arrival at Kishengunj a week later would lead to a series of incidents which, though Anandamayi seemed to find them only amusing, seriously disturbed the complacency of her followers. The first incident did not, of course, occur immediately. After his recent unpleasant experiences in Calcutta with His Holiness, who had taken revenge upon him for my defection, he was at first glad simply to enjoy the friendly, even convivial, atmosphere of the mango grove. Pandit-ji, moreover, knew well how to impress the young, and it was not long before Banerjee, who listened spellbound to the wily old scholar's discourses on Buddhism and the Vedanta, enthusiastically declared that he resembled the forest-dwelling sages of old. With Sudhir, who spent most of the day sleeping naked in the sun, he was soon on terms of familiarity. Friendships as a rule ripen quickly in India. Banerjee's eagerness to please, Pandit-ji's desire to impress, and Sudhir's wish to be allowed to doze undisturbed, were in themselves sufficient to ensure amicable relations. All three, moreover, were Bengalis, and, though Banerjee refused to admit the fact, the others had even before his arrival inferred from his name that like themselves he was a Brahmin.

Food, and all that relates to its preparation and consumption, occupying as it does a place of unique importance in the life of the orthodox Hindu, it was inevitable that Banerjee's first conflict with the ashramites should have been in connection with lunch.

At Anandamayi's invitation, Pandit-ji, Sudhir, and I had been staying on at the ashram after the morning session and taking this meal there. Space seemed to be limited, and I was not astonished when I was asked to squat on the north veranda of the main building, while Pandit-ji and Sudhir took their places in the long row of devotees on the veranda of the kitchen, a separate building immediately opposite. After a few minutes the woman who had turned round to look curiously at me on the day of my arrival bustled up with two leaf-plates, one of which she placed in front of me, the other a couple of feet away. After seeing that I had been served with rice, lentil soup, and curried vegetables, she took her place beside me. As she was of a communicative disposition I soon learned that she was not Kashmiri, but an Austrian – Blanca Schlaum – that she was the principal of a girls' school in Benares, and being greatly devoted to Anandamayi she was now spending her summer vacation at the ashram. When the meal was over, she brought me water for washing the hands, removed our two leaf-plates, smeared the corner of the veranda where we had eaten with cowdung and then washed it thoroughly with water. As she always looked after me and as, apart from the girl who served us, no other ashramite spoke to me, we soon became friends.

On the first day that Banerjee, too, was invited to stay for lunch, the question arose where he should sit. Pandit-ji, for some reason or other, was strangely insistent that he should join him and Sudhir on the kitchen veranda; Banerjee refused to be separated from me. As they spoke in Bengali I could not follow their argument, but both, I thought, had become unreasonably heated. Eventually, my friend seemed to gain his point, and a third leaf-plate was laid on the north veranda.

Only when we were again in the mango grove, and when Pandit-ji and Banerjee, who had argued violently all the way back, simultaneously tried to explain to me their respective points of view, did I discover that the matter was more serious than I had suspected. Though I had been kept in ignorance of the fact, the ashram was rigid in its observance of caste distinctions, especially as between Brahmins and non-Brahmins. All could, indeed, sit together in the hall, and all could join in the singing of the divine names; but the members of a lower were not permitted to eat with the members of a higher caste. The significance of the two verandas was now obvious. Blanca and I were being treated as Untouchables. She threw away our leaf-plates herself because no one else would have touched them. The cowdung was meant to purify the veranda, after we had polluted it by eating there.

Banerjee was furious that Pandit-ji had allowed me to be treated in this insulting manner. The old man, though agreeing that caste distinctions were absurd, was irritated that Banerjee, instead of quietly adapting himself to circumstances, had openly flouted the conventions of the ashram, thus creating an awkward situation for Pandit-ji himself and compromising, perhaps, the Vahini's chances of securing Anandamayi's patronage.

In the end, wearied by Banerjee's vehemence, Pandit-ji adopted a milder tone and related a long story of how he himself, more than half a century earlier, on returning home from his first trip to America had been compelled to stay in the cowshed for a week and undergo numerous ceremonies of expiation and purification before being readmitted to commensality with his kinsfolk. Did not the fact that such penalties were no longer imposed on those who ventured to cross the *kālāpānī*, the 'black water', he demanded – skilfully returning to his point – indicate that caste restrictions were on the decline? Indeed, the day of their final disappearance being in any case close at hand, should we not endeavour to hasten it by a tactful and sympathetic handling of those who still adhered to the old socio-religious taboos, rather than retard it by provoking a reaction? These arguments were not without their effect on my friend, who from the minute Pandit-ji adopted a more conciliatory attitude had begun to repent of his hasty actions and harsh words. He therefore apologized profusely for his rudeness, Pandit-ji delivered a little sermon on the necessity of compromise, and by the time we set out for the ashram to attend the evening programme, peace had been for the time being restored to the mango grove. But no argument could shake Banerjee's determination to eat with Blanca and me, and despite Pandit-ji's disapproval and to the infinite scandal of the ashramites, who for all his disclaimers knew he was a Brahmin, he continued to make a third with us on the north veranda, whence he cracked for their benefit embarrassing jokes about the 'Three Untouchables'.

Anandamayi being so obviously the queen bee of the ashram hive, we could not help speculating about the nature of her personal attitude towards the caste system. Pandit-ji assured us that, being in a state of constant communion with the Absolute, wherein all mundane distinctions are transcended, she certainly could not be considered as really believing in it. The ashram rules, as far as he knew, had been framed by Anandamayi's chief disciple and manageress, Gurupriya, a woman of the narrowest and most rigid orthodoxy, who was even then hastening to Kishengunj from Benares. Besides, he pointed out, however mistaken Anandamayi's Brahmin disciples might be, it would be wrong for her to hurt their feelings by offending their caste prejudices, since if out of disgust they left her their spiritual development might be retarded.

'But what about the feelings of the non-Brahmins?' demanded Banerjee. 'Aren't they entitled to some spiritual development too? At present they don't come to the ashram because they won't tolerate being treated worse than dogs!' The balance seemed too heavily weighted in favour of the Brahmins for Pandit-ji's arguments to sound convincing, and despite the air of long-tried patience the old opportunist assumed, we resolved to take up the matter with Anandamayi herself at the earliest opportunity.

This was not long in coming. Having heard from her disciples that Banerjee was really a Brahmin the Blissful Mother asked him whether, as was the orthodox custom, he wore his sacred thread and recited the Gayatri mantra thrice daily. This, we learned later, was a standard question, for she was strongly in favour of the strict observance of these practices by all Brahmins. The conversation being in Bengali, I was unable to appreciate the full force of Banerjee's reply; but he told me the gist of it afterwards, and from the outraged expressions that appeared on the faces of some of the disciples I could even then guess its tenor.

Without admitting in so many words that he came from a Brahmin family, he spoke in the most disparaging terms of 'that rope' as he called the sacred thread, saying that he had thrown it away long ago and had no intention of ever wearing it again. Besides, he was a Buddhist, having taken the Three Refuges and Five Precepts on the last Vaiśākha Pūrṇimā Day, and Buddhists did not believe in caste. As for the Gayatri mantra (the hearing of which by members of the lower castes was in ancient days punishable in a ghastly manner), he had taught it to a number of sweepers and made them recite it. If Anandamayi was a real Mata-ji, a real 'Holy Mother', he declared belligerently, she would not be so interested in trying to find out who was a Brahmin and who was not, but regard all equally as her disciples and children.

Whether this was the famous occasion on which he declared roundly that to him she was not a Mata-ji but only an old Calcutta Kali Ma (that is to say, a low-class fortune-telling medium), and that he had seen hundreds like her standing in the gutter waiting for customers, I do not remember. In any case, he had already said enough to infuriate the ashramites, who had punctuated the latter part of his tirade with angry shouts of protest. Pandit-ji looked intensely uncomfortable.

Anandamayi, however, who had been listening with the utmost unconcern, only laughed in her most captivating manner at his last outrageous words. What explanation she finally gave of her attitude towards the caste system was never clear, and though Banerjee recurred to the subject in subsequent conversations she could not be brought to admit either that she approved or that she disapproved of the restrictions observed in the ashram. Each time she extricated herself by adroitly covering philosophical evasiveness with an exercise of personal charm. The latter was of so extraordinary a quality that our dissatisfaction at her failure to give an unambiguous reply to our main question always ended by being subtly dissolved in the delight we could not help feeling in her fascinating presence.

This was no doubt precisely her intention. Quite soon after my arrival at Kishengunj I had noticed that she seemed to carry on with her disciples, male or female, young or old, a sort of spiritual flirtation. Such a procedure was quite in keeping with the ideals of Bengal Vaishnavism. Krishna had lured the cow-girls of Brindaban not with philosophy but by his flute; charmed them not by his wisdom but with his beauty; and they had gained emancipation, according to the Vaishnava scriptures, not through understanding but through love. So highly charged was the atmosphere surrounding Anandamayi, of so many eyes was she the cynosure, that her slightest word, look, or gesture could give rise to repercussions, and become the subject of animated discussion, for days and weeks afterwards. Devotees to whom she playfully tossed a flower almost swooned with emotion. Any special favour shown to one disciple threw the rest into paroxysms of jealousy. One neglected devotee, we were told, not so very long before had out of chagrin actually assaulted Anandamayi and knocked her down a flight of steps.

Not even Banerjee was prepared to go to such lengths as these in order to obtain an answer to our question! With our doubts periodically silenced by her captivating behaviour, but not permanently satisfied, we had no alternative but to infer Anandamayi's attitude towards caste from her actions, as well as from the actions of those who, since they derived their authority from her, might reasonably be supposed to be carrying out her directions.

We soon discovered that, after being divided from the non-Brahmins, the Brahmins themselves were subdivided into three groups, each of which ate separately. What the principle of this subdivision was I do not remember; but Anandamayi ate only in the presence of the first-class Brahmins, one of whom, usually either the untidy girl attendant or Gurupriya, had to feed her.

After lunch the Blissful Mother often sat on the front veranda of the ashram, where it was coolest. If she called for a glass of water non-Brahmins had to withdraw for a few minutes while it was poured down her throat. So much was it possible even for one who did not believe in them to be influenced by the atmosphere of the place where such restrictions were observed that when, once, I was allowed to remain – either because I was not sitting too near Anandamayi or because my unclean presence had gone unnoticed – I actually felt quite elated.

Blanca, who punctiliously withdrew on such occasions, stoutly maintained that Anandamayi had no personal objection to drinking anything touched by a non-Brahmin, affirming that she had herself once offered her water; but the ashramites pronounced this story apocryphal, and in any case, even if true the incident was so much the exception to the ashram's prevailing practice as to be of little consequence.

As the only European resident in the ashram poor Blanca was in fact the chief victim of orthodox malice. Several Brahmin youths, members of the inner circle, took a vicious pleasure in cruelly humiliating her on every possible occasion. Though she was twice their age, her devotion to Anandamayi usually enabled her to bear their insults with meekness; but occasionally she exploded.

Once, when one of her tormentors, a tall, fleshy young Bengali with a puffy, discontented face, was filling a bucket at the kitchen pump, Blanca happened to set her cup, which she was waiting to fill, on the top of the cement post, a few inches above the mouth of the pump.

'Now I'll have to throw all the water away,' he shouted angrily, suiting his actions to the words.

'But you only want the water for your bath!' wailed Blanca, as the water swirled round her bare ankles.

Muttering furiously to himself in Bengali, the youth clanged the bucket down in front of the pump.

'Let me fill my cup first,' pleaded the sorely tried woman. But with a venomous look the youth told her to go away before she caused any more trouble.

As it took half an hour to draw a bucket of water it would be a long time before Blanca could fill her cup, and she was in a hurry. After fifteen minutes, when the bucket was half full, she could bear it no longer. With a lusty Germanic imprecation she suddenly gave her tormentor a shove, lifted his bucket to one side, and before he could recover from his astonishment had filled her cup and marched off.

This incident I witnessed from the garden in front of the ashram. About another, which took place in the latrines at the back, Blanca herself told me.

The mother of the same youth, who had forgotten to take in with her the usual pot of water, was shouting to the women outside to bring one. Blanca obligingly did so. But when she heard Blanca's voice she refused to open the latrine door for the water and called out to another woman to fetch it instead. Blanca ruefully commented that her touch had made the water so impure that it was unfit for washing even the posterior of a Brahmin.

Banerjee's temperament being what it was, it was unlikely that he should endure the ashram's restrictions as meekly as Blanca usually did. Besides, there was a world of difference in their respective positions. A verse in the *Rāmacaritamānasa* by Tulsidas, the Bible of the Hindi-speaking people of north-western India, declares that a Shudra, a member of the fourth or lowest caste, should be despised even though possessed of all virtues; while a Brahmin, though committing all sins, should be worshipped. Blanca was not even a Shudra. She was a Mlechchha, lower than even the lowest Untouchable. However devout, or spiritually developed, she might be, she could not touch water or cooked food without polluting them. Banerjee, on the other hand, however bitterly he might rail, or however violently he might rebel, against the taboos of orthodox Hinduism, remained in the eyes of Anandamayi and the ashramites a Brahmin, and for all his protests as such they insisted on treating him. Since in modern (that is to say, in post-medieval) India it is practically impossible for a male Brahmin to repudiate his caste, no attempt at social reform, which in effect means the total abolition of the caste system, on the part of well-intentioned individual Brahmins, or indeed on the part of any Caste Hindu, can be of more than theoretical significance. Hence it was that Banerjee could utter with impunity blasphemies for which Blanca would have been expelled from the ashram. He could maintain not unfriendly relations with the redoubtable Gurupriya, a middle-aged female ascetic with a mass of tousled grey hair and the expression of a bulldog, with whom he at times behaved with such boisterous familiarity that her grim features relaxed almost into a smile. In fact he was on the whole tolerated, if not indulged, like a child who, for all his waywardness, is still a member of the family.

Leavings of food, or food that has in any way touched the lips, is called *jutha*, and no orthodox Hindu would consent to touch the *jutha* of a person of inferior caste. Food that has been ritually offered before the image of a divinity, to a saint, or to a teacher or highly respected elder, is termed *prasad*. Among the ashramites competition for Anandamayi's *prasad* was keen, and every day after lunch the untidy young attendant, momentarily a person of importance, would be besieged by importunate devotees as soon as she emerged from the kitchen with a few scraps left over from the Blissful Mother's meal. Sometimes there was no *prasad*, for Anandamayi, who by allowing herself to be given larger helpings could have supplied all the ashramites with *prasad* every day, evidently understood the art of increasing the demand by keeping down the supply. To be sent a morsel of food directly from her own plate, at her personal behest, was a signal mark of favour occasioning intense joy in the recipient and equally intense jealousy in everyone else. When, one day while the 'Three Untouchables' were lunching on the north veranda, *prasad* was brought with the awe-stricken comment that Anandamayi herself had sent it, we were obviously expected to be quite overwhelmed by such gracious condescension. The ashramites had yet to know Banerjee's strength of mind.

'I'm not going to touch that woman's *jutha*,' he said roughly, covering his plate with his hand. 'How do I know she hasn't got some foul disease?'

Incidents of this kind happened frequently. One of the most amusing took place not in the ashram but at Dehra Dun in the house of a devotee. All the ashramites, together with everyone in the neighbourhood who was in any way connected with, interested in, or even likely to be interested in Anandamayi had been invited to a feast. Anandamayi, as far as I remember, either did not come or came but did not eat anything. Banerjee and I were seated side by side; Pandit-ji and Sudhir elsewhere. As the custom is in India, the guests sat on the floor in long rows, men being segregated from women and children. In front of each person was a leaf-plate. The place on the other side of Banerjee, the last in our row, was empty.

We had just been served and were about to begin eating when a late arrival, an elderly man wearing a sacred thread, sat down in the empty place. Hearing Banerjee and me talking in English he leaned forward and gave me a suspicious stare. What he saw was apparently not reassuring, for he started fidgeting uneasily. Finally, bending towards Banerjee, he asked in a low voice, 'What is your caste?' My friend looked up from his plate with a mischievous expression.

'My caste?' he repeated in a loud, cheerful voice. 'I'm an Untouchable.'

The old gentleman sprang up as though he had seen a cobra. Presently we saw him a few rows away talking in an agitated manner to a group of ashramites and pointing towards Banerjee. The ashramites shook their heads. Evidently they were trying to explain that Banerjee was a Brahmin. A few minutes later, having been unable to find another vacant place, he returned and gingerly sat down again.

'Why didn't you tell me you were a Brahmin?' he demanded.

'I'm not a Brahmin, I'm an Untouchable,' again declared Banerjee, more cheerfully than ever. 'After all, I should know my own caste.'

The old gentleman was so obviously torn between fear of possible pollution and fear of missing his meal that neither of us could help laughing. Eventually, with a long dark look at Banerjee, he pulled the strip of matting at the end of the row out of alignment with that on which we were sitting, so that technically he would not be eating 'with' us, and slowly started on what was evidently a far from enjoyable meal.

With incidents of the type narrated occurring almost daily, it did not take Banerjee and me long to conclude that both Anandamayi and her more intimate followers not only tolerated, but actively encouraged, the observance of the caste system in all its rigid exclusiveness. Our findings were later corroborated by the accidental discovery that both Anandamayi and Gurupriya wore sacred threads. Since the custom of investing female Brahmins with this insignia of caste status had died out more than 1,000 years earlier, the fact of its revival indicated orthodoxy of the most pronounced type. Besides, Gurupriya wore the saffron robes of an ascetic, and according to the best Hindu tradition (which we encountered subsequently in South India) ascetics, whether male or female, are casteless, the sacred thread being one of the articles consigned to the flames at the time of initiation.

Nowadays holy men and ascetics, especially in North India, are often found retaining both thread and caste, and the punctilious observance of caste restrictions, even among themselves, is customary. Membership of certain Vedantic orders is indeed restricted to Brahmins. Once, when half a dozen monks belonging to the Ramakrishna Mission, members of which are known to eat even with Europeans, were given lunch at the ashram, we observed that they were carefully segregated from the more orthodox thread-wearing ascetics.

Having succeeded in coming to a conclusion on the subject of Anandamayi's attitude towards the caste system, it remained for us to attempt a general estimate of her true nature. In the electric atmosphere of the ashram, charged with an intensity of devotion verging on hysteria, it was impossible not to form an opinion on this engrossing subject, even if only by way of a refusal to accept the opinions of others. Gurupriya, the crane-necked youth, the knight of the bucket, and the rest of the 'inner group' asserted that Anandamayi was God Almighty in human form, and that the worship of 'Ma' (for which they afterwards coined the word 'Ma-ism') was the future religion of the world. Whether they made this staggering claim on Anandamayi's behalf because they belonged to the 'inner group', or whether they belonged to it because they made the claim, was a difficult question to determine. But I sometimes felt that an ashramite's spiritual development was held to be in direct ratio to the extravagance of his or her opinion of the Blissful Mother's 'true nature'. Such mutual backscratching of gurus and disciples is indeed so common in modern Hinduism that one cannot help wondering how much of the entire history of this religion is reducible to a congeries of dialogic processes, as the orientalist Max Müller called them, taking place within the framework of a relatively static social order. Some members of the 'inner circle' averred that there had been only two full incarnations of God: Krishna and Chaitanya. Anandamayi was the third. To the Buddha, for them a figure of quite minor importance, they grudgingly conceded the status of a partial incarnation.

Anandamayi herself was extremely reticent about her 'true nature', though she never repudiated any of the claims put forward on her behalf by the ashramites. But once, we learned, in response to the persistent questioning of Hari Baba, a thin, grey-bearded ascetic with a following of his own whom we often saw at the ashram, she had declared that she was '*Pūrṇa Brahma Nārāyaṇa*' – the absolute impersonal Reality of the 'Non-Dualist' Vedantins plus the incarnating personal God of the Vaishnavas. She was also reported to have declared more than once that her present existence was not the outcome of actions committed in past lives, that she had enjoyed uninterruptedly since birth full realization of the Truth, and that whatever *sādhanas* or spiritual exercises she had appeared to undergo had taken place spontaneously.

22

MEDITATIONS IN THE MANGO GROVE

However disinclined Banerjee and I felt to accept Anandamayi as God incarnate, we saw no reason to question the fact that she lived in a state of consciousness that transcended the waking state as much as the waking state transcends sleep, or that she possessed psychic powers of a high order. Gurupriya's seven Bengali volumes of reminiscences, running translations from which Banerjee sometimes gave for my benefit, related hundreds of anecdotes of *inedia*, levitation, telepathy, clairvoyance, prophecy, and other supernormal phenomena such as may be found in plenty not only in the biographies of the saints and mystics of all religions but even, occasionally, in the less illumined lives of ordinary men and women everywhere.

Several anecdotes related to phenomena witnessed not only by Gurupriya but by one or more of the other ashramites. But by the time we met Anandamayi such occurrences had become rare, and devotees of long standing in fact remarked that, though she still persisted in certain eccentricities, her behaviour was much more normal than it had been up to a few years earlier. We ourselves witnessed only one incident that might be regarded as being in any way out of the ordinary.

Towards the end of the afternoon Anandamayi, followed by an entourage that would have done credit to a queen, used to stroll a few furlongs up the road to a stretch of open ground on the right from which we could see, through the purple haze, first the tiny white cubes of bungalows high up on the hillside, and then, as evening deepened, the pinpoints of orange light that flashed from one building after another. The untidy girl always struggled along with a large bucket of water (no one else was allowed to touch it), as it was one of Anandamayi's minor eccentricities to perform in the open, among the bushes, functions usually reserved for a more private place. She would then sit on a low ridge enjoying the cool breeze that blew from the mountains. Often, while talking, she would shake down her long hair, then, with graceful coquettish movements of her hands (she could use them well enough for this purpose, it seemed, however useless they might be for eating and washing), twist it up into a topknot, then shake it down over her eyes, then toss it back, all the time casting at one or two favoured ashramites bewitching smiles and the archest of glances. Sometimes her hair would be admiringly combed by women devotees, who plucked out any grey threads they happened to find. Combings were of course piously treasured.

One afternoon, as we set out from the ashram, Anandamayi gave instructions that a large tray of fruits offered to her a few minutes earlier should be taken along with us. This was so unusual that several ashramites, divining a hidden significance in the order, asked her for what purpose the fruits were required; but as she often did when unwilling to answer a question, she only laughed.

A few hundred yards along the road stood the local branch of the Ramakrishna Mission. At the very moment that Anandamayi, who led the procession, drew level with the gate, out came four or five swamis. On seeing her they started back with every expression of extreme embarrassment. They seemed more embarrassed still when Anandamayi, kicking off her shoes, took the tray of fruits and with the greatest deference presented it to the seniormost swami. We afterwards learned that these monks, jealous of the greater popularity of her ashram, had been spreading ugly scandals about her and that she had decided, as it appeared, to teach them a lesson. The meeting at the gate could have been fortuitous. But never before had we seen the swamis going out together at that hour. And never before had a tray of fruits been taken with us on our walk.

According to the Buddhist tradition, it is the fourth *dhyāna*, or superconscious state, which is the 'base' for the development of supernormal powers, so that any person regularly manifesting such powers may be assumed to have made considerable progress in meditation (*samatha bhāvanā*). Despite our dissatisfaction with Anandamayi's attitude towards the caste system, Banerjee and I therefore decided, after long and earnest discussion, to seek her approval and advice regarding our own decision to take up the regular practice of *ānāpānasati*, or respiration-mindfulness. Whether the distinction between the exalted, but still mundane, states of superconsciousness that can be attained through continuous practice of the proper spiritual exercise, on the one hand, and the transcendental faculty of Wisdom (*prajñā*), in its distinctively Buddhist sense of an awakening to the true absolute nature of existence, through which alone Freedom and Enlightenment can be attained, on the other, was as clear to us then as it became subsequently, I would hesitate to affirm. But it was clear enough for me at least to conclude, not only from Anandamayi's social orthodoxy, which implied an absence of Compassion, the 'emotional' equivalent of Wisdom, but also from the banality of her sayings, a volume of which had been translated into English, as well as from her general outlook and, though to a less degree, from the whole atmosphere of the ashram, that though a great yogini she was neither 'Enlightened', in the Buddhist sense, nor even on the path to Enlightenment – except to the extent that *samatha*, though incapable of giving birth to *prajñā*, may yet constitute a basis for its eventual development. Consequently we had no intention of taking her as our guru or personal spiritual teacher. Like all Hindus the ashramites were unaware of the difference between a superconscious and a transcendental state, and since their bigotry made it impossible for us to confide our views to them they found our attitude towards the Blissful Mother unsatisfactory, especially as we only bowed and saluted her with folded hands, instead of falling prostrate at her feet as they always did.

Having made up our minds to ask Anandamayi's advice about meditation, we requested her to grant us a private interview. This took place the same night between 11 and 12. The ashramites had warned us that the Mother hardly ever granted such interviews, and then only for a few minutes, and the fact that the two black sheep of the ashram should be thus highly favoured so soon after their arrival gave rise to many murmurs and much heart-burning. 'I've been Ma's devotee for years,' complained more than one person bitterly, 'and she's never given me a private interview.' Even the crane-necked youth, we were astonished to learn, had not enjoyed this favour.

But we were too excited to take much notice of their reactions. Banerjee, who had no previous experience of meditation, was as eager to practise respiration-mindfulness as I was, for he already knew about my experiment with this method in Singapore. Anandamayi apparently had not heard of *ānāpānasati* before, but when, with Banerjee as interpreter, I explained in detail the successive stages of the practice, she nodded approvingly.

Most of the interview was devoted to hints of a general nature which, as we afterwards discovered, were matters of common knowledge. But one hint on how one-pointedness of mind that had been lost at a higher stage of the practice could be recovered at a lower stage proved useful during the whole of my subsequent practice of this method. At the conclusion of the interview Banerjee asked her to bestow on him a religious name. I was already known as Dharmapriya, 'Lover of the Law', having adopted the name in Calcutta. Anandamayi therefore named Banerjee Satyapriya, 'Lover of Truth'.

Both of us felt strangely moved and elated by this interview, which not only gave a final sanction to our decision to enter the path of meditation but stamped it as irrevocable, and it was with profounder bows than usual that we retired from Anandamayi's presence and walked in silence beneath the starry vastness of night back to the sleeping mango grove, where in the morning our practice was to begin.

For the next three or four weeks, in fact until the day of our departure from Kishengunj, Satyapriya (as my friend must now be called) and I meditated twice daily, at dawn and at dusk, in one of the small clearings in the strip of jungle running from the mango grove down to the canal.

One's first experience of meditation, like one's first love, retains in memory a virginal freshness too delicate and too delicious for words. We meditated for an hour at a time, sitting cross-legged, with spine erect, chin tucked in, and loosely closed hands resting, thumbs upwards, on our knees. Our meditation seats, each of which consisted of a folded blanket covered with a clean towel, were placed about twenty feet apart. If one finished a few minutes before the other, as usually happened, he uncrossed his legs and quietly waited for him to move. At Anandamayi's suggestion, each of us maintained a spiritual diary wherein, immediately after each meditation session, we recorded the degree of concentration attained, the kind of mental distractions that had arisen, and any unusual experiences that might have occurred.

At ten o'clock every morning, having breakfasted with Pandit-ji and Sudhir in the tent (we always slept outside), we ran down to the canal to bathe. The iciness of the swift-rushing waters, which roared so loudly between their narrow stone banks that we could hardly hear each other speak, contrasted with the intense heat of the mid-morning sun. Soon after Satyapriya's arrival I had adopted Indian dress, a white shirt and sarong, so that soaping myself in the open air was no longer the problem it had been in Ahmedabad. But I could not help feeling slightly embarrassed by the glance of a wandering goatherd, or the inquisitive looks of the village boys sporting naked downstream. Washing clothes was now the problem. Usually Satyapriya, after soaping them, slapped both mine and his on a big flat stone, swinging each one up into the air and then down with a sudden jerk of his powerful arm, as he considered mine too feeble for the strenuous work. We then went to the ashram. As the time of our meditation session coincided with that of the *bhajan* we stopped going in the evening. Instead, we passed the time quietly among the mango trees until Pandit-ji and Sudhir returned.

What experiences Satyapriya had in meditation I no longer remember, though each always showed the other his notebook. My own experiences were mostly in the form of visions. Once I saw the Virgin Mary, all in blue and white, as Murillo has depicted her. On another occasion Anandamayi appeared. Once, again, I had a vision of the Buddha, but as I gazed the nose suddenly became enormously elongated and his head turned into that of an elephant. When I asked Anandamayi the meaning of this strange occurrence she explained that the Buddha had given me the sign of *siddhi*, or success, the elephant-headed god Ganesha being regarded by Hindus as the remover of obstacles, both worldly and spiritual, and hence the giver of success in all undertakings. Presently I began to see beautiful landscapes, then as it were white birds flashing through brilliant blue sky, and finally kaleidoscopic geometrical patterns that seemed made of jewels. All these visions were remarkable for gem-like purity and brilliance of colour, as though one was being given glimpses of a higher and more beautiful world.

Since we now spent much less time at the ashram, Satyapriya had fewer opportunities of coming into conflict with the ashramites. After our interview with Anandamayi only a single such incident occurred.

One Sunday, perhaps in honour of Hari Baba's birthday, there was a feast, and at the conclusion of the morning programme practically the entire congregation was invited to remain for lunch. Since the guests were being fed in relays we naturally expected our own lunch to be served late. But first one, then two hours passed, and though almost everybody had finished eating the ashramites either ignored Satyapriya's enquiries as to when we would be served or curtly told him we would have to wait. Eventually, his face dark with rage, he said, 'Come on, let's go. These buggers are trying to make fools of us.' In vain I remonstrated that the ashramites were busy, and assured him we would be served within a few minutes. Knowing as well as I did that we were being subtly insulted, he strode angrily out of the gate, and I had no alternative but to follow.

Half an hour after we had reached the mango grove the knight of the bucket rushed up in a state of great agitation. Anandamayi was calling us, he said, and we were to return to the ashram immediately. Lunch was ready. Satyapriya, feeling that the advantage now lay on our side, smoothly replied that as we had just eaten a few mangoes our stomachs were full. Since we were practising meditation, he added, we ought not to overeat. When the youth had pleaded and expostulated long enough to assuage our wounded pride, however, we at last relented and returned with him to the ashram.

Anandamayi was looking out for us from the balcony of her room, and as we rather shamefacedly entered the gate she greeted us with an affectionate smile of unusual sweetness. Upstairs, where we had not been allowed before, she apologized with folded hands for the behaviour of the ashramites and begged our forgiveness, so skilfully making their fault her own (as indeed it was, ultimately) that we felt obliged to beg her forgiveness for the rudeness of our abrupt departure. She then called for fruits and sweets and gave them to us with her own hands. No one in the world, we felt, could be more charming than Anandamayi. When our lunch was at last ready she stood and watched us eat, keeping the ashramites busy running to and fro between the kitchen and the north veranda for fresh helpings of the delicacies she had ordered to be specially cooked for us. We subsequently learned that immediately after our departure she enquired if we had been given lunch, and on discovering how we had been treated had taken the ashramites severely to task for their behaviour.

This incident would, perhaps, have led to an improvement in our position at the ashram; but Anandamayi, who had for some time been showing signs of restlessness, had already spent six weeks at Kishengunj. A day or two later Gurupriya and a few other intimates were suddenly ordered to strike canvas, and she was gone.

23
THE DIVINE EYE

The Raipur Ashram stood on a knoll among trees beside an ancient whitewashed temple from which fluttered the orange pennant that showed it was dedicated to the god Shiva. From the foot of the knoll a path straggled to the village street below, while behind it, crossing the upper end of the street at right angles, ran a willow-fringed canal that cut straight through the fields as far as the eye could reach. At their point of intersection stood a small bridge. The surrounding countryside was comparatively flat and desolate.

The ashram consisted mainly of three buildings. A flat-roofed *bhajan*-hall stood opposite a dilapidated guest-house, on the same level. Between them was a small courtyard full of leaves. At each end of the *bhajan*-hall veranda a door opened onto a tiny room, not more than six feet square. Satyapriya stayed in one of these, I in the other. Pandit-ji and Sudhir shared the left-hand front room of the guest-house, immediately opposite my own miniature apartment. The two buildings were joined on that side by a parapet wall pierced by an opening from which a flight of steps twisted down to the ashram gate. On the other side, next to the *bhajan*-hall but on a higher level, the double-storey new building erected specially as a residence for Anandamayi rose dazzlingly white in the sunshine.

Twenty years earlier, I gathered, when phenomena of an extraordinary type occurred almost daily and when she was comparatively unknown, Anandamayi had spent a number of months at Raipur with her husband and the first (and according to her the greatest) of her devotees under conditions of extreme hardship, even privation. Since then she had not been near the ashram (though one or another of her disciples, who regarded it as a holy place, was always there), and the new residence had been erected, apparently, as a means of inducing her to pay a second visit and thereafter to make the place part of her regular itinerary. Pandit-ji, busy with schemes as ever, hinted that it was whispered among the disciples that the Raipur Ashram might become the Blissful Mother's permanent headquarters, for it was one of their dearest wishes that instead of spending a week here and a month there as the spirit moved her she would settle down in one place, preferably Benares, and allow them to organize around her a new religious movement.

Whether on our arrival from Kishengunj we found Anandamayi already installed in her new quarters, or whether she arrived a few days later, I no longer remember. At any rate, far from taking up permanent residence in the ashram, she stayed there for only a few days. My sole memory of the Blissful Mother at Raipur is of her climbing the steps to her room on the first floor of the new building and standing for a few minutes on the front balcony to look down into the courtyard at Satyapriya and me.

My recollections of the disciples and devotees who must have accompanied her are even vaguer. This may be because there were fewer of them than there had been at Kishengunj or because they all left at about the same time as Anandamayi. Or the hard feelings generated by an incident which had occurred within a day or two of our arrival might have caused them to avoid our company.

As at Kishengunj, the starting-point of the trouble was food, though its immediate occasion was a prejudice of a different but related kind. Pandit-ji, Sudhir, Satyapriya, and I had been allotted a wattle-and-daub kitchen, consisting of a single small, narrow room which, since it stood on the other side of the compound wall, was technically outside the ashram premises. Here Pandit-ji's squint-eyed Brahmin cooked for us, and here we ate. The quickest way from the *bhajan*-hall courtyard to the kitchen lay through a second courtyard, situated at the top of the knoll, where stood the diminutive Shiva temple, a single chamber containing a large phallus of black stone. Word was conveyed to Pandit-ji that while there was no objection to Satyapriya using this short cut I was on no account to pollute the sanctity of the temple by passing through the courtyard.

This order I did not dispute. However much I might disapprove of such narrow-minded intolerance, I was a Buddhist, not a Hindu, and my admission to a Hindu shrine was not a matter of right but only of courtesy. Satyapriya reacted with characteristic violence. There was a furious argument between him and the ashramites, one of whose pleas (quite baseless, as we afterwards discovered) was that the villagers might even stone me if they came to know that I had set foot in the temple courtyard. Their attempts to mollify his wrath by emphasizing that the prohibition did not apply to *him* had an effect quite contrary to what they had intended. 'If my friend can't enter your dirty temple I don't want to enter it either!' he shouted. 'I'll go and meditate in the latrine. That's a much purer and holier place, in my opinion. After all, everybody is allowed to go *there*.'

This outburst enraged the ashramites more than anything he had ever said at Kishengunj had done, and I believe he was mildly rebuked by Anandamayi for his intemperance. Thereafter, while Pandit-ji and Sudhir continued to use the short cut, Satyapriya and I had to go out of the ashram gate and then follow the compound wall round to the other side of the knoll where stood the kitchen.

After Anandamayi's departure, and the disappearance of the noisy, wrangling disciples, who had already begun to quarrel among themselves about who would be the owner of the Raipur Ashram and other institutions founded in the Mother's name after her death, there descended upon the place a peace all the more delightful in contrast to the tension by which it had been preceded.

Every morning Satyapriya and I rose at four, and after a hasty wash sat for meditation in the *bhajan*-hall, where we also slept. During the day Satyapriya studied Bengali translations of the Upanishads and the *Bhagavad Gītā*, while I read a few books on Hinduism that belonged to the previous occupant of my tiny room, an English-knowing ascetic, and wrote poems, articles, and letters.[28] Among the letters I wrote was one to the General Secretary of the Maha Bodhi Society, Devapriya Valisinha, protesting in the strongest terms against His Holiness's treatment of Miss Albers and urging him to do something about it. Years later I learned that my intervention had not been without effect, and that after Valisinha's return to Calcutta the inoffensive old creature had been made relatively comfortable until the time of her death. In addition to study and literary work, which occupied the greater part of the day, there were frequent discussions with Pandit-ji, who for all his chicanery was so learned and intelligent, and so affable and generous withal, that in private my friend and I often regretted his talents had not been devoted to more worthy ends. Though he had not followed Anandamayi, he proposed to do so soon, as it was rumoured that from New Delhi she would go up into the hills as far as Kasauli or even Solon, in both of which places Pandit-ji claimed to have good connections, and in one of which he hoped it would be possible for us to establish, under Anandamayi's patronage, a Buddhist education society. An elaborate prospectus for this venture I was then drafting.

Sometimes Satyapriya and I strolled down to the village, where my friend, who like most Bengalis was loquacious and sociable, was soon on terms of familiarity with the Bengali postmaster and his family, from whom he learned that Anandamayi's followers were not regarded in the village with unmixed approval. There were also walks along country lanes deeply rutted by the large wooden wheels of bullock-carts and with hedgerows on either side which reminded me of those which I had seen as a boy in Sussex.

Once or twice, crossing the wooden bridge, we walked for two miles along the opposite bank of the canal to where the waters of a famous mineral spring trickled down a wall of rock green with sulphur. In places where two or three trickles, uniting, made a cascade, men naked save for a rag between the loins were bathing. After walking for nearly an hour through open country in the blazing sunshine we were perspiring freely, and stripping off his clothes Satyapriya plunged beneath the nearest cascade. I still had too much English modesty in my make-up to follow his example. Besides, I had noticed four or five silent women unobtrusively filling large earthen pots. I therefore contented myself with washing face and hands in the waters of one of the shallow, cress-filled pools surrounding the approaches to the spring.

Another afternoon, without crossing the bridge, we followed the canal for a mile in the opposite direction. Midway we passed a kind of straggling village where the people seemed, from their extremely dark complexions and unkempt appearance, to belong to one of the scheduled castes or tribes. The entire male population, both men and boys, was fishing in the waters of the canal with English-style rods and lines. Though only a few small fish had been hooked, great was the excitement.

At six every evening we meditated in the back veranda of Anandamayi's room, the Mother herself having granted us this privilege. In the centre of her room, through which we had to pass, stood a large white bed. Leaning against the enormous bolster gleamed a life-size photograph of Anandamayi hung with a garland of large red flowers. Here, morning and evening, the only resident of the ashram – a quiet, elderly man – worshipped the Mother with the customary Hindu rites. When we passed through it in the evening the room was usually full of incense-smoke and the lamps still burning. Though Anandamayi had occupied the room for only a few days, it was pervaded by an unusual peace and tranquillity, so that on entering it we instinctively lowered our voices and moved quietly.

After meditating for an hour I would open my eyes to find the world a darker and a cooler place. An inch or two above the cement parapet of the balcony the ash-grey landscape swelled into a hardly perceptible convexity that stood out against a broad belt of luminous blue-grey sky. Between this belt and the blue-blackness that – aglitter with countless stars – already reigned in the zenith, lay banks of rosy cloud. Chirrupings from the trees told of birds returned to the nest.

More delightful still, perhaps, were the hours after supper when we sat silent on the moonlit roof of the *bhajan*-hall or listened from the courtyard to the sound of a distant party of villagers pouring out the feelings of their hearts in plaintive devotional songs.

This idyllic existence soon came to an end. After ten or twelve days Pandit-ji, Sudhir, and Satyapriya left for New Delhi, and I was alone in the ashram. The second night after their departure I had a most unusual experience. As already mentioned, Satyapriya and I always sat for our morning meditation in the *bhajan*-hall, where we spread our bedding on the cool marble floor and slept each beneath his mosquito net. Satyapriya, who was always the first awake, would sit up and rouse me with a shove.

On the night of which I am speaking, I felt this shove as usual, but being still more than half asleep did not immediately respond. Eventually, wishing that I could have slept on undisturbed instead of having to get up and meditate, I raised myself onto one elbow, lifted the mosquito curtain, and saw that my friend was already sitting with closed eyes apparently absorbed in meditation. Though we usually started sitting at the same time this was not in itself sufficient to amaze me. But the fact that gradually penetrated my sleep-drugged brain, giving rise to a vague bewilderment, even uneasiness, was that he was sitting naked to the waist on a string bed *that had not been there the night before.*

As I gazed, trying to puzzle out whence the bed had come and why he was sitting on it instead of on the floor, I suddenly recollected with awful clarity that Satyapriya had left for New Delhi two days earlier. In an instant I was wider awake than I had ever been in my life before. But he was still sitting there in meditation only three feet away. For several minutes I gazed intently, rubbing my eyes, yet still he was there. Eventually, convinced it was no hallucination – for he was there in front of me as undeniably as he had ever been – I decided to touch him and see what would happen. Slowly, very slowly, I stretched out my hand, intending to touch his shoulder. At the instant that the tip of my finger was about to make contact with his skin, he vanished, and the bed with him. I was left alone in the pitch-dark room, the wooden window-shutters all closed, unable to see even my own hand. Groping for our bedside clock, I held the dial close to my face and saw by the phosphorescent figures that it was two o'clock.

A few days later I received from Satyapriya a letter informing me that he, Pandit-ji, and Sudhir had reached New Delhi. Anandamayi, who never stayed at a private house, was living in a tent in the garden of a Jain multi-millionaire. On the night after their arrival, the second after they had left Raipur, he had talked with her until well after midnight and had not gone to bed until one in the morning. After tossing and turning for nearly an hour, unable to sleep for the sultriness of the atmosphere, he had sat up and meditated. In his meditation he had thought of Raipur and tried to visualize me sleeping. Had I felt anything? When we next met I asked him whether he had used a stringed bed in New Delhi and whether he had sat up to meditate. Both questions he answered in the affirmative.

Not all my experiences at the deserted ashram were of this unusual type. Pandit-ji having taken with him the squint-eyed Brahmin, I had now, for the first time in my life, to cook my own meals. Despite my ignorance, this was no hardship. Satyapriya had arranged for the postmaster's son, a lad of fifteen, to keep me supplied with rice, lentils, and potatoes from the village shop (onions were prohibited in the ashram), and Pandit-ji had left me not only a tin of tapioca and a bag of dried prunes but greatest help of all, a patent cooker.

At eleven every morning, therefore, I washed the rice and lentils, scraped the small yellow potatoes, mixed a handful of tapioca with a few dried prunes, and put them with just the right quantity of water into their respective containers. With the help of the postmaster's son I then kindled a charcoal fire in the burner, blew it into a clear red glow, and after sliding the burner drawer-like into position beneath the four containers, clamped them all together, washed the charcoal-dust from my fingers, and went back to my books and articles. At 12.30 lunch was ready. Both rice and lentils could be cooked to perfection by this method, and the tapioca and prunes, sweetened with a spoonful of sugar, made a tolerable dessert; but in the absence of oil and spices, in which vegetables are always fried in India, my unpalatable pieces of soapy legume could hardly be called a curry. Breakfast and supper consisted of bread and butter and tea.

As I never left the ashram, and as there were no visitors, the fortnight that elapsed before Satyapriya's return passed with so few interruptions from the outside world that my mode of existence might have won the approval of the most rigid anchorite. The only person to whom I ever spoke was the postmaster's son. Like most Hindus who have received a little education he believed that the marvels of modern science had all been anticipated by the ancient Hindu saints and sages and described in the Hindu sacred books. That the *Rāmāyaṇa* spoke of flying-machines proved that aeroplanes had existed in India thousands of years before their invention in the West. The magic throwing-discs of the *Mahābhārata*, which were capable of causing tremendous havoc, were of course atom bombs. Hindu customs, ceremonies, and superstitions, he was convinced, all had a scientific basis. The whole of modern scientific knowledge could be found in the Vedas and this, obviously, proved not only the truth of Hinduism but its superiority to all other religions. In vain I pointed out that archaeologists had failed to discover the remains of a single flying-machine at any excavated site, and that indulgence in flight fantasies was quite a different thing from scientific knowledge of flight mechanics. His belief gave him an emotional satisfaction that no argument could be allowed to disturb.

Though the more learned among them presented their case with more subtlety, and with a far greater refinement of sophistry, than lay at the command of the village postmaster's son, an astonishingly large number of Hindus, I afterwards found, maintain with varying degrees of vehemence that the saints and sages of ancient India found by yogic means all the truths known to modern science and that everything in Hinduism had a scientific foundation. The originators, or at least the popularizers, of this flattering thesis were the Theosophists. Mrs Besant, in a curious lecture, professes to find a scientific basis, hence a moral justification, for the practice of Untouchability – an attempt that won the immediate appreciation of her orthodox South Indian audience.

Despite the fact that I did not go outside the ashram I was not so much an anchorite as never even to look over the wall. Indeed, one of the vividest and most touching memories of my whole Raipur sojourn is of the flocks of black, white, and brown goats that I used to watch at five every afternoon. Beneath the horizontal beams of a sun that, though low in the pure blue sky, was still insufferably bright, they streamed in from the stony scrub where, all the long summer's day, they had nibbled and bleated, butted and skipped, under the watching eyes of the youthful neatherds and their dogs. Now udders were full, and the nanny goats, each with one or two gambolling kids, were pressed towards the milking-sheds with plaintive bleats that, from a distance, rang out almost like human cries.

24
THE GOING FORTH

Kasauli was so cold, and so full of damp white mist that came flying in over the fir tree tops as it were in large lumps, that I was reminded of Ghoom. Satyapriya had returned to Raipur for me and together we had travelled up into the Punjab hills; but though the gradual change of scene must have been of absorbing interest, my sole memory of the journey is of getting out of the ramshackle bus halfway between Kalka, the railway terminus, and Kasauli, and being violently sick owing to the sudden change of altitude. Pandit-ji and Sudhir, who had arrived a few days earlier, were waiting for us at the bus stand.

As the four of us walked through the streets of the small hill station, I could not help remarking on the extraordinarily large number of well-groomed and obviously wealthy Sikhs we saw, the stalwart bearded and turbaned men clad in beautifully tailored English suits, the plump women and girls wearing satin pyjamas, knee-length tunics, and with the two ends of the muslin scarf that covered their full breasts flung over their shoulders and floating out behind. Many had big new cars that flashed with chromium plate, and most, whether men or women, glittered with expensive jewellery. Pandit-ji explained that they were millionaire businessmen from West Punjab who, with independence approaching, and the division of the province between India and Pakistan imminent, had fled for safety to Kasauli, which was in East Punjab. So much was communal hatred already ablaze that some, fearing for their lives, had hastily crammed as many valuables as possible into their cars and driven away, abandoning house and furniture to the fury of the mob.

Whether because of this influx of moneyed refugees or for other reasons, there was a shortage of accommodation at Kasauli. Satyapriya and I were fortunate to find refuge in the guest-house of Lalla Pyarelal, a wealthy Punjabi businessman to whom Pandit-ji had introduced us. This gentleman's house was perched on the cliff-edge at the far end of the bazaar, up whose narrow cobbled streets, so steep they were almost stairs, we had to climb to visit Pandit-ji in the residential section of the town higher up. Fifty feet below the house was a narrow rocky ledge whereon stood the guest-house. To this we had access by a weed-flanked path that, descending from the main street of the bazaar, ran straight past Lalla Pyarelal's front gate and then, dropping sharply, looped round to meet the rocky ledge.

Within the loop, at a level halfway between the house and the guest-house, stood a large cement platform which, though roofed in, was enclosed only by stout wire mesh. In this structure, designed for fine-weather social and religious functions, Anandamayi had stayed for five days before going up to Solon, the capital of a small hill state of that name, the ruler of which was one of her devotees. Despite the Persian rugs with which the rich businessman had spread the floor and covered the wire mesh, Anandamayi's disciples had shivered; but the Mother herself, we were told, had shown remarkable indifference to the extreme cold. This we were by no means astonished to learn. In Kishengunj eye-witnesses had related how a truculent devotee once challenged her to show what difference there was between herself and an ordinary person. Calling for a shovelful of burning coals, she dropped one into her open palm and without the slightest change of expression in her laughing face allowed it to burn there for several minutes. 'Can you do this?' she mockingly demanded of the horrified devotee. On examination it was found that her hand had been badly scorched.

Despite the change of climate and atmosphere, the way in which Satyapriya and I passed our days did not greatly vary from the routine established at Raipur. Meditation, study, and (in my case) literary work continued to occupy the major part of our time. Thanks to the kindness of our host, we were spared the necessity of preparing so much as a cup of tea with our own hands. Twice a day, punctual to the minute, there came down from the house two trays each containing a stack of piping-hot chappatis, liberally smeared with ghee, half a dozen bowls filled with lentil soup and curries, a brass tumbler of hot milk, together with fruit and sweetmeats. So rich was the fare that, accustomed as I had been to a more spartan diet, I soon developed diarrhoea. Satyapriya, who boasted of having swallowed forty large sweetmeats at a time in his student days for a wager, remained unaffected.

At least once a day Lalla Pyarelal came down to enquire if we were comfortable and whether we needed anything. Though all Indians are by nature so warmly hospitable that it might appear invidious to make comparisons between the people of different provinces in this respect, Punjabi hospitality is overwhelming even by Indian standards. In the case of our present host, his modest, almost diffident manner added to his attentions a grace which mere lavishness could never have commanded. He was, moreover, a man of genuine piety, and when, during one of his visits, we confided to him our spiritual aspirations, they met with a deeply sympathetic response.

One thing only Lalla Pyarelal could not provide us with, and that was warmth. With a wall of wet rock behind and a billowing sea of damp white mist below, and with our quarters themselves all stone, cement, and corrugated iron, it was not astonishing that for all the blankets he heaped upon us we shivered by night and froze by day, our chapped hands so stiff the fingers would hardly open and our feet like blocks of ice.

Whether because of the cold, or by way of natural progression, there stole over our meditations a peculiar numbness. Often we spent the whole session in a dull, semi-conscious twilight state from which we were aroused only when our heads jerked forward heavily onto our chests. Later we learned that this experience, known as *yoga-nidrā*, or yogic sleep, is quite a common one. Beginners are warned not to mistake it for the superconscious state of *samādhi*. It corresponds, in fact, to the subtle-physical world, or astral plane, and with practice, shadows may be discerned moving about in it as though in depths of gloomy water.

Our only means of getting warm was a brisk walk into town, but rain and drizzle (and I believe hail) at times conspired to prevent even this respite from the cold. Pandit-ji we seldom saw. Our ties with him had in fact loosened. Though he was bursting with plans, and doing his utmost to coax from the pockets of Lalla Pyarelal, and other business magnates of the town, funds for his Anandamayi Boarding School (there was now no talk of Buddhism), the more clearly we saw how rapidly he was drifting away from our previous objectives the feebler grew our enthusiasm. Besides, we had made other friends, and though we still felt a quasi-affection for the aged adventurer, who on his part continued to treat us with great kindness, now that we were beginning to have an insight into the true nature of his activities, we could not help sometimes preferring their company to his.

The most valuable of our new acquaintances was Dr Gurukipal Singh, a devout Sikh working on malaria control at the Central Research Laboratory, the possession of which constituted the town's sole title to fame. My own connection with him was closer than Satyapriya's, and there were long conversations on Sikhism in which my friend did not participate.

Once he took us to a lonely place on the outskirts of the town and showed us a tiny hermitage perched in isolation on a spur of rock. Here, observing a vow of complete silence, had lived for many years a great ascetic whom Dr Singh regarded as his guru. The wild, deserted spot, which we saw late one afternoon through a veil of thick mist and fine rain, was silent with an intense silence of that eerie, strangely vibrant quality one finds in long-used cremation grounds far from any human habitation. As we stood there, thinking of the occupant of the hermitage, about whom were related many strange tales, I became aware that there existed between the old recluse and me a bond of profound sympathy, an occult understanding, and that there were wings fluttering within me yearning to spread themselves in the same infinite sky as that wherein, scorning all earthly ties, he had made his ascent.

Though I remember clearly only Gurukipal Singh, we must have made other friends who, from a distance of so many years, merge into an anonymous collectivity, for on Independence Day, 15 August 1947, I was invited to address the public meeting that was held at Kasauli, as at every other place, whether city, town, or village, throughout the length and breadth of the newly born subcontinent. That even in such a remote place everybody could think it right and natural that an Englishman should be asked to speak on the great occasion showed not only how little room for bitterness there was in Mother India's heart now that independence had been achieved, but also with what nobility of spirit the struggle for it had been waged.

By ten o'clock the populace had mustered 2,000 strong in the town square. Though the sky had been overcast since early morning, the rising of a high wind had eventually swept away the clouds so that, on standing up to speak, I found myself in the midst of a sunlit expanse of dazzling white shirts and colourful turbans. In undemonstrative but unmistakably cheerful groups at the back of the crowd stood more than a hundred English men, women, and children. As the Indian tricolour fluttered up the flagpole in front of the rostrum, and the mounting excitement of the crowd exploded in deep-throated cheers, the joy that was reflected in all faces made it impossible to feel that any considered themselves losers in the struggle for independence.

Three days later Satyapriya and I celebrated our personal 'Independence Day'. Even at Kishengunj we had noticed that although Anandamayi's devotees generally treated Pandit-ji with all the respect due to his age and learning, he seemed to command no confidence whatever in matters organizational and financial. Indeed, on the eve of our departure one of the devotees, a retired government official, had taken us aside and quietly warned us that the old man had long been notorious for his dishonesty and that we should on no account allow ourselves to become involved in any of his schemes. We were being used, he declared, simply as bait for Pandit-ji's latest traps.

Unwilling to believe that a scholar could be a cheat and a liar, we had at the time dismissed this warning as the outcome of prejudice, if not of hostility towards Buddhism; but in both Raipur and Kasauli we were often given cause to remember it. A number of small incidents revealed to us Pandit-ji's utter lack of principle. Though not ungenerous in spending money, he was obviously quite unscrupulous as regards the means of its acquisition. He had, on his own admission, neither regular income nor permanent headquarters (his wife was living in destitution in Calcutta), and it was with growing horror that we realized he spent his time moving from place to place collecting, on one plausible pretext after another, funds that were never used for the purpose for which they had been donated. Only the good nature, or perhaps the indolence, of his victims, had saved him from prosecution. After discussing the matter with Lalla Pyarelal, who had been duped by Pandit-ji several years earlier, we felt that in leaving the Maha Bodhi Society we had jumped out of the frying-pan into the fire.

Dharmapriya (with beard) addressing crowd on Independence Day, Kausali, 15 August 1947

There was only one way out. Religious societies, organizations, and groups, far from being a help to spiritual development were only a hindrance. However lofty the ideals with which they were founded, they had a natural tendency to degenerate, in the hands of selfish human beings, into instruments for the acquisition of money, position, power, and fame. Instead of trying any longer to work with them we would follow the example of the Buddha and sever at one stroke our connection with an incorrigible world. We would renounce the household life and go forth into the life of homelessness as wanderers in search of Truth. For the last few months we had only sat hesitantly on the shore of the vast ocean of the spiritual life. Now, casting aside all fear, we would plunge boldly in.

Having made this resolution, we lost no time putting it into effect. With the help of a handful of *gerua-mati*, the reddish-brown earth used since time immemorial by Indian ascetics, we dyed our shirts and sarongs the traditional saffron of the world-renunciant. Suitcases and watches were sold, trousers, jackets, and shoes given away, identification papers destroyed. Apart from the robes that we were to wear we kept only a blanket each and our books and notebooks. As for the last three months hair and beard had been allowed to grow we did not need shaving tackle.

On the eve of our departure we went to bid farewell to Pandit-ji. Though he had not been entirely ignorant of our intentions, the emotions that distorted his venerable countenance now that our defection had become a reality were horrible to behold. Gone was the urbane mask. In its place were astonishment, rage, indignation, baffled greed, frustrated cunning, guilt surprised, and despair, all in conflict. More dreadful still were his desperate attempts to regain his composure. Despite his efforts to smile, to be affable, to wave aside our resolution as a boyish fancy, the mask kept slipping from his face and we saw again and again the face of a monster.

Eventually, optimistic and fertile of invention as ever, he expostulated with us for our perversity, our ungratefulness even, in thinking of deserting him at the moment when his plans were on the verge of fruition, when a large building was about to be donated for the Anandamayi Girls' School, and when Lalla Pyarelal and other wealthy merchants were on the point of placing at his disposal large sums of money. If we left, the whole scheme would be jeopardized. Out of consideration for his feelings, if for no other reason, he pleaded, we should at least postpone our departure for a few weeks, even a few days. But though we could not help feeling touched by his appeals we now knew him far too well to place any further reliance on his protestations and remained firm in our resolve. At last, not without tears, he allowed us to go.

Next morning, after joyfully donning our saffron robes, we walked feeling shy and rather conspicuous through the bazaar to Dr Gurukipal Singh's house. Lalla Pyarelal and other friends, though regarding our aspirations with sympathy, did not feel at all happy about our decision, which in their opinion was rash. Only Dr Singh wholeheartedly approved. With him, therefore, we had agreed to take breakfast before leaving Kasauli. Apart from one of his sons, a stalwart youth who accompanied us part of the way, our worthy Sikh friend, whose deep emotion when he wished us success in our quest both humbled and heartened us, was the last person to whom we spoke before setting out on foot along the ten-mile road that led to the plains.

Tibetan Buddhists believe that the appearance of a rainbow is one of the most auspicious of signs, and the biographies of their saints and yogis are replete with references to this phenomenon. Whether our 'going forth' on 18 August 1947 may be considered an auspicious event I cannot say, but it was certainly signalized by the appearance not of one but of scores of rainbows.

As we left Kasauli it was raining, but, as in the course of our descent we emerged from the clouds into the bright sunshine below, we saw arching the road, at intervals of a few dozen yards, not only single but double and triple rainbows. Every time we turned a bend we found more rainbows waiting for us. We passed through them as though through the multicoloured arcades of some celestial palace. Against the background of bright sunshine, jewel-like glittering raindrops, and hills of the freshest and most vivid green, this plethora of delicate seven-hued bows seemed like the epiphany of another world.

25
A QUESTION OF IDENTITY

On the afternoon of our second day of freedom, Satyapriya and I reached New Delhi, where we caught the first train to Madras. Our plan was to study Buddhism in Ceylon. Throughout the whole of the 1,000-mile journey the third-class compartment into which we had fought our way was so densely packed with passengers and luggage that each night, when we wanted to sleep, my friend and I had to scramble up onto a luggage-rack of such narrow dimensions that even one of us could hardly have slept there in comfort. What with the glare of ceiling lights, the suffocating closeness of the atmosphere, and the slamming of doors, shouting of coolies, shrieking of passengers, and blowing of whistles at every station – not to speak of the excruciating discomfort of our position – we slumbered but fitfully, so that when on the morning of the fourth day we reached Madras, great was our relief.

Though they had not been unaware of my inclinations, the swamis of the Ramakrishna Math, Mylapore, to which we went straight from the station, were astonished to see the young Englishman who, only eight months earlier, had visited them in a white tropical suit, now reappearing in the saffron robes of an Indian sadhu. Whether they were pleased at the sight of this sudden transformation or not they were too subtle to allow me to discern. But they received us kindly, and after showing us round the library and dispensary attached to the math, which Satyapriya had not seen before, left us to sleep off our weariness in the guest-house in a manner that suggested we were their guests for the next few days.

We had time, therefore, to visit the headquarters of the Theosophical Society at Adyar, only a mile from the math – where, from the wooded river bank, we watched the sun go down over the estuary – as well as the famous Mylapore beach, a flat two-mile stretch of firm sand up and down which we strolled until long after nightfall with one of the younger swamis, now discussing questions of religion and philosophy, now pausing to listen to the hiss of the breakers as with moonlit white crests they raced far up the beach.

There were also exchanges with the President Swami, an unusually reserved and taciturn Bengali, and with the young and brilliantly intellectual editor of the *Vedanta Kesari*, a Travancorean with whom, as a regular contributor to the magazine, I had long been in correspondence. While the President Swami neither approved nor disapproved explicitly of the step Satyapriya and I had taken, he clearly felt misgivings; but whether on account of our youth and inexperience or because we were going to Ceylon to study Buddhism instead of remaining in India to study Vedanta it was difficult to be sure. Nityabodhananda the editor, franker and more communicative, not only approved our project but asked me a number of questions relating to Buddhist philosophy. Like most Hindus, he had been puzzled by the *anātman* doctrine, the doctrine that there is in man no permanent unchanging 'soul' independent of the evanescent psychic states and processes, and I therefore strove to elucidate it for him. The article which, in consequence of our discussion, he asked me to contribute to his magazine, gave rise to a controversy with an orthodox Vedantin that continued for several years.[29]

Though fellow passengers in the train had eyed us curiously from time to time, one or two of them going so far as to ply Satyapriya with questions regarding our caste and nationality, it was at Madras that we were made to realize the great change that had taken place in our status and the responsibilities which this entailed.

The incident that more than any other precipitated, or at least underlined, this realization, was at the time a source of great embarrassment to us. One afternoon, while we were reading at the big round table in the hall of the math, two visitors entered. Thinking that, as people often did, they had come to pay their respects to Sri Ramakrishna's image in the shrine upstairs, we went on reading. But instead of going towards the staircase they turned in our direction and, before we could prevent them, prostrated themselves at our feet. This they certainly did not do out of regard for our personal sanctity, for in any case they had no means of knowing who we were, what we did, or whence we had come. Their prostration was the formal expression of the respect traditionally paid to the wearer of the saffron robe.

Years later, when I had mixed much with robes of all hues, and had heard notoriously unworthy members of the Buddhist monastic order justifying their claim to be treated with the utmost deference by the laity on the grounds that 'respect is paid to the robe, not to the wearer of the robe,' I could not help wondering to what point this contradiction between appearance and reality could be carried without seriously undermining the whole structure of Buddhism. Surely it is incumbent upon the monk to respect the robe he wears by striving to be an embodiment of the ideal it represents, instead of merely demanding that the laity should show their respect for it by falling prostrate at his feet. As far as Satyapriya and I were concerned, our first experience of people making obeisance to us simply on account of our dress was not only a demonstration of the undiminished strength of Indian religious traditions, but a pertinent reminder of our own obligations.

At the end of an uneventful journey from Madras down the tip of the peninsula to Dhanaskuti and thence, by sea, to Colombo, we met with an unexpected setback. We were not allowed to land in Ceylon. In the extravagance of our zeal for world-renunciation we had destroyed all our papers and were without means of establishing our identity. Moreover, having come to the conclusion that nationalism was one of the greatest evils of the modern world and that, in becoming homeless wanderers, we had renounced not only all domestic ties and social obligations but all national loyalties, Satyapriya and I had vowed never to admit that we belonged to a particular nationality.

To the polite but puzzled Sinhalese immigration officer who came on board to inspect the documents of the passengers, we stated that we were sadhus and that we had come to Ceylon to study Buddhism and to take, if possible, ordination as *bhikṣus*. When he enquired our nationality we replied that having renounced the world we had none. This reply, however philosophical, was of course from the official point of view entirely unsatisfactory. After a brief interrogation, in the course of which we reinforced our position with quotations from the Buddhist scriptures, he told us that we would have to return to India by the next boat. As the boat was not due to leave until early the following morning we asked permission to visit Colombo; but this he refused to allow.

Though we eventually found it impracticable to maintain in all its uncompromisingness the attitude we had adopted, I still consider it logical and right, and though, owing to the exigencies of the modern state, accommodations have had to be made, I cannot even now feel that I owe an exclusive loyalty to any nation or race. A *bhikṣu*, a member of the Buddhist monastic order, is, or should be, a citizen of the world, and his sole allegiance is to the Buddha, the Dharma, and the Sangha. As an adherent of this view I was often saddened, in later years, by the blatant nationalism of some Buddhist monks, who evidently felt that they were Ceylonese or Burmese first, and *bhikṣus* a very long way afterwards.

The following afternoon Satyapriya and I found ourselves back in the camp at Mandapam where, two days earlier, we had been vaccinated before embarkation. The camp consisted of a few tents and hutments scattered on the loose, grassless yellow sand among the *margosa* trees. Sitting in the shade cast by the dense, feathery green foliage of one of these handsome trees, the twigs of which supply the South Indian with his morning toothbrush, we reviewed our position.

The collapse of our plan to study Buddhism in Ceylon did not unduly dismay us. Indeed, in the mood of spiritual exaltation which had persisted all the way from Kasauli we felt that it might turn out to have been providential – a feeling the cooler judgement of later years confirms. But now that the road to Ceylon was blocked where were we to go? Whose the idea was I do not remember, but we eventually decided to take the train back to Madura, go from there to Cape Comorin, the southernmost point of the whole peninsula, and then walk from Cape Comorin to the Himalayas, a distance of nearly 2,000 miles. Wherever we happened to halt for the night we would meditate as usual, for both of us were convinced that without regular meditation spiritual life was meaningless. Besides testing our powers of endurance and the strength of our renunciation, the venture would have the advantage of giving us constant opportunities of intimate contact with the Indian people.

26
ŚRAMAṆA VERSUS BRĀHMAṆA

Madura is one of the great pilgrimage centres of South India. Having left the station, Satyapriya and I were wandering in the streets of the town when we were accosted by a portly, rather light-skinned Tamil Brahmin wearing a spotless white sarong and with the upper part of his body bare save for a small, neatly folded towel over the right shoulder and a thick new sacred thread. The front half of his head had been shaved and the remaining hair dressed in a long, glossy bun. Addressing us in excellent English, with folded hands, he invited us in the most courteous manner to take lunch at his house. In South India some orthodox Brahmins consider it a sin to eat without having first fed a guest, and the more punctilious, if none happens to present himself, stand at the door looking for one or even, as in the case of our host, go out into the highways and byways in search of a guest to invite. Sadhus and religious mendicants of any kind are particularly sought after.

 Thus it was that, half an hour later, we found ourselves seated on the floor in a cool dark room eating rice and curries while our host, as the ancient Indian custom is, squatted before us driving the flies away with a palm-leaf fan. Despite our remonstrances, he refused to begin his own meal until we had finished. As our eyes grew accustomed to the gloom, we saw that the room in which we sat was spotlessly clean and absolutely bare. So clean was the black flagstoned floor that had our lunch been served on it instead of on the customary section of plantain leaf we could have raised no objection.

Only when all three leaf-plates had been removed, and the floor washed by an anonymous female who emerged from the kitchen for this purpose and silently retired as soon as her task was done, did our host, in the friendliest manner, enquire who we were and whither we were bound. We returned the same answer that we had given the Sinhalese immigration officer, adding only that we were going to Cape Comorin with the intention of travelling on foot from there to the Himalayas. His curiosity not satisfied, for he was obviously doubtful whether I was a European or an unusually fair-complexioned North Indian, he therefore put to us, with apparent casualness, questions that were obviously designed to give him a clue to our nationality. Despite our manifest reluctance to reveal this all-important secret, his questions gradually became so pointed that the issue could no longer be evaded. We therefore frankly told him that it was improper to question a sadhu about his *pūrvāśrama* or 'previous stage of life'. With this blunt statement he at once agreed, and the matter dropped. Our uncommunicativeness did not prevent an exchange of views on less personal topics, and we soon discovered that our host, though limited by the prejudices of his caste, was pious, intelligent, and informative. As he urged us not to leave Madura without seeing the famous temple, promising to accompany us thither next morning, we eventually accepted his invitation to stay with him for two or three days.

One cannot be long in Madura before hearing the name of Tirumal Nayak. This seventeenth-century monarch, the greatest and most famous of his line, not only constructed the present temple for Minakshi, the 'Fish-Eyed' goddess, and her consort Somasundara, the 'Moon-Beautiful', but built a palace for himself and excavated a bathing-tank for the people as well. Even in South India, where taste traditionally favours an almost Egyptian architectural gigantism, these structures are remarkable no less for their beauty than for their colossal proportions. Guidebooks doubtless give the height of the *gopurams*, or gate-towers, through which we passed, courtyard by courtyard, into the inner precincts of the temple; but in place of facts and figures, all that remains in my mind are vague recollections of a morning spent in exploring a Brobdingnagian world of architecture and sculpture of such ponderous floridity, such massive exuberance, that I felt simultaneously overwhelmed by its size and wearied by its opulence. More precious were the moments when, after being led by our host through narrow passages seemingly chiselled out of the rock, we emerged from the darkness into a blaze of lights and found ourselves in the inmost sanctuary of the temple. So heavily were they loaded with jewels and flower-garlands, to which we added our own (one of the priests offering it on our behalf), that we could see no more than the painted staring eyes of the two images. Flowers and split coconuts littered the floor. The atmosphere of the place was strangely heavy as if with the vibrations of a supernatural presence.

Though smaller, in the sense of covering fewer acres of land, Tirumal Nayak's palace was, by reason of its unornamented severity of style, even more imposing. Experts, I believe, consider it one of the finest specimens of Hindu civic architecture in the whole of India. To me the simplicity of its enormous white columns and lofty horseshoe arches stood in as striking a contrast to the temple's riot of ornamentation as a statue of a young Greek god by Praxiteles does to a painting of a group of naked Flemish Bacchantes by Rubens.

Even simpler, and no less beautiful of its own kind, was the tank a quarter of a mile square, in the midst of which stood an island green with trees where, as a refuge from the heat, the king had built for himself, his queens, and his concubines a two-storeyed pavilion of white stone.

On our return from the island, where we had spent half an hour on the pavilion roof enjoying the cool breeze, we saw coming from the direction of the temple a milling mass of people in the midst of which, like a queen bee in the midst of a swarm of workers, rode a small palanquin containing, we were told, the lavishly bejewelled images of the two presiding deities. Evidently it was one of the more important of those festivals, so popular in South India, when images are treated to an airing by their worshippers, for the crowd appeared to be at least tens of thousands strong. As it passed quite close to the tank we were soon caught up in its less densely packed fringes, but so vast was the crowd, and so tightly jammed together its nucleus of excited devotees, that we found it impossible to get within a hundred yards of the palanquin. Abandoning the struggle, we stood aside and watched the hawkers who had set up their stalls in the midst of the crowd which, now that there was no room for the palanquin to advance, was slowly milling round it like a great wheel revolving on its hub. On a ridge barely clear of the crowd a man was selling what appeared to be enormous white dolls with red hair and black eyes. These, we were informed, represented Sitala, the dread goddess of smallpox, a fresh figure of whom, for purposes of domestic worship, or rather of propitiation, was bought by the people of the locality every year on the occasion of this festival.

Before we left Madura our introduction to some of the forms assumed by popular South Indian Hinduism was complemented by an initiation into certain aspects of South Indian religious psychology. Our host was undoubtedly a very worthy person, but not many discussions had taken place between us when we realized that he was the victim of an odd kind of inferiority complex that is, I now believe, peculiar to a certain type of Hindu. Our suspicions were not all at once excited. When he expatiated on the strictness with which he performed his religious duties, how punctiliously he worshipped his household gods, how regular he was in prayer, meditation, and scriptural study, how generous to the poor, how pure in conduct, we felt that these rather naive revelations indicated merely frankness and simplicity of heart. At every fresh confession of goodness and piety we therefore nodded our concurrence. Even when, encouraged by our approval, he declared that he in fact lived like a sadhu and that his house was really an ashram we did not demur. Only then was what had been all the time at the back of his mind allowed to escape his lips.

'Then what difference is there between you and me?' he demanded. 'How can you consider yourselves better than I am?'

No sooner had our host spoken these words than there ensued between him and Satyapriya, who took the questions as a personal challenge, a long, inconclusive, and at times almost acrimonious argument. My own views on the subject have remained unchanged. That a man's intrinsic worth is not dependent upon his profession, and that, in any religion, individual laymen may be better men than certain of the priests or monks to whom, by virtue of their office, they are obliged to pay formal respect, seems a truth so obvious as to be hardly deserving the dignity of explicit statement.

What Satyapriya and our host were really arguing about, though neither fully realized it, was whether world-renunciation was indispensable to higher spiritual development. Their divergent attitudes represented a continuation, in modern times, of the mutual antagonism between *brāhmaṇa* and *śramaṇa* – that polarization of spiritual life between the twin ideals of world-fulfilment and world-renunciation – between the principles of immanence and transcendence – to which the Theravādin Pāli scriptures bear witness, and which was finally resolved only by the Mahāyāna in its ideal of the infinitely wise and boundlessly compassionate bodhisattva. For though, since the time of Shankara, the great non-dualist philosopher and reformer, Hinduism has incorporated elements derived from Buddhist monasticism, many South Indian Brahmins, especially those who cling to the ancient traditions of their caste, tend to look upon the existence even of Hindu holy men and ascetics as a threat to their own supremacy.

It was, perhaps, in an attempt to 'contain' monasticism that they formulated in medieval times the doctrine that world-renunciation – according to their scheme of an ideal society the fourth 'stage of life' – should be entered upon only by Brahmins who had spent twenty-five years in each of the three previous 'stages of life'. Kshatriyas or members of the warrior caste might proceed only as far as the third stage, retirement to the forest; Vaishyas or merchants and traders as far as the second, that of family life; while Shudras or serfs, who constituted the lowest caste, were entitled to the second only, excluding the first stage, that of scriptural study, which was open only to members of the three highest castes. Though this scheme could not always be rigidly enforced, even under the most orthodox Hindu kings, it was nevertheless the basis of a vigorous attempt to restrict world-renunciation to members of the Brahmin caste, thus in effect making the ascetic merely a species of Brahmin. In the course of our wanderings Satyapriya and I were more than once to encounter Brahmins who showed respect only to Brahmin ascetics.

Our host, of course, did not go as far as this. Despite the radical difference of opinion that had been disclosed, he continued to treat us with generous hospitality, and when the time came for us to set out on the next stage of our journey his last farewells had all the courtesy, and many times the warmth, of his first greeting.

Between Madura and Cape Comorin lies the town of Tinnevelly, headquarters of the district of that name. Here we had our first experience of South Indian sanitary habits. Having risen before dawn, as we wanted to catch the first bus, Satyapriya and I, *lota* in hand, stole while it was still dark to the river bank, for South Indian houses, as we had already discovered at Madura, are not provided with latrines. Whoever it was had accommodated us for the night obligingly showed the way.

We were still crouching on the sandflats when dawn broke and the broad river, hitherto unseen, returned a grey gleam to the sky. Rising to our feet, we saw on every side along the whole length of the river, thousands of men, women, and children squatting almost elbow to elbow on the sand, all with a brass *lota* at their side. Most were simultaneously cleaning their teeth with *margosa* twigs. At the river's edge some, with garments hitched, were dashing water between their buttocks; while others, further out, stood waist-deep in it either scraping their tongues with loud hawking noises or saying their morning prayers with faces turned towards the now risen sun. Whether there exists, in South Indian music or poetry, an *aubade* consonant with the mood of this very characteristic scene I do not know; but we did discover, on returning to the town, that the Tamil name for this befouled stretch of water meant 'The Golden River'.

27
THE TEMPLE OF THE VIRGIN GODDESS

Cape Comorin presented a very different spectacle from Tinnevelly. On descending from the bus, which had halted on a ridge less than a hundred yards from the seashore, we rubbed our eyes in amazement. At our feet lay a vast expanse of violet water. Above, shading from palest cornflower blue at the horizon up to deep indigo in the zenith, stretched pure and cloudless a sapphire infinity of sky. Poised between sea and sky there hung in the west the flamingo-red globe of the setting sun, in the east the golden-white disc of the rising full moon. Their reflections, making a dazzling track across the intervening oceans, merged in one indistinguishable blaze of splendour. Mild silver and furious gold celebrated nuptials on the violet water. For nearly an hour we watched. Sea and sky grew one darkness, relieved above by a million scintillating stars, below by innumerable fragmentary silver reflexes of the moon which, as it climbed higher, threw long black shadows behind us onto the white sand.

    Apart from its temple, the place wherefrom we had decided to set out on our trek to the Himalayas was little more than a village, so that our descent from the bus had been marked by practically the whole population. On returning from the beach we were therefore intercepted by five or six persons who, after making the usual enquiries, conducted us to a small library and reading room nearby. Here, having served us coffee in tiny brass tumblers, they brought various Tamil delicacies on plantain leaves for our supper and made arrangements for us to pass the night on the floor. So kind were these new friends, at whose invitation we stayed at the library for four or five days, that I regret not being able to remember a single one of them individually. Perhaps, as I was then new to the South, the extreme blackness of their complexions, so many shades darker than those of the North Indians, made them look all alike to me.

The temple of Kanya Kumari, the Virgin Goddess, is a place of no architectural pretensions. When, escorted by our friends, Satyapriya and I walked there the next morning over a stretch of loose silver sand, we found ourselves beneath a massive wall painted with alternate red and white vertical stripes. Compared to those of Madura, the *gopurams* were mean and rudimentary. At the entrance, as the custom is in South India, we removed our shirts, it being considered disrespectful to appear before the Deity with the upper half of the body covered. Mindful of my experiences at Dakshineshwar and Raipur, I had enquired on the way, through Satyapriya, whether the temple was open to everybody. There were certainly restrictions, our friends admitted. Low-caste Hindus, Christians, Muslims, and Europeans were prohibited from entering the sacred precincts. But these restrictions, they hastened to add, did not apply to us, for we were sadhus and as such superior to all distinctions of caste and nationality.

On passing through the gate, which seemed to be a side entrance cut in the wall, we found ourselves first in a series of gloomy passages and then, after we had groped our way down flights of stone steps, in a dark tunnel lit by flares placed at intervals along the walls. Such was the atmosphere of the place that I felt as though I was in the Labyrinth or the Catacombs or even, as we advanced farther and made another descent, in the very bowels of the earth. Simultaneously, with so strong a sense of incredible ancientness was I affected, that I felt borne not only downward in space but backward in time – back thousands, even hundreds of thousands, of years, to the time when, at the dawn of the Stone Age perhaps, men had first worshipped the Virgin Mother on this spot.

These impressions were intensified as we emerged from the tunnel into a square chamber which, in the red glare of wall-torches, appeared hollowed out of rock. Presently, however, when my eyes had become accustomed to the gloom, I noticed that the roof was supported by rude pillars. We were, I reflected, not so far underground as I had imagined;

perhaps the chamber ... But before reflection could dissipate my original impressions, a kettledrum started throbbing and a hautboy wailing with such violence that the reverberations, in that confined space, were deafening. Fifteen or twenty people, their black bodies glistening with oil, now stood expectantly before the small door opposite. Most waited with folded hands; the lips of some moved as though in prayer. When the weird, savage, yet strangely imploring racket of drum and hautboy had continued for fifteen minutes there was a sudden awful silence in which the devotees with moving lips could be heard praying with loud voices. The small door flew open. Everybody fell prostrate in adoration. Within, amidst a blaze of lights, stood the black stone goddess, while a priest stationed to the left of the altar rotated before her face a ceremonial lamp with five flames.

Afterwards we were told that in the centre of the goddess's forehead was an enormous diamond of such brilliance that when, on stormy nights, the inner and outer gates of the temple, which faced south, were thrown open, it served as a beacon for ships far out at sea. Either because this jewel was part of a head-dress used only on special occasions, or because it had been stolen centuries earlier, or simply because of the weakness of our faith, we failed to perceive it.

Having seen the temple, we had exhausted the man-made attractions of Cape Comorin. But nature's attractions of sea and sky were inexhaustible. Much of our time was spent down at the beach, either bathing or scrambling over the rocks that separated the sand-strewn bays, or simply sitting near the edge of the water watching the dancing-in of waves and listening to the thunder of the surf. Sometimes the sea was rough, sometimes smooth, but whether rough or smooth it always boiled dangerously among a group of rocks situated perhaps a hundred yards from the shore. The last of these was known as Vivekananda's Rock, as it is said that the famous apostle of Vedanta once swam out to it and spent the day there.

No sooner did he hear of this exploit than Satyapriya was fired by a spirit of emulation. Despite my expostulations, he plunged into the breakers and was soon swimming strongly out to sea. Five minutes later, to my relief, I saw a black head bobbing out of the foamy water that swirled round the base of the rock and a pair of brown arms struggling to get a purchase on its sheer side. Hauling himself up to the top of the rock, he afterwards told me, had been far more difficult and exhausting than swimming out to it. Eventually, however, he succeeded, and as he stood on the highest point waving his hand I heard above the roar and crash of waves a faint halloo. Not caring to spend the day on the rock like his famous predecessor, he sat there until he was rested and then swam back.

On one of our expeditions along the beach we discovered a knot of men extracting salt from sea-water by primitive methods that must have been in use for thousands of years. Large canvases were loosely suspended on all sides from four-foot stakes so that they sagged in the middle to form a receptacle. Into this receptacle were emptied buckets of sea-water which, seeping through the bottom, left behind a grey deposit. This unpromising product was then refined, by processes no less crude, into row upon glistening row of salt-mounds that rivalled the sand in whiteness.

When not down on the beach we were in the library, which had become our abode, and whither our meals were brought. One morning, over the coffee and plantains, our friends told us that they were so fortunate as to have a *jivanmukta* living in Cape Comorin. Now a *jivanmukta*, according to the Advaita Vedanta, is one who, by realizing his essential non-duality with the attributeless *brahman*, has in this life won complete freedom from all the illusions and passions that make for rebirth. Satyapriya and I therefore insisted on going to see the liberated one immediately.

On the way our friends told us all that they knew about him. Of unknown antecedents, he had lived at Cape Comorin for several years. No one had ever seen him either eat or drink, though he smoked country cigarettes – and he dwelt under a tree. Utterly indifferent to heat and cold, summer and winter he wore only a *langoti* or jock-strap. Except to demand cigarettes, he never spoke. From the manner in which these descriptions were given, it appeared that the holy man was held in high esteem, and Satyapriya and I felt our excitement rising. But a disappointment awaited us. The *jivanmukta* was sitting beneath his tree, smoking a cigarette. Body and hair were covered with dust, so that it was difficult to judge his age; but he might have been fifty – or thirty-five or sixty. His features were coarse, his expression dull and bestial. He took no notice of us whatever. After gazing at him for a few minutes, as at an animal in a zoo, we returned to the library. He was, perhaps, a *hatha yogi* who, by means of certain psycho-physical exercises, had developed the power of living without food; but having made the acquisition of this power an end in itself had sunk to the level of a brute.

More interesting than this half-animated corpse was a photograph hanging inside the library above the door. Satyapriya and I often looked at it. The turbaned, sword-begirt figure in knee-length black coat and white breeches was obviously that of one accustomed to rule. But the face, though intelligent and resolute, showed a puffiness under the dark-ringed crafty eyes that gave to it a slightly sinister, almost cruel cast which, despite the full lips and noble brow, was not reassuring. One day Satyapriya and I asked our friends whose the photograph was. Our ignorance was greeted with exclamations of astonishment. Did we not recognize Sir C. P. Ramaswamy Iyer, maker of modern Travancore, twelve years Dewan, saviour of Hinduism, the brilliant legal intellect, the bold administrator, the profound philosopher, the orator of unrivalled eloquence? For several minutes the library rang with the great man's praises. But the praises were not unmixed with laments. Only the day before our arrival, we were informed, an attempt had been made to assassinate 'Sir C. P.' (as everybody called him), and though he had escaped with only a knife-wound in the cheek, the experience had so unnerved him that, conscious that he had more enemies in the state than friends, he had relinquished all his offices and left by plane.

During our year and a half's stay in Travancore we met many people who, while granting Sir C. P.'s ability, represented his character in darker colours than our Cape Comorin friends, all of whom were Tamils and most, like their hero, Tamil Brahmins. Christians, particularly, could not paint him black enough, for he had not only stemmed the tide of conversions by means of the famous Temple Entry Proclamation and the Hindu Mission but had also, most unforgivable offence of all, ordered the greatest of their banks to be closed. The figure that finally emerged from these conflicting reports was what, after seeing the library photograph, one might have expected. Sir C. P. was evidently a bold, brilliant, efficient, unscrupulous, amoral autocrat whom absolute power had corrupted absolutely. Wherever we went in Travancore, we found no improvement, and few mischiefs, for which he had not been responsible.

Before we set out from Cape Comorin, Satyapriya procured for us two six-foot bamboo poles. So long as we travelled by train and bus the two bundles with which we had left Kasauli seemed not only small and light, but the absolute minimum of luggage; but with the prospect of walking hundreds of miles before us we began to realize that despite our world-renunciation we still possessed much that was superfluous. The heaviest part of our load being books, we presented a few volumes to the library. Satyapriya's idea was that when our arms were tired the bundles could be suspended over our shoulders from the poles. The poles would also serve to support our steps and as a defence against village curs, wild beasts, and robbers.

Five days after our arrival, therefore, we bade farewell to our kind friends, who had assembled at the library to see us off and, shouldering our poles and bundles with light hearts, stepped out briskly along the road to Trivandrum, the capital of Travancore, fifty miles away.

28
THE ROAD TO TRIVANDRUM

Satyapriya had estimated that, travelling by easy stages and allowing time to visit places of religious importance on the way, it might take us two years to reach the Himalayas. Such a prospect we did not find in the least daunting. With the open road before us, and the consciousness that our life as wandering ascetics had at last truly begun, we were in fact both in a highly elated mood. The period of false starts and delays was over. We now had a definite objective, the attainment of which was only a matter of time. This knowledge gave fresh meaning to our existence, directing all our energies into a single channel, and adding, as it were, wings to our feet.

For the first hour the going was pleasant enough. But as the sun ascended we began to feel hot and tired. Our bundles, so small and light to the eye that morning, felt heavy as lead, and for the first time in my life I wished that I possessed fewer books. When my arm started aching, I slung the bundle over my shoulder, and when the heavy bamboo began chafing my collar bone I transferred the ever weightier bundle now to my right hand, now to my left. As, with each change of position, my arm started aching, and my collar bone paining me more quickly than before, I was soon shifting the bundle every few minutes. Meanwhile, my feet had blistered and I started to limp. Satyapriya, though stronger and sturdier than I, was also feeling the strain. In this sorry state we entered our first village. It had been our intention to allow ourselves a short rest, but as we plodded wearily past the single row of mean huts, the inhabitants, who from their dress we recognized as Muslims, shouted and jeered at us with such obvious ill-nature that we did not stop. Late that night we staggered into the town of Nagercoil.

In the public hall at Nagercoil, as in the library at Cape Comorin, we awoke beneath the dark-ringed eyes of Sir C. P., whose picture occupied the place of honour here also. They greeted us every morning for a week, for in Nagercoil we made numerous friends, some of whom not only invited us to their houses but made arrangements for me to deliver, in the same hall, a series of lectures on Indian philosophy and religion. Yet the town must have been less interesting than Cape Comorin for, like the frescoes of a ruined temple of which, after centuries of exposure to the elements, there remains but half a pensive face, a fragment of upraised arm, a patch of darker background, whatever impressions I had of it have long since faded. My most vivid recollection is of having my blistered foot attended to in the 'dispensary' (as a doctor's surgery is called in India) of a medical practitioner who was attending the lectures.

Nagercoil, though falling within predominantly Malayalam-speaking Travancore, was a Tamil-speaking town, and we were not in it many days before becoming aware that there existed throughout the state a strong feeling of hostility between the two groups; the Tamils, who originally hailed from Madras, being regarded by the Malayali majority as interlopers and aliens. Antagonism between Brahmins and non-Brahmins was also pronounced. Like most South Indian towns, Nagercoil had its Brahmin street, and my second most vivid recollection is of being taken to view this sociological curiosity.

Undeniably it was the neatest and cleanest street in town, and the most picturesque. The fronts of the tiny houses were painted with red and white vertical stripes like a temple (Brahmins being considered 'gods on earth'), while the broad cowdung-smeared space in front of each door was covered with an astonishing variety of delicately beautiful geometrical designs executed in a white paste made from powdered rice. Until recent times, we were told, non-Brahmins were prohibited by law from passing through this street, and though the legal sanction had been withdrawn, so strong was the force of religious tradition that, with few exceptions, non-Brahmins even now continued scrupulously to respect this absurd prohibition.

In Suchindram, halfway between Nagercoil and Trivandrum, we spent only one or two days. Much smaller, older, and quieter than Nagercoil, it was a curiously lifeless place. Bathing in the deep green waters at the bottom of an ancient stone tank, from whose crumbling sides grew tufts of grass and small bushes, we felt alone in a noiseless world.

Most of the afternoon was spent exploring the adjacent temple, a fine old building where in a kind of cloister, from which opened several small chapels, we discovered stone slabs bearing inscriptions in archaic characters. Against the pillars stood life-size female figures who cupped their hands against protuberant breasts to make receptacles for the oil in which lighted wicks were placed at night. We also discovered several multiple columns, polished to such smoothness that it felt as if one was fingering human flesh. When struck, their different sections emitted various musical notes.

In ancient times, we were told, a *devadasi* would dance from the temple gates up through the hall between these columns to the doors of the sanctuary. As they could be played upon like a musical instrument, the accompaniment would be taken up on each pair of columns as she passed between, so that the dancer seemed to be carrying the music with her as she advanced. Both music and dance were, of course, for the entertainment of the Deity living in the temple. Who this was I have forgotten: probably it was a goddess; but I remember we were told, by the same informant, that she was famous throughout South India for her enormous appetite. Forty maunds, or more than one and a half tons, of rice were cooked every day and ritually offered to her.

The Ramakrishna Mission literature I had read, and swami friends with whom I had discussed the subject, emphasized that no Hindu worshipped images: images were merely symbols of the Absolute. Both, following Swami Vivekananda, pointed out to the ignorant Westerner that the Hindu's respect for an image was analogous to a son's respect for his father's picture, and that only the most ignorant confused the symbol with the thing symbolized. However much this rationalistic explanation may suffice for image-worship in certain schools of Buddhism, it is a complete distortion of Hindu beliefs and observances. The image in a Hindu temple, once consecrated, is invariably regarded as a living being. The temple is its personal abode, and the daily ritual worship consists simply in offering it whatever is necessary to life. Like a king, it must be awoken in the morning with music. It must be bathed, clothed, and decorated with flower-garlands and jewels. It must be entertained with song and dance, taken for periodical outings (as at Madura) and on ceremonial visits to other gods. Above all, it must be fed. Whenever an image is installed, Brahmin priests perform a *prāṇapratiṣṭhā* or 'life-giving' ceremony. Those responsible for the establishment and endowment of the temple are then informed what quantity of cooked food will be required to sustain the life thereby infused into the image. The more *jagrat* or 'awake' it is, the more sustenance must be given. South Indian temples were endowed with vast estates by ancient Hindu kings simply in order to satisfy, out of their produce and revenues, the inordinate appetite of their deities. What really happened to the enormous food offerings we discovered only in Trivandrum.

Meanwhile, we continued our journey. This took us to a hill known as Silver Mountain, sacred to Murugam, the ancient Tamil god of war, where we spent two days with a Hindu ascetic, and to Padmanabhapuram, the ancient seat of the rulers of Travancore. Of the latter there remained little more than the old palace, a magnificent structure built entirely of wood. We spent several hours exploring the finely carved chambers. In one stood a couch of black marble for the hot weather; in another, two full-length silver mirrors, so tarnished that they showed only fragments of our reflections. Most interesting of all was the long, low first-floor gallery with the 'elephant windows' through which the monarch used to step onto the back of the tusker standing in the courtyard below. Other places too we visited; but as though in a dream. Eventually, footsore and weary, we reached the capital.

29
WHAT HAPPENED TO THE OFFERINGS

Though not strikingly beautiful, Trivandrum, with its trees and gardens and open spaces, is certainly one of the most attractive cities in India. But at the time of our arrival we had no eye for its charms. Our first thought was for accommodation. This we eventually found in an outlying suburb under the hospitable roof of the local branch of the Ramakrishna Mission. What the two resident swamis thought when they first saw us I do not know, but we were given a courteous reception and assigned quarters in an unfinished building of bright red laterite blocks. After a bath and a meal we talked. When our hosts discovered that Satyapriya and I were well known to their brethren at Belur Math and elsewhere, and that I was familiar with the whole of the Mission literature, their courtesy warmed into cordiality, and the conversation, which had been confined to generalities, took a more serious, personal turn. Though by no means saints, both were pious, learned, and cultured men with a firm faith in the regenerating power of India's ancient spiritual ideals. One indeed, I already knew by name as the author of a biography of Sarada Devi, Sri Ramakrishna's wife, whose disciple he had been. Friendly relations were therefore soon established. Besides being mines of information about the history, religion, culture, politics, and communities of Travancore (all of which were closely interconnected), they were able to advise us what places of interest there were to be seen in Trivandrum.

Every afternoon for the next few days, therefore, after an early lunch, we walked to the nearest bus stop and caught a red single-decker bus into town. When the conductor handed us our change we saw that it included several small unfamiliar coins. Travancore had its own currency which, though interchangeable with that of India, circulated only within the state. When we wanted to dispatch letters to Cape Comorin and Nagercoil we discovered that it was also served by its own postal system, called the Travancore Anchal, and issued a series of stamps bearing the head of the Maharaja. A feeling of quasi-independence from the newly born Indian Union – accession to which Sir C. P. had done his best to prevent – was indeed quite strong, and never, during our lengthy sojourn in the state, did we hear any of its inhabitants refer to himself as anything but a Travancorean.

The sights of Trivandrum were soon exhausted. After we had visited the miniature zoo, and the art gallery – where the small but representative collection, arranged by Dr James Cousins, revived for a few moments all my love of art – we had little to do but stroll down the wide avenues beneath flame-of-the-forest trees or take our ease on a bench in the public gardens. A visit to the public library was of interest only for a sign of the times that could be seen there: a life-size marble statue of Sir C. P. lying broken beside its pedestal in the courtyard. One afternoon, as we were munching buns after paying a second visit to the lions and hippopotamuses, Satyapriya suddenly proposed that we should call on the Maharaja and the new Dewan. After briefly discussing the matter we walked to the Dewan's residence, which was not far from the gardens, and an appointment was made for ten o'clock the following morning.

In taking this step we were actuated not by mere respect for formalities, much less still by a desire of meeting the great. Our motive was strictly practical, stemming directly from the exigencies of the life to which we had so recently dedicated ourselves. Our chief desire was to meditate. But our experience during the previous three weeks had demonstrated, on our own minds and bodies, that the regular practice of meditation cannot be combined with a daily trek of ten or twelve miles. Due to fatigue and other reasons, since our departure from Cape Comorin we had not once sat for meditation as we had been doing in Kishengunj, at Raipur, and at Kasauli. Prior to this débâcle we had entertained no suspicion that – as further experience abundantly confirmed – for all save the highly advanced, a life of meditation and a life of strenuous physical, or even externally directed activity, are mutually exclusive. After discussing our problems with the swamis, who listened sympathetically, we had therefore decided to interrupt, if not to abandon, our plan of walking to the Himalayas and instead to search in Travancore itself for a quiet corner where, undisturbed, we might continue the practice of *ānāpānasati*. It was these ideas which, simmering in Satyapriya's brain, had suddenly boiled over in his proposal that we should call on the ruler of the state and the head of administration.

Next morning, after waiting for a few minutes in the vestibule among pots of palms, we were ushered into the Dewan's office. A rather short, stout, grey-haired man rose from his desk to receive us. When we were all seated a pleasant conversation ensued. The Dewan, who was a Hindu though not a Brahmin, seemed not only interested in religion but well informed regarding the various cults which flourished in Travancore. From him we first heard of Ayyappan, a god whom many regarded as being in reality the Buddha. This of course greatly interested us, and we promised to devote ourselves to making researches into the subject. The main object of our visit being to safeguard our meditations from possible interruptions, we then enquired whether there would be any objection to our spending a few months in Travancore. There was no objection at all, the Dewan told us; we could stay as long as we liked. As for meeting the Maharaja, about which we had also asked, arrangements would have to be made through his private secretary.

This functionary, a little man of about sixty, half gnome and half bird, we met in his office at the palace. Having been installed during Sir C. P.'s regime he was, of course, a Tamil Brahmin. His gay, almost frisky manners, were in great contrast to the dignified politeness of the Dewan, and we were soon chatting like old friends. We told him our history, from the time that we had left Kasauli, and though I do not know how his name came up, it transpired that he knew Pandit-ji. Five or six years earlier the old scholar had descended on Trivandrum with elaborate plans for a Hindu religious and cultural organization, wheedled funds from Sir C. P., and then vanished. During the next few years we heard this story so often, and in so many places, that in the end we thought it wiser never to mention Pandit-ji's name. Conversation then turned to Ayyappan. When we repeated the Dewan's remark that this popular divinity was really the Buddha, the private secretary's little claw-like hands were at once raised in protest. Certainly not, he declared, shaking his big bald head, Ayyappan was a Tamil god, the guardian of the fields.

Presently, with canary-like fervour, he started singing the Maharaja's praises. The young ruler, it seemed, was the best of princes, handsome and intelligent, and of so spiritual a disposition that though thirty-five years old he was not only still unmarried but a celibate. After this paean Satyapriya and I were more eager than ever to meet the Maharaja, whose sympathy we thought might contribute to the success of our new plan. But when we raised the question of an audience the little private secretary shook his head firmly. Owing to recent political developments in the state it was not considered advisable for His Highness to meet anyone from outside for another two or three weeks. We must have looked disappointed, for he immediately added that, if we liked, arrangements could be made for us to have a glimpse of the Maharaja in the Padmanabhaswami Temple, whither he repaired every morning to pay his respects to the tutelary deity of the ruling family. With this concession we had to be content.

At 9.30 next morning we took up our station to one side of the pillared hall through which the Maharaja would have to pass on his way to the inner sanctuary of the temple. With us on duty stood an official of the Ecclesiastical Endowments Department, to whom the private secretary had given us a letter of introduction. While we waited, this official explained that Padmanabhaswami was a form of Vishnu, and that the founder of the dynasty having once gifted to him all his domains, the rulers of Travancore were in theory only the representatives of the god, who was the *de jure* owner of the state.

He also related a story about Sir C. P. which, he said, was characteristic of the man. A fire had broken out inside the temple, and it was feared that the images would be destroyed. Two young English police officers in the service of the state volunteered to rescue them; but the priests objected, for in their eyes this would have involved the desecration of the images and the pollution of the whole temple. Sir C. P., who was as good a Brahmin as they, silenced their objections with the remark, 'Let the images be rescued first. You can perform the purification ceremonies afterwards.' He also rewarded the two volunteers handsomely for their bravery.

Punctually at ten o'clock, amidst much saluting of police inspectors and bowing low of temple officials, the Maharaja made his appearance, and, preceded by a file of dignitaries, one of whom bore the ceremonial fly whisk, walked with rapid steps towards the sanctuary. Fair-skinned, of medium height, and well built, he wore only a voluminous white dhoti, and his hands were clasped to his naked breast as though in prayer. As the little procession advanced, he glanced from side to side as if searching for someone, seemed to recognize us, and without pausing bowed deeply in our direction. Probably his private secretary had told him we would be there. The next moment he was within the sanctuary, through the door of which we saw him first circumambulate the god thrice, then chant a hymn before the altar while the priests performed the ritual. Not being a Brahmin, he was not entitled to perform it himself.

Later, having seen the Maharaja make his exit, we found out what happens to the food-offerings made in South Indian temples. Our friend of the Ecclesiastical Endowments Department, who had constituted himself our guide, led us through courts and colonnades to a large pillared hall where, in rows on the stone floor, sat not fewer than a thousand Brahmins – adolescents, grown men, and dotards – all with sacred threads, half-shaven crowns, and either pigtails or buns. In front of each was a plantain leaf. As we watched, servitors started running up and down the rows with brass buckets, pausing an instant in front of each man or boy to deposit on his leaf a generous helping of rice, lentils, or curry. The buckets, we saw, were filled from a dozen gigantic cauldrons standing together in one corner. On going over to look at them Satyapriya and I found that most of them were not less than six feet in diameter. The contents of each were of the richest type, such as middle-class Indian families can afford to prepare only on the occasion of weddings. As our guide remarked, only the best could be offered to God. From the loud smacking and sucking noises with which the thousand Brahmins were tackling their daily free meal it seemed they would have concurred heartily in this statement.

With Hinduism so obviously organized to the social and economic advantage of the Brahmins, it was natural that some of those who declined to recognize them as 'gods on earth' should also repudiate the religion that accorded them this exalted status. Nearly half the population of the state was Christian. Nairs, though still nominally Hindu, were on the whole strongly anti-Brahmin. Among the Eazhavas, a large and important Untouchable community, there was a definite movement in the direction of Buddhism. These facts were elicited from our first Eazhava friend, a grizzled, middle-aged man who accosted us a few days later as we were walking in the city and enquired if we were *bhikkhus*. We were not *bhikkhus*, we told him, but we were Buddhists; in fact, we were *anagārikas*, or homeless wanderers, who hoped by leading such a life for a couple of years to qualify themselves for ordination as *bhikkhus*. Delighted by this reply, he at once invited us to his house, which stood in a grove of incredibly tall coconut palms outside the city.

Though describing himself as a Buddhist, our host seemed to have no knowledge whatever of the Buddha's teaching. About his passion for Buddhism, however, there could be no doubt. Twenty years earlier, he told us, when a Malayalam translation of *The Light of Asia* had aroused the interest of many Eazhavas, he had founded a Buddhist organization and brought a *bhikkhu* from Ceylon to preach the Dharma. Unfortunately, the *bhikkhu* had shown more concern for his own creature comforts than enthusiasm for his pastoral duties, and his demands eventually became so unreasonable that he had to be sent back to Ceylon. Twenty years earlier! In twenty years, if the *bhikkhu* had been of the right type, an organization could have been built up in Trivandrum that would have diffused the influence of Buddhism throughout the entire state. Instead, our friend's organization had foundered, he himself lost confidence in the sangha, and opportunity, not having been seized by the forelock, thereafter presented a bald noddle. So many variations on this theme did I afterwards hear, in different parts of the country, that I eventually concluded that *bhikkhus* from South-east Asia often did more harm than good to the cause of Buddhism in India.

After our failure to meet the Maharaja, or to interest our co-religionist in the starting of a new Buddhist organization, we realized the impossibility of presuming any longer on the hospitality of the Ramakrishna Ashram, where we had already spent ten days. At the suggestion of the swamis, who had followed all our moves with kindly interest, we decided to make our way north to Kalady, the birthplace of Shankara, where the Mission had another branch. The swami-in-charge, they thought, who was single-handed, might welcome our cooperation and allow us to stay in his ashram.

The days which followed our departure from Trivandrum possess, in recollection, a curiously dream-like quality. My most vivid memory is of the middle part of our journey, which saw us make the fifty mile boat trip up through the famous Travancore backwaters from Quilon to Alleppey. On green islands and strips of beach on either hand grew grove upon grove of coconut palms. Every few hundred yards we passed a fishing village, each comprising a group of bedraggled palm-leaf huts. Sometimes we saw the fishermen, shapely black figures naked but for the usual *langoti*, casting their finely-woven nets into the water from the prows of small boats. After every two or three villages appeared a large whitewashed building with a bright red roof which, though not out of place among the coconut palms, we instinctively felt was not of the soil. Only when a bell rang out from one of them did we realize they were churches. The Untouchable fisher-folk had been Christianized. Occasionally there drifted by a tangled mass of water-melons so dense as to seem like a green floating island, and once, towards evening, we glimpsed behind the palm groves on the western bank the sunlit waters of the Arabian Sea.

There remain also fainter, more fragmentary pictures.... A river wherein grew pink lotuses.... A house where we stayed two days and were given for breakfast a kind of roll made of ground rice and desiccated coconut steam-cooked in a bamboo and eaten with plantains.... Quiet little old-world towns where everybody seemed to know English.... Then eventually, after a period of blankness, we are found hesitating outside a small grey building flanked by a quaintly gabled shrine where, it being the time for evening service, there was in progress much ringing of bells and waving of lamps by light-skinned, intelligent-looking Brahmin boys with little pigtails and sacred threads: the Kalady Ashram.

Swami Agamananda, the incumbent, was a tall, elderly man with the rounded shoulders and pronounced stoop of the scholar. Though his eyes were small and close-set and his mouth somewhat large, the expression of his fair-complexioned face, with its plump, almost rubicund cheeks, was one of immense cheerfulness. As the Trivandrum swamis had guessed, he was in need of assistance, and welcomed us if not with open arms certainly with marked cordiality. The assistance was needed, though, not so much at Kalady as at Muvattupuzha, a town thirty miles distant, where the Mission had an ashram that had been long unoccupied. When he told us that, if we liked, we could go and stay there, we gratefully accepted his offer.

Two days later, having visited the temple of Sarada, the Goddess of Learning, which is said to mark the spot where Shankara was born, and with two or three books from the swami's well-stocked library under our arms, with lighter hearts we left for Muvattupuzha. The swami had not told us that the ashram had remained unoccupied because it was haunted.

30
THE TOWN OF THE THREE RIVERS

Muvattupuzha means 'the town of the three rivers'. A few minutes after entering the suburbs we rattled over a bridge and ground to a halt in front of a long rambling structure of wood and corrugated iron. This belonged to Ramaswami Iyer, the town's most prominent businessman, to whom Swami Agamananda had given us a letter of introduction. We met him in his office, a badly lighted room pervaded by the strong, almost sickening smell of lemon-grass oil, where five or six clerks were at work among ancient typewriters and dusty racks full of dog-eared files. Tins of kerosene were stacked against the wooden partition wall on the left. Ramaswami Iyer, who occupied a desk facing the door, was in complexion, dress, and hairstyle the typical Tamil Brahmin; only in his vocation was he atypical. Though the expression with which he greeted us was bland and affable to the point of smugness, I noticed in all his movements a distinct nervous agitation. When we had finished explaining the circumstances that brought us to Muvattupuzha, and the purpose for which we wished to stay at the ashram, he not only expressed approval but promised sympathy and support, and after offering us some light refreshments sent a man with us to show us the way.

The road, which was in reality a broad track of beaten earth, followed the course of one of the rivers, the waters of which we sometimes glimpsed at the bottom of the flights of uneven steps that ran down to its banks in between the high mud walls of the houses on our left. Sometimes we passed well-timbered structures standing back from the road in spacious compounds. *Jak* trees were plentiful, their enormous lumpy green fruits, often as big as small bolsters, hanging in clusters just out of reach on the stalwart trunks and sturdy branches. At the confluence of the three rivers the road turned right and passed through the cool, shady precincts of the Brahmin quarter. Opposite this, on the other side of another river, stood the ashram; but as it could not be forded at that time of year we had to make a detour and cross by Muvattupuzha's second bridge further down. We were now fairly out of town. The road, which had become broader and dustier – for buses and bullock carts passed that way – ran between coconut groves and green paddy fields with here and there a modest house or row of thatched huts. On either side of the road ran a deep ditch.

On our way through the town, people had stopped dead in their tracks and gaped at us with undisguised curiosity; bands of naked children had run yelling behind us for a few dozen yards. Now a stranger thing happened. Two black figures, whether male or female we could not tell, who had been coming towards us from the opposite direction, suddenly flung themselves into the ditch and remained cowering there with their hands over their heads until we had passed. They were outcastes who, since there was no place for them in the rigid Hindu social system, were treated by members of the higher castes not only as Untouchables but as 'Unseeables'. The mere sight of them in the distance brought pollution. Recognizing us as sadhus, who were almost always of high caste, they had hastened to avoid the sin of bringing visual pollution upon us by concealing themselves as best they could in the ditch.

A few minutes later we saw the ashram. It stood among trees on the brow of a small laterite hill, the vivid redness of which contrasted admirably with the blue-greens and yellow-greens of the paddy fields at its foot. We turned left. The sharp red gravel cut the tender soles of our bare feet as we trudged along the stony path past the rice field at the corner, then past a plot of waste ground, and finally beneath the low, crumbling laterite wall of the ashram compound, which stood at a slightly higher level on the right, with a cashew nut tree or two peering over into the path below. Instead of a gate there was a gap in the wall barred by two stout moveable bamboos which fitted into rough sockets on either side. Removing the top one and stepping over the other we found ourselves at the lower end of a long rectangular compound, hardly more than an acre in extent, which sloped steeply from the entrance.

Halfway up it was divided into almost equal parts by an enormous step, nearly six feet high, in the centre of which a flight of normal size steps had been cut to connect the upper and lower terraces. The soil of the lower terrace seemed too rocky for cultivation, and apart from mango and cashew nut trees only periwinkle, with its bright pink flowers and dark glossy leaves, grew among the untidy heaps of red laterite rubble. As we climbed the steps we saw, on the upper level, great dark bushes of crimson hibiscus and deep red China rose, as well as other kinds of flowering shrubs. Beyond them, high on a cemented plinth, squatted the ashram.

While Ramaswami's man went in search of the caretaker, who occupied the small kitchen building lower down on the left, Satyapriya and I explored the place that henceforth would provide us not merely with shelter but with the seclusion and quiet that, as we had been made to realize, were indispensable conditions for the practice of meditation.

It was a small, gable-roofed building the greater part of which was taken up by a hall thirty feet long and twenty feet wide. A broad open veranda ran along the front of the building. Another, enclosed by a parapet wall, ran down the right-hand side. The latter opened into a porch, fifteen feet square, similarly enclosed. Both the floor of the side veranda and the floor of the porch were of beaten earth. Grilled folding doors at the far end of the hall opened into a small shrine where photographs of Swami Vivekananda, Sri Ramakrishna, and the Holy Mother stood side by side on the second step of a low, three-tiered cement altar. The left-hand side of the building was occupied by two small rooms separated by a veranda that gave access on one side to a door opening into the hall and on the other to a short flight of steps leading down into a tree-bordered courtyard in the centre of which was a well surrounded by a circular laterite wall. Though not more than twenty-five years old, the ashram was so dilapidated as to seem ancient. In a number of places the cement facing had crumbled away, revealing the large-pored red laterite beneath. Tiles were missing from the roof, and on looking up through the crossbeams and rafters (there was no ceiling) we could see blue sky through the holes. In place of glass the windows were fitted with stout wooden bars and heavy shutters. Except for two clumsy wooden benches and an empty bookcase in the first of the two small rooms there was no furniture. But after three months of peregrination Satyapriya and I were well content; the very defects of the place seemed beauties, and it was not without a sigh of relief that we set down our bundles (the bamboo poles had been discarded in Trivandrum) and tried to accustom ourselves to the idea that we could in future lie down at night without the necessity of taking thought as to whither we would go on the morrow.

Within a few days a routine had been established which gave us the feeling of having always lived in the ashram. At five in the morning, while it was still dark, we were awoken by the noise of a hautboy and drum playing outside the temples in the Brahmin quarter half a mile away across the river. These were the same raucous instruments that had deafened us in the temple of the Virgin Goddess at Cape Comorin, but heard from such a distance, in the hush that preceded dawn, they made the business of waking up delightful. As there were two temples, we heard them twice. When, after a five-minute interval, they sounded for the second time, we rose from the hard teak benches, on which we slept without mattress or pillow, and washed in water that had been drawn from the well the previous night. We then meditated for an hour in the hall. Except on days when our meditation lasted longer than usual, it was still dark when, *lota* in hand and a change of robes over our shoulder, we went down to the river to bathe.

To me this was the least enjoyable part of the day. The water was cold and dirty, and until I grew accustomed to it the sound of people hawking on the opposite bank and spitting into the water was not reassuring. Satyapriya, good swimmer that he was, plunged in and out like a seal. Usually I sat on the rough pier formed by half a dozen huge teak logs that projected from the bank into the water and douched myself with the *lota*. During our first week at the ashram the logs were almost submerged; but in the hot weather the water level receded until they were two or three feet clear of the surface. Eventually, I took my bath a few dozen yards further down, nearly opposite the bathing-ghat below the temples, where, to my intense disgust, I once saw lumps of yellow excrement floating past only a couple of feet from my knees.

Back in the ashram, we hung our wet clothes out to dry, washed our feet with the water we had brought from the river in our lotas before entering the hall, and then prepared for the morning puja or ceremonial worship. The question to what extent a Buddhist could show respect to non-Buddhist religious teachers at that time hardly occurred to me, for not being a member of the sangha, or living among Buddhists, I had not to consider the possibility of such respect being misconstrued as actual worship of the teacher concerned or as indicating approval of all his teachings. If to me such a question *did not*, to Satyapriya it *could not*, occur. Holding, as he did, the view that Buddhism and Hinduism were in essence one, it was a matter almost of indifference to him whether he worshipped the Buddha or Ramakrishna. As we agreed in thinking that, since we were enjoying the hospitality of the ashram, it was but right and natural for us to assume responsibility for the decent upkeep of the shrine, the difference at first seemed immaterial.

Every morning Satyapriya washed the cement floor and the altar, while I gathered hibiscus, China rose, jasmine, and other flowers in a basket. Even the humble periwinkle was not disdained, though orthodox Hindu friends afterwards warned me that wild flowers, as well as 'English' flowers (including the rose!) were impure and could not be offered to the Almighty. Usually I spent more than half an hour arranging my flowers on the altar. This came to be regarded as evidence of great devotion. In truth the feelings which inspired me were aesthetic – if indeed it is possible to separate the aesthetic from the devotional. When the photographs had been anointed on the forehead with sandalwood paste, and two or three joss-sticks and the tall brass temple lamp lit, so still and pure was the atmosphere of the clean, flower-adorned shrine that all I had ever felt about the importance of such aids to devotion was confirmed afresh.

Our ministrations did not, of course, constitute puja in the orthodox Hindu sense, and perhaps I was glad they did not. I was perfectly content arranging flowers. Later on when Satyapriya, following his unitarist views to their logical conclusion, procured by post from Calcutta a Sanskrit-Bengali manual of the elaborate ritual worship of Sri Ramakrishna as an incarnation of God, and started performing the puja according to its directions, my heart turned as cold against the idea as it had done against that of Anandamayi being '*pūrna brahma nārāyaṇa*'. While prepared to respect both teachers for certain moral qualities, I could not, as a Buddhist, worship them as the incarnations of a deity in whose existence I did not believe. Though our disagreement on this point was felt rather than expressed, it was symptomatic of a divergence of views that, towards the end of the following year, more than once threatened to become acute. Meanwhile, I sat with my friend while he recited mantras, scattered flowers and water, and waved various kinds of lamps, and I continued to decorate the altar; but now that this act had been invested, by implication, with a significance I did not feel, for me the joy of it was poisoned.

After the puja, at about eight o'clock, we hurried down to the kitchen for breakfast – which introduces the subject of food. For the first three weeks we ate nothing except dried tapioca. Those for whom the word means a kind of sweet pudding (as in my boyhood it did for me) may be interested to learn what it meant for us. On the morning after our arrival, Raman Nair the caretaker, who had constituted himself our cook, placed before each of us on the cement floor an enamel dish piled with what looked like wood-chips. They tasted like wood-chips too. When we enquired of him what they were, he only gibbered and gesticulated like an ape, for he was little more than a half-wit, though as I remarked to Satyapriya when we knew him better, he was very cunning on his own level of intelligence. Eventually, in the jabber of Malayalam, we distinguished the word tapioca. At first we thought we had misheard him; but when we repeated the word, pointing to the wood-chips as we did so, our cook nodded his white head vigorously and his eyes shone with delight. Tapioca it was. Subsequently we discovered that, for several months of the year, this tuberous root was the staple diet of the poor. When the crop was lifted at the end of the rainy season the greater part of it was cut into small pieces and dried, the 'wood-chips' thus produced giving the cultivators something on which to live during the cold weather. The ashram land, though seemingly uncultivable, was not too rough for the hardy tapioca plant. Sackfuls of wood-chips were stowed away above the smoke-blackened rafters of the kitchen. Of course they were boiled before being eaten, but this made no more difference to their consistency than the addition of a little salt made to their taste. Lest we should find the diet monotonous, Raman Nair served them sometimes dry and sometimes floating in the water in which they had been boiled.

Much of the time during the morning, after our tapioca breakfast, as well as during the afternoon, after our tapioca lunch, was spent in study. Besides the books we had brought from Kasauli I had the *Yoga-Vāsiṣṭha* and the first volume of Śāntarakṣita's encyclopaedic *Tattvasaṅgraha*, or 'Compendium of Principles' – a masterpiece of eighth-century Indian Buddhist dialectics – which I had borrowed from Kalady. There were also the commonplace books into which I had copied, ever since my arrival in India, passages from books I read. These provided me with much material for reflection, and I developed the habit of pacing up and down the long side veranda – which thus became a kind of ambulatory – turning over in my mind various matters that were still not clear to me. In the back of one of these books, which is still in my hands, are ten poems bearing various dates in the month of November 1947.[30] All are expressive of intense spiritual aspiration. At the same time I started writing an article on our recent experiences entitled 'From the Himalayas to Cape Comorin'.[31]

While I occupied myself in this way, Satyapriya was busy improving his English. At my suggestion he started keeping a diary, for though he could speak the language fluently, if not very correctly, the weakness of his grammar and the limitations of his vocabulary became apparent whenever he tried to write on religion and philosophy, in which field he was indeed ambitious to distinguish himself. Unfortunately, he fell into the same trap from which the well-meaning English teacher had once striven to rescue me. Whatever he wrote he handed to me saying, 'Please pomp it up a bit. You know, put in a lot of bombastic words.' This was said in all seriousness. 'Bombastic' was to him a word of praise, expressive of the highest stylistic excellence. For this error, or rather perversion, of taste, the vicious influence of the older prose style of his own vernacular was responsible. Bengali, like most other modern Indian languages, had long struggled beneath the incubus of Sanskrit; until very recent times that style was considered best which said nothing in a Bengali word of two syllables which could be said in a Sanskrit word of ten. Among Hindi 'purists' the bombastic style flourishes even now, and their fanatical preference for fantastic compounds of Sanskritic origin has indeed produced, since Independence, a growing volume of hostility to the Indian official language on the part of millions of non-Hindi-speaking people. What Satyapriya, an unconscious victim of such influences, was really asking me to do was to latinize his style, substituting for his monosyllables my polysyllables. He wanted to write Johnsonese. When I explained that this style was obsolete, and that simplicity and directness were now the qualities most admired, he accused me of being unwilling to help him. For a long time the topic was a bone of contention between us. Like many novices, he could not understand that if he wrote correctly and had something to say, a style consonant with his personality would automatically develop.

For the time being, therefore, I had simultaneously to supply him with *sesquipedalia verba* and correct his grammar.

Such minor differences apart, the latter part of the day passed no less uneventfully than the earlier. In the evening, after a wash, we again meditated for an hour and recorded our progress in the manner Anandamayi had suggested. At eight o'clock we went down to the kitchen and by the light of a coconut-oil lamp ate our third meal of wood-chips. Having read for half an hour, or paced the ambulatory, we stretched ourselves out on our benches, which were scarcely eighteen inches wide, and were soon asleep.

31
'WHAT IS YOUR CASTE?'

There was still half a sack of wood-chips left when Swami Agamananda sent an emissary to see how we were getting on. Swami Dharmananda, who had called in at the Kalady Ashram while we were there, was a short, dark, slightly corpulent man of about forty, clad in a saffron-coloured shirt that reached almost to his ankles. It was soon evident, from the turn he contrived to give the conversation, that the motive of his visit was less altruistic than we had supposed, and that he was interested not so much in our welfare as in our identity. Some months later we discovered that he was reputed to be an agent of the secret police. But this was not necessarily the explanation of his curiosity.

In India, particularly in South India, people rarely feel at ease with a stranger until they know his caste, language, income, marital status, and family history. Should this information not be immediately forthcoming, they do not drop the matter, as people in most other countries would do, but press it in a manner so vigorous and aggressive as to suggest that they have a right to know. The original reason for this extraordinary behaviour is to be found in the caste system. Hindu society consists of about 2,000 castes. Every Hindu belongs by birth to one of them; a casteless Hindu is a contradiction in terms. Relations between castes are regulated by the socio-religious manuals known as *Dharma Śāstras*. Until a Hindu knows a man's caste he is uncertain whether or not he may eat and drink with him, or even touch him. So acute is the discomfort created by this state of uncertainty that orthodox Hindus, especially Brahmins, will go to almost any lengths of rudeness in order to wrest from the uncommunicative this vital secret. Though during recent years the rigidity of the caste system has been slightly relaxed, especially in towns and cities, and the practice of Untouchability made a penal offence, much of the personal inquisitiveness that was necessitated, originally, by the requirements of the caste system, is still operative in the make-up of people who believe themselves devoid of caste prejudice.

Malabar (that is to say, Travancore and the adjacent Malayalam-speaking areas) we found even worse in this respect than Tamilnad. Once we had told a Tamil Brahmin that a sadhu possessed neither caste nor nationality the matter could usually be regarded as closed. Not so with the Malayalis. They insisted on pursuing the argument to the bitter end. Though Swami Dharmananda was less obstreperous than many whom it was our misfortune to encounter, he certainly made up in resourcefulness what he lacked in vehemence. But having spent several days bruising himself in vain against the wall of our resolution he apparently decided that direct methods were of no avail and thenceforward allowed the discussions to flow into normal channels.

When he stopped playing the inquisitor, we discovered that his company was by no means uncongenial. Not that he was a saint, but he was shrewd, sensible, and well-informed and knew much about Travancore that we were desirous of learning. Having been so reticent about our own caste and nationality, we could hardly question him concerning his antecedents. From his undisguised hostility to Brahmins, however, as well as from the darkness of his complexion, we concluded him to be a member of the Nair community. Moreover, in order to encourage communicativeness on our part he had confided to us that he had once belonged to the Ramakrishna Mission. He also seemed to have been somehow connected with the Maha Bodhi Mission in Calicut, in what was then known as British North Malabar. Now, he told us, he spent most of his time travelling up and down the state delivering lectures. The Malayalis had an inordinate passion for attending lectures. Travancore was, in fact, the only place in India where people were so addicted to this form of entertainment that they paid the lecturer not only his travelling expenses but a fee for his speech. Like many sadhus, Swami Dharmananda explained, he made several hundred rupees a month by this means. Not being deeply interested in religion, he preferred to speak either on politics or on social questions such as the abolition of the caste system. But he had no objection to lecturing on religion, for this was still the most popular and lucrative topic. Before returning to Kalady he predicted that we would soon be inundated with invitations to address meetings.

After this prediction, we were not astonished when, a few days later, arrangements were made for us to speak at a public meeting in Muvattupuzha. Swami Agamananda, who had evidently been apprised of our determination to remain at the ashram despite the wood-chips, came over for the day to preside. So great was the Malayali's love of lectures, and so intense the curiosity that had been excited by our arrival, that practically the entire literate population of the town turned up to hear – and see – the two young ascetics. Though he was not unaware of our feelings in the matter, Swami Agamananda introduced Satyapriya as a Bengali and me as an American. This gave him an opening for a vigorous attack on the Christian missionaries, his avowed enemies, whom he ridiculed for trying to convert Indians to Christianity when cultured Westerners were voluntarily adopting Hinduism. (To him Buddhism was a caste-cum-sect within the Hindu fold.) Satyapriya and I then spoke for about half an hour each. Swami Agamananda concluded by appealing to the public of Muvattupuzha to support the ashram and cooperate with its new incumbents. On our return to the ashram a committee was set up with Swami Agamananda as president, Anagarika Satyapriya as secretary, Anagarika Dharmapriya as assistant secretary, and Mr Ramaswami Iyer – who, with about a dozen other gentlemen, had walked back with us – as treasurer. Ramaswami promised ten rupees a month. The others pledged one rupee each. A list of subscribers, potential and actual, was drawn up, and Satyapriya and I were instructed to go from house to house for subscriptions at the beginning of every month.

From the first of December, therefore, our daily routine underwent an important modification. Every morning after breakfast we crossed the bridge into Muvattupuzha and made the rounds of as many houses as possible, returning to the ashram at about midday. In the beginning we had assumed it would be possible for us to collect the subscriptions of all the members of the ashram, as they were styled, within two or three days. But as our list grew longer, and the town apparently more extensive, the work lingered on into the first, into the second, and finally even into the third week of each month. Members were not always at home when we called, and even if they were they sometimes asked us to call again later as they happened to be without money just then. Moreover, with most of the subscribers on our list, who at the peak of our activity numbered nearly a hundred, we were soon on terms of friendship, even, in a few cases, of familiarity. For this development Satyapriya's extreme sociability was mainly responsible. In consequence we acquired the habit of visiting certain houses more often, and staying much longer, than our business required. This was no doubt of greater benefit to us than spending the whole of our time at the ashram. Apart from getting more exercise, we became closely acquainted with Muvattupuzha and its people, and learned much about the manners and customs, the beliefs and practices, of the various castes and communities of the state.

Like Trivandrum, Muvattupuzha contained more open spaces than houses and more trees than people. The three rivers which gave the town its name made a rough T that trisected it into three unequal segments. These segments were connected by two bridges, the first of which crossed the river forming the left arm of the T about a mile before it reached the confluence, while the second crossed the river forming the upright about the same distance down from the confluence. By far the greater portion of the town lay under the left arm of the T between the two bridges. In the middle of this segment, equidistant from the bridges, stood a small conical hill. After crossing the bridge from the ashram we turned right in the direction of the town. Presently the road forked. One could reach the first bridge by going either round to the right of the hill through the Brahmin quarter or round to the left past the Roman Catholic church, the Government Hospital, the Anchal Office, the Anglican church, the toddy shop, the Courts, and a row of Western-style shops which in the course of a year nearly doubled in length. Usually we went into town by one route and returned by the other. Sometimes, crossing the first bridge and turning right, we made our way through the crowded bazaar quarter to the sandy shores of the confluence, where we crossed over to the ashram bank of the river in a country-boat which, on market days, was so overloaded that it almost foundered. During the rains the confluence measured nearly a mile across; but in summer the rivers shrank within their channels to such an extent, and the water became so shallow, that after hitching our robes above our knees we could wade from one bank to the other without much difficulty.

Only at the centre (not the geographical centre) of the town, at the two ends of the first bridge, and in the bazaar, did one see a few rows of shops and houses built end to end after the Western pattern. Practically all the other houses, including those scattered up and down the hillside, as well as government offices and public buildings, stood four-square in their own compounds, in every one of which slim white coconut palms reared themselves fifty and sixty feet high, their gently swaying heads crowned with a mass of nodding green plumes. One could hardly tell where the town ended and the countryside began. When one reached the suburbs paddy fields started appearing in between the low compound walls; but even in the heart of the town, where houses were thickest and compounds smallest, we occasionally found that a short cut from one house to another led through a field of grain or across freshly-ploughed land.

The houses with the most character were the tiled, heavily timbered red laterite mansions of the traditional Malabar type. Some of the older, and perhaps more purely indigenous, specimens were built entirely of teak that had grown black with age. A few were thatched instead of tiled. Not a pane of glass, not a single nail or screw or hinge, had been used in their construction. The small, low windows were closed with stout wooden bars. Massive folding doors, of four-inch thick teak, turned on wooden pegs that fitted into sockets in the door-frame, and were barred on the inside by a heavy teak sliding-bolt. The floors were paved with black stone. A dusty table and a chair or two, obviously unused except by visitors, were usually the only concessions to modernity. On the walls, among garish lithographs of the blue Vishnu astride his bird-mount Garuda, with one arm round each of his plump, homely spouses, and a medley of other Hindu gods and goddesses, hung large framed portraits of various members of the British royal family from Queen Victoria down to King George VI. Though dark, the interiors of these old houses were delightfully cool, and after a long walk in the hot bright sun Satyapriya and I found it pleasant to relax in a dusty chair and allow our eyes to become accustomed to the gloom, while our host, who was generally a Nair, disappeared into the yet darker back premises to fetch us one of the traditional cold drinks.

For the first two or three months that we went out on our rounds we were often pestered by enquiries concerning our caste and nationality. Though we found them rather trying, neither of us could help laughing at the ridiculous, even comical manner in which they were sometimes made. A perfect stranger, passing us in the road, would stop, fix us with a fish-like stare, and without a word of explanation demand of us, in hollow, sepulchral tones, 'What ... is ... your ... nationality?' Our favourite reply was that we were sadhus and had none. If the questioner was deficient in effrontery, or in English, he would look us up and down very deliberately in silence for a few minutes and then move slowly off, keeping us fixed with the same fish-like stare as he did so. When asked 'What is your caste?' we replied (or rather Satyapriya replied) that we were Buddhists and as such did not believe in this institution. This almost always led to an argument. Everybody had a caste, we were told, and among the orthodox our reticence in this important particular told against us, for to them it was a matter of common experience that the lower a man's caste the more reluctant he was to reveal it. Attempts to explain that there were countries outside India, and religions other than Hinduism, which knew nothing of caste, were met, on the part of the semi-literate, by an incredulous silence. The more persistent type of questioner, vexed by our uncommunicativeness, would proceed to ask such subtle leading questions as 'Where were you born?' and 'What is your mother tongue?' To the latter question Satyapriya replied that he knew thirteen languages, which was true in a sense. Being a much less gifted linguist I said nothing. Some questioners became argumentative. 'Why shouldn't a sadhu tell his nationality?' they would demand belligerently. 'He can be universal at heart.'

If we happened to be in a hurry we generally left such people arguing in the middle of the road. Had their enquiries been conducted with greater reasonableness we might have felt tempted to break the resolution we had made on leaving Kasauli. As it was, the fact that nothing about us seemed to interest them so much, or concern them so deeply, as our caste, made us all the more determined to lesson them in the minor importance of such distinctions by firmly adhering to the principles we had adopted. Eventually, when our attitude became generally known, the persecution ceased. Thereafter, whoever stopped and fixed us with a fishy stare we knew must be a stranger to the town. When Satyapriya was in a jovial mood he would sometimes be the first to put the well-known question, imitating with great success the tone in which it was usually asked. Spluttering with suppressed mirth we would then escape, leaving the would-be questioner looking after us with a sagging jaw and an expression of bewilderment.

Despite the success of these light-hearted methods with members of the public, a day came when it seemed that our reticence regarding our antecedents would get us into serious trouble with the authorities. We received a summons to the police station. Unlike the people of Muvattupuzha, who took equal interest in us both, especially in our caste, the station superintendent seemed concerned exclusively with me and my nationality. All foreigners, he explained, were now required to register with the police, and since it was suspected that I belonged to this category of persons I had been called for interrogation. Would I kindly state my nationality. Had I replied that I was English all would have been well, for the registration order did not apply to citizens of the United Kingdom and other Commonwealth countries, who were not classified as foreigners. Official suspicion had, in fact, been excited only by Swami Agamananda's unfortunate description of me as an American. But as Satyapriya and I had insisted for three or four months that as sadhus we had neither caste nor nationality, stoutly resisting all attempts to extract from us the much-prized information, we felt we could now hardly retract. Perhaps there was also a grain of obstinacy in our attitude. Fortunately the station superintendent took a lenient view of the case, merely remarking, after a few supplementary questions, that he would have to report to headquarters that a person suspected of being a foreigner was residing in the vicinity and had refused to declare his nationality.

A few weeks later came a second summons. On our arrival at the police station we found that the station superintendent had been transferred. His successor, a strapping, handsome young Nair of about my own age, was the son of one of our ashram members, a teacher in the local Middle School, and we had already met him at his father's house before his appointment. This of course made things much easier for us. After he had put me the same questions as his predecessor, and I had given the same replies, we enrolled him as a member of the ashram and collected his first subscription. Thereafter the police station was included in our regular monthly itinerary. On one of our visits the young superintendent showed us the lock-up, where we saw, behind bars, half a dozen desperate-looking characters who were awaiting trial on charges of theft and murder. For several days afterwards we speculated whether this gesture was meant to be taken as a hint; but as no further official interest was taken in us we eventually dismissed the suspicion as unfounded. The authorities, it seemed, were more easily satisfied than some of our acquaintances.

32
THE THREE LAWYERS

We had not been long in Muvattupuzha before discovering that apart from the Untouchables and Unseeables almost everybody owned at least half an acre of land. Boundary disputes between the owners of adjacent plots were, therefore, extremely common. A man could hardly go away for the weekend without finding, on his return, that one of his neighbours had shifted the fence a foot or two to his own advantage. Such incidents led to interminable litigation. Going to law was, in fact, the most popular local pastime – and the most ruinous. Most of our members were involved, either as plaintiffs or defendants, in two or three suits every month. Under such favourable conditions lawyers flourished. One of the most typical sights of the town was that of a *vakil*, or solicitor, in rusty black coat and ready-made white turban, making his lordly way to the Court at 9.45 in the morning followed by a train of obsequious clients not one of whom but had what Judge Jeffreys would have called a hanging face. Knots of no less villainous-looking characters could be seen gathered about the entrances of the various court-rooms. When we enquired who they were and what they wanted we received the cynical reply, 'They are witnesses waiting to be hired. They'll swear to anything for eight annas.' Later we learned that there was a tacit agreement between *vakils* to limit the number of false witnesses produced at any single hearing. More than eight or nine for each side, it was felt, would tend to defeat the ends of justice.

So great was the amount of litigation that went on, and so urgent the demand for lawyers, that the legal profession seemed to have absorbed an abnormally high percentage of the more highly educated middle class. How many *vakils* and advocates were enrolled as members of the ashram I no longer recollect. But it was certainly no coincidence that though we made friends among practically all professions, trades, and occupations, more friends followed the law than any other vocation, while of the three closest of all our friends in Muvattupuzha two were *vakils* and one an advocate. That the former should have been Nairs, and the latter a Brahmin, was also hardly a coincidence, for these were the two most influential and educated Hindu communities.

Kumaran Nair lived at the top of a flight of steep laterite steps on the left-hand side of the hill; Kesava Pillai on the river bank halfway between Ramaswami's office and the Brahmin quarter. We must have made their acquaintance simultaneously, for their boyhood friendship had lasted without diminution into middle age and they were inseparable companions. Indeed, I can no more think of them separately than I can think of Tweedledum apart from Tweedledee. Not that as men they had much in common. Physically and mentally they were contrasting types. Kumaran Nair was tall, thin, shrewd, suspicious, and cynical; Kesava Pillai short, stout, trustful, affectionate, and cheerful. The former had a deep cleft between the brows; even when his face became animated, which it usually did in discussion, he never entirely lost his half-worried, half-querulous expression. The latter, even when grave, could never suppress for more than a minute or two the smile that lurked in the corners of his mouth. One was quick and bird-like in his movements, the other slow as a tortoise. In matters of religion, if Kumaran Nair was what the Hindus call a *jñānin*, or one whose approach to Reality is intellectual, Kesava Pillai was definitely a *bhakta*, or devotee.

Between them they monopolized two-thirds of the entire legal practice of Muvattupuzha. This meant that they frequently appeared for opposite parties. When this happened, neither spared the other in his argument. Kumaran Nair, we were told, excelled in attack, Kesava Pillai in defence. Each being a match, but no more than a match, for the other, the two friends lost and won an even number of cases, thus dividing the forensic honours of the town between them. Their courtroom brawls, far from resulting in any ill feeling, seemed not only to strengthen their friendship but to give it an added zest. Perhaps one cannot love a man without knowing his strength, and it is difficult to know his strength without having wrestled with him. They never discussed the merits of a case outside the Court. When one of them had won a case, however, he sometimes pointed out flaws in his own arguments that had escaped his friend's notice.

The nest reveals the bird, and the homes of the two *vakils* were characteristic of their respective owners. Kumaran Nair's, perhaps, was less so. It was a new house; in fact, when we made his acquaintance it was still under construction. Like practically all new middle-class houses it was built of blocks of red laterite and the walls were faced with cement. In the sitting room, where he usually received us, stood a small table and three or four chairs. However often we called, he greeted us cheerfully and at once started talking. In the course of the discussion his son Radhakrishnan, a college student, and nephew Menon, who ran a radio shop, would sometimes come in and stand with folded arms listening to what was being said. In Malabar it was not good manners for a young man to sit in the presence of his elders. Sometimes, when they had stood for more than an hour, Kumaran Nair would tell them, in a testy manner, to sit down. 'Just look at the young rascals!' he would exclaim to Satyapriya and me, 'They're more old-fashioned than I am!' But the young men merely smiled, casting their eyes down as they did so, and remained standing. When they felt tired they leaned against the wall, drawing one bare foot up behind them and pressing the sole against the cool cement. Despite their modesty, which became them very well, Radhakrishnan and Menon were not shy; indeed, subject to the formalities imposed by convention, their intercourse with Kumaran Nair was quite easy. After a decent interval they joined in the discussion, neither of them hesitating to differ from the older man. With Menon, indeed, Kumaran Nair argued and expostulated as with an intimate, and the exchanges between them at times grew quite heated.

Like most Hindus, especially the English-educated intellectual type, Kumaran Nair dearly loved to discuss philosophical topics such as the nature of Reality. But as with so many of his co-religionists he never defined his terms and pursued no line of thought to its conclusion, with the result that his contribution to the discussion was generally a stream of ideas as brilliant but as inconsequential as successive trails of sunlit foam on a river. Theism and pantheism, mysticism and hedonism, the inevitable Vedantic story of the snake and the rope and parables from the New Testament, wholesale praise of Hinduism that might have been ironical and equally wholesale denunciation that seemed deliberately to negate itself by overstatement, were all mixed and jumbled together in astounding confusion. Twenty times in the course of a single argument he shifted his ground. If in replying to something he had said we proceeded upon the same assumptions that he had done he would interrupt the argument to question these assumptions. Every few minutes he scratched his head and suddenly flew off at a tangent. Our philosophical discussions in fact usually went round and round in circles until we were dizzy. Satyapriya was still Hindu enough to enjoy these noisy debates; but to me the meaningless argumentation soon became distasteful.

Much more interesting were the occasions on which Kumaran Nair spoke of local manners and customs. He was a staunch opponent of the caste system. That is to say, he criticized it vehemently. Though I had not then succeeded in grasping the fact, for a modern Hindu it is quite easy to practise a thing and to criticize it without any sense of inconsistency. One day he told us the exact number of feet up to which the members of various inferior castes had been allowed to approach a Nair house. Untouchables could not enter the compound. Eazhavas, or those of the toddy-tapping caste, could enter the compound but had to stand at least thirty feet from the door.

Ambiguous as was our friend's attitude toward caste, however, his hatred of the Brahmins – who treated the Nairs almost as contemptuously as the Nairs treated the Eazhavas – was undoubtedly sincere. Probably it was he who translated for our benefit a Malayalam proverb meaning 'If you meet a Brahmin and a cobra, kill the Brahmin first.' He also told us about a famous Vishnu temple not far from Muvattupuzha where, on a certain day each year, one hundred Brahmins were ceremonially fed. According to a legend invented by 'those threaded rascals', as he always termed members of the priestly caste, one of the Brahmins thus fed was always the god Vishnu in disguise and to partake of his *prasad* was a certain cure for leprosy. When the meal was over the leaf-plates containing the leavings of the hundred Brahmins were thrown onto the rubbish heap, whereupon the lepers, who gathered there every year from all over the state, fought over them like dogs in the hope of getting a scrap of the precious *prasad*. Even Nairs, he told us in a tone of disgust, sometimes sank so low as to partake of the leavings of the 'threaded rascals' in this humiliating manner.

When neither discoursing on the nature of Reality nor denouncing the Brahmins Kumaran Nair usually railed bitterly against his profession. In the mouth of a Malayalam-speaking person the words 'lawyer' and 'liar' are homonymous. Both Kumaran Nair and Kesava Pillai made much of this coincidence, asserting that they were compelled to speak in Court nothing but unmitigated falsehood. The former often declared himself utterly disgusted with so dishonest a calling, and periodically announced his intention of retiring from practice immediately. At first we admired him for his loftiness of spirit, but eventually we perceived that he was well content with his profession and railed against it only as a married man rails against marriage.

Kesava Pillai lived in surroundings much more old-fashioned than those of his friend. His house was old and stood in a small compound the gate of which consisted of two or three sliding bamboos. The interior of the front room, where we always sat and talked with him, was dark and dusty, with a predominance of gloomy black woodwork. From the walls hung torn old calendars and bunches of grimy papers on spikes. Unlike Kumaran Nair, who at home wore an English shirt and a silk sarong, Kesava Pillai never received us wearing anything more than a small piece of cloth round the waist; his face was usually covered with white stubble. From a black band round his neck hung a small square phylactery of gold. He, too, always made us welcome, standing with bowed head and folded hands, the familiar smile lurking in the corners of his mouth, until Satyapriya and I had taken our seats. Except once or twice when he was seriously ill, his mood was invariably one of cheerful composure.

Though he was much less talkative than his friend, we enjoyed his conversation; there was often a great deal behind his short but shrewd observations. But our visits were never allowed to interfere with the day's work. At intervals he would walk slowly over to his clerk, who scribbled steadily in a cubby-hole on the right of the entrance, and quietly give him a few brief instructions. Every half an hour he prepared himself a fresh wad of pan, which he was, like most Malayalis, greatly addicted to chewing. The jaws of many of the people we knew seemed never to rest from this exercise. While we talked, half a dozen very small children, quite naked, would run laughing in and out of the room: some were his own offspring, others his daughter's. More than once our old friend, who was about fifty-six, told us with a rueful smile that in order to give his youngest children as good an education as he had given their elder brothers and sisters he would have to go on working until he was well over seventy.

Despite their great difference of temperament, Kumaran Nair and Kesava Pillai had one major characteristic in common: both were, and for many years had been, very heavy drinkers. As soon as we found this out, Satyapriya and I did our utmost to persuade them to give up the habit, which had done neither of them much good. Kesava Pillai, in fact, who was the heavier drinker of the two, suffered from a variety of gastric and other complaints due to alcoholic poisoning. On Kumaran Nair our persuasions were wasted. After admitting that drinking was an evil habit, he would launch into pseudo-philosophical generalizations that made the admission meaningless. We therefore concentrated on Kesava Pillai, whose doctor had already warned him more than once that unless he gave up his regular evening potations they would kill him. But though he, too, admitted drinking was a great evil, and often wished himself rid of a habit that might easily prove fatal, for a middle-aged man to break all at once the chains that had bound him practically for a lifetime was no simple matter. But eventually, after several months of argument, exhortation, and expostulation on our part, break them he did, though by the time he had nerved himself for the act even so drastic a remedy could not counteract the effect of the poisons that were now rapidly undermining his whole system.

Since they drank only at night after dinner, whereas we called on them only in the morning, we had never seen either of the two friends ever looking the worse for drink; though had we been more experienced we might have wondered why the hands of one trembled so badly when he lit a cigarette and why the eyes of the other were so red.

One evening, however, between 7 and 8, we unsuspectingly went to see Kumaran Nair on urgent ashram business. We found him in the kitchen with a wooden keg at his side. To our astonishment he greeted us incoherently (he had removed his false teeth) and in a foolish, hiccoughing manner began excusing himself for being drunk and telling us how ashamed he felt, and how repentant, that we had discovered him in such a condition. Having said this, he assured us, very volubly, and with many asseverations, that he was *not* drunk and that we would be committing a great mistake, and doing him a great injustice, if we thought he was. He then proceeded to pick a quarrel with Menon, to whom he spoke not in Malayalam, as he usually did, but in English, and ended by shedding a few tears.

After a few minutes his head seemed to clear a little, and he launched into one of his usual philosophical harangues, in the course of which he declared, at great length and with many supporting arguments, that Hinduism was a universal religion, according to which all paths led to God and that if he chose to find God through the path of drunkenness why should he not? Satyapriya and I were amazed not by the novelty of this thesis, which was the sort of thing we were accustomed to hear from him, but by the brilliance of his language. Normally he spoke English very well; but that evening his speech was almost poetry. Menon afterwards told us that when drunk his uncle never spoke anything but English even to those members of his household who knew only Malayalam, and that he often expressed himself just as brilliantly. Thereafter, whenever we saw Kumaran Nair in the morning we would jokingly ask him how well he had been speaking English the evening before.

Venkateshwara Iyer, Advocate, the third of our three closest friends, was a Tamil Brahmin who drank nothing stronger than coffee. At least once a week we visited him at his house in the Brahmin quarter, stepping over the sliding bamboos and climbing up a short but very steep flight of steps to his ever-open portals. On the way up we passed a small green cocoa tree, the only one I ever saw, among whose branches there hung one month, to my intense delight, three-inch pods like purple Chinese lanterns.

On stepping over the raised wooden threshold we invariably found Venkateshwara Iyer sitting cross-legged on the black stone platform, six feet in breadth and a foot high, which filled the rear half of the room. Except on chilly mornings, when he donned a shirt, he wore no more than Kesava Pillai, while across his left shoulder, conspicuous against the brown skin, hung the brahminical thread. He never sat without a book in his hand or a wad of pan in his mouth. Sometimes we found him reading Burke or Macaulay, sometimes a Sanskrit philosophical work, and sometimes the cheapest type of detective fiction: they were all grist to his mill. Whatever the book might be, he laid it aside as we entered, looked up at us over the steel rims of his spectacles, which he wore far down his nose, shifted the pan to the opposite side of his mouth, and without either rising from his place or folding his hands in greeting called out a welcome in his customary harsh, strident tones. At first we were a little disconcerted by this uncivil reception, so different from anybody else's, but we soon grew used to his ways. When Satyapriya and I had settled down on the edge of the stone platform, where reed mats had been spread for us – sitting at opposite ends, and leaning against the woodwork – conversation would begin. Sometimes it was sparked off by the book we had found the old Brahmin reading, sometimes by current ashram affairs, sometimes by an incident of socio-religious interest we had recently witnessed, or which had been reported to us. Whatever the starting point might have been, violent differences of opinion soon arose. Most of these clashes were between Venkateshwara Iyer and Satyapriya, and most of them were connected, in one way or another, with the ubiquitous subject of caste.

On one of our first visits, quite by chance, we had remarked how great an injustice it was that Untouchables were not even allowed to use the road that led past the temples of Shiva and Ganesha a few hundred yards away. To our astonishment, Venkateshwara Iyer not only bluntly disagreed with us, but stoutly upheld the traditional prohibition, maintaining that Untouchables were Untouchables and should be treated as such. This was too much for Satyapriya, who at once leaped into the fray. The pitched battle that followed set the pattern for many others in the course of the next fifteen months. If Satyapriya excelled in volubility and indignation, Venkateshwara Iyer was more than a match for him in dialectical acumen and rock-like immovability of conviction. As discussion grew more and more heated, I gradually ceased to participate. In any case I agreed and disagreed with both parties. Satyapriya believed that the caste system was evil and that it was not really part of Hinduism, being a later corruption. Venkateshwara Iyer believed that the caste system was good, being in fact a sublime, God-given institution, and that it was of the aboriginal essence of Hinduism. I believed that the caste system was evil and that both practically and theoretically it was part of Hinduism, which was one of the reasons why I was a Buddhist and not a Hindu. For me, however, the subject of caste was not the highly emotive one that it was for my two friends. So violent did their exchanges sometimes become that a permanent breach seemed unavoidable. But fortunately they always managed to check themselves in time, and though we continued to be shocked by some of the more outrageous manifestations of his unabashed orthodoxy,

Satyapriya and I remained on good terms with Venkateshwara Iyer. Outspokenness such as his was in any case a welcome change from the equivocations of the average Hindu, and in the end we started almost liking him for his intransigence. For his part, the old reactionary had no objection to being anvil to the hammers of our youthful idealism, and in the end adopted towards our persistence an attitude of almost paternal indulgence. Once, indeed, he unbent so far as to offer us coffee. Despite ourselves, we could not help feeling highly honoured. When his wife brought the coffee, however, we saw that she had served it in silver tumblers. Silver, being a pure metal, could not be polluted whoever drank from it.

Stimulating though our discussions with Venkateshwara Iyer were for both Satyapriya and me, they tended to have a disrupting effect on our own personal relationship. Whenever the old Brahmin had been more than usually militant, Satyapriya would be at pains to assure me that he was only an old-fashioned eccentric, one of a breed now virtually extinct. On no account should I regard his views as those of Hinduism. If I did so, he warned me, I would be doing that great religion a grave injustice. Despite his expostulations, I remained unconvinced. So far as I could see the only difference between Venkateshwara Iyer and other orthodox Hindus was his outspokenness. What all believed and practised he was not ashamed or afraid of proclaiming from the housetops. As I knew only too well, Satyapriya's real concern was to minimize the differences between Buddhism and Hinduism. For if Hinduism could be equated with caste, whereas Buddhism could not, then he would be forced into the position of having to choose the latter religion and reject the former, and for so drastic a change he was not yet ready.

That Hinduism could, in fact, be equated with caste, transpired from one of the longest and most interesting of all our discussions, on account of which Venkateshwara Iyer failed to attend Court that morning and Satyapriya and I were late for lunch.

Satyapriya had happened to refer, in passing, to the Hindu Mahasabha's definition of a Hindu as one who regarded India as Holy Land or who followed a religion the founder of which had been born in India. This was, of course, much too broad, and Venkateshwara Iyer instantly objected. If such a definition was accepted, he argued, one would not only have to regard Buddhists, Jains, and Sikhs as Hindus, which was bad enough, but even unclean people beyond the sea. Satyapriya having failed to satisfy him with the Mahasabha's definition, I tried out on him a more traditional one. A Hindu, I suggested, was one who believed in the authority of the Vedas. To our amazement, this definition was rejected as peremptorily as the first. Belief in the authority of the Vedas, growled the old man, did not make one a Hindu. What grounds he gave for this assertion I no longer recollect, but it was certainly not due to lack of respect for the Vedas. Indeed, his was the only Brahmin house in South India in which we found a copy of the Vedas, and he often lamented the fact that Vedic studies were nowadays generally neglected by the Brahmin community. 'What about the *Rāmāyaṇa* and the *Mahābhārata*?' demanded Satyapriya. They were universally popular scriptures. Wasn't a Hindu one who believed in them? No, he wasn't. 'The *Bhagavad Gītā*, then?' That was even more widely read than the two great epics. But the *Gītā*, for all its popularity, fared no better than the Vedas. By this time Satyapriya and I were feeling distinctly puzzled. 'All right,' we said at last, 'You tell us. What is a Hindu?' 'A Hindu', our friend replied with the greatest imperturbability, 'is one who observes the caste system, including Untouchability.'

Not all our discussions were confined to the subject of caste, or even to that of religion. We also talked about politics, law, English literature, the Tamil classics, and local manners, customs, and traditions. One day Venkateshwara Iyer told us a strange story about a Brahmin woman who had suffered various misfortunes due to the fact that in her previous existence, when she had belonged to a low-caste family, she had once struck a cat in a fit of rage and killed it. Greatly interested, we enquired how it had been possible to find out that her misfortunes were the consequences of that particular action. 'By means of astrology, of course,' replied Venkateshwara Iyer, as though stating the obvious. We must have looked surprised, for he went on to explain that in the Tamil country there was a well-known branch of astrology that was concerned exclusively with tracing present misfortunes back to sins committed in previous existences. Once the offence had been identified, the appropriate penances could be performed, and the sufferer freed from the consequences of his past misdeeds. In the present instance, the Brahmin woman had been advised to feed a certain number of cats every day, as well as to perform the ritual worship of Sri Krishna. On our again looking surprised Venkateshwara Iyer added that cats were said to be particularly fond of Sri Krishna, and that in South India the god was, in fact, sometimes depicted with a cat standing on his shoulder.

On another occasion, calling out to his son to bring the key, our friend showed us his library, which was housed in an outbuilding. All the major English classics were there, many of them in splendid bindings. Pointing to one particularly magnificent set, his son exclaimed, 'I borrowed those books eleven years ago!' We could not help wondering how many of Venkateshwara Iyer's books had been acquired in the same manner, but he said nothing to enlighten us, merely beaming on his first-born with paternal pride and satisfaction. Not that Sundaram Iyer, as he was called, seemed much to be proud of. Unlike his father he was small, unhealthy, and totally devoid of character, and having failed to complete his studies now stayed at home. More surprisingly still, he was not a particularly good Brahmin, and according to Muvattupuzha gossip was not averse to a glass of toddy. Perhaps Satyapriya was right and Venkateshwara Iyer's breed was dying out after all.

Though we had many discussions with Venkateshwara Iyer, and though he expressed himself forcibly on all occasions, one of his sayings in particular stuck in my mind. 'A regulated life gives strength.' With its daily ritual baths, its constant repetition of mantras, its fasts and dietary restrictions, its seasonal religious observances, and above all its social prohibitions of every kind, the life of the orthodox Brahmin was certainly regulated. But as our friend demonstrated in his own person, such regulation was an abundant source of physical and mental strength – how that strength was used was another question. As I look back on my days in Muvattupuzha, the figure of the bigoted old Tamil Brahmin with his red-rimmed eyes, and mouth like a steel trap, looms before me like an Epstein bronze, harsh and rigid of feature indeed, but not without a certain beauty of its own.

33
OTHER FRIENDS

While Kumaran Nair, Kesava Pillai, and Venkateshwara Iyer were our closest friends in the Town of the Three Rivers, there were a number of other people with whom we were on almost equally friendly terms and whom we saw almost as frequently. Nairs of course predominated, they being in any case the majority community. Indeed, not only did we have many Nair friends but many Nair friends with exactly the same name and surname. There were three or four Raman Nairs, and at least five or six Krishna Pillais.

Our principal friend among the Krishna Pillais was the Anchal Master, that is to say, the officer in charge of the Muvattupuzha branch of the Travancore internal postal service. He was important to us because he was an ardent devotee of the god Ayyappan, and we had many talks with him on the subject. According to Krishna Pillai, Ayyappan was, in fact, a form of the Buddha. Although, as we knew, this hypothesis was by no means universally accepted, it could not be denied that between the Ayyappan cult and Buddhism there were a number of interesting parallels, parallels that seemed almost too close to be coincidences. Devotees of Ayyappan recited *Ayyappan saraṇam*, 'Ayyappan the Refuge' or '(Take) refuge in Ayyappan', in much the same way as Buddhists recited *Buddhaṃ saraṇaṃ gacchāmi*, 'I go for refuge to the Buddha.' Unlike other Hindu gods, with the possible exceptions of Karttikeya and Ganesha, Ayyappan was a strictly celibate divinity. Moreover, on their annual pilgrimage to Sabarimalai, in central

Travancore, where Ayyappan had his principal shrine, devotees of the god not only observed an ethical code remarkably similar to the five precepts of Buddhism but, more extraordinary still, while actually on pilgrimage did *not* observe caste distinctions of any kind. This last fact was all the more significant inasmuch as the pilgrims were of all castes and communities including, so we were assured, even a few Muslims and Christians. The picture of Ayyappan which Krishna Pillai presented to the ashram, and which we hung in the shrine, depicted a youthful, two-armed figure, white in colour, and with a smiling face, squatting on his heels and wearing round his knees what appeared to be a meditation band. He was adorned, in princely fashion, with silks and jewels, and was flanked by various wild animals. To me this picture, which was the standard one, did not appear to bear a very close resemblance to any of the traditional representations of the Buddha, though subsequently, after I had left Muvattupuzha, it occurred to me that Ayyappan might well have been one of the great bodhisattvas, such as Mañjuśri or Avalokiteśvara. Be that as it may, it was significant not only that so many people in Travancore believed that Ayyappan was a form of the Buddha but that they wanted to believe. It was as though, through the familiar but unorthodox figure of the god of Sabarimalai, they were in fact reaching out to the Buddha and Buddhism.

Next to the Nairs, the two biggest communities in Travancore were the Eazhavas, or toddy-tappers, and the Christians. Our main Eazhava friend was Mr Krishnan, the local Conservator of Forests, whose jurisdiction extended over a third of the entire state. As its highest-ranking central government officer he enjoyed considerable prestige in the town, and was the means of introducing us to a number of people. Tall, slim, fair-complexioned, and almost completely Westernized, in his khaki shorts and solar topi he looked much more like an English tea planter than an Indian government servant. He could not forget his origins, however. Indeed, Travancore being what it was he would not have been allowed to forget them. Whenever we saw a brown figure in a loincloth shinning up a coconut-palm he would exclaim, with good-natured irony, 'There you are, that's what I am! I'm a toddy-tapper!' His official duties being what they were, Mr Krishnan was always having to go out on tour, and always urging us to accompany him. Occasionally, when we felt like an outing, we did so. On one of these excursions we watched a tract of jungle being cleared. Scores of elephants were at work, removing enormous logs of wood in their curled trunks. Sometimes we passed the night at a government bungalow, sometimes with relatives of Mr Krishnan. All his relatives were completely Westernized. Their houses were furnished in Western style, complete with antimacassars. Womenfolk spoke English as well as the men, and joined freely in the conversation. All, despite their 'low caste', were as light-skinned as Mr Krishnan.

The Christians of Muvattupuzha were divided into Syrian Christians, Anglicans, and Roman Catholics. Swami Agamananda having introduced us in the manner that he did, it was not surprising that they at first regarded us with deep suspicion, not to say hostility. Eventually, however, we succeeded in gaining the confidence of some of them. One or two we even enrolled as members of the ashram. If Christians could regularly approach Hindus for subscriptions, we said, why should Hindus and Buddhists not approach Christians? This argument appealed to the more broad-minded, and laughingly they paid up.

Our principal Christian friend was the Anglican postmaster, a man of about thirty with a cheerful golliwog face who wore a Western-style jacket and trousers during working hours and a plain white shirt and white sarong at home. He was keenly interested in English literature, and despite Satyapriya's manifest disapproval the pair of us occasionally discussed Shakespeare and Milton. Other Christian friends included the local Subdivisional Officer and the local Member of Parliament, both of whom were Syrian Christians. From the former we once heard an interesting anecdote. Before being posted to Muvattupuzha, he had been in charge of a subdivision in the interior of the state. One day, while checking revenue accounts in a remote village, he had heard in the distance an extraordinary sound, which for our benefit he did his best to imitate. It sounded like 'Hoooooooo-in! Hoooooooo-in!' with the emphasis falling sharp and short on the last syllable. On his enquiring from the clerks what it meant, they told him that it was a member of one of the 'Unseeable' castes warning high-caste Hindus of his approach.

Partly on account of the caste system and partly on account of some of the more bizarre manifestations of popular devotion, all our Christian friends had, we found, a strong antipathy toward Hinduism. Indeed, as we got to know them better, and as they felt they could be more open with us, some of them confessed to feelings of horror and loathing. It was as though they really sensed, in Hinduism, something evil, even diabolical, for which they were unable to account but which they both feared and hated. Such being the case, it was all the more surprising that several of them were strongly drawn to Buddhism. Varghese, the Member of Parliament, indeed admitted that as a student he had been deeply influenced by *The Light of Asia*. Whether our Christian friends had any real understanding of either Hinduism or Buddhism is another question. What they feared in Hinduism was the strength of its chthonic irrationality. Conversely, what attracted them in Buddhism was its apparent rationality, as well as the presence of a spiritual ideal which, on the ethical level, could be superficially assimilated with that of Christianity.

Despite their numerical inferiority to the Nairs, Eazhavas, and Christians, the Brahmins were, or had been, a highly influential community and were still of great social and religious consequence. They were divided into two groups, that of the Tamil Brahmins, who were more or less recent immigrants from the Madras Presidency, and the Malayali Brahmins, who were indigenous. Apart from Ramaswami Iyer and Venkateshwara Iyer, we had few friends among the Tamil Brahmins of Muvattupuzha. Among the Malayali Brahmins we had no friends at all. We had, however, one acquaintance. The manner in which we met him throws an interesting, if lurid, light on the more recondite workings of the caste system in Travancore.

Among the members of the ashram was a Nair woman, a distant relative of Kumaran Nair, who lived in a substantial house of the traditional type set in a spacious compound crammed with coconut trees. She knew a little English, and when we called for her monthly subscription we sometimes stayed for a chat. There were five or six children in the house, but no man. Her husband, apparently, was always out. One day, however, we found a handsome, fair-complexioned young man lounging against the railing of the veranda with his arms folded across his chest. On our entering into conversation with him, he told us that he was the father of the children, and that he had come to see their mother, who was his concubine. He was a Nambudiri Brahmin. Among the Nambudiris, he explained, only the eldest son was allowed to marry a Nambudiri woman and inherit the ancestral property. The younger sons, while they had the right to live at home at the family's expense, were not permitted to marry. Instead, they had to keep Nair women as concubines and visit them in their own homes. Caste restrictions, however, were still observed. With a rueful smile he told us that he was not permitted to touch his children, nor take so much as a glass of water under his concubine's roof.

Other friends subsequently filled in for us the details of this strange picture. Such was the prestige of Brahmins in general, and Nambudiri Brahmins in particular, that an alliance of this kind still reflected great honour on the family of the Nair women concerned. Indeed, the system extended even to the ruling family of Travancore, the present Maharaja himself being the product of a liaison between the previous Maharaja's sister and a Malayali Brahmin. These unequal unions were facilitated by the fact that Nair society was organized on a matrilineal basis, with property passing not from father to son, but from maternal uncle to nephew. The system was not without its disadvantages. Nambudiri girls were treated with extreme strictness, not to say harshness. If a girl so much as looked at a strange man, she was finished. Public announcements would be made of her crime, with the information that on a certain day, at a certain hour, she would be expelled from the parental home. As the time drew near, men of various castes and communities would gather expectantly outside the back door of the girl's house. Suddenly the door would fly open, the girl would be flung out, and the door again closed. The men would then fight for possession of the girl. Whoever seized hold of her first had the right to carry her off. Henceforward she belonged to him. Being fair-complexioned, which by Indian standards automatically meant beautiful, such girls were in great demand, especially among Muslims.

The Nambudiris were certainly a remarkable community. Judging by what we heard of them they were distinguished mainly for their extreme socio-religious orthodoxy and for the extent of their philanderings. According to a Malayalam proverb a Nambudiri Brahmin took three ceremonial baths a day and enjoyed four women. Another Nambudiri characteristic was that they had no inhibitions about nudity. Instead of taking water with them to the latrine, as everybody else did, they would wander about looking for it afterwards, all the time keeping their dhoti hitched up in such a way that they were indecently exposed. One of the commonest sights of the day in villages of the interior, we were told, was that of a group of Nambudiri Brahmins squatting after their bath under the *mandapa*, or covered stone platform in front of the temple, all deep in discussion, and all stark naked. Mindful of the fact that Shankaracharya, the great non-dualist philosopher, had been a Nambudiri Brahmin, I enquired what it was they usually discussed. 'Sex,' I was told, 'nothing but sex.' Perhaps it was in circles such as these that works like the *Kāma Sūtras* had originated. Even among the Nambudiris, however, the old order was changing. Younger sons were growing restive, and a number of them had, in fact, become Communists.

Most of our friends we met in their own homes. Hardly any of them ever visited us at the ashram. Krishna Varrier was one of the exceptions. Indeed, the old man was exceptional in many ways. Not only was he the sole representative of the Varrier community in Muvattupuzha, but he never wore anything other than the briefest of loincloths and a string of *rudrākṣa* beads. What he lacked in clothing, however, he more than made up for with what Satyapriya and I jocularly termed war-paint. Forehead, arms, and chest were streaked with white ash, liberally applied, as well as spotted with pink and yellow sandalwood paste. Since he lived alone, and had no regular occupation, he was a fairly frequent visitor. Emerging from the shrine after the morning puja we would find him sitting in our room, shaven head sunk on his chest, and white-stubbled visage creased in a toothless grin. Despite his broken English, and our still more broken Malayalam, we were soon on familiar terms. One day we asked him where the Varriers stood in the caste system. 'Higher than Brahmins,' he replied with a chuckle. At first we thought he was joking. For orthodox Hinduism 'higher than Brahmins' was a contradiction in terms: the Brahmins, by definition, were the highest. Nevertheless, our old friend persisted in his assertion.

Afterwards, talking the matter over between ourselves, Satyapriya and I wondered if the Varriers had any connection with Buddhism. They were a small community. It was said there were only a few hundred of them in the entire state. Like Krishna Varrier himself, who had been initiated into the secrets of the Tantric goddess Rājarājeśvarī, all were good Sanskrit scholars, and well versed in traditional religious, medical, and occult lore. Possibly, like the Vajracharyas of Nepal, they were the laicized descendants of Buddhist monks of the late Tantric period. This would explain the claim to be 'higher than Brahmins', and also, perhaps, the definite connection with Tantrism. However, we were unable to investigate the matter further, and the origins of the Varriers remained, for us, one of the unsolved mysteries of Travancore.

34
OUTINGS AND ACTIVITIES

Much as we enjoyed meeting our friends and familiarizing ourselves with the manners and customs of the various communities, Satyapriya and I were happiest at the ashram, which indeed had become our spiritual home. Except at the beginning of the month, when we were out collecting subscriptions, in accordance with our original intentions we spent more and more time in meditation, and also started observing silence. After our evening meditation, which now ended quite late, we would not speak again until after puja the following morning.

There were other changes. Raman Nair left, and at Swami Agamananda's suggestion was replaced by Shankara Pillai, a thin, active retired clerk of about forty. As Shankara Pillai was a more imaginative cook than his half-witted predecessor, wood-chips, dry or in water, were soon replaced by a more nourishing diet. For breakfast and supper there was rice-gruel, eaten with the help of a *jak*-leaf spoon, and for lunch rice and chutney, the chutney consisting of pounded coconut and red chillies. Sometimes there was a dessert, usually either sticky yellow valves of the *jak* fruit or a few bananas. Occasionally, as a special treat, we had poppadam, or rice-flour cakes of wafer thinness, which Shankara Pillai bought ready made in the bazaar. This, however, presented a problem. There was caste in poppadoms. One could buy Brahmin poppadom, Nair poppadom, Eazhava poppadom, and Christian-Muslim poppadom, but in Travancore there was no such thing as a casteless poppadom. What were we to do? In the end we left it to Shankara Pillai, which probably meant that we ate Nair poppadam.

Before many months had passed the ashram wore a neater, less neglected look. Besides being a cook, our new manager was also a cultivator. As with most Malayalis, indeed, cultivation of the soil was in his blood, and he soon had the ashram land well in hand. He watered the flowering shrubs on the upper terrace every day, so that they bloomed more profusely than ever, and cleared the wasteland further down in readiness for tapioca. Nor was the ashram itself forgotten. On Satyapriya's instructions, he had missing roof-tiles replaced, exposed brickwork recemented. Finally, in confirmation of his managerial status, he was allowed to employ an Untouchable old woman as sweeper. Clad in only the briefest of loincloths, and with her white hair tumbling about her shoulders, she would creep noiselessly into the compound every morning and sweep up the fallen *jak* leaves that littered the courtyard outside our room. For this service we paid her two rupees a month.

For someone of my temperament, conditions at our ridgetop retreat were now ideal. When not actually meditating or studying, I was content simply to sit on the low veranda wall watching the way in which the rubbery green leaves of the plantain flapped and shivered in the seemingly motionless air, or listening to the rise and fall of the lilting, yodelling cry with which, throughout the day and night, a cultivator worked the Persian wheel in rice-fields half a mile from our gate. Sometimes, when I had been deeply moved by the beauty of the scene or by my own reflections, words and descriptive phrases would rise unbidden from the depths, occasionally forming themselves into lines of verse, into poems. For Satyapriya, however, this idyllic existence was not enough. Even with our excursions into the town, most of which I would quite gladly have forgone, a life of meditation and study did not provide him with sufficient outlets for his abounding energies, and he was soon casting about for something else to do. Eventually, he decided to organize the distribution of powdered milk to the children of the locality, a number of whom were clearly under-nourished.

At four o'clock every afternoon, therefore, the ashram was invaded by twenty or thirty boys and girls of all ages, from toddlers to teenagers, each carrying a brass tumbler, or perhaps a coconut-shell cup. Before their arrival the milk powder, which we obtained through the local branch of the Red Cross, would be mixed with water by Shankara

Satyapriya (photo from 1949)

Pillai in an outsize cooking-pot. On the very first day of distribution we noticed that the children instinctively separated themselves according to caste, and try as we might it was almost impossible to get them to mix. The Untouchable children, who were darker and dirtier than the others and more ragged (when they wore clothes at all), at first would not even come as far as the porch of the side veranda, where the milk was distributed, but insisted on clustering at the foot of the front steps. Only after several weeks of persuasion would they come as far as the veranda, an encroachment to which the other children reacted by automatically edging away. Another problem was that many of the children had been instructed not to drink the milk on the ashram premises but to carry it home for the family coffee. Satyapriya and I therefore had to make sure that every drop was drunk up on the spot, a proceeding that involved a great deal of mock serious threatenings on our part and a great deal of laughter on theirs. Despite their early exposure to caste prejudices the children, though at first somewhat shy, were on the whole lively and friendly enough, and we were glad to see their numbers growing and their health showing signs of improvement week by week.

Encouraged by the success of the milk distribution, Satyapriya started a Sunday morning *bhajan* session at which he sang devotional songs to the accompaniment of a pair of small cymbals, the congregation joining in the chorus in the prescribed manner. At the conclusion of these sessions *prasad* or sacramental food would be distributed. As I had a poor ear, and was in any case not particularly moved by the praises of Rama or Krishna, I did not join in these performances. Originally the *bhajan* was intended to provide the ashram members with the equivalent of a Sunday morning service, but adults soon stopped coming, and with only children attending, mainly for the sake of the *prasad*, it eventually became, like the milk distribution, an exclusively junior occasion. Not that Satyapriya minded this. With a crowd of children clapping hands and gleefully joining in the choruses he could let himself go to a greater extent than in the presence of their more critical elders, bawling out the hymns as lustily – and as unmusically – as he pleased. Adults came only for more solid spiritual nourishment. Occasionally, therefore, we organized public meetings and lectures at the ashram.

One of the most successful of these was held on the first Christmas Day after our arrival, when I spoke on Buddhism and Christianity. Over a hundred people attended, including our friend the Postmaster and one or two other Christians. In Travancore, of course, it was unheard of for a Christian to enter a Hindu place of worship, and we were told that this was the first time a non-Hindu had ever set foot inside the ashram premises; but I had deliberately chosen a provocative subject, and sure enough, the fish had risen to the bait. Towards the end of my lecture I summarized the evidence for Buddhist influence on early Christianity. Though I knew quite well that such influence was only a possibility, and that there was no direct proof, I carefully marshalled all the relevant facts and stated my case as strongly as I could. Christianity in Travancore being an extremely militant faith, I wanted to stage if not a full-scale 'counter-attack from the East' at least a small diversionary skirmish. Sure enough, as I drove home my points, referring now to Aśoka's missions to the West in the third century BCE, now to the Essenes, and now to the parallels between Buddhist and Christian parables, I saw a look of dismay pass across the cheerful face of the good Postmaster, who was standing at the back of the audience. Subsequently, we had several discussions on the subject, and though I could never bring him to admit so much as the possibility of Buddhism having ever influenced Christianity, at least he was willing to discuss the subject, and that in my view was the main thing. Our Hindu friends were of course extremely pleased with the lecture. They accepted all my arguments without question, and regarded my case as proved, which of course it was not. However, I did not grudge them their satisfaction. Hinduism having been so long on the defensive in Travancore, I felt that they were entitled once in a while to enjoy a small booster to their morale.

Sometimes we participated in functions held in the town. Five weeks after my lecture on Buddhism and Christianity there occurred in New Delhi an event that sent a thrill of horror through the entire country, indeed through practically the whole world, and which, being felt in Muvattupuzha no less deeply than elsewhere, involved us in the biggest public meeting held in the town during our sojourn there. On 31 January 1948 Mahatma Gandhi was assassinated. On our way through Delhi, only six months earlier, Satyapriya and I had debated whether or not to go and see him. Now, to my intense regret, the opportunity was gone for ever. At first people were simply stunned by the news. Then there were fears of large-scale communal riots between Muslims and Hindus – it being at first widely assumed that the Mahatma must have been assassinated by a Muslim. When it was known that the assassin was Nathuram Godse, a Brahmin, people's reaction was one of relief. 'Thank God it was a Hindu,' they said. Public grief was intense. Newspapers appeared with heavy black borders, and for once Satyapriya and I read them.

A week later I was invited to preside over the condolence meeting that had been organized to give expression to the town's sense of grief and bereavement. The meeting was held in the evening, in the grounds of the local high school. By the time the proceedings started darkness had fallen, and the stars had come out in the deep blue sky above the dark tops of the coconut-palms. The only illumination was that of a small oil lamp standing on the table before me, with its soft golden light shining on the faces of the first two or three rows of the densely packed crowd squatting at my feet. The rest of the meeting was plunged in darkness. To my surprise, at the back of the gathering I saw the red pin-points of a dozen or more cigarettes, while from the people standing behind me, among whom were most of the leading citizens of the town, I perceived a strong smell of liquor. Several people, I subsequently learned, had come to the meeting straight from the toddy-shop. In my presidential speech I took the culprits severely to task, whereupon the red pin-points abruptly vanished, and two or three of the figures behind my chair silently melted into the shadows. Mahatma Gandhi had only been dead a week, I said, but it seemed that people had already started forgetting his teachings.

Of incomparably less importance, though of great interest to all sections of the Christian community, was the garden party that was held at the local Anglican church in honour of a visiting Anglican bishop. To this function Satyapriya and I were invited through the good offices of the Postmaster. As the bishop was an Indian by birth, I had hoped it would be possible for us to have some discussion with him. Indeed, in my innocence I had even imagined that he would welcome the opportunity of meeting representatives of another faith. But a discussion with two saffron-robed ascetics, one of them apparently a Westerner, was the last thing the bishop wanted. On our being introduced to him he coldly shook hands and turned away without a word. Before many minutes had passed he had made his position clear. Replying to the address of welcome, he referred to Travancore as 'this Christian land' as though the Hindus of the state, who after all outnumbered the Christians two to one, simply did not exist. Some of the Hindus present, among whom was Kumaran Nair, waxed extremely indignant at this affront, but as usual they only muttered among themselves and did nothing.

Conscious as we were of the need for seclusion, Satyapriya and I did as little as possible to attract the attention of the outside world. Nevertheless, despite our precautions word of our presence in Muvattupuzha spread to the surrounding area, and before long we were being inundated with invitations from lecture-hungry Malayalis all over the state. These invitations were couched in the most flattering terms and were at first usually addressed to me, as the superior attraction, but coming to understand that they could not have one of the strange, casteless, nationality-less ascetics without the other, the organizers soon learned to include Satyapriya too in their arrangements.

One of the most extraordinary of these meetings took us some distance from Muvattupuzha. Thousands of people had assembled, and what seemed to be a fair was in progress. Rather to our surprise, we were not due to speak until midnight, but this was apparently the usual practice. Meanwhile the crowd was being entertained by the antics of five or six dancing elephants, all elaborately painted and caparisoned and with gilded tusks. To the deafening sound of drums and hautboys the great beasts would rise slowly and majestically on their hind legs and then move from side to side in time with the music. When they had risen to their full height half-naked figures perched on the top of their enormous heads would perform fantastic acrobatic dances, at the same time waving in semaphore-fashion what seemed to be enormous flag-shaped fans. With pitch darkness all around, and only the red glare of torches fitfully lighting up the scene, altogether it was a magnificent spectacle. Our lectures, I felt, would be an anticlimax.

So far as my own lecture was concerned my fears were justified – though not on account of the elephants. Satyapriya, who spoke first, concluded his lecture by telling the audience that I would be speaking next and that I would be saying exactly what he had just said, and that the two lectures would be absolutely identical. The only difference, he assured them, would be that I would be putting the matter in slightly different words. Besides making things difficult for me, this naive announcement caused Satyapriya to look ridiculous, and I was mortified to see derisory smiles appearing on the faces of the more sophisticated members of the audience. Swami Dharmananda, who was on the platform with us, having also been invited to speak, could not forbear a chuckle. However, I spoke as though nothing had happened, and did my best to retrieve the situation. Satyapriya certainly had no intention of making my lecture an anticlimax to his own. Knowing that we disagreed on certain issues, he was only anxious that our differences should not be obvious to the audience and that we should create an impression of unanimity.

On another occasion we visited Varkala and Thackalay, the two main centres of the movement started by Narayana Guru at the beginning of the century. As we already knew from a pamphlet given us by one of our friends, Narayana Guru was a Hindu religious teacher and social reformer of great integrity who, despite the severe handicap of having been born an Eazhava, by the time of his death had become a widely respected and highly influential figure not only in Travancore but throughout a great part of South India. At Varkala, the social headquarters of the movement, we attended a meeting held in the spacious inner courtyard of what seemed to be an ashram. But nothing much happened. Indeed, there was a sense of unspoken differences, even of silent controversy, in the air. It was as though opposing forces were cancelling each other out and preventing anything being done, so that the whole place had a curiously inert, lifeless atmosphere. However, we were able to exchange a few words with Nataraja Guru, Narayana Guru's best-known disciple, a man in the prime of life who, with his grizzled shoulder-length locks and flowing robes of pale yellow silk, seemed half monk and half layman.

At Thackalay, which was the movement's religious headquarters, there were no meetings, and we spent our time quietly. One afternoon, in an octagonal building of red laterite that stood out vividly against the lush greens of the surrounding countryside, we met eight or nine members of the monastic order founded by Narayana Guru and had a long discussion with them about Buddhism. Unlike Nataraja Guru they were all shaven-headed and wore the saffron robes of the orthodox Hindu ascetic. Nevertheless, there seemed to be something wrong, or at least not quite right. It was as though they did not really feel themselves to be monks at all, and were only acting a part. Possibly this was because being Eazhavas they knew that they were not recognized as monks outside their own community. We were also shown two temples, one dedicated to the goddess Saraswati, the other to the god Shiva. The movement did not recognize the Hindu deities, we were told, but Narayana Guru had authorized the worship of Saraswati, patroness of learning, as the symbol of pure Beauty, and of Shiva, lord of ascetics, as the symbol of Renunciation. Unlike more orthodox places of Hindu worship, the two temples were spotlessly clean, well lit, and colourful.

Despite daily milk distributions and weekly *bhajan* sessions, and even our occasional outings, the energies Satyapriya had left over from meditation and study were still far from having found a satisfactory outlet. Eventually, after much fretting and chafing and many discussions with our friends, especially those on the ashram committee, he decided that it would be a good idea for us to raise funds for the purchase of a number of hand-looms and open an industrial section of the ashram. Children of poor parents would be given training in weaving, basket-making, and other cottage industries and in this way enabled to earn a living. At first it was proposed to house the industrial section in the porch and side veranda, but these were too small to accommodate more than five or six looms, and in the end we decided against this. Besides, the continual racket of the looms would have completely destroyed the peaceful atmosphere of the ashram, and Satyapriya was as desirous as I was that this should be avoided.

Fortunately, happening to examine the title-deeds of the ashram, we discovered that on the opposite side of the path running past our front gate was about half an acre of unfenced and uncultivated land that belonged to the ashram. Though nobody had known about this plot, and though it had of course been encroached upon, with the help of Kumaran Nair and other legal friends we had no difficulty in establishing the ashram's title to possession. Why should the industrial section not be located here? Why should there not be not just an industrial section of the ashram but an independent Industrial School? Why should we not construct a special building for it? In his mind's eye Satyapriya already saw an imposing edifice with dozens of teachers and hundreds of pupils from all over the state. People would come to look at it and admire it, from all over India.

Within a matter of days the land had been cleared and levelled and blueprints prepared. Money also started coming in. As the Industrial School was to be quite separate from the ashram, with its own committee, and as its function was purely social and educational, we did not hesitate to approach even people who had no interest in the religious activities of the ashram and ask them to contribute towards the cost of construction. On all sides the scheme met with warm approval.

Satyapriya was delighted. From morning till night he was busy with builders' estimates, with specifications for looms, with accounts, as well as with discussions and consultations of every kind. At last he had found an outlet for his energies.

Preparations were in full swing when fortune favoured us again. Having discovered that we had land for the Industrial School we found that we had building materials as well. Beneath a thin layer of topsoil the ridge-end on which the ashram stood was a solid block of laterite. Soon a coolie with an axe was excavating twenty-inch slabs in the bottom half of the compound, the soft porous stone coming up looking for all the world like freshly cut red Gruyère cheese.

This coolie was an Untouchable, son or grandson of the old woman who swept our courtyard, and father of two or three of the dusky toddlers who came for afternoon milk. The whole family, consisting of seven or eight persons, inhabited a tiny clearing in the jungle halfway between the ashram and the river, and Satyapriya and I often passed them on our way down to our morning bath. Plastered with black mud, the wretched hovels in which they lived looked more like the dens of wild beasts than human habitations. Famished curs, all ribs and eyes, slunk about with their tails between their legs, while red-eyed black swine rooted for scraps in the surrounding mire. There were no amenities of any kind. The Untouchables themselves were thin, black, and furtive, with unwashed bodies and frowzy hair, and were at first extremely embarrassed that we should have detected their shameful unclean presence.

Our young laterite-cutter, however, was strikingly different from the rest. Hardly more than twenty, he had a copper-coloured, almost golden body, finely proportioned, while his face, which was extraordinarily beautiful, wore an expression of angelic innocence. I could not help wondering if Nambudiri philanderings extended even to the huts of the Untouchables. Being accustomed to hearing only orders or abuse, he was extremely shy with us, and it proved impossible to enter into conversation with him. The only response we got was an amiable, though foolish, grin. Besides, he was often drunk, and looked at us uncomprehendingly with bloodshot eyes. Nevertheless we did eventually learn his name. It was Panglin, he told us, rubbing his arm across his forehead with embarrassment.

What Panglin meant we were unable to fathom. It was certainly not a Sanskrit word, and it did not even sound like a Malayalam one. Eventually Kumaran Nair enlightened us. Panglin and Tanglin were names of wild birds. In Travancore, as in other parts of India, Untouchables were not allowed to use the ordinary Hindu personal names. Instead they were known either by the names of birds or beasts or by such denominations as Dirty, Ugly, Stupid, Thief, and Rascal. If an Untouchable was asked what his name was, therefore, he would have to reply, for example, 'My name is Stupid,' or 'I am called Ugly.' The reason they were not allowed to use Hindu names was that these usually incorporated the name of a god or goddess, and the names of gods and goddesses were much too sacred to be defiled by association with the Untouchables. Once again I was forcibly reminded of Swami Vivekananda's famous exclamation, when travelling in the same part of the country half a century earlier. Malabar was a mad-house! But if orthodox Hinduism was mad in its treatment of the Untouchables, here as elsewhere in India there seemed to be a cruel method in its madness.

On our learning the meaning of Panglin, Satyapriya promptly 're-christened' the young stone-cutter. Henceforth his name would be Rama, he told him. But Rama only looked up from his work with a fuddled grin, and though Satyapriya afterwards got him to respond to the name it was clear that the change meant very little to him.

As Swami Agamananda was president of the ashram committee, we naturally had to consult him with regard to our new project. This involved several trips to Kalady. On one of our visits we arrived late at night and were alarmed to find the whole ashram surrounded by an armed guard of about sixty policemen with rifles, so that after establishing our identity we had to creep along the bank of the river and make our way in through the back entrance. Swami Agamananda was having one of his periodic affrays with the local Roman Catholics, and apparently this time their blood was up. Not only had he attacked the Virgin Mary in his magazine, saying that she was no better than she should have been and that Christ was the illegitimate son of a Roman soldier, but he had even had the effrontery to acquire, through the State Government, a plot of land that the Catholics had wanted for a new church. Roused to fever pitch by their priests, an infuriated mob was now bent on lynching Swami Agamananda and burning the ashram to the ground. Satyapriya and I were far from approving Swami Agamananda's abuse of the Virgin Mary, but we knew that he was only retaliating for the attacks that Christians of all denominations (except the Syrians) had long been in the habit of making on the morals of Sri Krishna and other Hindu gods, and in reason they could hardly complain if he considered that sauce for the goose was surely sauce for the gander. Inside the ashram we found him cheerful and unrepentant. Indeed, having scored over his enemies, he was in a merry mood. Roman Catholics were an excitable lot, he told us, his eyes twinkling. Always up in arms about something or other. Never mind, they would learn, they would learn....

35
THE PATH WITHIN

The rainy season had come and gone, and our angel-faced stone-cutter had excavated some 2,000 blocks of red laterite, when Satyapriya abruptly called off the whole Industrial School project. For several months he had thought of little else. Leaving me to give the children their free milk, he had frequently spent the whole day in town, returning only at about six o'clock in time for the evening meditation. Now the tide had turned. A strong reaction had at last set in. He was tired of social work, tired of having to meet people. He did not want to have anything more to do with blueprints and builders' estimates. All he wanted to do was meditate. Industrial schools were all very well in their own way, but to provide them was no part of the duty of one who had renounced the world and dedicated himself to the spiritual life. His duty, indeed his sole duty, was to realize the Truth.

Acting on this new-found understanding, Satyapriya promptly drew up an ambitious programme of meditation, hatha yoga exercises, and scriptural study that would keep him busy from early in the morning until late at night. It was, indeed, one of his most outstanding characteristics that he did nothing by halves. Everything was to him either black or white, and he could therefore commit himself to whatever happened to be his current conviction or enthusiasm without hesitation, reservation, or qualification. Doubts were traitors. Fears were liars. Having wound up the Industrial School committee, and discontinued the daily milk distribution and the weekly *bhajan* session, he therefore plunged into full-time spiritual practice as wholeheartedly as he had previously plunged into social work. Visitors were discouraged. Soon there descended upon the ashram a silence that was hardly ever broken by the sound of intruding footsteps.

Though the rapidity and completeness of Satyapriya's volte-face took me by surprise, it did not at first make any significant difference to my own routine. Study, meditation, and literary work were my only real interests, and these I had diligently pursued ever since our arrival in Muvattupuzha. During the three or four months that my friend had been preoccupied with plans for the Industrial School, his repeated absences from the ashram had indeed given me additional time for reflection, and a number of things had become clear to me. Six years had passed since I had first read the *Diamond Sūtra* and the *Sūtra of Wei Lang* and realized that I was a Buddhist. During that time I had read much, not only about Buddhism but about Hinduism and other spiritual traditions. I had also had the opportunity of coming into personal contact with both Buddhists and Hindus. Very much to my regret, I had to admit that so far I had been more fortunate in my contacts with Hindus than with Buddhists. Among the Buddhist monks I had met there was none who could be compared with the Yoga Swami of Jaffna, or with Anandamayi. Bhikkhu Soma was perhaps comparable with Swami Pavitrananda, but on the whole such Theravādin monks as I had encountered had impressed me as less active, less cultured, and less spiritually alive than their counterparts in the Ramakrishna Mission. But for all these disappointments I was more of a Buddhist than ever. Indeed, so firmly was I convinced of the truth of Buddhism, that even had I never met another Buddhist whom I could respect, or had I been the only Buddhist in the world, it would have been quite impossible for me to follow any other path. My present isolation in the midst of a completely Hindu environment served only to intensify my awareness of Buddhism. Encounters with one or another manifestation of the harsh and divisive spirit of the caste system reminded me of Buddhism's compassionate concern for the welfare of all sentient beings. Pious references to God, or to the Supreme Self, recalled its rejection of a Supreme Being and of an unchanging immortal soul.

Partly as a result of this conflict with Hinduism, partly as a result of its own natural development, at this period my faith in Buddhism underwent a significant change. From being a quasi-instinctive attraction, a sort of spiritual falling-in-love, it became more of the nature of a reasoned conviction that included understanding as well as emotion, clarity as well as passion. While in Calcutta I had immersed myself in the writings of D.T. Suzuki, particularly in his *Outlines of Mahāyāna Buddhism* and *Essays in Zen Buddhism*, both of which had given me further tantalizing glimpses into the magical world of the Mahāyāna. Now, relying mainly on Bhikkhu Silacara's translation of the first fifty discourses of the *Majjhima Nikāya*, or Collection of Middle-Length Discourses of the Buddha, and on Mrs Rhys Davids's Home University Library book on Buddhism, I started exploring colder and clearer regions of the spirit. Three of the Buddha's teachings in particular drew my attention. These were the doctrine of conditioned co-production, the four noble truths, and the three characteristics of conditioned existence. Previously, though they were all well known to me, I had given them very little systematic attention. Now they occupied my mind virtually to the exclusion of everything else. Besides reflecting on them during the day I meditated on them at night. Or rather, as I meditated, flashes of insight into the transcendental truths of which they were the expression in conceptual terms would sometimes spontaneously arise.

Something of this concern with the fundamentals of what, for want of a better word, we call Buddhist thought, appears in the articles I wrote at this time. Several of them deal, in one way or another, with the doctrine of *anattā*, which represents the Buddha's realization of the fact that the 'soul' (*attā*) is not an entity but a process, so that if one's definition of reality involves the notion of permanence the soul is necessarily unreal.[32] One of these articles, entitled 'The Goal of Life's Endeavour',[33] was the cause of serious unpleasantness with Satyapriya. It had been written specially for the Silver Jubilee souvenir published by the local printing press, the proprietor of which was an ashram member. After Satyapriya had read it I pointed out to him that the structure of the article corresponded to that of the four noble truths. Instead of being pleased with this device, as I had expected, he became almost insane with fury. I was trying to propagate Buddhism by underhand methods. I was trying to undermine Hinduism, he shouted. He would expose me, he would denounce me to the authorities, he would see that I was imprisoned. It was an hour before he calmed down. Eventually, he admitted that even though I was seriously at fault he ought not to have become so angry, and declared that since his fault balanced mine he would forgive me for what I had done to him even though, with my usual intransigence, I refused to acknowledge that I was in the wrong.

Despite the fact that the peace and tranquillity of the ashram were occasionally shattered by outbursts of this kind, which more often than not he bitterly regretted, Satyapriya adhered faithfully to the programme he had set himself and soon had more than made up for lost time. With hatha yoga, the traditional Indian system of physical exercises, he was already familiar, having practised it in his youth. Now, with renewed enthusiasm, he not only brushed up what he already knew but wrote off to Bombay for a series of bulky modern treatises on the subject, as well as for translations of the classical Sanskrit texts. Some of these volumes I too read, including the well-known *Hatha Yoga Pradīpikā* and *Gheraṇḍa Saṃhitā*. Under Satyapriya's guidance, I also took up various exercises and, while showing no great aptitude for the subject, eventually succeeded in mastering eight or nine elementary *āsanas* or postures. Though I knew that in modern India hatha yoga was often treated as an end in itself, rather than as a means to an end, the importance for the spiritual life of physical health and vigour was obvious, and there seemed to be no reason for not utilizing the ancient discipline in the manner originally intended.

One day, probably in connection with some new exercises about which Satyapriya had been reading, the question of fasting arose. After discussing the matter thoroughly, and informing ourselves of the precautions to be taken, we decided to experiment, first with a two-day fast, then with one lasting a whole week. Fasting was, we knew, a time-honoured spiritual discipline. Ancient sages had sometimes fasted for months on end. Even in these degenerate modern days, Mahatma Gandhi had more than once fasted for several weeks (admittedly for political rather than spiritual reasons), while among ordinary people fasting on the anniversary of the death of one's father or mother, or at certain phases of the moon, was still a common practice. Fasting helped to destroy craving, not only craving for food, but for material things in general. It enabled one to recognize the strength of one's attachments. It was conducive to peace and serenity of mind. Moreover, fasting was good for health. It expelled toxins from the body, and purified the whole system.

With all this ringing in our ears, we started our experiment. The two-day fast went off smoothly enough, and after allowing a week to pass we told Shankara Pillai that for the next seven days he would be cooking only for himself. Before we actually started, the idea of fasting for a whole week seemed slightly suicidal. It was as though, in depriving ourselves of food for so long a period, we were deliberately taking a look into the face of death. But we need not have worried. On the third day, as the stomach reached the limit of its contractions, we felt extremely hungry, and visions of ravishing dishes danced before our eyes. Occasionally there was a slight fever and dizziness (due, I learned later, not to bodily weakness but the expulsion of toxins). These were the only discomforts we experienced. Towards the end of the week, especially, we felt light, almost weightless, as though we hardly belonged to the world at all. The mind, once its initial reactions had subsided, became calm and bright. There was no desire to do anything, and no desire not to do anything. We sauntered about the courtyard, or sat in our room, silent, aware, content.

During these and subsequent fasts we consumed only water, with perhaps a few drops of lime juice. Tea in any case we never took. Since our arrival in Muvattupuzha we had eschewed both tea and coffee. Whether at the houses of our friends, or in the ashram, we drank either water or one or another of the traditional Malayali thirst-quenchers. Among the latter were a preparation of whey flavoured with salt, fresh ginger, green chillies, and a local green herb; a mixture of molasses and water; and jeerum-vellum, a popular drink made from a kind of seed and taken hot after meals. Partly on principle, partly for reasons of economy, we lived a life of extreme simplicity. For a long time we did without soap, this being esteemed a luxury in the villages of South India, and as such not suitable for those who had given up the world. Toothbrushes and toothpaste had been replaced by the cheaper and no less effective *margosa* twig and rolled mango leaf. As for clothes, we were still wearing the gerua-stained shirts and sarongs in which we had left Kasauli more than a year ago and these, having been laundered almost daily in the Indian manner, were now becoming in places more than a little threadbare.

Since the day that Satyapriya had called off the Industrial School project neither he nor I had gone outside the ashram compound. Indeed, to save time we had discontinued the practice of going down to the river every morning for our bath and instead now took it standing in the stone cistern beside the well. After the thick well-rope had run through our fingers there would be a faint splash as the bucket hit the surface of the water sixty or seventy feet below. Then, when a sudden drag on the rope had signalled a full bucket, the long slow haul to the top would begin. Even in the hottest weather, the water was always icy cold, and I finished quickly, ladling only one or two bucketfuls of water over me to Satyapriya's four or five.

One morning I had an extremely unpleasant experience. As I picked up my towel from the edge of the cistern something suddenly stung me in the wrist. It was a scorpion. Within minutes the venom had spread all the way up my left arm, which rapidly became puffed and swollen. The pain was excruciating. On hearing my calls, Satyapriya and Shankara Pillai came rushing to my assistance and were soon vigorously rubbing the affected arm with ashes, this being the traditional local remedy. Fortunately, the scorpion was not fully grown, otherwise the sting might have proved fatal. As it was, my arm remained swollen and painful for a whole week and I felt very feverish.

What with meditation and hatha yoga, as well as study and literary work – not to speak of fasting – the weeks slipped by almost without our noticing. One day it occurred to us that well over a month had passed since we had last called on the ashram members, and that subscriptions were long overdue. What was to be done? Unless we took prompt action, some of the subscriptions might lapse, in which case the ashram finances would suffer. Formerly, Satyapriya would have leaped to his feet, seized his account book and been out of the gate and on the road into town in a flash. Now, however, he flatly refused to go. Worldly people were all hypocrites, he declared. Despite their nauseating protestations of piety and devotion they were mean and deceitful in the extreme, the slaves of every imaginable kind of weakness and depravity. Worst of all, they wallowed day and night in the mire of sensuality, and he wanted to have nothing whatever to do with them. In future, I would have to go out and collect the monthly subscriptions by myself. People liked me, he averred – rather equivocally in the circumstances – whereas they disliked him for his honesty and straightforwardness, and they would be glad to see me on my own. The latter part of his statement, unfortunately, was only too true. On some people, Satyapriya's rough speech and overbearing manner, as well as his morbid quickness to take offence, had made a distinctly unfavourable impression. Others, recognizing his fundamental goodness of heart, were able to overlook the less attractive manifestations of this sturdy independence of spirit. Besides, Hinduism had a long and highly respectable tradition of hot-tempered sages and it was not difficult for them to assimilate him to some peppery Vedic original.

At first the ashram members and other friends whom I visited clearly thought that, with Satyapriya out of the way, they would be able to extract from me the precious secret of my caste and nationality without much difficulty. But to their disappointment I proved no less intractable than he had been. If anything, I was more difficult to handle. Instead of reacting to the more impertinent enquiries with angry impatience, as he had sometimes done, I stonewalled them with a joke, with one of their own favourite philosophical generalizations, or with a bland smile. Despite such intransigence, however, the fact that I now came to see them on my own, without Satyapriya, soon put my relationship with many of the ashram members on a more friendly footing. Previously Satyapriya had always done most of the talking, while I either remained silent or contributed to the discussion no more than an occasional remark. This led to my acquiring an entirely undeserved reputation for taciturnity, if not downright unsociability. In the eyes of some of our friends, of course, taciturnity was a sign of spirituality. Others believed that I spoke so little not from choice but from necessity, my English being less perfect than that of my friend.

The truth of the matter was that I knew from repeated bitter experience that if Satyapriya thought I was giving people the impression that I knew something that he did not know, especially about philosophy or religion, or if they showed the slightest sign of paying greater attention to me than to him, or of valuing my opinion more, there would be trouble. On one occasion, thinking that I was about to speak, Kumaran Nair had interrupted him with the words 'Be quiet, Swami-ji is going to say something.' The repercussions of this unfortunate incident lasted for days. In the end I learned that trouble could be avoided and peace preserved only by my saying as little as possible and ensuring that, in any conversation or discussion, Satyapriya always occupied the centre of the stage. Had I been a Christian such self-effacement would doubtless have been regarded as providing a lesson in humility. Being a Buddhist I took it as an exercise in mindfulness.

Not only did I have to watch carefully over what I said, when I did say anything, but also to observe the effects of my words on other people, especially on Satyapriya. Good for me though this training undoubtedly was, it was a strain to have to keep it up for so long, and for such reasons. Indeed, it was only after I had started collecting the ashram subscriptions on my own, and could once more talk freely with people, that I realized how great the strain had been. For their part, the ashram members could not help noticing the change, and not only eagerly plied me with questions but asked for advice on various personal matters. Though the last thing I wanted to do was to give the impression of having been held in check by Satyapriya, they clearly felt that now that I was on my own a barrier had been removed, and once I had made my position clear on the burning topic of caste and nationality we were able to have a number of serious and worthwhile discussions.

Satyapriya himself, however, was not by any means very happy about these developments. On my departure from the ashram he would warn me not to waste time talking to people, especially the Christians, and on my return always cross-examined me closely as to whom I had met and what had been said. Sometimes, indeed, he acted as though I could not be trusted, and that if he was not careful I would enter into a conspiracy with the Christians against him.

36
'KRISHNA HAS COME!'

One day, while I was out on one of my subscription-collecting expeditions, there occurred in my absence an incident which, while not unprecedented in my experience, was unusual enough to provide us with food for thought for some time afterwards. On returning to the ashram, shortly before one o'clock, I found Satyapriya and Shankara Pillai waiting for me at the top of the steps leading up to the front veranda. Both were in a state of subdued, even suppressed, excitement. Before I could open my mouth Satyapriya exclaimed, 'Shankara Pillai, tell Swami-ji what I told you half an hour ago!' Half amused, half embarrassed, Shankara Pillai related how, thirty minutes earlier, Satyapriya, who had been meditating, called out to him to serve lunch for four people, instead of for three as usual, as he had heard me coming along the road beneath the compound wall talking to one of the ashram members, whose voice he had recognized. To their surprise, however, neither of us turned up, and when Shankara Pillai, anxious that the rice should not get cold, had gone to the gate to see what had become of us, there was nobody to be seen. Suspecting what might have happened, Satyapriya had then repeated word for word to Shankara Pillai the conversation that he had overheard between me and my companion, an unsuccessful Nair lawyer whose invalid son I sometimes visited. To my astonishment, and Satyapriya's jubilation, it transpired that the conversation was the very one I had had with the friend in question, at his house on the outskirts of the Brahmin quarter, exactly half an hour earlier. I had taken nearly half an hour to walk back to the ashram, and I had come alone without speaking to anybody on the way. Clearly it was a case of clairaudience. Meditating, and probably with the thought of me somewhere at the back of his mind, Satyapriya had actually 'overheard' me talking with my friend more than half a mile away.

Once our initial elation had subsided, we felt not a little awed and impressed, perhaps even slightly shaken. Strict silence about the matter having been enjoined on Shankara Pillai, Satyapriya and I returned to our meditations with renewed alacrity and vigour. While we were well aware that supernormal faculties such as clairvoyance and clairaudience were at best only by-products of the spiritual path, and that they were in themselves no indications of real spiritual progress, it was at least encouraging to know that such powers did actually exist, and that the accounts given of them in the Buddhist scriptures were not wholly mythical. Moreover, if the scriptural accounts of the supernormal faculties could be believed, as we now knew they could in part, it was all the more possible to accept their testimony as to the existence of even higher, purely transcendental, states.

This was not, of course, my first encounter with the supernormal. Nor was it the first time that I had experienced it in connection with Satyapriya. Had I not 'seen' him in Raipur when he was hundreds of miles away in New Delhi? It was not even the first time that something out of the ordinary had occurred at the ashram. The ashram was indeed a strange place, with a strange atmosphere. Some months after our arrival we had got into the habit of sleeping in the hall. Summer had begun, and our own small room was hot and stuffy. On our second or third night in the hall, we were awoken, at about two in the morning, by the sound of footsteps on the side veranda, which ran the whole length of the building. The footsteps passed up and down, coming now from one end of the veranda, now from the other, rather as though someone was using the place as an ambulatory. What was stranger still, the sound was not that of bare feet, but as it were of large, heavy, hobnailed army boots, such as no one in Muvattupuzha ever wore, and so loud as to be absolutely unmistakable. As soon as we opened the door and looked out onto the veranda, however, all was silent. There was nobody to be seen. Thereafter we heard the same footsteps every night, or whenever we happened to wake up at about two o'clock. They seemed to continue for half an hour, and then ceased. Friends to whom we discreetly mentioned the matter told us that the ashram was popularly believed to be haunted, and that local people would not pass near it at night. In ancient times, it was said, a temple of the dark powers had stood on the spot, and sacrifice, even human sacrifice, had been offered there.

Later on something even stranger happened, this time only once, and to me alone. At ten o'clock one evening, having finished my meditation, I opened my eyes to find myself surrounded by seven or eight tall black figures. I was sitting cross-legged at the back of the hall, in the left-hand corner, and the figures stood round me as though in a semicircle of light. They were six or seven feet tall, naked, and as it were tubular in shape, being uniformly not more than ten or twelve inches wide. What was more remarkable still, each of the figures possessed a pair of enormous white saucer eyes, and with these eyes they were all looking down at me. Their whole appearance and attitude, but particularly their eyes, were expressive of an indescribable mournfulness, of an infinite hopelessness and sadness such as I had never seen, and which I had never imagined could exist. How long we remained looking at each other I do not know. Perhaps it was five minutes. Perhaps it was half an hour. Eventually, as the effect of the meditation started wearing off, I began feeling slightly uneasy. Rising to my feet, I walked straight through the figures and out onto the little veranda in between our own room and the storeroom, on the courtyard side of the ashram. It was absolutely dark. Satyapriya was still meditating in the shrine, behind the grilled doors. Shankara Pillai, I knew, was doing something in the kitchen. After remaining on the veranda for a couple of minutes I returned to the hall, sat down in my corner, and looked…. There was nothing there. Later I concluded that the figures I had seen must have been those of *pretas*, or hungry ghosts, a class of beings who, according to traditional Buddhist cosmology, inhabit one out of the five or six spheres of conditioned existence, the others being occupied respectively by gods, titans, animals, tormented beings, and men. Though I did not know it at the time, I ought to have spoken to the *pretas* and asked them what the matter was and whether I could do anything for them.

In retrospect it seemed strange that I had not felt afraid of my ghostly visitants. No less strange was the fact that, on another occasion, when confronted by something of a more definitely spiritual nature, I did feel afraid. Perhaps the psychic is nothing to be afraid of, whereas the spiritual is.

The incident in question took place in the shrine. As was my custom, having swept the place clean I was decking the altar with fresh flowers in readiness for the morning puja. Along the edge of each of its three cement steps I placed great scarlet hibiscuses, using forty or fifty of the trumpet-shaped blossoms. On the treads of the steps, as well as on the floor round the base of the altar, I scattered the small, dark, brittle leaf of the sacred *bel* tree mixed with white jasmine. Hibiscuses were also placed on top of the framed photographs of Sri Ramakrishna, the Holy Mother, and Swami Vivekananda (on special occasions they were garlanded) and their foreheads marked with fresh white sandalwood paste as though they were living persons. There were no vases, as fresh offerings had to be made each morning, nothing being kept from the previous day. Suddenly, while I was thus engaged, the figure of Sri Ramakrishna appeared in mid-air above the altar, four or five feet from the ground. Though considerably larger than life, he appeared sitting in the usual cross-legged posture, looking exactly as he did in his photograph. He remained there for some time, certainly for at least several minutes, looking straight ahead as though unaware of my existence.

Besides seeing the figure of Sri Ramakrishna, I also had an indescribably intense feeling of his actual presence, as though Thakur, as his disciples called him, was there in the room, and as though I was in close proximity to an incalculable spiritual force. It was this sense of presence and proximity that made me feel afraid. Indeed, I felt my hair stiffen at the roots, while shivers passed up and down my spine. It was an unnerving experience and I was at a loss to account for it. The devotion which I had felt towards Sri Ramakrishna in Colombo had long since evaporated, and I certainly never meditated upon him or invoked his name. Could the apparition have been a kind of thought-form created by the power of the regular ritual worship performed by Satyapriya and his predecessors at the ashram? Or had the ritual only evoked a spiritual presence that was there all the time, only waiting for a favourable opportunity to manifest itself? Was it not possible that after the death of his physical body Sri Ramakrishna had continued to exist in a glorified spiritual form that might, under certain circumstances, become visible to his devotees? Was something of this sort the explanation of the Resurrection of Christ?

Questions of much the same sort were raised by yet another incident, which like the incident of the clairaudience involved Satyapriya,

Shankara Pillai, and myself. It also involved a fourth resident at the ashram, a new arrival. Satyapriya and I being fully occupied with study and meditation, the care of the ashram, including the ashram land, had been left to Shankara Pillai. He was a willing enough worker, but what with planting tapioca in the lower half of the compound, and supervising the picking and skinning of cashew nuts in the upper half, it was only natural that he should feel the need of an assistant. It was also only natural that he should eventually select for the post a poor orphan boy whose father had recently died and whose mother was unable to support him. Indeed, Shankara Pillai related, the poor little fellow was in danger of actual starvation, and even if he had not needed an assistant it would have been our bounden duty to take him in. It was still more natural that the boy in question should be Shankara Pillai's own nephew, though this we did not know until later on.

As soon as we saw our faithful manager leading him by the hand up the path Satyapriya and I took a liking to the boy. His expression was one of unusual friendliness and intelligence, and when we questioned him he replied without hesitation, his face breaking into a charming smile. His name was Krishna, he said, and he was eight years old. With his large dark eyes and dusky complexion, and with a strip of scarlet cloth for his only clothing, he indeed looked a little Krishna. All that was needed to complete the effect was a peacock feather in his hair. Before long he was making himself useful, and Satyapriya and I could not help smiling whenever we saw the little dark figure in the scarlet jock-strap trotting round the ashram at the heels of Shankara Pillai.

One evening, before meditation, Satyapriya abruptly announced that Krishna was too good a boy to be allowed to lead a worldly life and that he was going to make him his disciple. He would initiate him that very instant, and in future he would sit with us when we meditated. Calling the boy, he told him his plans and said he was going to give him a mantra. Krishna's eyes sparkled with pleasure. Taking him into the hall, Satyapriya then told him to recite the well-known Hari mantra, in which now the name of Rama, now the name of Krishna, is interwoven with that of Hari or Vishnu, the second member of the Hindu Trinity, whose earthly 'incarnations' Rama and Krishna are traditionally believed to be. Satyapriya had learned this mantra as a boy, and we had often heard it sung at Anandamayi's ashram at Kishengunj in the course of the evening *bhajan* sessions. Having initiated him, Satyapriya told Krishna to sit in the hall and repeat his mantra to himself while we meditated. If he did this properly, he declared, Krishna would appear to him.

By the time we got started that evening it was seven o'clock. At about ten, having finished our meditation, Satyapriya and I rose to our feet. To our astonishment, Krishna was still sitting at the upper end of the hall, in the right-hand corner, exactly where we had left him. He was sitting cross-legged on the bare floor, with his hands folded in his lap, and was gazing fixedly ahead. Satyapriya called him, but he did not stir and we went down to the kitchen without him. At eleven o'clock he was still sitting there. By this time Satyapriya was beginning to feel worried. The mantra was supposed to be a very powerful one. Suppose it had been too much for the boy. Suppose he had gone into some kind of trance. Suppose he should be unable to regain normal consciousness and should go on sitting there indefinitely.... By this time Shankara Pillai, whom we had told about the matter over dinner, had come and joined us, bringing with him a coconut-oil lamp. Drawing up mats, the three of us sat down near Krishna, and awaited developments. He was smiling gently, and his breathing was deep and regular. Satyapriya called him again, more loudly than before, but he continued gazing ahead with wide open eyes and gave no sign of having heard.

At twelve o'clock Satyapriya decided that something would have to be done. He had heard that a person who had gone into trance could be brought back to ordinary consciousness by repeating in his ear the same mantra that he had been repeating prior to his going into trance – if, of course, this was known. Satyapriya, Shankara Pillai, and I accordingly started reciting the Hari mantra. At first we recited it softly, but as this had no effect we started repeating it more and more loudly, until in the end we were shouting it into Krishna's ear with all the force of our lungs. It was a bizarre scene. Round the ashram, darkness and silence. Inside, the sound of the Hari mantra, the glow of the coconut-oil lamp on the bare walls, the unconscious figure of the small boy, the anxious faces of the three adults. At one o'clock we were still shouting – the raucous sound could hardly be called chanting. From time to time, in desperation, Satyapriya slapped Krishna or shook him bodily. But none of these drastic measures produced the slightest effect. Krishna had gone limp, however, and Satyapriya, who was sitting cross-legged on the floor, was cradling him in his lap, with the boy's head resting in the crook of his arm. Suddenly there flashed on me a picture of something

I had seen many years before, on the Monkey Hill at London Zoo. It was a picture of a female baboon sitting clasping her dead infant to her breast, refusing to give it up, though it had been dead many days, and refusing to allow anyone near. But Krishna was not dead yet, and the hoarse, desperate sound of our shouting continued to be heard. Anyone passing by the ashram that night would have thought it was haunted indeed, and that tormented spirits were wailing their agonies to the four winds of heaven. Satyapriya shouted loudest of all. By this time he was almost frantic with anxiety and bawled out the mantra as though Krishna's very life – and his own too – depended on his exertions.

At two o'clock the boy suddenly drew a very deep breath and sighed. We redoubled our efforts. Before long Krishna drew another deep breath, then another. The trance was coming to an end. He was returning to normal consciousness. Shankara Pillai, who had been much less worried than Satyapriya and myself, spoke to him in a cheerful, encouraging tone. Eventually, the boy blinked his eyes and looked up at us with an expression of happy recognition. It was as though he had just awoken from a deep, refreshing sleep, and was pleased to see familiar faces round his bed. Shankara Pillai spoke to him again. This time he responded instantly, in his usual clear, distinct tones. Seeing that the boy was apparently none the worse for his experience, Satyapriya at once started questioning him. What had happened? Had he seen anything? Rather shyly, Krishna confessed that he had seen his divine namesake and that they had played together. Had he enjoyed playing with him? Oh yes, very much indeed. The smile that accompanied this statement was more expressive than any words. 'And in what form did Sri Krishna appear to you?' Satyapriya finally demanded. 'He was a little boy,' came the reply, 'just like me.'

This was too much for the overwrought nerves of my friend. Already half crazed with relief after the tensions of the night, Satyapriya now suddenly leaped to his feet and started gyrating wildly round the hall, hopping now on this foot and now on that and shouting, 'Krishna has come! Krishna has come!' in a loud voice hoarse with hysteria. He seemed to think that since the boy had seen Sri Krishna the latter had quite literally visited the ashram. Shankara Pillai and I looked on in amazement. Satyapriya seemed to have gone quite mad. Round and round the hall he went, leaping and dancing, shouting and sobbing, a grotesque and slightly alarming sight. I was irresistibly reminded of the scene I had once witnessed at Anandamayi's ashram, when devotees collapsed on the floor shrieking and foaming at the mouth. Such was the violence of Satyapriya's movements that after a few minutes his sarong fell off, but he took no notice, and continued dancing naked round the room, his arms raised above his head and his black hair streaming behind him. The yellow lamplight shone on his stalwart bronze body, by this time gleaming with sweat, and threw onto the walls and up among the rafters an enormous black shape whose movements were even more fantastic than his own. Within half an hour his emotion had exhausted itself. Sobbing for breath, he dropped to the ground, and as soon as he had recovered himself we went to bed.

During the next few days the dramatic consequences of Krishna's initiation were the main topic of conversation at the ashram. Shankara Pillai was inclined to treat the whole matter lightly, saying that such experiences were common enough and of no more significance than a vivid dream. Satyapriya and I were not so sure. According to the books on Bengal Vaishnavism I had read during my first visit to Calcutta, when still in the army, the subtle forms of Sri Krishna and his consort Radha eternally sported in the celestial Brindaban, while according to Mahāyāna tradition the Buddha eternally proclaimed the Dharma in his 'Body of Glory' on the spiritual Vulture's Peak. Was there, then, a world of divine archetypes underlying or overlaying or interpenetrating the realm of material existence, and did Krishna's experience represent a glimpse of this world through the tinted lenses of a Hindu upbringing? Again, had his experience been simply the result of his childish belief in Satyapriya's words, or was it the more or less spontaneous manifestation of a disposition innately spiritual? Would it be wise to allow him to go on repeating the Hari mantra? The last question at least was answered for us. Before we could make up our minds what to do, Krishna's mother, whom we had not seen before, appeared one morning on the ashram steps and declared that she was taking him home with her. What Shankara Pillai had told her we never knew, but it was plain she did not want her son to be Satyapriya's disciple or to become a monk. Having touched our feet in farewell, Krishna left the ashram as cheerfully as he had come. The last we saw of him was a smile and a flash of red jock-strap as, ducking between the bamboos, he disappeared through the gate.

With Satyapriya, Shankara Pillai, and I on our own again, and with life once more flowing in its old channels, many of the questions raised by the latest incident at the ashram soon lost much of their significance. For me at least, however, one question remained as urgent as ever. If anything, indeed, it gained rather than lost in urgency as the days went by. This question concerned Satyapriya. Ever since the night of Krishna's vision – or whatever the experience might have been that the boy had had – I could not get out of my mind the picture of my friend gyrating wildly round the hall completely overcome by hysteria, nor could I help wondering whether his mental balance, precarious at the best of times, had not been seriously affected by the prolonged strain of our ascetic way of life as well as by the still more rigorous discipline to which he had recently subjected himself. Indeed, there were moments when I doubted his sanity altogether. Despite undoubted achievements in meditation, ever since he had given up the Industrial School project his constitutional unreasonableness and irritability had grown steadily worse, and his liability to periodic outbursts of insane fury more and more pronounced. Once or twice, indeed, his lack of self-control had culminated in actual violence. Talking in the semi-darkness of the veranda one night after dinner, we happened to find ourselves disagreeing over something. Knowing how sensitive Satyapriya was, and how impatient of contradiction, I at once saw the danger and stopped pressing my point, but it was too late. Despite all my efforts to pacify him, my friend insisted on enlarging the difference as much as possible and working himself up into one of his usual terrible rages. It was as though he wanted to be angry. This time, however, pausing in his tirade, he suddenly struck me a tremendous blow in the face with his fist. No sooner was the blow struck than his anger left him. By the time Shankara Pillai, hearing me cry out, had come running up to the veranda, Satyapriya was dabbing my bleeding cheek with his shoulder-towel and rocking me in his arms in an agony of remorse. Though he told Shankara Pillai that I had accidentally banged my head against a pillar in the dark, and though I confirmed this story as best I could, our manager was not to be deceived. Not only was he well acquainted with Satyapriya's irascibility, but he had heard his voice raised in anger for some minutes before the supposed accident occurred. As a result of the blow, I had a black eye for a week, while the left side of my head remained practically devoid of sensation for years.

On another occasion it was Shankara Pillai who was the victim, or very nearly the victim, of Satyapriya's lack of self-control. Unexpectedly going through the household accounts one night, and meticulously checking the cost of each bunch of bananas and every ounce of cooking oil, my friend discovered that the cash was short by the equivalent of nearly a shilling. After prolonged inquisition, Shankara Pillai tremblingly confessed that over the past two months he had, by instalments, misappropriated the amount from the money that he had been given for the purchase of provisions from the bazaar. Further inquiry revealed that the reason for the theft was his secret addiction to bidis or country cigarettes. Shocked and indignant, Satyapriya took the culprit severely to task, and despite his tears and entreaties gradually became more and more incensed. Eventually, seizing a heavy stick, he made to grab him by the scruff of his neck and administer a good thrashing. But Shankara Pillai was too quick for him. With a shriek of terror he darted through the kitchen door and out into the darkness. Now thoroughly roused, Satyapriya dashed after him. Over the compound wall went Shankara Pillai. Over the compound wall went Satyapriya. As it was a dark night, with no moon, it was some minutes before either of them was able to get his bearings, and I could hear the sound of bodies crashing about among the *lantana* bushes. At last Shankara Pillai found the path. Guided by the sound of his footsteps, Satyapriya found it too, and soon the sound of two pairs of running feet, as well as the imprecations of the pursuer and the supplications of the pursued, died away in the distance.

Half an hour later, his intended victim having given him the slip, Satyapriya reappeared. For two days we had to do without a manager. Then, through the intercession of one of the ashram members, with whom he had taken refuge, Shankara Pillai returned, humbled himself at Satyapriya's feet, apologized, professed repentance and reformation, and was at length magnanimously forgiven, though not without stern warnings of what would happen if the offence was ever repeated.

Satyapriya's lack of mental balance, as well as his increasing inability to control his temper, was in my mind not unconnected with a set of exercises he had learned from his books on hatha yoga. These were not ordinary physical exercises, but a form of *prāṇāyāma* or breath control. As I knew very well from my own experience, and as all the books on the subject I had read repeatedly emphasized, exercises that involved the control of the breath, as distinct from simply watching it, had an extremely powerful effect on the nervous system and could therefore be highly dangerous. They should be practised only under the personal guidance of a fully qualified teacher. According to popular belief, unsupervised practice of *prāṇāyāma* heated the brain. All this I pointed out to Satyapriya as soon as I discovered what he was doing, but with his usual self-confidence he brushed aside my pleas for caution and carried on as before. Indeed, so ardent was his desire for spiritual progress that he went so far as to practise the breath-control exercises in a particularly extreme form. He also lengthened his periods of silence and started fasting for weeks on end. But apart from reducing him to a state of extreme physical weakness and emaciation these drastic measures produced not the slightest effect. The periodic insane outbursts of rage continued, and to our mutual distress the personal differences between us became more and more acute.

By this time we had been at the ashram more than a year. Already, for the second time since our arrival, the air was filled with the sound of 'Ayyappan Saraṇam!' as bands of devotees who had started the long and arduous pilgrimage to Sabarimalai made their way through the town. Krishna Pillai the Anchal Master, and other friends who were devotees of the god, strongly urged us to accompany them this time and see for ourselves the wonders of the timber-built mountain shrine that was the holy of holies of the cult. Promising to look after us on the way and render us every possible assistance, with friendly importunity they hung round our necks the basil-wood rosaries that were the traditional insignia of those who had vowed to undertake the pilgrimage. But though we wore the rosaries and often talked of going, and though in a sense we wanted to go, the situation at the ashram was such that, not knowing what to do, we allowed the weeks to go by without coming to a decision. In the end, unable to wait any longer, our friends had to leave without us. By the time they returned the situation had changed and Satyapriya and I had begun to see a way out of our difficulties. Developments had taken place that not only carried us a stage further along the path within but resulted in our making a journey that took us even farther afield than Sabarimalai. Indeed, they resulted in our leaving Travancore altogether.

37

RAMDAS, THE SERVANT OF GOD

Among the two or three books which, at the time of our arrival, were all that remained of the ashram library, was a tiny volume entitled *Mother Krishnabai*. It was about a saintly Hindu lady who had, apparently, lived quite recently. But though well written the book made no great impression on me at the time and having once read it through I thought no more about it. Some time later, however, when Satyapriya was busy with the Industrial School project, I undertook the parallel responsibility of building up the library by writing to a number of well-known Indian authors asking them to donate copies of their works. The response was good, and before long the ashram library was richer by several dozen volumes. One day, having exhausted the better-known names, I remembered the little book on Mother Krishnabai. The author was Swami Ramdas, of Anandashram, Kanhangad, and he had apparently written other books as well. Without delay I wrote to him with my usual request. Almost by return of post came a parcel containing four or five books, as well as the latest issue of the *Vision*, a monthly magazine founded by Swami Ramdas and published by the Anandashram.

One of the books was entitled *In Quest of God*. This was Swami Ramdas's account of his early life, especially of his spiritual experiences from the time of his leaving home to the time of his final realization of the Truth. Though his renunciation of worldly things had been unqualified, and though in the course of his search he had endured terrible hardships, there was nothing in his account to suggest conscious austerity, or even a sense of effort. As the narrative danced happily along, and one highly entertaining episode succeeded another, the character that emerged from its pages seemed more like a playful, affectionate child than a hoary sage or a frigid ascetic. Both Satyapriya and I read the book through several times, and were profoundly affected. We also read the other books in the parcel, as well as the hitherto neglected *Mother Krishnabai*. The saintly Hindu lady, it transpired, was Ramdas's disciple, and according to him had also realized the Truth. For the guru to write about the disciple was, of course, highly unusual; but Ramdas, it seemed, was no ordinary guru, and Krishnabai, indeed, no ordinary disciple.

Deeply moved though Satyapriya and I were by Swami Ramdas's story, the possibility of our actually meeting him never occurred to us. As my letter had been acknowledged by the manager of the ashram, and as the events described had clearly taken place many years ago, it was not even certain if the swami was still alive. We therefore read *In Quest of God* much as we might have read *Tibet's Great Yogi Milarepa*, or the *Life of Sri Ramakrishna*. Uplifting and inspiring though it was, it had all happened a long time ago, and the marvellous events it described did not occupy a plane coterminous with that of our own lives. Some months later, however, when Satyapriya had almost exhausted himself with his austerities, we heard that someone from Muvattupuzha had been to see a great saint who lived near Mangalore and had returned a changed man. Kesava Pillai heard about it too. The saint was Swami Ramdas. Though now advanced in years, he was still very much alive, and devotees flocked to him at Anandashram from all over India, particularly from Bombay and the north-west.

The news affected us like an electric shock. We were living in the same world with one who had realized the Truth. It was possible for us to see him, to talk to him. Perhaps it would be possible for him to help us in our spiritual development, in particular to resolve the difficulties that had arisen between Satyapriya and myself. There was no time to be lost. Kanhangad was only four or five hundred miles away up the coast, and we could easily go and spend a few days with Swami Ramdas, returning to Muvattupuzha within the week. Kesava Pillai, whom we took into our confidence, warmly approved. Indeed, he announced his intention of accompanying us. Conscious as he now was of the brevity of human existence, the idea of having the *darshan* or 'sight' of a great saint strongly appealed to his devotional nature.

Anandashram, the 'Abode of Bliss', was an unpretentious place. Situated at the foot of a hill about two miles out of town, it consisted principally of a small *bhajan*-hall with a few bungalows and other buildings scattered round about among the trees. Our first meeting with Swami Ramdas took place in the *bhajan*-hall. Shaven-headed, and simply dressed in white cotton shirt and sarong, he appeared considerably older and stouter than in the frontispiece of his book. Rimless pince-nez on his nose, and carpet slippers on his feet, as he beamed at us from the armchair he was the very picture of grandfatherly benignity. The only unusual thing about him were his ears, with lobes of extraordinary length, so that I was irresistibly reminded of traditional images of the Buddha. Though the feelings of reverence with which we approached him were not unmixed with awe, not to say dread, his childlike simplicity of manner and radiant good humour soon put all three of us completely at ease. Within a matter of hours we had been accommodated in one of the bungalows, had attended our first *bhajan* session, and had started addressing Ramdas as 'Papa' like everyone else.

During the next few days the favourable impression produced on us by our reading of *In Quest of God*, as well as by our reception at the ashram, was not only confirmed but reinforced a hundredfold. The majority of the fifteen or twenty devotees then staying at the ashram were very ordinary people, but the atmosphere of genuine friendliness and devotion that pervaded the place far exceeded anything that I had yet experienced. Though like Anandamayi both Ramdas and Krishnabai were Brahmins by birth, no discrimination on grounds of caste was practised within the ashram precincts. Indeed, none was allowed to be practised. 'Ramdas is militant against caste,' Papa told us one day, when we raised the question. Though he made the declaration without any loss of his customary benignity, there was no doubt that he meant it. Indeed, the more we saw of life at Anandashram the more it struck us that here, at least, there was no compromise between spiritual ideals and mundane exigencies. Swami Nityaswarupananda had not hesitated to call in hooligans to drive tenants by force from the building the Ramakrishna Mission Institute of Culture wanted to occupy. Ramdas, however, had recently given away several acres of ashram land to some families of landless labourers. 'We don't really need so much land,' Mother Krishnabai had told him, and he had agreed.

Soon our confidence in Ramdas was complete. Approaching him one morning after the *bhajan* session, we therefore asked for a private interview. The request was immediately granted. Pausing only to give instructions to some workmen, Ramdas led us to a secluded room in one of the adjacent bungalows where we would not be disturbed, and the meeting from which we were expecting so much began.

Constituting himself the spokesman for both of us, Satyapriya gave a full and frank account of our joint history from the time of our first meeting in Singapore down to the time of our decision to visit Anandashram and meet Ramdas. Nothing of importance was omitted. Our disillusionment with the Maha Bodhi Society, our contact with Anandamayi and her caste-conscious disciples, the circumstances that led to our leaving Kasauli as wandering ascetics, the failure of our attempt to enter Ceylon, the troublesome questions of identity, the breakdown of our plan of walking from Cape Comorin to the Himalayas, and our decision to settle in Muvattupuzha for the sake of our meditation, were all included. If Satyapriya happened to leave something out, I intervened and supplemented his recollections with my own.

Throughout the recital Ramdas listened attentively, without saying a word. But when Satyapriya came to his outbursts of anger, as well as the austerities we had practised, particularly his own prolonged fasts, Ramdas's face took on an expression of the deepest concern. Indeed, shaking his head as if unable to credit his ears, he exclaimed on our foolhardiness with sympathy and sorrow. Eventually, when Satyapriya had finished, he hastened to point out to us the error of our ways. Austerities which endangered one's health were sheer madness, he declared emphatically. On no account should we commit the mistake of thinking that they could facilitate the process of spiritual development. The one thing needful was wholehearted love and devotion towards the spiritual ideal. From that everything would follow. Health and strength were to be preserved by all reasonable means. Without them, spiritual practice was difficult, if not impossible.

At that moment, as though to emphasize his last point, Mother Krishnabai came in with a tray of medicines. Changing in an instant from the serious to the comic, Ramdas broke into mock lamentations for his own total neglect of his health during the period described in *In Quest of God*. On no account should we follow his example, he warned us, wagging an admonitory finger. If we did, we would regret it.

Swami Ramdas, Anandashram

He certainly regretted it. In his old age he not only had to suffer from all sorts of aches and pains, but to submit to being periodically dosed by Mother Krishnabai, who bullied him unmercifully. As he said this he glanced up at Krishnabai with an expression of archness, as though he was in truth a naughty child being made to swallow unpleasant medicines by a stern mother. Krishnabai, serene and not unsmiling, said nothing.

When the door had closed behind her, Ramdas turned to the subject of *prāṇāyāma*. To practise this without a teacher, as Satyapriya had done, was the height of folly. No wonder he had developed such an ungovernable temper! It was lucky that he had not gone mad. On our enquiring whether the traditional warnings were to be taken literally, and whether one could actually become insane as a result of practising *prāṇāyāma*, Ramdas replied with a decided affirmative. Cases of people losing their mental balance due to forcible methods of breath control were by no means uncommon, he declared, especially in South India. Devotees who had gone astray in this way were often brought to him for treatment. Sometimes he was able to help them, sometimes not. On prudential grounds alone, therefore, leaving aside the theoretical objections, he strongly disapproved of *prāṇāyāma*, and did everything in his power to discourage the practice. For the vast majority of people, constant repetition of the name of God was far more beneficial.

Though he took us severely to task over the question of austerities, and though his language left us in no doubt that we had acted very foolishly, Ramdas's response to our joint history was far from being wholly discouraging. Warmly commending our spirit of renunciation, he assured us in the most emphatic terms that our decision to give up the world and lead a spiritual life had been the right one and that we should persist in our chosen course until Enlightenment had been attained. His blessings were always with us. Pleased and heartened though we were by these words, even if Ramdas had done nothing but scold us and point out our mistakes we would not have minded in the least. Praising or blaming, every word he spoke was not only uttered in a heartfelt manner expressive of the deepest interest and concern but seemed to come from an unfathomable depth of love and compassion.

By the time the interview was over, and Ramdas had spoken at length on the need for brotherly love between us, we felt that we were in another world. All our difficulties had vanished. Indeed, from the minute

Satyapriya had started telling the story of our life and experiences together it had seemed that we were making confession of all our weaknesses and imperfections, that this confession was being received by Ramdas, like the ocean receiving into its pure depths the sullied waters of a river, and that having made our confession we were now free from the past and could begin afresh. Indeed, thanks to Ramdas, we could not only begin afresh but begin at a higher level than before. With feelings of profound gratitude we prostrated ourselves at his feet. As we did so he pulled out his watch, exclaiming with mock alarm that if he was not soon back in his quarters he would catch it from Mother Krishnabai, who would be waiting for him with his lunch.

The remainder of our visit passed only too quickly. When we were not talking with Ramdas in the *bhajan*-hall, or at the head of the ashram steps, we were busy exploring the neighbourhood in various directions. More than once we climbed to the top of the hill behind the ashram, and from its windy heights we could see in the distance the long blue line of the Arabian Sea. We had only one cause for anxiety, and that was Kesava Pillai. Our first meeting with Ramdas had affected our old friend profoundly. Indeed, he had flung himself full length on the ground at Ramdas's feet, and remained there without moving for several minutes, his whole frame racked by sobs and his eyes streaming with tears. Some nights later he was taken seriously ill. Satyapriya and I did what we could to relieve his sufferings, but his normally dark face was so ashen, and his breath seemed to come with so much difficulty, that we eventually called the ashram doctor. In these circumstances there could be no question of our prolonging our stay, even had we wanted to do so. But neither Satyapriya nor I felt this as a deprivation. Not only had the week at Anandashram more than fulfilled all our hopes, but it had been made clear to us that we were free to return whenever we liked.

By way of a parting present, Ramdas gave us a mantra. This was so unexpected as to take us completely by surprise. Though we had felt for some time past that devotional repetition of a mantra would help us, and though Satyapriya had once mentioned this to Ramdas, we had not formally asked for initiation. Indeed, despite my confidence in Ramdas I was more than doubtful about the advisability of our taking such a step. Being a Buddhist, I wanted a Buddhist mantra, and Ramdas, I knew, was a great believer in the efficacy of the Rama mantra. This was the mantra into which he had been initiated by his father, whom he regarded as his guru, which he had himself constantly repeated. It appeared on the cover of every issue of the *Vision*, was regularly chanted at the morning and evening *bhajan* sessions, and was the one into which he invariably initiated his disciples. Apparently he had never been known to initiate anyone into any other mantra.

However, I need not have worried. On our entering the *bhajan*-hall one morning, shortly before our departure, we found Ramdas reading *The Light of Asia*. As soon as he saw us he jumped from his chair, and raising his right hand as though in an initiatory gesture exclaimed, 'Your mantra is *oṃ maṇi padme hūṃ!*' With this mantra, the mantra of the great bodhisattva Avalokiteśvara, the embodiment of Compassion, I was well content. Indeed, though I did not then know it, it was the starting-point of a whole network of symbolic associations that gradually came to occupy a central position in my spiritual life.

On our return to Muvattupuzha we began to realize the extent of the change that had taken place in us. While the current of our existence did not flow quite so smoothly as that of the river in which we again took our morning bath, much of the old tension was gone, and contact with Ramdas having reactivated all that was positive in our relationship, both Satyapriya and I found the ashram a happier and more peaceful place. Meditation and ritual worship continued as before, but Satyapriya relaxed his austerities, and gave up the practice of *prāṇāyāma* altogether. As for our newly-acquired mantra, we not only recited it to ourselves at frequent intervals, but chanted it aloud in unison to a tune of Satyapriya's devising.

Taking advantage of the mild weather, we also went for long walks down the country roads on the other side of the ashram, hitherto unvisited, where there were ditches full of dead leaves, and where the late afternoon sunshine, striking through the giant *jak* trees onto the dusty track, threw a warm golden light into the dim interiors of wayside huts. Sometimes, making the journey into town more frequently than we had done for a long time, we renewed acquaintance with old friends. Nevertheless, it was not long before our feeling that our days in Muvattupuzha were numbered crystallized into a definite decision to leave. A longer stay at Anandashram was clearly the next stage of our spiritual journey. Besides, we had spent long enough in the South, and the time had now come for us to continue our long-delayed journey to the North, to the Himalayas, and to start thinking, perhaps, in terms of formal ordination as Buddhist monks.

Having experienced so much kindness in Muvattupuzha, we could not think of leaving without taking the ashram members and all our other friends into our confidence and telling them the reason for our departure. House by house, this was eventually done. Sorry though they were to see us go, everybody understood that as wandering ascetics we could have no attachment to any particular place and that, as some of them remarked, they were lucky to have enjoyed the benefit of our presence at the ashram for so long. For our part, we had found shelter when we needed it, and an opportunity to consolidate our meditation, and for this we were profoundly grateful.

On the eve of our departure we formally relinquished charge of the ashram, Satyapriya handing over to the committee a detailed statement of income and expenditure for the whole period of our tenure. The ashram was now in good repair, he told them, and there remained in hand more than 1,000 rupees in cash, as well as 2,000 laterite blocks. It was up to all of them to continue the work we had started. Our friends, who had assembled in force for the occasion, then thanked us for all that we had done, and after placing garlands of marigolds round our necks handed us an envelope containing 360 rupees that they had collected among themselves towards the expenses of our journey.

Next morning, wearing new saffron robes, and feeling very naked about our freshly shaven heads, we boarded the ramshackle bus outside Ramaswami's office and soon the Town of the Three Rivers was lost to sight behind thick clouds of yellow dust.

38
AT THE 'ABODE OF BLISS'

The first thing we did on arriving at Anandashram was to hand over all our money to Ramdas and ask him to let us stay for as long as it lasted or until he thought it was time for us to be on our way. The next was to devise a routine for ourselves. Now that we had come to live within the radiant orbit of two beings who had realized the Truth, conditions for spiritual practice were even more propitious than they had been in Muvattupuzha, and we wanted to make full use of our opportunity. Satyapriya would have had us go into complete seclusion, cutting off all contact with the other inmates of the ashram, but of this Ramdas did not approve. However, we were allocated one of the more remote bungalows and had our meals brought to us instead of taking them in the communal dining-hall as on our first visit.

Rising before dawn each morning, we devoted the first hours of the day to meditation. After breakfast we went for a walk. The purpose of the walk was twofold: besides giving exercise, it provided us with an opportunity for learning by heart the verses of the *Dhammapada*. Stepping briskly out along the road, we flung to the breezes of the North Malabar coast the deathless words that had not been heard there for 1,000 years. Originally it had been our intention to memorize the whole work, Satyapriya having calculated that as there were twenty-six chapters, and as we could easily memorize one chapter a day, it would be possible for us to have the entire *Dhammapada* at the tip of the tongue within a month. As neither of us knew Pāli we had to learn the verses parrot-fashion, with only a general idea of their meaning. Progress was therefore much slower than we had hoped. Though Satyapriya did rather better, I thought I was doing quite well if I committed one verse to memory each day.

By the time we returned to the ashram everyone would be ready for the mid-morning *bhajan*. With Ramdas sitting in an armchair, and the devotees ranged in a semicircle at his feet, this was a simple, homely occasion, almost like family prayers. A young man with a fine voice who had been nicknamed the Nightingale of the Ashram sang two or three devotional songs, including a setting of a long English poem by Ramdas, the devotees chanted the Rama mantra in chorus, and sweets that had been converted to *prasad* by Ramdas's touch were distributed to young and old alike. Afterwards Ramdas remained seated in his armchair. Anyone who wanted to speak to him could then do so. As at least two or three people always stayed behind for this purpose, and as one question invariably led to another, a general discussion soon arose. In response to a specific request, or in order to illustrate a particular point that he wished to make, Ramdas frequently related anecdotes from his own past experience. Many of these we already knew, being familiar with them from our reading of *In Quest of God* and its sequel *In the Vision of God*. But funny as the anecdotes were to read, they were infinitely more funny when heard from Ramdas's own lips. Such was his excellence as a raconteur, and so great were his gifts of humour and mimicry, that when he related some old favourite the most serious-minded devotee could not help smiling, while others, more susceptible, burst into roars of laughter or rolled helplessly on the ground. The most mirth-provoking anecdotes were often the most meaningful. One related to the occasion when, waking up one morning in his mountain cave after years of wholehearted devotion, he found that his ego had disappeared. 'Ramdas searched high and low,' he declared amidst laughter, suiting his actions to the words with indescribably comic effect, 'but he couldn't find the fellow anywhere – and he hasn't been able to find him since!'

With Ramdas constantly regaling the devotees with anecdotes of this kind, Anandashram, the Abode of Bliss, indeed lived up to its name. If Anandamayi's method was that of spiritual flirtation, Ramdas's was that of transcendental comedy. At the same time, his fundamental seriousness was never in doubt. Glad as he was to help people laugh their way to God, he was firm, even strict, in his adherence to principles, and the decided enemy of all weakness and compromise. One day a devotee asked why it was that, while so many embarked on the spiritual life, so few seemed to make any real progress. Ramdas's reply was unequivocal. They failed to make any progress for two reasons, he said. Firstly, because they had no clear idea of the goal they wished to reach. Secondly, because they had no clear idea of how to get there. This was a warning to all happy-go-lucky aspirants, and conscious as we were of the danger of allowing ourselves simply to drift, Satyapriya and I took it very seriously indeed.

Before many mornings had passed some of the devotees had started speaking to us after the *bhajan* and inviting us back to their quarters for a cup of coffee. Satyapriya at first was inclined to rebuff these friendly advances. Though better-tempered than before, he was still quick to imagine that people looked down on him and that they were out to expose his lack of knowledge, or to humiliate him in some other way. In the atmosphere of Anandashram, however, doubts and suspicions of this kind could not last for long. Soon we had not only accepted the invitations but started making friends among the devotees. Most of them were elderly and retired, and several had brought their families with them. Nearly all came from north-western India. One in fact was the ruler of Porbunder, in Gujerat, the state in which Mahatma Gandhi had been born. With his military moustache, erect bearing, and dark Western suit, he cut rather an odd figure at the ashram, but there was no doubting the depth of his devotion to Ramdas. Reserved, almost diffident, in manner, he very rarely spoke, and I got the impression that he was by nature rather shy. Our chief friend was a retired college principal, a Sindhi, who wanted to give up the world and become a monk but whom Ramdas discouraged from taking this step. Thin, silver-haired, and bespectacled, he was a sweet-natured person, with unusually intense feelings. While talking he often adopted an attitude of ecstatic devotion, falling on one knee, clasping his hands and gazing fervently upwards. This attitude, which he sometimes maintained for minutes on end, at first struck us as rather artificial, not to say theatrical, but we eventually realized that it was not only quite genuine but, for our good friend, the perfectly natural expression of his feelings.

One of the most interesting figures at the ashram was a thin, black-skinned youngster of thirteen or fourteen known as the Boy Yogi. As he spoke only Tamil we could not talk to him, but he grinned at us good-naturedly whenever we met, and one day Ramdas told us his story. His father had wanted to become a monk but being forced by his family to get married had transferred his spiritual ambitions to his son. By the time the boy was four he had not only taught him to meditate but had constructed for him, at the bottom of the garden, a kind of underground cave. In this cave the boy lived. Most of his time was spent practising *prāṇāyāma* and similar exercises. As the years went by, the fame of the spiritual prodigy who lived in the underground cave started to spread, and the young ascetic became widely known in the Tamil-speaking areas as the Bala Yogi, or Boy Yogi. By the time he was eight, an ashram had grown up round the mouth of the cave, and there were a number of devotees. The Boy Yogi became a guru. The father's ambitions were fulfilled. Eventually, however, outraged nature started to take her revenge. Mainly on account of the prolonged practice of *prāṇāyāma*, the Boy Yogi suffered a nervous breakdown, went mad, and after two or three years of acute mental distress had recently been brought to Ramdas for treatment. Since his arrival at the ashram his condition had improved considerably, Ramdas told us, but it would be a long time before he was restored to normality.

No less interesting than the Boy Yogi was an elderly ascetic who lived at the foot of the hill in a cave formed by a cleft in the rock. Though he came only occasionally to the ashram, and did not talk much with anyone, he always greeted Satyapriya and me in a friendly, almost conspiratorial fashion, as if there was a secret understanding between us. Apart from a scanty saffron loincloth, his principal clothing consisted of row upon row of *rudrākṣa* beads, which he wore hanging round his neck and twisted round his arms and waist. With him in the cave lived a huge cobra, who not only shared the milk with which the ashram supplied him, but coiled up beside him at night on the rude stone couch that was the cave's sole furniture.

Only a few yards from the *bhajan*-hall stood the bungalow that housed the ashram library. Our Sindhi friend, who was known to everyone as Dada-ji, or Grandfather, was the librarian. Every two or three days Satyapriya and I would spend half an hour browsing round the shelves and looking for something to take with us back to our bungalow. Though most of the books dealt with religion and mysticism, they had been donated by different people at different times, and formed a very miscellaneous collection. Among the old favourites that I was happy to meet, and read again, were Zhuangzi and Liezi. New discoveries included *The Religion of No-Religion* by Frederic Spiegelberg, with the main thesis of which I found myself deeply in sympathy. Spiegelberg, a professor from Stanford University, California, had visited Anandashram, and Ramdas spoke of him with high regard. Besides reading, I continued my old practice of making extracts from what I read. Indeed, shortly before our departure from Muvattupuzha, Satyapriya had had made for each of us at the local press a specially bound notebook. These notebooks we had asked Ramdas to inscribe for us. Playing on the names Dharmapriya and Satyapriya, and at the same time teaching us a profound spiritual lesson, in mine he had written 'Love Dharma, for Dharma is Truth,' and in Satyapriya's 'Love Truth, for Truth is Dharma.'

Into my own notebook, thus blessed, I not only copied extracts from my past and present reading, but transcribed one complete work. This was Suzuki's translation of Aśvaghoṣa's *Awakening of Faith in the Mahāyāna*. Though I had read it before, the compactness of its style and the profundity of its teaching now impressed me more than ever, and I copied it out not only for practical reasons, so that I might have it always by me, but also as an act of merit. Both Buddhists and Hindus have long regarded the mindful transcription of sacred texts as being in itself a religious practice, and I had seen in the ashram office a number of exercise books completely filled with the Rama mantra. This was the second time in my life that I had taken the trouble of making a copy of a work that I admired. The first time was when, at the age of thirteen or fourteen, I copied from Swinburne's *William Blake: A Critical Essay* the whole text of *The Marriage of Heaven and Hell*, or as much of it as Swinburne had given. On the present occasion, it was not only a matter of producing for myself a copy of a work not otherwise procurable, but of imprinting every word of it on my consciousness.

Among the books that I had borrowed from the library were Ramdas's collected articles and letters, in some of which he discussed the time-honoured themes of Indian philosophic thought with remarkable assurance and penetration. So acute was his understanding, indeed, and so clear and confident his exposition, that I could not help thinking that though he customarily spoke the language of devotion he was at heart not so much a *bhakta*, a devotee of God, as a *jñānin*, a knower of the Absolute. With some of his assertions, however, I could not agree.

One that particularly troubled me was to the effect that the enlightened man, having transcended morality, was capable of acting either in a 'moral' or 'immoral' manner. He could even take life. When I raised the question with Ramdas he not only confirmed that this was, indeed, so, but having refuted all my arguments enlarged upon the theme with his usual lucidity and radiant good humour. Finally, he insisted that in the case of the enlightened man the taking of life would be not a negation of compassion but an expression of it, and summed up his position with the vigorous and uncompromising declaration, 'Love can kill!'

This placed me in a dilemma. I was unable either to accept Ramdas's proposition or to say that Ramdas himself was wrong. According to the Theravādin Pāli scriptures, the Buddha had stated categorically that the *arahant*, the liberated soul, was incapable of the deliberate taking of life. This seemed to me not only true in principle but advisable in practice, so that had anyone but Ramdas told me that love could kill I would have at once concluded that far from being enlightened he was, in fact, labouring under a gross delusion, and that his so-called love was only a form of attachment. But in Ramdas's case such a conclusion was hardly possible. The assertion that love could kill was being made by one who was himself the undoubted embodiment of love. If the liberated soul was incapable of the deliberate taking of life, but if at the same time love could kill, the only conclusion that could follow was that love and Enlightenment were mutually exclusive. Yet, as I well knew, according to the Mahāyāna scriptures Compassion was coordinate with Wisdom and both together made up Perfect Enlightenment or Buddhahood. Moreover, certain passages in the Mahāyāna scriptures suggested, or seemed to suggest, that the bodhisattva, the living embodiment of the Will to Perfect Enlightenment, could out of compassion for sentient beings abrogate the rules of morality, including even that which forbade the deliberate taking of life. Was Ramdas a bodhisattva, then? Were the Pāli scriptures wrong and Ramdas and the Mahāyāna scriptures right? Did the Buddha of the Theravāda contradict the Buddha of the Mahāyāna? Struggling with these and many other similar questions I only impaled myself more firmly than ever on the horns of the original dilemma. Indeed, I was to remain impaled there for many years.

Every now and then in his conversations with us Ramdas would speak of the various saints and sages he had met in the course of his early wanderings. The one for whom he felt the greatest veneration was

Ramana Maharshi, whose blessings he had sought at the outset of his quest. For Sri Aurobindo too, whom he had not met, he entertained feelings of great regard. As Ramana Maharshi lived at Tiruvannamalai, and Sri Aurobindo in Pondicherry, while Ramdas himself lived at Kanhangad, he used to refer to the three of them as the Trimurti of the South, the Trimurti or trinity in question being, of course, that of the three principal deities of the Hindu pantheon – Brahma the Creator, Vishnu the Preserver, and Shiva the Destroyer. Ramana Maharshi was Vishnu, he declared. Firm and immovable as the central axis of the cosmos, he remained ever in one place and supported all. Sri Aurobindo was Shiva. He was the Great Yogi, ever absorbed in contemplation. As for himself, he was Brahma. Naturally active, like a child, he did nothing but play.

One day, when we had been at the ashram for about six weeks, Ramdas told us that having seen one member of the Trimurti it was time we started thinking of seeing the other two. A date was accordingly fixed for our departure. Though sorry to leave, we knew it was Ramdas's regular practice not to allow anyone to settle down at the ashram. Occasional visits, during the whole period of which one felt uplifted and inspired, were in his opinion of far greater value than a protracted stay in the course of which one gradually reverted to more worldly attitudes. In our case, we had benefited enormously from our contact with Ramdas and Krishnabai, and having received so much it was surely now incumbent upon us to give it effective expression in the life to which we had dedicated ourselves. Since we had no money, we had decided to walk all the way to Tiruvannamalai, a distance of about four hundred miles. When we went to pay our last respects to Ramdas, however, he handed us two third-class railway tickets and told us firmly that we were to go by train.

39
THE VISION IN THE CAVE

In contrast with the lush greenness of the Malabar coast, the Tamil country was harsh and desolate of aspect. As the train carried us from west to east across the vast plateau of the Deccan, and we passed through the straggling hutments of one sun-baked township after another, it was as though the earth was being stripped bare of vegetation, and as though the fewer the trees and bushes that were left, the more stunted and withered they became. With the landscape the people too changed, becoming thinner, darker, and less pleasing of feature. By the time we reached Tiruvannamalai we were in another world. It was sand rather than soil that we trod underfoot on our way to the ashram, and huge boulders, weathered by the millennial action of sun, rain, and wind into perfect smoothness and whiteness, that we saw on either side of the road rather than human habitations. In between rocks, as well as on wind-eroded hillocks and the level ground, tiny whitewashed shrines sprouted as though from thickly sown seed. Thorn bushes sprouted too, while cactus hedges half concealed mud huts shrouded in withered bines. Beyond, greyish-brown paddy fields bordered with areca palms stretched in uneven patchwork to the horizon, where low hills, blue with distance, were just visible through the haze. In this prehistoric world the only things that flourished were the big shady trees which, judging by the freshness and abundance of their leafage, had found beneath the barren rock sources of nourishment known only to themselves.

The ashram which had grown up round Ramana Maharshi during the previous half-century was not only bigger than the one that had grown up round Ramdas but run on very different lines. We noticed this as soon as we took our seats for lunch. Down the middle of the dining-hall ran a partition which, stopping short of the wall at the far end, divided the greater part of the place into two sections. One section was reserved for Brahmins, the other for non-Brahmins. Despite our saffron robes, and the fact that as ascetics we were beyond caste distinctions even according to orthodox Hindu tradition, Satyapriya and I were relegated to the non-Brahmin section, where we took our seats on a narrow strip of matting that ran the whole length of the hall. Scurrying along the closely packed rows, bare-legged attendants hastily deposited on the leaf-plates dollops of rice and curry and small puddles of chilli-and-onion soup and buttermilk. I noticed that the leaf-plates were not large rectangles of freshly cut plantain leaf, green and rubbery, as in Malabar, but consisted of small withered leaves pinned together with thorns into rough discs hardly bigger than a doily. At a signal from the far end of the hall, everybody started eating, and soon the loud slurping, sucking, and smacking noises of Hindus in hearty enjoyment of a good meal was all that could be heard. Was it my fancy, or were the noises that came from the other side of the partition, where the Brahmins were eating, even more resounding than those that came from our own side? Glancing up from my plate, I saw through the forest of bowed heads and rhythmically moving right arms a dark dignified figure in what looked like a pair of white briefs seated at the far end of the hall at right angles to the rows of eaters. Close-cropped white hair gave him an alert, almost military look. His eyes seemed to miss nothing. It was the Maharshi. From where he sat he could look down either side of the partition and see both Brahmins and non-Brahmins. Both Brahmins and non-Brahmins could see him and, what was even more important, the Brahmins could neither see the non-Brahmins nor be seen by them.

After spending a few days at the ashram, where we slept in a barrack-like dormitory with several dozen other male visitors, and a few days with friends in one of the bungalows outside the ashram gate, Satyapriya and I started looking for a quieter and more convenient place to stay – somewhere near enough for us to be able to see the Maharshi regularly and far enough away to ensure freedom from disturbance. We did not have to look very far. Behind the ashram rose the twin peaks of Arunachala, the Hill of Light, sacred throughout the Tamil country, the mere name of which had strangely, magically drawn the seventeen-year-old Ramana to the spot more than fifty years earlier. Untold ages ago, in the Satya Yuga, the Age of Truth, it had been a great pillar of light, the top and bottom of which even the gods had been powerless to discern. With the passage of time, and the gradual deterioration of the universe, the hill too had changed. In the Treta Yuga it had become a heap of rubies, in the Dvapara Yuga a heap of gold, and now, in the Kali Yuga, the Dark Age, it was a heap of stones. But even as a heap of stones Arunachala had its charms. On the tree-covered slopes, where bands of monkeys roamed at will, shrines had been set up on precipitous ledges and caves excavated wherever there were natural holes and clefts in the rock. Most of the caves were occupied, but a few were empty, and in one of these we established ourselves. Before doing so we sought the approval of the Maharshi. Intercepting him on his way to the bathroom, which was not really allowed, we cast ourselves on the sand at his feet and asked for his blessing on the step we were about to take. Leaning heavily on his stick, and with body painfully bent, the frail old man listened gravely to what we had to say. Then, in two or three short simple sentences, and with an expression of great kindliness, he not only assured us that we were doing the right thing, and had his blessing, but urged us to persevere in our efforts to realize the Truth.

    The cave we had selected was known as the Virupaksha Guha, and it was situated on the south-east slope of the hill, overlooking the spacious courtyards and lofty *gopurams* of the Tiruvannamalai Temple, at the end of a short sandy track that branched off from the main path up the hillside. Beyond the cave, where water slowly trickled down a dark crevice, a tangle of pink oleanders, seven or eight feet tall, made a pleasant contrast with the sunlit grey rock. Inside the cave, which was big enough to shelter four or five persons, it was surprisingly warm and dry. Indeed, despite the good ventilation, the warmth was almost oppressive. Much of the space was occupied by a raised stone structure on which we slept at night. This was the tomb of the saint after whom the cave was named, who had lived there five or six hundred years ago, and had been buried there. The place was also associated with the early life of the Maharshi. Two years after his arrival in Tiruvannamalai he had abandoned the shrines and temples in which he had stayed till then and started living on the hill itself. The Virupaksha Guha was the cave to which he had resorted first and in which he had stayed longest. Whether on account of the presence of the dead saint, or its association with the living one – or simply because it was a cave – the place had an atmosphere of peculiar intensity. According to popular belief the mantra *om* could be distinctly heard there. Neither Satyapriya nor I ever heard either this or any other mantra, but there was no denying that at times the vibrations of the cave were of such intensity that we seemed to hear a kind of buzzing or humming sound. We heard other sounds as well. For the first few days of our stay we had to share the cave with a young Tamil, so thin and black and saucer-eyed as to seem like one of the hungry ghosts I had seen at Muvattupuzha. Since we did not know Tamil, and he spoke neither Hindi nor English, we were unable to talk to each other, but at night there was no lack of communication – from his side at least. His food, which he cooked outside the entrance of the cave, consisted principally of red chillies, with the result that he was a chronic sufferer from flatulence. At intervals during the night Satyapriya and I would be woken up by reports like pistol-shots which, in the confined space, crashed and rolled around us for minutes on end.

In our way of life, and even in our appearance, we were now virtually indistinguishable from all the other hermits and ascetics who dwelt on the sacred hill. Like them we rose before dawn, like them we meditated until the early morning sun glittered clean and bright above the white ground mist, and like them, having taken the prescribed bath, we descended on the town of Tiruvannamalai for alms. Most of the sadhus actually begged from door to door. In our case, the friends with whom we had been staying at the bungalow had arranged for us to take our one meal of the day at a house in the Brahmin quarter of the town, where they had entered into an agreement with the occupier. Our host, an elderly Tamil Brahmin, fed us generously, but he was apparently quite unable to understand that non-Tamil throats, stomachs, and intestines were simply incapable of dealing with the same huge quantities of red chillies to which he was accustomed. Every meal was therefore agony. Gulping water at frequent intervals, we ate with streaming eyes and noses and burning throats while our well-meaning host, convinced that we must be enjoying it, stood over us with brass pot and ladle warmly urging us to take another helping.

On our way back to our cave we usually took the short cut through the Tiruvannamalai Temple, skirting the second of the three massive walls that girdled the inner precincts. Strict rules governed the right of entry into the place. Untouchables could not enter at all. Indeed, they were not permitted even to pass too close to the outermost wall of the temple. Those who, though not actually Untouchables, were still of low caste, could enter, but only as far as the grassy space between the second and third walls, where our own short cut lay. High-caste Hindus could pass at will through the gates of all three walls, though Brahmins alone enjoyed the ultimate privilege of access to the holy of holies. Knowing that as a Mlechchha I ranked even lower than the Untouchables, and that I was not really entitled even to enter as far as I did, I had no intention of trying to penetrate further into the temple. What the Hindus did in their own places of worship, and who they admitted there, was for them to decide, not me.

One day, however, despite my reluctance, Satyapriya insisted on our exploring the whole temple complex. To our surprise we found that the inner precincts, within the third wall, were more spacious than we could have imagined. Shrines and Shiva-lingams stood everywhere, while stone canopies floated on forests of slender columns, yet such were the dimensions of the place that there was no sense of crowding. Indeed, the gate-towers through which we had just passed seemed so far away that it was difficult to believe that they were part of the same building. Worshippers with trays of offerings came and went. Ascetics, black and near-naked, squatted on the steps of shrines or lay motionless in the shade of trees. Humped sacred bulls, white and placid, stood munching discarded marigold-garlands beside their stone brethren. Nobody took the slightest notice of us, or even appeared to see us. Eventually, having negotiated a maze of courtyards and corridors, we found ourselves leaning against a stone barrier and looking through doorway on doorway into the black recesses of the inmost shrine.

As it was still winter, and by Indian standards not very hot, much of our time was spent out of doors. Having recovered from the immediate effects of our meal in town, we usually passed the remainder of the day until nightfall in a shady spot not far from the mouth of the cave. Amid the primal simplicities of Arunachala books seemed out of place, and though we had borrowed a few volumes from the ashram library, we dipped into them only occasionally, for inspiration rather than information. Indeed, with the possible exception of the *Song of Dattatreya* the only work that made any impression on me at all at this period was Evans-Wentz's *Tibetan Yoga and Secret Doctrines*, a copy of which had been presented to the ashram by a Western devotee, and with which the Maharshi was well acquainted. Most of our time we spent simply looking at the scene spread out before us, or walking slowly up and down the sandy paths. Within the diminished rectangle of the Tiruvannamalai Temple, into which we now looked as the gods must have looked from Mount Ida down at the walls of Troy, even the biggest shrines had shrunk to insignificance, while human figures swarmed like ants. As night fell, and the gate-towers rose shadowy and insubstantial in the gloom, there would float up to us, faint with distance, the noise of conches calling to evening worship, the long-drawn-out wailing note suddenly shattering itself in an angry explosion of sound. As though in reply, drums and gongs would start beating, their rhythms gradually becoming more and more insistent. Then, when the sound had been built up into a crescendo and the climax of the worship finally reached, there would be a sudden blaze of lights in the middle of the rectangle, where the shadows were deepest. Momentarily revealed by the blaze, we would see round the doorway of the main shrine, all stretching out their hands to the lights, and struggling to get in, a dense crowd of people. As we watched, and as shouts and cries rose confusedly into the night air, something of the tumult and excitement of the worship would communicate itself to us across the intervening spaces. Soon, however, it would all be over. The temple would return to darkness and silence, and Satyapriya and I would be left alone on the hillside watching the sky grow brighter and brighter with stars until, with the rising of the mists, we were forced to retire into the dry warm depths of the cave.

Long before dawn, as well as at intervals throughout the day and night, we heard the temple bell. Perhaps it was my imagination, but I seemed always to hear the temple bell. It was not really one bell but two bells that I heard, the first being higher in pitch than the second, but the twin strokes came so close together, and were at once so well contrasted and so well harmonized, that they constituted for me a single experience. As a single experience I referred them to a single origin, and thought of the sound as being produced by one bell, or rather by a kind of double bell which was struck, perhaps, either by two hammers in one place or in two places by one hammer. The bell sounded louder than any of the instruments that accompanied the evening worship, louder than all of them combined. It was so loud that it penetrated rock as easily as air, so loud that it made no difference whether we were inside the cave or outside it. When we were inside the cave, indeed, it was as though the great bell swung not somewhere inside the temple but up in the air, directly outside the cave. Sometimes I heard it in my dreams. Hour after hour it seemed to toll, incessant and insistent, wave after wave of brazen sound breaking upon me like the repeated thunder of surf on the sea shore. Sometimes it was as though the bell, swinging outside, was striking against the hill, and that the hill was the bell and the bell itself the hammer that struck the bell. Again, the hill was not bell but anvil, and the bell the hammer that, stroke after sonorous stroke, smote upon the anvil. The point of impact, the point where the hill and bell met, where hammer smote anvil, was the cave, was me. Between the hill and the bell, between the anvil and the hammer, I was being reshaped, was being beaten into something, I knew not what. I was being changed....

Every two or three days Satyapriya and I went to the ashram, finding our way along the network of footpaths that skirted the lower slopes of Arunachala. In the early morning sunshine, it was a pleasant walk. Past shrines and hermitages we went, some freshly whitewashed, others so tumbledown as to resemble heaps of stones, past tangles of scrubby bushes and clumps of grey-green cacti with yellow flowers. At one point our way led through a small secluded valley lying in between the main hill to the north and two or three small foothills to the south. In this spot I regularly experienced an intensity of silence and tranquillity that I did not find in the ashram, even at the Maharshi's feet. It was as though someone even greater than the Maharshi had once dwelt there, and as though the whole valley was still filled with his invisible presence. Nevertheless, *darshan* at the ashram was truly a memorable experience. By the time we arrived the Maharshi was generally established in his usual place on the couch at the far end of the hall, where he would either recline against a bolster or, though more rarely, sit up cross-legged. Sometimes we arrived early enough to hear the chanting of the Vedas by a group of Tamil Brahmins, with which the morning *darshan* began. What with the harsh, unmusical sound of the chanting, and the hard, unsympathetic faces of the Brahmins, I could not help thinking of Venkateshwara Iyer. After the chanting was over, and the Brahmins

Sri Ramana Maharshi and Arunachala Hill

had filed out of the hall, not much seemed to happen. The Maharshi sat on his couch. From time to time someone would approach him with a question or a request, would receive a brief reply, sometimes no more than a look or gesture, and would then return to his place. That was all. The rest of the time the sixty or seventy people sitting in the hall either simply looked at the Maharshi, which was what the word *darshan* literally meant, or else closed their eyes and meditated. Talking was by no means prohibited, and muted greetings would sometimes be exchanged between new arrivals and friends in the congregation, but for the most part the devotees sat quiet and motionless hour after hour and a great silence reigned in the hall. One could not sit there for long without becoming aware that this silence was not mere absence of sound but a positive spiritual influence, even a spiritual force. It was as though a light breeze blew down the hall, or as though a stream flowed through it, a stream of purity, and this breeze, this stream, seemed to emanate from the silent, nodding figure on the couch, who did nothing in particular, only reading the letters that were brought to him or glancing, every now and then, at some member of the congregation with keen but kindly eye. Sitting there in the hall with Satyapriya I felt the stream flow over me, felt it flow over body and mind, over thoughts and emotions, until body, mind, thought, and emotion had all been washed away, and there remained nothing but a great shining peace.

Since our excursions to the ashram were intended solely for the purpose of *darshan*, we did our best to avoid spending time in merely social contacts, and took as little notice as possible of the new arrivals who were constantly turning up, many of whom would have been only too glad to find out more about us. One new arrival, however, it was impossible for us to ignore. This was no less a person than the same amiable Shankaracharya of Puri whom I had met in Ahmedabad two years earlier, and with whom I had afterwards corresponded. Entering the hall one morning we found there not only a slightly larger concourse of people than usual but the little Shankaracharya himself, in full regalia, seated at the far end of the hall on a level with the Maharshi. A throne with a tiger-skin draped over it had been set up for him at the foot of the Maharshi's couch, and there he sat, impassive, his silver staff of office firmly gripped in his right hand, the ancient confronting the modern representative of Advaita Vedanta. As everybody in the ashram appreciated, it was an historic occasion. Shankaracharyas of Puri did not usually go out of their way to show respect to other dignitaries, even of their own school, and the visit was an honour indeed.

When we paid our respects to him in the tent in which, for reasons of orthodoxy, he had been accommodated, I found him no less frank and liberal-minded than on the occasion of our first meeting. Why should he not pay the Maharshi a visit, he asked, even if he was Shankaracharya of Puri? He had heard much about him, and wanted to see him. Other statements reflected the same mild unorthodoxy. He maintained the external trappings of his position, he declared, and observed all the orthodox socio-religious taboos, because this was what the majority of his followers expected of him. He himself, however, attached very little importance to them. Since our last meeting I had come to learn that there was another Shankaracharya of Puri in existence, and that this rival claimant to the office was in physical possession of the math, or monastic headquarters of the line, at Puri in Orissa. Were there in fact two Shankaracharyas of Puri, I asked, and if so how had the division arisen? The little Shankaracharya laughed. 'The regalia is with me,' he said simply. As we could see, with him it was, and that apparently settled the matter.

Though Satyapriya and I kept ourselves free of all social contacts, we were certainly interested in whatever spiritual activities might be going on within the sphere of the Maharshi's immediate influence. One day we visited the little colony of ascetics that had sprung up to the west of the ashram. Huts and hermitages alike were built on the smallest scale, like dolls' houses, and from the simplest materials. Silver-grey mud walls were crowned with palm thatch of faded greyish brown, while cowdung-ochred courtyards were enclosed by wattle-and-daub fences in which every stick stood out beneath the thin coating of mud, like ribs and veins beneath the skin. Despite the perfect neatness and cleanliness of the place there was no sign whatever of human life. The diminutive buildings might well have been the work of ants or bees, or of some shy, delicate-handed pygmy race that, scenting the approach of man, had silently melted into the ground.

In one of the tiny courtyards, no more than eight or ten feet in diameter, stood a papaya tree, the top of its straight slender trunk as thickly hung with fruits as the Diana of Ephesus with breasts. Satyapriya pushed open the low wattle-and-daub gate. Then, crossing the courtyard, he quietly pushed open the light wooden door. Inside was a single small room, completely bare, and inside the room, almost directly facing us, there sat, meditating, the most beautiful young man I had ever seen. Slim and fair-complexioned he sat there, with closed eyes, beautiful not only on account of his perfectly proportioned body, naked save for a small cloth but, even more so, on account of the beatific smile that irradiated his face. He was quite oblivious to our presence. Unable to take our eyes off him, we stood there for several minutes. Then, having closed the door behind us even more gently than we had opened it, we slowly made our way back to the ashram.

Despite frequent changes of abode, during the previous few months Satyapriya and I had not neglected our own practice of meditation. Wherever we might happen to be, we sat without fail morning and evening. While we were at Anandashram this had led, in my case, to some interesting side effects. One afternoon I discovered I had a temperature. Though it was alarmingly high – so high that Satyapriya, on feeling me with his hand, at first wanted to call the doctor – I did not feel the least unwell. Indeed, I felt blissful, almost ecstatic, while the heat itself seemed to envelop the whole body in a melting sensation of infinite warmth, comfort, and security. The experience lasted two days; when we told Ramdas about it he pointed out that *tapasya*, the ancient Sanskrit word for spiritual practice, literally meant the generation of heat, and said that the experience signified the burning up of all impurities. Now that we were staying at the Virupaksha Guha, and devoting most of our time to meditation, even more extraordinary experiences were only to be expected, nor was it astonishing that some of them should seem to indicate the course of future developments.

One night I found myself as it were out of the body and in the presence of Amitābha, the Buddha of Infinite Light, who presides over the western quarter of the universe. The colour of the Buddha was a deep, rich, luminous red, like that of rubies, though at the same time soft and glowing, like the light of the setting sun. While his left hand rested on his lap, the fingers of his right hand held up by the stalk a single red lotus in full bloom and he sat, in the usual cross-legged posture, on an enormous red lotus that floated on the surface of the sea. To the left, immediately beneath the raised right arm of the Buddha, was the red hemisphere of the setting sun, its reflection glittering golden across the waters. How long the experience lasted I do not know, for I seemed to be out of time as well as out of the body, but I saw the Buddha as clearly as I had ever seen anything under the ordinary circumstances of my life, indeed far more clearly and vividly. The rich red colour of Amitābha himself, as well as of the two lotuses, and the setting sun, made a particularly deep impression on me. It was more wonderful, more appealing, than any earthly red: it was like red light, but so soft and, at the same time, so vivid, as to be altogether without parallel. In the course of the next few days I composed a series of stanzas describing the vision. Contrary to my usual practice, I failed to write them down afterwards, with the result that they gradually faded from my mind. But the experience itself never faded. Nearly a quarter of a century later, the figure of the red Buddha is as clear to me, in recollection, as it was the next morning in the Virupaksha Guha.

With the approach of summer, the atmosphere of the cave had by this time not only lost its freshness but become quite stuffy. Satyapriya and

I therefore decided to move to a square stone-built shrine that stood lower down, at the very foot of the hill. Better ventilated than the cave, and extremely cool, it consisted of a single chamber about six foot square divided into two sections. One section was occupied, from wall to wall, by a low stone platform, on which one of us slept at night, while in the other a lingam of polished black stone, eight or ten inches high, had been let into an anvil-shaped yoni sunk in the middle of the floor. Though involving such a short distance, our removal from the higher to the lower slopes of Arunachala was not without significance. The vision in the cave had convinced me that our two-years' apprenticeship to the holy life had come to an end, and that we must now retrace our steps to North India and seek formal ordination in one of the Buddhist centres there. My desire for ordination had indeed become unbearably intense. In waking fantasy I saw myself living as a monk at Sarnath, where the Buddha delivered his first discourse, and thought that if only I could live there sweeping the temple steps every morning it would be the height of happiness. The truth was, perhaps, that after living so long in the midst of Hinduism, I was now homesick, as it were, for Buddhism, and wanted not only to experience it in my own life but to see it in tangible form all about me. Our removal from the cave to the shrine seemed the first step in this direction.

Before we could be permitted to leave Tiruvannamalai, however, Arunachala had a few more experiences in store for us. The black stone cubicle that we shared with the sacred lingam was not only cooler than the cave but more accessible to visitors, and in the course of the ten or twelve days that remained Satyapriya and I became objects of interest to some of the more eccentric members of the local ascetic community. Our most persistent visitor, who ended by calling several times a day, was a thin, dark, active woman with straggling iron-grey hair who lived in a small shrine dedicated to the goddess Durga on the road to Tiruvannamalai. We called her Tehsildah's Mother. This was because she was constantly impressing on us, in her broken English, that she had a son, and that this son was not only a very good boy but had done extremely well for himself, being now a Tehsildah, or subdivisional officer, somewhere in Andhra. Her speech and gestures were habitually wild, almost crazy. Whenever she came to see us she brought various titbits that she had cooked for us and insisted on feeding us with her own hands. Once she decorated us as though we were sacred images, anointing our foreheads with sandalwood paste, tucking flowers into the tops of our waist-cloths and, finally, planting a generous kiss full on our lips.

Another regular visitor was an ancient, saffron-clad ascetic whom we nicknamed Swami Ek So Aat or Swami 108. 108 was the sacred, or at least auspicious, Hindu number. There were 108 Upanishads, 108 places of pilgrimage, 108 beads to a rosary, and even, as we had discovered when we were invited to a wedding feast in Muvattupuzha, 108 chutneys. There were also 108 Sris before the name of any extraordinarily holy or auspicious personage, though instead of actually writing 'Sri' 108 times, which would take up a lot of space, one could write the figure 108 instead. The old ascetic in question, who had the plausible air of the professional impostor, informed us early in our acquaintance that he was entitled to this distinction, and that when we wrote to him after our departure which he seemed to think we were bound to do, we should be sure to address the letter to Swami Sri 108 Blank. We therefore called him Swami Ek So Aat. Among his disciples, he told us, there were a large number of princesses. All these princesses had realized the Truth. How had they realized it? Simply by their devotion to him. Whenever he stayed with them in their palaces in north-western India they waited on him personally, he declared. Such was their devotion to him, that no service was too mean or too humble for them to perform. They even washed his *kaupin*. The *kaupin* was the narrow strip of cloth traditionally worn as a jock-strap by Hindu ascetics and an old one, hanging up to dry, was not a particularly attractive sight. Since there were no princesses around in Arunachala, Swami Ek So Aat was for the time being having to wash his own *kaupin*, but any woman, he averred, who washed it for him every day for two years, or at the most three years, would be sure to realize the Truth.

Though we at first listened to these claims in silence, after the third or fourth repetition Satyapriya could not forbear asking for further details of the princesses' devotion, thus leading the old man into such absurdities that eventually, unable to contain ourselves, we both burst out laughing. Tehsildah's Mother was more direct. On being told that it was high time that she, too, started thinking of realizing the Truth, she roundly declared that she would rather not realize it at all than realize it by such means. When Swami Ek So Aat retorted that she was lacking in devotion, she retaliated by calling him an old fraud. In the noisy altercation that followed Tehsildah's Mother won an easy victory, at least verbally, and the old man was forced to concede the field. He did not retire from the conflict, however, without a parting shot. Anxious to wash his *kaupin*, two or three young and beautiful princesses were at that very moment on their way to Arunachala, he shouted angrily. When they arrived, she would see with what devotion they served him. Tehsildah's Mother tossed her grey locks. Oh yes, she said, with a scornful laugh, she would see. Strange to relate, a few days afterwards we noticed that Swami Ek So Aat did have quite a number of female disciples with him; but whether they were princesses, and whether they washed his *kaupin*, we never discovered.

The third and last of our regular visitors was perhaps more truly representative of the ascetic community. Shaven-headed, and wearing only a small white loincloth, he passed our door every morning in the course of his daily circumambulation of the sacred hill, and soon got in the habit of stopping for a chat. Though he could not have been more than thirty-five, he was thin and emaciated in the extreme, like an old man, and it was soon apparent that he hardly ever took any food. He was not interested in food. This was due not to excessive asceticism, as we at first supposed, but to reasons of a very different nature. Like so many other Hindu ascetics, our friend was an inveterate smoker of ganja or Indian hemp. Ganja enabled one to see God (*ganja se Shiv-ji ka darshan milta hai*), he told us simply, in response to our enquiry.

One day, when we were out for a walk, we happened to see him sitting in the shade of a tamarind tree not far from the road. At his invitation we joined him. With him were three or four other ascetics, of various ages, all raggedly clad in different shades of saffron. Though less emaciated than our friend, they were of a dull and bestial appearance, and looked at us, if they looked at all, with glazed eyes. That they saw God there was no evidence apart from the fact that they were smoking ganja. After we had sat there for a few minutes one of them offered a little of the herb first to Satyapriya, then to me. We both refused it, saying that we did not smoke. An expression of surprise flickered for a moment on their faces. One of them remarked that if we did not smoke ganja we were not true sadhus, then relapsed into indifference.

Perhaps he was right. Perhaps we were not true sadhus, after all. In any case, we were now on the point of departure from Tiruvannamalai, and had no time to pursue the matter further.

40
THE ONE-EYED GURU

During the fifteen months that Satyapriya and I spent at Muvattupuzha three lawyers had been our closest friends. In Bangalore, where we stayed for a much shorter period, it was two railway engineers. Like Kumaran Nair and Kesava Pillai, they had known each other since they were boys, had worked together all their adult lives, and though equally religious-minded and the closest of friends, were of completely different temperaments. Narayan was quiet and reserved, not to say withdrawn, and apparently found it difficult to communicate with people. Though he had been married for a number of years, and had four or five children, he even found it difficult to communicate with his wife. Indeed, he never actually spoke to her. Whenever he wanted to say anything to her he told his mother, who passed on the message. His mother, of course, lived with them and it was she who managed the household. Rajgopal, on the contrary, was a lively, cheerful extrovert who experienced no difficulty whatever in getting on with people. He was on the best of terms with his wife and bevy of teenage daughters, who indeed treated him more like a favourite elder brother than as a husband or father.

Our first few days in Bangalore were spent with Narayan in a spacious colonial-type bungalow that evidently dated from the highest and palmiest days of the Raj. We had met our new friend at Tiruvannamalai, where having inspected a section of railway track he was taking the opportunity of paying his respects to the Maharshi, and at his invitation we had accompanied him back to Bangalore. Our original plan had been to visit Pondicherry, on the east coast, and see Sri Aurobindo, but on learning that he gave *darshan* only four times a year we had abandoned the idea. As we were still undecided what to do next when we met Narayan, his invitation seemed providential, especially as Bangalore, 200 miles distant from Tiruvannamalai, lay directly on the road back to North India. We therefore accepted the invitation with alacrity, and in a matter of hours were sitting in the good railway engineer's special bogie and heading north to Bangalore, the Middle Country and, perhaps, ordination.

Despite the presence of his family and the servants, Narayan's bungalow was very quiet. Apart from Rajgopal, whom we met soon after our arrival, there were no visitors, and Satyapriya and I were able to continue our meditations almost as usual. At night our host played us records of Subbalakshmi, the Nightingale of the South, of which he had an extensive collection. Neither Satyapriya nor I had ever heard this celebrated songstress before, and were more than a little doubtful as to the propriety of our listening to anything so worldly as popular film music. However, Narayan was a passionate admirer of the singer's talent, and not wishing to spoil his enjoyment by raising objections we said nothing. Subbalakshmi had, indeed, a glorious voice, and whatever reservations we might have about film music it was impossible to deny that she sang devotional songs in a way that was extraordinarily moving.

When Narayan had to go out on tour again it was arranged that we should stay with Rajgopal. The change was so great as to be almost a shock. It was like being swept from some quiet but stagnant backwater, shaded with trees, out into the middle of the main stream, where gaily painted river-craft raced up and down in the bright sunshine, oars dashed and sails billowed, and where people hailed one another joyfully from carved and gilded prows. Though smaller and less spacious than Narayan's, Rajgopal's bungalow behind the railway station was the scene of constant activity. In addition to Rajgopal himself, and his wife and daughters – all of whom were gay and lively enough – there was a constant stream of visitors, all cheerful and communicative, all interested in religion, and all expected to stay for a meal.

The place was busiest in the evening. In the lounge, where Satyapriya and I slept, at least fifteen or twenty people would gradually assemble, the men either in Western dress or the traditional white, the women without exception in colourful silk saris with borders of heavy gold or silver brocade. After general religious discussion, much music, and many devotional songs, Rajgopal would perform the *arati*, or ceremonial waving of lights, in front of the framed lithographs at the far end of the room, after which sweetmeats would be distributed. Sometimes he scandalized the more orthodox by performing *arati* not in a sarong, as tradition prescribed, but in his customary trousers and shirt. Many of the devotional songs were in praise of the god Shiva. One of them was in praise of the Shiva-lingam. Satyapriya and I could at first hardly believe our ears when we heard the rich soprano voice of Rajgopal's eldest daughter hymning the size, splendour, and omnipotence of the divine phallus, but from her rapt expression it was plain that she was quite unconscious of the actual meaning of the words. So far as she was concerned, and so far as her audience was concerned, she was simply singing the praises of Shiva.

We had not been many days under Rajgopal's hospitable roof before discovering that the whole family, and many of their friends, were deep in Spiritualism. Sessions with the Ouija board were held almost every day. Their spirit guide, Rajgopal told us, was Swami Vivekananda, with whom they were in constant communication and whom they consulted on every aspect of their lives. True to his earthly reputation, the swami was irascible in the extreme, and not only abused and scolded them incessantly but frequently lost his temper. He was also in the habit of ordering the whole family to take a purificatory bath, sometimes making them do this as many as seven or eight times a day. Rajgopal's only son, a bright and impudent schoolboy of sixteen, happened to be a natural medium, and sometimes they relied on him rather than the Ouija board as their means of communication with the unseen.

As soon as Satyapriya heard about the Ouija board he was on fire with impatience to try it. We would invoke the spirit of the Buddha, he exclaimed excitedly, and consult him about our future! This sacrilegious proposal I flatly refused to countenance. Indeed, much as my curiosity had been roused, I did not want to have anything to do with Spiritualism. It was not that I dogmatically disbelieved in it, but rather that the atmosphere surrounding it seemed unhealthy. In the end, at Satyapriya's urgent entreaty, I reluctantly agreed to an experimental session. Four of us participated. Sitting round the table on which the Ouija board rested, we touched the traveller very lightly with the tips of our fingers. Rajgopal invoked the spirit of the legendary hero Rama, popularly regarded as the seventh incarnation of the god Vishnu, and put a question. Almost immediately, after a brief preliminary shudder, the traveller darted off on its ball-bearings, and moving swiftly from one letter of the alphabet to another spelled out the answer to his question. Rajgopal put another question, then another, and received further answers in the same way. Though they were all acceptable enough, none of the answers was really in any way remarkable. What was remarkable was the fact that the traveller seemed to possess a will of its own, that it was activated by a force far in excess of the very insignificant pressure that we were exerting on it through our fingertips. So powerful was this force, indeed, that far from it being any unconscious impulse on our part that set the traveller in motion, it seemed rather as though our fingers were being dragged hither and thither against our will.

Satyapriya was deeply impressed. Trembling with suppressed excitement, he asked Rajgopal to invoke the spirit of Mahatma Gandhi and, when communication had been established, put the question that he had in readiness: 'Now that the country has been left without a leader, who will take your place?' Like millions of other Indians, what my friend wanted to know was whether it was Jawaharlal Nehru, Rajendra Prasad, Vallabhbhai Patel, Abul Kalam Azad, or even some individual as yet entirely unknown, who was going to succeed to the national leadership. Again moving swiftly from letter to letter of the alphabet, the traveller spelled out an answer that was completely unexpected by any of us: 'The whole people.' It was the whole people that would take Mahatma Gandhi's place, the whole people that would succeed to the national leadership! So unexpected was this answer, indeed, and so remote from our own assumptions, that in the first shock of astonishment it really did feel as though we were in contact with a discarnate intelligence independent of our own minds. Satyapriya, wildly excited, was ready to devote his life to Spiritualism. Sessions with the Ouija board would have to be held every day, he declared. With the help of Mahatma Gandhi, Swami Vivekananda, and other spirit guides, it would be possible to solve the social and economic problems of India, indeed of the whole world. Moreover, we would be able to obtain regular guidance not only on the practice of meditation but on every other aspect of the spiritual life.

Little by little I managed to calm him down. The interest aroused by Spiritualism could, I perceived, be extremely dangerous, and I privately resolved that whatever Rajgopal and his friends might do neither Satyapriya nor I should participate in any more experiments with the Ouija board. That we were in contact, through the traveller, with a psychic force independent of our own conscious volitions I was quite prepared to grant; but there was no evidence whatever, so far as I could see, that the force in question was identifiable with the discarnate personality of Rama, or Mahatma Gandhi, or Swami Vivekananda. There was not even any guarantee that it was of a genuinely spiritual nature, or beneficent, or even that it was spiritually more advanced than we were ourselves. Such being the case, there could be no question of our surrendering ourselves to it absolutely, or of our obeying implicitly any instructions it might give. These arguments, together with my absolute refusal to participate in any further sessions with the Ouija board, soon had the desired effect. Satyapriya's enthusiasm subsided, and he began to feel more than a little ashamed of himself. Fortunately, even before I had succeeded in convincing him of the undesirability of our getting involved in Spiritualism, there had occurred the first of a whole chain of events that was to be of far greater value to us, spiritually speaking, than any number of sessions with the Ouija board. Indeed, they were to constitute the most interesting and worthwhile part of our stay in Bangalore, and an important stage of our pilgrimage.

On our first or second Sunday in Rajgopal's house, in the morning, four or five young men came to see us. In this there was nothing unusual. What was unusual, however, was the way in which they paid their respects to us. Instead of the usual salutation with folded hands, or more or less perfunctory touching of the feet, each of them in turn went through an elaborate full-length prostration that lasted several minutes and was quite different from anything we had ever seen before. Arms were raised above the head and lowered again, body was spread-eagled on the floor, head turned from side to side, arms extended and withdrawn one after the other in wide sweeping movements, the whole exercise being performed slowly and with great concentration. More remarkable still, all the young men wore Western dress and all were 'educated', that is to say, could read, write, and speak English.

When the prostrations had been completed we entered into conversation with them, making the standard Indian enquiries, and it transpired that they were disciples of an ascetic popularly known as Yalahankar Swami. Yalahankar, they told us, was the name of a small town some thirty miles from Bangalore, where the swami had his ashram, and where he usually stayed. On hearing that we were staying with Rajgopal he had told them to go and pay their respects to us. The young men themselves lived in Bangalore, where, it seemed, they all had good jobs. When we asked them the meaning of their unusually elaborate prostrations they explained that according to Yalahankar Swami the majority of people, even religious people, were full of egotism. On account of this egotism they generally paid their respects to ascetics and holy men in a casual, hasty, and perfunctory manner. Since the purpose of the custom was to help curb egotism, to pay one's respects in this sort of way was of no value whatsoever. Indeed, by making people think how religious they were, or how humble, it could even intensify egotism. The swami had therefore devised for the use of his disciples the long and elaborate type of prostration we had just witnessed, and insisted that whenever they met a sadhu they should pay their respects to him by making it a number of times. Sometimes, they added – not without smiling – he even sent them to meet visiting sadhus with the special object of giving them extra practice with their prostration – and, of course, further experience in curbing egotism.

Delighted with this explanation, Satyapriya and I plied the young men with further questions. Yalahankar Swami seemed more original in his methods than the ordinary run of Hindu gurus, and we wanted to learn as much about him as possible. For their part, the young men were only too happy to tell us whatever they knew, and in the course of this and subsequent visits we heard from them a number of anecdotes that threw further light upon the methods and the temperament of their extraordinary master. Among other things he was a strict disciplinarian – so much so, indeed, that the disciples felt for him a respect bordering on actual terror. One young man, on going to see him one Sunday morning, had been ordered to take off all his clothes, sit down stark naked, and meditate. This was extraordinary enough, but there was more to come. He had just seated himself in front of the guru, he told us, and was about to close his eyes, when he saw slithering straight towards him across the floor an enormous cobra. Terrified, he was about to leap to his feet, when the swami, with a menacing look, shouted, 'Don't move! I'll look after that! You just carry on with your meditation!' So great was his fear of the guru, he confessed – far greater than his fear of the cobra – that he had sat there, unable to move, while the cobra not only slithered right up to him but coiled itself up in his lap. 'Meditate!' the swami shouted again. As he closed his eyes he suddenly lost consciousness of his surroundings, his ego dissolved, and he found himself in a state of *samādhi* or superconsciousness such as he had never experienced before. When he 'came to', he and the swami were still sitting alone together in the room, the cobra had vanished, and the time was some hours later. Subsequently there had been much discussion among the disciples as to the true nature of the incident. According to some, the cobra was a real one, and had either appeared by accident or been specially summoned by the swami. According to others, it was not a real cobra at all, and what the young man had in fact seen was a magical illusion conjured up by the swami in order to test his faith and his powers of concentration. The narrator of the incident professed himself unable to say which of these explanations was correct, and of course nobody dared ask the swami.

Even more extraordinary was an anecdote related by another disciple, a stout, dark-complexioned elderly woman who spoke nothing but Tamil, and was illiterate. According to the swami, she was the most advanced of his disciples, the young men being less spiritually developed. Apparently she was particularly experienced in meditation, and had great powers of mental absorption. One day the swami had asked her, 'How's the *samādhi* getting on?' When she replied that it seemed to be getting on fairly well he said, 'All right, let's see!' Making her place her hand palm uppermost on a wooden board, he had thereupon seized a hammer and with two or three well-directed blows had driven a large iron nail right through her hand and into the board. When she neither flinched nor cried out he exclaimed, 'That seems to be all right!' and pulled the nail out again. On this occasion there seemed no reason to doubt that the nail was a real nail, and not an illusory one, for she still had a small scar on her hand where it had gone through. When Satyapriya and I asked her if she had experienced any pain she replied, laconically, 'Not much.'

What we had heard from the disciples about Yalahankar Swami stimulated rather than satisfied us, and in between their visits we applied for further information to Rajgopal, who had himself met the swami a number of times. Unlike most ascetics, our friend told us, he was more concerned with the quality than with the quantity of his disciples, and tended to treat newcomers in so outrageous a fashion as to discourage further visits altogether. High-ranking government officials, who in most ashrams were received with semi-divine honours, fared no better than anybody else. If they showed the slightest trace of arrogance or condescension he would start abusing them the minute they appeared in the doorway. 'What do you want here?' he would shout roughly. 'Think you're doing us an honour in coming here, don't you? Think you're a big man! Well, we don't want your bigness here. You can get out – quick!' Only if he survived this fusillade was the visitor permitted to enter and asked to sit down. So fierce was the swami's manner, however, and so violent his abuse, that the majority of visiting dignitaries simply turned and fled. Sometimes, knowing his reputation, and anxious to escape rough treatment, visitors would deliberately adopt an attitude of profound humility. But for tactics of this sort the swami was more than a match. Springing to his feet, he would welcome such people with every mark of deference, saying how greatly honoured he felt by their visit, and what a blessing it was for his ashram to have such an embodiment of sanctity within its walls. As soon as they were seated in the place of honour, and had been pressed to take tea, or pan, or a cold drink, he would beg them, with folded hands, to give him and his disciples the benefit of their extraordinary wisdom. On their protesting their unworthiness, as of course they invariably did, he would only redouble his demonstrations of respect until in the end they collapsed in agonies of embarrassment and begged for mercy.

Another of the swami's practices, Rajgopal said, was to clean people's shoes. For this purpose he always kept by him a good stock of shoe polish of various kinds, as well as brushes and dusters. On days when there were more people at the ashram, and hence a motley collection of footwear lying outside the door, he would sometimes remove to his own room all the shoes, sandals, and slippers in sight and then spend a couple of hours not only scraping them free from dirt but carefully brushing and polishing them until the worn leather shone like glass. According to orthodox Hindu ideas it was absolutely unthinkable that a person of higher socio-religious position should touch the shoes of one of lower position, much less still actually clean them, and those unaccustomed to the swami's ways would react with feelings of mingled horror, astonishment, and outrage. The swami himself would remain unmoved.

'You come here to have your souls cleaned, don't you?' he would demand, still polishing. 'You don't seem to object to me doing *that*. If

I can clean your souls, why can't I clean your shoes too? Your souls are much more dirty!'

A similar line of reasoning seemed to underlie another of the swami's practices. Besides the shoe-cleaning equipment, he also kept in his room a municipal scavenger's uniform. This consisted of a pair of blue cotton shorts, blue shirt, and blue Gandhi cap. Once or twice a week he would lay aside his saffron robes, don his scavenger's uniform, and seizing the stiff reed broom used for such purposes would go and spend the day sweeping out all the latrines in the neighbourhood.

Although it was not difficult to detect a method in all this madness, the figure that emerged from the anecdotes of Rajgopal and the disciples, while striking and powerful enough, seemed bizarre and eccentric in the extreme. Yet bizarre and eccentric as it was, there was something about Yalahankar Swami more extraordinary than anything Satyapriya and I had yet heard. He was at least 600 years old! When Rajgopal at last told us this he did so with unaccustomed diffidence, as if expecting not merely astonishment but incredulity and even laughter. He need not have worried. Astonished indeed we were, but while unwilling to accept without question everything that we were told, neither my friend nor I was prepared to go to the opposite extreme of rejecting a statement like Rajgopal's out of hand simply because it was in conflict with currently received notions of what was possible and what impossible. All over the world there were traditions of wise men who had lived for many hundreds of years, and if such longevity had sometimes been achieved in the past it did not seem unreasonable to suppose that it might occasionally be achieved in the present as well. Had I not already met the Yoga Swami of Jaffna? True, he was only 150 years old, but if a man could live for 150 years why not for 600? Why not indefinitely?

Pleased that his story had not been derided as an old wives' tale, Rajgopal told us more. There was continuous reference to the swami in local records for the last 600 years, he said, and the fact of his extraordinary longevity was both well known and widely accepted. Knowing how little reliance could be placed even on evidence of this kind, I could not help wondering if all the records of which Rajgopal spoke did, in fact, explicitly refer to one and the same person, or whether there had not been a succession of Yalahankar Swamis whom folklore and legend had subsequently identified, much as Buddhist tradition had at times confused Nāgārjuna the Mādhyamika metaphysician with the much later Nāgārjuna who was a Tantric initiate. Whatever reservations either Satyapriya or I had about the fact of the swami's longevity, as distinct from the principle of its possibility, what Rajgopal had told us made both of us more eager than ever to see him, and at our urgent entreaty he promised to consult with the disciples and see if a meeting could be arranged. As we already knew, the swami was not an easy person to approach, he warned us, and if we were not to be greeted with a shower of abuse it would be necessary to proceed with caution.

While we were still waiting to hear the outcome of Rajgopal's consultations with the disciples, Satyapriya and I discovered that for all his devotion our lively and good-natured host was not above playing a practical joke on us. Knowing our eagerness to meet ascetics and yogis of every kind, he suddenly told us, one Sunday afternoon, that he was taking us to see one of the most celebrated gurus in the whole of South India. 'Why didn't I think of it before?' he exclaimed, slapping his forehead with cheerful vexation. Suspecting nothing, we at once asked for further information. Rajgopal was only too ready to oblige. The guru in question, he told us, as we drove through the broad sunlit streets, was the object of special devotion to millions of Tamil-speaking people and ashrams had been established in his name not only in the Madras Presidency, where he had been born, but throughout the whole of the adjacent area as well. His principal ashram, however, was in Bangalore, in the heart of the city, and it was there that we were now going. We would not be the only visitors. Every Sunday afternoon devotees came to pay their respects to the great guru from all over the city, and from even farther afield, and the place was usually crowded. With luck, however, we would be able to get a glimpse of him. His name? He would tell us that when we had made his acquaintance, but he was sure we had heard it before. A few minutes later the car halted in front of a large two-storey building that stood several yards back from the road. It did not look very ashram-like, but there were certainly plenty of visitors. Saying we might have to wait, our friend dispatched his son to find out if the guru was at home. While the lad was gone Satyapriya and I tried to read the blue and white signboard that spanned the entire front of the building. As it was in Tamil, neither of us had much success, and we were still struggling with the angular, unfamiliar letters when Rajgopal's son reappeared. 'The guru is at home,' he announced with a flourish, 'and sends you this *prasad* with his blessing!' On our undoing the leaf-wrapped packets he handed us our nostrils were pleasantly assailed by a warm, spicy fragrance, as of something hot and savoury. 'Guru Masala Dosai!' shouted Rajgopal, delighted with the success of his joke. 'Three cheers for Guru Masala Dosai, the greatest guru in the whole of South India!' Though Satyapriya did not usually appreciate a joke against himself, neither of us could help sharing Rajgopal's merriment and laughing at the way in which we had been taken in. We had certainly heard the name of the guru before. Masala *dosai* was a favourite Tamil delicacy, and the 'ashram' to which our friend had taken us was famous for the excellence of its *dosais* all over South India. Even before we had finished our second packet of *prasad*, Satyapriya and I told Rajgopal that Guru Masala Dosai fully deserved his reputation and that we were prepared to enrol ourselves as his disciples on the spot.

Soon after making the acquaintance of Guru Masala Dosai we met Yalahankar Swami. The meeting took place not at the Yalahankar Ashram, as we had expected, but in an ancient, stone-built ashram somewhere in the interior where the swami, it seemed, was temporarily staying, and where the disciples and their wives had arranged to spend the weekend with him. Arriving on Saturday evening with Rajgopal and his family, Satyapriya and I found some two dozen people quietly chatting in a large room with bare grey walls of undressed stone. Every now and then someone glanced expectantly, not to say apprehensively, towards a low arched doorway set in the middle of the right-hand wall that seemed to be barred and bolted from within. This was the entrance to the swami's private quarters, where it was assumed he was still meditating. At any rate, the door had been closed when the earliest arrivals came, in the middle of the afternoon, and nobody had yet seen or heard anything of him. Knowing his ways, however, they showed no astonishment, and settling down in little groups on the bare stone floor simply waited for him to emerge in his own good time. As it turned out, they had to wait longer than they expected. Three hours went by, then four, then five, and there was still no sign of the swami, neither could any sound of him be heard from behind the door. Since he had not given them any previous instructions as to what they should do nobody dared to start cooking, and nobody dared to go to bed. By twelve o'clock the disciples were feeling not only tired and hungry but distinctly anxious. Perhaps they had offended the swami in some way. Perhaps he was angry with them. Perhaps he would not come out of his room at all and they would have to go away without seeing him.... Or perhaps it was a test....

At precisely three o'clock in the morning there was a sound of bolts being withdrawn, the small door opened, and the swami emerged from his confinement. Taken by surprise despite their long vigil, and not knowing quite what to expect, the disciples struggled to their feet and greeted him as best they could. Having advanced a few steps into the room, the swami paused, his sturdy saffron-clad figure lit up by the rich yellow glow of the oil-lamps. With a shock of surprise, I saw that he had only one eye, and though it was not situated in the middle of his forehead it gave his features, already grim and terrible enough, so startlingly villainous a cast that they seemed more appropriate to some notorious highwayman or pirate of the old days than to a celebrated ascetic. At the same time – and all this registered instantaneously – Yalahankar Swami had an expression of compassion such as I had seen on no other human face. As for his age, I did not find it difficult to imagine that he was 600 years old or more. He had an immemorial look, like that of some ancient hill, and though he had the outward appearance of a man of fifty-five it was as though he had been fifty-five for a very long time. Barely had we finished exchanging greetings when he started issuing his orders. All the womenfolk were to start cooking immediately. It was time everybody had something to eat and since we had been fasting since noon the previous day the meal should be as large and as elaborate as possible. In fact it should be a regular feast. Despite the lateness, or rather earliness, of the hour, and the relative scantiness of provisions, no one ventured to demur, and the disciples' wives all obediently trooped off to the kitchen, where cauldrons of rice and curry were soon bubbling on the squat, cowdung-plastered kitchen ranges.

In less than two hours the feast was ready. Before allowing anyone to sit down to it, however, the swami announced that the disciples would all have to take a bath, or rather, would be given a bath. The women would bathe the men. He himself, assisted by the old Tamil woman, would bathe the two sadhus. Before we well understood what was happening, Satyapriya and I found ourselves in the steaming bath house, divested of our robes, with Yalahankar Swami and his chief disciple vigorously soaping us one after the other. Both were extremely gentle in their ministrations but also extremely thorough. When the job had been completed to their joint satisfaction we were conducted to the kitchen and seated there in readiness for the meal. From the bath house came the sound of loud splashing, mixed with the indistinct murmur of voices. Suddenly we heard the voice of Rajgopal raised in a shout of protest – a protest that was quickly cut short by the gruff tones of the swami and shrieks of merriment on the part of the women. Afterwards our friend told us that coming back into the bath house from the kitchen and finding him being soaped down by two of the wives, who were already tittering with suppressed mirth, the swami had pulled off his jockstrap with the remark that they should do the job properly. According to a widespread Indian belief, shame, in the sense of sexual modesty, was one of the very last fetters to be broken by the disciple in his quest for spiritual enlightenment, with the result that those who practised religious nudity were traditionally held in high esteem by both Hindus and Jains. Either out of respect for our position as ascetics, or because we had been judged unready for such a renunciation, Satyapriya and I had been suffered to retain our jockstraps, but from Rajgopal, apparently, a higher degree of emancipation was expected. When we asked our friend what his feelings were when he suddenly found himself stark naked in the hands of two giggling women he replied that, rather to his surprise, he had felt just like a small child.

Next morning (or it may have been two or three days later) we had a second meeting with Yalahankar Swami, this time in his room at the Yalahankar Ashram. Since Satyapriya remained strangely silent throughout practically the whole interview, and since Rajgopal, usually so loquacious, was on this occasion content to function mainly as interpreter, conversation was almost entirely between the swami and me. As the pair of us talked, and as the single eye was bent sternly but kindly now on me and now on Rajgopal, I could not help thinking of the great Buddhist teacher Āryadeva, the disciple of Nāgārjuna, and the founder, next to him, of the Madhyamaka School. Like Yalahankar Swami, Āryadeva had only one eye, and was a native of South India. According to legend he had also lived for several hundred years. Indeed, according to some accounts he had mastered the secret of longevity and was still alive somewhere in South India. Was Yalahankar Swami, perhaps, none other than Āryadeva? Buddhism having disappeared from the area five or six centuries ago, and Hinduism having taken its place, for the great teacher to appear in the guise of a Hindu ascetic would be fully in accordance with the compassionate spirit of the

Mahāyāna, which believed in being all things to all men, so that haply some at least might be led in the direction of Enlightenment. Judging by his extant writings, however, Āryadeva had been in some ways a typical high-caste Indian intellectual, and the swami did not seem like an intellectual at all. On the contrary, in his outward appearance, as well as in the earnestness and simplicity with which he spoke of his methods, he appeared more like a skilled workman who, knowing his job, could talk about it in a detached, matter-of-fact manner, without intellectual pretensions of any kind. Though the blue cotton uniform, complete with Gandhi cap, hung from a hook by the door, and though shoes and sandals of various sizes, recently polished, stood in shining rows against the wall, it was difficult to imagine that the thick-set figure now so quietly talking to me was the subject of the extraordinary tales we had heard from the disciples.

As the conversation ebbed and flowed, with Rajgopal occasionally stopping to ascertain whether he had correctly understood our meaning, the swami impressed upon me that the only real obstacle to the realization of Truth was egotism. Once that had been overcome, he insisted, the religious aspirant would automatically achieve a state of unconditioned spiritual freedom. This was of course standard Vedantic, not to say Buddhist, doctrine: I had heard it often before. But Yalahankar Swami spoke with a conviction and authority I had rarely if ever encountered. Moreover, unlike many exponents of Vedantic metaphysics, his approach was not theoretical but practical. Egotism could be overcome only by the prolonged experience of *samādhi*, by which he meant, not meditation in the ordinary sense of the term, but a superconscious state in which all sense of separative individual selfhood was transcended. In the training of his disciples, he said, his sole concern was to eradicate egotism by inducing the *samādhi* experience. Since there were two different forms of egotism, pride and humility, he had two different methods of dealing with people. With those who were proud he behaved more proudly still; with those who were humble, with even greater humility. Thus both were made to realize how egotistic they actually were. 'However high you go,' he concluded, addressing me directly, 'I shall always be above you. However low you go, I shall always be below you.' The idea that humility was just as much a form of egotism as pride represented an important new insight for me, and I never forgot the swami's words.

Among the disciples who had accompanied us to the stone-built ashram in the interior, as well as to Yalahankar, was a small dark Kannada-speaking Mysorean named Krishna who invariably wore not only a Western-style jacket and trousers, both rather crumpled, but also an unironed white shirt, collar, and tie. Sometimes he also wore a khaki-coloured pith helmet. Though not much more than thirty, he was already the owner of one of the small fleets of inadequately serviced motor coaches which, jolting and rattling along the hundreds of miles of dusty country roads, were the principal means of long-distance transport within the state. Every few weeks he personally inspected one or another of the main routes, some of which it took several days to traverse. Not long after our second meeting with Yalahankar Swami he suggested that we might like to accompany him on his next excursion, which would include Belur and Halevid, with their famous temples, Sringeri, seat of the Shankaracharya of that name, and the Jain hilltop shrine of Sravana Belgola, with its colossal standing figure of Gomateshwara. Krishna's offer had, it seemed, Yalahankar Swami's approval, if it had not been actually inspired by him, and in our eagerness to see more holy places, perhaps meet more holy people, Satyapriya and I accepted with alacrity. Within a few days we had left Bangalore, the jungles of Mysore had closed behind us, and we were on the first lap of our journey.

41

SANDALWOOD COUNTRY

The jungle through which our road lay, and which we saw from the front seat of Krishna's coach, was not of the lush green tropical variety but, for the most part, dry, brown, and dusty. Indeed it was bush rather than true jungle. On either side of the deeply rutted track, so thick with white dust that we could be said to plough rather than drive our way through, medium-sized trees, many of them practically leafless, rising sparsely out of a tangle of undergrowth, stretched as far back as the eye could see. Sunshine and dust seemed to cover all. Every twenty or thirty miles came a halt, when there would be a general climbing in and out of passengers, besides much loading and unloading of baggage, and when Krishna would bring us little brass tumblers of tea and strange Mysorean delicacies wrapped in banana leaves. At night we stayed in the local Government Bungalow or with friends of Krishna's.

As on previous occasions when the travelling arrangements were in somebody else's hands, and I had no decisions to make, I relaxed in my seat and became simply the spectator of the scenes through which we passed. If these were monotonous, or of no special interest, I withdrew into myself and became absorbed in my own inner experience. Thus our ten- or twelve-day trip was for me a kind of waking dream, a dream from which I emerged only at intervals, when something of particular significance claimed my attention, and I can give of it, therefore, no connected account. All that remains are isolated images, the exact sequence of which it is no longer possible to determine. But though the sequence of the images may have been forgotten, the images themselves are still fresh and vivid, emerging with archetypal brilliance from the nondescript jungle of my dreams.

The temples of Belur and Halevid, built under the Hoysala Dynasty in the twelfth and fourteenth centuries, were quite different from those of Madura, Cape Comorin, Suchindram, and Tiruvannamalai. Their forms were more compact and more rounded. Here were no fortress-like walls, no spacious courtyards, no soaring gate-towers. Everything was on a smaller and more intimate scale. If the shrines that dominated the flat bare landscape of the Tamil countryside needed to be systematically explored, those that now rose to meet us out of the jungles of Mysore could be taken in at a single glance. If those were sublime, these were beautiful. There the gate-towers and the capitals of pillars were splendidly sculptured indeed, but here everything was covered, inside and outside, with carving as bold as a bunch of fruit and as delicate as lace. On the outside walls, bands of sculpture extended from top to bottom, the horizontal courses making a pleasant contrast with the full, not to say bulbous, outlines of the buildings. Despite the appeal of the divine and semi-divine figures so gloriously sculptured in the panels of the middle and upper bands, my attention was drawn chiefly by the bottommost band, where a procession of diminutive elephants ran round the base of the entire temple, which seemed almost to float on their backs. Though there must have been hundreds of elephants, each one was different, and all were astonishingly alive.

One of the temples seemed to have no windows. The only natural light came in at the door through which we had just entered. As we struggled to make out the dim shapes by which we were surrounded, the broad yellow beam of a spotlight suddenly stabbed upwards into the dome above our heads. As it crept slowly round, scene after richly sculptured scene was revealed to our gaze, the swarms of black stone figures standing out sharply in the glare. Eventually, having traversed the dome and picked its way carefully down the wall the spotlight came to rest on a free-standing female figure of smoothly polished black basalt near the door. So languidly beautiful were the limbs, so voluptuously sweet the face, that none who had once beheld her could easily turn away. It was Mohini the Deluder, embodiment of all feminine witchery, in whose infinitely charming form the god Vishnu had tempted Shiva himself from his asceticism and caused him to beget, for the salvation of the world, a hero to destroy demons and resuscitate Dharma....

Having torn ourselves from the embrace of Mohini, and said goodbye to the temples of Belur and Halevid, we passed through more jungle, some of it denser and greener than any we had yet seen, through coffee plantations, through vast tracts of sandalwood forest, and through yet more jungle. Somewhere in the jungle there was a mountain, and somewhere on the side of the mountain a cave. In the cave lived four or five people, the devotees of a female ascetic who lived not in the cave itself but in an underground chamber beneath the floor of the cave, emerging for only half an hour each day. When Satyapriya and I arrived at the cave with Krishna it was about noon, and Mother Lakshmi, as she was called, was expected to come out within the next ten or fifteen minutes. While we were waiting we asked the devotees for further information about her. Eight years ago she had taken a vow to observe complete silence for the next twelve years, which meant that only four more years now remained. What she would do after that they did not know. Perhaps she would speak, perhaps she would take another vow of silence. At present most of her time was spent in meditation. The only reason she left her underground retreat even once a day was to answer the calls of nature and take a little food. From the way in which the devotees spoke it was clear that though they saw so little of her they regarded it as a great privilege to be able to live in such close proximity to her and minister to her needs.

While we were talking Mother Lakshmi's grey head appeared through a hole in the floor, and with the gentle assistance of the devotees she slowly emerged into the cave. After steadying herself on her feet, the frail, white-clad figure turned her head in the direction of Satyapriya and myself and advanced towards us with hands outstretched in welcome, on her face a smile of tenderness and affection. Though nothing was said, her quiet, graceful gestures, as well as the way in which she gazed up into our faces and stroked our cheeks, were far more expressive than any words. When we had been given something to eat she indicated, with more gestures, that we were to go one at a time down the hole and have a look at her underground chamber. After descending a short flight of rough stone steps I found myself crouching in a cell not more than four feet square and of about the same height. Small as Mother Lakshmi was, it would have been impossible for her either to stand upright or to stretch out full length on the floor. There was no ventilation other than that provided by the stairway, while the sole illumination came from a tiny oil-lamp placed on the floor. Apart from Mother Lakshmi's meditation mat, and a tiny altar with two or three religious pictures, the chamber was completely bare. It was also completely silent. For all the sound that could be heard from the cave upstairs, the people there might have been a million miles away. In that chamber one really was alone. I could not help wondering what it was that enabled Mother Lakshmi to sit there for more than twenty-three hours out of the twenty-four and gave such ethereal sweetness to her smile.

Two or three days later I was speculating about the inner experiences not of a comparatively unknown female ascetic but about one of the most prominent figures in the orthodox Hindu ecclesiastical establishment. Travelling through still more jungle, we had come to the little riverside town of Sringeri, which was situated only a few miles from the coast and marked the westernmost point of our whole excursion. Sringeri, as I well knew, was the seat of the Shankaracharya of that name. More than 1,000 years earlier the original Shankaracharya, founder of the Advaita Vedanta school of Indian philosophy, had established in different parts of the subcontinent a series of maths or monastic centres for the dissemination of his own special interpretation of the Upanishadic tradition as well as for the revival of orthodox Hinduism. Four of these maths, including that of Puri – with one of whose Shankaracharyas at least we were already acquainted – had in course of time attained to a generally acknowledged ascendancy, and among these four Sringeri was undoubtedly pre-eminent. If not the Vatican of Hinduism, as guidebooks sometimes claimed, it was by far the wealthiest of the maths, with a long tradition of Sanskrit learning, impeccable socio-religious orthodoxy, ecclesiastical dominance, and political influence.

Since admission to the math was strictly limited to members of the two highest castes, there was of course no question of our being accommodated within its precincts. Indeed, it seemed doubtful if we would get so much as a glimpse of the place from the inside. The original Shankaracharya was even now venerated by the orthodox as the destroyer of the hated Buddhists and the exterminator of their pernicious faith and we could hardly expect much of a welcome at the seat of his principal successor. A surprise, however, was in store for us. Though we could not be accommodated in the math, thanks to Krishna's influence room was found for us in the modern, Western-style guest house which it maintained for the benefit of high-ranking government officials, princes, millionaires, and others who, though their unclean presence could not be tolerated within the actual math area, were important enough for the math authorities to be anxious not to offend them by too unceremonious a reception. The guest house was situated on the roadside quite near the math. Looking across the river from the window of our second floor room, we could see among the flame-of-the-forest trees on the opposite bank the whitewashed buildings of the Forbidden City of the Shankaracharyas.

Fortunately it did not remain forbidden for long. Also staying at the guest-house was a tall, portly Tamil Brahmin in the traditional white sarong and shoulder-towel who lost no time in introducing himself to us. He was staying there, apparently, on a semi-permanent basis, having been seconded to Sringeri as administrator of the math from the Ministry of Home Affairs in New Delhi. The math had vast landed properties in every part of India, he explained, properties that had been gifted by kings and merchant princes over a period of many centuries, and its annual income amounted to millions. Among other things, it owned practically all the sandalwood forests in Mysore. Unfortunately, in recent years there had been repeated complaints about the administration of the math estates, and the spending of its revenues, and the matter having become practically a public scandal the Central Government had been forced to intervene and he himself had been appointed administrator. For the last year or more he had been engaged in cleaning out whatever was the Hindu mythological equivalent of an Augean stable of inefficiency, mismanagement, and downright corruption. Now, however, something like order had been introduced into the chaos. Collection of revenues had been entrusted to reliable persons, a proper system of accounting had been established and, above all, expenditure had been brought under control, so that some at least of the math's resources were now being utilized in accordance with the original intentions of the donors instead of being used to provide dowries for Telugu Brahmin girls and pay for the *upanayanam* ceremonies of Telugu Brahmin boys.

Not understanding how the Telugu Brahmin boys and girls came into the picture in this way, and seeing that our new friend was inclined to be communicative, Satyapriya and I asked for further information on the subject. The administrator at once obliged. Perhaps we did not know it, he said, but despite the fact that the original Shankaracharya was a Nambudiri Brahmin from Malabar, for some centuries past the Shankaracharyas of Sringeri Math had been drawn exclusively from a particular sub-caste of Telugu Brahmins living in the Andhra country, on the east coast. As a result of this custom, the office of Shankaracharya had become in effect the private appanage of that community, the members of which considered themselves entitled to dip into the math's treasury as frequently as they pleased. Whenever a daughter was married, the math was called upon to provide the dowry; whenever a son was invested with the sacred thread, the math was called upon to meet the expenses of the ceremony. As every Brahmin family had at least five or six children, and as 1,000 rupees was the least that was expected on such occasions, there was thus a perpetual drain on the math's resources. Indeed, dowries and *upanayanam* ceremonies had swallowed up the greater part of the revenues every year, so that very little was left over for other purposes. Some of the Brahmin families, on one pretext or another, had lived entirely off the math, doing no work at all of any kind. But now, he declared with evident satisfaction, the flow of money was beginning to dry up. The math was no longer subsidizing an entire sub-caste of Telugu Brahmins. Its revenues were being devoted to more worthy purposes. A Sanskrit College had been built. Vedic education was being encouraged.

By this time both Satyapriya and I were wondering what part the Shankaracharya himself played in the affairs of the math. Was he the unwilling spectator of the corruption, or part of it? Did he support the administrator's reforms, or was he opposed to them? Above all, was he a spiritual personage in his own right or just a particularly high-ranking Hindu ecclesiastical dignitary? At the mention of the Shankaracharya's name (for these thoughts were soon put into words) our informant's expression changed from virtuous triumph to rapt devotion. The Shankaracharya was a saint, he exclaimed. He knew absolutely nothing of what was going on around him. He was immersed in perpetual *samādhi*. Some members of his entourage had spread a report that he was mad. Some of them even wanted to get rid of him. But he was not mad, he was perfectly sane, or if he was mad it was with the madness of God-intoxication. He was a liberated soul, a *jivanmukta*. On no account should we leave Sringeri without having the blessing of his *darshan*. He himself would arrange an interview. It was not usual, of course. Only Brahmins and Kshatriyas were permitted to enter the math, and only Brahmins of unblemished orthodoxy could come within speaking distance of the Shankaracharya or actually converse with him, and though we had been strangely reticent on the subject he knew perfectly well that one of us, at least, was a non-Brahmin – possibly something even less acceptable to the orthodox. But never mind. He asked no questions. For him it was quite enough that we were sadhus, ascetics, who had nothing to do with the caste system. If we would accompany him to the math the following morning he would not only show us the temples, and other places of interest, but station us where we would have the opportunity of seeing the Shankaracharya on his way to his ceremonial ablutions, perhaps of exchanging a few words with him. He could assure us categorically that, much as his entourage might disapprove, the Shankaracharya himself had no objection whatever to speaking with anyone.

The administrator's offer having anticipated our own wishes, next morning Satyapriya and I rejoiced to find ourselves crossing the ancient whitewashed bridge that was, apparently, the sole means of access to the math from the guest-house side of the river. On the way our guide proved no less communicative than before, and not only told us more about the math and its inmates, but also, consciously and unconsciously, revealed more of himself. With his combination of theological acumen and administrative vigour, of orthodox piety and worldly shrewdness, he evidently belonged to a class of Brahmins who in ancient times had advised kings and administered kingdoms and of whom, in the present century, the notorious Dewan of Travancore, Sir C. P. Ramaswamy Iyer, was perhaps the most illustrious example. Like other men of business whom we had met, and whose protestations we had once believed, he professed to be thoroughly disgusted with the world and to long only for the peace of the hermit or the freedom of the wandering ascetic. If only he could have had his own way, he exclaimed, in a voice that might have been called a sigh if it had not been so loud, he would have spent the first half of his life studying the *Rig Veda* and the second half of his life meditating upon it! In this *Veda*, from one of the inspired authors of which he was himself descended, there were to be found all the truths that had ever been taught by all the philosophies and all religions of the world – and much more beside. Surprised as we might be to hear it, he added, even the vaunted discoveries of modern science were not discoveries at all but only borrowings from this priceless work, though for reasons best known to themselves – perhaps on account of feelings of national pride – Western scientists had so far not cared to acknowledge their indebtedness to the sages of ancient India.

Before I had time to question this assertion, with which I knew Satyapriya was inclined to agree, we had entered the math premises and our loquacious friend had changed the subject. With temples and other buildings all about us, it was not surprising that he should start expatiating on the power and splendour of the Shankaracharyas of Sringeri Math. Whenever they went out, which was not often, they rode in golden palanquins on the backs of elephants and were attended by a numerous retinue. On their arrival at the borders of such states as acknowledged their spiritual overlordship, of which only Travancore, Cochin, and Mysore now remained, the ruler of the state thus honoured was compelled by ancient custom to welcome them in person and make offerings amounting to millions of rupees – though if he was not of sufficiently high caste he was not permitted actually to approach the Shankaracharya. From the relish with which he recounted these facts it was clear that despite his reformist zeal our friend's imagination had been stirred by what the editor of the *Children's Encyclopaedia* would have called 'The Romance of the Shankaracharyas'. But it was also clear that enthusiasm for the past had not been permitted to blind him to the realities of the present. Times had changed, he declared. Much of the old pomp had gone, and the present Shankaracharya did not care even for what little was left. Among other eccentricities, he steadfastly refused to wear his regalia, which was of solid gold, studded with enormous precious stones, and worth hundreds of millions of rupees. He even refused to wear it on ceremonial occasions, and on this account the members of his entourage were extremely displeased and dissatisfied with him. Indeed, they were displeased and dissatisfied with him on a number of accounts. So much so was this the case, in fact, that besides spreading the story of his madness they had recently compelled him, very much against his will, to consecrate as his successor a young man more after their own hearts.

By the time we had learned all this, and heard the history of the various temples round which our good-natured guide insisted on conducting us, the hour of the Shankaracharya's mid-morning bath had struck, and he was on his way to the river for the second ceremonial ablutions of the day. Stationing us on the steps of a small temple near the water, with instructions to wait there until the Shankaracharya passed by, the worthy administrator hastened away to join the little procession that escorted the Shankaracharya to the screened-off section of river where, assisted by his personal attendants, he took his bath out of the sight of profane eyes. Though we did not have to wait many minutes, there was time for a number of thoughts to pass through our minds. Was the Shankaracharya a saint, as the administrator appeared to believe, or was he mentally unbalanced? Would we be able to speak to him, or would the members of his entourage object? As we were asking ourselves these questions, a slight, saffron-clad figure came into view round the corner of a nearby building and started moving slowly and unsteadily in the direction of the river. Behind him, no less slowly, came an untidy procession of attendants and math officials in white dhotis and sacred threads. Some of them, among whom was the administrator, walked quite close to the Shankaracharya, as if in readiness to catch him if he staggered or fell. Whatever its significance might be, whether spiritual or pathological, the frail, elderly man at the head of the procession was clearly in no ordinary state of mind. Scarcely conscious of his surroundings, he moved like a sleepwalker or a drugged person, or as though in a trance. When he was nearly abreast of us, Satyapriya and I, descending the temple steps, came forward and waited in the middle of the path, the administrator moved to the Shankaracharya's side and whispered a few words of explanation, the procession halted, and we stood face to face. After we had saluted the official head of the Advaita Vedanta tradition, and received his blessing, he asked us one or two questions, and a brief conversation ensued. Though he was undoubtedly in a state of semi-abstraction from the world, and though he spoke with a hesitancy that was almost fearfulness, whatever he said was perfectly rational, while there was no mistaking the genuine kindliness and gentleness of his disposition. Somewhat to our surprise, he spoke in English, as of course we did too, the administrator helping out with a murmured translation whenever my accent was unintelligible to him.

After we had bidden farewell to the Shankaracharya, and seen his procession escort him as far as the bank of the river, we stayed behind for a few minutes to say goodbye to the administrator and thank him for all the trouble he had taken. As we did so along came the Shankaracharya's successor-designate, or the Junior Shankaracharya as he was called, walking at the head of a little procession of his own with what could only be described as a military swagger. About twenty-five years of age, handsome and well built, it was clear that when the time came he would have no objection whatever to wearing the regalia.

For some time after we had crossed the bridge and made our way back to the guest house I could not help thinking of the frail saffron-clad figure and vacant kindly face of the unwanted Shankaracharya – and wondering what was the nature of his experience. He seemed like a man who was still recovering from some terrible shock. Was this shock the impact of undiluted spiritual Reality, or was it something more mundane? Was he, perhaps, a sensitive person of genuine spirituality who, not being strong enough to withstand the various pressures to which he was subjected by his entourage, had simply cracked under the strain? I was still asking myself these questions when, next morning, we left Sringeri for Sravana Belgola. Not until some years later, when the Sandalwood Country had long ceased to occupy my thoughts, did I learn, quite by accident, that the Shankaracharya was dead. He had drowned while taking his bath, the math authorities said, and the Junior Shankaracharya had been installed in his place.

The last of the images that rose upon me from the jungles of Mysore was a perfectly nude male figure standing immobile, his arms at his sides, his face expressionless, and his eyes gazing into the far distance. Gomateshwara! Lord of Sacred Mother Cow! As we approached Sravana Belgola we saw him in the far distance, white against the blue sky, standing at the top of a small hill, the lower part of his body hidden by the surrounding buildings. Less than an hour later we stood beside the massive feet, looking up past the well-rounded thighs, past the flaccid, wrinkled penis the height of a man, past the broad sweep of the breast and the firm chin up to the serene face and the eyes which, oblivious of our presence, continued to gaze out into the endless distance. Who Gomateshwara was and how he came to be standing there I did not know. According to Jain tradition he had lived in very ancient, even in prehistoric times, being a disciple of one of the legendary predecessors of Mahavira, the founder of Jainism. Leaving his father's kingdom for the forest, he had stood absorbed in meditation for so long that plants had grown round his legs as though round the trunks of trees. Sure enough, up the side of each enormous leg climbed a tendril, so tall that it rose above our heads, so short that it reached only halfway up to the smoothly jointed knees. With his eyes fixed on Infinity, Gomateshwara not only rose out of Nature, but transcended her.

From the upper galleries of the buildings that surrounded the courtyard in which the giant figure stood it was possible to see the great oval of its face from waist level, but so majestically calm was its expression, so uncompromisingly distant its gaze, that one felt no nearer than before. Lower down the hill, on either side of the irregular flights of stone-cut steps, stood a number of unpretentious temples, monasteries, and other buildings. In one of them a learned Jain scholar, a layman, showed us a rich collection of Sanskrit palm-leaf manuscripts. Sravana Belgola was, in fact, one of the most ancient and celebrated centres of Jainism in Mysore, perhaps in the whole of India, and an important place of pilgrimage. According to Jain tradition it had been founded by Chandragupta Maurya, the grandfather of the Emperor Aśoka, who was said to have ended his days there as a Jain ascetic, committing religious suicide in the most approved manner by starving himself to death. Every twelve years, we were told, the hill was the scene of a great festival, to which tens of thousands of devotees came from all over the country. At the climax of the festival hundreds of buckets of milk, curds, and clarified butter were emptied on to the head of the image from a specially constructed platform and allowed to trickle all the way down to his feet. The Jains being a wealthy community, hundreds of thousands of rupees were spent in this way.

42
'TIGER, TIGER ...'

Though our excursion with Krishna had not lasted much more than a week, on our return to Bangalore we found that during our absence changes had taken place. The Ouija board, formerly so much in request, now stood idle. In fact, Rajgopal told us, he had decided to give up Spiritualism altogether. After our departure the demands of their spirit guide, Swami Vivekananda, had become so incessant and so outrageous that they threatened to disrupt the whole tenor of their existence. He himself had found it impossible to attend to his official work, his son had been unable to go to school, and his wife had had no time for her domestic duties. Swami Vivekananda wanted to take them over completely, and for this, he admitted with cheerful frankness, they were not yet ready. Sessions with the Ouija board had therefore been discontinued, and he now relied for spiritual guidance on holy men with whom he was in actual physical contact.

With the Ouija board out of the way, Rajgopal's bungalow was a much quieter place, and I would not have minded passing the remainder of our time in South India under his friendly and hospitable roof. But this was not to be. Before our departure for the North we had a second excursion to make, though one of rather different character from the first. Having heard from Krishna a full account of our journey, Yalahankar Swami suggested that it would be a good idea for us to spend some time in the Divyagiri range of mountains, somewhere to the north of Bangalore, where many ancient sages had lived, and where some of them were reported to be still residing. No sooner was this suggestion conveyed to us than Satyapriya was impatient to be off. We had wasted far too much time in the company of worldly people, he exclaimed, and listened to their worldly talk long enough, and it would be good for us to get away for a few weeks. Indeed, since we ourselves had been talking far too much, he intended to observe complete silence during the whole of our stay in the sacred mountains. *I could do whatever I liked.*

Arrangements for the journey were soon made, and a day or two later we were in a coach with Krishna and some of the other disciples and heading north. Two miles from the foot of the mountains, in the midst of a vast expanse of fields, stood a double row of mud houses, one of which seemed to be a shop. Here the motor road came to an end. Leaving the coach parked in the shade of a tree, we made our way in single file through the fields, Krishna leading. Within half an hour the fields had given place to trees and boulders, and we were climbing steeply. Like Arunachala, Divyagiri seemed an enormous heap of stones, the only difference being that here the stones were not grey but black. The trees, which appeared to cover the entire mountainside, were all *bel* trees, sacred to the god Shiva. So thickly did they grow that, even though their leaves were nearly all fallen, it was at times difficult to get more than a glimpse of the cloudless blue sky. On the ground, embedded in the fallen leaves, lay thousands upon thousands of smooth-shelled green and yellow *bel*-fruits, some of them almost as large as coconuts. Many were so ripe that they had split open, exposing the viscous orange meat within, and their astringent, medicinal odour filled the air. When we had climbed steadily for two or three hours, the trees started to thin out, the sun shone more and more hotly in our faces, the smell of the fallen *bel*-fruits became almost overpowering, and with a gasp of relief we emerged onto a kind of rocky terrace 2,000 feet above the plain. To our left, backing onto the mountain, was a long, irregular structure of rough stone slabs. To our right was a low parapet wall. Having rested a while, and having warned us that the mountain was full of leopards and that we should be sure to shut ourselves in every night, Krishna and his friends started on their journey back down the mountainside, and Satyapriya and I were left alone.

As soon as the sound of footsteps had died away my companion drew a deep breath. What bliss! At last we were free from the idle and impertinent chatter of worldly-minded fools. At last we could be silent. For the next two or three weeks he was going to devote himself entirely to meditation, and under no circumstances should I disturb or interrupt him by speaking. If, in my foolishness, I attempted to do so, he gave me fair warning that it would be difficult for him not to lose his temper, and anything of an untoward nature that happened as a result of this would therefore be entirely my fault.

Our first few days on the sacred mountain were occupied in settling down into a routine that would leave us as much time as possible for meditation. Such domestic chores as were unavoidable even in our hermit-like state were reduced to an absolute minimum. Once a day, usually at ten o'clock in the morning, we silently prepared *kichuri* from the rice and lentils that Krishna had left with us, eating the mixture with our fingers out of the same earthenware pot in which it had been cooked. Whatever was left over we had cold at night. This, with water from a nearby rock pool to assuage our thirst, was our sole means of sustenance. Once or twice, indeed, we sampled the fallen *bel*-fruits, but even the ripest of them were so extremely bitter that we were unable to swallow more than a few mouthfuls. Cooking and eating once out of the way, our only other employments were gathering sticks for the fire, washing our robes, and bathing. The rest of time we were free to meditate.

By the evening of the third day our silent routine was well established, and it seemed that we could look forward to two or three weeks of peaceful contemplation, perhaps of ever-deepening spiritual experience. Having just finished a session of meditation, we were seated, as was now our custom, cross-legged on the broad flat slabs of the parapet wall. Satyapriya was seated at the far end, where the parapet joined an enormous boulder, on a raised stone platform rather like a throne. I was seated at a lower level. 2,000 feet beneath us stretched the plain, its fields forming a green, yellow, and brown patchwork in the fading light. Here and there a black and white dot moved imperceptibly in the direction of the pall of thin blue woodsmoke that betokened the village. Everything seemed peaceful and serene. Sitting there on the parapet one might well have written an Indian version of the opening stanzas of Gray's 'Elegy'. Suddenly there was an abrupt movement above my head, and I heard Satyapriya exclaim 'I can't stand it any longer! I'll go mad if I don't speak!'

Looking up, I saw my friend gazing down at me with a comical expression of distress, his mouth still half open. 'Come on,' he said with an embarrassed laugh, 'You must speak too.'

Despite his appeal, however, I did not feel like breaking my silence. The spell of the evening was still on me, and I would gladly have adhered to our original compact. Moreover, after the way in which Satyapriya had warned me against disturbing or interrupting him I could not resist the temptation of teaching him a small lesson. But I soon realized it would not be wise to continue the lesson for too long. On my failure to respond instantly to his appeal, Satyapriya's brows had contracted dangerously, and seeing that he was about to lose his temper I broke my silence and asked him what had happened.

From the time that he had started observing silence, he said, he had not had a minute's peace. His mind had been an absolute whirlpool of thoughts. At first he had done his best to stem the flood, but this had proved quite impossible and in the end he had been completely overwhelmed. So great had been the tension that he had thought he would either explode or go mad. Now that we had been talking for a few minutes the flow of thoughts was subsiding, the pressure diminishing, and he already felt much better.

For the remainder of the week meditation was therefore combined with discussion. Occasionally, still restless, Satyapriya explored the mountainside. From one of these expeditions, in the course of which he penetrated almost to the top, he returned pale and shaken. He had seen a hyena emerging from its lair beneath a rock, he told me. Luckily, the beast had not seen him, and the wind not being in the right direction it had not smelt him either. But in future we would have to be more careful than ever at night. While we had little to fear from the leopards we heard snuffling at our door after dark, or snarling on the flat stone roof, a hyena was a very different matter. Unless they were cornered, leopards rarely attacked human beings, but the hyena, a killer born, had no such inhibitions.

Though our breach of silence brought relief to Satyapriya, for me the change was not without its disadvantages. Discussion might give rise to a difference of opinion, and a difference of opinion, I well knew, was something Satyapriya was quite unable to tolerate, or even to understand. If you disagreed with him you were his enemy, you were trying to humiliate him, to destroy him, and his wrath and fury knew no bounds. Well as I understood this, and keenly as I realized the unwisdom of provoking my irascible friend, I did not always find it possible to soften an honest difference of opinion to the point of acceptability.

Indeed, Satyapriya was so morbidly sensitive, and so quick to take offence, that he seemed to imagine differences where none existed. It was as though he had to create a difference in order to give himself an excuse for losing his temper.

Something of this sort happened two or three days after we had stopped observing silence. We were bathing in the icy waters of the pool, eight or ten feet across and very deep, that lay beneath an overhanging fragment of rock, a few yards along the cliff face from the temple. Something I said, which he interpreted as expressing a difference of opinion, upset him, and despite all my efforts to calm him down he succeeded in gradually working himself up to a pitch of murderous fury such as I had never before witnessed, even in Muvattupuzha. He had had enough of me, he hissed, his eyes bloodshot with rage. He had allowed me to torment him with my unreasonable behaviour too long already. Now he was going to kill me. He would drown me in the pool. No one would ever know. He would tell them that I had died accidentally. Looking at him, I knew that he meant it. For the first time in my life I was actually face to face with death. Strange to say, though I was frightened, I had no intention whatever of withdrawing the offending remark. On the contrary, I became aware of the existence within me of a rock bottom of obstinacy that made it utterly impossible for me to retract or disown any opinion which I genuinely believed to be true even to save my life. How the episode ended I no longer recollect. At one stage Satyapriya was clutching me by the arm and preparing to hold me down under the dark water until I drowned.

With my companion liable to what seemed like fits of homicidal mania, I was glad when, a day or two later, we were visited by Krishna and some of his fellow disciples. At first, however, their presence threatened to make the situation worse instead of better. Yalahankar Swami sent his greetings, they told us. In fact, he had charged them to convey them to us in a highly peculiar manner they did not profess to understand and of which they were only the faithful transmitters. They begged us not to take offence. 'To the English saint,' the swami had said, 'you are to convey, from me, 2,673 prostrations. As for that Bengali fellow who is with him, you can give him two or three prostrations too, if you like!'

When we had recovered from the initial shock of this extraordinary message, the meaning of which we understood only too well, Satyapriya and I took counsel with Krishna and arranged for him to come again the following weekend and take us back to Bangalore. Three days afterwards, therefore, having spent less than two weeks at Divyagiri, we found ourselves picking our way through the *bel* trees down to the plain. A few hundred yards from the foot of the mountain the two coolies Krishna had engaged to carry what was left of the rice and lentils suddenly halted. Running beside the path, clearly visible in the loose, sandy soil, were the impressions of two enormous pairs of paws. A leopard, we enquired? No, said the coolies, in scared tones, a tiger. He had passed that way only a few hours earlier. We had better hurry.

43
DISAPPOINTMENT AT SARNATH

The road that ran through the jungle from Borivli to the Kanheri Caves was not so much a road as a broad sandy track. As we did not leave the town before noon, and as it was almost the hottest time of year, Satyapriya and I had not walked above a mile or two before the loose drifts of silver sand became a burning marl that was agony to our bare feet. We limped along as best we could, however, and after a few more miles had the satisfaction of seeing in the distance not only the low-lying ranges of the Kanheri Hills but also, as the road made a bend, the naked grey cliff face with the indentations that we knew were the Kanheri Caves. A few days earlier we had arrived in Bombay, and the friend with whom we were staying, a devotee of Swami Ramdas, had undertaken to show us various places of interest. Whether or not I had heard of the Kanheri Caves before I no longer recollect, but as soon as I learned that they were only five miles from Borivli, and that Borivli was only thirty-five miles from Bombay, I was eager to pay them a visit. For two years I had had virtually no external contact with Buddhism, and I now felt for it the same desire that a starving man feels for food, or that a lover, long absent, feels for the sight of his beloved.

As we picked our way from terrace to terrace, up and down the cliff face, I could not help feeling that it was worth waiting two years to see the Kanheri Caves. About a hundred in number, and dating from the early centuries of the Common Era, they were of practically all shapes and sizes. Some were big enough to accommodate four or five hundred people, and had obviously been used as assembly halls by the resident monastic community, while in others there was room only for a pair of inmates, perhaps two friends, or a senior monk and his disciple. Two or three of the biggest and grandest caves had façades thirty or forty feet high, with enormous 'mushroom head' pillars that were almost Egyptian in their squatness, strength, and simplicity. Many of the smallest, on the other hand, had porticoes of almost contemporary design. Large or small, simple or ornate, all the caves were well supplied with drinking water. The intricacy and completeness of the water supply was, indeed, one of the marvels of the place. But most marvellous and impressive of all to me, at that time, were the two colossal standing Buddhas, twenty feet or more in height, that stood in decorated niches at either end of the vestibule of one of the biggest caves. Right hands hanging at their sides, palm outwards, in the gesture of supreme generosity, left hands holding up to shoulder level the scalloped edges of their robes, they stood there in supernatural strength and solidity, the massively proportioned trunks and limbs clearly visible through the clinging draperies. As I stood beneath them, my head not much above the level of their ankles, I felt as though I was once again under the protection of Buddhism.

As the result of walking on scorching hot sand the soles of our feet were so badly blistered that for two or three days we were unable to go out. Our friend, who though a goldsmith, also had some knowledge of traditional medicine, massaged them with clarified butter, as well as with a copper disc on which were inscribed various magic diagrams. He also gave us an account of his domestic troubles. He was in his early forties, he said, his wife had been dead for some years, and there were no children. With him lived his younger brother, who was about twenty-five, and who helped him in the business. This brother had recently married. Though his wife was both beautiful and well-behaved, and though the young couple were quite happy together, he himself could not get on with his sister-in-law. Any mistake she happened to commit irritated him intensely, and he was often so angry with her that he beat her. In fact, he confessed, up to the time of our arrival he had been thrashing her every day. The young husband, who was of a gentle and submissive disposition, out of respect for his elder brother made no effort to interfere. Satyapriya, ever an upholder of the right of the weaker sex to masculine protection, took our pious friend severely to task for his brutality, but it was evident that there were psychological complexities here beyond the reach of moral exhortation.

When the soles of our feet had healed we were taken out to other places of interest. One of these was the temple of Mumba Devi, the goddess to whom Bombay is dedicated, and of whose name the word Bombay is in fact a corruption. To our astonishment we found the *sanctum sanctorum* so densely packed with an excited, jostling mass of Gujerati businessmen that we could hardly see anything at all. I noticed, though, that the walls were thickly plastered with rows of silver rupees. As we edged our way in the direction of the image, said to be of solid silver, a Gandhi-capped worshipper pressed a two-rupee note into my hands with the entreaty 'You are a holy man. Please pray to the Goddess that I may do well on the Stock Exchange today!' Bombay was, of course, the commercial and financial capital of India, the Indian Stock Exchange was located there, and Mumba Devi herself, originally the patroness of the local fisher-folk, was now popularly regarded as a form of Lakshmi, the Hindu goddess of wealth.

Though Satyapriya and I had come from Bangalore to Bombay, our real destination was Sarnath, and after we had spent ten days with our goldsmith friend we felt it was time for us to be on our way. It was already mid-April, according to the Indian reckoning the month of Vaiśākha had begun, and at the back of both our minds there was the hope that on the Vaiśākha Pūrṇimā or full moon day – anniversary of the Buddha's Enlightenment – it would be possible for us to be ordained. On our way to Sarnath, however, we still had one more call to make. As he put into our hands the third-class railway tickets that would carry us on the next stage of our journey, our kind host strongly urged us to get down at a certain station near Lucknow and spend a few days at the ashram of a well-known Vedantic swami, whose name he gave us. The swami, he said reverently, was a Brahma-jnani, a 'Knower of the Absolute'.

Our curiosity naturally aroused, after more than a day and a night in the train Satyapriya and I accordingly alighted at the station indicated and found our way to the swami's ashram, which was a small building situated on the banks of the Ganges at some distance from the town. Within minutes of our arrival we discovered that whether or not the swami was a 'Knower of the Absolute' he was certainly a Non-Dualist Vedantin of the most virulent type. The world was nothing but an illusion, he declared. Spiritual practice was completely unnecessary. Since one was already in truth the Brahman, the Absolute, there was nothing whatever to realize.

'Have you realized Brahman?' demanded Satyapriya belligerently.

'I've already told you that there is nothing to realize,' snapped the ascetic, with evident irritation. 'I *am* Brahman. So are you.'

This reply failed to satisfy my friend, who promptly returned to the attack, and for the next two hours argument and counter-argument flew back and forth until the ashram fairly rang with the conflict. The swami was by far the more experienced dialectician, and successfully maintained his position against all assaults; but in strength and stentoriousness of performance Satyapriya was more than a match for him. As the debate proceeded, the swami showed his irritation at what he clearly considered my friend's obtuseness more and more plainly, until finally the latter, descending to personalities, truculently demanded to know how it was possible for a *Brahma-jñāni* to give way to anger.

'No one has given way to anger!' shouted the swami. 'There's no such thing as anger. It's all an illusion.'

That night we stayed at the ashram, but after the unpleasantness of the debate, and the swami's subsequent scoffing references to our lack of spiritual development, the atmosphere of the place was so uncongenial that next day we left. Wandering along the banks of the Ganges, we came to a broad stretch of silver sand which, scattered as it was with burnt-out funeral pyres, we at once recognized as a cremation ground. Here we decided to stay. The landscape could hardly have been more simple or more austere. Above us there was nothing but the dazzling blueness of the sky, from the midst of which the sun shone down with blinding brilliance; around us, nothing but the whiteness of the bare sands, through which the river, shrunken but still gigantic, rolled down its jade-green waters to the sea. Apart from ourselves, the only living things to be seen were the small, stunted trees that grew a few dozen yards from the bank. Not one of them stood more than ten feet from the ground. With their crooked, even contorted, branches, and light green feathery foliage, most of it at the top, they looked like rudimentary umbrellas with bent handles, broken ribs, and tattered silk. Here and there four or five of the umbrellas stood closer than the rest, their scanty foliage running together into a single canopy-like strip of green. Beneath one of these canopies Satyapriya and I took shelter from the heat.

As soon as we had sat down, we became aware that for all the apparent barrenness of the place we were, in fact, surrounded by a whole world of life and activity. Striped tree-rats raced up and down the trunks of the trees, or peered round them at us with bulging eyes and palpitating breasts. Cicadas shrilled invisible from the thin grass. Bees, deeply humming, flew heavily in and out of the pink or white blossoms of shrub after flowering shrub. But above all there were the peacocks. There seemed to be hundreds of them living among the trees. Every few moments, either from near at hand or far away, a harsh bell-like call, not unlike a greatly amplified miaow, would ring loud and clear through the hot afternoon air, to be almost immediately answered by another. Lodged in the forks and lower branches of the trees were scores of huge, untidy nests, none of them more than five or six feet from the ground. On most of the nests, looking much too splendid for so humble a task, sat the cock birds, the magnificent, many-eyed trains of their tails hanging over the nest-edge and practically brushing the sandy soil below. Occasionally, we would see a sudden vivid flash of gold, blue, and green as one of the stately creatures, tail feathers streaming out behind like an enormous bunch of ribbons, would launch himself in clumsy horizontal flight among the trees. None of them took the slightest notice of us.

When it was dark, and the heat of the day had abated, we returned to the cremation ground, scrambling down the bank to the stretch of soft silver sand that was now part of the foreshore but which, once the rainy season began, would soon be part of the river bed. After we had plunged about for a few minutes, ankle-deep in the warm white drifts, we settled down among the shadowy shapes of the burnt-out funeral pyres for our evening meditation. When we opened our eyes some hours later we found ourselves in another world. An electric white full moon was in the sky, and the whole landscape lay steeped in an unearthly silver radiance so bright that we could hardly bear to look at it. Away on our right the river ran glittering beneath the luminous blue of the sky, while all around us the low mounds of ashes and charred wood cast shadows black as ink onto the white sand.

In the morning we made our way back to the ashram, and from there to the station. Though we had been deeply moved by the idyllic beauty of the spot, the full moon had reminded us that it was now only twenty-eight days, or one lunar month, to the Vaiśākha Pūrṇimā Day, and we wanted to be in Benares as soon as possible. Before leaving the cremation ground we spent half an hour rummaging among the heaps of ashes and charred wood looking for pieces of cloth. According to Buddhist tradition, the best and most suitable robe for a Buddhist monk was one made entirely of fragments of material picked up in a cremation ground, and in view of our forthcoming ordination both Satyapriya and I thought it would be a good idea if, taking advantage of our present opportunity, we were to collect the necessary fragments and provide ourselves with this highly desirable type of robe. Unfortunately we were disappointed. Though we succeeded in uncovering numerous fragments of charred bone, both large and small, very little was forthcoming in the way of cloth. At the end of our search all we had found was three or four fragments, none of them more than two inches in width, and all so badly charred at the edges that we were left wondering how the ancient worthies had ever managed to stitch them together, even assuming that they had been able to collect a sufficient number of pieces for their purpose.

On our arrival in Benares, we went straight to the local branch of the Ramakrishna Mission, where we hoped to be able to stay for a few days before making our way to Sarnath. After we had given our names, and been asked to wait for a few minutes, a youthful novice ushered us into the president's office. To our astonishment, the smiling, saffron-clad figure who rose behind his desk to receive us was none other than our old friend Buddha Maharaj, whom I had last seen two and a half years ago in Singapore. After returning to India and enjoying a period of rest and recuperation in the Himalayas, he had been posted to Benares, where he was now responsible for the management of the Mission's hospital and dispensary.

Within minutes of this unexpected meeting, Satyapriya and I were chatting with Buddha Maharaj as easily as if we had never parted, and had not only given our older and more experienced friend an up-to-date account of our adventures but confided to him our aspirations for the future. Having spent two years as wandering ascetics, we declared, and having convinced ourselves of our ability to fulfil all the requirements of the monastic life, we were now desirous of formally dedicating ourselves to the following of the Path to Nirvāṇa and receiving ordination as Buddhist monks in the traditional manner. For this purpose we were going to Sarnath, where there was a branch of the Maha Bodhi Society, and where we hoped it would be possible for us to be ordained as *śrāmaṇeras* or novice monks. Imperturbable as ever, Buddha Maharaj received these confidences with the same cheerful benignity that he had exhibited in Singapore, and neither approved nor disapproved of our plan. One suggestion, however, he did make. Since we were in Benares, he said, and since Benares was not only one of the oldest cities in India but the spiritual headquarters of Hinduism, it would be a pity if we did not visit at least some of its innumerable shrines and holy places. When Sri Ramakrishna had come on pilgrimage he had seen the whole city as made entirely of gold, while above it, in the clouds, he had seen the god Shiva, the Lord of Benares, receiving into heaven the souls of all who died within its precincts. If we were lucky we too might be vouchsafed a glimpse of the splendours of the Heavenly City – of that Eternal Benares of which, according to orthodox Hindu belief, the earthly Benares was but a pale reflection.

Impatient though we were to reach Sarnath, Satyapriya and I accordingly spent the next few days sightseeing. Although with the exception of the odd gilded dome or pinnacle, the narrow streets and crowded insanitary dwellings of the old city were to our eyes far from being made of gold, and though the swarms of beggars, holy men, pilgrims, and prostitutes seemed assured of anything but salvation, our excursions were by no means devoid of interest. Besides seeing the celebrated ghats, where hundreds of pilgrims were taking a ceremonial dip in the greasy waters of the Ganges, we found our way to such widely different places as the newly-built Anandamayi Ashram and the Benares branch of the Theosophical Society. The Anandamayi Ashram was a large building, beautifully situated on the banks of the river, but as Anandamayi was elsewhere it was practically deserted, and we wandered from room to room looking at the large framed photographs of the Blissful Mother and the gaudy oleographs of Sri Krishna and Chaitanya. We also visited Bharat Mata Mandir or 'Temple of Mother India'. This was a large, rather unsightly modern building, said to have been inaugurated by Mahatma Gandhi. Instead of an image, the main hall enshrined an enormous relief map of India. Though not modelled strictly to scale (the Himalayas were shown many times higher than they should have been) it nevertheless gave one a good idea of the main geographical features of the subcontinent, besides furnishing a striking example of what Rabindranath Tagore called 'the idolatry of geography'.

As was usually the case with Satyapriya and me, our sightseeing included not only places but people. In the course of our visit to the Theosophical Society we discovered that the well-known Theosophist Bhagavan Das, whose books I had read in Singapore, was a resident of the holy city, and at once decided to go and see him. The venerable old scholar, who was then well over seventy, received us on the veranda of his spacious suburban bungalow, and before long we were deep in Indian philosophy and religion. Rather to our astonishment, we found that for all his veneer of Theosophical universalism he was at heart almost as orthodox a Hindu as Venkateshwara Iyer. For Buddhism he had, it seemed, very little sympathy indeed, while he clearly had no sympathy at all either for the life we had been leading as wandering ascetics or for our desire to receive ordination as Buddhist monks. As for our determination not to identify ourselves with any particular nationality, this was to him mere youthful eccentricity, and as such beyond the comprehension of the wise. However, on our departure he presented us with an autographed copy of his book *The Essential Unity of All Religions*, which I knew was highly esteemed in Theosophical circles.

After spending three or four days exploring the highways and byways of Benares, Satyapriya and I decided that we had had enough of sightseeing. It was now the hottest time of year in one of the hottest parts of India, and since we had no money – having stopped handling it ever since our stay at Anandashram – we not only had to go everywhere on foot but also to spend the whole day without refreshment of any kind. Not that we really minded this. The real reason for our decision lay much deeper. Despite our having acted on Buddha Maharaj's suggestion in good faith, we had been feeling the pull of Sarnath more strongly each day, and in my case at least, contact with Hinduism had served only to intensify my longing for Buddhism. Early in the morning, therefore, while it was still only moderately hot, we said goodbye to our inscrutable swami friend, and together set out on the ten- or twelve-mile walk to Sarnath.

Ever since I had started reading about Buddhism the name of Sarnath had been familiar to me, and for the last few months in particular it had been as it were ringing in my ears. It was the place where, only two months after his attainment of Perfect Enlightenment, the Buddha had sought out the five ascetics who had been his companions in self-mortification in the days when he was still searching for the Truth and where, in the peaceful seclusion of the Deer Park, he had communicated to them the essentials of the newly discovered Dharma. After strong initial resistance they had accepted him as their teacher, had realized the truth of his teaching for themselves, and had become the nucleus of the spiritual community which, in the course of the next few months, rapidly sprang up around him. The road along which we were now walking was the very one, perhaps, which the Buddha himself had trod, 2,500 years ago, on the last stage of his journey from Bodh Gaya. There were the same blue sky overhead, the same straggling suburbs, the same mud-walled huts, the same bands of naked children playing in the dust, the same creaking bullock carts, the same level fields on either side of the road, and the same sun blazing more and more fiercely down on it all.

After we had walked for a couple of hours and more the road, which hitherto had meandered uncertainly, started to run very straight, as though it now knew exactly where it was going. Trees appeared at intervals on either hand. Before long Satyapriya and I found ourselves walking in the welcome shade of a broad avenue of fine mango trees, their glossy green foliage contrasting sharply with the dusty brown of the surrounding fields. Presently, on our right, we saw through more mango trees the dilapidated shell of a small railway station, whose outbuildings were little more than heaps of rubble. On the opposite side of the road, to our left, rose an enormous pile of bricks surmounted, most incongruously, by an octagonal kiosk of Mogul design. This, I knew, was all that remained of the Chaukambhi Stupa, said to mark the spot where, on his arrival at Sarnath, the Buddha actually met the five ascetics. We were nearing our destination. Suddenly we saw above the tree-tops, about a mile away, the pinkish-grey pinnacle of the Mulagandhakuti Vihara, the new Sinhalese temple constructed about twenty years earlier. We were there! After a few hundred yards the road turned sharply to the right and as though in a dream we saw before us the park-like prospect of Sarnath.

The next few days were among the pleasantest and the most painful of my entire existence. Since it was the height of the hot season, when pilgrims were few, we had the whole place practically to ourselves, and after the congestion and clamour of Benares, the spaciousness and peace of Sarnath, with its green lawns, flowering trees, and cool, well-kept shrines, was delectable indeed. Though we saw practically everything of interest, the main object of our attention was, of course, the polished granite column set up by the Emperor Aśoka to mark the exact spot where the Buddha taught the five ascetics. This column, or what was left of it, stood in a roofed-in enclosure of its own in the midst of several acres of ruined temples, monasteries, and votive stupas, all of which had been uncovered in the course of excavations, and were now carefully preserved. The famous lion capital by which it had originally been surmounted was kept in the museum. Yet beautiful as Sarnath was, I knew it had not always been so. Muslim invasion and orthodox Hindu revival had between them levelled it to the ground, and for hundreds of years the very name of the place was virtually unknown. At the end of the last century it was being used as a breeding ground for pigs. In the course of the last few decades, however, a great change had taken place, and with the establishment of temples and monasteries, and the provision of facilities for pilgrims, Sarnath had been restored to a modest semblance of its former glory. From my contact with the Maha Bodhi Society in Calcutta I knew that all this was due to the initiative of Anagarika Dharmapala, who had started there a branch of the Society and built the Mulagandhakuti Vihara. Dharmapala himself had died nearly twenty years earlier, but his work was being continued by Sinhalese monks, some of whom had been his personal disciples. It was from these monks that we were hoping to receive ordination.

Rarely in the history of Buddhism can two candidates for admission to the sangha have been more quickly or more cruelly disappointed. Though we were allowed, rather grudgingly, to stay in the vast, empty Rest House, from the very first the attitude of the five or six resident monks towards us was clearly one of incomprehension, suspicion, and hostility. Our going barefoot might have been overlooked, and even our interest in meditation excused, but to be altogether without money was, we were made to feel, the unforgivable offence. Indeed, when we confessed that we had been trying to practise the precept of not handling gold and silver, the observance of which was of course incumbent on *śrāmaṇeras* and *bhikṣus* alike, and that for the past few months we had not possessed as much as a single anna between us, they reacted rather as though we had told them we had leprosy. From that moment our fate was sealed. In the eyes of these representatives of 'Pure Buddhism' we were no better than beggars, and it was clear they wanted nothing whatever to do with us. They were even unwilling to give us a little food. When, in response to the bell, we turned up at the dining-hall, we heard one of them murmur angrily, 'Why do they come without being asked?' After the open-handed hospitality of the Hindu ashrams we had visited such an attitude came as a shock indeed.

Nevertheless, we decided not to be discouraged. In the case of a step so important as the one we now wanted to take, difficulties were bound to arise, and the best thing we could do was to treat them as tests. Accordingly, at the first opportunity, we acquainted the monks with our religious history and made the formal request for ordination. After listening to our account in silence, they said they would consult among themselves and let us know their decision. It was not long in coming. They were all members of the Maha Bodhi Society, they explained, and in view of the fact that the Society would be responsible for the maintenance of monks ordained under its auspices, they were not permitted to ordain anyone without the consent of the General Secretary. Since the Society was at present very short of funds, they were sure that in our case this consent would not be forthcoming.

Though we had known what the verdict would be, the shock when it came was none the less acute. All our plans were laid in ruins, all our hopes destroyed. Bitterly disappointed, we returned to Benares.

44
THROUGH THE CURTAIN OF FIRE

The week that followed was a period of bewilderment, uncertainty, and confusion. During the last few months the idea of being ordained at Sarnath had taken such complete possession of our minds – we had dreamed so much about it, built so much upon it – that the likelihood of our meeting with a refusal, and being denied something that was for us already a reality, had entered our consciousness only as the remotest and most abstract of possibilities. Difficulties we had been prepared for, even trials; but certainly we had never expected that in Sarnath, of all places, we should meet with downright hostility and incomprehension, or that our request for ordination should be rejected with flimsy excuses which, as we afterwards discovered, were no better than lies. Yet the unlikely, the virtually impossible, the unexpected, had actually happened. Our application had been rejected. We had been refused ordination as śrāmaṇeras. Once again we were just two homeless wanderers, with the difference that this time we had nothing to look forward to and nowhere to go. Back at the Ramakrishna Mission, where even Buddha Maharaj could not wholly disguise his astonishment at our return, we felt as though the bottom had dropped out of the universe and that we now hung aimless and directionless in a void.

For me the situation was doubly upsetting. In addition to my own disappointment, which was keen enough, I had to cope with the consequences of Satyapriya's and be not only the confidant but the scapegoat for the violent anger and resentment that burst from him as soon as he had recovered from the initial shock of our rejection. Who were these monks of Sarnath, he demanded, furiously, and what right had they to refuse ordination to two candidates who, for aught they knew, were spiritually far more advanced than themselves? They were not monks at all. They were no better than caretakers in yellow robes, making a living out of the pilgrims, and furtively grubbing together a few wretched possessions. He knew what they were really like. He had talked with the Indian servants. Things were as bad at Sarnath as they had been in Calcutta, if not worse. The Maha Bodhi Society stank. Sinhalese monks were thoroughly corrupt. Buddhism itself was corrupt. He was glad that his eyes had been opened in time and that he had been prevented from taking a step he undoubtedly would have regretted all his life. Far from being disappointed that we had not been ordained, he was delighted. He felt as though he had had a lucky escape. His only regret was that he, an Indian, had been forced to beg for ordination from a set of Sinhalese rascals who had received their religion and their culture from India and who, before that, had been no better than monkeys. For this humiliation, so painful to his self-respect, he had me to thank. Had it not been for my insidious influence he would have had nothing to do with Buddhism, nothing to do with the filth and corruption of the Maha Bodhi Society. But that was how it always was. Due to his association with me he had been repeatedly humiliated. He had stood it long enough. In future he intended to have nothing whatever to do with Buddhism. The Sinhalese monks could keep their ordination. He was quite happy to remain what he had been born, a Hindu. There were plenty of Hindu monks who would be only too glad to have him for a disciple. If the worst came to the worst, he could always join the Ramakrishna Mission. They might not be very spiritual, but at least they did good social work. India needed social workers....

When he had raged and stormed in this way on and off for a couple of days, my friend's fury gradually subsided, and before long I was able to talk him into a more reasonable frame of mind. However un-Buddhistic the behaviour of the monks at Sarnath might have been, I urged, as aspirants to Enlightenment it was our duty not to give way to feelings of resentment. On the spiritual path difficulties and disappointments were bound to arise, but if we regarded them as tests of our sincerity then they would strengthen rather than weaken our determination to reach our goal. Despite these pious words, however, in my heart of hearts I could not help recognizing the justice of much that Satyapriya said. True it was that we ought not to cherish resentment, and that the disappointment we had experienced should be regarded as a test, but no amount of spiritual whitewashing could disguise the fact that the monks at Sarnath were a worldly-minded lot, without the faintest spark of enthusiasm for spiritual things, and that in refusing our request for ordination they had been activated by mean and unworthy motives. Indeed, I had to admit that both the fact and the manner of their refusal had hurt me far more deeply than it had hurt Satyapriya. Besides being disappointed as a candidate for ordination, I was mortified as a Buddhist, and disgusted as a human being. Only my faith in Buddhism remained unshaken. Not for one instant did I consider seeking ordination elsewhere than in the spiritual community founded by the Buddha. The greater were the shortcomings of the latter-day disciples, the more they heightened the sublimity of the ideal and the more, indirectly, they intensified my devotion to the ideal. Suppressing my own disappointment, I therefore did my best to assuage my friend's resentment and convince him that the monks at Sarnath were not the only ones in India, and that though we had failed to get ordination the first time there was no reason why a second or third attempt should not be more successful. In any case, it was clearly impossible for us to stay at the Ramakrishna Mission much longer. We had already stretched their hospitality to the limits. Since we would have to go somewhere, we might as well go wherever there was the possibility of our being ordained as *śrāmaṇeras*.

These arguments were not without their effect on my friend, who in any case was reproaching himself for the violence of his reaction. But to which of the holy places should we now make our way? Where would it be possible for us to get ordination? These were the questions that had to be answered, and answered immediately. We had spent several hours deep in earnest but ineffectual discussion, and were beginning to feel quite desperate, when Satyapriya suddenly recollected that one of the monks at Sarnath, the sole Indian member of the community, had mentioned to him the name of the well-known monk-scholar Bhikkhu Jagdish Kashyap, who for a number of years had been teaching Pāli and Buddhist Philosophy at the Benares Hindu University. We would go and ask his advice. He would be able to help us. Even if he did not give ordination himself, he would certainly be able to tell us where to go and whom to approach for this purpose.

In a matter of hours we had walked to the university, located Bhikkhu Kashyap's modest residence in a distant corner of the vast campus, and been whisked up a flight of bare cement steps into his presence. We at once saw that here was a completely different type of person from the monks at Sarnath. Extreme corpulence gave him an air of mountainous imperturbability. At the same time, the expression of exceptional intelligence that played upon the strongly-marked features of the dark-brown face created an impression of vivacity, even as the look of gentle benignity that beamed from them seemed to invite confidence and trust. In less than an hour we had acquainted him with much of our joint history, especially with its most recent chapter, that of our disappointment at Sarnath. Having listened in sympathetic silence, Bhikkhu Kashyap pondered deeply for a while. Then, rolling the words up from the depths of his enormous frame with a slowness that gave them a special emphasis, and speaking with evident warmth and sincerity, he advised us to go to Kusinara, the place where the Buddha had passed away into final Nirvāṇa. There we would find U Chandramani Mahāthera, the seniormost Theravādin Buddhist monk in India. He had many disciples. In fact, he was well known for the generosity with which he gave ordinations. Provided we were able to convince him of our sincerity, there was no reason why he should not give us ordination too.

These words filled us with fresh hope, and we decided to leave for Kusinara without delay. Since we had no money we would have to walk, but so great was our desire for ordination that if necessary we would have prostrated ourselves the whole distance, as Tibetan pilgrims sometimes did all the way from Lhasa to Bodh Gaya. When we told our friends at the Ramakrishna Mission what we proposed to do they were horrified. Kusinara was well over a hundred miles from Benares, they protested, and it was the hottest time of year. We would never reach our destination alive. The dreaded hot wind from the deserts of western India had already started blowing, and every day the newspapers carried reports of people dropping dead from the heat. Why not stay in Benares a few weeks, and leave as soon as the early monsoon rains had cooled the air? This was sensible advice, and in any other circumstances we would have heeded it. Having just spent several hours walking to the university and back in the furnace-like heat of midday we knew only too well what awaited us at almost every step of our journey. A curtain of fire hung between us and our goal. Nevertheless our minds were made up. There was no time to be lost. Through the curtain of fire we would go, or perish in the attempt.

Early next morning we set out for Sarnath. Being north-east of Benares it lay directly in our path, and with its hallowed associations it was obviously the best point for our journey to begin. While the monks of the Maha Bodhi Society could hardly be said to welcome us, they were much less unfriendly than on our first visit. Indeed, once we had made it clear that we were on our way to Kusinara, and would not be staying, two or three members of the community, better-natured than the rest, became quite cordial. One of them, the same Indian monk who had mentioned the name of Bhikkhu Jagdish Kashyap, turned out to be not only a native of Deoria, the district in which Kusinara was situated, but a personal disciple of U Chandramani, from whom he had received his *śrāmaṇera* ordination. On hearing that we were going to Kusinara in quest of ordination he gave us two letters of introduction, one to U Chandramani himself, and one to his seniormost female disciple. What Kashyap-ji had told us about the Mahāthera's generosity in granting ordinations was perfectly true, he said, and we were almost certain to get what we wanted. Another monk, a Sinhalese, who as one of the Joint Secretaries of the Maha Bodhi Society was in charge of its institution and activities in Sarnath, was even kinder. Taking us aside, he told us in a friendly, even affectionate, manner, that he strongly sympathized with our aspirations and wished us the best of luck. We should not take it too much to heart, he added, that on our previous visit he and his brother monks had refused to grant us ordination. It was extremely difficult to know who was sincere and who was not. Hundreds of people came to Sarnath asking for ordination. Most of them were Hindus who only wanted to be supported. After a number of painful experiences, he and the other *bhikkhus* had learned to exercise extreme caution.

These friendly attentions, together with the fact that we had been invited to take our midday meal in the refectory, not only raised our spirits but disposed us to look more charitably on the shortcomings of the Sarnath monastic establishment. True, none of the monks could be described as spiritually-minded, and some seemed barely religious. For them Buddhism was evidently not the path to Enlightenment, but simply part of the national culture of their land, a culture in which they had been born and brought up, and to the external requirements of which they instinctively conformed. But at the same time it was clear that they were not bad fellows at heart and wished us no harm. What we had taken for hostility was in fact only defensiveness. We had descended on them out of the blue, and they had reacted to us in much the same way as a bevy of Anglican cathedral clergy would have reacted to a ragged and barefoot African Christian who, having sold all his possessions and given the money to the poor, had suddenly appeared at a Deanery tea-party wanting to know what he should do next. Now that they had had time to recover from the shock, and had been assured that we were taking our eccentricities elsewhere, they had no objection to wishing us success in our mission. With their benedictions ringing in our ears, we therefore left Sarnath more light-hearted than we had arrived. Before our departure Satyapriya warned me that this would be definitely our last attempt. If we failed to obtain ordination in Kusinara he would give up Buddhism altogether and become a Hindu monk and I would have to follow his example. Against such an idea as this my whole soul rose in revolt. For me there could be no second choice. Come what might, it was ordination as a Buddhist monk I wanted and nothing else. However, not wishing to provoke an argument at the outset of the journey I kept my thoughts to myself.

 For the next eight days we were on the road. Or rather, we were on the railway track, for having met the branch line over the first ridge out of Sarnath we had decided that, since we had no map, it would be best to follow it for as far as we could. From village to nondescript village ran the gleaming silver rails, from town to ramshackle town, straight through the flat brown landscape, over the beds of dried-up streams, past field after withered field, with only the telegraph wires for company and nothing but the long green line of the occasional mango grove to lend a touch of colour to the scene. In most of the villages and towns through which they passed there was a temple or an ashram of some kind and here we usually spent the night. Since the heat was all that we had been led to expect, and more, we tried to get the greater part of the day's walking done by noon. Rising before dawn, when the stars had not yet faded from the sky, and quickly stuffing our scanty belongings into the small cloth bag that was all each of us now carried, we carefully picked our way through the gloom, found the railway line, and headed north. By the time the sun was up we were well on our way. One morning, when we had risen even earlier than usual, we saw in the soft earth at the side of the track the imprints of a tiger's enormous paws. They were not more than an hour old and continued for several hundred yards. Evidently we were not the only ones who followed the railway track.

After walking for two or three hours we stopped and had breakfast, generally halting beside a river so that we could take our bath at the same time. Breakfast consisted of *chatua*, or roasted barley flour, a small bag of which had been given us by a friendly Hindu ascetic with whom we had passed the second night of our journey. Mixed with water, and kneaded into a soft cake, it was not unpalatable, and sufficed to keep us going until our next meal. As soon as we were rested and refreshed we set off again. All this time the sun had been growing steadily hotter, and by nine o'clock the perspiration would be not only pouring from our faces but trickling down our bodies and soaking into our robes as well. Sometimes, especially when the hot wind was blowing, the heat was so intense that we had to walk along with a wet towel wrapped turban-wise round the head for protection. Yet great as the discomfort was we pressed on without slackening our pace. At every step we took, white dust rose in suffocating clouds, then drifted away like smoke. Only when the sun was at its zenith, and the shadows had been swallowed up in the broad noonday glare, did we start looking for shelter. By this time even the brave shrilling of the cicadas had died away among the scorched-up grass, while the landscape quivered and danced in the heat as though behind a veil. From the cracks in the ground exhalations shot up like flames.

Our favourite shelter was a mango grove, where the dense foliage provided a shade that, after the heat outside, was so exquisitely cool as to be voluptuous. If no mango grove was forthcoming we generally took refuge, as at night, in a temple or an ashram, where more often than not a friendly ascetic or sympathetic villager would bring us something to eat, and where, if local curiosity or local sympathy proved sufficiently strong, Satyapriya would become involved in discussion. In one or two places the villagers were so hospitable, and in the course of a few hours became so warmly attached to us, that on their insistence we stayed till the following day. Once, indeed, we were passed on, as it were, to a son in a village further up the line, who promptly proved himself to be truly a chip off the paternal block by entertaining us as lavishly as his father had done the day before. Usually, however, we left our place of midday refuge at about five o'clock, when the heat had abated, and after finding our way back to the railway track continued our journey until nightfall. In this way we generally covered twelve to fifteen miles a day. Once, either to make up for lost time or because we were feeling particularly energetic, we covered twenty-nine miles.

Most of the temples and ashrams at which we spent the night, or where we stayed for a few hours during the day, were of either the Vaishnavite or the Shaivite persuasion, and in most the only vestige of spiritual activity we saw was the smoking of ganja or Indian hemp. In one at least, restrictions based on distinctions of caste were, so we found, strongly insisted on. It was on the fifth day of our journey, and at nightfall we had reached Mau. This was the biggest place we had seen since leaving Benares, and judging from the number of shops and houses being run up – apparently by refugees from East Pakistan – it was in process of vigorous, if chaotic, expansion. On the outskirts of the town, next to the railway, stood a fairly large ashram. Here we decided to halt. For some time nobody took any notice of us, and from the noise and bustle that surrounded us we concluded that, far from being a centre of quiet contemplation for those who had renounced the world, it was a place of ecclesiastical business, where people came to pray – and pay – for success in worldly undertakings. Eventually, when we were thinking of leaving, the head of the ashram approached us. He was a tall, thin old Vaishnavite ascetic, shaven-headed, and wearing the customary string of tiny basil-wood beads. Though at first inclined to be sarcastic, after a short conversation he became quite friendly and offered us some sweetmeats. He himself smoked ganja. We were then shown to the veranda of the Shiva temple next door, where we spent the night in the company of an elderly monk, an orthodox Advaita Vedantin, whose leg had been broken when he fell down on the railway track one night while under the influence of ganja.

The following morning, while we were sitting on the veranda with the crippled monk and a few other people, an old *dhobini* or washerwoman came and sat down nearby. As we had decided to leave somewhat later than usual that day, we asked her if it would be all right for us to come to her house for our midday meal. Shocked and dismayed at the idea, she explained that since she belonged to a very low caste indeed it was quite impossible for us to take cooked food from her hands. If we liked she would give us some uncooked things instead. This was not what we wanted. Determined to break the orthodox taboo, we persisted in asking her for at least one roti or cake of unleavened bread apiece, at the same time doing our best to convince her that one caste was as good as another. Our arguments proved not altogether without effect. Though the poor old creature continued to protest that it was quite impossible for holy men like ourselves to accept cooked food from members of the Dhobi caste, it was clear that her resistance was weakening, and that she was in two minds about the matter. All the time we were talking, however, the crippled monk had kept up a stream of threats and abuse. If she dared to pollute the holy men by giving them cooked food with her unclean washerwoman's hands, he warned her, he would see to it that she was given a sound thrashing as soon as they had left the place. These harsh words turned the scale. Wiping a tear from her eye, the old woman got up and crept silently away. Apparently the fact that the holy men themselves had no objection to being polluted did not matter. But we had not seen the last of our downtrodden friend. Some time later she reappeared, bringing with her some sweetmeats for Satyapriya and me and a handful of ganja for the crippled monk and his companions. Far from being mollified by her devotion, however, that pillar of orthodoxy continued to scoff and jeer at her in the most heartless fashion. Nevertheless, he smoked the ganja she had brought.

On the sixth day of our journey we said goodbye to the railway track and started heading in a more easterly direction. We had not gone many miles when we came to the great river Saraya or Sarabhu. The only means of crossing was by the ferry-boat, and for this we had to wait an hour. The ferry-boat belonged, we discovered, to the mahant or abbot of the local math or orthodox Hindu monastic establishment, and before its departure the mahant's disciple, a fat monk dressed in white like a householder, came and collected the fares from the passengers, not sparing even the poorest of them, who paid up with many groans and much grumbling. Since we were ascetics the fat monk was good enough to excuse us from paying, but as soon as he found out that we were Buddhists he could not resist the temptation of airing his views on the innate superiority of Brahmins, especially Brahmin monks and holy men, to which category, judging by the sacred thread that hung round his neck, he himself belonged. Naturally, we were not backward in giving our own views on the subject of caste, views with which all our fellow passengers who were not themselves either Brahmins or Kshatriyas seemed to be in hearty agreement. By this time the ferry-boat was more than full. Having extorted the last anna from the last reluctant passenger, the mahant's disciple waddled back to the math, and with long thrusts of the boatman's poles the unwieldy craft moved off.

The concluding stages of our journey were the worst, and had it not been for the hope that every step was bringing us nearer to the goal of our desires it might have been difficult for us to carry on. It was still early May, and the heat, having risen in fiery crescendo to its terrific climax, now seemed likely to remain there indefinitely. Not a drop of rain fell. Day by day the hot dry wind from the desert, laden with dust, blew more strongly and more scorchingly than ever upon the hard, sun-baked earth, which by this time had become criss-crossed with a network of innumerable cracks and fissures, some of them several inches wide. Travelling during the less hot hours of the day, and taking advantage of every scrap of shade, grimly and wearily Satyapriya and I plodded on from temple to temple and from ashram to ashram, mile after mile across the heat-stricken land. In some of the temples and ashrams at which we halted we were given a cordial welcome, in others our reception was more reserved. Towards the end of our journey our stops became more and more frequent. At one place we took our bath in a pond full of lotuses. At another, where we came across an unusually well-kept ashram standing within a secluded mango grove, a friendly Nanak Panthi, or follower of Guru Nanak, not only put us up for the night but treated us with exceptional kindness.

On our last morning we were less fortunate. Indeed, this was the least fortunate part of the whole journey. We had intended to halt for an hour or two at the Buddhist Rest House which had been built, so the Nanak Panthi had informed us, not half a dozen miles from our destination. On our arrival there we found that the Rest House had been converted into a school, and the headmaster received us in a very unfriendly fashion. We had no alternative but to set off again at once. Before long we were heartened by the sight of the dome of the Mahaparinirvana Stupa rising majestically from behind a cluster of trees in the far distance, and leaving the road we cut straight across the fields towards it. I could not help thinking with what exultation, only ten or twelve days earlier, we had seen the pinnacle of the Mulagandhakuti Vihara rising above the tree-tops of Sarnath. Did Kusinara hold a similar disappointment in store for us? Or were we destined to receive here the ordination on which we had set our hearts?

45
AT THE SHRINE OF THE RECUMBENT BUDDHA

The place at which we had arrived with so much hope, and where we were to spend the next two weeks, was one of the most famous and ancient Buddhist shrines in India. With Lumbini, Bodh Gaya, and Sarnath it was, in fact, one of the four principal places of Buddhist pilgrimage, to which devout followers of the Enlightened One came to worship, to meditate, and to make offerings from all over the Buddhist world. Like Sarnath, it had been sacked at the time of the Muslim conquest, like Sarnath it had remained derelict and deserted for more than 600 years, and like Sarnath it had been reoccupied around the turn of the century after being disinterred by the spade of a British archaeologist. Like Sarnath, too, in addition to its two stupas it consisted mainly of a monastery and guest-house, a temple, a school, and an archaeological area. Unlike Sarnath, however, it was rather off the beaten track, and despite its importance was therefore a smaller and shabbier place, and much more rural in character. Indeed, with its weed-choked paths and shrub-infested masonry it had an air of having only partly emerged from the surrounding jungle. In atmosphere, too, Kusinara was unlike Sarnath. Though both were exceptionally peaceful places, at Sarnath the peacefulness was touched with joy, as of glad tidings imparted to mankind, whereas here it was tinged with solemnity, even with sadness, as of a great loss sustained. After all, Kusinara was the scene of the Great Decease, and though nearly 2,500 years had passed, the vibrations of the sublime pathos of the occasion still seemed to linger in the air.

As might have been expected, the resident monastic community of Kusinara was even smaller than that of Sarnath. In fact it consisted of only U Chandramani himself and an Indian monk, his disciple. There were, however, five or six shaven-headed, yellow-robed *anagārikās*. Though faithful observers of the ten precepts, these devoted women were not technically nuns, indeed could never be nuns, for according to the Theravāda, the form of Buddhism predominant in South-east Asia, the tradition of ordination for women had died out many centuries ago and could not be revived. In addition to their personal religious duties, the *anagārikās* cooked and swept for the monks and did the rest of the menial work. The oldest and seniormost of them was a frail little old woman of about sixty-five known as Mother Vipassana, and it was to her that one of our letters of introduction was addressed. A Nepalese Brahmin by birth, and for many years a widow, she had been drawn to Buddhism through her contact with U Chandramani and for the last few years had lived in retirement at Kusinara. Apart from keeping a motherly eye on the other *anagārikās*, all of whom were much younger than herself, she devoted her time to the study of the Pāli texts and to meditation. Though it may have been less radiant, the smile that lit up her worn features had the same peculiar sweetness as that which had illumined the face of Mother Lakshmi, in the Sandalwood Country. From the very first she took a great liking to Satyapriya and me, and could never do enough for us. No sooner had she read the letter of introduction than she set about preparing us a meal, had a room in the guest-house swept out, showed us where we could take a bath and, most important of all, arranged for us to see U Chandramani.

The interview took place the following morning at the Chapter House, in the dim, practically unfurnished ground-floor room that was evidently both sitting room and study. U Chandramani sat up cross-legged on an old cane-bottomed armchair, the only chair in the room; Satyapriya and I, who on entering had made the traditional three prostrations, knelt before him on the strip of worn and frayed carpet that one of the *anagārikās* had pulled out for us. As usual, Satyapriya acted as spokesman for us both. Once my eyes had become accustomed to the gloom, I was therefore free not only to take in our surroundings but to study the personage to whom we had been directed, and on whom all our hopes now centred. Draped in the dull orange robes of the Burmese sangha, which left his right shoulder bare, U Chandramani was an impressive figure. Though he was well over seventy, and looked his age, his frame was sturdy and robust, while the deeply furrowed Mongoloid face with the sagging jowl and remarkably long ear-lobes expressed both strength and determination of character. As he sat there gravely listening to Satyapriya's highly circumstantial account of our joint history from the time of our meeting in Singapore down to the time of our disappointment at Sarnath he looked for all the world like the statue of a Lohan, or traditional Chinese representation of an *arahant*. He sat impassive as a statue too. Only when my friend happened to dwell more on my own particular career did he glance in my direction, and I saw that his face, which had seemed stern at first, in fact wore a benevolent, even a fatherly expression.

'So you want to be ordained, do you?' he said with a chuckle, apparently by no means displeased at the idea, when Satyapriya had at last finished. 'Well, well, we shall have to see.' For the next hour we were therefore subjected to an interrogatory which, though kindly, was extremely searching. What U Chandramani particularly wanted to know was whether we had been properly initiated into Buddhism by taking the Three Refuges and Five Precepts from a monk in the traditional ceremonial manner, for unless this had been done, and we were already *upāsakas* or lay brothers, it would hardly be possible for us to be ordained as *śrāmaṇeras* or novice monks, which represented the next highest degree of initiation. Fortunately neither of us had any difficulty in satisfying U Chandramani on this point. I had taken the Refuges and Precepts, five years earlier, from the scholar-monk U Thittila, then working as a stretcher-bearer in London; Satyapriya, less fortunate, had taken them two years ago in Calcutta from His Holiness. When he learned of my connection with U Thittila, who like himself was Burmese, U Chandramani showed both surprise and pleasure. Indeed, he seemed to regard it as a good omen. The rest of the interrogatory was concerned with questions of a more general nature. How many precepts had we been observing? What was our understanding of the Doctrine? Which method of meditation were we practising and what results had we achieved? Eventually it was all over. If we had not passed with flying colours, we had at least not done too badly, and judging by the nods of approval that he had given from time to time U Chandramani was not dissatisfied with our replies. He would consider our request, he now told us, and let us know in a few days' time whether or not it was

*U Chandramani
Mahathera,
Sangharakshita's first
preceptor*

possible for him to accept the responsibility of giving us ordination. Meanwhile, we could make ourselves comfortable at the guest house, the *anagārikās* would see to our meals, and we could explore the sacred site at our leisure. There was much that was worth seeing. With a good-humoured wave of his hand he dismissed us. Scarcely able to believe that our application had not been rejected out of hand, we prostrated ourselves three times and withdrew.

For the next few days we followed U Chandramani's advice and explored Kusinara. Our first halt was naturally at the Mahaparinirvana Stupa which, according to tradition, marked the spot where the Buddha, coming to the end of his last journey, had laid himself down on a stone couch in the sal grove of the Mallas and allowed his Enlightened consciousness to dissociate itself from the physical body. Though smaller than the Dhamekh Stupa at Sarnath, it was in a much better state of repair, having in fact been practically rebuilt by U Chandramani with the help of funds donated by Burmese Buddhists. On completion of the work, the whole dome had been gilded, but that was years ago, long before the war, and now all that remained of this evidence of devotion were a few patches of gold leaf that gleamed in the morning sunlight. Not far from the Stupa was the Temple of the Recumbent Buddha. This was a place of no architectural pretensions whatever. Indeed, it was nothing more than a whitewashed brick shed, long and narrow, with a barrel roof that had been put up to protect the celebrated image which, next to the Stupa itself, in the heyday of Kusinara had been the principal object of worship at the sacred site. This image, which belonged to the Gupta period, was about thirty feet in length, and represented the Buddha at the time of the Great Decease. One foot on top of the other, head supported on right hand, stiff and solemn he lay there in his gilded robe, the great face serene and majestic in the hour of bodily death as ever it had been during life. Though the temple was so small that there was barely room to circumambulate the image, to me, at least, the dimensions of the place were exactly right. As we knelt there in the gloom, with only two or three lighted candles flickering between us and the placid features of that enormous face, so deep was the silence, and of such inexpressible solemnity, that we seemed to be present at the very deathbed of the Master. Before many days had passed, the Stupa and the Temple had become the twin centres of our spiritual existence. Every evening, at sunset, we sat and meditated in front of the Stupa, stirring only when it loomed a black shape against the star-filled depths of the sky. Every morning, long before dawn, having chanted our praises in that unsleeping ear, we sat and meditated beside the stone couch of the Recumbent Buddha. During the rest of the day we studied, talked with Mother Vipassana and, of course, continued our explorations.

Next to the Mahaparinirvana Stupa and the Temple, and apart from the excavated ruins that made up the archaeological area, the most interesting relic of Kusinara's glorious past was the Angar Caitya, the mound marking the spot where the earthly remains of the Buddha had been cremated. Interesting as this was, however, we had not gone more than halfway round it before we came upon something more interesting still. Near the Caitya grew an enormous peepul tree, and high up in the tree, half hidden by the dense foliage, there was perched a strange figure in a saffron-coloured loincloth. As soon as he caught sight of us he let out a loud whoop, apparently of welcome, and with amazing agility swarmed chuckling and gibbering down the tree until he stood balancing himself only a few feet above our heads. We then saw that he was Chinese, and that his arms, shoulders, and chest, which were bare, were covered with a multitude of burns. Though he seemed to know a little Hindi, his pronunciation was so uncouth that it was impossible for us to make out more than a few words. In response to his gesticulations, however, we looked up into the tree, and eventually saw among the branches a kind of rough platform, so clumsily put together from half a dozen planks as to seem like the nest of some enormous bird. It was here that the strange figure lived. As we afterwards learned, he had lived in the tree for a number of years, and though he moved about freely among the branches he never set foot on the ground. Periodically he applied lighted candles to different parts of his body and allowed them to burn down into the flesh. This was, of course, an extension of the Far Eastern Buddhist practice of burning wax cones on the head at the time of ordination, as a sign of one's willingness to suffer for the sake of Supreme Enlightenment, and was not without precedent in traditional Chinese Buddhism – or indeed, without canonical sanction in the *White Lotus Sūtra*. Whatever visiting Buddhists may have thought of these bizarre practices, the local Hindus were full of admiration, and Cheenia Baba, as they called him, was held in high esteem. Some of the villagers, indeed, would bring him candles to burn on himself in the belief that whatever prayers they offered up while he was doing so were sure to be granted.

A less eccentric figure than Cheenia Baba, and of more importance for the history of modern Kusinara, was one whom it was no longer possible to see in the flesh. This was Mahavir Swami, a faded full-length photograph of whom, discoloured by damp, hung in a worm-eaten frame on the front veranda of what had formerly been the main vihara. A veteran of the Indian Mutiny of 1857, he had settled in Kusinara towards the end of the last century after being ordained in Ceylon. At that time Kusinara was completely in ruins. So desolate was the place, indeed, that it was popularly believed to be haunted, and no one dared go anywhere near it. Undeterred, Mahavir Swami had built a bamboo hut and then, in 1902, the first Buddhist monastery to be erected in modern India. Unfortunately, by the time Satyapriya and I visited it the building was somewhat dilapidated, and Mahavir Swami's portrait looked down on cracked cement floors and crumbling brickwork that was rapidly becoming covered by green mould. U Chandramani had come and joined Mahavir Swami in 1901, the year before the vihara was built, and had not only resided there without interruption ever since but continued his predecessor's work of restoring the ruined shrines of Kusinara and making the place once more a living centre of Buddhism. Half a century of service to the Dharma! Half a century of single-minded dedication! When we had finished exploring Kusinara, and seen all that the old man had achieved, we could not help thinking that even if we had visited all the Buddhist centres of India we could hardly have found a more suitable person to ask for ordination.

But to ask was one thing, to be given quite another. Some days had now elapsed since our first interview. Vaiśākha Pūrṇimā, the thrice-sacred anniversary of the Buddha's Supreme Enlightenment, was drawing near. Moreover, from remarks let fall by Mother Vipassana, we gathered that at least one person in Kusinara was not happy at the idea of our receiving ordination from U Chandramani. The Indian monk, it seemed, had objected to it on the grounds that if we were ordained we would become entitled to a share of the vihara property after the Mahāthera's death! But we need not have worried. When the moon that rose every night above the shadowy dome of the Mahaparinirvana Stupa was almost full, U Chandramani called us to his room and with his customary affability told us that he was prepared to accede to our request. We would be ordained immediately after breakfast on the morning of the Vaiśākha Pūrṇimā Day. It would have to be clearly understood, however, that in giving us the *śrāmaṇera* ordination, he would not be accepting any responsibility for our future training, nor would it be possible for us to stay with him at Kusinara. As we could see for ourselves, the resources of the vihara were limited, and he was not in a position to support two more disciples. But if it was only ordination we wanted, he said, with evident warmth and sincerity, then he would ordain us with the greatest pleasure and we could have his blessing, too, into the bargain.

Ex-Brahmin that he was, Satyapriya was at first shocked by the idea of our being ordained after breakfast, and not before it, while still fasting. But after breakfast it was definitely to be. Buddhism attached no importance whatever to ritual purity and impurity, we were reminded, and an empty stomach was no more holy than a full one. At nine o'clock on Thursday, 12 May 1949, therefore, after we had eaten our breakfast in the old vihara, we received the long-expected summons to the Chapter House. Here U Chandramani handed us our robes, tied up in a bundle, and told us to go and take a bath and put them on. Our heads had already been shaved the previous day. The robes for which we now exchanged the informal saffron of the last two years were of the regulation size, shape, and colour, and along with the rest of the permitted articles – girdle, water-strainer, needle, and razor – had been presented to us by Mother Vipassana and the other *anagārikās*, who in order to have them ready in time for the ceremony had, in fact, sat up stitching the complicated seams until late at night. U Chandramani himself had presented us with our begging-bowls. On our returning to the Chapter House, duly 'robed and bowled' as the texts have it, we were made to squat on our heels with our elbows resting on our knees and our hands joined together at our foreheads. This was an extremely difficult and uncomfortable position. Indeed, after a few minutes the pain in various parts of my body became excruciating. As I afterwards realized, the position we were made to adopt was that of the child in the womb, for the ordination represented the process of spiritual rebirth, and 'at the birth of a child or a star, there is pain'.

Having to remain in such a position throughout the ceremony was by itself ordeal enough, but for me at least the difficulties of ordination were by no means over. The Three Refuges – the Refuges in the Buddha, the Dharma, and the Sangha – had not only to be repeated thrice each but repeated in both Pāli and Sanskrit. This was to make sure that the novice monk was able to distinguish between the two kinds of pronunciation, for in the early days of Buddhism, when the Buddha's Message was preserved and transmitted exclusively by oral means, the slightest carelessness in matters of phonetics could in the course of time result in a serious distortion of the letter of the teaching leading, perhaps, to eventual loss of its spirit. Try as I might, however, my English tongue could not manage to reproduce the elusive Indian sounds. U Chandramani, for his part, was determined that the requirements of tradition should be scrupulously respected. Time and again he intoned the sacred formulas, patiently coaching me in the production of aspirated consonants, nasalized terminations, and palatal sibilants. After much effort on my part, and much exercise of patience on his, I eventually succeeded in repeating the Refuges to his complete satisfaction in both Pāli and Sanskrit and we were able to pass on to the next part of the ceremony, which consisted in the taking of the ten *śrāmaṇera* precepts. This time reciting in Pāli only, and with less regard to pronunciation, Satyapriya and I undertook to abstain from injury to living beings, from taking the not-given, from unchastity, from false speech, and from intoxicants, as well as from untimely meals, from song, dance, instrumental music and indecent shows, from garlands, perfumes, unguents and other worldly adornments, from large and lofty beds, and from handling gold or silver. All these precepts we were already observing, but the kindly, simple, and good-humoured manner in which U Chandramani explained each one gave them a fresh significance, and we felt that we would die rather than be guilty of the smallest infringement. The more formal part of the proceedings ended with the Mahāthera solemnly adjuring us in the last words which the Buddha had addressed to his disciples, as he lay on his deathbed in the Sal Grove, only a few hundred yards away: 'With mindfulness strive on!'

We were now fully-fledged *śrāmaṇeras*! The desire of our hearts had been fulfilled! We had been spiritually reborn! The ordination ceremony was over! But not quite over, it seemed. Having been born anew, we had to be given new names. As we relaxed our cramped limbs, U Chandramani asked us on which day of the week we had been born. Neither of us knew. Well, well, murmured the old man, mildly astonished at such ignorance, but evidently not disposed to be over-strict about a matter of secondary importance, he would have to manage as best he could without the information. In Burma each day of the week was associated with certain letters of the alphabet, and a monk's name had to begin with one of the letters belonging to the particular day of the week on which he had been born. In our case, since it would not be possible for him to follow this procedure, he would have to name us at random, as he himself thought best. Satyapriya would be known as Buddharakshita. Dharmapriya would be known as Dharmarakshita. With these names, which placed us under the protection of the first and the second Refuges, we were well content. Whether on account of the forgetfulness of old age, however, or for some other reason, U Chandramani had overlooked the fact that he already had a disciple called Dharmarakshita. This disciple was the same Indian monk whom we had met at Sarnath, the one who had given us our letters of introduction, and he was even now in Kusinara, having arrived shortly before our ordination. On hearing that I had been given the same name as himself he came rushing over to the Chapter House. If there were two Dharmarakshitas, he protested, there would be endless confusion. People would not know which of us was which. My letters would be delivered to him. What was worse, his letters would be delivered to me. Neither of us would ever know where we were. 'Oh well,' said our preceptor, dismissing all this fuss and bother about names with a gesture of good-humoured impatience, 'Let *him* be Sangharakshita!'

In this unceremonious manner was I placed under the special protection of the sangha, or Spiritual Community, rather than under that of the Dharma, or Teaching. Even before the matter of names had been sorted out, however, Mother Vipassana and the other *anagārikās* were thronging round us not only to offer congratulations but to salute our feet in the traditional manner, just as we had already saluted the feet of U Chandramani and the other monks. These symbolic acts served to remind us that our ordination had not only an individual but also a social significance. As *śrāmaṇeras* we belonged to a community, to a spiritual community, the community of the spiritually reborn. In this we had a definite place, and our relationship with other members of the community, lower or higher than ourselves in the hierarchy, was not only clearly defined but governed by a strict protocol. With Mother Vipassana our relationship was of a very special kind. Next to our preceptor, she was for us the most important person at Kusinara. In the absence of our own mothers, who in a Buddhist land would have taken a prominent part in the proceedings, she had constituted herself our Dharma Mata or Mother in Religion, and besides organizing the preparation of our robes, she offered the customary ceremonial meal to U Chandramani and all the other monks at Kusinara including, of course, Buddharakshita (as I must now call him) and myself. Indeed, as we afterwards learned, when the Indian monk had objected to our ordination she had spoken up strongly and warmly on our behalf. But for her, therefore, we might not have been ordained at all.

Though it meant so much to us, for most of the people who had come to Kusinara for the Vaiśākha Pūrṇimā our ordination that morning was only a very minor incident in the events of the thrice-sacred day – if, indeed, they knew of it at all. What mainly interested them was the procession that took place in the afternoon when, strung out behind the glittering instruments of the brass band, a long line of orange-robed monks with red Burmese parasols, white-clad laity with black umbrellas, and schoolchildren with books or handkerchiefs on their heads, wound their way through the fields from the vihara to the neighbouring villages. Unfortunately, before the brass band had got more than halfway there the sky became overcast, thunder crashed and boomed, lightning flashed, and the rain came down in such torrents that the procession had to be

With Buddharakshita, after śrāmaṇera ordination at Kusinara, May 1949

abandoned, together with the rest of the day's programme. The rainy season had begun!

Buddharakshita and I had intended to leave Kusinara on the fourth day after our ordination. The bowls we had been given were of iron, and before we could use them they had to be lacquered to prevent rust. U Chandramani himself showed us how this was done. After being coated with a certain kind of oil, very thick and dark, the bowls were baked for a couple of hours in a specially constructed oven. The whole process had to be repeated eight or nine times. Even so, the results were not very satisfactory, and far from presenting the smooth, black, glossy appearance of some bowls we had seen ours looked as though they had been coated with cheap brown varnish. When the lacquering was finished, however, and we were ready to set out on our travels again, Bhikkhu Dharmarakshita asked us to stay for two more days and join him and the rest of our fellow disciples in celebrating U Chandramani's seventy-third birthday. We could hardly refuse his request. Indeed, though it meant a slight readjustment in our plans, we were glad to have an opportunity of showing how much we appreciated our preceptor's achievement, and I undertook to compose a poem in honour of the occasion.[34] This time the day's celebrations were not interrupted by rain, and the procession and the public meeting passed off as planned. At three o'clock the following afternoon, having paid our respects to U Chandramani and the other monks, and said goodbye to the *anagārikās*, Buddharakshita and I left Kusinara. U Chandramani had asked us to go and preach the Dharma to his disciples at Butaol and Tansen, in southern Nepal, and both he and Mother Vipassana had provided us with letters of introduction. On the way we could visit Lumbini, where the Buddha had been born, which was just across the Indo-Nepalese border. From Tansen we hoped to go up to Pokhara, in central Nepal, and from there perhaps to Muktinath, the sacred mountain that was a place of pilgrimage for Buddhists and Hindus alike. It might even be possible for us to penetrate into Tibet. Equipped with our robes and our bowls, as a bird with its two wings, there was now no limit to where we might go.

46
'HERE THE BLESSED ONE WAS BORN'

The first thing we did after leaving Kusinara was to get lost. In fact, though we did not really have far to go, our journey that day was difficult in a number of ways. Since for the time being we had decided to head due west, we had the sun shining in our faces all the time. Moreover, there was no proper path, and the people of the villages through which we passed always seemed to misdirect us. One man, indeed, refused to direct us at all. When we stopped and asked him the way he only looked at us with surly suspicion and inquired, none too politely, who and what we were. We were Buddhist monks, we told him, and were on our way from Kusinara to Lumbini. 'Oh,' he exclaimed, turning away with a hostile sneer, 'You are the people who have dismembered Dharma as the Muslims have divided India into Hindustan and Pakistan!' He was, of course, a Brahmin. Eventually, after walking for twelve or thirteen miles, we reached the village of Raggerganj, on the outskirts of which there was situated the hermitage of an ascetic. Though the place was not much more than a ganja club, the ascetic himself was quite friendly, and not only offered us sugar-water but allowed us to sleep under a tree in the courtyard. In the middle of the night a storm blew up, and we were forced to retreat into the porch of the hermitage. We did not pass a very restful night.

Our main preoccupation next morning was to find a place where we could start putting our begging-bowls to the use for which they were intended and go for alms. Now that we were *śrāmaṇeras* we were resolved to do this in strictly traditional fashion. We would beg from door to door until we had obtained enough cooked food for our one meal of the day, not skipping so much as a single house. We would not accept people's invitations, nor would we even sit down inside a house in order to eat the food that we had collected. After walking from 5.30 until 10.30, with only a little *chatua* to sustain us on the way, we were feeling rather hungry. But at the first township to which we came we found the atmosphere so forbiddingly commercial that our courage failed us and tired as we were we decided not to stop there. Luckily there was a village only a mile further on. Before reaching the village proper, which was called Barspar, we halted at a well and asked a woman who was drawing water there to pour some into our lotas or brass pots. Respectfully she refused. She belonged to the Chamar or leather-worker caste, she explained, and for high-caste holy men like ourselves contact with anything that she had touched would mean pollution. Buddharakshita and I could hardly believe our ears. The woman at the well was saying exactly the same thing as the Mātaṅgī woman had said to Ānanda, cousin and personal attendant of the Buddha, 2,500 years ago, and saying it in exactly the same circumstances. History was repeating itself. Making exactly the same reply as Ānanda had done, we told the woman that what we wanted was water, not caste. Whereupon she gladly filled our lotas. India had not changed much since the days of the Buddha, it seemed.

Having quenched our thirst, we made our way to the woman's hut, which was situated nearby, on the outskirts of the village, and stood silently in front of the door with our bowls in our hands. Before very long a man came out and after looking at us in a rather puzzled manner asked us what we wanted. When begging at orthodox Buddhist doors, of course, a monk never spoke, but here there seemed to be no alternative, and we therefore told the man that we had come for alms. On hearing this he went inside and quickly returned with a small quantity of paddy or unmilled rice. This we refused, saying that we accepted only cooked things. He thereupon offered us money; but this too we refused. Either there was no cooked food in the hut or, what was more likely, he was afraid to give it on account of his caste. Not wishing to cause him further embarrassment, we quietly departed.

On entering the village we took our stand at the entrance to what was probably either a Brahmin or a Kshatriya house, where a number of people had assembled on the veranda. After gazing at us for some time with undisguised astonishment they asked us what we wanted, to which we again replied that we had come for alms. Like the man in the hut, they at first wanted to give us some paddy, but on being told that we accepted only cooked food they eventually dropped into our bowls a handful of puffed rice, which, having been parched, was not in orthodox Hindu eyes cooked food in the technical sense that boiled rice was. From the buzz of comment that rose from the veranda it was clear that astonished as they were by the unfamiliar cut and colour of our robes, and by the fact that we stood holding our bowls in silence instead of shouting out 'Give alms!' as the Hindu ascetics and holy men did, the villagers were still more astonished by our insistence on accepting only cooked food. In their experience, holy men were strict observers of the caste system, and avoided the risk of pollution by accepting as alms only uncooked food. Since from our complexion, dress, and deportment we were, so far as they could see, high-caste holy men, they were completely mystified by our disregard of the conventional code. For our part, we could now see that by obliging his homeless disciples to beg from door to door without regard to caste, and to accept only cooked food, the Buddha had initiated a social revolution – a revolution that had been checked, in the end, by the forces of brahminical reaction.

Our next stop was at a Muslim house. On learning what we wanted, the sarong-clad occupant told us to go round to the back door. If the Hindus saw him giving us alms, he said, he would be in danger of a beating. Who was it that had really divided India, we wondered. Besides giving us alms himself, this friendly son of the Prophet accompanied us to all the other houses we visited and his explanations saved us a lot of trouble. Indeed, thanks to his exertions we were able to complete the remainder of our almsround in silence. Some of the people at whose doors we stood were sympathetic, others sarcastic. One well-to-do Brahmin asked us to come in and sit down, saying that since he had just finished eating and there was nothing left he would prepare a meal specially for us. This kind offer we refused, as we already had something in our bowls, and our refusal impressed him more than ever. Another Brahmin, who had also just eaten, poured into each of our bowls a pint of milk, in which the puffed rice, boiled rice, curried vegetables, fruits, curds, pickles and all the other things we had been given were soon afloat. Before long we had more than enough for our requirements, and we therefore made our way to a mango grove on the outskirts of the village. Since this was the first time we had gone out begging in the traditional Buddhist manner, the occasion was one of unprecedented importance in both our lives, and it was with a sense of elation that we sat down in the deep, cool shade of the handsome trees. Apparently it was something of an event in the life of the village too, for we were followed to the mango grove by a crowd of about a hundred people who, with the dull curiosity of sheep or cows, stood staring at us from among the trees as though they intended to do so for the rest of the day. Feeling a little uncomfortable under all those eyes, and wishing to be left in peace, we asked them to go away until we had finished our meal. This they eventually did, though not without much urging on the part of our Muslim friend and many backward glances at us over their shoulders.

As soon as they had gone we put our hands into our bowls, kneaded the contents into a uniform if rather sticky mess, and started on our meal. While we were eating someone came running up with an enormous tray piled high with rice, curries, and lentil soup. Although we already had all that we really wanted, we accepted a small quantity, and asked that the rest should be distributed as *prasad*. According to the scriptures, the first time the future Buddha had tried to eat almsfood he had nearly vomited with disgust. Either we had been brought up less delicately than he had, or we were more fortunate in what we had collected. Far from feeling any disgust, as soon as we got used to the idea of eating everything mixed up together we thoroughly enjoyed our meal. What was left over we scattered at the foot of a tree for the birds. When the villagers saw that we had finished they started drifting back to the mango grove, whereupon, having collected them together and made them sit down on the ground, Buddharakshita addressed them on the necessity of leading a moral life and the importance of observing the five precepts of ethical behaviour. Though this was probably drier spiritual fare than that to which they were accustomed, they listened attentively, and we had the satisfaction of repaying them for their hospitality by preaching the Dharma in the traditional manner. At three o'clock we left for Maharajgunj, a village about a dozen miles away.

Our second experience of begging our food in the traditional manner was not unlike our first. Having spent the night at Maharajgunj, where we slept on a stone platform under a tree, we set out again before six o'clock and after walking all the morning, and passing through four or five villages, some large and some small, we eventually made our way to the village of Tehri with the intention of going for alms there. As we entered the place we saw an aged Vaishnava ascetic with a big rosary round his neck sitting on a bedstead making a *kamandalu*, the special waterpot carried by orthodox Hindu monks. Without pausing in his work, he called out to us rather roughly and asked us what we wanted. When we explained that we had come for alms he told us, none too politely, that he could not give us anything. The first house outside whose door we stood did not give us anything either, but at all the remaining houses the womenfolk proved wonderfully kind and generous. On hearing that we were willing to accept cooked food from them even though they belonged to the Aheer or dairy farmer caste, a very low caste indeed, they gave us rice, unleavened bread, vegetable curries, lentil soup, and curds in such profusion that both our bowls were quickly filled.

Since there was no mango grove at Tehri, we had to finish our second meal of almsfood in whatever shade was available, after which we walked a short distance along the riverside until we came to a fine shady mango tree where we rested for a while, and where an old woman brought us drinking water. We then continued our journey, following the river for a few miles until we came to another village. Though late afternoon, it was still scorching hot, and having quenched our thirst at the Forestry Department pump we were glad to sit down for a few minutes at the edge of a grove of sal trees. Shortly after this, for the second time since leaving Kusinara, we lost our way. In the absence of any road, we had been forced to try and find our way across the fields, with the result that before long we found ourselves wandering round in circles uncertain in which direction we ought to go. We were still wandering in this manner when we stumbled, quite by accident, upon a small village, where an old Shaivite devotee received us with the greatest respect and insisted on giving us sugar-water to drink. He and a Muslim neighbour then not only directed us which road to take but were also good enough to accompany us for a short distance so as to make quite sure that we did not miss it. From then onwards we had no difficulty. After being given more sugar-water to drink, this time by a sympathetic shopkeeper, we met up with our old friend the railway line, and after following it eastward for a mile, reached the township of Nautanwa.

On our arrival at the Lumbini Rest House, a tiny building not far from the centre of the town, we were at once warmly welcomed by the thin and elderly, but extremely active and energetic, Sinhalese monk who had been posted there by the Maha Bodhi Society to look after the needs of pilgrims on the last stage of their journey to the birthplace of the Buddha. Despite his great seniority in the Order, Venerable K. Sirinivas Nayaka Mahāthera was no stickler for protocol, and seeing how hot and tired we were, cheerfully set about lighting a fire and preparing tea. What if we were only *śrāmaṇeras*, and he an elder, he declared, brushing aside our protests. We obviously needed a cup of tea, and since the servant had gone home for the night and would not be back until morning, he would prepare it.

Two days later, having passed the time pleasantly enough in the company of our friendly and communicative host, we left Nautanwa for Lumbini. With us were Brahmachāri Munindra, a Barua Buddhist whom we had met at Sarnath, and two young friends of his, Arun Chandra, an Indian, and U Thaung Aung, a Burmese, all of whom had arrived late the previous night, long after Buddharakshita and I had finished talking with Venerable Sirinivas and gone to bed. Since Aung was travelling with a certain amount of luggage, a coolie had to be engaged in the bazaar, a process which occasioned some loss of time and no little trouble. Eventually we were all ready to start. After walking for nearly two miles we came to the river that marked the boundary between India and Nepal. At this time of year it was a river bed rather than a river, and we had no difficulty in wading through the sluggish trickle of muddy water that still flowed in the deepest part of the channel. On the other side a broad dirt-track led through the sparse jungle of the Terai, and following this we traversed two villages, at the second of which Munindra and Aung stopped for a drink of milk. On the way we saw a black antelope and a small herd of red deer browsing among the sal trees. Lumbini was now quite near, the coolie told us. Quickening our pace, we traversed two more villages, and before long could see in the distance two mounds of earth surmounted by small brick towers with a diminutive temple in between.

During the couple of days that we spent at Lumbini our feelings were divided between joy at being at the very spot where the future Buddha had first seen the light of day, and a sense of regret, even outrage, at the desolate and neglected appearance of the sacred place. It was as though the tide of Buddhist revival, which flowed strongly at Sarnath, and none too feebly at Kusinara, had as yet hardly touched

Lumbini. The only modern building to be seen was the Rest House erected by the Government of Nepal for the benefit of pilgrims, where we installed ourselves soon after our arrival, and where the caretakers provided us with a meal. Those other than pilgrims found it convenient to use the Rest House, however. Either because there was no other accommodation, or because in this land of autocracy even the lowest representative of authority was accustomed to behave in a high-handed manner, touring government officials regularly treated it as a sort of caravanserai. On the evening of our arrival a police inspector turned up with twenty of his men and soon the peace and silence of the place were lost in uproar. Next day it was even worse. While their master was busy squeezing money from the local landlords, who from time to time arrived on elephants, bearing with them the customary gifts, some of the inspector's men slaughtered a goat in the compound and without removing its hair, hide or anything else cooked it whole over an open fire. Though Munindra, Arun Chandra, and Thaung Aung were by no means vegetarians, on seeing this gruesome sight all five members of our little party felt like making a strong protest. But on reflection we decided not to do so. The police inspector had been drinking since early morning, and to judge from the way in which he was behaving with the landlords he was not the sort of person who would be amenable to reason. All the same, we could not help thinking how sad it was that the First Precept, the precept of abstaining from injury to any living being, should be so flagrantly violated in the very birthplace of the Buddha.

Apart from the two mounds, which rose like two volcanic islands out of a perfect sea of loose bricks, and seemed to have once formed the lower half of twin stupas, the only ancient building of which any trace remained above ground was the Rummindei Temple. This was so small as to be a chapel rather than a temple, and in an extremely dilapidated, not to say ruinous, condition. On our first visit to the place, soon after our arrival, we found the door locked, and it was not until the evening of our second day at Lumbini that it was opened by the old Hindu woman who kept the key and was responsible, so it seemed, for the rudimentary worship that kept alive the religious traditions of the place. The interior of the temple was disappointing. The only object of interest was a stone slab so well worn, and so thickly smeared with vermilion, that the figure of Mahāmāyā holding on to the branch of a sal tree as she stood giving birth to the future Teacher of Gods and

Men was barely discernible. On our questioning the old woman it soon became clear that she had not even heard of the Buddha or of Buddhism and that she was under the impression that the temple was dedicated to a Hindu goddess.

More easy of access was the Aśoka Pillar nearby, which stood beneath the open sky behind a low iron railing. On its highly polished surface the ancient Brahmi letters were cut deep and clear, and we could still spell out the announcement 'Here the Blessed One was born.' For some reason or other, I felt even more deeply moved here than I had done either at Sarnath or Kusinara. The truncated stone shaft stood so calmly and so simply beneath the cloudless blue sky; it seemed so unpretentious, and yet to mean so much. Lingering behind when Buddharakshita and the others had moved on in the direction of the mounds, I gathered some small white flowers and with a full heart scattered them over the railing at the foot of the column. As I did so I heard Buddharakshita's voice. 'What are you messing about with those flowers for?' he shouted roughly. 'Come on, we can't wait for you all day!'

The following morning our party broke up. Munindra and his two young friends returned to Nautanwa with their coolie; Buddharakshita and I set off through the jungle for Butaol. With us went three or four local people who were also travelling part of the way and who were glad, it seemed, to make the journey in the company of two ascetics – probably because of the belief that holy men are never attacked by wild animals. In the course of a few hours we passed through two villages, at the second the last of our companions left us, and Buddharakshita and I refreshed ourselves with a quick bath. We then had to pass through a stretch of thick forest, but though we took the wrong turning more than once, and had to retrace our steps, we managed to find our way along the narrow jungle tracks and after passing through two more hamlets eventually emerged at the prosperous Tharu village of Farsatirka Bazaar. Here we had our third experience of going for alms. At the first house we got nothing. At the second, a buxom young woman sprawling on a string bed just inside the door jeered, 'Wearing spectacles, are you? Think you're very high and mighty, don't you?' Then, her voice rising in a shriek of fury, 'Go on, why don't you go and work for a living.' Out of the corner of my eye I saw that my friend's face had flushed purple with rage, but controlling himself with an effort he repeated the customary benediction and we moved on to the next house. In rural

Nepal, as in rural India, it seemed, spectacles were still regarded as a species of jewellery, as were fountain pens and wristwatches, and as such could fittingly be worn only by worldly, semi-Westernized young men of some social pretensions.

The women of the other houses to which we went were more sympathetic, and our bowls were soon almost full. At the last house of all, indeed, the old woman who came to the door was so amazed at our willingness to accept cooked food from such a low-caste person as herself that, tremulous with joy, she hurried back into the house and returned with all the rice, lentil soup, and curds that we needed. We then sought out a secluded spot at the far end of the village and ate our meal sitting inside a cowpen. All around us were the pleasant signs of rural prosperity. Cows were fatter and sleeker than any we had yet seen. Barns were overflowing with fodder. Under the projecting eaves of the mud-walled houses rows of enormous earthenware jars, each one higher than a man and of corresponding girth, stood brimming with grain. The people, too, though not yet Mongoloid of feature, seemed stronger and healthier than those of India. While we were eating, Buddharakshita expatiated on our encounter with the young woman on the string bed. He was overjoyed that she had abused us, he declared. Not for anything in the world would he have missed the experience. Now, and now only, could we consider ourselves monks indeed. We had been found worthy to share in the insults that had rained not only on the head of the Buddha himself but on the heads of all his worthy disciples down the ages.

Having rested for a while under a tree some distance from the village, we set off once more and, though the jungle became much thicker, succeeded in passing through three more villages without losing our way too often. Ever since our departure from Lumbini the type of vegetation had been changing, from subtropical to temperate, and by this time the whole countryside was not only far greener but full of brooks and streams. What with the softness and springiness of the turf, the shafts of sunlight that came slanting down through the big leafy trees, the coolness, and the quiet that was broken only by the clear, fluting calls of birds, it seemed as though we were passing through a stretch of English woodland rather than through a region of the Nepal Terai only a few miles from the foothills of the Himalayas. For a moment I fancied I was a boy again, wandering among the bluebells and bracken in the depths of Wimbledon Common. For the last two or three miles of our journey the path ran beside a broad river fringed with reeds and water-flags, and as soon as we could find a suitable spot Buddharakshita and I stopped and took a dip in the clear, ice-cold current. Soon afterwards we saw rising up like a grey-green wall before us the first range of foothills. Below the foothills, on the banks of the river higher up, there stretched in ugly perspective row upon row of corrugated iron roofing of every conceivable variety of rust and in every stage of decay. We had reached Butaol.

47
WITH THE NEWARS IN NEPAL

The Newars of Nepal belonged to the same ethnic group as the Tibetans and the Burmese. Most of them lived in the Kathmandu Valley, which until the Gurkha conquests of the eighteenth century had been the seat of one or more independent Buddhist kingdoms, and despite pressure, not to say persecution, on the part of the state religion, Hinduism, most were still Buddhists. Apart from the Vajracharyas, the hereditary Tantric priests, the majority of 'high-caste' Newars were either craftsmen or traders, and though the bulk of the Newar population was concentrated in and around Kathmandu itself, as well as in Patan, small Newar communities existed in many parts of the country – wherever, in fact, there was the possibility of trade. During the previous decade several Newars had gone to Ceylon and Burma to study the Pāli scriptures and be ordained there, and at least one Theravādin Buddhist monk from Ceylon had visited Nepal. A minor revival of Buddhism was, in fact, in progress among them. This revival was not unconnected with the political aspirations of the Newars, who felt themselves to be a subject people in their own homeland, and it was therefore regarded with grave suspicion by the Rana despotism which, about a century earlier, had usurped the royal authority and now governed the country with harsh efficiency. When U Chandramani asked us to go and preach the Dharma to his disciples in Butaol and Tansen he knew exactly what he was doing. These disciples were Newars, and the presence among them of two foreign monks would undoubtedly encourage them in their efforts to preserve their religious and cultural identity. At the same time the experience would be of great value to Buddharakshita and myself. In Kusinara all our contacts had been with *bhikkhus* and *anagārikas*. Now that we were with the Newars of Nepal we would be meeting ordinary lay members of the spiritual community, and besides preaching the Dharma to them would be acquainting ourselves with the traditional observances and the etiquette customarily observed between monks and lay people.

We were soon made to realize how inexperienced we were, and how much we had to learn, even on the most elementary level. One of the rusty roofs we had seen belonged to the Padmagarbha Vihara, and it was to this tiny outpost of Buddhism that, on our arrival at Butaol, we had made our way and where we had been put up for the night. Early next morning, just after we had completed our devotions, we were surprised by the arrival of eight or ten Newar women of various ages, all swathed in voluminous white muslin saris and with rows of tiny gold rings glittering in the rims of their ears. Since they spoke very little Hindi, and we did not understand Newari, which was a monosyllabic language unrelated to any Indian tongue, we could not at first make out what they wanted. Eventually, however, after much laughing and giggling on their part, and a certain amount of cross-examination on ours, it transpired that they had come to take the Three Refuges and Five Precepts from us in the traditional ceremonial manner. This put us in a quandary. Though we had learned the Salutation to the Three Jewels in Kusinara, and recited it every day, we had not as yet been called upon to administer the Refuges and Precepts to anyone. What were we to do? After a quick consultation, we decided that the best course for us to take would be perfect frankness. Through one of the older women, who understood a little more Hindi than the rest, Buddharakshita therefore explained that we were newly ordained and had no experience of performing ceremonies but that, if they had no objection, he would read out the appropriate Pāli formularies from the book. They had no objection at all. In fact, they were touched by our frankness and overjoyed at having the opportunity of taking the Refuges and Precepts, and it was with smiles of satisfaction that they settled down on their knees, joined their hands together, closed their eyes, and prepared, with every evidence of devotion, to intone the sacred words of the responses after my friend. Being a Brahmin by birth, and accustomed to chanting in Sanskrit from an early age, Buddharakshita had no difficulty in playing his part in the proceedings, which were therefore gone through without a hitch and terminated amidst general satisfaction. During the six weeks that we spent in Nepal one or the other of us was called upon to administer the Refuges and Precepts at least once a day, so that we soon became proficient in this simple but basic ceremony and able to perform it without reference to the book.

On our first day in Butaol some of the women who had taken the Refuges and Precepts brought our pre-midday meal to us at the vihara. On the second day, by general request, we went with our begging-bowls to all the Newar houses in the neighbourhood. We had made known our intention of leaving for Palpa-Tansen early next morning, and everybody wanted to have an opportunity of 'making merit' by feeding us before we went. Since it was known beforehand that we were coming there were none of the difficulties that we had to face in our quest for alms in the villages through which we had passed after leaving Kusinara. Conducted as we were from house to house by a small procession of men and boys, our 'going for alms' was in fact not so much a begging-round as a triumphal progress for the collection of the offerings of the faithful. At every one of the ten or twelve houses to which we were led we found the white-clad women waiting for us on their doorsteps with rice, vegetable curries, lentil soup, curds, milk, sweetmeats, and pickles in such generous quantities that in a very short time our two bowls were filled to the very brim. Judging from the joy with which they received us, and the devotion with which they made their offerings, it was a new experience for them to give alms in this way, and one which they deeply appreciated. Though the handful of Newar monks who had been trained in Ceylon had introduced a number of Theravādin customs they had not, it seemed, as yet introduced the almsround. On returning to the Padmagarbha Vihara we emptied our bowls of more than half their contents and distributed this quantity among the young people present as *prasad*. Even so, we were unable to finish what was left, with the result that for once in their miserable lives, the lean, mange-ridden curs that skulked in the neighbourhood of the vihara enjoyed a good meal.

Since we still went barefoot, we could not help noticing how filthy were the narrow, unpaved streets of the little town. There was no sanitation or garbage collection of any kind. Rubbish was simply thrown out of doors and windows into the street, where it rotted and decomposed in heaps, or was fought over by stray dogs. By-lanes and alleys, in fact any convenient wall, gutter, or patch of waste ground, were evidently used as public latrines. Flies buzzed everywhere. Stench filled the air. Besides the lack of sanitation there was, we found, an absence of some of the basic amenities of life. There was no hospital and no school. When we went out for a walk in the evening a room in a ramshackle wooden building was pointed out to us. This was the library, we were told. Or rather, it had been the library. After functioning for only three months it had been closed down by the authorities and the founder arrested and imprisoned. Not without reason, perhaps, the Government of Nepal believed that education fomented discontent. Potentially subversive institutions such as schools and libraries were therefore not encouraged.

Despite the kindness with which we had been received, Buddharakshita and I were not sorry to abandon Butaol for the cleaner air of the mountains. Though we left early, most of the Newar population not only came to the vihara to see us off but walked with us as far as the tree that marked the boundary of the town. At this tree we halted a few minutes, and with the exception of the two young men who were to accompany us to Tansen everybody bade us a friendly and affectionate farewell. We had not been climbing for more than an hour, and lungs and leg muscles had hardly begun to feel the strain, when something happened which not only interrupted our journey for that day but suggested that the hardships of the last few months had not been without their effect on my health. Since four o'clock in the morning I had been suffering from a pain in the stomach, a pain I had at first attributed to diarrhoea, and it was now so severe that I was hardly able to walk. Massage brought only temporary relief, and after we had pressed on again for half an hour the pain returned with such violence that having vomited a number of times I lay down at the side of the road almost wishing I could die on the spot. With great difficulty Buddharakshita and our two young companions got me to a hut a few hundred yards further on, where I lay exhausted on the veranda. For the next two or three hours the pain not only continued without respite but grew steadily worse. Luckily, a man who happened to pass by suggested that the juice of a certain root would cure me of the complaint, and the old woman who lived in the hut was good enough to go off into the jungle and get it. The juice of that root was the bitterest thing I had ever tasted. After I had drunk it, however, the pain gradually subsided, and I sank into a deep and refreshing slumber. When I awoke two hours later I found that the pain had disappeared, and after fortifying ourselves with Tibetan buttered tea – the first I had tasted – the four of us continued on our journey.

Whether because surcease of pain made me feel more alive, or because of the invigorating effect of the mountain air, I not only stepped out as smartly as the rest but started looking about me with fresh interest. Since my visit to Darjeeling three years earlier I had seen nothing so magnificent as the scenery through which we were now passing. On our right, overhanging the stony track that girdled the base of the mountain, towered an enormous mass of rock, and down its precipitous face streams of water were pouring in a number of places and even cascading across the path. On our left, far below, raced the pale green foaming waters of the river, which roared so loudly along their boulder-strewn course that at times we could hardly hear ourselves speak. After crossing a plank suspension bridge, and traversing a pleasant valley, we found our way up to the shoulder of the next range of foothills and continued steadily climbing for nearly four hours. All around us, tier upon tier, rose the steep tree-clad slopes, and the sound of streams was continually in our ears. Apart from a fat woman being carried in a sling between two coolies, the only signs of human existence that we came across were the occasional wayside hovel and the small patches of cultivation that clung precariously to the hillside. The higher we climbed the colder it grew. Mist swirled across our path, and eventually became so thick that we could hardly see our way. Buddharakshita and I shivered in our thin cotton robes. As soon as we reached the top and entered the village of Mashyam, however, the mist started clearing, and we could see the masses of red and purple dahlias glimmering through the slowly thinning clouds from window-boxes on either side of the road. Since Mashyam marked the highest point of our journey, Buddharakshita and I at first thought of spending the night there, but the presence of a number of sepoys, as well as a well-armed party of bandits, made us change our minds. Besides, our two young friends assured us that Tansen was not very far away and that we could easily reach it that night. When they had consumed the usual enormous heaps of rice and curry, and had prepared some sherbet for us (though we had missed our pre-midday meal owing to the pain in my stomach, as *śrāmaṇeras* my friend and I could not eat after twelve o'clock and so would have to fast until the morning), our little party therefore made haste to leave Mashyam and after walking a short distance started descending into the valley below.

Although the upward climb had been difficult enough, the subsequent downward scramble proved to be harder still. Moreover, night fell more quickly than we had expected, and the small electric torches of our companions were of little avail against the almost total darkness by which we were soon engulfed. For about two hours we groped our way along dangerous ledges, down precipitous slopes, and round awkward bends, with loose stones constantly slipping and rolling beneath our feet and the sheer drop into the stream below uncomfortably close. By the time we reached the village of Dumrai, Buddharakshita and I were so exhausted that we decided to spend the night in a Newar house there. The night was far from peaceful. At about ten o'clock the pain in my stomach returned, and since the whole place was in darkness, making it difficult to extract the juice of the old woman's root, my friend gave me a piece to chew. It was so bitter that I vomited. Buddharakshita therefore went and begged some water from the next house, which was situated several dozen yards further down the cliff, almost immediately below us, and where judging from the sounds that floated up to us through the cold night air a party was in progress. On his return Buddharakshita reported, in tones of the deepest disgust, that the place was full of prostitutes – 'prostitute' being in his vocabulary any woman not conforming to the strictest Hindu notions of feminine propriety. Despite the darkness he somehow managed to crush the root between two stones and after mixing the juice so obtained with a little of the water he had begged gave it to me to drink. This time it was not very effective, and it was two o'clock before the pain had subsided sufficiently for me to be able to sleep.

Next morning we left Dumrai as soon as it was light and after a pleasant walk through well-cultivated valleys came to the outermost bastions of the next range of mountains and started on the stiff climb up to Tansen. Having eaten nothing for two days we felt a little weak, and frequent rests were necessary. Moreover, the sun was now high in the sky and shone so hotly that we were soon drenched in perspiration. Fortunately the pain in my stomach was no more than a dull ache, and for this at least I was thankful. At about nine o'clock we at last reached Tansen, and went straight to the Ananda Vihara, where we were warmly welcomed by the Venerable Shakyananda, the resident monk, who immediately offered us tea, sweetmeats, and fruit. After the unexpected difficulties of the journey we were glad to have reached our destination and to have the opportunity of meeting one of the more senior disciples of U Chandramani. We were also glad to be within reach of medical aid. Such aid was in fact soon forthcoming. Shortly after our arrival a *vaidya*, or indigenous physician, happened to visit the vihara, and on our explaining to him the nature of my complaint he said that it was due to lack of nourishment and advised me to keep the stomach filled. Though I had no appetite, I therefore ate something, and after sleeping for an hour or two felt much better.

In the afternoon, when Buddharakshita and I were both sufficiently rested, we climbed through a maze of narrow cobblestoned streets to the Mahachaitya Vihara, situated at the upper end of the town, where it had been settled we should stay. Like the Padmagarbha Vihara and the Ananda Vihara, this was no more than a narrow oblong chamber with an image-table at the far end between two cupboards. In one important respect, however, the Mahachaitya Vihara differed from the other viharas. Outside, in the middle of the courtyard, stood a *caitya* or stupa seven or eight feet in height. This whitewashed monument with the brass finial, after which the vihara was named, was not the modern Theravādin type, as might have been expected, but a genuine product of traditional Nepalese Buddhism. From the image-table inside the vihara, the Ceylon- and Burma-trained revivalists had banished all the Buddhas except the historical Śākyamuni, to say nothing of all the bodhisattvas; but outside, from their niches in the four sides of the *caitya*, the transcendental Buddhas, Amoghasiddhi or 'Unobstructed Success', Ratnasambhava 'the Jewel-Born One', Akṣobhya or 'the Imperturbable', and Amitābha 'the Infinite Light' still looked out upon the four quarters of space – Vairocana 'the Illuminator', the Buddha of the centre, being hidden within the body of the monument. In the absence of a resident monk, care of the vihara had been entrusted to Anagārikā Sushila, a tiny, intense woman, neither young nor old, with a cropped turnip head and rows of tiny holes in the rims of her rather prominent ears. She and the other Newar Buddhists of the neighbourhood gave us an even warmer welcome than the one we had received at the Ananda Vihara, and after we had sat talking with them for an hour or two they took us to see the lending library that had been established nearby.

With Buddharakshita (right) and Shakyananda (centre) at the Mahachaitya Vihara, Tansen, Nepal, 1949

We were still looking at the 200-odd volumes when the pain in my stomach returned and in the course of the evening became increasingly severe. Fortunately medical aid was again forthcoming. Among the people who came to see us was a Calcutta-trained Bengali doctor. According to him what I was suffering from was not lack of nourishment but something much more serious. It was what the local people called *gunnaw*, he said. *Gunnaw* was a ball of wind that formed in the intestines as a result of drinking the hard mountain water and it was extremely difficult to dislodge. He would get a mixture made up for me, and after fasting completely for twenty-four hours I should take it three times a day until I was cured. Though I took the mixture as directed, it was more than a fortnight before the ball of wind was dispersed and I was entirely free from pain. Moreover, to make matters worse, before I had been cured of one complaint I developed another. A painful ulcer appeared on my right foot which not only made it difficult for me to walk but required daily dressing. What with the *gunnaw* and the ulcer it was not easy for me to get about, and though Buddharakshita was often out visiting I therefore spent practically all my time at the vihara.

In less than half a week we had slipped into the placid routine of the orthodox Theravādin monk, and the ceremonious rhythm of our days was broken only by the larger rhythms of the recurrent lunar festivals. Rising at dawn, we chanted the praises of the Three Jewels and sat for a while in meditation. As soon as it was fully light the more devout Newar women and girls would assemble and one of us would administer the Refuges and Precepts. This was followed by the ceremonial worship of the Buddha, after which the women came forward one by one and measured out in front of each of us in turn a small portion of unmilled rice. What with triple prostrations on their part and repeated blessings on ours this part of the proceedings lasted nearly an hour, and it was often quite late before Buddharakshita and I were able to have breakfast. Moreover, the women did not always come together, and on some mornings we had to administer the Refuges and Precepts two or three times. We also discovered that in Nepal it was possible to perform one's devotions without entering the vihara. Suddenly, as we were sitting there, a handful of rice and small change would come flying through the air, narrowly missing us, and land with a crash on the image-table. Sometimes it would hit the Buddha full in the face. Looking up, we would see through the door a stout, white-clad figure with a small basket under her arm hurrying off to the next place of worship. Apparently it was an old Newar custom to make an early morning round of all the temples, viharas, and wayside shrines in the neighbourhood, worshipping at each one, and a busy housewife did not have much time to spare.

The two or three hours after breakfast were generally spent in study. At eleven o'clock came lunch. For the first two or three days this was provided by one or another of the Newar families living in the neighbourhood, but in a society as caste-ridden as that of Nepal anything even remotely connected with food and drink was bound to give rise to difficulties. Hindu neighbours noticed that the Newar women not only took cooked food to the two foreign monks at the vihara but brought the dirty dishes home after they had eaten and washed them. Since one of the monks was evidently a Mleccha, a man from across the 'black water', this involved instant pollution not only for the women themselves but for all who came in contact with them, and the neighbours therefore threatened to report the matter to the police. This was no idle threat. In Nepal the caste system had the force of law, and any infringement of its provisions was punishable by a fine or imprisonment or both. It was therefore arranged that in future we should have our lunch in Anagarika Sushila's schoolroom, which was only a few doors away. She was a nun, declared the intrepid little woman, and so far as she was concerned caste restrictions did not apply to her. In any case, law or no law, no power on earth was going to stop her doing her duty by the monks of her own religion.

At eleven o'clock every morning we therefore made our way to the big upstairs room where, with the assistance of another *anagārikā*, Sushila taught two or three dozen Newar girls of various ages, and where she also lived. As a result of these visits we got to know her quite well. Buddharakshita, indeed, was soon making fun of the way in which she spoke Hindi with the boisterous jocularity that was his nearest approach to humour. Her principal fault, in the eyes of the purist, lay in the fact that when referring to her own actions she often forgot to inflect her verbs according to the sex of the speaker. This fault Buddharakshita was constantly correcting. She spoke Hindi as though she was a man, he told her, which was most improper. One day, with a flash of impatience, she told him she was tired of all this business of masculine and feminine. Since she was a nun, and was supposed to have discarded worldly conventions, she didn't think it mattered much whether she spoke like a man or like a woman. On another occasion she told us what had led her to become an *anāgarika*. She had had a younger brother, of whom she was extremely fond. This brother had died suddenly. For a long time she could not put the thought of him out of her mind. Then one night, when she was meditating, she saw him as a skeleton, white and shining, and all attachment had at once disappeared. Realizing that worldly things were impermanent, she had decided to devote herself to the spiritual life.

When we had ceremonially given thanks to Sushila and her assistant for our meal, we returned to the vihara and after a brief rest settled down to our studies again. Since it was the hottest, the afternoon was also the quietest time of day, and we could usually count on not being disturbed for at least four or five hours. While Buddharakshita ploughed his way through Hindi translations of the Pāli canon, I renewed my acquaintance with *Some Sayings of the Buddha*. I also did a little writing, and besides maintaining the journal I had been keeping since our departure from Benares, worked on verse translations of the hymn, 'Salutation to the Three Jewels', and the five most popular *paritrāṇa sūtras*, or canonical texts recited as a means of blessing and protection. At five or six o'clock someone would bring us a cup of tea, and people would start assembling for the evening worship. Buddharakshita and I laid aside our books and engaged in conversation. From a Western point of view the atmosphere was a curious blend of the religious and the domestic, the formal and the familiar. Buddharakshita and I sat cross-legged on either side of the image-table, on the pallets where we slept at night and where we meditated. In front of us on the floor were the empty tea cups. Men, women, and children – practically all of them Newars – arrived singly and in small family groups. Some busied themselves at the image-table arranging the big purple, crimson, and yellow dahlias and lighting little paper twists of acridly sweet incense. Others sat quietly chatting. All, on their arrival, saluted each of us in turn with the traditional threefold prostration. Children seemed to take a particular delight in doing this properly. Babies had their heads bumped on the floor at our feet, which sometimes made them cry. When everybody had assembled or when the flow of new arrivals seemed to have stopped, and when all those who wanted to talk to us had done so, candles would be lit and the worship begin. On special occasions, such as the full moon and new moon days, and the 'eighths' of the waxing and waning halves of the lunar month, the men devotees would gather in force and devotional songs would continue until far into the night. Some of these songs were of great beauty, and though for sheer emotional appeal they far surpassed anything I had heard in India, the note of hysterical abandon which had so repelled me at Anandamayi's ashram was completely lacking. Consequently, despite the fact that according to the most rigid Theravādin interpretation of the precepts, the enjoyment of music, even devotional music, was forbidden to monks, I never tired of listening to the rising and falling of the great wave of melody that carried one, in a mood of serene ecstasy, nearer and ever nearer to the shining lotus feet of the Buddha.

Devout Newars were by no means the only people who came to the vihara. Apart from the Bengali doctor and the Bihari headmaster of the local high school, both of whom were frequent visitors, there was the town's second doctor, also Calcutta-trained, a plump energetic Nepalese of the Malla caste who despite his Western education and his comparative youth, still wore the traditional Mogul-type dress of the country. His ancestors had been Buddhists, he told us, and he was descended from the Mallas of the Pāli scriptures, who had been among the most faithful of the Buddha's followers, and in whose territory the Master had died. In the Middle Ages his family had ruled Nepal. Besides having a dispensary in town, he was physician-in-ordinary to the Commander-in-Chief, whom he saw every day. The Commander-in-Chief was not well enough to see us personally, it seemed, but we gathered from Dr Malla that he knew of our arrival and had no objection to our staying at the vihara as long as we wished. This was welcome news. Usually foreigners were not allowed to stay more than three days in one place, and in any case we had entered the country without official permission. Unfortunately, the Commander-in-Chief's goodwill seemed to take rather a long time to permeate the lower levels of the administration, and we continued to see at the vihara a number of visitors of a less welcome type. These were the various plain-clothes police agents whom, ever since our arrival, we had noticed reclining against the wall, their looks of undisguised suspicion contrasting oddly with the reverential demeanour of the Newars. Two of them, in fact, took the trouble of coming several times a day. Only much later, after the overthrow of the Rana regime, did I learn that the Commander-in-

Chief himself was at that time an object of suspicion to the authorities in Kathmandu, and that an Assistant Commander-in-Chief had been appointed to keep an eye on him.

One evening an incident occurred that shed further light on conditions in Nepal. Happening to look up from his book, Buddharakshita saw a man standing outside the vihara door and in his usual imperious manner at once invited him in. At first the man refused, but on my friend's insistence he eventually sidled diffidently into the room, clasping his cap to his chest with both hands. He was a tailor, and according to the laws of Nepal all those who followed what orthodox Hinduism regarded as 'low-caste' occupations were prohibited from entering any place of worship or public assembly. This meant that a Buddhist goldsmith, or a Buddhist tailor, for example, was unable to enter the viharas and temples of his own faith. Venerable Shakyananda, who was sitting with us at the time, told us that when a 'low-caste' Buddhist woman had wanted to take the Refuges and Precepts from him he had had to perform the ceremony outside the vihara as she was not allowed inside. Later on we had several more opportunities of observing the workings of the caste system in Nepal. For about a week a party of some twenty uniformed police were bivouacked in the vihara courtyard. On the night of their arrival Buddharakshita and I, looking out of the window, saw a dozen different cooking-fires burning. There were a dozen different castes in the contingent, we were informed, and all of them cooked and ate separately from the rest. Some nights later, however, we saw only two cooking-fires. What had happened to everybody's caste, we wondered. One of the Newar devotees cleared up the mystery for us. On previous nights the policemen had cooked rice. Tonight they were cooking roti or unleavened bread. There was caste in rice, but not in roti. Not long afterwards we received a still more bizarre reminder of how the caste system functioned in the 'Land of the Four Colours and the Thirty-Two Castes'. In the early hours of the morning we found a man of Gurung or Magar caste on the vihara doorstep in a state of great distress. On his way back from Butaol he had been taken seriously ill and had been confined to bed for three days at an inn. One of his travelling companions, a man of much lower caste, had stayed behind and looked after him while the rest of the party went on. Since he had eaten food cooked by this man he had forfeited his caste, and his wife, fearful of pollution, refused to allow him into the house. Could he stay at the vihara for a few hours? As soon as the police station was open he would go and tell them what had happened, pay the necessary fine, and obtain a certificate stating that he had regained his caste. He would then be able to go home to his wife.

The description of Nepal as the 'Land of the Four Colours (*varṇa*) and Thirty-Two Castes (*jāti*)' we found in Part v of the *Laws of Nepal*. This part, which had been published some years before, during the Prime Ministership of Maharaja Yudha Shumshere Junga Bahadur Rana, contained the laws governing religion. Since it was written in Nepali (Gurkhali) neither my friend nor I was able to read it, but the young man who had brought it along for us to look at provided a running translation of some of the more crucial sections. Like the *Laws of Manu*, on which it was probably based, it enumerated the different hereditary castes and subcastes, defined their respective duties, and regulated, not to say restricted, social intercourse between them, paying particular attention to who could touch or not touch, eat or not eat, marry or not marry, with whom. Penalties for infringements of the code were also prescribed, some of them harsh in the extreme. As in India, the whole system weighed most heavily and oppressively on the lower castes. Besides being unable to intermarry and interdine with those of higher caste, which may not have been a very great hardship, they were also denied admittance to temples and schools. What was more serious still, perhaps, they were prohibited from opening a shop or from engaging in any form of business, which, in a country where trade was the only means of acquiring wealth, meant they were denied all means of bettering themselves economically. Power of every kind – social, political, economic, religious, and intellectual – tended to be concentrated at the top of the pyramid where, indeed, it was meant to be concentrated. In all this there was nothing strange. Hindu Nepal was only following in the footsteps of Hindu India. What was strange was the way in which the Newars and other Buddhist groups had been forcibly incorporated into the orthodox Hindu caste structure and compelled, under the threat of fines, imprisonment, or even death, to conform to a system that was in direct opposition to the tenets of their own religion. No criticism of the established order was permitted. Only two or three years ago, so Venerable Shakyananda told us, one of the Ceylon-returned monks had been flogged by the then Prime Minister with his own hands for daring to say that the caste system was incompatible with the teaching of the Buddha and ought not to be followed.[35]

Some of the laws of Nepal were clearly designed not only to force the Newars into the rigid framework of orthodox Hindu society but also to discourage the cultivation of the Newari language and literature and, indeed, to stamp out Buddhism itself altogether. Books, magazines, and newspapers could not be published in the Newari language without prior permission of the Government, and usually this permission was withheld. While the conversion of Buddhists to Hinduism was permitted, even encouraged, a Buddhist monk who administered the Refuges and Precepts to a non-Buddhist could be sent to prison for six years or subjected to any other punishment, including capital punishment, as the Prime Minister thought fit. Moreover, no one could be ordained as a Buddhist monk in Nepal. Should a Nepalese subject receive ordination abroad, and should his parents report the matter to the Government after his return, he would be forced to return to lay life and might be fined, imprisoned, or otherwise punished according to the wishes of the Prime Minister.

With laws like these on the statute book, it was only to be expected that foreign monks who gave moral support to the Newars and preached the Dharma were not particularly welcome to the authorities. We had been in Tansen for two weeks, and were becoming accustomed to the ceremonious routine of our days, when we were suddenly summoned to the local office of the Government of Nepal and questioned with regard to our intentions. Our original idea had been to go on pilgrimage to Muktinath, we explained, but owing to illness and to the onset of the rains we had been forced to abandon this plan. As soon as the ulcer on my foot was sufficiently healed we would be returning to India. This explanation was apparently considered satisfactory, and no further questions were asked. However, we were told that we would have to leave Tansen within two or three days. After returning to the vihara and discussing the situation with the devotees we therefore decided to go and see the Assistant Commander-in-Chief and ask for an extension. This gentleman was a Brahmin, and an orthodox one at that. In fact, he had the title of Purohit Guru, which meant that he was one of the main pillars of the ecclesiastical establishment and wielded a great deal of influence. Venerable Shakyananda and two or three of the devotees accompanied us to his house. After we had waited a considerable time a message came that we should stand in the middle of the street and that the Assistant Commander-in-Chief would speak to us from the fourth or fifth storey veranda. In this godlike manner, apparently, Nepalese Government officials were accustomed to interview members of the public. Tearing a leaf from my journal, I at once wrote a note. According to Buddhist tradition, I said, it was not proper for a monk to speak to a layman from a lower level. We must speak together on the same level or not at all. When Venerable Shakyananda and the devotees learned what I had written they were aghast. Such effrontery would land us all in jail, they protested – and fled. However, the servant returned after a few minutes and asked us to come upstairs. In a room on the first floor we found a thin, elderly man in a white dhoti and sacred thread sitting on a mattress surrounded by a perfect horde of small children. It was the Assistant Commander-in-Chief. As he did not salute us, we did not salute him, and as he did not ask us to sit down, we sat down without being asked. Whether because he was afraid of assassination, or of ritual pollution, or whether (what was most likely) because we had put him at a disadvantage by addressing him in English, which he understood but did not speak very well, the Purohit Guru seemed extraordinarily nervous and ill at ease. Our business was therefore soon concluded. When we had explained why we were in Tansen, emphasized that we had no interest in politics, stressed our desire to return to India as soon as possible, and shown him my foot, he muttered something to the effect that it would be all right for us to stay in Tansen until my ulcer had healed and I could walk properly. Whereupon we thanked him for his kindness and left.

Despite the success of our interview, Buddharakshita and I knew that we could not stay in Tansen much longer. Indeed, we had no real wish to stay. The rainy season had begun, and though as novices we were not obliged to observe the 'Rains Residence' that was incumbent on all fully-ordained *bhikkhus*, having preached the Dharma to U Chandramani's disciples as best we could we were now eager to return to India and find a place where it would be possible for us to go 'into retreat' for a few months. The last two weeks of our stay passed more rapidly than the first. Now that the ulcer was healing, and I could walk more easily, our time tended to be divided between the Mahachaitya Vihara at the top end of the town and the Ananda Vihara at the bottom, and the accelerated rhythm of our days included sermons and celebrations at both places. One afternoon, after a new moon day function at the Ananda Vihara, we set off with a party of devotees and scaled the heights behind Tansen. Though it was a stiff climb, and though Buddharakshita and I were perspiring freely when we reached the top, the view that met our eyes would have made far greater efforts worthwhile. Brilliantly white against the blueness of the sky, the gigantic masses of the Himalayas rose in the distance before us sheer and awful as the walls of heaven. Through the smoke-blue valleys at their feet drifted flock upon flock of small white clouds. One of our companions, more knowledgeable than the rest, pointed out some of the principal peaks. To the west was Dhaulagiri, to the east Annapurna, while in between, almost due north from Tansen, rose a peak the Nepalese name of which meant 'Fish Tail'. For a time we stood motionless, conscious of nothing but the silent sublimity of those immaculate heights and the coolness of the breeze that blew straight down from them on to our perspiring bodies. Then our attention was diverted to things nearer at hand. On an eminence to the east huddled a small group of buildings. They had mud walls and roofs of thatch and were completely encircled by a rough stone perimeter wall. This was Shrinagar, whispered the devotees, the residence of the Commander-in-Chief. To me it looked more like a Stone Age fort than the home of one of the most powerful men in Nepal. Though there must have been quite a number of people inside, there was no sign of life whatever. As we already knew, the Commander-in-Chief lived in virtual isolation. He never went out, and except for Dr Malla, who seemed to act as a kind of intermediary, nobody from the town ever came to see him. As I looked across at the little hilltop settlement I could not help feeling that its quietness was the quietness of those who watch, and its inactivity the inactivity of those who hold themselves in readiness for an attack.

A day or two later we left Tansen. Several dozen people, including Venerable Shakyananda and the two *anagārikās*, accompanied us down into the valley as far as a small wayside shop, where the last photographs were taken and where we said goodbye. Though we had spent only four weeks in their town, everybody seemed to be deeply affected by the parting, and as they rose to their feet after making their final prostrations, or pressed into our hands small packets of sugar-candy, many of the devotees wept. Wanderers though we were, we felt sorry to be bidding farewell to so much love and devotion. The journey back to Butaol passed without incident. Or rather, it passed without incident until we were within a mile of our destination. At this point the light drizzle which we had encountered on our way down from Mashyam turned into heavy rain, and we were forced to take shelter in a fisherman's hut. This hut not only overlooked but actually overhung the river which, swollen by the monsoon rains, was now roaring more loudly than ever. By nightfall, however, we were safe in Butaol, and soon the same devotees who had seen us off four weeks earlier were busy making us comfortable at the Padmagarbha Vihara.

48
ACADEMIC INTERLUDE

The Benares Hindu University campus was several square miles in extent and criss-crossed by broad tree-lined avenues along which plied a small army of brightly painted cycle-rickshaws. Some distance behind the trees, and usually at considerable intervals, rose the red sandstone blocks of the university buildings, all of them in the 'neo-Hindu' style of architecture, and all of enormous size. 'Buddha Kuti', Bhikkhu Jagdish Kashyap's modest two-storey residence, was situated in a quiet corner just inside the perimeter wall, not far from the university post office, and several miles from the red sandstone splendours of the main entrance. Buddharakshita and I had not been long in Benares before we went to pay our respects to our kind adviser and inform him of the successful outcome of our mission to Kusinara. We were staying, not very happily, at the Burmese Rest House in the city, where the two harsh-voiced, rough-mannered Burmese monks jeered at us for being vegetarians. 'Not eat meat!' they exclaimed angrily. 'You *must* eat meat! If you don't eat meat you're not Buddhists, you're Hindus!' Though the rainy season was now well advanced, we were still no nearer to finding a place in which to spend the Rains Residence than we had been in Nepal. Buddharakshita was strongly in favour of our making another attempt to enter Ceylon, where we would be able to study and where we could take the higher ordination. Partly because I was without means of identification, and partly because I did not feel well enough to embark on further wanderings, I was against this plan. It was Bhikkhu Kashyap who resolved the dilemma. With characteristic generosity he made it clear that, if it would be of any use, there was room for one of us at Buddha Kuti, but only for one, and that he would be happy to provide not only board and lodging but instruction. This of course meant the end of the partnership between Buddharakshita and myself, which had now lasted uninterruptedly for two and a half years. After prolonged discussion, my impetuous friend suddenly announced that his mind was made up. He would go to Ceylon. I should stay in Benares with Bhikkhu Kashyap. Since I was unfit to travel, and needed a bit of looking after, this was clearly the best arrangement. In any case, he added, unable to resist a parting shot, it was me that Bhikkhu Kashyap wanted as a disciple, not him. Within twenty-four hours I had moved into Buddha Kuti and Buddharakshita was on his way to Calcutta.

Though I was sorry to lose my warm-hearted but irascible companion, once the actual parting was over my predominant feeling was one of relief. Living with Buddharakshita had at times been a nightmare, and it was only now that I was once more on my own that I realized how great the strain had been. True, since our ordination he had been easier to get on with. The deference and submissiveness of the Newars had been as balm to his soul, and seeing him better-tempered than he had been for a long time I had begun to entertain hopes that the demon by which he was periodically afflicted had been permanently exorcized. These hopes were soon shattered. While we were at the Padmagarbha Vihara there arrived in Butaol a young Newar monk who had just spent two years in Ceylon. Not content with exhibiting his accomplishments to an admiring circle of friends and relations, and covering the walls of the vihara with the Sinhalese posters of all the lectures he had given, he tried to treat Buddharakshita and me as he thought newly-ordained *śrāmaṇeras* ought to be treated by a fully ordained monk who had just spent two years in the very citadel of orthodoxy. Buddharakshita bore it for a couple of days, then after an altercation which did credit neither to him nor to his antagonist he exploded. The young monk's grandmother did her best to assuage my friend's wrath. 'Take no notice of him,' she confided. 'He's the fool of the family. We only sent him to Ceylon to become a monk because he wasn't bright enough to be of much use in the family business.' But the damage had been done. The demon was back. Yet despite the tensions of our life together, and my relief at finding myself once more on my own, I was far from failing to appreciate the many sterling qualities that Buddharakshita undoubtedly possessed. But for him I might never have spent two years as a wandering ascetic, might never have made the difficult transition from the old way of life to the new, and for that I was deeply grateful.

In less than a week I was feeling perfectly at home in my new surroundings, and had embarked on a course of study that was to keep me busy – almost without interruption – for seven of the quietest and happiest months I have ever known. Life at Buddha Kuti was simple in the extreme, and there were no distractions. Apart from a bookcase filled ceiling-high with books my room contained only a string bed, a table, and a chair. Bhikkhu Kashyap's room, which was next door, and communicated with mine, contained no more – not even a piece of carpet on the floor, or a picture on the wall. As I soon realized, it was not that my new preceptor attached any special importance to asceticism: he simply did not bother with material things. Except for two or three students reading Pāli for their BA, who came once a week, there were no visitors, and even the married nephew who lived downstairs was rarely seen or heard. Other than Bhikkhu Kashyap, the only person with whom I had any contact was the servant, a thinner, darker, less sprightly version of Shankara Pillai who had the distinction of being the illegitimate son of a Sinhalese monk.

Our day began at dawn. After we had breakfasted on tea and toast (the latter saturated with ghee and sprinkled with sugar) I read Pāli, Abhidhamma, and Logic with Bhikkhu Kashyap, then returned to my room and did the exercises he had set me. This kept me busy until noon, when we had the usual rice-and-curry lunch. Bhikkhu Kashyap, mindful of the Indian equivalent of 'an apple a day keeps the doctor away,' always rounded off the meal by chewing a couple of cloves of raw garlic. In the afternoon, having enjoyed a brief siesta, I either studied on my own, referring to my teacher occasionally if necessary, or engaged in literary work. When it was dusk Bhikkhu Kashyap took his stick and we went for a walk. Every time we drew abreast of one of the big *margosa* trees that lined the broad avenues through which we passed I was struck by a strong current of vitality. Perhaps it was only the sun's heat radiating from the rough grey trunks, but I could not help feeling that the trees were alive, even as I was alive – that they were living presences, almost personalities. The first time we went out Bhikkhu Kashyap confessed that only a year ago he was so fat that he could not walk. If he tried to do so the insides of his thighs chafed so badly that he bled. For the last year, however, he had been following naturopathy, and having succeeded in reducing his weight by about a third was now a firm believer in that system of medicine. A few weeks later, when I fell ill with jaundice, he persuaded me to follow naturopathy too. On our return to Buddha Kuti I took a glass of hot milk (strictly speaking against the rules, but Bhikkhu Kashyap insisted) and carried on with my studies. At ten or eleven o'clock I paid my respects to my teacher in the traditional manner, asking forgiveness for whatever offences I might have committed in the course of the day, and retired for the night to my string bed.

The three subjects that I read with Bhikkhu Kashyap (or Kashyap-ji, as he was generally known) were all quite new to me and I cultivated them with varying degrees of success. Not having much of a gift for languages, I had the greatest difficulty with Pāli, the ancient Indian language in which the Theravāda redaction of the Buddha's teaching had been preserved. According to Kashyap-ji, who besides being trained in Western academic disciplines was a pandit of the old type, and had learned everything by heart at an early age, Pāli grammar was child's play, and he did his best to encourage me with the reminder that in Pāli there were only 700 rules, whereas Sanskrit had 3,000. I was far from finding Pāli child's play. Though I did my exercises every day, and committed to memory long lists of conjugations and declensions, I did so with grim determination rather than with the gay abandon that Kashyap-ji seemed to think appropriate to the subject. Sometimes I felt dull and bored. Luckily my teacher was not one of those who believe that you first have to learn the grammar of a language thoroughly before being allowed to look at a text, and before many weeks had passed I had been introduced to the Tipiṭaka. Some of its books were composed in ridiculously simple Pāli, explained Kashyap-ji, and a smattering of grammar was all that was needed to understand them. Starting with these books, and progressing gradually to others more difficult, one could easily get through the forty-five volumes of the Royal Thai edition of the Tipitaka in a twelvemonth. Why, it was not even a volume a week! Though I did not live up to these expectations, and though my knowledge of Pāli never went much beyond the smattering necessary to carry me through such works as the *Dhammapada* and the *Udāna*, the delight of being able to study the Buddha's teaching in what many

Buddhists believed were his own words more than compensated for the difficulties of learning the language in which it had been imparted.

With both Abhidhamma and Logic I fared rather better, especially with Logic. Though in my early and middle teens I had read quite widely in philosophy, for some reason or other I had completely neglected this ancient and venerable partner of metaphysics, ethics, politics, aesthetics, and rhetoric. It was therefore with some trepidation that I set about making good the omission. But I need not have worried. Once I had emerged from the thorny thickets of Formal Logic I found myself in one of the most fascinating and enjoyable stretches of the intellectual terrain in which it had ever been my lot to wander, and with companions among the most delightful it had ever been my good fortune to meet. Bradley, admittedly, was a little forbidding, but Mill and Carveth Read I found exhilarating in the extreme, while F. C. S. Schiller's *Formal Logic*, a Radical Empiricist's brilliant exposure of the aridities and absurdities of the subject, as traditionally expounded, was undoubtedly one of the most hilarious books I had ever encountered. While I was reading it there escaped me from time to time chuckles – even guffaws – which Kashyap-ji, in his room next door, never heard when I was studying Pāli.

However conventional Kashyap-ji's teaching methods might have been, his manner of teaching was unconventional enough. When I entered his room (the communicating door was always left open) it was generally to find him stretched out on his string bed like a stranded whale, sound asleep, for though he could work day and night when necessary he could sleep day and night too with equal ease. As Professor of Pāli and Buddhist Philosophy his duties were minimal, and much of his time was therefore spent on the string bed, which creaked protestingly from time to time, and where he slept without benefit of either mattress or pillow. On my coughing, or murmuring 'Bhante!' a single eyelid would twitch, whereupon I would put my question, which was generally on some knotty point of Pāli grammar, or Abhidhamma, or Logic, which I had not been able to unravel by myself. Without opening his eyes, and without moving, Kashyap-ji would proceed to clear up the difficulty, heaving the words up from the depths of his enormous frame and rolling them around on his tongue before releasing them in slow, deliberate utterance. Sometimes he rumbled on for only a few minutes, sometimes for half an hour. Whatever he said was clear, precise, and to the point. If I asked about a particular passage of text, he always knew whereabouts it came, what had come before, and what followed. Yet all the time he had hardly bothered to wake up. As I returned to my room I would hear behind me a sigh and a snore and before I had settled down at my table Kashyap-ji would be sound asleep again.

The intercourse between us was not always of this kind. When not stretched out on the string bed, Kashyap-ji could be both animated and entertaining, with a pleasant touch of the unsophisticated humour of his Bihari peasant ancestry. Sometimes he spoke about his experiences in Ceylon, where he had studied at the Vidyalankara Pirivena (where I had seen him at the 1944 Convocation, when he came to receive the title of Tripitakācārya), and where he had been ordained. Though he had enjoyed his stay, he did not have a very high opinion of the Sinhalese Buddhists. Monks and lay people alike were narrow-minded and unintelligent. Formalism was rife. Once, when he was returning from his almsround, his robe had come undone, and in order to adjust it he had put his begging-bowl down on a patch of grass. 'Just look at the Indian monk!' shrieked an old woman who saw him. 'Supposed to be a scholar! He doesn't even know how to respect his bowl!' According to tradition, begging-bowls should never be placed on the bare ground. On another occasion he was lecturing on the well-known Buddhist doctrine of *anattā*, literally 'no self' or 'no soul'. In order to understand the meaning of *anattā*, he had declared, one had first to understand the meaning of *attā*, 'self' or 'soul'. For unless one knew what particular concept of 'self' or 'soul' the Buddha was negating how could one possibly know what his teaching of 'no self' or 'no soul' was meant to convey? This was apparently beyond the Sinhalese Buddhists. There were angry shouts of protest from the audience. 'We don't want you bringing your Hindu philosophy here!' yelled the monks. 'Sit down! Sit down!' In vain Kashyap-ji tried to explain that it was not his intention to defend the detested *attā* doctrine. He was not allowed to continue his lecture. Some of his experiences had been of a more amusing kind. Sinhalese monks were always wanting to know which *nikāya* or sect of the monastic order he belonged to. In fact, said Kashyap-ji, they were no less inquisitive on this score than orthodox Hindus were on the subject of caste. His usual reply was that he belonged to 'Buddha Nikāya'. One group of monks, not satisfied with this, had asked him whether he covered his right shoulder with his robe when leaving the monastery or whether he left it uncovered, the point of the enquiry being that some *nikāyas* followed one practice, some the other. 'When it's cold,' Kashyap-ji had replied, 'I cover both shoulders. When it's hot, I keep one shoulder uncovered, and when it's very hot I don't wear any robe at all!' One day, when he had gratefully acknowledged the part played by Ceylon in the preservation of the Pāli scriptures, my preceptor delivered himself of his considered opinion of the Sinhalese Buddhists in the following memorable words. 'Sangharakshita-ji,' he said, speaking slowly and deliberately, and with evident feeling, 'they are a set of monkeys ... sitting on a treasure ... the value of which ... they do *not* understand.'

Much as Kashyap-ji's anecdotes reflected on the Buddhists of Ceylon, there was nothing in his attitude to suggest either self-righteousness or censoriousness, and he was capable of telling a story against himself with equal relish. Before being appointed professor at Benares Hindu University he had spent some time in Penang, where there was a large and wealthy Chinese business community, and a flourishing Buddhist movement. Whenever he performed his devotions in the magnificent temple they had built he saluted the image of the Buddha but, being a Theravādin, he did not salute the images of Kuan Yin and the other attendant bodhisattvas. One day the Chinese Mahāyāna Buddhist with whom he was staying gave him for lunch nothing but rice. When Kashyap-ji, mildly astonished, enquired what had happened to the curries he was told that the rice was the main thing. 'Of course the rice is the main thing,' agreed Kashyap-ji, 'but the curries are also necessary.' 'Just so,' retorted his host. 'The curries are also necessary, as you say. Similarly, the Buddha is the main thing – no one doubts that; but the bodhisattvas are necessary too.' After this homely lesson, said my teacher, he was always careful to salute the bodhisattvas.

Though Kashyap-ji definitely preferred the 'rationalism tinged with mysticism' of the Theravāda to the 'mysticism tinged with rationalism' of the Mahāyāna, and though his main interest in life was the revival of Pāli studies in India, he was an exceptionally tolerant and open-minded person with a real respect for the right – and duty – of the individual to think for himself. For him, the born teacher, teaching represented not a process of indoctrination but a sharing of knowledge, a pooling of intellectual resources, and while he was always ready to answer my questions he never made the slightest attempt to influence my thinking. On the contrary, in after years he was fond of maintaining that in some respects he had learned as much from me as I had from him. While it was not for me to contradict my preceptor on such a point as this, whatever exchange there might have been between us must have been very unequal – 'the price of a hundred oxen for the price of nine'. Besides sharing with me his vast knowledge of the Pāli scriptures, especially the Abhidhamma, Kashyap-ji was the means of introducing me to some of the less well-known branches of Indian religious tradition. Among these were Jainism, and the heterodox (i.e. non-Vedic, even anti-Vedic) post-medieval mysticisms, some of which were believed by scholars to have been continuous with the last phases of Tantric Buddhism. In addition to the texts of my regular trivium I read with him the Jaina Apabhramsa equivalent of the *Dhammapada* (with which, as he pointed out, it had a number of verses in common), and a riddling, esoteric work by Kabir known as the *Bijak*. For all members of the *śramaṇa* as distinct from the *brāhmaṇa* group of Indian religions, Kashyap-ji indeed had a strong sympathy, a sympathy that was by no means confined to books. On our rare expeditions into Benares, when I accompanied him on visits to Jain monk-scholars and Kabir Panthi ascetics, I could see for myself how cordial his relations with them all were, and how much they, on their part, loved and venerated him.

As might have been expected, during the whole of the time that I was with him Kashyap-ji made no attempt to restrict my freedom, in particular my freedom to read and write what I pleased. All his books, as well as his ticket to the university library, were at my disposal, and he never questioned the use I made of them. Indeed, it did not seem to occur to him to question it. When not occupied with Pāli, Abhidhamma, and Logic I therefore read more widely than I had done for several years. As the mood seized me, I also wrote. After being confined to works that I had come across more or less by accident, it was delightful to be able to range at will through all the fields of literature, ancient and modern, Eastern and Western, sacred and profane. But delightful though it was, such freedom was not without problems of its own. More clearly than ever before, it brought out into the open a conflict in my interests, perhaps a conflict in my nature itself, which the circumstances of my wandering life with Buddharakshita had tended to obscure.

The nature of this conflict was well illustrated by two letters which I received during the second half of my stay at Buddha Kuti. One was from the redoubtable Bhikkhu Soma. He had already taken me very

Bhikshu Jagdish Kashyap, Sangharakshita's first Buddhist teacher

seriously to task for 'gadding about' instead of settling in one place and getting down to serious work, and having seen some of my recent contributions to the Buddhist magazines of Ceylon he now wrote to put me to rights as regards my literary work. When I could write such excellent articles on Buddhist philosophy, he demanded, why did I waste my time writing those foolish poems? By a strange coincidence the other letter, which was from a Sinhalese Buddhist laywoman, arrived on the same day, and expressed exactly the opposite point of view. When I could write such beautiful poems on Buddhism, she asked, why did I spend so much time writing those dry, intellectual articles? The truth of the matter was that I agreed – and disagreed – with both correspondents. The conflict was not so much between the philosophically-inclined monk and the poetry-loving laywoman, as between Sangharakshita I and Sangharakshita II. Sangharakshita I wanted to enjoy the beauty of nature, to read and write poetry, to listen to music, to look at paintings and sculpture, to experience emotion, to lie in bed and dream, to see places, to meet people. Sangharakshita II wanted to realize the truth, to read and write philosophy, to observe the precepts, to get up early and meditate, to mortify the flesh, to fast and pray. Sometimes Sangharakshita I was victorious, sometimes Sangharakshita II, while occasionally there was an uneasy duumvirate. What they ought to have done, of course, was to marry and give birth to Sangharakshita III, who would have united beauty and truth, poetry and philosophy, spontaneity and discipline; but this seemed to be a dream impossible of fulfilment. For the last two and a half years Sangharakshita II had ruled practically unchallenged. Aided and abetted by Buddharakshita, who strongly disapproved of poetry, he had in fact sought to finish off Sangharakshita I altogether, and but for the timely intervention of Swami Ramdas, who firmly declared that writing poetry was *not* incompatible with the spiritual life, Sangharakshita I might well have died a premature death in Muvattupuzha.

However, despite the bludgeoning that he had received he had not died, and after leading a furtive existence in Nepal he was now coming into his own again at Buddha Kuti. Kashyap-ji's dealings were of course mainly with Sangharakshita II, but he had no objection to Sangharakshita I being around, and even spoke to him occasionally. Soon Sangharakshita I was feeling strong enough to demand equal rights. If Sangharakshita II devoted the afternoon to *The Path of Purity*,

Sangharakshita I spent the evening immersed in the poetry of Matthew Arnold, which for some reason or other exerted a powerful influence during this period. When the former wrote an article on Buddhist philosophy, or edited the second edition of Kashyap-ji's *Buddhism for Everybody*, the latter composed poems. Sometimes, while one self was busy copying out extracts from the books he had been reading, the other would look idly out of the window and watch the falling of the rain. One day there was a violent clash between them. Angered by the encroachments of Sangharakshita I, who was reading more poetry than ever, and who had written a long poem which, though it had a Buddhist theme, was still a poem, Sangharakshita II suddenly burned the two notebooks in which his rival had written all the poems he had composed from the time of their departure from England right down to about the middle of their sojourn in Singapore. After this catastrophe, which shocked them both, they learned to respect each other's spheres of influence. Occasionally they even collaborated, as in the completion of the blank verse rendition of the five *paritrāṇa sūtras* that had been started in Nepal. There were even rare moments when it seemed that, despite their quarrels, they might get married one day.

Though the months at Buddha Kuti passed quickly enough, and though the rainy season ended and winter began without any change in my way of life, I was not so remote from the world, nor so deeply immersed in my studies, as to be altogether beyond the reach of outside influences. To begin with there were letters from Buddharakshita, who after spending a short time with Bhikkhu Soma was now staying with the German monks at Dodanduwa, in southern Ceylon. Though he was making good progress with Pāli, his Hindu prejudices were evidently receiving a tremendous hammering and he seemed to be suffering from a species of cultural shock. From within India there was the news of the fierce and bitter controversy raging round the proposed Hindu Code Bill, in connection with which I first heard the name of the Scheduled Castes leader Dr B.R. Ambedkar, then Law Minister in the Government of India. Owing to the opposition of orthodox Hindu elements within the ruling party itself, the Bill was eventually passed only in a fragmented and mutilated form, and in disgust Ambedkar resigned from the Cabinet. In later years I came to know him personally, and after his death in 1956 was deeply involved in the movement of mass conversion to Buddhism that he had initiated among his Untouchable followers. From Benares itself came the news of the arrival of the Sacred Relics of the *arahants* Śāriputra and Maudgalyāyana, the Buddha's two 'Great Disciples'. After spending ninety years in the Victoria and Albert Museum they had been returned to India at the beginning of the year, at the request of the Maha Bodhi Society, and were now being taken round various parts of India, as well as to some of the Buddhist countries, and exposed for the veneration of the people. Everywhere they went they had been received with tremendous enthusiasm. In Benares, however, the welcome was comparatively muted. Kashyap-ji and I went and paid our respects to the relics at the Vizianagaram Palace, where we found them enshrined in the Throne Room on a solid silver chair. To the right of the relics stood a dozen or so yellow-robed monks, among whom I soon detected the gleaming pate and vulturine features of His Holiness from Calcutta. On seeing me he gave a violent start, and biting his lip turned away without a word.

Finally, only a few weeks before my departure from Benares, there was an unexpected visit from Venerable M. Sangharatana Thera, Secretary of the Maha Bodhi Society at Sarnath. A wall had just been built round the Maha Bodhi Rest House at Bodh Gaya, he announced in his usual voluble fashion. The work had cost 2,000 rupees and the amount had been donated by one of the richest and most important High Priests in the whole of Ceylon. The High Priest himself and a dozen other monks were even now at Bodh Gaya. All the week they had been chanting, in a special bamboo pavilion constructed inside the hall of the Rest House, and in two days' time the wall would be solemnly consecrated. He would of course have to attend the ceremony and accept the wall on behalf of the Maha Bodhi Society. Would I care to accompany him? Though I was not particularly keen on seeing the wall, despite the glowing accounts Venerable Sangharatana gave of it, I was very eager indeed to see Bodh Gaya, the site of the Buddha's Supreme Enlightenment. Sarnath, Kusinara, and Lumbini I had already seen earlier in the year, but Bodh Gaya, the most important of the four great holy places, was as yet unvisited. With Kashyap-ji's permission, I therefore accepted the invitation our good-hearted friend had so warmly extended.

Bodh Gaya! Bodh Gaya! How many people have come to you in the course of ages! How many pilgrim feet have trodden the dust of your groves, how many pairs of hands been joined in silent adoration beneath the wide-spreading boughs of the Tree of Enlightenment, how many heads touched in profound thanksgiving the edge of the diamond throne! Bodh Gaya! Bodh Gaya! How beautiful you are in the morning, with the sunlight streaming on the renovated façade of your great temple as it rises four-square against the cloudless blue sky! How beautiful in the evening, when in the shadowy depths of the deserted temple courtyard a thousand votive lamps glitter like reflections of the stars! Bodh Gaya, I shall always remember how beautiful you were the first time I saw you, when my heart was young, and you made me your own!

The shrines of Sarnath, Kusinara, and Lumbini had all been destroyed in the twelfth century, and both the Mulagandhakuti Vihara and the Temple of the Recumbent Buddha had been built in modern times. Since they had been built by Buddhists, their management was naturally in Buddhist hands. At Bodh Gaya the situation was different. The Maha Bodhi Temple, or Temple of the Great Enlightenment, restored by General Sir Alexander Cunningham in 1870, was substantially the one built in the second century on the remains of an earlier Aśokan structure. In the course of two millennia the level of the surrounding countryside had risen by twenty or thirty feet, with the result that the entire temple complex, including the bodhi tree and the diamond throne, now stood in an enormous rectangular well. Until earlier that year, management of the temple had been in the hands of the Hindu mahant, or abbot, of Bodh Gaya, then the second biggest landowner in the state of Bihar, one of whose predecessors had somehow gained possession of it in the sixteenth century. As an orthodox Brahmin, the mahant's main interest was in the offerings of the pilgrims, who in recent centuries had been making their way to Bodh Gaya in ever-increasing numbers. Under an Act of the State Government, however, management of the temple had now been transferred to a committee, but as the constitution of the committee had been so framed as to ensure a permanent Hindu majority things were not much better than they had been in the mahant's time. Images of the Buddhas and bodhisattvas were still being smeared with vermilion, and in a shed-like structure near the main entrance five of them were being palmed off on a gullible Hindu public as representations of the five Pandava brothers, legendary heroes whose exploits were described in the *Mahābhārata*. To assist the deception, the images had been draped with pieces of dirty cloth, so that only their faces were visible. Venerable Sangharatana was furious. 'Just like the bloody Hindus!' he exploded, tearing the cloths from the images and flinging them violently on the floor. 'Always trying to assimilate Buddhism to their own dirty religion! Always trying to get a bit more money out of the stupid pilgrims! Pilgrims? Bah! Superstitious idiots! They deserve to be robbed!' Though rather taken aback by this un-monk-like outburst, I could not help sympathizing with Venerable Sangharatana's feelings. As I well knew, he was a personal disciple of Anagarika Dharmapala, and for more than thirty years Dharmapala had tried without success to gain for the Buddhists some say in the management of their own most sacred shrine.

In the holy of holies, a pleasingly simple chamber lit only from the door, it was even worse. A stone lingam, or phallic symbol of the god Shiva, had been let into the middle of the floor in front of the offering-table, just where one was likely to trip over it in the semi-darkness. Long-legged Brahmins clambered like monkeys all over the altar, passing backwards and forwards in front of the great sedent image of the Buddha, and vociferously insisted on doing the pilgrim's worshipping for him – for a consideration. Nothing we were able to say could still their clamour or convince them that we did not require their services. We were Buddhist monks, we protested. We were quite capable of worshipping the Buddha ourselves. They took absolutely no notice. 'We are Brahmins,' they choroused, jumping down off the altar and grabbing us by the arm. 'We are the priests here. We will make all the offerings. We will pray to God for you. How much will you pay us?' In circumstances like these it was not easy to concentrate on the great golden figure in the background, or to feel that I was in the place where the Buddha had gained Supreme Enlightenment. Had it not been for the Tibetan pilgrims, indeed, I might not have really felt it at all, and my most vivid memories of that first visit to Bodh Gaya would have been of evading the clutches of mercenary Brahmin 'priests' and consecrating boundary walls.

As it was, the Tibetans were my salvation. They were poor, they were ragged, they were dirty, and the other pilgrims looked down on them, but they had walked all the way from Tibet, some of them with babies on their backs, and now they came shuffling in through the gate with their prayer-wheels and rosaries in their hands and expressions of ecstasy on their upturned faces. For them history did not exist. They knew nothing about the mahant, nothing about the management of the temple. They did not even see the Brahmins. As they circumambulated the temple, as they prostrated themselves before the diamond throne, as they lit butter-lamps round the bodhi tree, they saw only the naked fact of the Buddha's Supreme Enlightenment, and through their eyes, even if not with my own, I could see it too.

49
IN THE LAND OF THE GREAT DISCIPLES

Spring had come to the plains of Bihar, and the beauty of the landscape as it lay in the bright morning sunshine beneath an expanse of soft blue sky was such as to melt the heart of artist and farmer alike. In all directions, far as the eye could see, stretched the chequer-work of the fields, their dusty brown soil now flushed with the lighter or darker green of rice, wheat, pulse, potatoes, and other early crops. On either side of the road stood huge shady peepul trees, like that beneath which the Buddha gained Enlightenment, and tamarinds with gnarled boughs and light, feathery foliage. Beyond, in the middle distance, mango groves brooded like banks of cloud. Some of the fields were edged by smooth-stemmed areca palms, or else by squat, clumsy-looking date palms with deep notches in their trunks where they had been tapped for toddy. Nearer at hand grew clumps of graceful bamboos, sahajan trees whose straight slim branches were white with bloom, and another tree which, though devoid of leaves, was decked out with enormous scarlet flowers that, according to Kashyap-ji, were traditionally likened to lumps of raw meat. After the rains that had fallen during the night the air was fresh and clean and full of the sweet scent of the sulphur-coloured mango blossom. On the horizon to the south, ten or twelve miles away, the hills of Rajgir loomed grey and purple through the mist.

We had left Benares a week earlier, on the last day of January. Kashyap-ji had decided to take a holiday. After twelve years at the Hindu University he was badly in need of a change. He was tired of the caste-ridden atmosphere of the place, tired of its undisguised hostility to Buddhist studies, tired of having so little to do. As he had already confided to me, he was there very much on sufferance. Dominated as it was by orthodox Brahmins, the university had not wanted to have a Professor of Pāli and Buddhist Philosophy at all, and Kashyap-ji's appointment had been due to the insistence of the multimillionaire philanthropist Jugal Kishore Birla, a benefactor whose wishes the university could not afford to ignore. But though the university had been forced to appoint a Professor of Pāli and Buddhist Philosophy it was not obliged to supply him with pupils. In fact it made it as difficult as possible for him to get any. Under university regulations, no one could take Pāli without also taking Sanskrit. In other words Pāli and Buddhist Philosophy were not allowed to become alternatives to Sanskrit and Hindu Philosophy. One could take Sanskrit and Pāli, or only Sanskrit, but under no circumstances could one take only Pāli. So effectively did these tactics limit the number of Kashyap-ji's students that he never had more than three or four, sometimes none at all. For someone as devoted to his subject as he was this was a bitter disappointment. He had accepted the professorship only because he hoped it would enable him to make some contribution to the advancement of Buddhist studies and thus, indirectly, to the cause of Buddhism; but as it became more obvious every year that Pāli and Buddhist Philosophy were unwelcome guests at the Benares Hindu University, he had come to the conclusion that he was wasting his time there and he was now thinking of resigning. Before taking this drastic step, however, he wanted to get away from the university for a while and think things over. We would both have a holiday. He would show me some of the holy places of Bihar, and from there, perhaps, we would go up into the foothills of the eastern Himalayas, to a place called Kalimpong.

For the past week, therefore, we had been in Bihar, in the land of the Great Disciples. The disciples in question were Śāriputra and Maudgalyāyana, the two principal followers of the Buddha, who like Kashyap-ji himself had come from that part of India. They had both been born, in fact, not far from Nalanda, and it was towards the ruins of the great monastic university that had subsequently grown up on this spot that we were now making our way. Outwardly at least the seven days that we had so far spent in Bihar had been more eventful than seven months in Benares. In Patna, the ancient Pataliputra, where our tour had started, we were constantly accosted in the streets by young men who asked us if we were Buddhist monks and who, when we replied in the affirmative, begged us to establish a Buddhist temple there and propagate the teaching of the Buddha. Only a few months earlier the relics of Śāriputra and Maudgalyāyana had been received all over the state amidst scenes of tremendous popular enthusiasm, and demands for the revival of the faith that had brought so much glory to Bihar were very much in the air. In Bihar Sharif, where we addressed two meetings, we had spent the night at the local college, which was said to be built on the site of the ancient monastic university of Odantapuri – as, indeed, was the whole town. From Bihar Sharif we had walked to the village of Dipnagar, and from Dipnagar, where we had addressed another meeting the previous night, we had decided to walk to Nalanda. For Kashyap-ji this was quite a feat, but the interest and enthusiasm that surrounded us at every stage of our journey – so different from anything he had encountered in Benares – was having a tonic effect on him and he felt equal to any exertion, even that of walking.

He also felt that he was a monk again. For the last two days we had been 'going for alms' in the traditional manner, a thing he had not done since leaving Ceylon. Like the monks at Sarnath, he had taken it for granted that this was no longer possible in India. Unlike the monks at Sarnath, however, he was willing to make the experiment, and to find out for himself whether the success Buddharakshita and I had had with our begging-bowls in the villages between Kusinara and Lumbini had been simply a happy accident or whether it was, in fact, still possible for a Buddhist monk to subsist on alms in the India of the twentieth century. As one of us at least had expected, the experiment was entirely successful. Both in Bihar Sharif and in Dipnagar we had each collected enough food for half a dozen monks, and townsfolk and villagers alike had given not only with devotion and joy but with the consciousness that we – and they – were reviving a tradition that had been dead for six or seven hundred years. Kashyap-ji was delighted. A great problem had been solved. No longer was it necessary to depend for one's maintenance on educational institutions unsympathetic to Buddhism or worldly-minded Buddhist organizations more interested in collecting money than in preaching the Dharma. As in the days of old, a monk could rely for his support directly on the people. In his mind's eye he saw himself walking from village to village with his begging-bowl all over Bihar, teaching Pāli and Buddhist Philosophy wherever he went.

Nalanda was only three miles south of Dipnagar, on the Rajgir road, and exhilarated as we were by the beauty and freshness of the morning and by a new-found sense of freedom it did not take us much more than an hour to get there. After taking tea with Venerable Fu Chin Lama, an ancient Chinese monk, in the tiny Rest House he had built just behind the railway station, we went for alms to the nearby village of Kul, which according to the accounts of the seventh-century Chinese pilgrim Xuanzang, was the birthplace of Maudgalyāyana. Our presence naturally created some excitement among the inhabitants and when we had finished our meal we were invited to address a small crowd of about a hundred persons that had gathered nearby. In the afternoon we set out for Bargaon, a large village that had originally belonged to the ancient monastic university of Nalanda. Here we put up at the Svetambar Jain Dharmasala, that is to say, a Rest House belonging to the 'white-robed' – as distinct from the Digambar, 'sky-clad' or naked – sect of the Jains. Nearby, in the midst of the open fields, was a large bodhisattva image, fairly well preserved, and with a lengthy inscription on its halo. Having been unearthed by a local farmer, it had been set up beneath a tree and was now being worshipped as a sort of guardian deity of the fields. We also visited a temple dedicated to Surya, the Sun God, outside which stood two large and beautiful images of polished black stone, one of the Buddha, the other of the Hindu goddess Parvati. Though Surya had been greatly honoured in Vedic times, such temples were rare, and I did not remember having seen one before. That evening a public meeting was held, but although about one hundred people attended it the response was not, for some reason or other, quite so enthusiastic as in other places.

Early next morning, accompanied by the Curator of the Nalanda Museum, we went to see the ruins of the ancient monastic university. For close on a mile heaps of dark red brick rose at intervals from the ochre-coloured plain in a way that, from a distance, seemed vaguely Mexican rather than Indian. As we approached the huge walls of the principal monastery buildings, and saw the many-storeyed stupa towering above our heads, grand even in decay, a picture of Nalanda Maha Vihara as it lives in the vivid pages of Xuanzang rose involuntarily before our mind's eye. How easily we could imagine the great Chinese pilgrim approaching the lofty portals of the then spiritual metropolis of the far-flung Empire of Buddhism! Those were the spacious days when 10,000 students and more than 1,000 teachers thronged the cells and cloisters of its dozen nine-storeyed monastery buildings, when daily one hundred lectures were delivered, when its three great libraries treasured up the accumulated wisdom of more than 1,000 years of Buddhist religion and culture, and when the aged and venerable Silabhadra, at whose feet Xuanzang sat for many years, presided over the studies and directed the spiritual practices of monks of more than fifty nationalities. Now the place was deserted. 800 years ago Nalanda had been sacked by the iconoclastic fury of the Muslim invader, its monks slaughtered, its treasure carted away. For six whole months the palm-leaf manuscripts in the three libraries had burned. As we paced along the cool corridors, and peered into the secluded cells, Kashyap-ji and I could not help wondering what it had been like to be a monk at Nalanda and whether, now that Buddhism was returning to India, it would ever be possible for a new Nalanda to rise from the ashes of the old.

From Nalanda to Rajgir was a distance of only seven or eight miles, but the exertions of the last few days were beginning to tell on Kashyap-ji and when, twenty-four hours later, we left the Nalanda area, it was not on foot but seated in one of five or six tiny railway carriages behind a brisk little engine of the local branch line. We had gone for alms in the village of Sarichak, which according to some scholars was the birthplace of Śāriputra, and given two more lectures, and it was time for us to be on our way.

In Rajgir we stayed at the Japanese Buddhist Temple, a modest two-storeyed building which was situated almost at the foot of the Vipula range and faced west towards the site of the Veḷuvana or Bamboo Grove, where the Buddha had often stayed. In the absence of the Japanese monks, who had either left for Japan just before the war or been interned, there was the usual Hindu cuckoo in the Buddhist nest, the cuckoo in this case being a long-bearded ascetic who had once belonged to the Ramakrishna Mission. Though he came to meet us at the station, and though he made us welcome enough, he was clearly more interested in naturopathy than in Buddhism. In the shrine upstairs the images on the altar were inches deep in dust and cobwebs. Shocked by the sight, Kashyap-ji and I at once set to work and cleaned things up, carefully putting to one side the grimy photographs of Sri Ramakrishna and Swami Vivekananda that had usurped the place of honour. Though most of his time was taken up by his naturopathic practice, the good swami was not altogether neglectful of the religious traditions of the temple, which belonged to a branch of the Nichiren sect. For half an hour every evening he banged away at the big Japanese drum, bawling as he did so the words of the great mantra *namu myōhō renge kyō* – 'Salutation to White Lotus Sūtra!'

Our first expedition was to the site of the Bamboo Grove, which lay on the other side of the road not far from the foot of the Ratnagiri Range. Not a single bamboo was to be seen. In fact, there was hardly any vegetation, and what with the heaps of rubble that were lying all around, the appearance of the place was drear and desolate. A few yards south of the site, however, there was a training camp for *gram sevaks*, or village workers, from the Patna and Gaya Districts of Bihar. In response to their invitation we addressed them on Buddhism, Buddhist culture, naturopathy, Untouchability, and other subjects almost daily during the next two weeks. Another expedition took us to the Pippala Cave, which was not a cave at all but a huge, fortress-like structure built entirely of enormous blocks of roughly-dressed stone. According to tradition it had been occupied by Mahākāśyapa, whom the Buddha had declared to be the foremost of his disciples for ascetic practices, even as Śāriputra was the foremost in wisdom and Maudgalyāyana the foremost in psychic powers. On this expedition we were not alone. With us were Reverend Riri Nakayama, a dignitary of the Shin School of Japanese Buddhism who had come to India for a pacifist conference, and Venerable Amritananda, a rising young Newar monk who had received his training in Ceylon. On another occasion we were accompanied by a strange young American who had adopted the Vaishnava faith. Awkwardly clad in a white dhoti, and with the tiki or crown-lock of the orthodox Hindu, he was more than a little eccentric, and I could not help wondering whether, in the inscrutable ways of 'Providence', this transatlantic travesty of the genuine Indian article was not meant as a warning to me. Every five or ten minutes he assured us, in broken Hindi, and at great length, that he was a strict vegetarian, and that his motto was 'Only pure food, from a pure hand, in a pure house.' By 'pure' he of course meant vegetarian. He also informed us that he would like to hold *satsangh* or spiritual communion with us, and that we were free to ask him any question. Whenever Kashyap-ji asked him anything, however (I declined to do so), he at once adopted an expression of intense self-satisfaction, cast up his eyes, and declared '*That* is a secret between me and my guru!' Less ecstatic than the American Vaishnava, but more open to discussion, was the priest in charge of the local Roman Catholic mission, with whom Kashyap-ji and I had a long 'comparative' talk about mysticism, Christian and Buddhist. Since my teacher had never been inside a Christian place of worship, we spent a few minutes in the mission chapel. It was strange to see the red light that indicated the presence of the Blessed Sacrament burning in such a place. When we left, the priest handed me two books by Thomas Merton, an author whose name I had not heard before. The two books were *Seven Storey Mountain* and *Seeds of Contemplation*. Perhaps I could find time to read them, he said.

I certainly could. Devouring the books back at the Japanese temple I discovered that Thomas Merton was an Irish-American Catholic who, as a young man, had become a Trappist monk. *Seven Storey Mountain*, which was his autobiography, did not appeal to me very much. It was pervaded by an atmosphere I disliked – the stifling atmosphere of Roman Catholic domestic piety. *Seeds of Contemplation*, however, a collection of essays, appealed to me more strongly than might have been expected. Despite the author's predominantly theistic idiom, several of his insights appeared strikingly relevant to my own spiritual situation, even to my own spiritual needs. For some time past I had been greatly preoccupied with the question of the ego, not only with the theoretical question of what it was, or was not, but with the more practical one of how to get round it, or get rid of it, or get beyond it. Meditation did not seem enough. Something more drastic and more down-to-earth was needed, something that could be practised every hour of the day, something that would provide a constant check to the unruly motions of the egoistic *will*. In *Seeds of Contemplation* I found what I wanted, or at least a clear enough indication of it. The disciple should surrender his will absolutely to the will of his spiritual superior. In small matters as in great he should have no will of his own, not even any personal wishes or preferences. This was the secret. This was the way to subjugate the ego, if not to destroy it completely. Though the idea was certainly not unfamiliar to me, it had never struck me so forcibly before, and I resolved to apply it forthwith to my relations with Kashyap-ji. In future his wishes would be my law. I would have no wishes of my own. Whenever he asked me if I would like to do something, as in the goodness of his heart he often did,

I would reply that I had no preference in the matter, and that we would do just as he wished. For the remainder of the time that we were together I faithfully adhered to this resolution. As a result, I had no troubles, and experienced great peace of mind. What the priest at the mission would have thought, had he known that *Seeds of Contemplation* had helped me in this way, I cannot imagine. Still less can I imagine what Father Merton would have thought. Perhaps he would not have been greatly surprised. In later years he became deeply interested in the spiritual teachings of the East, particularly in Taoism and Zen Buddhism, and in fact died in a Buddhist monastery in Bangkok – from an accident caused by a faulty electrical connection. I have sometimes wondered if there was a moral to be drawn from the bizarre and tragic manner of his end.

Our most important expedition – indeed, the climax of our travels in the Land of the Great Disciples – took us to a place that was not only farther away and higher up than either the Bamboo Grove or the Pippala Cave but of even greater spiritual significance. Taking advantage of a sudden change in the weather, which since our arrival in Rajgir had been cold, windy, and rainy, we set out one Sunday afternoon for the Gṛdhrakūṭa or Vulture Peak. Our way led through the hill-encircled valley where the old city of Rājagṛha, capital of the kingdom of Magadha, had once stood. As we entered the opening known as the North Gate we at once became aware of the pin-drop silence of the place. The road, which must have existed in the time of the Buddha and King Bimbisāra, ran southward through a dense jungle of huge white-flowered cactus trees that were branched like candelabra, ragged thorn bushes, and clumps of slim yellow bamboo. After walking for about half an hour in the hot sunshine we passed the ruins of the Manniyar Math, a Jain temple which had originally been a seat of snake-worship. Soon after this we came to the site of Bimbisāra's Jail. Here it was that the aged king had been imprisoned by his son Ajātaśatru. Only the foundations of the building remained. According to Buddhist tradition the unhappy monarch used to gaze from his cell window eastward towards the Vulture Peak where he could see the Buddha, conspicuous in his yellow robe, walking up and down. It was in these circumstances that the Buddha, appearing in a spiritual body to the devoted consort of the dethroned king, preached for her consolation the Mahāyāna *sūtra* known as 'The Meditation on the Buddha of Eternal Life'.

Shortly afterwards the road branched off towards the east and before long we were ascending the lower slopes of the Ratnagiri Range. As we climbed up we could not help admiring the almost cyclopean strength and skill of the ancient engineers who had paved the road with such huge flat stones and built up giant steps at regular intervals. Small brick structures, now in ruins, marked the points where King Bimbisāra had descended from his chariot and where he had dismissed his retinue before making the final ascent. At both of these Kashyap-ji and I rested for a few minutes and enjoyed the cool breeze that came sweeping across the mountain-top. The Vulture Peak itself was an enormous mass of rock which some primeval convulsion of the earth's crust had flung up with such violence that, as the almost vertical lines of its strata plainly showed, it was now standing practically on end. At the foot of the rock the road narrowed to a path which, having spiralled round the peak from east to west past a succession of caves and grottoes, finally thrust upwards and emerged at a square platform whereon stood the ruins of a brick structure once occupied by the Buddha. From here one could see the whole valley at a single glance. To the west lay the Golden Range, Sonagiri, to the north-west the Brilliant Range, Vaibhāragiri, to the south the Ample Range and the Jewel Range, Vaipulyagiri and Ratnagiri, and to the north the Uplifted Range, Udayagiri. Hither the Buddha had been accustomed to retire from the comparative noise and bustle of the Bamboo Grove. Here he had spent the pleasant spring days and starry summer nights plunged in profound meditation. From this dizzy eminence, he had gazed down on the many-storeyed mansions, the busy streets, the crowded markets, of the great and ancient city of Rājagṛha. Most important of all, here on the wind-swept heights of the Vulture Peak – at the summit, as it were, of mundane existence – he had revealed to the most receptive of his disciples the transcendental splendours of the *White Lotus Sūtra*, his ultimate teaching, the *sūtra* in which is enacted the Drama of Cosmic Enlightenment, the great drama in which all the different 'ways' of the Buddha's teaching are shown to be comprised in the Great Way, the One Way, the Way of the Buddha, and in which the Buddha himself is revealed not only as a historical figure but as an eternally active spiritual principle – the principle of Enlightenment.

As we gazed, even as the Master must have gazed, first at the valley 1,000 feet below – once a populous city, now an impenetrable jungle –

then at the blue encircling hills, and finally beyond the hills to the green and fertile fields, the mud-walled villages, the pleasant mango groves, of ancient Magadha, the modern Bihar, a prayer went forth from my heart. I prayed that not only in this land, the Land of the Great Disciples, but in every land, men might hearken to the Voice of the Buddha, as it sounded from the unseen heights of the spiritual Vulture Peak. I prayed that they might set their feet on the Path leading to their own and others' Enlightenment. Finally, I prayed that I too might one day be enabled to help in some way towards this end. Though I did not know it, the last part of my prayer was to be granted sooner than I expected.

50
FACING MOUNT KANCHENJUNGA

A quarter of a mile upstream, the graceful white arch of Teesta Bridge floated like a dream between the steep tree-clad slopes. Within a few minutes we were across, and the jeep that had been sent to fetch us from Siliguri Station was shooting up the mountainside along a succession of hairpin bends that lifted us several hundred feet above the river every few minutes. Already the figures on the bridge looked no bigger than ants, while the river itself lay like a ribbon of grey-green jade between the mountains. Every time we swung round a bend new perspectives opened up before us, each one vaster and more awe-inspiring than the last. Behind us, to the west, loomed the mauve and indigo masses of the Darjeeling hills, while across the River Rungeet, to the north, the mountains of Sikkim flowed in ridge upon smoke-blue ridge to the far horizon. Soon the air grew quite cold, though the sky was a vivid blue and the sunshine more brilliant than ever. We were above the clouds. Looking down, we could see them drifting in fleecy white masses down the valley, following the course of the river. With the change of altitude came a change of vegetation. Sal forest gave way to fir and pine, while the bamboo became smaller and less frequent. Every few hundred yards an explosion of pure scarlet proclaimed the presence of the giant poinsettias. Thatched cottages flashed past. Shops, shrines.... When we were seven or eight miles from Teesta Bridge, and nearly 3,000 feet above sea level, thatched cottages began to change into English bungalows with tiled roofs and trim gardens and soon, strung out along the saddleback before us, I saw the town of Kalimpong.

It did not take Kashyap-ji and me many days to realize that we were in a new world. On our arrival we had been accommodated in a two-storey building just above Ninth Mile, and every day we walked through the main street to Tenth Mile, where a Newar merchant whom Kashyap-ji had once met in Calcutta gave us our morning meal. Most of the shops that were jammed up against one another on either side of the road seemed to belong to Indians, but the people passing up and down were of a dozen different national origins. By far the greater number were Nepalis of various castes and tribes, many in traditional Mogul-type costume, with kukris thrust into their waist-bands and enormous wicker baskets on their backs. Indians were well represented, though, and included Marwari merchants in saffron-yellow headgear, turbaned and bearded Sikhs, Bihari sweepers with long crown-locks, and Bengali clerks. There were also stocky Bhutanese in striped knee-length gowns, a few Chinese – the older generation in black silk trouser-suits – and a sprinkling of small, shy Lepchas from the forests of Sikkim. There was even the occasional pink-faced European, more often than not with a big black bible clutched beneath the arm.

Most striking of all, however, were the Tibetans, who so far as numbers went were second only to the Nepalis. Tall and barrel-chested, with gowns kilted up to the knee, ten-gallon hats thrust far back on their heads, and short swords dangling at their sides, they swaggered down the main street looking as though they owned the place. In a sense of course they did own it. Kalimpong owed its undoubted prosperity to the fact that it was the focal point of the trade with Tibet, exporting such things as cigarettes, kerosene, fountain-pens, and wristwatches to the Land of the Lamas, and receiving in exchange wool, yak-tails, and musk. In the absence of motorable roads, everything had to be transported on the backs of mules. As we approached Tenth Mile, Kashyap-ji and I often saw forty or fifty of the heavily-laden beasts coming along the road in a great cloud of dust to the accompaniment of a tuneful jingle-jangle of mule bells and much cheerful shouting and whip-cracking on the part of the red-cheeked muleteers. Whether they were arriving or departing we had no means of telling, but men and beasts alike seemed in good condition, while the leader-mule tossed his red plumes proudly as he stepped out at the head of the caravan.

But much as Nepalis and Indians, Bhutanese and Sikkimese, Europeans and Tibetans, contributed to the colourfulness of the scene, it was not simply on account of their presence that Kalimpong was a new world. The whole atmosphere of the place was different. Coming as we did from the plains, where only too often life stagnates in its accustomed channels, we experienced everything as being not only fresher and cleaner but more sparkling and alive. It was like drinking ice-cold champagne after warmed-up soup. People went about their perfectly ordinary affairs in a perfectly ordinary manner, but whether on account of the altitude, or for some other reason, there was a sense of exhilaration in the air, as though it was the festive season, or as though they were all on holiday. Missionaries alone excepted, there was a smile on every face, and while it would be an exaggeration to say that there was a song on everybody's lips we could hardly put our head out of the window without hearing, loud and clear in the distance, the cheerful melody of the latest popular film song. And the colours! On account of these alone Kalimpong would have been a new world. From the blues and purples of the mountains to the reds and yellows of the flowers in the Nepali women's hair, they were all preternaturally vivid, as in a Pre-Raphaelite painting. Sometimes, indeed, they glowed with such intensity that everything seemed to be made of jewels. And all the time, above the mirth and the music, above the life and the colour, above the steadfastness of nature and the security of civilization – above everything – there were the snows.

On the morning of our arrival they had been veiled, and we had seen nothing of them, but since then they had shone forth every day, and often for the whole day. With the blue of the valleys at their feet and the blue of the sky above their heads, the shimmering white masses stretched from end to end of the horizon majestic beyond belief. Since the building where Kashyap-ji and I were staying faced north, we had an uninterrupted view of Mount Kanchenjunga, the second highest peak in the entire Himalayan range and the third highest in the world. In the early morning it was particularly beautiful. Looking out of the window just before dawn, I would see it glimmering ghostly in the blue twilight, more like ice than snow. Then, as the sun started rising, the bluish tip of the summit would be flushed by a fiery pink that, in a matter of minutes, had travelled all the way down the peak. Soon the whole range would be a mass of pink embers glowing against the pale blue sky. Pink would change to crimson, crimson to apricot, apricot to the purest, brightest gold. Finally, as the sun cleared the horizon, gold

Mount Kanchenjunga

would change to silver and silver to dazzling white. On particularly fine days the mountain wore a white plume, almost like a plume of smoke. According to the experts, this was caused by a strong wind blowing the loose snow from its summit. But whether it wore its plume or not, and regardless of the time of day, I was never tired of looking up at Mount Kanchenjunga as it sat enthroned in the sky. Totally absorbed in itself though it was, and utterly oblivious of my existence, the great white peak nonetheless seemed to speak to me. What it said, I did not know, but perhaps, if I stayed in Kalimpong long enough, and looked hard enough, I would come to understand.

Though I did not then know it, I was to stay there for the next fourteen years. After weeks of indecision, Kashyap-ji had finally made up his mind not to return to the Benares Hindu University. Instead, he would spend some time meditating in the jungles of Bihar, where a yogi whom he knew had a hermitage. Perhaps, as he meditated, it would become clear to him what he ought to do next. Meanwhile, I was to remain in Kalimpong. 'Stay here and work for the good of Buddhism,' he told me, squeezing himself into the front seat of the jeep that was taking him to Siliguri. 'The Newars will look after you.' There was little that I could say. Though I did not really feel experienced enough to work for Buddhism on my own, and though I doubted whether the Newars were quite so ready to look after me as Kashyap-ji supposed, the word of the guru was not to be disobeyed. Bowing my head in acquiescence, I paid my respects in the traditional manner, Kashyap-ji gave me his blessing, and the jeep was off.

I was left facing Mount Kanchenjunga.

APPENDICES

The Rainbow Road from Tooting Broadway to Kalimpong has had a somewhat colourful publication history. How the author came to write this first volume of memoirs, and how they came to be published minus the first ten chapters as *The Thousand-Petalled Lotus* (Heinemann, London 1976), as well as the later appearance of the 'amputated' chapters as *Learning to Walk* (Windhorse Publications, Glasgow 1990) was explained by the author in an Introduction to the latter. That Introduction is included here as Appendix 1.

Sangharakshita wrote his first volume of memoirs in two phases, one in the late 1950s and early 1960s when he was based in Kalimpong, India, the other in 1972–3 in England. During the second phase he revised some of the earlier material, especially Chapter 1, 'Giants and Dragons', which was 'cut and rearranged to such an extent' that it was decided to include the original, unrevised version as an appendix in *Learning to Walk*. We have included it here as Appendix 2.

Appendix 1
INTRODUCTION TO *LEARNING TO WALK*

'Why don't you write *your* autobiography?'

The speaker was the burly, forty-year-old English doctor who, for the last five or six months, had been staying with me at the Triyana Vardhana Vihara, the monastery I had founded on the outskirts of Kalimpong, a small town in the foothills of the eastern Himalayas, some two years earlier. During those months he had, at my suggestion, written his autobiography, to which he had given the title *Out of the Ordinary* (he was a transsexual and a former disciple of the notorious Lobsang Rampa), and now he was suggesting that I should write *my* autobiography.

'But what would be the point?' I protested. 'I haven't had nearly such an interesting life as you. In fact, my life has been quite ordinary, and even if I did manage to write my autobiography who on earth would want to read it?'

'Nonsense!' retorted my friend, in his usual brusque fashion. 'You've had a very interesting life, and if you were to write your autobiography a lot of people would want to read it. It might even become a bestseller.'

I remained unconvinced. I had suggested that Jivaka (at his request I had given him a Buddhist name shortly after his arrival) should write his autobiography because there were, I suspected, things he needed to get off his chest, and writing his autobiography seemed a good way for him to do this.[36] In my own case no such consideration applied. There was nothing of a personal nature of which I particularly wanted to disburden myself. However, Jivaka returned to the attack, pointing out that I was not very busy just then, and the following morning I therefore sat down at my desk and cast my mind back to my childhood in faraway Tooting.

This was in 1959, and in the course of the next two years I produced about 100,000 words. Not that the work of producing them proceeded uninterruptedly. During the same period I undertook a number of extensive lecture tours in the plains, some of which kept me away from Kalimpong for months together. Then in 1962 I was invited to contribute the articles on Buddhism to the *Oriya Encyclopaedia* and put aside other literary work in order to concentrate on this project. In the course of writing, these articles far outgrew their original purpose, and the first of them was eventually published as *The Three Jewels*[37] and the second as *The Eternal Legacy*[38]. A third article, on the sects and schools of Buddhism, was never completed. Early in 1964 I was asked to write the chapter on Buddhism for the new edition of *The Legacy of India*[39] and later that same year, having written my chapter, I left Kalimpong for England, which I had not seen for twenty years. The visit was to have lasted four months. Instead it lasted more than two years and eventually resulted in a permanent change of domicile, from India to England. It also resulted in a change of direction in my own life and in the lives of many other people.

Only in 1972, when it had been put aside for ten years, was I able to resume work on my autobiography. By that time I had founded the FWBO and WBO and was living in a flat at Muswell Hill. Though continuing to grow, the FWBO was homeless at the time, and for several months I had fewer classes to take than usual and could devote more time to writing. Not that I found it easy to reconnect with the autobiography. A lot had happened to me in the interim, and the man who took it up again in London in 1972 was in some respects a very different person from the man who put it aside in Kalimpong in 1962. I was also farther away by ten years from the period about which I had last written, and laboured, moreover, under the disadvantage of having to reconnect with the work right in the middle of a chapter—the chapter entitled 'The Three Lawyers'. But reconnect I did, and in the course of the summer produced about 25,000 words. 1973 was the year of my sabbatical. I spent most of it in a chalet on the coast of Cornwall, where I produced some 50,000 or so words more, and in 1976 *The Thousand-Petalled Lotus* appeared under the Heinemann imprint.

The title was not exactly of my own choosing. Or rather, it was not my *original* choice. My original choice, at least as a working title, was *The Rainbow Road*. The publishers did not like this; they asked me to think again; I submitted a list of five possible titles and from these they eventually selected 'The Thousand-Petalled Lotus'. They also insisted on my lopping off the first ten chapters of the book, dealing with my early life, on the grounds that this part of the story was of little or no general interest.

Strange to relate, more than one reviewer wondered why I had not written about my life prior to my arrival in Colombo at the end of 1944, while during the last fourteen years friends to whom the existence of the ten amputated chapters was known have increasingly urged me to have them published. This I am now doing—not entirely without misgivings. When, at Jivaka's suggestion, I started writing my autobiography I did so quite lightheartedly, without much regard either for the arrangement of my material or for literary style. Only after I had written quite a few tens of thousands of words did I realize the significance of what I was doing and start taking the work more seriously. For this reason the earlier chapters of the (original) *Thousand-Petalled Lotus* are, I think, less well written than some of the later ones—though here opinions may differ, an author being not necessarily the best judge of his own work. I also realized that I was not, in fact, writing my autobiography at all, that is, not writing my auto-biography: I was writing my *memoirs*. In the words of the unrevised version of the first of the ten amputated chapters the work on which I was engaged was 'less a collection of facts than an evocation of memories, from the degree of whose distinctness the more delicately perceptive may gauge both the relative intensity of the experiences whose impressions they are and the nature and ultimate extent of the influence exerted by those experiences on the development of character and formation of opinion in the narrator.'

The lopping off of the first ten chapters of my memoirs naturally necessitated a few adjustments in the text of *The Thousand-Petalled Lotus* as published. These adjustments were of a minor character, and did not extend to the material now being brought out as *Learning to Walk*. In any case, that material had already been subjected to a fairly thorough revision in 1973. This was particularly the case with the first chapter, which was cut and rearranged to such an extent that I have decided to include the unrevised version as an appendix. I should also mention that the ten chapters now entitled *Learning to Walk* were typed for me in Kalimpong by Jivaka, and that in typing them he exercised his blue pencil pretty freely on what he termed my 'book lists', that is, my rather lengthy accounts of my reading. Fortunately or unfortunately, these accounts are no longer recoverable.

It only remains for me to thank [those who have contributed to this publication], and to hope that the friends who have been urging me to have these recollections of my early life published will not be disappointed when they read them.

Sangharakshita
Sukhavati
London
20 May 1990

Appendix 2
CHAPTER ONE: ORIGINAL VERSION

From *Learning to Walk*

I
GIANTS AND DRAGONS

Apart from my refusal to cry when born, the strangest circumstance of my most recent appearance in this world on 26 August 1925 is that it took place in a nursing home in south-west London only a few hundred yards from the spot where, two years earlier, had died Allan Bennett, otherwise Ananda Maitreya, the first Englishman to take the yellow robe in the East and return to teach the Dharma in his native land.

My parents at that time occupied the upper part of a house in Tooting which belonged to my grandmother. Brick-walled and slate-roofed, with green privet hedge, a pair of highly polished front doors – one for the upstairs the other for the downstairs flat – and lace-curtained windows, it was one of the hundreds of thousands which, standing back to back in interminable rows, help to make up that vast maze of mutually intersecting streets which is suburban London.

What I take to be my earliest memory, however, finds me not outside but inside the house. Lying at night in the great double bed in my parents' room, which was at the front of the house, I used to stare up at the foliated ceiling piece, the size and shape of a cartwheel, from the centre of which hung the light. As motors passed up and down the main road which was at the bottom of our street, their headlights, reflected onto the ceiling, swung slowly round the centrepiece light great bright spokes around a shadowy hub. If the motors were going south, towards the coast, the spokes swung clockwise; if north, to the city's heart, in the opposite direction. With the clanging of the distant tram bells and the low roar and rumble of the other traffic in my ears I used to lie in the darkness and watch the spokes turning now this way, now that, and now both ways simultaneously as two motors passed each other, until lulled to sleep. In later years, when I slept in my own bedroom, I used to experience the sensation of being whirled round and round into a great golden light which gradually engulfed me and I knew no more. Whether the later experience, which continued until I was five or six, was connected with the earlier, I do not know; but for quite long time after it had ceased I took for granted that everyone fell asleep in the same manner.

As I grew older I naturally became dissatisfied with passive contemplation: 'Mother, can I go out and play?' was my constant cry. The natural playground of the London child is, of course, the street, but there I was not allowed to play until after I had started school. In the meantime, therefore, I played on the black and white tiles of the porch and behind the dusty privet with my sister, fifteen months younger than myself, and a girl of my own age who lived down the road at no. 1 (our house was no. 23) a game of our own invention called Old Mother Witchie. Sometimes we played so noisily that 'the lady downstairs', a kindly old soul who used to send us up jelly and trifle in tumblers, had to tap gently on the window of her front room to silence us, for although we did not know it her husband, who died not long afterwards, was seriously ill.

When it rained, or when I was not allowed to play 'out in the front', my refrain was 'Mother, can Frances come in to play?' Usually she could. Our favourite game was 'dressing up', for which we ransacked the house for old lace curtains. As a special treat we were sometimes allowed to borrow the embroidered veil in which my father and I had been christened, and then great was our joy, for instead of playing Fathers and Mothers, as we usually did, we could play at weddings. I was the bridegroom, Frances the bride, and my sister sometimes the bridesmaid and sometimes the officiating clergyman. This love of dressing up persisted much longer in my case than it did in that of the girls, and even at the age of eight I could spend hours in front of the long mirror in my parents' bedroom experimenting with different styles of dress. Jersey and knickerbockers were not my real costume, I felt sure, and almost desperately I swathed and draped myself in lengths of material, searching in vain for my true vesture. The only times I felt satisfied was when, with the help of a Red Ensign, I achieved, more by accident than design, a toga-like effect which, though not exactly right, was to some extent what I desired. Then, gravely holding my grandfather's silver-mounted amber cane, I would stand gazing at my reflection which solemn pleasure for several minutes.

On days when I had no playmate I used to crawl beneath the dining room table and amuse myself by scrawling on its underside with coloured crayons. How often my mother left me alone in the house while she went out shopping I no longer recollect, but I remember her solemn adjuration not to open the door if anyone knocked and the precipitation with which, in anticipation of some terrible visitor, I used to take refuge beneath this table as soon as she had gone. On her return she would usually find me still crouching there, my heart pounding with terror. Experiences of this sort gave rise to frequent nightmares, frightful variations on the theme of waking dread. In one, great heavy footsteps would drag slowly up the stairs, along the passage, and into the room, until from my refuge I could see, as it were, the feet of the unknown evil and woke screaming. In another the tramp of an approaching army would come closer and closer upon me, full of infinite menace and horror, while I would be rooted with terror to the spot, unable to move. For several years I was afraid to go to bed, and still more afraid to sleep. Memory of the nightmares made me yet more terrified if my mother left me alone during the day, and perhaps it was not altogether without dread that I played underneath the table while she was at home.

A much less unpleasant memory of this friendly piece of furniture is of being called out from underneath it one morning to be told that Uncle Tom, my godfather, was dead. This red-faced, white-haired old gentleman, with a rough and hearty manner and a savage temper, used to call me to his knee on my birthday and other state occasions and make me hold out my hand while he counted into it as many half-crowns as he was in a humour to give. He lived across the road with his niece, a thin, meek, rheumy-eyed woman whom he treated with great harshness, believing that she cared for him only in the hope of being left his money. On the wall of the room where I sometimes visited him hung a glass case containing a stuffed red fox with a pigeon in its mouth. From the day I saw it I coveted this wonder, and I believe I had been promised it. As soon as I heard the news of my godfather's death I therefore eagerly inquired: 'Now shall I get the fox?' Though this brutally direct question for the moment horrified my parents, they were too sensible to take serious exception to a child's lack of feeling. Besides, my enquiry was not unjustified. From conversations which I had overheard I knew that Uncle Tom, who was not related to us in any way, had several times proposed marriage to my grandmother, promising, as an additional inducement, to make me his heir if she would accept him. My grandmother, who had already buried two husbands, told him plainly that she had no desire to bury a third and that it was his duty to leave his money to his niece; but as she and Uncle Tom were still friends and often went on excursions together, it was generally assumed that he had probably remembered me in his will. In the end the wilful old man left all his money to very distant relations and neither the niece nor I got anything – not even the fox!

My grandmother, who occupied a place in my affections hardly second to that of my parents, lived in Southfields in another house which belonged to her. Among my earliest recollections is that of my father taking us to see her on fine Sunday mornings in the perambulator, with its cream-coloured awning. When I was old enough to walk we went by tram to Earlsfield station, whence we strolled through the side streets to the quiet road, more select than ours, where she lived. As soon as my father swung open the iron front gate, I used to run up the path and rattle the shining brass letter box until either Nana, as I always called her, or Auntie Noni, came to let us in, all the time peering eagerly through the stained glass panels of the big dark green front door. The hall never failed to interest me, and never did I pass through it without pausing to look up at the Nepalese kukris and Chinese swords and chopstick-sets with which the walls were decorated, and rarely could I refrain from ringing the Tibetan ritual handbell that stood in a corner behind the door.

But what drew my attention most of all was the big Chinese picture on the left-hand wall. This my father had lifted me up to see ever since I was a baby and it was thus among the most familiar objects of my childhood. Almost square in shape, it depicted an august and mysterious personage seated cross-legged on a kind of throne. He was arrayed in loosely flowing robes and behind his head was a nimbus. His features, which were markedly oriental, with slant eyes that gazed far into the distance, were expressive of a remarkable combination of benignity and power. This enigmatic being was surrounded by half a dozen figures, some making offerings, others playing on musical instruments, and all not more than a tenth of the size of their master, whom, for this reason, I called the Giant.

Running into the sitting room, at the far end of which glass doors opened into the conservatory where one of the cacti, so my father assured me, bore a single red rose-like flower every seven years, I found objects to gaze at and even handle which were hardly less wonderful than those in the hall. The Chinese cloisonné vases, which there were several pairs, were as fine as any which, in later years, I saw in Tibetan temples and at the houses of Chinese friends, and the shape of some has been in my experience unique. One great flagon-shaped pair with gold dragon handles depicted houses, gardens, and human figures. Even now, at a distance of thirty years, I can see a favourite figure in blue gown and black cap, standing pensively among the toy hills. Round each of the other vases, all of which were a deep rich blue, coiled a five-clawed imperial dragon, with liver-coloured body, yellow head, red horns, black eyes, purple mane, and scales picked out in gold. Each dragon had its jewel and spat flame as if in its defence. Of these mysterious beasts it never occurred to me to feel afraid, and certainly they were never for me, as they are for the Christian tradition, symbolic of evil, so that it was without astonishment that I learned, in later life, that to the Chinese the dragon had been for thousands of years the symbol of the yang, the bright, masculine, creative principle of the universe, even as the phoenix, with which I was unacquainted, was the symbol of the yin, the dark, feminine, destructive principle. Was it because of this early acquaintance with dragons that I have never been afraid of snakes, but even as a child longed to stroke their smooth silken bodies – neither cold or clammy, as those who ignorantly shrink from them imagine – and have them coiling about my hands – that, in fact, I had a strange love for all reptiles, even the common toad? Children are animists to whom nothing is dead, and to me my dragons were not pictures on vases but friendly shapes with whom I played whenever I went to my grandmother's house, and with whom, perhaps, in some luminous underground chamber of my mind, I am playing still.

On the white marble mantelpiece, between the Westminster chime clock and the flagon-shaped vase on the right, was a small sedent bronze image which, when able to talk, I called the Empress Dowager. When

I shook it, it rattled. Now I know that the figure my baby fingers clutched, the features of which I can remember as well as any human face, represented not the last imperial ruler of China but the 'Goddess of Mercy', Guanyin, the feminized Chinese version of the bodhisattva Avalokiteśvara, one of the most popular figures of the Indian Buddhist pantheon. The rattling noise must have been produced not, as I then supposed, by a stone, but by one of those holy relics that the Buddhists of China, like those of Tibet, frequently seal in images. Strange it is that in those days I should have met an image of the great spiritual being who, in later years, became to me a living presence!

But in what mysterious way did the Buddha, the dragons, and the Chinese goddess come to make their appearance in that English household? How was it that a boy of three or four could be in a position to make so free with the name of the last Empresses? At this point an English family chronicle and Chinese history intersect.

In Nana's dining room there hung, on opposite walls, the portraits of two men, one in naval the other in military uniform. The man in the first, which was considerably larger, wore a walrus moustache and must have been about thirty. The man in the second picture, which was slightly yellowed, had a small trim moustache and seemed to be in his early twenties. It puzzled me very much in that time to be told that both men were my grandfather for, as from Uncle Tom's courtship it has already transpired, my grandmother had been twice married and moreover had had four children, first my father, then my Auntie Noni and then, after an interval of several years, another boy, my Uncle Charles, who, like Auntie Noni, still lived with her, and a girl, Dorothy, who had died young and whom I never saw.

It was her second husband, about whom I gathered little more than is recorded here, who was responsible for the introduction into the house of the exotic objects described. Of partly Portuguese descent, he had travelled widely, at one time serving in the Merchant Navy. At the time of the Boxer Rebellion he was working for the Imperial Government of China as a commissioner of railways and, having a mania for curios, took advantage of the opportunity afforded by the sack of the Summer Palace at Pekin to add to his collection. Though the greater part was dispersed after his death, as my grandmother disliked having to dust grass skirts and polish spears every day, and my father objected to living with the cases of live shells on the wall, much remained, most of which passed to

Uncle Charles. Among the things that she kept were three of the Empress's bedspreads of yellow silk worked with gold dragons, tiny butterfly shoes, and a number of embroidered silk robes. These and the cloisonné vases had come from the Summer Palace; the picture in the hall, the figure of Kwan Yin, and the bell behind the front door, from the Lama Temple.

Grandfather was also a photographer, it seems, for there was an album of photographs taken at the time of the rebellion. Kneeling on the ground with their hands pinioned behind their backs were rows of naked rebels, some with their severed heads already at the executioner's feet. My sister and I spent many happy hours looking at these pictures, which were kept at the bottom of a curio cabinet, until one day Nana realized that they were not the most suitable thing for children to see. Years later I found them with Uncle Charles who, being sadistic and acquisitive, had eventually laid claim to them.

About Nana's first husband, albeit he was my own grandfather, I knew hardly as much as I did about her second, partly, perhaps, because he had died so young that my father had no recollection of him to share with me. He came, I gathered, of a good Suffolk family and was the youngest of eight brothers. How he met Nana, the daughter of a Norfolk farmer, I do not know. But perhaps he married her against the wishes of his parents, for never, to my knowledge, did my father have any dealings with his paternal aunts and uncles. Only years later and when, just before I left England, they started dying off at a ripe old age – leaving what was left of the money they had inherited from their mother, who had been an heiress, to be shared among my father, Auntie Noni, and a cousin – did I even hear their names.

After their marriage Nana and grandfather lived at Woolwich where, in 1899, my father was born. Grandfather was then working at the War Office, where he made out the officers' commissions which went to the Queen for signature. Years later, in the Natural History Museum at South Kensington, Father showed me the famous War Office cat, as large as a bull terrier, on which as a very small boy he had been given rides. Grandfather also handled foreign dispatches, for when, shortly after being himself commissioned, he died suddenly after a short illness, the family physician attributed his death to germs which had been transmitted through these papers. Nana believed that he died of pneumonia.

Be the cause what it may, his death left Nana to support two small children, one of them still a baby. But being a woman of very decided character she met the situation courageously and resolved to work. From odd reminiscences of hers in later years I gathered that at different times she had been a cleaner, a parlourmaid, and a housekeeper. Probably it was for the sake of security that, after five or six years of this hard life, she married for the second time and thus came to live at Tooting. She once told my mother, whom she loved as her own daughter, that she remembered her first husband much better than her second, from which the romantically inclined may conclude that she has loved him much more. To my mother's question, 'Doesn't your first marriage seem rather vague to you after so many years?' she at once replied with a joyous expression, 'Oh no, it's as fresh as if had happened yesterday!' Whatever the difference in her feelings about her two husbands might or might not have been, their memories were honoured equally, and thus it was throughout my childhood and adolescence my two grandfathers continued to regard each other across the dining room table.

Between my father and his sister, who was also my godmother, existed a very deep and strong affection; in fact they were in many ways much alike. Besides inheriting Nana's heavy eyebrows, blue-grey eyes, and aquiline nose, they were both, like her, outspoken in opinion and firm in adherence to principle. But whereas Auntie Noni was exceptionally self-possessed and could make the deadliest remarks with the utmost coolness – especially to my mother, who would sometimes be reduced to helpless fury or to tears, both of which Aunt Noni regarded with equanimity – my father was, or at least in his youth had been, as I knew from his own confession, hot-tempered in the extreme and almost morbidly quick to take offence. But being of a generous and forgiving nature his anger never lasted long, and by the time I was born his temper was more or less under control, only an occasional flash showing that there was still lightning in the cloud. He was in fact on the whole an unusually good man, and apart from the Indian and Tibetan saints I afterwards met I never knew anyone to whom unselfishness was so natural, or who so cheerfully put the pleasure and happiness of others before his own.

Aunt Noni hero-worshipped him, which was natural, but unfortunately could not refrain from singing his praises to my mother who, however much she loved my father, could hardly have enjoyed being told, as she frequently was, what a good man she had married and how lucky she was to have married him. This last remark was always conveyed in a tone which suggested that having such a man for a husband was a miracle for which my mother should go down on her unworthy knees and render thanks to heaven.

Aunt Noni was herself unmarried. Her fiancé, my father's best friend, had been killed in the Great War, and so much did she cherish his memory that she preferred to remain single.

Unlike Mother, both my father and Auntie Noni had a very lively sense of humour and were excellent raconteurs. If at home my cry was: 'Auntie, tell me a story,' Auntie Noni's stories were all about a little boy called Dicky Doughnut and Mrs Jellybottom, his aunt, and always ended disastrously for poor Mrs Jellybottom who, by the mischievous contrivance of Dicky, would be unexpectedly deluged with blancmange, or precipitated head first into a bowl of cream. At the climax of these stories I would clap my hands in excitement and shriek with delight. My father, a glass of wine in his hand and a sausage roll before him (the customary last refection) would laugh good-naturedly and Nana would wipe the tears from her eyes, for they all enjoyed these stories. When I was an adolescent Uncle Charles used to tease me telling his small son to call me Dicky Doughnut, it having been generally understood that the hero of Aunt Noni's stories was in fact none other than myself.

My father's stories, which he told me when I had been put to bed, were of two kinds, true and imaginary. Most of the true stories were about his own life, especially his schooldays and experiences as a soldier in the trenches during the Great War. The imaginary stories, in the telling of which he must have drawn upon a great many sources of inventiveness, as he had to tell me a new one every night for a number of years, were all tales of adventure. In fact his secret ambition, which circumstances did not permit to be fulfilled, was to be a writer, and I attribute his subsequent connivance at my own literary aspirations to the feeling that his youthful ambition might one day be realized in the person of his son.

The then vivid and exciting stories are now only a very vague and general impression from which his accounts of how he gave a false age to be able to enlist, lived under shellfire, saw comrades blown to bits, and was himself wounded and woke up in a hospital tent without the use of the right hand, which was permanently disabled, project like hilltops above the surrounding mists. Little did he think, as he told me these stories, that when I was his age I would have war experiences of my own to relate!

In the Church Lane Hospital, Upper Tooting, where he convalesced, he met my mother, who worked there as a member of the Voluntary Aid Detachment. One of his more amusing stories was about her helping him clamber over the hospital wall at night when he had stayed out after hours. They were married in 1919. My father was then nineteen, my mother perhaps twenty. I say 'perhaps' because mother subsequently declared she was younger than Father, a claim that he refuted by recalling how, in the early years of marriage, she tried to settle any difference of opinion between them by saying that she was a year older than he was and ought to know better. But as Father was always rather a wag I am not quite sure whether this story is to be classified as true or imaginary. After their marriage they lived for a short time at Merton Park, just over the border of Metropolitan London, removing thence to the house at Tooting when, on the death of her second husband, Nana shifted to Southfields.

The road in which the house was situated ran from east to west about half a mile. At the corner that our side of the street made with the main road stood the dairy, from which every afternoon at four o'clock the dog belonging to 'the lady downstairs' could be seen carrying home in his mouth his daily bar of Nestlé's chocolate. To this dairy my sister Joan and I were sometimes sent for butter or eggs, and while waiting to be served we would feel the coldness of the marble counter with our foreheads and look wonderingly at the rows of stoppered glass jars filled with wafer biscuits wrapped in varicoloured silver paper. When she was in a good mood the proprietress would give us each a pair of cardboard Oxo spectacles. Often, while there, we would turn round at the sound of the bell to see hobbling in the familiar figure of the incredibly ancient crone dressed from head to foot in rusty black with the yellowest parchment-like face I ever saw. But the most familiar thing about her was neither her face nor her clothes but her odour, which we could have recognized with our eyes shut and which was so bad that I can still smell it when I think of her. On the opposite corner stood a pet shop, in the window of which could be seen little day-old chicks and white rabbits, and, next door to the pet shop, a sweet shop of which Joan and I were regular patrons for many years, running there whenever we had a copper to spend.

Less than half way up the street on the other side of the road rose the grey stone and yellow brick mass of the school that my father had attended as a boy and to which at the age of four I, too, was sent. The building was by no means unfamiliar to me. Had I not seen its green cupolas against the sky and heard its bell ringing twice a day ever since I could remember? But so frightened was I on the day of my admission that at the first opportunity I ran home. This reluctance to study did not last long, and four not unhappy years did I spend in the infants' department – the longest period of continuous schooling I was ever to receive.

From the confused whirl of impressions belonging to that time some stand out with special vivedness: the beautiful swans which, when we were in the bottom class, we were taught to draw on the blackboards; the much hated afternoon siesta on folding cots in the hall; the brass bell on the headmistress's desk; the cup of hot cocoa which, on a cold winter's day, my mother handed me through the iron railings at playtime – an act of indulgence for which she was duly rebuked; the paper lunch-bags pencilled with our names which were kept in the wastepaper basket until the morning break when the names were read out and the bags redistributed; dear old Mrs Davies my teacher's flowered housecoat and the alarming manner in which her eyeballs bulged as she threaded a needle; the agony of not being allowed to go outside to the lavatory and the shame when bowels could no longer be controlled and when, after letting out a sudden howl in the middle of a lesson, I was led off home in tears; the day on which my mother, washing me for afternoon school, saw on my arm the weal of the slapping I had received in the morning from a new teacher, and going on to complain to the headmistress, who found her desk besieged by a score of indignant mothers with the same complaint; the tall flowers in the school garden which, since they were known to us as red-hot pokers, I thought would burn me if I touched them; the breaking-up party with its buns and lemonade at which I appeared as a Red Indian and Joan as a fairy; the headmistress's shoes each with three straps and each strap fashioned with a button; the kiss I exchanged under the desk with a little girl when I was in the top class; the potted aspidistras in the hall which the older pupils considered it a great distinction to be asked to water; the unutterable boredom of spelling and arithmetic lessons when it seemed the period would never end; the uproarious delight with which, the minute the 'going home' bell rang, we would tumble pell-mell out of the classroom, round the lobby for our hats and coats, and out of the gate home to tell our mothers what had happened during the day.

None of these seem to be of any special significance, but an autobiography, unlike a biography, is less a collection of facts than an evocation of memories, from the degree of whose distinctiveness the more delicately perceptive may gauge both the relative intensity of the experiences whose impressions they are and the nature and ultimate extent of the influence exerted by those experiences on the development of character and formation of opinion in the narrator. If this is disputed it will at least be conceded that, in weaving the fabric of autobiography the warp of significant incident can hardly be woven except upon the woof of its less interesting counterpart. In this field it is surely unreasonable to expect every common bush of anecdote to be afire with divine significance.

After tea on weekdays, all day on Saturday (though not usually on Sunday), as well as practically every day during the holidays, we were free to play in the street. Frances, Joan, and I always shared our games, for though we knew many other girls and boys, we formed a self-contained little confederacy and were happiest playing with one another. Frances, who was uncommonly quick and intelligent, often defeated me and I remember with what sorrow in my heart I went to her house with a whole bagful of marbles to ransom a particularly large glass favourite she had won from me.

We never played all our games in one day. In fact as I look back it appears that our games had their cycles and that the investigating anthropologist would very likely find that conkers and marbles, tops and hopscotch, came and went in accordance with laws as immutable as those of economics. Conkers were available only in autumn. But there was no observable reason why, at one time, for weeks on end we should do nothing but lash tops, and at another devote ourselves exclusively to yo-yos, both of which could always be bought at the toyshop.

An anthropologist might be able to tell me why, with the same infallibility of instinct with which a bird starts building its nest at the proper season, all the children of the district would begin making grottoes on or about a certain date in August, any attempt to set them up earlier or prolong their existence for more than three weeks being regarded as extremely reprehensible.

These grottoes, which were always built on the pavement against a wall, consisted of shells or small stones arranged in the form of a square, within which could be set flowers, small pieces of crockery, and any bright or curious object. After constructing the grottoes we had the right to sit by them and demand coppers from the passers-by. Rarely were we disappointed. In the evening the grottoes were dismantled, being set up again next day from the same materials in another place. As we got older Frances, Joan, and I used to make our grottoes not only in our own street but in the neighbouring streets too, setting them a yard or so apart against the same wall.

Another event which loomed large in our year was Derby Day, when throughout the afternoon and evening and until late at night a continuous stream of cars, buses, coaches, and horse-drawn carts and carriages, all packed with happy and excited racegoers, would be flowing along the main road between London and Epsom. Waving red, white, and blue streamers and holding to their mouths an instrument of wood and oiled paper which, when blown, would not only emit a raucous blare but, suddenly uncoiling to its full length, strike full in the face the unwary person at whom it was pointed, swarms of excited children would be standing on the kerb, their parents generally hovering behind to see that they did not fall under the wheels of the vehicles. When, races over and bets lost and won, the stream of traffic set more and more steadily in the homeward direction, our excitement reached its climax. Each brightly lit coach that swung slowly past us would be greeted by a shout of 'Throw out your mouldies!' whereupon the beerily jovial occupants would respond by flinging into our midst a handful of coppers for which we scrambled and fought until the next coach came along. At intervals, with the crack of a whip and the jingle of beribboned harness, there would pass by, in all the glory of innumerable gleaming pearl buttons, a Pearly King and Queen. They were always stout, elderly, and smiling, and the Queen, who was generally stouter than the King and who smiled more broadly and laughed with greater heartiness, invariably wore a black hat with enormous ostrich plumes that nodded and danced at every step the pony took.

After putting Joan and me to bed my parents would go for a drink at the Trafalgar, a public house named in honour by of the famous victory of good Lord Nelson who had lived at Merton, outside which, as outside every other pubic house in London that night, would be jammed a solid mass of people trying to elbow their way into the suffocating atmosphere of the bars.

Yet another annual event was Guy Fawkes Day. One year, when I was seven or eight, Mrs Davies wrote on the blackboard:

> Please to remember the Fifth of November,
> Gunpowder, treason and plot.

Though another boy could read 'please', I was the only member of the class who could read 'remember' and 'November'. Reading never gave me any trouble. But whether they could read the words or not, it was unlikely that anyone would forget to celebrate Guy Fawkes Day. For more than a week we had all been busy making our guys from pairs of old trousers and jerseys stuffed with straw and tied together with string. Father would make the head with a ball of rags and a piece of white cloth and paint on it a face complete with eyes, nose, and mouth. When the guy was ready, which was sometimes as much as a week before it was due to be burned, it would be taken from street to street in a small handcart or propped against a wall with a pipe in its mouth and passers-by would be implored to 'Spare a penny for the old guy'. With the money we collected we bought fireworks.

On November the fifth, as soon as it was dark, Joan and I, Mother and Father, and sometimes Nana and Auntie Noni too, would file downstairs into our tiny backyard where the guy had already been propped up in the middle of the cement floor. After Father had sprinkled him with petrol he was set on fire, whereupon the flames would leap up, the smoke swirl, and the darkness be lit up with a glare of ruddy light in which our faces would glow red and even our voices sound different. Sparklers, which we could run about with in our hands, and roman candles and golden rain, which had to be set at a distance on the ground, would then be ignited. Catherine wheels would go whizzing round, broadcasting a shower of rainbow sparks, and rockets go whizzing up into the night. Squibs and crackers exploded at our feet.

In less than half an hour our Guy Fawkes would be blazing merrily; ten more minutes and its head, with charred features no longer recognizable, would fall into the flames, sending up a shower of orange gold sparks. Within the hour the bonfire would have burned itself out and the last flame subsided, leaving only a mass of glowing embers; and standing silent there in the darkness, our shouts and laughter hushed, we would look up through the misty air and see that the stars had come out in the chill November sky.

To what extent London children keep up these old customs I do not know, but I am sure that all their radios, cinemas, and television sets do not give them half the pleasure that we derived from the playing of traditional games and making grottoes and celebrating Derby Day and Guy Fawkes Night.

At this period I never went to the cinema but once. The film was one of the old, silent Wild Westerns, and I remember how, whenever the hero used his six-shooters, an invisible attendant would fire a blank cartridge. The expected report was usually heard half a minute after we had seen the guns silently spitting fire on the screen.

Our only radio was a long black box with numerous knobs and dials. Once or twice, when my father allowed me to put on the headphones, I heard the voice of Uncle Bob, the first of a long line of *Children's Hour* uncles.

Do London children now ever hear the bell of the muffin-man in distant streets, or see the roast-potato man wheeling his portable brazier round the corner on a cold day? Perhaps they still see the knife grinder trundling his grinding wheel or the rag-and-bone man pushing his long coster's barrow on which are the tortoises and goldfish he is willing to give in exchange for scrap iron, old clothes, old newspapers, broken china, and any other household refuse.

But I am sure they never see the lamplighter on his rounds. Even before we left the house at Tooting the old gas streetlights, which on rainy days were reflected in a strange iridescence from the wet pavements, had been replaced by electric standards. As late as eight o'clock in the height of summer and as early as four o'clock in the depths of winter, the old lamplighter would come down the street. Having set his ladder against the arm of the lamp-post he would climb up, open the window of the glass shade, light the mantle, adjust the flame and climb down, shoulder his ladder, and be off down the street to the next lamp-post. I am sure that there is nothing lonelier in the world than a deserted street in a big city, dimly lit at intervals by gas lamps.

Not that Joan and I were ever allowed out alone after dark. But sometimes in the summer when it was fully light at six o'clock my mother would send us to the Broadway to meet my father. Tooting Broadway, with its huge statue of King Edward VII in royal robes dominating the latrines and coffee stalls from its marble pedestal in the centre of the traffic island, round which trams would lumber with a dreadful grinding of wheels and screeching of brakes, was to us the hub of the universe. It is, indeed, one of the biggest junctions and busiest shopping centres in the whole of London, though my father could remember how, at the beginning of the century, the High Street had been a country road with green fields on either side.

By the time we were the age he was then, the nearest field had retreated several miles, though of course there were Tooting Bec Common and Clapham Common, those green islands in a sea of brick and mortar, where we were taken sometimes in parties to play. There was also Figge's Marsh, where under a charter granted by Queen Elizabeth, an annual fair with swings, roundabouts, and coconut shies had been held for more than three hundred years. Farther afield was Mitcham Common, at the verge of which the Blue House stood in isolation against the sky as though at the end of the world, and Wimbledon Common, where my father had shown me Caesar's Well, with its old Latin letters and figures cut deep into the stones, and where we had tea and plum cake at the Windmill before going down to Queensmere to feed the swans.

As we stood in the vestibule of the tube, waiting for Father to come through the barrier, Joan and I used to feast our eyes on baskets of apples, oranges, plums, pears, peaches, and strawberries, and on the bunches of grapes and bananas displayed in the window of Walton the Fruiterers. Every time a strong gust of hot air blew across the vestibule from the escalator shaft, which meant that a train had come in, we peered eagerly over the barrier, searching for my father among the crowd that had started pouring through the gate. Sooner or later we would see him, bareheaded and attaché case in hand, coming towards us with his rolling, rather nautical stride, whereupon we would dash forward, seize hold of a hand apiece and lead him home in triumph.

Once in the kitchen, I would open his case and take out the newspaper, which was always *The Daily Herald*, for unlike the rest of the family he was a staunch supporter of the Labour Party, for which he invariably voted. His only concession to Conservatism was to take the *Sunday Express*, a paper Nana also read. Later on, I do not know why, he changed to the *People*. My own interest in the *Daily Herald*, which I read spread out on the floor, it being far too big for me to hold at arm's length, was strictly non-political. I was interested in following the adventures of Bobby Bear. Only after informing myself of the latest activities of this hero did I turn to the news. It was from Father's newspaper, I think, rather than any school primer, that I learned to read.

The first real book I ever handled must have been the old family Bible, so big and heavy I could hardly lift it, with tooled leather cover and gilt clasp which, imitating my father, I called grandmother's Bible, the old volume having belonged to his maternal grandmother. The illustrations with their rich blues, reds, and yellows, depicting Daniel in the lions' den kneeling among skulls and ribs, and Samson with the jawbone of an ass in his hand, had long been familiar to me. One rainy day when I was five or six years old, it occurred to me that instead of merely looking at the pictures I could read the text, and I promptly spelled my way through the first and second chapters of Genesis.

If the Bible gave me my first experience of prose, it was from a prayer-book that I had my first taste of poetry. Inside a cupboard in the sitting room among my father's books, I discovered at the age of six or seven a volume entitled *Prayer and Praise for Eventide*. From the inscription on the flyleaf I gathered that it had been presented to my paternal grandfather by his mother. Opening it, I came upon the lines

Stay, pilgrim, stay!
Night treads upon the heels of the day.

This was the first time I had ever met a metaphor and I can still recall the shock of delight the experience gave me. Though I read the rest of the volume, even the prayers, none of it had for me the magic of those first two lines.

Nana visited us once a week on the day she came from Southfields to Tooting to see her old friends, collect her rents, and do a little shopping. Aunt Noni came less often. With the exception of Father's friends and their wives, nearly all the other visitors were Mother's relations. The most frequent and regular of these were Auntie Kate and Auntie Jessie, who came once every three weeks, usually on a Friday and invariably together.

Only the creator of the aunts in *The Mill on the Floss* could have done them justice, though they had neither of them the formidability of Aunt Glegg nor the airs and graces of Aunt Dean. Except that Aunt Jessie was taller, in form and features they resembled each other. In fact the family likeness between all the brothers and the sisters was amazing.

Auntie Kate, who could not quite be called stout, had a watery blue eye with a twinkle in it and wore her hair in a bun kept in position by large hairpins which I always tried surreptitiously to pull out. Her nose, which being the family nose could only be called long, was red at the end and shiny, for despite the expostulations of Aunt Jessie and Mother she refused to powder. Their epithet for her was 'old-fashioned', which hardly was matter for astonishment since she was the eldest of the sisters and had already married and given birth to a son when my mother, who was the youngest, was still in the cradle. Aunt Kate was in fact an old-timer in many ways. She liked a thing no worse for having a patina on it, and invariably preferred the old to the new. Even the sweets she brought us were of a kind which must have been on the market in Dickensian times. Her ginger biscuits were the hardest and hottest I have ever tasted and usually had to be broken with a hammer. Her sense of humour, too, was rather ripe, not to say ribald, and while on holiday at Brighton she used to send all her friends and relations rather broad picture postcards depicting enormously fat women in bathing costumes with exaggeratedly prominent posteriors; so broad, indeed, both pictures and letter-press sometimes were, that old Mrs Bareham at Shoreham, with whom both my parents and Auntie Kate stayed at different times, once told my father, 'My dear, I'm afraid to pick them up off the mat in case I burn my fingers!' Yet Auntie Kate was a victim of melancholia, and in later years used to spend her evenings reading murder mystery stories after which she would put out the light and sit in darkness for hours on end. She also talked of committing suicide. But at that period of which I am speaking she was a cheery soul and I looked forward immensely to her visits. For many years she was the only aunt whom I suffered to kiss me or whom I consented to kiss for, despite my intense dislike of this form of salutation, I could never resist the breezy way in which she offered her cheek with a 'Come on, lad, give us a banger!'

Auntie Jessie's epithet was 'stately', even as Auntie Lil's was 'refined' and Mother's 'vivacious'. She had a full bosom, kind brown eyes, a musical voice, and was always redolent of scent and powder. Moreover she was quiet and gentle, with a touch of sadness in her expression. Unlike Auntie Kate she relished a ribald joke well enough to laugh at one but not well enough to tell one, and while laughing she always put her hand up to her mouth as if to hide either a blush or her rather prominent false teeth. It was she, not my mother, who amidst the giggles and titters of the sisters would slap at Aunt Kate with her glove and cry, 'Oh, don't, Kate!' when the latter's broad stories went too far.

On their visiting days they usually arrived early in the afternoon; but sometimes they came at eleven o'clock, on which occasions Auntie Kate would scandalize my mother and Auntie Jessie by producing her own lunch, which usually consisted of bread, cold meat or cheese, and pickles from a paper bag. Perhaps my mother's cooking was not old-fashioned enough! Both of them were always very well dressed. After taking off their gloves but not their hats, they would settle down with my mother to discuss clothes and husbands, during which proceedings numerous cups of tea would be drunk. It was one of the mysteries of my boyhood how they could talk for so many hours without stopping. From what I overheard of their conversations I gathered their husbands were rather deplorable creatures, though Aunt Katie and Aunt Jessie were both unanimous that my mother had been much more fortunate in that respect than themselves.

Auntie Kate's husband, Uncle Dan, was an Irish Catholic. He was six foot tall with steel-grey eyes, craggy jaw, and ruddy face, and he smelt very strongly of pipe tobacco. His temper was extremely violent, and he had treated Mother, when she had lived with him, and Auntie Kate before her marriage, with great brutality. A well-known trade unionist, he played a prominent part in the General Strike. My father, rather diffidently, once asked him whether Lord Beaverbrook's accusation that the Communists had promised him £25,000 to engineer the strike, was true, but he only laughed, puffed at his pipe and replied, 'If they did I haven't seen any of the money yet'. When I was much older, he offered to get me into the cooperative movement, and thence push me through the trade unions into politics.

Uncle Charlie, Aunt Jessie's husband, was a sporting type, with light brown hair, features inflamed with drink, and a thick utterance. He was related to the proprietor of a chain of butchers' shops in one of which he worked as manager. Unfortunately he could not resist the temptation of levying an unauthorized tax on the daily takings, in which connection he had several times been in serious trouble.

When they had last finished discussing the merits and demerits of their husbands the three sisters would try on one another's hats, for they all frequently bought new ones, and at each meeting at least one hat was produced which at least one sister had not seen. This ritual accomplished, Auntie Kate and Auntie Jessie would pull on their gloves, pick up their handbags, and, after kisses all round, depart to catch the tram which would take them home.

At that period Auntie Kate lived, as she had always done, at Fulham and Auntie Jessie a little further afield at Hammersmith. Perhaps twice or thrice a year Mother took me by tram to Fulham, which seemed a very long journey, and on one occasion she left me to stay with Auntie Kate for a whole week. Of this visit, which belongs to my fourth or fifth year, I remember only the pranks I played. Besides pulling out Auntie Kate's hairpins, I tied her to the armchair in which she had her afternoon nap, locked her in the kitchen, opened the door of the chicken coop so her white hen escaped over the wall into a neighbour's garden, and no doubt committed a score of other villainies. But whatever I did Auntie Kate never minded. In fact she always laughed, for out of the abundance of her good nature she was indulgent to the point of actually enjoying my naughtiness.

But though this is the oldest of my Fulham memories it is not the clearest. Much vivider is our alighting from the tram and hurrying over Wandsworth Bridge. Somehow it always seemed to be raining, or if it was not raining the sky would be gloomy and overcast and there would be the suspicion of drizzle in the air. In fact I do not remember that we ever had fine weather when we went to see Auntie Kate. Even if we got on the tram in sunshine, we would be sure to have to get down from it in the fog. A blue sky at Tooting Broadway meant black clouds over Wandsworth Bridge.

As we crossed the river we entered what was almost another world. It was not the barges moored at the water's edge, nor the tall white cranes that loaded and unloaded them from the shore, neither the grey gulls wheeling above our heads, but something deeper than all these yet inclusive of them, which made me feel that the atmosphere of Fulham was as different from that of Tooting as that of London was from Pekin's. In what that atmosphere consisted, or how it should be best described, even now I cannot tell. But as I write these lines the dreary, sooty, mournful, decayed, and desolate atmosphere of the Fulham streets comes palpable upon me, and once again I hear the sound of a tugboat siren in the distance like the wail of a lost soul.

Once over the bridge we were not far from Auntie Kate's house. As we passed, block by block, those rows of sordidly respectable houses where, at six o'clock on a cold December night, one might well be tempted to murmur

> The winter evening settles down
> With smell of steaks in passageways.

Mother would point out to me one house, bigger than the rest, that occupied a unique place in her affections. This was the house where she was born, and in which she had lived with her brothers and sisters until, on the death of their father, the family had been broken up.

The sight of the old house sometimes revived memories and Mother would begin to talk about her grandfather who had been born in Hungary and who could speak only a little broken English and in whose sweetshop she had sometimes helped as a girl. Father, to whom she always related these memories, used to tease her by saying that she had surely eaten more sweets than she had ever sold, an accusation which Joan and I always laughingly supported. But Mother's tenderest memories were of her father who, she wistfully recalled, had called her his little fairy. This reminiscence, too, made us shout with laughter and we professed to be unable to understand how anyone could ever think of describing Mother as a fairy. But without heeding us she would go on to relate, with a kind of dreamy pleasure, how when he was resting on the sofa after lunch she would receive permission to slip her hand into his pocket for a penny. However often she asked, she averred, she was never refused. At this point we would declare our conviction that Mother used to take advantage of his drowsiness to extract not the penny to which she was entitled but sixpence. 'Oh no,' she would say, 'Never!' Why we laughed at her so much when she indulged in these pathetic memories I do not understand. Perhaps unconsciously we wanted to disguise the fact that Mother's feeling for her father had really moved us very much. Like many English folk, we tended to shrink from all exhibition of emotion, especially of the tender sort, and to camouflage our susceptibility to it with an affectation of callousness. This grandfather, whom I never saw, for he died when Mother was fourteen, was a celebrated clarinettist and one of her earliest recollections was of being seasick during the Channel crossing when she accompanied him to a continental recital.

Most of her other memories related to her brothers and sisters of whom, including herself, there were fourteen. Uncle Bert, the eldest, was employed as a departmental manager in a famous London store. Between him and Auntie Kate, the next sister, there was no intercourse as she refused to speak to him because of his culpably unfilial behaviour at the time of their father's death.

Uncle Dick, who with the exception of my mother was the youngest, was a clarinettist like his father. At the age of sixteen he went to India, where he joined the staff of the Governor of Bengal and married. He was the innocent cause of the cruellest disappointment of my boyhood. When I was six he returned to England on leave. The news of his arrival threw me into a fever of excitement, for I assumed he would be accompanied by a whole retinue of Indian servants and, never having set eyes on an Indian before, I therefore looked forward to his coming to the house with the keenest anticipation. But as the sitting room door opened I craned my neck forward for a glimpse of the

> Dusk faces with white silken turbans wreathed

which I hoped to see beaming over his shoulder, all I saw was the very European features of Uncle Dick, Auntie Dolly, and my two cousins. When, a year later, Uncle Dick returned to Calcutta, he left behind a trail of unpaid bills which, to salve the family credit, Auntie Kate and Uncle Jack paid, and it was a long time before any of his brothers or sisters heard of him again.

Uncle Jack, who was the second youngest surviving brother, was accountant in a City firm. He had at one time suffered from a kind of religious mania, which took the form of falling on his knees in the street and praying aloud and of calling out to the passers-by that the Second Coming was at hand. By the time I began to be acquainted with him he had recovered from his harmless affliction, but still taught in Sunday School, and it was he who presented Joan and me with our first Bibles, a green one for me and a plum-coloured one for her. He was a good, kind, gentle soul, though quite ineffectual, and as the years went by he became more and more prone to fits of absentness from which he could only with difficulty be recalled.

His wife, Auntie Hilda, was plump and very pretty, and of a disposition almost angelic. Their only child had died very young and the bereaved pair often used to calculate when Joan's age or mine was mentioned, how old 'ours' would have been if he had lived.

Of Uncle Tom and Uncle Harry, neither of whom I ever saw, I know only that the former was killed in the Great War and that the latter emigrated to Australia and became a sheep farmer. About the twins who died not long after my mother's birth, I know nothing at all.

By the time we reached Auntie Kate's door I would have absorbed a good deal of Mother's family history.

The interior of the upstairs flat which she occupied (her son and his red-headed wife lived downstairs) was, like Auntie Kate herself, old-fashioned. The curtains were old-fashioned, the tablecloth was old-fashioned, and even the dog and the cat, an enormous tabby, were old-fashioned. Several years later she and Auntie Jessie went to live in the upper and lower flats respectively of a house down a quiet turning nearby, not far from their old home. But despite the comparative modernity of this house, to such an extent was Auntie Kate successful in impressing her old-fashionedness on her surroundings that to go upstairs to her flat after visiting Auntie Jessie, who had an electric cooker, was like stepping into H. G. Wells's Time Machine and going into the Victorian past.

At Christmas time representatives of both Father's and Mother's families would be invited to the house, but Mother often used to complain that 'her side' was being neglected. Father's family, which for practical purposes consisted of Nana and Auntie Noni, being not only more compact but geographically more accessible, was, in fact, more frequently invited, for whereas Mother's sisters and their husbands came to tea or dinner in rotation, Nana and Auntie Noni came every time. Of course there was never any serious disagreement between my parents on this point, but I was always conscious of the fact that in my mother's mind at least a certain amount of tension existed between the claims of the two 'sides'.

Preparations for Christmas usually began with the purchase of large quantities of holly and mistletoe from a barrow in the vicinity of Tooting Broadway, where the brightly lit shop windows already glittered with tinsel and where, during Christmas week, the slow-moving crowds of cheerful shoppers thronged the pavements more and more densely every night. The peak period was, of course, the last Saturday before Christmas, when, with the help of Nana's expert eye, we bought the turkey, and when the last stir was given to the Christmas pudding, on which Joan and I had already been working for weeks as hard as we could.

In the kitchen and sitting room Father would put up paper chains, which we sometimes made ourselves from slips of coloured paper, Chinese lanterns, bunches of balloons, and paper bells. There was always a Christmas tree, which we decorated with iridescent globes of coloured glass saved from year to year, candles of red, blue, green, and yellow wax, and strings of tinsel. The lower branches hung with presents, while at the top of the tree glittered a large tinsel star. One afternoon shortly before Christmas, Joan and I would be taken to one or other of the large department stores, such as the Co-op at Upper Tooting and Holdron's at Balham, where, at the end of our ride through Fairyland, Father Christmas would give each of us a parcel, a pink one for Joan and a blue one for me.

When we were very young we firmly believed in the existence of this mythical personage, every year making out for his benefit a list of the presents we wanted. This list, accompanied by a letter, we posted up the chimney, down which, we were assured, he would come sliding on Christmas Eve to fill the stocking we had hung up before going to sleep. At what age I found out that Haldron's Father Christmas was only one of the shop assistants dressed up, I do not remember, but certainly neither of us was any the better for the discovery.

Whatever the source of our presents, which after our disillusionment were inscribed with the name of the giver, the first thing we did when we awoke in the morning was empty our stockings, in the toe of which there was always a tangerine, and open the parcels heaped on a chair at our bedside. I do not remember that anyone in the house went to church on Christmas Day, though Nana probably did, but when I was fourteen or fifteen Mother and Father went to the midnight service. The morning was spent in the sitting room, where there were dishes of nuts and fruit and packets of figs and dates and where, at midday, Joan and I would be given a glass of wine to drink with our mince pie.

Due to the length of time required for cooking the turkey, which had to be roasted for several hours, Christmas dinner was a late meal, being served usually not before two o'clock. Flushed and triumphant, Mother would emerge amidst clouds of steam from the kitchen, where there had been anxious consultations with Nana as to the precise moment at which the succulent fowl should be taken from the oven, bearing the turkey – a spring of holly stuck in its breast – before her on a large oval dish.

After dinner, which lasted for upwards of two hours, we adjourned to the sitting room, where the presents were untied from the tree and distributed. Sometimes Father played his favourite gramophone records, among which I remember an operatic aria sung by Caruso of whom he was very fond, and Gershwin's *Rhapsody in Blue* which, from the way in which the clarinet climbed up the scale in the opening bars, I called 'the aeroplane'.

Boxing Day was always spent at Southfields, where we ate what was really a second Christmas dinner, complete with pudding. In her younger days, when Father was still a lad, Nana had cooked five or six Christmas puddings every Christmas, keeping the extra ones for birthdays; but now she did not feel equal to making more than one a year. Her speciality, though, was cakes, jellies, and trifles, of each of which there would be nearly a dozen varieties at tea-time, besides savouries.

The best Christmases, of course, were those on which there was a fall of snow and when, on Father's opening the front door for us to go out and make snowballs, our eyes would be struck by the dazzle of whiteness that made us blink. But whether we were at home or at Nana's the evening would be spent around the fire where glasses of wine stood warming on the hearth and where chestnuts fizzled and popped in a shovel between the bars of the grate.

A few days later came New Year's Day, which as a boy Father celebrated by ringing the Tibetan ritual hand-bell and exploding crackers outside the front door, a tradition which he would have kept up if Nana and her Southfields neighbours, who were more elderly and more definitely middle class than those of Tooting, had been prepared to tolerate the racket.

Birthdays were celebrated in the same way, though on a much less lavish scale, turkey and Christmas pudding being replaced by the cake with an appropriate number of candles and our name embossed in coloured icing, and instead of the assembly of grown-ups there would be a small gathering of children. But for me Christmases and birthdays always ended in disaster, for I would get keyed up to such a pitch of excitement that however tired I was I could not bear the thought of going to bed, with the result that Father had to exert his authority and send me off to my own room in tears. Even so early in life did I have to learn that

Every sweet with sour is tempered still.

NOTES

1. The autobiography of Ayya Khema (1927–1993), *I Give You My Life,* was published in 1997. That of Chögyam Trungpa (1939–1987), *Born in Tibet,* appeared in 1966.
2. One of eight Reveries and Reminiscences in *A Moseley Miscellany,* Ibis Publications, 2015 (*Complete Works* vol. 23).
3. Introduction to *Learning to Walk,* see Appendix 1.
4. *A Stream of Stars,* Windhorse Publications, Birmingham 1998, p. 15.
5. See *Complete Poems 1944–1994,* Windhorse Publications, Birmingham 1995, pp. 23–90ff. (*Complete Works,* vol. 25) and *Early Writings 1944–1954,* Ibis Publications, Ledbury 2014 (*Complete Works,* vol. 7).
6. *The History of My Going for Refuge,* Windhorse Publications, Glasgow 1988, sections 2–5, pp.19–33 (*Complete Works* vol. 2).
7. Peter Avery and John Heath-Stubbs (trans.), *The Rubáiyát of Omar Khayyaám,,* Allen Lane, London 1979, p. 49.
8. T. S. Eliot (1888–1965), Prelude 1 from *Prufrock and Other Observations* (1920).
9. John Milton (1608–1674), *Paradise Regained* (1671), book 4, line 76.
10. Edmund Spenser (1552/3–1599), sonnet 26 from *Amoretti and Epithalamion* (1595).
11. A. E. Housman (1859–1936), *A Shropshire Lad* (1896). These lines from the second of 63 poems.
12. William Sharp, *Dante Gabriel Rossetti: A Record and a Study,* Macmillan & Co, London 1882.
13. William Wordsworth (1770–1850), 'November 1806' (published 1807).

14 Percy Bysshe Shelley (1792–1822), 'Ode to the West Wind' (1820), canto 3.

15 *Abhijñānaśakuntala*, a play in Sanskrit based on an episode from the *Mahābhārata*, composed by Kālidāsa (flourished fourth–fifth centuries CE).

16 From ch. 11, 'The Book of Religion by the Heavenly Perfections', Edwin Arnold (1832–1904) (trans.), *The Song Celestial or Bhagavad Gītā*, published 1885.

17 Both these articles can be found in *Early Writings 1944–1954*, Ibis Publications, Ledbury 2014 (*Complete Works*, vol. 7).

18 Sangharakshita writes about this novel in 'A Room with a View' in *A Moseley Miscellany*, Ibis Publications 2015, pp. 51–2.

19 'Heaven-Haven' (1918) by Gerard Manley-Hopkins (1844–1889); 'The Haystack in the Floods' (1858) by William Morris (1834–1896); *Non Sum Qualis eram Bonae Sub Regno Cynarae* (1894) by Ernest Dowson (1867–1900).

20 Ascribed to Sufi poet and musician Ab'ul Hasan Yamīn ud-Dīn Khusrau (1253–1325 CE).

21 Included in the collection *Early Writings 1944–1954*, Ibis Publications, Ledbury 2014 (*Complete Works*, vol. 7).

22 Sangharakshita wrote about this experience in an article, 'An Occidental Ear Listens to Indian Music' published in 1946. See *Early Writings 1944–1954*, Ibis Publications, Ledbury 2014, pp. 95–7 (*Complete Works*, vol. 7).

23 Sangharakshita writes about Walpola Rahula (whom he met several times), and discusses the Sri Lankan monk's political-cum-religious views and their impact in 'Religio-Nationalism in Sri Lanka' in *Alternative Traditions*, Windhorse Publications, Glasgow 1986, pp. 69–91 (*Complete Works*, vol. 13).

24 *Ratnagotravibhāga* 1, verse 73, quoted in E. Conze et al (eds.), *Buddhist Texts Through the Ages*, Harper & Row 1964, p. 130.

25 Sangharakshita went on to write a substantial article on this theme during his stay in Benares in 1949: 'Philosophy and Religion in Original and Developed Buddhism'. See *Early Writings 1944–1954*, Ibis Publications, Ledbury 2014, pp. 208–225 (*Complete Works*, vol. 7).

26 Sangharakshita wrote an article called 'The Ramakrishna Mission in Malaya' on behalf of the Swami Buddha Maharaja, which describes the Mission's history, including what happened to it during the war. The article is included in *Early Writings 1944–1954*, Ibis Publications, Ledbury 2014 (*Complete Works*, vol. 7).

27 One such lecture was later written up and published as

'A Modern View of Buddhism' which is included in the collection *Early Writings 1944–1954*, Ibis Publications, Ledbury 2014 (*Complete Works*, vol. 7).

28 One of the poems written at this time was 'Meditation' (see *Complete Poems 1941–1994*, Windhorse Publications, Birmingham 1995, p. 31 (*Complete Works*, vol. 25).

29 See 'A Note on Anatta' in *Early Writings 1944–1954*, Ibis Publications, Ledbury 2014, pp. 226–32 (*Complete Works*, vol. 7).

30 The author recalls today (2016) that the poem 'Rain' was among them.

31 This article has not survived. It was sent to the editor of the *Vedanta Kesari* (see p. 228) but was not published.

32 See 'Attavāda and Anattāvāda' (date of composition not clear), and 'A Note on Anattā' in *Early Writings 1944–1954*, Ibis Publications, Ledbury 2014 (*Complete Works*, vol. 7).

33 This article was published in the *Mannam Souvenir* but no copy survives.

34 This poem has not survived.

35 The monk was Mahaprajna, who appears (disrobed) in Sangharakshita's second volume of memoirs, *Facing Mount Kanchenjunga*. The Prime Minister who flogged him was Mohan Shumsher Jang Bahadur Rana (1885–1967), the last Prime Minister of the Rana regime in Nepal (1948–1951).

36 The story of Jivaka is recounted in *Precious Teachers*, Windhorse Publications, Birmingham 2007, ch. 5 (*Complete Works*, vol. 22).

37 See (*Complete Works*, vol. 2).

38 See (*Complete Works*, vol. 14).

39 The request came from Raghavan Ayer whom Sangharakshita met through his friends B. P. and Madame Wadia. The first edition of *The Legacy of India* was published by the Oxford University Press in 1937. After submitting his chapter for the new edition Sangharakshita, hearing nothing further for many years, decided to include it in a new, American edition of *A Survey of Buddhism* (Shambhala, Boulder 1980, pp. xix–xlix). It was included similarly as an 'Introduction' in all subsequent editions (i.e. seventh, eighth, and ninth). The chapter was also published as a booklet by Sinhanad Publications, Pune, in 1990 as part of their *Dhammamegha* series under its original title, *A Bird's Eye View of Indian Buddhism*. The piece is also included in *Complete Works* vol. 7.

INDEX

Introductory Note

References such as '178–9' indicate (not necessarily continuous) discussion of a topic across a range of pages. Wherever possible in the case of topics with many references, these have either been divided into sub-topics or only the most significant discussions of the topic are listed.

Abhidhamma 444, 446, 449
Advaita Vedanta 240, 343, 367, 372
Adventurer 19, 51
Aeschylus' tragedies 51
Agamananda, Swami 253, 255, 263, 265, 269, 284, 288, 298
Agra 111
Ahmedabad 172, 179–80, 182, 208, 343
Ainsworth, H. 18
Akṣobhya 430
Albers, A.C. 167, 169–72, 213
Alf 140–1
Alice 95
Alice in Wonderland 15–16
All-India Religions Conference 172–3
alms 109, 338, 414–16, 418, 421, 426, 459–61
almsfood 417–18
almsround 416, 426, 447
altars 33, 121, 127, 251, 259–60, 311, 455, 461
Ambedkar, B.R. 452, 522–3
Amitābha 345, 430
Amoghasiddhi 430
anagārikās 403, 405, 409, 411, 413, 425, 433–4, 440

Ānanda 415
Ananda Maitreya 4, 101, 480
Ananda Vihara 429–30, 439–40
Anandamayi Ashram 182, 184–5, 312, 315, 435
Anandamayi Ma 179, 182–213, 215–16, 220, 259, 262, 321–2, 387
Anandamayi's ashram 182, 184–5, 312, 315, 435
Anandashram 319–23, 325–6, 328–30, 332, 344, 388
ānāpānasati 144, 206–7, 249
anattā 302, 447
Angar Caitya 406
Anglican church 20, 40, 42, 48, 70, 266, 293, 397
Aparokṣānubhūti 113, 125
aphorisms 522, 524
arahants 85, 333, 404, 453
Arjuna 164
army 88, 94, 96–7, 105, 154–5, 159, 191, 315
  corporals 92–7
  fatigues 93–4, 97, 155–6, 248
  life 92, 95, 110, 114, 153, 157
  NCOs 94, 98, 138
  rifles 92–5, 97, 106, 155, 157, 170

Arnold, M. 452
Arnold, Sir Edwin 62, 128
art master 31, 39, 48
art school 35–6
Arthur, Uncle 84
Arunachala 337, 339, 341, 346–8, 376
Āryadeva 361–2
ascetics 202, 235, 336, 338–9, 353–5, 358, 361, 414
 five 388–90
 Hindu 246, 295, 347–8, 361, 398, 416
 wandering 243, 322, 327, 370, 386, 388, 444
ashes 174–5, 305, 385–6, 461
Ashok 180–1
Aśoka 191, 292, 374, 390
Aśoka Pillar 421
astrology 280
atheism 39–40
Audrey, Aunt 132–3, 159–60
Aurobindo, Sri 334, 350
austerities 320, 322, 324, 326
Avalokiteśvara 2, 283, 326, 485
'Avalon, Arthur' 148
Awakening of Faith in the Mahāyāna 332
Ayyappan 249–50, 282–3

Bach, J.S. 72–3, 100, 155
Bacon, Sir Francis 46
Baker, Mrs 56–7, 59–60, 62
Bamboo Grove 461–2, 464–5
Banerjee, R. K. 146, 152–3, 158–63, 165–72, 192–7, 199–201, 204, 206–7; *see also* Buddharakshita; Satyapriya
Bangalore 349–50, 353–4, 358, 363, 375, 380, 383
Baptist Church 21, 41–2, 48
Barnstaple 46, 48, 51–4, 60–1, 68
Barspar 415
Barua, B. M. 124, 135, 166
bathing 214, 239, 245, 377, 379
Batty Tatty 95
Baudelaire, C. P. 72, 113
bazaars 111, 185, 190, 220, 226, 267, 288, 317
beaches 33, 116, 118, 228, 237, 239–40, 252
Beatrice 84
beds 14, 16–19, 24, 26, 88, 92–4, 216, 314–15
 string 216, 421–2, 444–7
Beethoven. L. van 68, 72–3, 155
beggars 109–10, 127, 387, 390
begging 415, 417

begging-bowls 143, 409, 414, 426, 447, 459
bel trees 311, 376–7, 380
bells 99, 139, 253, 340–1, 390, 486, 489, 494
Belur Math 129, 131, 135, 141, 162, 247, 363, 365–6
Ben 43
Benares 194, 196, 386–9, 391, 395–6, 442–3, 452–3, 458–9
 Hindu University 394, 442, 448, 458, 470
Bengal 138, 169, 171, 184, 501
Bengal Vaishnavism 188, 197, 315
Bengalis 119–20, 167, 184, 186–7, 193–4, 196, 198–9, 261
Besant, A. 148
Besant, W. 18
Besthorpe 24, 83
Bhagavad Gītā 61–2, 111, 164, 175, 213, 280
bhajans 187–91, 291, 296, 300, 312, 321–2, 326, 329–30
Bharat Mata Mandir 387
bhikkhus 121–2, 162, 166–7, 169, 252, 396, 425, 439
bhikṣus 101, 229–30, 390
Bible 9–10, 44, 61, 199, 496, 501
 classes 41–2, 45, 70
Bideford 51, 54
Bihar 454, 457–60, 462, 466, 470
billeting officers 46–7, 52–3
billets 48, 50, 53
Bimbisāra 464–5
birthdays 14, 18, 75, 106, 179–80, 413, 482, 504
black water 195, 433
Blanca, *see* Schlaum, B.
Blavatsky, H. P. 64, 85
blessings 45, 324, 334, 337, 356, 358, 369, 372
Blissful Mother 179, 183, 186, 196, 198, 200, 202, 212
Blitz 53, 67–70, 99, 102
boats 23, 33, 131, 230, 253, 401
Bodh Gaya 389, 395, 402, 453–5
bodhisattvas 124, 235, 283, 333, 430, 448, 454, 521–2
 Avalokiteśvara 2, 326, 485
Bombay 173, 180, 303, 320, 381, 383
bonfires 8, 162, 493
bookshops 32, 51, 62, 82–4, 107, 113, 117
 second-hand 32, 51, 82, 88
Borivli 381
Bose, Subhas Chandra 141, 146, 153
Boswell, J. 51

Botticelli, S. 24, 26
bowls 134, 221, 413, 415–18, 422, 426, 447, 488
Boy Yogi 330–1
Boys' Brigade 40–2
Bradley, F. H. 446
Brahma 334
Brahmin quarter 256, 258, 266, 272, 277, 308, 338
Brahmins 193–6, 198–202, 235, 249–51, 274, 285–7, 336, 414–16
  by birth 321, 425
  Malayali 285–6
  Nambudiri 285–7, 369
  Nepalese 403
  orthodox 231, 281, 454, 458
  Tamil 241, 249, 255, 277, 281, 285, 338, 341
  Telugu 368–9
breakfasts 16, 217, 253, 260, 265, 398, 408, 432–3
breath control 125, 317–18, 324
bridegrooms 182, 481
Bridges, R. S. 124
Brontë, C. 18
Browne, Sir Thomas 84
Browning E.B. 36
buckets 33, 198–9, 202, 209, 251, 305, 374
Buddha 282–3, 345–6, 388–90, 415–17, 419–22, 453–5, 457–62, 464–6
Buddha Kuti 442–5, 449, 451–2
Buddha Maharaj 141, 143, 146, 149, 386–8, 392
Buddharakshita 410–13, 415, 421–2, 425–34, 436, 439–40, 442–4, 451–2; *see also* Banerjee, R. K.; Satyapriya
Buddhist monks 115, 121, 386, 388, 395, 397, 455, 459
Buddhist philosophy 122, 228, 394, 446, 451–2, 458, 460
bungalows 115, 185, 204, 321, 331, 336, 338, 350
  government 284, 364
Bunyan, J. 44
Burke, E. 277
Burmese 102, 230, 403–5, 419, 424
buses 28, 51, 59, 95, 182, 235, 237, 241
Butaol 413, 421, 423–7, 436, 441, 443

cake-wallah 110–11, 115
Calcutta 128–31, 134–6, 158, 161, 168–70, 192–3, 390, 393
Cameron, C. 87, 100, 103, 150

canals 108, 185, 207–8, 211, 214
candles 12, 14, 67, 115, 142, 407, 434, 503–4
  roman 8, 493
Cape Comorin 230, 232, 235, 237, 239–41, 244, 248, 258
caretakers 185, 257, 260, 393, 420
caste 198–9, 201–2, 263–4, 266–9, 278–80, 399–400, 415–16, 436–7
  low 196, 284, 339, 399, 418, 436–7
  prejudices 196, 264, 291
  restrictions 195, 202, 285, 433
  system 195, 197, 200–2, 263–5, 278, 280, 284–5, 436–7
cave, vision in the 335–48
ceremonies 67, 73, 175–7, 181, 190, 195, 368–9, 409
Ceylon 116–17, 124, 144, 227–30, 252, 424, 442–3, 447–8
Chaitanya, Sri 185–6, 188, 202, 387
Chakravarty, G. 184
Chamberlain, N. 46
Chandra, Arun 419–20
Chandragupta Maurya 374
Chandramani, U 396, 403–5, 407–11, 413, 424, 430
chanting 36, 313, 341, 426, 453
Chapter House 403, 408–10
Charing Cross Road 82–4
Charles, Uncle 56–8, 67, 99, 104–5, 485–6
Cheenia Baba 407
Chelliah 121
chess 39–40
children 3, 7, 29, 35, 200–1, 285–6, 291, 484–6
  London 5, 481, 494
Children's Encyclopaedia 15, 22–3, 27, 109, 371
China 2, 22, 140, 144, 257, 259, 485
Chinese Buddhists 142–3
Chinese friends 2, 142, 147, 484
Chinese monks 142, 149, 460
Chowrasta 132–3
Christ 20, 23, 44, 150, 298, 311
Christianity 20, 71, 150, 173, 265, 285, 291–2
Christians 61, 64, 238, 241, 283–5, 291–3, 306–7, 463
Christie, A. 64
Christmas 12, 14–15, 36, 97, 502–4
  dinner 14, 503–4
  morning 15–16, 36
  pudding 12, 14, 502, 504
Chu Ta-Kao 87
Churchill, W. 49
cigarettes 154, 240, 276, 293, 317, 468

INDEX / 511

cinemas 91, 493–4
clairaudience 309, 311
clairvoyance 204, 309
Clapham Common 32, 88, 495
classical music 72, 140, 155
Clement 40, 46–52
Cleopatra 27, 39
coal office 64–5
cobras 201, 274, 331, 354–5
coconut palms 116, 118, 161, 252–3, 256, 283, 285, 293
coffee 81, 132, 237, 240, 277, 279, 304, 330
Colombo 116–18, 122–3, 126, 128–30, 135, 141, 229–30, 311
communities 247, 266, 282–3, 285–8, 295, 394, 396, 411
 spiritual 389, 394, 411, 425
Comorin, Cape 230, 232, 235, 237, 239–41, 244, 248, 258
compassion 149, 206, 324, 326, 333, 360, 521
composers 31, 70, 72
concentration 67, 73, 207, 353, 355
concubines 233, 285–6
confessions 79, 234, 325, 487
conflict 20, 25, 194, 208, 348, 357, 449, 451
Confucius 23
congregations 42–3, 45, 187–9, 209, 291, 342–3
Congress 146, 190–1
Connaught Circus 112–13
consciousness 61, 64, 73–4, 98, 204, 243, 332, 392
 normal 313–14
consent 135, 175, 190, 192, 200, 391
contemplation 334, 463–4
 passive 5, 481
 peaceful 377
control 4, 122, 131, 166, 317, 368, 487
Cook, Miss 75–6, 79–82
cooked food 199, 246, 399–400, 415–16, 418, 422, 433
cooks 47, 57, 119, 149, 167–9, 216, 260, 289
coolies 227, 297, 380, 419, 421, 428
corporals 92–7
corruption 83, 278, 368–9, 383, 393
Coué, Dr 21
courtyards 127, 211–13, 215, 232, 246, 248, 337, 344
 temple 213, 454
cousins 12, 76, 84, 160–1, 415, 486, 501
Cousins, J. 248
craving 19, 41, 303

Creighton, M. 32
cremation ground 384–6
Cultural Heritage of India 160–1
culture 70, 112, 119–20, 130, 153, 158, 393, 396
cunning 94–5, 225, 260
Cunningham, General sir Alexander 454
curds 374, 416, 418, 422, 426
curiosity 122, 147, 184, 232, 256, 263, 265, 351
curries 119–20, 217, 221, 231, 251, 336, 360, 448
 vegetable 194, 416, 418, 426
curtain of fire 392, 396

Daily Herald 9, 495
Dakshineshwar 131, 238
Dalada Maligawa 126
dance 37, 64, 132–3, 189, 245, 409
Dante 84
Darjeeling 132, 428, 467
darshan 320, 341, 343, 350, 369
Das, Bhagavan 388
daughters 3, 20, 35, 179, 275, 349–50, 369, 486–7
 adopted 168
Dave 159
death 142, 213–14, 303–4, 374, 483, 485–6, 489, 500–1
deference 184, 205, 229, 356, 443
Defoe, D. 37
Dehra Dun 179–80, 182, 190, 200
Delhi 109–11, 115–16, 118, 120, 122, 125, 140, 142
Delius, F. 72
demons 366, 443
devotion 44, 126, 128, 259, 321–2, 329–30, 347–8, 425–6
devotional songs 184, 186–7, 215, 291, 329, 350–1, 435
Dewan 241, 248–9, 370
Dhammapada 115, 122, 328, 445, 449
Dharma 332, 407, 409, 411, 413, 424–5, 438–9, 521
Dharma Parishad 172–3, 178
Dharmananda, Swami 263–4, 294
Dharmapala, Anagarika 168, 390, 455, 522
Dharmapriya 207, 224, 265, 410
Dharmarakshita 410, 413
Diamond Sūtra 85, 101, 301
diamond throne 454, 456
Diana of Ephesus 344
Dick, Uncle 12, 109, 132, 157, 159–60, 501
Diderot, D. 51
dining-halls 91–2, 328, 336, 390

dinner 14, 57, 101, 119, 181, 313, 316, 502–3
Dipnagar 459–60
disappointments 12, 41, 240, 301, 306, 392–5, 401, 404
disciples 186–7, 196–7, 212, 353–63, 393–5, 410, 424, 462–3
  female 348, 396
  Great Disciples 453, 458, 464, 466
  personal 390, 396, 455
discipline 56, 86, 97, 128, 130, 155, 316, 451
disgust 133, 140, 159–60, 187, 196, 258, 274, 417
Divyagiri 375–6, 380
doctors 15, 17–18, 24, 26, 152, 276, 435, 444
Dolly, Aunt 12, 84, 501
Donne, J. 100
Donnelly, I. 32
dowries 368–9
dragons 1–2, 473, 480, 484–5
  five-clawed imperial 2, 484
  gold 2, 484, 486
dreams 74, 157, 246, 315, 341, 364–5, 389, 451
drums 134, 189, 239, 294, 340, 462
Dumrai 429
Durga 134, 346
Dutt, N. 135

eastern Himalayas 458, 475, 522
Eazhavas 251–2, 274, 283, 285, 295
Eckhart, Meister 161
Eddie 96
education 18, 22, 38, 56, 153, 217, 427, 435
ego 329, 355, 463
egotism 78, 84, 152, 354, 362
Ek So Aat, Swami 347–8
elephants 208, 283, 294, 365, 371, 420
  pink 115
Elizabeth I 27, 37, 495
Elizabeth of York 27
emotions 44–5, 92, 108, 188–9, 197, 225–6, 302, 343
enjoyment 20, 56, 72–3, 86, 121, 350, 435
Enlightenment 206, 324, 333, 393, 396, 453, 457, 465–6
  Perfect 333, 388
Ernie 91–100, 105, 107–8, 111, 140, 153, 157
evacuees 46, 48, 50, 52
Evans-Wentz, W. Y. 340
evening meditation 288, 300, 385
evening worship 340–1, 434

Everyman 62, 86
evil 22, 147, 152, 276, 278, 284, 482, 484
excitement 12, 14, 123, 127, 187–9, 488, 501, 504
exhilaration 45–6, 469
experience 10, 72–4, 248, 314–17, 345–6, 421–2, 425, 481
  spiritual 85, 176, 377
experiments 23, 27, 37, 39, 97, 125, 303, 459
explosions 101, 103–4, 467
Ezalda, Cousin 84

faith 44, 86, 239, 247, 293, 301, 332, 355
fame 121, 222, 225, 331
family 28, 46–7, 59–60, 162–3, 181, 330–1, 350–1, 500
family life 159, 235
Fanny, Auntie 24
fasting 281, 303–5, 318, 322, 360, 408, 432
Father 3–5, 8–10, 18–22, 24–9, 67–71, 88–90, 104–6, 502–4
fatigues 93–4, 97, 155–6, 248
Faust 49
festivals 12, 162, 233–4, 374
Fingal's Cave 72
fish 148–9, 192, 215, 292
Fish 96
Five Precepts 102, 196, 404, 417, 425–6, 432, 436, 438
flowers 35, 42, 100, 102, 127, 187, 197, 259
food 109–10, 140, 149, 200, 303–4, 348, 415, 417
forgiveness 30, 209, 445
formal ordination 327, 346
Frances 5, 7, 481, 491–2
freedom 23, 31, 64, 98, 153, 168, 206, 449
French, L. 86
French, Mary 60
French, Mr 60
French, Mrs 60, 65, 67
Freud, S. 82
friendship 76, 142, 147, 153, 193, 266, 272
Fu Chin Lama 460
Fulham 11, 28, 499
funeral pyres 384–5

Gandhi, Mahatma 179, 292–3, 303, 330, 352–3, 387
Ganesha 121, 208, 278, 282
Ganges 179, 383–4, 387

ganja 348, 399–400
gardens 26, 34, 46, 51, 92, 115, 119, 247–8
garlands 62, 127, 134, 215, 327, 409
Gayatri mantra 196
Gemmell, W. 85
George V 27
George VI 267
Ghoom 133, 219
Gillian, Cousin 132
girls 5, 29–30, 75–6, 78–9, 194, 286, 481, 490–1
Gladys 159
God 41, 43, 110, 202, 277, 319–22, 329, 348
goddesses 115, 175, 245, 253, 267, 298, 383; *see also individual names*
    Virgin Goddess 237–8, 258
gods, *see also individual names*
    Hindu 122, 267, 282, 299, 383, 421
    incarnations of 202, 259, 352
Goethe, J. W. 49
going forth 226
gold 2, 60, 67, 121, 127, 385, 387, 469
    dragons 2, 484, 486
Gomateshwara 363, 373
Gouranga 188; *see also* Chaitanya, Sri
government bungalows 284, 364
grammar 261–2, 445
Grandfathers 2–3, 5, 10, 12, 482, 485–7, 496, 500
Grandmothers 1–2, 9, 480, 483–5, 496
Grant, J. 37
Gray, T. 377
Gṛdhrakūṭa 464
Great Disciples 453, 458, 464, 466
Great War 4, 47, 488, 501
Gretton, Miss 76–7, 80, 82
grottoes 7, 465, 491–2, 494
guest-houses 211, 220, 227, 368, 370, 373, 402–3, 405
Gujerat 179, 182, 330
Gujerati 173–5
gunnaw 432
Gurukipal Singh 222, 226
Gurupriya 196, 198, 200–2, 204, 210
gurus 177, 202, 206, 320, 326, 331, 354, 358–9; *see also individual names*
Guy Fawkes Day 8, 492–4
Gwen 60, 65, 67, 69

Halevid 363, 365–6
Halford, Corporal 93, 97–8
hand-drums 186–7
Hardy, T. 36, 52

Hari Baba 203, 209
Hari mantra 312–13, 315
harmonium 44, 187, 190
Harmsworth, A. 22
Harry 'the Ticker' 95
Hartmann, F. 63
hatha yoga 303, 305, 317
hautboys 239, 258, 294
Haydn, F. J. 73
headmasters 38–9, 50, 401, 435
health 53, 75, 77, 88, 291, 303, 322, 427
heat 107, 110, 113, 345, 384–5, 395, 397–8, 401
Hegel, G. W. F. 70, 83, 107
Heine, H. 46
Henry VIII 27
Hercules 23
hermitages 222, 341, 344, 414, 470
Herod 48
heroes 9, 19, 51, 146, 241, 366, 488, 494–5
Herrick, R. 100
Hilda, Aunt 104, 501
Himalayas 128–9, 230, 232, 237, 243, 322, 327, 386–7
    eastern 458, 475, 522
Hindu ascetics 246, 295, 347–8, 361, 398, 416
Hindu gods/goddesses 122, 267, 282, 299, 383, 421
Hindu monks 117, 393, 397, 418
Hindu philosophy 164, 447, 458
Hinduism 158–9, 174, 217–18, 265, 277–9, 284–5, 301–2, 387–8; *see also* Brahmins; caste
    orthodox 199, 287, 298, 367, 436
Hindus 123–4, 173–4, 178–9, 217–18, 249, 272–4, 278–80, 292–3
    orthodox 194, 200, 263, 279, 447, 462
history 22–4, 27–8, 31–2, 37, 39, 247, 249, 407
'History of the Reign of Queen Elizabeth' 37
Hitler, A. 47
Hokkien 143, 149
holidays 7, 11, 88, 95, 457–8, 469, 491, 497
holly 12, 14, 502–3
Holy Mother 121, 136, 196, 257, 311
Holy War 44, 61
Homer 49
Hoole, J. 51
Hornung, E.W. 18
hospitality 50, 180, 221, 235, 252, 259, 391, 394

hospitals 4, 15–17, 77, 88, 91, 136, 427, 488–9
hostility 97, 223, 244, 261, 264, 390, 392, 397
Hotspur 19, 22
Housman, A. E. 36
humility 123, 128, 306, 356, 362
humour 4, 11, 329, 433, 447, 488, 497, 524
Humphreys, T. C. 100–3, 150
hungry ghosts 310, 338
hymns 35, 43–5, 71, 251, 291, 434
Hypatia 18–20
hysteria 202, 314, 316

idiosyncrasies 94–5
Ilfracombe 51–2
Iliad 49
image-worship 245
In Quest of God 319–22, 329
incarnations of gods 202, 259, 352
independence 59, 83, 146, 153, 173, 179, 219, 222–3
Independence Day 222–4
Indian National Army 142, 146, 153
Indian National Congress 146, 190–1
Industrial School 296–7, 300–1, 304, 316, 319
initiations 67, 202, 234, 325, 404
Isis Unveiled 54, 63–4, 85, 147
Iyer, Ramaswami 255, 257, 265, 272, 285, 327
Iyer, Sir C. P. Ramaswamy 241, 370
Iyer, Sundaram 281
Iyer, Venkateshwara 277–82, 285, 341, 388

Jack, Uncle 104, 501
Jackson, R. L. 101
Jainism 279, 361, 363, 373–4, 449, 460, 464
Jane Eyre 19–20
Japanese Army 141–2, 150, 155
Japanese officers 138, 154
Jason 23
Jessie, Aunt 10–11, 26, 28, 496–9, 502
Jivaka 475–8
jivanmukta 240, 369
jñānin 272, 332
Joan (sister) 5, 7–9, 33–5, 72, 88–9, 104–5, 489–95, 500–3
Jock 118
John Watkins 85–6
Johnson, S. 18, 46, 51, 53
journeys 191–2, 326–7, 375–6, 395–401, 418–19, 421, 423, 427–8
Julian, Emperor 61

jungle 157, 207, 297, 363–7, 373, 381, 421–2, 427
jutha 200

Kalady 252–3, 260, 263, 265, 298
Kalimpong 58, 458, 467–70, 473, 475–6, 478–9, 522
Kanchenjunga, Mount 467, 469–71
Kandy 126, 128, 143
Kanhangad 319–20, 334
Kanheri Caves 381
Kant, I. 61, 70
Kantaraj 130–1, 134–7, 141, 158, 160, 162–3
Karttikeya 282
Kasauli 214, 219–20, 222–3, 226, 230, 241, 248–9, 260
Kashyap, Bhikkhu Jagdish 122, 394–6, 442–9, 453, 457–9, 461–3, 465, 468–71
Kate, Aunt 10–11, 26, 28, 33, 71, 496–502
Kath, Auntie 46, 57–8, 60, 67, 99, 105
Kathmandu 424, 436
kaupin 347–8
Keats, J. 36
Kheminda 144
Kierkegaard, S. O. 124
kindness 60, 171, 220, 222, 327, 427, 439
Kingsley, C. 18
Kishengunj 182, 184–6, 192–3, 196–7, 207, 210, 212–13, 220
kites 109–10
knowledge 23–4, 39, 56, 64, 243, 252, 445, 448–9
Kollupitiya 116–17
Krishna (child) 313–15
Krishna (Mysorean) 363–4, 366, 375–7, 379–80
Krishna, Sri 164, 187–8, 197, 202, 280–1, 291, 299, 314–15
Krishnabai, Mother 319–22, 324–5, 334
Krishnan 283–4
Kshatriyas 235, 369, 400, 415
Kul 460
Kumari-Puja 135
Kusinara 395–7, 401–3, 405–8, 410–14, 418–19, 421, 425–6, 453–4
Kwan Yin 2, 448, 486

'Lady of Shalott' 29–30, 56
Lakshmi 383
   Mother 366–7, 403
Lamb, C. and M. 56
landladies 50–2, 56

INDEX / 515

Laṅkāvatāra Sūtra 74
Laotzu 23
latrines 82, 161, 177, 199, 213, 235, 286, 357
laughter 8, 143, 159, 183, 291, 329, 493, 500
Laurie 95
Lawrence, D. H. 82
Laws of Nepal 437
lawyers 164, 180–1, 271–2, 275, 308, 349, 476
Laxminarayan Temple 114–15
Leadbeater, C. W. 148
Leatherhead 91, 94, 100, 105
lectures 121–2, 124, 135, 148–9, 244, 264–5, 291–2, 294–5
lentils 194, 216–17, 221, 377, 380, 417–18, 422, 426
leopards 376, 378, 380
Levy, Mrs 47
Li Po 61
Liezi 332
life, spiritual 117, 119, 123, 230, 300, 303, 324, 326
Life of 37, 51
Life of Johnson 51
'Life of Siddhartha Gautama the Buddha' 37
Lil, Aunt 497
Lodge meetings 149–50
London 46–7, 49, 53, 58–60, 67–70, 101, 492, 499–500
  children 5, 481, 494
lotas 235–6, 258, 415
Lumbini 402, 413–14, 418–20, 422, 453–4, 459
lunch 57, 59, 194, 198, 200, 209, 231, 433
lunch hour 76, 78, 81–2

Macaulay, T. B. 277
Mackenzie, Dr 24
madness 83–4, 92, 298, 324, 331, 369, 371, 377–8
Madras 116, 177, 227–9, 244, 285, 358
Madura 230–2, 234–5, 238, 245, 365
Maha Bodhi Society 162, 165, 167–8, 386, 390–1, 393, 396, 453
Maha Bodhi Temple 454
Mahābhārata 217, 280, 454
Mahachaitya Vihara 430–1, 439
Mahākāśyapa 462
mahants 400–1, 454–5
Mahaparinirvana Stupa 401, 405–6, 408
Maharaja of Travancore 248–52, 286

Maharshi, Ramana 334, 336–7, 340–4, 349
Mahasabha 146, 279–80
Mahavir Swami 407
Mahaweera, Ven. M. M. 143
Mahāyāna 143–4, 235, 302, 315, 332–3, 362, 448, 523
Maitreya 134
Maitreya, Ananda 4, 101, 480
Malabar 264, 273, 298, 335–6, 369
Malayalam 244, 252, 260, 264, 274–5, 277, 286–7, 297
Malayali Brahmins 285–6
Malayalis 244, 264, 275, 289, 294
Malays 138–40
Malla, Dr 435, 440
Mallas 405, 435
mango groves 193–5, 204, 207, 209, 397–8, 401, 416–18, 457
mantras 281, 312–14, 325–6, 338
Māra 114
Margaret (mother's friend) 71
Marx, K. 82–3
Mary Queen of Scots 27
Mashyam 428–9, 441
maths 131, 175, 227–8, 343, 367–70, 401
Mau 399
Maudgalyāyana 453, 458–60, 462
meat 11, 148–50, 442, 457, 498
medicines 16, 152, 322, 324, 445
meditation 143–6, 204–8, 215–16, 248–9, 308–10, 312–13, 326–8, 377–8
  evening 288, 300, 385
Medusa 23
Menon 273, 276–7
mental balance 316–17, 324
Merton, T. 463
Messengers From Tibet and Other Poems 103
Michelangelo 24
Middle Way, The 87, 100–1
Mike 95
Milarepa 151, 320
milk 60, 162, 291, 297, 331, 416, 419, 426
  distributions 291, 296, 300
  hot 221, 445
Milton, J. 36, 284
Minakshi 232
mist 58, 133–4, 219, 221–2, 338, 340, 428, 457
Mitcham Common 27, 495
Mitcham Lane 42
Mohini 365–6
monasteries 117–18, 128, 134, 136, 143, 390, 402, 407

monastery buildings 460–1
money 51–2, 223, 225, 388, 390, 395, 397, 482–3
monks 128–30, 143–4, 390–1, 393–6, 411, 447, 459, 461
　Buddhist 115, 121, 386, 388, 395, 397, 455, 459
　Chinese 142, 149, 460
　crippled 399–400
　foreign 424, 433, 438
　Hindu 117, 393, 397, 418
　novice 387, 404, 409
　Sinhalese 121, 143, 149, 390, 393, 419, 444, 447
　Theravādin 143, 301, 432
monsoon 109, 154, 395, 441
Mookherjee, S. 135
moon 126–7, 181, 237, 303, 317, 385, 408, 435
Mother 4–5, 8–12, 53–4, 56–8, 69–72, 88–90, 496–500, 502–3
mountains 126, 205, 366, 375–7, 380, 427–9, 467, 469
Mozart, W. A. 73
Mulagandhakuti Vihara 389–90, 401, 454
Müller, F. Max 85, 202
Mumba Devi 383
Munindra 419–21
Murugam 246
music 31, 68, 72–3, 120–1, 128, 133, 245, 435
　classical 72, 140, 155
musical instruments 1, 188, 245, 484
Muslims 131–2, 159, 166, 169–70, 238, 283, 286, 292
Muvattupuzha 253–6, 265–6, 271–2, 281–5, 287, 294, 320, 326–8
Myers, L. H. 111
Mylapore 227–8
Mysore 363–5, 368, 371, 373–4
mystical experiences 73
mysticism 36, 63, 86, 273, 331, 448–9, 463

Nag, K. 135
Nāgārjuna 61, 357–8, 361, 524
Nagercoil 244, 248
Naidu, Sarojini 113
Nair, Kumaran 272–7, 282, 285, 293, 296, 298, 306
Nair, Raman 260, 282, 288
Nairs 251, 267, 269, 272, 274, 282–3, 285
Nakayama, Rev. Riri 462
Nalanda 458–61
Nambudiri Brahmins 285–7, 369

Nana (grandmother) 2–4, 8–10, 26, 56–8, 66–7, 485–9, 495–6, 502–4
Nanak, Guru 115, 401
Narayan 349–50
Narayana Guru 295
Nataraja Guru 295
nationality 142, 228–9, 232, 238, 264, 267–9, 306–7, 388
naturopathy 445, 461–2
Nautanwa 418–19, 421
NCOs 94, 98, 138
Nehru, J. 190–1, 352
Nelson, H. 37
Nepal 419–20, 422, 424–7, 431–3, 436–8, 440, 442, 451–2
　government 420, 427, 438
New Delhi 114–16, 182, 190, 214–16, 227, 292, 309, 368
Newars 424–5, 434–5, 437–8, 443, 471
Newman, T. H. 46
Nietzsche, F. W. 68
nikāyas 447–8
Nityabodhananda 228
Nityaswarupananda (Secretary Swami) 160–1, 163–4, 166, 321
Nixon, R. 184
non-Brahmins 194, 196, 198, 244, 336, 370
Noni, Aunt 3–4, 8, 26, 28, 99, 485–8, 493, 502
Norah 35, 104
Northcliffe, Lord, *see* Harmsworth, A.
notebooks 35, 88, 105–6, 208, 225, 332, 452
novice monks 387, 404, 409
nurses 16–18, 91

offerings 1, 115, 246–7, 251, 311, 339, 426, 454–5
officers 40–1, 94, 97–8, 105, 141, 154, 282, 486
　billeting 46–7, 53
　Japanese 138, 154
ordination 143–4, 386, 388, 390–7, 401, 403, 407–13, 442–3
　formal 327, 346
Orphanage 166–70
orthodox Brahmins 231, 281, 454, 458
orthodox Hinduism 199, 287, 298, 367, 436
orthodox Hindus 194, 200, 263, 279, 447, 462
Ouija board 351–3, 375
owl clock 18, 22

Padmagarbha Vihara 425–6, 430, 441, 443

Padmanabhaswami 250
pain 279, 305, 324, 355, 409, 427–9, 432
Pakistan 168–9, 219, 414
  East 399
Pāli 102, 122, 409, 444–6, 448–9, 452, 458, 460
  grammar 445–6
  scriptures 144, 235, 333, 424, 434–5, 448–9
Pallis, M. 151
Pandit-ji 178–86, 190–7, 201, 208, 211–17, 219–21, 223, 225
Panglin 297–8
Pannasiha 144
Paracelsus 63
parades 40–2, 70, 92, 95, 110, 118, 138, 155
Paradise Lost 36, 72
Parkes' Coal Company 58–60, 64
Patel, Sardar Vallabhbhai 191, 352
paternal grandfather 10, 496
patients 16–17
Patna 458
Pavitrananda, Swami 128–9, 301
Peaks and Lamas 150–1
Perseus 23
personal disciples 390, 396, 455
Pete 96
philosophy 61, 63, 70, 72, 124, 128, 446, 451
  Buddhist 122, 228, 394, 446, 451–2, 458, 460
  Hindu 164, 447, 458
  Indian 117, 119, 122, 244, 367, 388
Phoe Thay, Ven. 143
phoenix 2, 484
Phyllis 35, 104
pilgrimages 82, 126, 282–3, 318, 347, 353, 374, 387
pilgrims 10, 115, 387, 389–90, 393, 395, 419–20, 454–5
Pillai, Kesava 272, 275–7, 282, 320, 325, 349
Pillai, Krishna 282–3, 318
Pillai, Shankara 113, 119, 125, 252–3, 288–9, 304–5, 308–10, 312–17
Pinkie 95
Pippala Cave 462, 464
Pirates of Penzance 37
poetry 29–30, 35, 63, 72, 87–9, 101, 108, 451–2
police 19, 159, 166, 170, 250, 269, 420, 433
  secret 142, 263
politics 136, 143, 146, 153, 158, 161, 163, 167–8

pollution 162, 201, 250, 256, 415–16, 433, 436, 439
Ponnabalam 122
poppadoms 288–9
poverty 109–10, 113, 130
power(s) 190–1, 225, 241, 309, 311, 355, 433, 437
  psychic 86, 204, 462
prāṇāyāma 125, 317–18, 324, 326, 331
prasad 186, 200, 274, 291, 329, 358–9, 417, 426
Praxiteles 233
prayers 10, 18, 21, 40, 43–5, 71, 466, 496
  extempore 42, 44
preceptors 43, 405, 411, 444, 448–9
precepts 390, 403–4, 410, 420, 425–6, 432, 435–6, 438
  Five Precepts 102, 196, 404, 417, 425–6, 432, 436, 438
prejudices 147–8, 212, 223, 232, 452
Prem, Sri Krishna 61, 184
pretas 310
Price, A. 101, 150
pride 209, 281, 362, 371
priests 22, 121, 131, 233–4, 239, 250–1, 455, 463–4
princesses 347–8
Pringy 156
privations 167–8, 212
processions 136–7, 181, 205, 251, 365, 372, 411, 413
Proclus 81
prostrations 229, 353–4, 379, 403, 432, 434, 440
protests 16, 38, 56, 163, 197, 199, 361, 419–20
psychic experiences 85
Public Health Department 74–5
public houses 21, 71, 88, 90, 101, 106, 492
public meetings 222, 265, 291–2, 413, 460
pujas 134–5, 259–60, 288
Purcell, H. 31
purity 33, 120, 128, 145, 149, 183, 208, 342
Purohit Guru 438–9
Pyarelal, Lalla 220–1, 223, 225–6

Radha 175, 188, 315
Radhakrishnan 273
Radhakrishnan, Dr 122
radios 57, 72–3, 493–4
Rahula, Walpola 121, 143
rainbows 226
rainy season 260, 300, 385, 413, 439, 442, 452

Raipur 211–13, 216, 218–20, 223, 238, 248, 309
Rājagṛha 464–5
Rajgir 457, 460–1, 464
Rajgopal 349–59, 361–2, 375
Raleigh, Sir Walter 37
Rama 187, 291, 298, 312, 353
  mantra 325, 329, 332
Ramakrishna, Sri 117, 121, 124, 131, 257, 259, 311, 320
Ramakrishna Math 227
Ramakrishna Mission 117, 119, 124, 148, 202, 245, 247, 392–5
Ramana Maharshi 336, 342
Rāmāyaṇa 217, 280
Ramdas, Swami 319–26, 328–34, 336, 345, 381, 451
Rana, Maharaja Yudha Shumshere Junga Bahadur 424, 435, 437
rationalism 448
Ratnagiri Range 462, 465
Ratnasambhava 430
Read, Carveth 446
Rechabites 21
Refuge 404, 409–10, 425–6, 432, 436, 438, 522, 524
Reg 41, 44
regalia 175–7, 343–4, 371, 373
Reggie 52
relics 2, 453, 459, 485
religious duties 102, 234, 403
renunciation 128, 159, 230, 296, 319, 324, 361
respiration-mindfulness 206–7
rest houses 390, 401, 420, 453, 460
rheumatic fever 17
Rhys Davids, C. 302
rice 119–20, 216–17, 377, 380, 417–18, 426, 428, 448
  unmilled 415, 432
Rie 147, 149
rifles 92–5, 97, 106, 155, 157, 170, 298
Rimbaud, A. 113
rivers 255–6, 258, 266, 325–7, 370–2, 384–5, 418–19, 467
robes 225, 229, 386, 408, 411, 413, 416, 447–8
  saffron 202, 226–7, 229, 295, 327, 336, 357
  yellow 115–16, 127, 136, 143, 165, 173, 393, 403
rocket 103–4
Rolland, R. H. 117
Rossetti, D. G. 36, 51
Rover 19
Rubens, P. P. 233

rudrākṣa beads 174–5, 287, 331
Rummindei Temple 420

Sabarimalai 282–3, 318
sacred threads 196, 201, 231, 251, 253, 369, 372, 400
sadhus 229, 231–2, 234, 238, 264, 268–9, 348, 354
saffron robes 202, 226–7, 229, 295, 327, 336, 357
sages 185, 193, 217–18, 303, 306, 333, 371, 375
St John of the Cross 161
saints 200, 204, 217–18, 320, 333, 337–8, 369, 372
salmon-pink robes 118, 175
Salome 48
salvation 43–4, 164, 365, 387, 455
samādhi 85, 221, 355, 362, 369
sand 110, 228, 236, 240, 335, 337
  silver 238, 381, 384–5
Sandalwood Country 364, 373, 403
sangha 230, 252, 258, 390, 409, 411
Sangharatana, Ven. M. 453–5
Sanskrit 61, 187, 261, 297, 409, 426, 445, 458
Sanyal, Phani 136, 160
Sarada 253
Sarada Devi 121, 247
Saradananda, Swami 124
Saraswati 295
Sarichak 461
Sarkar, Benoy Kumar 135
Sarnath 383, 386–90, 392–7, 401–5, 419, 421, 453–4, 459
Saroj 163–4
Satyapriya 211–17, 238–43, 273–81, 287–98, 300–20, 324–30, 348–55, 357–61; *see also* Banerjee, R. K.; Buddharakshita
scheduled castes 214, 452
Schiller, F. C. S. 446
Schlaum, B. 194–5, 198–200
schools 18–19, 29, 39–41, 46, 48, 50, 58–9, 427
Schopenhauer, A. 61, 83
scriptural study 143, 234–5, 300
scriptures, Pāli 144, 333, 424, 435, 448–9
sea 108, 112, 116, 141, 146, 229, 237, 239
secret police 142, 263
secrets 22, 64, 67, 84, 191, 264, 287, 463
Seeds of Contemplation 463–4
self 177, 301, 447, 452
Seneca 61

servants 48, 50, 118, 123, 138, 142, 439, 444
Set Room 99, 102–3, 108, 110, 138, 154
Seven Storey Mountain 463
sex 82, 96, 287, 433
Shakespeare, W. 51, 56, 61–2, 284
Shakyananda, Ven. 430–1, 436–40
Shankara Pillai 113, 119, 125, 252–3, 288–9, 304–5, 308–10, 312–17
Shankaracharyas of Puri 175, 343–4
Shankaracharyas of Sringeri Math 369, 371–2
Shaw, G. B. 39
Shiva 162, 174–5, 211, 278, 295–6, 334, 351, 376
  temples 212, 399
shock 10, 49, 125, 350, 352, 360, 391, 397
shoes 30, 79, 97, 110, 115, 131, 356–7, 362
shops 60, 74, 84, 111, 117, 124, 140, 467–8
Shoreham 33, 497
Shrine of the Recumbent Buddha 402, 405–6, 454
shrines 125–7, 135–6, 165, 169–70, 259, 337, 339–41, 346
Shudras 199, 235
Shylock 37
Siak Kiong Hiup, Ven. 142–3, 149–50
Sid (Boys' Brigade) 41–4
Sid (Mother's friend) 74, 89, 99
Siddhatmananda, Swami 119, 121–2, 124, 130
sidesmen 41, 43, 45
Sikhs 115, 140, 189, 219, 222, 226, 279, 468
Sikkim 467–8
Silacara, Bhikku 302
silence 313, 318, 340–2, 347, 378, 406, 416, 420
  complete 222, 366, 376
  intense 74, 222
  observation of 288, 378–9
silver 5, 16, 109, 112, 126–7, 237, 279, 470
  sand 238, 381, 384–5
  staff 175, 177, 343
simplicity 95, 128, 133, 233–4, 261, 304, 321, 339
sincerity 86, 393, 395, 408
Singapore 105, 137–9, 148, 150–4, 156–8, 161, 207, 386–8
Singh, Dr Gurukipal 222, 226
Sinhalese 142–3, 396
  Buddhists 447–8, 451

monks 121, 143, 149, 390, 393, 419, 444, 447
sins 30, 114, 163–4, 199, 231, 256, 280
Sirinivas, Ven. Nayaka Mahāthera 419
Sitala 233
sitting rooms 2, 10, 12, 14, 160, 163, 496, 501–3
Skipper 40–3, 71
Smeed 95
Smith, Corporal 93
Smith, Mr 47, 49
Smith, Mrs 47–50
Smoky Joe (Smoker, William) 31–2, 37–9, 56
social contacts 343–4
social work 21, 300–1, 393
Soma, Bhikkhu 144–5, 157, 301, 452
Somasundara 232
songs 17, 31, 150–1, 186–7, 245, 340, 409, 469
  devotional 184, 186–7, 215, 291, 329, 350–1, 435
Sonia 78–9, 83–4, 87–8, 106
soul 92, 96, 302, 356–7, 387, 397, 443, 447
  liberated 333, 369
South India 119, 124, 230–6, 238, 244–6, 280–1, 358–9, 361
south-west London 1, 37, 480
spectacles 59, 76, 79, 84, 133, 188, 237, 421–2
speeches 47, 49, 120, 129, 153, 173–6, 264, 277
Spenser, E. 36
Spiegelberg, F. 332
spiritual communities 389, 394, 411, 425
spiritual development 196, 202, 225, 234, 320, 322, 384, 524
spiritual experience 85, 176, 377
spiritual life 117, 119, 123, 230, 300, 303, 324, 326
Spiritualism 21, 351–3, 375
spirituality 122, 124, 128, 306, 373
śrāmaṇeras 387, 390, 392, 394, 404, 410–11, 414, 419
Sravana Belgola 363, 373–4
Sri Dharmarajika Vihara 136
Sri Sri Sri Ma Anandamayi Ashram 182, 185
Sringeri 363, 367–9, 371, 373
Sten 147, 149
strain 53, 68–9, 77, 90, 98, 144, 155, 307
Strindberg, A. 68
string beds 216, 421–2, 444–7
Subbalakshmi 350

Subhas Chandra Bose 141, 146, 153
subscriptions 265, 269, 284–5, 288, 305, 307–8
suburbs 116–17, 145, 255
Suchindram 244, 365
Sudhir 178–80, 182–5, 193–4, 201, 208, 211–13, 215–16, 219
Suez 108
sugar-water 414, 418
Sullivan, A. S. 31, 37
Summer Palace, Beijing 3, 485–6
summers 8–9, 46, 67, 83, 85, 88, 123, 494
sun 100, 110, 112, 115–16, 127, 345, 397–8, 469
Sunday school 20, 41, 43–4, 109, 501
Sundays 28, 32, 35, 45, 51, 102, 105, 358
  afternoons 28, 58, 60
  mornings 1, 21, 42, 48, 354, 483
superconscious state 205–6, 221, 355, 362
supernormal faculties 309
suppers 215, 217, 237, 288
Śūraṅgama Sūtra 73
Surya 460
Sushila, Anagarika 430, 433–4
sūtras 85, 301, 434, 452, 465, 523, 525
  Diamond Sūtra 85, 101, 301
  Laṅkāvatāra Sūtra 74
  Śūraṅgama Sūtra 73
  Sūtra of Wei Lang 85, 301
  White Lotus Sūtra 407, 465
Suzuki, D. T. 302, 332
swamis 116–19, 121–3, 128, 130–1, 162–3, 252–4, 354–62, 383–4; *see also individual names*
Swedenborg, E. 60, 64
sweetmeats 120, 221, 351, 399–400, 426, 430
sweets 10, 14, 52, 59, 186, 497, 500, 504
Swinburne, A. C. 76, 332
Sybil 48
Symonds, J. A. 32
sympathy 20, 152, 222, 226, 250, 322, 332, 388
Syrian Christians 284
Systems of Buddhistic Thought 101

Tagore, R. C. 387
Tamil Brahmins 241, 249, 255, 277, 281, 285, 338, 341
Tamil country 280, 335, 337, 365
Tamils 119–23, 241, 244, 250, 330, 338, 355, 358
Tan Keng Lock 142–3, 147, 149–50

Tansen 413, 424, 427–9, 431, 438–40
Tantric Buddhism 449
Taoism 61, 87, 464
tapioca 217, 260, 289
Tchaikovsky, P. I. 73
Tehri 418
Tehsildah's Mother 346–8
Telugu Brahmins 368–9
temper 4, 29, 317, 351, 377–9, 487, 498
Tennyson, A. 29, 56
tents 154–5, 185, 208, 216, 230, 343
Thackalay 295
Thakur 311
Thaung Aung, U 419–20
Thelma 75, 79–80, 87
Theosophical Society 147, 168, 228, 387–8
Theravāda Buddhism 144–5, 333, 403, 424, 426, 435, 445, 448
Theravādin monks 143, 301, 432
Thittila, U 102–3, 404
Thomas, D. 82
Thousand-Petalled Lotus 473, 476–7
threads, sacred 196, 201, 231, 251, 253, 369, 372, 400
threats 58, 93, 235, 400, 437
Three Jewels 425, 432, 434, 476, 522
Three Refuges 102, 196, 404, 409, 425
Thus Spake Zarathustra 100
Tibet 2, 103, 134, 144, 413, 455, 468, 485
Tibetan Buddhism 86, 151, 226
Tibetan temples 2, 134, 484
Tibetans 162, 424, 428, 455, 468
Tinnevelly 235, 237
tinsel 12, 502–3
Tirumal Nayak 232–3
Tiruvannamalai 334–5, 337–8, 346, 348–50, 365
  Temple 337, 339–40
Tojo, H. 150
Tom 97–9, 105
Tom, Uncle 482–3, 501
Tomo Geshe Rimpoche 134
Tooth Relic Temple 126
Tooting 3–4, 8, 10, 20–1, 487, 489, 494, 496
Tooting Broadway 9, 12, 27, 71, 73, 88–9, 499, 502
Torquay 53–5, 57–8, 60–1, 66–72, 88, 99
trains 9, 46, 101, 106, 109–10, 227–8, 230, 334–5
trams 9, 89, 95, 103, 483, 494, 499
trance 72, 124, 313–14, 372

INDEX / 521

Travancore 241–2, 247–9, 264, 282–3, 285–8, 292–3, 295, 370–1
trees, mango 185, 208, 389
Trimurti 334
Trivandrum 242–4, 246–9, 252–3, 258, 266
Trollope, A. 81
Truman, H. S. 150
truth 217–18, 300–1, 319–20, 332, 337, 346–7, 388–9, 451
turkey 12, 14, 502–4
Tut 37

Udāna 445
ulcers 432, 438–9
uncles, *see individual names*
unmilled rice 415, 432
Unseeables 256, 271, 284
Untouchables 193, 195, 199–201, 271, 278, 280, 297–8, 339
Upanishads 62, 213, 347

Vairocana 430
Vaiśākha Pūrṇimā 129, 156, 180, 196, 383, 385, 408, 411
Vaishnavism, Bengal 188, 197, 315
vakils 271–3
Valisinha, Devapriya 168, 213
valvular disease 17, 19
Varkala 295
Varrier, Krishna 287
Vedas 217, 280, 341, 370
vegetable curries 194, 416, 418, 426
vegetarianism 101, 120–1, 148–9, 420, 442, 462
Victoria, Queen 267
viharas 136, 407–8, 411, 426–7, 430, 432–8, 443
violence 73, 150, 169, 239, 315–16, 394, 427, 465
Vipassana, Mother 403, 406, 408–9, 411, 413
Vipulananda, Swami 119–23, 131
Virgin Mary 208, 298
Virupaksha Guha 337–8, 345
Vishnu 250, 267, 274, 312, 334, 352, 365
vision in the cave 335–48
Vivekananda, Swami 117, 121, 125, 136, 168, 245, 351–3, 375

Vivekananda Society 117–18
Vivekananda's Rock 239
Vulture Peak 464–6

wages 59, 65–6
wandering ascetics 243, 322, 327, 370, 386, 388, 444
Wandsworth Bridge 11, 499
war 45–6, 49, 137–8, 142, 150, 153–5, 157, 161
water 198–9, 214, 258, 260, 286, 288–9, 304–5, 428–9
weekends 60, 88, 97–9, 271, 359, 380
Wei Lang 85, 301
Wellawatta 117–18
White Lotus Sūtra 407, 465
Williams, Mr & Mrs 50–3, 59, 64–5
Wimbledon Common 27–8, 32, 99, 423, 495
wine 488, 503–4
winters 8, 35, 58, 123, 240, 339, 452, 494
wisdom 23, 54, 78, 85–6, 197, 206, 461–2, 522–3
women 75, 77–8, 80, 199, 360–1, 415, 425–6, 432–4
  Nair 285–6
  Newar 425, 433
Wong Mou-Lam 85
wood-chips 260, 262–3, 265, 288
Woodroffe, Sir John 135, 148
Wordsworth, W. 49
world-renunciation 225, 229, 234–5, 242
worship 259, 292, 295, 339–40, 402, 406, 433–4, 436

Yalahankar Swami 353–5, 357, 359–63, 375, 379
Yashoda Ma 184
yellow robes 115–16, 127, 136, 143, 165, 173, 393, 403
yoga, hatha 303, 305, 317
Yoga Swami of Jaffna 123, 131, 301, 357
yogic sleep 221

Zen Buddhism 302, 464
Zhuangzi 332
Zoroaster 23, 61, 173

A GUIDE TO THE COMPLETE WORKS OF SANGHARAKSHITA

Gathered together in these twenty-seven volumes are talks and stories, commentaries on the Buddhist scriptures, poems, memoirs, reviews, and other writings. The genres are many, and the subject matter covered is wide, but it all has – its whole purpose is to convey – that taste of freedom which the Buddha declared to be the hallmark of his Dharma. Another traditional description of the Buddha's Dharma is that it is *ehipassiko*, 'come and see'. Sangharakshita calls to us, his readers, to come and see how the Dharma can fundamentally change the way we see things, change the way we live for the better, and change the society we belong to, wherever in the world we live.

Sangharakshita's very first published piece, *The Unity of Buddhism* (found in volume 7 of this collection), appeared in 1944 when he was eighteen years old, and it introduced themes that continued to resound throughout his work: the basis of Buddhist ethics, the compassion of the bodhisattva, and the transcendental unity of Buddhism. Over the course of the following seven decades not only did numerous other works flow from his pen; he gave hundreds of talks (some now lost). In gathering all we could find of this vast output, we have sought to arrange it in a way that brings a sense of coherence, communicating something essential about Sangharakshita, his life and teaching. Recalling the three 'baskets' among which an early tradition divided the Buddha's teachings, we have divided Sangharakshita's creative output into six 'baskets' or groups: foundation texts; works originating in India; teachings originally given in the West; commentaries on the Buddhist scriptures; personal writings; and poetry, aphorisms, and works on the arts. The 27th volume, a concordance, brings together all the terms and themes of the whole collection. If you want to find a particular story or teaching, look at a traditional term from different points of view or in different contexts, or track down one of the thousands of canonical references to be found in these volumes, the concordance will be your guide.

1. FOUNDATION

What is the foundation of a Buddhist life? How do we understand and then follow the Buddha's path of Ethics, Meditation, and Wisdom? What is really meant by 'Going for Refuge to the Three Jewels', described by Sangharakshita as the essential act of a Buddhist life? And what is the Bodhisattva ideal, which he has called 'one of the sublimest ideals mankind has ever seen'? In the 'Foundation' group you will find teachings on all these themes. It includes the author's *magnum opus, A Survey of Buddhism*, a collection of teachings on *The Purpose and Practice of Buddhist Meditation*, and the anthology, *The Essential Sangharakshita*, an eminently helpful distillation of the entire corpus.

2. INDIA

From 1950 to 1964 Sangharakshita, based in Kalimpong in the eastern Himalayas, poured his energy into trying to revive Buddhism in the land of its birth and to revitalize and bring reform to the existing Asian Buddhist world. The articles and book reviews from this period are gathered in volumes 7 and 8, as well as his biographical sketch of the great Sinhalese Dharmaduta, Anagarika Dharmapala. In 1954 Sangharakshita took on the editing of the *Maha Bodhi*, a journal for which he wrote a monthly editorial, and which, under his editorship, published the work of many of the leading Buddhist writers of the time. It was also during these years in India that a vital connection was forged with Dr B. R. Ambedkar, renowned Indian statesman and leader of the Buddhist mass conversion of 1956. Sangharakshita became closely involved with the new Buddhists and, after Dr Ambedkar's untimely death, visited them regularly on extensive teaching tours.

From 1979, when an Indian wing of the Triratna Buddhist Community was founded (then known as TBMSG), Sangharakshita returned several times to undertake further teaching tours. The talks from these tours are collected in volumes 9 and 10 along with a unique work on Ambedkar and his life which draws out the significance of his conversion to Buddhism.

3. THE WEST

Sangharakshita founded the Triratna Buddhist Community (then called the Friends of the Western Buddhist Order) on 6 April 1967. On 7 April the following year he performed the first ordinations of men and women within the Triratna Buddhist Order (then the Western Buddhist Order). At that time Buddhism was not widely known in the West and for the following two decades or so he taught intensively, finding new ways to communicate the ancient truths of Buddhism, drawing on the whole Buddhist tradition to do so, as well as making connections with what was best in existing Western culture. Sometimes his sword flashed as he critiqued ideas and views inimical to the Dharma. It is these teachings and writings that are gathered together in this third group.

4. COMMENTARY

Throughout Sangharakshita's works are threaded references to the Buddhist canon of literature – Pāli, Mahāyāna, and Vajrayāna – from which he drew his inspiration. In the early days of the new movement he often taught by means of seminars in which, prompted by the questions of his students, he sought to pass on the inspiration and wisdom of the Buddhist tradition. Each seminar was based around a different text, the seminars were recorded and transcribed, and in due course many of the transcriptions were edited and turned into books, all carefully checked by Sangharakshita. The commentaries compiled in this way constitute the fourth group. In some ways this is the heart of the collection. Sangharakshita often told the story of how it was that, reading two *sūtras* at the age of sixteen, he realized that he was a Buddhist, and he has never tired of showing others how they too could see and realize the value of the '*sūtra*-treasure'.

5. MEMOIRS

Who is Sangharakshita? What sort of life did he live? Whom did he meet? What did he feel? Why did he found a new Buddhist movement? In these volumes of memoirs and letters Sangharakshita shares with his readers much about himself and his life as he himself has experienced it, giving us a sense of its breadth and depth, humour and pathos.

6. POETRY, APHORISMS, AND THE ARTS

Sangharakshita describes reading *Paradise Lost* at the age of twelve as one of the greatest poetic experiences of his life. His realization of the value of the higher arts to spiritual development is one of his distinctive contributions to our understanding of what Buddhist life is, and he has expressed it in a number of essays and articles. Throughout his life he has written poetry which he says can be regarded as a kind of spiritual autobiography. It is here, perhaps, that we come closest to the heart of Sangharakshita. He has also written a few short stories and composed some startling aphorisms. Through book reviews he has engaged with the experiences, ideas, and opinions of modern writers. All these are collected in this sixth group.

In the preface to *A Survey of Buddhism* (volume 1 in this collection), Sangharakshita wrote of his approach to the Buddha's teachings:

> Why did the Buddha (or Nāgārjuna, or Buddhaghosa) teach this particular doctrine? What bearing does it have on the spiritual life? How does it help the individual Buddhist actually to follow the spiritual path?... I found myself asking such questions again and again, for only in this way, I found, could I make sense – spiritual sense – of Buddhism.

Although this collection contains so many words, they are all intent, directly or indirectly, on these same questions. And all these words are not in the end about their writer, but about his great subject, the Buddha and his teaching, and about you, the reader, for whose benefit they are solely intended. These pages are full of the reverence that Sangharakshita has always felt, which is expressed in an early poem, 'Taking Refuge in the Buddha', whose refrain is 'My place is at thy feet'. He has devoted his life to communicating the Buddha's Dharma in its depth and in its breadth, to men and women from all backgrounds and walks of life, from all countries, of all races, of all ages. These collected works are the fruit of that devotion.

We are very pleased to be able to include some previously unpublished work in this collection, but most of what appears in these volumes has been published before. We have made very few changes, though we have added extra notes where we thought they would be useful. We have had the pleasure of researching the notes in the Sangharakshita Library at 'Adhisthana', Triratna's centre in Herefordshire, UK, which houses his own collection of books. It has been of great value to be able to search among the very copies of the *suttas*, *sūtras* and commentaries that have provided the basis of his teachings over the last seventy years.

The publication of these volumes owes much to the work of transcribers, editors, indexers, designers, and publishers over many years – those who brought out the original editions of many of the works included here, and those who have contributed in all sorts of ways to this *Complete Works* project, including all those who contributed to funds given in celebration of Sangharakshita's ninetieth birthday in August 2015. Many thanks to everyone who has helped; may the merit gained in our acting thus go to the alleviation of the suffering of all beings.

Vidyadevi and Kalyanaprabha
Editors

THE COMPLETE WORKS OF SANGHARAKSHITA

I FOUNDATION

VOLUME 1 A SURVEY OF BUDDHISM / THE BUDDHA'S NOBLE EIGHTFOLD PATH
A Survey of Buddhism
The Buddha's Noble Eightfold Path

2 THE THREE JEWELS I
The Three Jewels
Going for Refuge
The Ten Pillars of Buddhism
The History of My Going for Refuge
Was the Buddha a Bhikkhu?
Forty-Three Years Ago
My Relation to the Order
Extending the Hand of Fellowship
The Meaning of Conversion in Buddhism

3 THE THREE JEWELS II
Who is the Buddha?
What is the Dharma?
What is the Sangha?

4 THE BODHISATTVA IDEAL
The Bodhisattva Ideal
The Bodhisattva Principle
The Endlessly Fascinating Cry

5 THE PURPOSE AND PRACTICE OF BUDDHIST MEDITATION
The Purpose and Practice of Buddhist Meditation

6 THE ESSENTIAL SANGHARAKSHITA
The Essential Sangharakshita

II INDIA

VOLUME 7 CROSSING THE STREAM: INDIA WRITINGS I
Early Writings 1944–1954
Crossing the Stream
Buddhism in the Modern World
Ordination and Initiation in the Three Yānas
Buddhism in India Today
A Bird's Eye View of Indian Buddhism
The Meaning of Orthodoxy in Buddhism

8 BEATING THE DHARMA DRUM: INDIA WRITINGS II
Anagarika Dharmapala and Other 'Maha Bodhi' Writings
Dharmapala: The Spiritual Dimension
Beating the Drum: Maha Bodhi Editorials
Book Reviews

9 DR AMBEDKAR AND THE REVIVAL OF BUDDHISM I
Ambedkar and Buddhism
Lecture Tour in India, December 1981– March 1982

10 DR AMBEDKAR AND THE REVIVAL OF BUDDHISM II
Lecture Tours in India 1979 & 1983–1992

III THE WEST

11 A NEW BUDDHIST MOVEMENT I
The Buddha's Victory
The Taste of Freedom
Buddha Mind
Human Enlightenment
New Currents in Western Buddhism
Buddhism for Today – and Tomorrow
Ritual and Devotion in Buddhism
Great Buddhists of the Twentieth Century
Articles and Interviews

VOLUME 12   A NEW BUDDHIST MOVEMENT II
Previously Unpublished Talks

      13   EASTERN AND WESTERN TRADITIONS
Buddhism and the West
The FWBO and 'Protestant Buddhism'
Buddhism, World Peace, and Nuclear War
From Genesis to the Diamond Sūtra
Dialogue between Buddhism and Christianity
Aspects of Buddhist Morality
Buddhism and Blasphemy
Buddhism and the Bishop of Woolwich
Buddhism and the New Reformation
Alternative Traditions
Creative Symbols of Tantric Buddhism
Tibetan Buddhism
The Essence of Zen

      IV COMMENTARY

      14   THE ETERNAL LEGACY / WISDOM BEYOND WORDS
The Eternal Legacy
The Glory of the Literary World
Wisdom Beyond Words

      15   PĀLI CANON TEACHINGS AND TRANSLATIONS
Dhammapada (translation)
Karaniya Mettā Sutta (translation)
Living with Kindness
Living with Awareness
Mangala Sutta (translation)
Auspicious Signs (seminar)
Tiratana Vandanā (translation)
Salutation to the Three Jewels (seminar)
The Threefold Refuge (seminar)
Further Pāli Sutta Commentaries

VOLUME 16   MAHĀYĀNA MYTHS AND STORIES
The Drama of Cosmic Enlightenment
The Priceless Jewel (address)
Transforming Self and World
The Inconceivable Emancipation

17   WISDOM TEACHINGS OF THE MAHĀYĀNA
Know Your Mind
Living Ethically
Living Wisely
The Way to Wisdom (seminar)

18   MILAREPA AND THE ART OF DISCIPLESHIP I
The Yogi's Joy
Milarepa and Rechungpa Seminars

19   MILAREPA AND THE ART OF DISCIPLESHIP II
Milarepa and Rechungpa seminars

V MEMOIRS

20   THE RAINBOW ROAD FROM TOOTING BROADWAY TO KALIMPONG
The Rainbow Road from Tooting Broadway to Kalimpong

21   FACING MOUNT KANCHENJUNGA
Facing Mount Kanchenjunga
Dear Dinoo: Letters to a Friend

22   IN THE SIGN OF THE GOLDEN WHEEL
In the Sign of the Golden Wheel
Precious Teachers
With Allen Ginsberg in Kalimpong 1962 (essay)

23   MOVING AGAINST THE STREAM
Moving Against the Stream
1970: A Retrospective
Moseley Miscellany Writings

VOLUME 24   THROUGH BUDDHIST EYES
Travel Letters
Through Buddhist Eyes

VI POETRY AND THE ARTS

25   POEMS AND STORIES
Complete Poems 1941–1994
The Call of the Forest
Moseley Miscellany Poems
Adhisthana Poems
How Buddhism Disappeared from India: A Satire
The Cave
The Artist's Dream
The Talking Buddha
The Antique Dealer
The White Lotus
The Two Roses
The Healer

26   APHORISMS AND THE ARTS
Peace is a Fire
A Stream of Stars
The Religion of Art
In the Realm of the Lotus
The Journey to Il Convento
St Jerome Revisited
A Note on the Burial of Count Orgaz
Criticism East and West
Book reviews
Urthona articles and interviews

27   CONCORDANCE AND APPENDICES

WINDHORSE PUBLICATIONS

Windhorse Publications is a Buddhist charitable company based in the UK. We produce books of high quality that are accessible and relevant to all those interested in Buddhism, at whatever level of interest and commitment. We are the main publisher of Sangharakshita, the founder of the Triratna Buddhist Order and Community. Our books draw on the whole range of the Buddhist tradition, including translations of traditional texts, commentaries, books that make links with contemporary culture and ways of life, biographies of Buddhists, and works on meditation.

To subscribe to the *Complete Works of Sangharakshita*, please go to: windhorsepublications.com/sangharakshita-complete-works/

THE TRIRATNA BUDDHIST COMMUNITY

Windhorse Publications is a part of the Triratna Buddhist Community, an international movement with centres in Europe, India, North America and Australasia. At these centres, members of the Triratna Buddhist Order offer classes in meditation and Buddhism. Activities of the Triratna Community also include retreat centres, residential spiritual communities, ethical Right Livelihood businesses, and the Karuna Trust, a UK fundraising charity that supports social welfare projects in the slums and villages of India.

Through these and other activities, Triratna is developing a unique approach to Buddhism, not simply as a philosophy and a set of techniques, but as a creatively directed way of life for all people living in the conditions of the modern world.

For more information please visit thebuddhistcentre.com